Business Analytics and Artificial Intelligence

Business Analytics and Artificial Intelligence provides an in-depth exploration of the intersection of business analytics (BA), machine learning, and artificial intelligence (AI). Tailored to undergraduate, graduate, and professional learners, it equips readers with the knowledge and skills needed to leverage data-driven insights and AI technologies for strategic decision-making, operational optimization, and innovation in a dynamic global business environment. This book bridges the gap between theory and practice by:

- Introducing the foundational principles of business analytics and AI
- Demonstrating the integration of advanced AI techniques into business analytics processes
- Providing a unified guide to business analytics and machine learning with a focus on real-world applications
- Presenting a clear, practical, and accessible framework to harness AI and machine learning for solving complex business problems, optimizing operations, and driving innovation
- Exploring the ethical, legal, and social implications of AI in business contexts
- Presenting case studies and real-world applications from diverse industries to showcase best practices

The textbook combines foundational concepts, advanced techniques, and hands-on applications, catering to readers with varying levels of technical expertise. It includes global perspectives on BA and AI, case studies, practical examples, and coding snippets (in Python or R) to help readers implement AI-driven solutions in their organizations. Topics span predictive analytics, machine learning, data visualization, natural language processing, and decision support systems, emphasizing how these tools empower businesses to stay competitive and ensure operational sustainability.

Zabihollah Rezaee is the Thompson-Hill Chair of Excellence and Emeritus Professor of Accountancy at the University of Memphis and has served a two-year term on the Standing Advisory Group of the Public Company Accounting Oversight Board (PCAOB). He is currently a Visiting Professor of AI, Sustainability and Governance at Corvinus University of Budapest.

Joseph H. Zhang is the Department Chair and the Robert W. and Patricia A. Maurer Family Distinguished Endowed Professor in the Department of Accounting and Management Information Systems at Bowling Green State University (BGSU) in Ohio, USA.

Salem Lotfi Boumediene is the Department Chair and Associate Professor in the Department of Accounting, Economics, and Finance at the University of Illinois Springfield (UIS) in the College of Business and Management.

Nick J. Rezaee is a graduate student in the Computational Biology and Quantitative Genetics program and programmer at the Harvard T.H Chan School of Public Health.

Business Analytics and Artificial Intelligence

Concepts, Skills and Real World Application

Zabihollah Rezaee, Joseph H. Zhang, Salem Lotfi Boumediene, and Nick J. Rezaee

Routledge
Taylor & Francis Group
NEW YORK AND LONDON

Designed cover image: Getty Images

First published 2026
by Routledge
605 Third Avenue, New York, NY 10158

and by Routledge
4 Park Square, Milton Park, Abingdon, Oxon, OX14 4RN

Routledge is an imprint of the Taylor & Francis Group, an informa business

For Product Safety Concerns and Information please contact our EU representative GPSR@taylorandfrancis.com. Taylor & Francis Verlag GmbH, Kaufingerstraße 24, 80331 München, Germany.

ISBN: 978-1-041-12402-3 (hbk)
ISBN: 978-1-041-12400-9 (pbk)
ISBN: 978-1-003-66455-0 (ebk)

DOI: 10.4324/9781003664550

Typeset in Times New Roman
by SPi Technologies India Pvt Ltd (Straive)

Access the Support Material: www.routledge.com/9781041124009

Dr. Rezaee wishes to honor the memory of his late parents Fazlollah and Fatemeh, his sister Monireh, his brother Heshmat, and his cousin Mohamad Reza Rezaee, and dedicates this book to his wife Soheila and children Nick and Rose.

Dr. Joseph Zhang dedicates this book to his parents, his wife Julia, and his two daughters, Wenjing and Susan.

Dr. Salem Boumediene dedicates this book to his parents, his wife Salma, and daughters, Synda and Cyrine.

Mr. Nick Rezaee dedicates this book to his mother Soheila and sister Rose. He would also like to thank his partner Ana for the support she has given him.

Contents

Figures

Tables

Preface

In a world increasingly shaped by data and algorithms, business leaders and professionals face both extraordinary opportunities and unprecedented challenges. The convergence of artificial intelligence (AI), data analytics, and ethical imperatives is reshaping how decisions are made, products are built, and organizations compete. This textbook offers a comprehensive guide to understanding, implementing, and leveraging AI and business analytics (BA) in business. It bridges foundational theories and real-world applications, equipping students, professionals, and decision-makers with the knowledge and AI-powered tools, and BA-driven methodologies necessary to lead in a data-driven, ethically responsible future. Covering core technologies, BA-assisted tools, strategic implementation, and emerging trends, the book also includes timely chapters on responsible AI, generative AI, Agentic AI, and Gemini AI Enterprises.

This textbook is conceived as a comprehensive and accessible guide to understanding the transformative power of AI and BA in business. It is intended for readers from diverse backgrounds, including students entering the field, professionals seeking upskills, and executives exploring digital transformation strategies. Whether you are a student, a data scientist, a business analyst, or a corporate decision-maker, this book will equip you with the foundational knowledge, applied tools, and critical thinking required to thrive in a data-driven, knowledge-based economy.

Our approach balances technical insight with business practicality. Each chapter builds progressively from basic concepts of AI and BA to real-world applications and simulation cases, with an emphasis on strategy, ethics, and accountability. We explain how AI and BA platforms work and explore why they matter and how they can be deployed responsibly and effectively. As the fields of AI and BA continue to evolve, the need for ethical, data-driven leadership becomes more essential and relevant. This book aims to support that leadership by empowering you with both technical competence and moral clarity. AI and BA technologies are transforming industries and capturing the public imagination in profound ways. While excitement and opportunities around these technologies are widespread, their inherent characteristics present a host of ethical challenges, including data insecurity, bias, hallucinations, and misinformation. As awareness of these risks grows, professionals must draw on the expanding body of real-world learning and expertise to develop and apply AI and BA systems that are ethical, humane, and sustainable.

This textbook equips readers with the development of the skills to implement ethical frameworks and governance strategies effectively in real-world applications of AI and BA platforms. This book is ideal for professionals across multiple industries who are responsible for developing or deploying AI and BA systems. Ultimately, this book addresses the most critical needs of understanding AI and BA systems in both business education and professional practice today and is designed as a comprehensive and forward-looking resource that integrates core principles of AI and BA for students and practitioners; focuses on fairness, transparency, and governance of data-driven decision-making; and presents hands-on illustrations and simulation cases across many industries including finance, marketing, healthcare, manufacturing, and sustainability. Unlike existing texts that focus either narrowly on technical algorithms or broadly on management concepts, this textbook examines both the technical and strategic dimensions of AI and BA. Readers will learn how machine learning, natural language processing, predictive analytics, and optimization can be applied across industries and how to design and implement AI and BA strategies that align with organizational goals, foster innovation, and ensure long-term growth. This book offers valuable insights into how AI and BA platforms can be purposefully directed to build a resilient, inclusive, and thriving world by challenging readers to think beyond technological advancement alone and to consider the responsible implications of AI and BA systems. We hope you find this textbook relevant to your educational pursuits, career developments, and aspirations in building a sustainable future through the power of AI and BA technologies.

Acknowledgments

This book has also benefited, *inter alia*, from permission to quote from several references and publications of a variety of professional organizations and standard-setting bodies, including the Securities and Exchange Commission (SEC), the Public Company Accounting Oversight Board (PCAOB), the Financial Accounting Standards Board (FASB), the International Accounting Standards Board (IASB), the American Institute of Certified Public Accountants (AICPA), the International Sustainability Standards Board (ISSB), Sustainability Accounting Standards Board (SASB), Global Reporting Initiative (GRI), the Big-Four public accounting firms (Deloitte & Touche, Ernst & Young, KPMG, and PricewaterhouseCoopers), Google, National Institute of Standards and Technology (NIST), IBM, European Commission (EC), and OpenAI.

Many people have generously contributed their time, knowledge, and talents during the development, writing, revisions, and production stages of this book. We are most grateful to all of them, and without their valuable assistance and contributions, this book would not have come to fruition. We thank Professor Ranik Raaen Wahlstrøm of the NTNU Business School for carefully reviewing earlier drafts of all chapters and for providing constructive and insightful comments. We appreciate the support of our colleagues at the Corvinus Institute for Advanced Studies of Corvinus University of Budapest, particularly Dean Zoltán Oszkár Szántó and Professor Peter Baranyi, as their work is supported by AI NEXTHURIZONTPROJECT2025-2026NKFIH–2024-1.2.3-HU-RIZONT-2024-00030 and contributes to our book. We also extend our sincere appreciation to the editorial staff of Routledge, especially Jessica Rech and Michelle Rynkewicz, for their guidance and support throughout the publication process.

We are grateful to our graduate assistants, Carrie (Qiuting) Gui and Sail (Zhifeng) Xu, for their hard work, dedication, and invaluable assistance. Finally, our heartfelt thanks go to our families for their constant love, patience, and encouragement: Zabi Rezaee's family—his wife Soheila, son Nick, and daughter Rose; Zhang's family—his wife Julia and daughters Wenjing and Susan; Boumediene's family—his wife Salma and daughters Sinda and Cyrine; and Nick Rezaee's family—his mother Soheila and sister Rose for their unwavering support throughout this journey.

1 Introduction to Business Analytics and Artificial Intelligence

Learning Objectives

- Learn the modern business landscape with technological advances
- Understand how organizations are increasingly leveraging BA and AI to gain global competitive advantages
- Learn AI-powered technologies of machine learning, deep learning, and other cognitive computing AI-powered tools and techniques
- Describe how prescriptive analytics and AI-driven analytics enable businesses to make proactive decisions based on real-time data
- Contrast Human Intelligence (HI) with Artificial Intelligence (AI)
- Learn the role of AI and BA in modern business

1.1 Introduction

Business Analytics (BA) has evolved significantly over the past decades from operations research (OR) and descriptive analytics focused on historical data to advancements in computing and data storage, where predictive analytics enables organizations to forecast trends and improve decision-making. Today, prescriptive and Artificial Intelligence (AI)-driven analytics allow businesses to make proactive decisions using real-time data. AI involves the simulation of human intelligence (HI) in machines, enabling tasks such as learning, reasoning, and problem-solving. Overall, BA focuses on generating insights that guide business planning, whereas AI encompasses techniques such as machine learning (ML) and deep learning (DL) that can be applied within BA. The integration of BA and AI is reshaping how organizations operate in the global market. As businesses adopt these technologies, their effective understanding and application become essential for executives, boards, and corporate stakeholders to drive innovation and strategy. Ultimately, this chapter provides an overview of the technologies and methodologies shaping modern business decision-making by bridging traditional practices with advanced analytics, showing how data-driven insights enhance performance.

DOI: 10.4324/9781003664550-1

1.2 Evolution of Business Analytics and Artificial Intelligence

1.2.1 Business Analytics Evolution

This section presents the evolution of BA from OR to data analytics (DA) and now to BA. This evolution can be traced back to OR, which emerged during World War II to improve military logistics and strategy through the application of mathematical models, statistical analysis, and optimization techniques.[1] The application of these methodologies paved the way for systematic decision-making within complex environments. Initially, OR focused on deterministic models, which assumed precise outcomes based on known variables. This foundational period laid the groundwork for the application of mathematical tools in operational decision-making across various sectors. Main attributes and characteristics of OR are (1) primary focus on mathematical modeling and optimization; (2) emphasis on efficiency and decision-making in operations; (3) reliance on structured data and well-defined problems; (4) limited use in engineering, logistics, and industrial systems; and (5) limited by computational capacity and data availability.[2]

Organizations began to recognize the importance of DA as part of a broader strategic framework.[3] The advent of digital computing, database systems, and networked information systems in the late twentieth century led to the development of DA with a massive increase in data generation and storage.[4] Initially, the focus was on basic descriptive analytics, which involved summarizing historical data to understand trends and patterns. Traditional tools such as spreadsheets and basic statistical software facilitated this process.[5] During this period, the use of databases became prevalent, and organizations began collecting and storing data more systematically. Coupled with the advent of decision support systems (DSS), organizations attempted to harness this growing wealth of data to improve decision-making and efficiency.[6] Key attributes and characteristics of DA are as follows: (1) focus on the systematic analysis of historical data to uncover patterns, trends, and correlations; (2) emphasis on descriptive and diagnostic analytics; (3) use in strategic planning by offering insights into past performance; (4) utilizing tools such as SQL, spreadsheets, and business intelligence (BI) platforms; (5) focus on data mining, reporting, and dashboard visualization. Overall, the revolution from OR to DA reflects a move from prescriptive precision to probabilistic discovery, where historical data becomes a guide for anticipating what may come next, rather than merely understanding what came before. Building on the foundations of both OR and DA, BA emerged as an integrative framework that unites descriptive, predictive, and prescriptive techniques to drive strategic and operational decisions in real time.

In recent years, organizations have increasingly recognized the strategic value of data and the importance of data-driven decision-making. Thus, BA has emerged as a strategic initiative that integrates the core principles of OR and DA while leveraging modern technologies such as big data, ML, and cloud computing to drive predictive and prescriptive insights.[7] The evolution of BA is characterized by its multi-dimensional approach, which empowers organizations to make informed decisions that enhance operational efficiency and competitive positioning. Key attributes and characteristics of BA are (1) combining descriptive, diagnostic, predictive, and prescriptive analytics; (2) using advanced statistical methods, AI, and ML, DL to forecast trends and simulate outcomes; (3) enabling real-time decision-making and strategic planning; (4) allowing highly interactive business processes through dashboards and DSSs; (5) reflecting a cultural transformation where data-driven decision-making is central to achieving competitive advantage; and (6) empowering organizations to become intelligent, agile, and proactive in an increasingly competitive and data-saturated world.

Figure 1.1 illustrates the evolution of early OR into DA, BA, and now AI-powered BA. This figure suggests four phases of BA evolution as it has undergone a profound and continuous evolution, reflecting advances in mathematics, computing power, data availability, and organizational decision-making needs. Its earliest foundations lie in OR, which emerged in the mid-twentieth century and focused on applying mathematical optimization, linear programming, queuing theory, simulation, and decision theory to solve well-defined operational problems. OR models were largely deterministic, rule-based, and assumption-driven, designed to improve efficiency, cost minimization, and resource allocation in stable and structured environments such as manufacturing, logistics, scheduling, and inventory management. OR models required clearly specified objectives, constraints, and parameters, which limited their applicability in dynamic and uncertain business contexts.

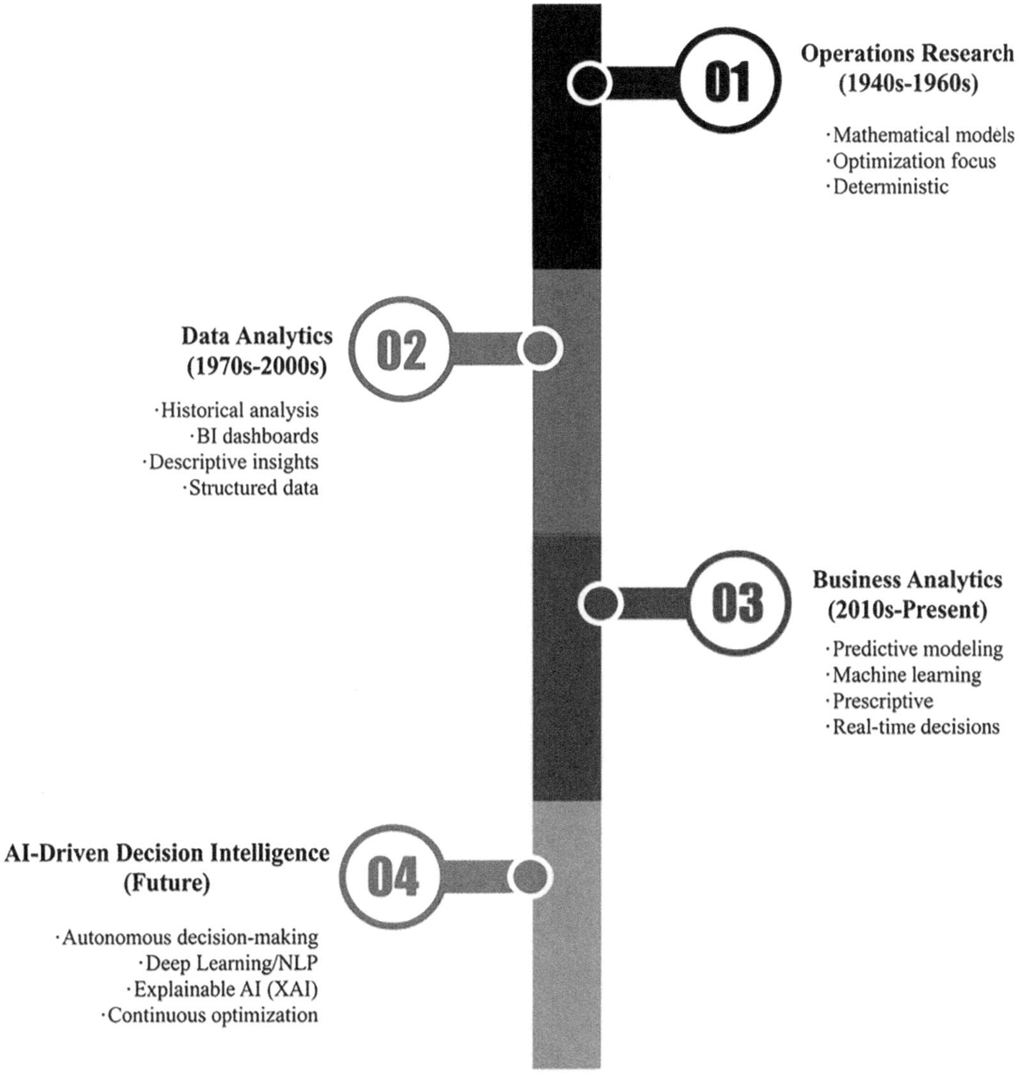

Figure 1.1 Evolution of Business Analytics.

In its second phase, as organizations digitized their operations and information systems, BA expanded into what became known as DA, enabled by advances in databases, enterprise systems, and statistical computing. This phase shifted the focus from optimization under fixed assumptions to extracting insights from historical and real-time data. DA emphasized descriptive analytics (what happened), diagnostic analytics (why it happened), and predictive analytics (what is likely to happen), using statistical inference, econometrics, data mining, and early ML techniques. The availability of large-scale transactional, financial, and customer data allowed firms to identify patterns, trends, and correlations that were previously inaccessible. However, decision-making remained largely human-driven, with analysts and managers interpreting outputs, defining models, and translating insights into action.

The third and fourth phases are characterized by the emergence of AI-driven analytics, which represents a fundamental shift from insight generation to intelligent and adaptive decision support. AI-driven analytics integrates advanced ML, DL, natural language processing (NLP), computer vision, and generative and agentic AI to analyze vast volumes of structured and unstructured data, including text, images, audio, and streaming sensor data. Unlike traditional analytics, AI systems can continuously learn from new information, update models autonomously, and operate effectively in complex, uncertain, and rapidly changing environments. Generative AI enables the creation and interpretation of narratives, explanations, and scenarios, while agentic AI extends analytics by planning, reasoning, and executing actions across interconnected tasks and systems with limited human intervention.

In summary, BA has evolved from the optimization-focused foundations of OR, emphasizing deterministic models in structured problems to DA that leverage statistical methods to generate descriptive, diagnostic, and predictive insights. More recently, this evolution has culminated in AI-driven analytics, which integrates advanced techniques to move beyond insight generation toward adaptive, real-time, and increasingly autonomous decision support. Unlike earlier approaches relying on predefined rules and retrospective analysis, AI-driven analytics continuously learn from new data, interact with complex environments, and augment managerial judgment through foresight, scenario simulation, and strategic action at scale.

1.2.2 AI Evolution

The evolution of AI has been transformative in reshaping businesses and industries and redefining how organizations are operating, making decisions, and delivering value. In the early stage, during the 1950s–1980s, the concept of AI was developed by pioneers like Alan Turing and John McCarthy as symbolic reasoning and rule-based systems, whereas BA was largely manual, based on statistical methods and spreadsheets, and decision-making was driven by historical data and intuition.

During the 1990s and 2000s, AI was employed to automate repetitive and data-heavy reporting tasks with the use of early-stage ML and robotic process automation (RPA). AI-powered tools have been developed to automate the collection and aggregation of data from disparate financial systems, identifying inconsistencies in large datasets to ensure compliance with accounting standards, to increase efficiency in producing financial reports, but have a limited ability to collect and analyze nonfinancial information. BI tools such as SAP, Oracle, and later Tableau and Power BI emerged by allowing businesses to visualize data and generate insights.

During the late 2010s and early 2020s, AI enabled the expansion of advanced analytics by leveraging predictive analytics for deeper insights. AI technologies, including advanced ML models, NLP, and data visualization tools, enable organizations to assess and predict risks related to financial health and stability, regulatory compliance, and environmental, social, and governance (ESG) issues. AI-powered tools such as automated narrative generation software were used to prepare financial and sustainability reports. During this time, the concept of big data was advanced to enable the exploration of data from social media, IoT devices, and other sources, which created a need for advanced analytics, and businesses moved beyond descriptive analytics to predict future outcomes) and prescriptive (recommending actions) analytics.

In recent years (2020s and beyond), AI-powered real-time data reporting and monitoring technologies, such as NLP, computer vision, IoT, and DL, enable the use of databases like Refinitiv, MSCI, and Bloomberg to generate financial and ESG reports. NLP tools analyze stakeholder sentiment from news, investor communications, and social media to improve corporate disclosures. The integration of AI and IoT enables real-time tracking of emissions, energy use, and waste management, as well as the identification of anomalies in financial disclosures to detect potential fraud and material misstatements. Generative AI is expected to play an important role in transforming how companies communicate sustainability initiatives to stakeholders. AI-powered tools, including Generative AI (e.g., ChatGPT), advanced neural networks, Agentic AI, and Gemini AI Enterprise, can tailor financial and sustainability reports for stakeholders, such as shareholders, creditors, regulators, employees, suppliers, and consumers.

To understand AI's potential, it is beneficial to break it down into its key subfields, as depicted in Figure 1.2. ML is a subset of AI that enables systems to automatically learn and improve from experience without explicit programming. The fundamental objective of ML is to develop algorithms that can analyze data, identify patterns, and generate predictions or decisions based on input data. This involves training a model on a dataset, from which it derives rules or features that enable it to make predictions on unseen data. AI encompasses a broad spectrum of techniques designed to emulate human cognitive functions. ML is centered on the creation and utilization of algorithms that can learn from and generate predictions based on data patterns. Statistical modeling often involves the application of mathematical frameworks to explain relationships within datasets and predict future outcomes. Although ML techniques can arise from statistical methods, they fundamentally differ from traditional statistical modeling in that ML prioritizes predictive accuracy and the ability to learn from vast amounts of data, often involving complex, nonlinear relationships that traditional statistical models can struggle to handle effectively.

Figure 1.2 illustrates that AI has evolved through several distinct yet interrelated phases, each expanding the scope, capability, and impact of intelligent systems in business and society. Early AI systems were largely rule-based and symbolic, relying on programmed logic, expert systems, and heuristics to emulate human reasoning in narrowly defined domains. While effective for structured problems, these systems lacked adaptability and struggled with uncertainty, scale, and unstructured data. This limitation led to the rise of ML, shifting AI from rule-driven logic to data-driven learning. ML algorithms enabled systems to identify patterns, make predictions, and improve performance over time by learning from historical data rather than relying solely on predefined rules. Within ML, neural networks represent a breakthrough by mimicking the interconnected structure of the human brain through layers of artificial neurons. Early neural networks showed

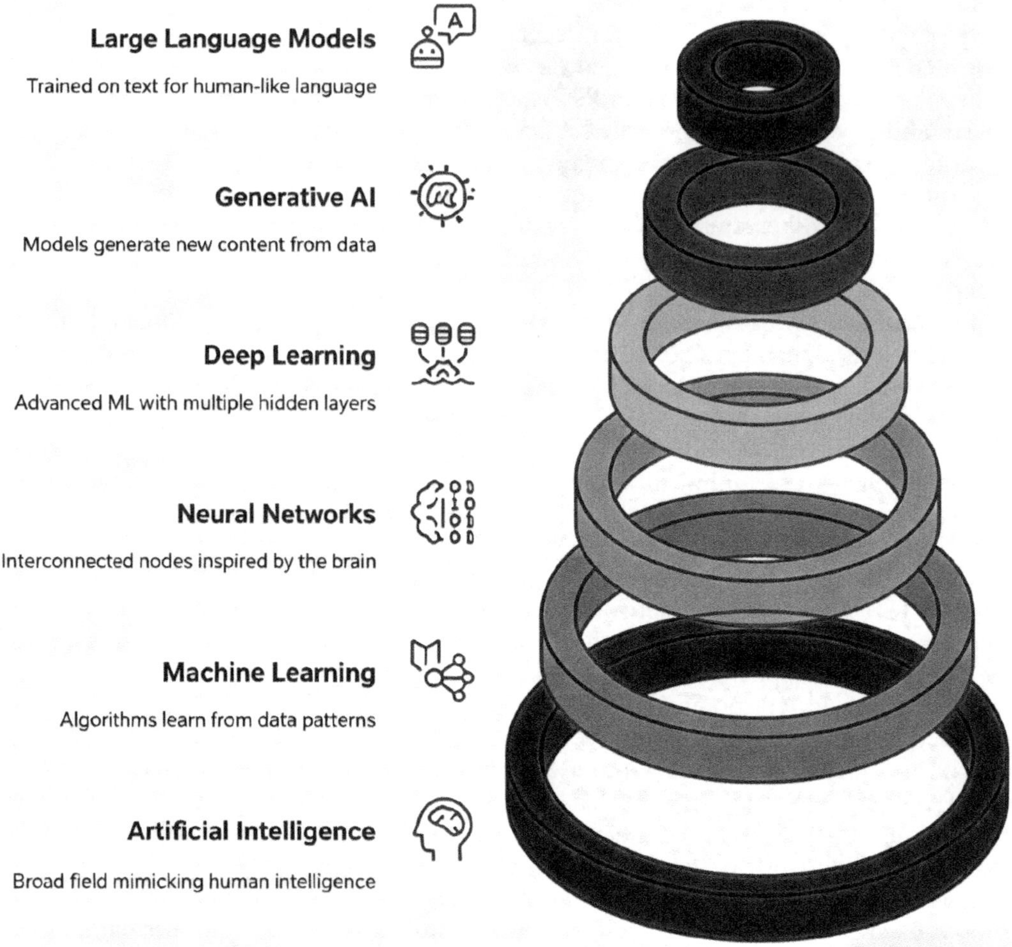

Figure 1.2 Artificial Intelligence and Key Subfields.

promise but were constrained by limited computational power, insufficient data, and training challenges. These barriers were overcome with the emergence of DL, which introduced multi-layer neural architectures capable of learning complex, hierarchical representations from large datasets. Advances in Graphics Processing Units (GPUs), cloud computing, and big data fueled DL's success in areas such as image recognition, speech processing, natural language understanding, and recommendation systems, marking a turning point where AI performance began to rival or exceed human capabilities in specific tasks.

Building on DL, generative AI introduced a new paradigm in which systems not only analyze and predict but also create content, including text, images, code, audio, and video. Generative models learn the underlying structure of data distributions and produce outputs that are coherent, contextually relevant, and increasingly human-like. This shift transformed AI from a primarily analytical tool into creative and interactive technology, enabling applications such as content generation, design, simulation, and decision support. At the core of this transformation are large language models (LLMs), which leverage transformer architectures and vast textual data to understand, generate, and reason with natural language. LLMs have significantly enhanced human–AI interaction through conversational interfaces, contextual understanding, and domain-specific reasoning across professional and organizational settings.

The evolution continues with Agentic AI, which extends beyond content generation to autonomous, goal-oriented behavior. These systems can plan, reason, make decisions, invoke tools, coordinate workflows, and adapt dynamically based on feedback and changing environments. Rather than responding passively to prompts, they actively pursue objectives, manage multi-step tasks, and collaborate with humans and other systems. This marks a shift from AI as an assistant to an active participant in organizational processes, supporting complex decision-making, operations, and strategy execution. At the enterprise level, these advancements converge in platforms such as Gemini AI Enterprise, integrating generative and agentic AI into a secure, scalable, and governed environment. It combines multimodal capabilities across text, code, images, and data with enterprise-grade security, compliance, and integration across cloud infrastructure, analytics platforms, and productivity tools, enabling organizations to embed AI into core workflows while maintaining oversight, transparency, and responsible governance.

1.3 Fundamentals of Artificial Intelligence

AI is the simulation of HI in machines programmed to think and learn like humans with more consistency and objectivity. However, there are some differences and similarities between HI and AI with cognitive qualities that capitalize on the distinct advantages of both HI and AI. There are key notions of the constraints of HI: the possibility of multiple forms of general intelligence beyond human-like AI, and the potential of narrow AI applications that should be considered in evaluating the importance of "Intelligence Awareness" to optimize human–AI collaboration, advocating for educational frameworks to help humans understand AI's unique strengths and limitations.[8] There is a need to move beyond human-like AI and focus on leveraging narrow AI to complement human limitations. It helps to better understand the real meaning of AI by focusing on training tools, methods, and content that are flexible and adaptive enough to be able to keep up with the rapid changes in the field of AI and with the wide variety of target groups and learning goals.[9] AI-powered tools and techniques are transforming businesses and industries, particularly the field of BA, to analyze and organize data to gain better insights, identify new opportunities for the organization, and, ultimately, improve decision-making. Advanced AI-powered tools and techniques enable organizations to expand the boundaries of traditional data analysis and provide a better understanding of the available information, streamline the entire business processes, improve decision-making, and develop more efficient strategies to gain a competitive edge in the market.

AI, ML, and DL are typically used interchangeably in literature. However, there are significant differences among them, such as static AI systems using fixed rules or formulas, whereas adaptive AI systems incorporate learning capabilities, such as ML models. AI refers to any technique that enables machines to mimic HI, encompassing reasoning, learning, and improving over time. ML is a subset of AI, which reflects the idea that systems can learn from data, identify patterns, and make decisions with minimal human intervention through algorithms that enable computers to learn from and make predictions or decisions based on data. DL is a subset of ML that uses neural networks to simulate the behavior of the human brain by allowing the machine to learn from large amounts of data in advancing fields like NLP, computer vision, and audio recognition.

1.3.1 Components of AI

AI is built upon several key components that work together to enable machines to perform tasks that typically require HI in a consistent and objective manner. These components include algorithms, data, and computing power, as AI systems for prediction, decision support, and other applications are developed by applying algorithms to data using computational resources. AI consists of a diverse set of technologies and methodologies that enable intelligent behavior in machines. One important component is ML algorithms, which allow systems to learn from data and improve over time without explicit programming. NLP enables machines to understand, interpret, and generate human language, supporting applications such as chatbots and virtual assistants. Computer vision allows AI to interpret and analyze visual information, enabling image recognition, facial detection, and autonomous navigation. Expert systems use rule-based logic to simulate decision-making in specialized domains, while robotics integrates AI with physical machines to perform complex real-world tasks. Data, knowledge representation, and reasoning allow AI systems to store and manipulate information for informed decision-making, while planning and optimization enable efficient problem-solving. Learning mechanisms, including supervised, unsupervised, and reinforcement learning, play a crucial role in adapting AI to different tasks. Together, these components form the foundation of intelligent systems, enabling AI to function across a wide range of applications and industries.

1.3.1.1 Algorithms

AI algorithms are the foundational mechanisms that enable machines to mimic HI, learn from data, and make decisions or predictions. These algorithms range from simple rule-based systems to complex models like deep neural networks, which are inspired by the structure and function of the human brain. AI algorithms process large volumes of data to identify patterns, extract insights, and improve over time through techniques such as ML, NLP, and reinforcement learning. For example, supervised learning algorithms learn from labeled datasets to make accurate predictions, whereas unsupervised learning uncovers hidden structures in data without explicit labels. Reinforcement learning allows AI systems to learn optimal behaviors through trial-and-error interactions with their environment, often achieving remarkable performance in dynamic settings like robotics or game playing. Modern AI applications such as facial recognition, autonomous vehicles, medical diagnostics, fraud detection, and personalized recommendations rely heavily on these algorithms to operate effectively and efficiently. With the integration of AI into various tasks in many industries, algorithmic fairness, transparency, and interpretability have become critical considerations, prompting ongoing research into ethical AI design and the prevention of bias. As computational power and data availability continue to grow, AI algorithms are expected to become even more powerful, adaptive, and integral to decision-making processes.

Algorithms are step-by-step procedures or formulas for solving problems by processing data, making decisions, and learning from patterns.[10] There are several types of algorithms, including (1) supervised learning algorithms that learn from labeled data and make predictions based on that data (e.g., linear regression, decision trees, and support vector machines); (2) unsupervised learning algorithms that find hidden patterns or intrinsic structures in input data that are not labeled (e.g., k-means clustering, principal component analysis, PCA); and (3) reinforcement learning algorithms, which learn by interacting with an environment and receiving rewards or penalties that are presented in next few chapters.[11]

Models are an integral component of AI systems, as a component of algorithms, serving as mathematical and computational structures that learn from data and make decisions or predictions. Indeed, AI models represent the relationship between inputs and outputs by allowing the system to generalize from past experiences to new, unseen data. Models can take various forms, ranging from simple linear regression models to highly complex deep neural networks with millions of parameters. During the training process, these models adjust their internal parameters based on patterns found in the training data, optimizing their performance according to a specific objective intended for AI systems, such as minimizing prediction error or maximizing accuracy. Types of AI models are commonly used depending on the task and its intended purpose. For example, classification models are used for sorting data into categories, regression models are designed to predict numerical values, and generative models are utilized to create new content. The choice of model significantly affects the system's performance, interpretability, and scalability. Furthermore, as AI technologies become more sophisticated, models are increasingly being designed to incorporate ethical considerations, handle uncertainty, and provide explanations for their decisions. Overall, models are the engine that drives the learning and decision-making capabilities of AI systems, enabling them to perform tasks ranging from language translation to medical diagnosis.

Models that are mathematical representations of real-world processes created by training algorithms on data to make predictions, recognize patterns, and make decisions based on new input data. There are several types of AI models including (1) ML models of linear regression, logistic regression, decision trees, random forests, and support vector machines used for tasks like classification, regression, and clustering; (2) DL models that are neural networks with multiple layers capable of learning complex patterns in data (e.g., convolutional neural networks (CNNs) for image processing, recurrent neural networks (RNNs) for sequential data, and transformers for NLP; and (3) ensemble models that combine multiple models to improve performance and robustness (e.g., bagging, boosting, and stacking create ensemble models). These models should be continuously trained and evaluated using algorithms to minimize prediction errors and assess the model's performance using accuracy, precision, recall, and F1 score metrics. These models should also be continuously developed and maintained by monitoring the model's performance over time, retraining it with new data as needed, and updating it to improve accuracy and adapt to changing conditions.

1.3.1.2 Data

Data plays a vital role in AI systems by serving as the foundation upon which intelligent behavior is built. AI algorithms rely heavily on data to learn patterns, make predictions, and improve performance over time. In ML, for instance, data is used to train models so they can recognize trends, classify information, or forecast outcomes based on historical inputs. The quality, quantity, reliability, and diversity of data directly impact the accuracy and robustness of AI outputs. High-quality, well-labeled, and representative datasets lead to more effective and unbiased AI models. Data fuels various AI applications such as speech recognition, image analysis, fraud detection, and recommendation systems, allowing them to adapt to user behavior and environmental changes. Furthermore, real-time data enables AI to operate dynamically in applications like autonomous vehicles and financial trading. However, the use of data also raises important concerns about privacy, security, and ethical usage, making responsible data governance a critical component of AI development. Thus, without data, AI systems would lack the context and information needed to function intelligently or evolve over time.

Data is the foundation of AI as AI systems require large amounts of data to learn and make accurate predictions, and their performance is substantially affected by the quality and quantity of data. There are several types of data including (1) structured data such as databases and spreadsheets that are organized in a tabular format (e.g., customer information, transaction records, sensor readings; (2) unstructured data that is not organized in a predefined manner, such as text, images, audio, and video (e.g., social media posts, emails, and medical images); and (3) data processing that processes data before it is fed into AI models, including cleaning, normalizing, and transforming data to ensure it is in the right format and quality for analysis. Data processing in AI involves collecting, cleaning, and structuring data to make it suitable for analysis, including handling missing values, removing outliers, and converting data into a format that the algorithms can perform efficiently.

1.3.1.3 Computing Power

Computing power is a pivotal component of AI systems, providing the infrastructure needed to process large volumes of data and execute complex algorithms at high speeds. Advanced AI techniques, including deep learning, NLP, and computer vision, require substantial computational resources to train and deploy models effectively. High-performance hardware such as GPUs, TPUs (Tensor Processing Units), and distributed computing clusters enable parallel processing and significantly accelerate tasks that would otherwise be time-consuming or infeasible. Cloud computing platforms have become integral, offering scalable and cost-effective access to powerful computing environments for AI development. Sufficient computing power supports the training of large-scale models, such as those used in image recognition and generative AI, improving accuracy and responsiveness. Real-time AI applications, including self-driving cars, financial trading systems, and medical diagnostics, depend on robust computing capabilities to deliver fast and reliable decisions. As AI evolves, the demand for greater computational efficiency and energy-conscious processing has driven innovations in hardware design and optimized algorithms, ensuring computing power remains central to the scalability of AI technologies. Overall, adequate computing power is essential for training and deploying AI models to process large datasets and perform complex calculations. Key computing resources include (1) Central Processing Units (CPUs) for general computing tasks; (2) GPUs, designed for parallel processing to handle intensive neural network computations; and (3) TPUs, specialized processors developed by Google for optimized ML training and inference.

1.3.2 Types of AI Systems

AI systems can be classified as narrow, general, super, and human AI categories, which provides a framework for understanding their capabilities and potential future development. (AI) across its various forms, including Artificial Narrow Intelligence (ANI), Artificial General Intelligence (AGI), Artificial Superintelligence (ASI), and Human-Level Intelligence (HLI).[12] These AI classifications have their own attributes and challenges in terms of security, fairness, energy consumption, and controllability, with definitions, relationships, and evolution as described in the following subsections. AI systems can be categorized into different types based on their capabilities and functionalities, which help in understanding their complexity and range of applications.

1.3.2.1 Artificial Narrow Intelligence (ANI)

ANI, also known as weak AI, is designed and trained to perform a specific task, such as facial recognition, language translation, or spam filtering. These systems operate under a limited set of constraints and are the most common type of AI in use today, including applications like Siri, Alexa, and recommendation engines. Narrow AI, also known as ANI, refers to AI systems that are designed and trained to perform a specific task or a limited range of functions and a limited set of tasks with high efficiency and accuracy. It is intended for a specific task and usually operates within a limited predefined range or set of contexts, such as speech recognition systems (e.g., Siri or Alexa, recommendation systems on Netflix or Amazon, and facial recognition technologies. Unlike general intelligence, ANI does not possess consciousness, self-awareness, or genuine understanding and operates within a predefined set of parameters and excels at executing focused tasks such as facial recognition, language translation, recommendation systems, or autonomous driving. These AI systems are usually built using ML algorithms and large datasets, enabling them to learn patterns and improve performance over time. However, ANI lacks the flexibility to adapt beyond its programmed purpose, making it fundamentally different from AGI, which aspires to replicate human cognitive abilities across a broad range of activities. Despite its limitations, ANI has become deeply integrated into everyday life and business processes, powering many of the AI-driven technologies in use today.

Unlike AGI, which aims to replicate the broad cognitive abilities of humans, ANI operates within a constrained domain and cannot function beyond its programmed purpose. Examples of ANI include voice assistants like Siri and Alexa, recommendation algorithms on platforms like Netflix and Amazon, spam filters in email systems, facial recognition software, and autonomous navigation systems in self-driving cars. These systems rely on ML and data-driven models to perform their tasks, often outperforming humans in speed and precision within that narrow scope. However, they lack general reasoning abilities, self-awareness, or adaptability outside their specialized functions. Despite these limitations, ANI has become deeply integrated into daily life and industry, driving advancements in automation, healthcare, finance, customer service, and more. It represents the current stage of AI development and serves as the foundation for ongoing research into more advanced forms of intelligence.

1.3.2.2 Artificial General Intelligence (AGI)

AGI refers to a form of AI that can understand, learn, and apply knowledge across a wide range of tasks at a level equal to or exceeding that of humans. Unlike narrow AI, which is designed for specific applications such as image recognition or language translation, AGI would possess the cognitive flexibility to perform any intellectual task a human can, including reasoning, problem-solving, learning from experience, understanding abstract concepts, and adapting to new situations without task-specific programming. AGI would be capable of transferring knowledge across domains, exhibiting common sense, and making decisions in complex, unfamiliar environments. While its development represents a major milestone in AI research, it also raises significant technical, ethical, and societal challenges. Achieving AGI will require breakthroughs in areas such as ML, neural networks, memory architecture, and potentially consciousness modeling. At present, AGI remains a theoretical concept. Its potential benefits range from accelerating scientific discovery to addressing global challenges, but its risks, if not developed and governed responsibly, must also be carefully considered. As such, general AI (or strong AI) continues to represent the long-term goal of AI research and development.

1.3.2.3 Artificial Superintelligence (ASI)

ASI refers to a hypothetical form of AI that surpasses HI in all aspects, including creativity, problem-solving, decision-making, emotional intelligence, and even social and moral reasoning. It is currently representing a hypothetical stage of AI development in which machines surpass HI across all aspects, including intellectual, emotional, creative, and even social capabilities. Unlike AGI, which matches human cognitive abilities, ASI would be capable of outperforming the best human minds in every field, from scientific discovery and strategic thinking to artistic expression and interpersonal communication. The concept of ASI is often associated with advanced self-learning systems that can continually improve themselves without human intervention, leading to an exponential increase in intelligence.

1.3.2.4 Human-Level Intelligence (HLI)

HLI refers to an advanced form of AI that can match the cognitive abilities of a typical human being, with capabilities such as reasoning, learning, understanding language, perception, problem-solving, and even emotional awareness, where machines possess cognitive abilities comparable to those of a typical human being. This includes the capacity to learn from experience, understand complex concepts, reason logically, communicate effectively, perceive the environment, and adapt to new situations across a wide range of domains. HLI is often considered synonymous with AGI, as both involve a level of flexibility and general-purpose understanding that allows machines to perform intellectual tasks with the same competence as humans. Achieving HLI would mark a transformative milestone in AI, enabling machines to autonomously carry out diverse activities such as scientific research, creative writing, strategic planning, and emotional interaction. However, replicating HI also requires addressing challenges such as consciousness, self-awareness, moral reasoning, and emotional understanding, including areas where current AI systems still fall short. The development of HLI has profound implications for society, economy, ethics, and human identity, and it necessitates careful consideration of safety, transparency, and alignment with human values to ensure it benefits humanity. HLI is intended to replicate the breadth and depth of human intellectual performance across diverse domains. Achieving HLI would allow machines to perform any intellectual task that a human can do more effectively, efficiently, and timely, potentially working alongside or even replacing humans in complex decision-making roles. While current AI systems have made impressive strides in specialized tasks, they still lack the general adaptability and contextual understanding that characterize HI. The pursuit of HLI continues to drive AI research and practice, with significant focus on interdisciplinary approaches that combine cognitive science, neuroscience, ML, and ethics to create truly human-like artificial agents.

1.4 AI-Powered Business Analytics Transformation

AI has revolutionized the field of BA by enabling organizations to harness vast amounts of data in real-time, generate deeper insights, and make faster, more accurate decisions. The transformation from traditional analytics to AI-powered analytics represents a fundamental shift from descriptive and diagnostic approaches to predictive and prescriptive models that can anticipate outcomes and recommend optimal actions. The shift from traditional BA to AI-driven decision intelligence marks a fundamental evolution in enterprise decision-making by enabling organizations not only to interpret data but also to act intelligently and autonomously, turning uncertainty into strategic advantage. As AI technologies mature, decision intelligence will become a cornerstone of digital transformation, driving smarter, faster, and more responsible business actions. This transformation is not just technological but also strategic, reshaping how businesses perform, compete, operate, and innovate. AI-powered BA transformation is redefining competitive advantage in the digital economy. By leveraging the power of AI, businesses can unlock new levels of agility, efficiency, and innovation. The future of analytics is not just about understanding what has happened but predicting what will happen and prescribing what to do next.

1.4.1 Role of AI in Business Analytics

The exponential growth of big data in terms of data volumes, complexity, and velocity has exposed the limitations of legacy analytics systems. Organizations now require advanced AI tools that can process unstructured data, detect subtle patterns, and adapt to dynamic environments. AI, particularly through ML, NLP, and deep learning, enables a new generation of BA that goes beyond human capabilities.

1.4.2 The Emergence of AI-Driven Decision Intelligence

In the past decade, there has been a rapid transition from traditional BA to the use of AI in BA and now to AI-driven decision intelligence. Decision intelligence represents a move forward by integrating AI, ML, optimization algorithms, and human expertise into decision-making processes. It turns data into intelligent actions by creating systems that can learn from data, understand context, simulate outcomes, and make or recommend decisions with minimal human intervention. The key components of decision intelligence are (1) data integration of aggregating structured, semi-structured, and unstructured data from various internal and external sources; (2) the use of ML models to predict outcomes, detect anomalies, and uncover hidden patterns; (3) application of decision models of applying rules, simulations, and reinforcement learning to evaluate and choose among alternatives; and (4) human engagement of involving human in the decision-making process and incorporating human expertise, judgment, and ethical considerations into AI systems.

Table 1.1 presents the main differences between traditional BA and AI-driven analytics and decision intelligence. The differences are in their focus, data type used, speed, automation, and intelligence. Overall, AI-driven analytics and decision intelligence are expected to produce faster and more accurate decisions, enhanced customer and operational insights, increased agility and resilience, and improved return on investment (ROI) on data and technology investments.

1.5 Artificial Intelligence (AI) and Business Analytics (BA) Integration

The integration of AI and BA is revolutionizing how organizations make strategic decisions, optimize operations, achieve financial, economic, and nonfinancial ESG performance, and drive innovation and growth. AI enhances BA by enabling more advanced data processing capabilities, such as ML, NLP, and predictive modeling, which allow organizations to extract deeper insights from vast and complex data sets. This synergy empowers businesses to transition from traditional descriptive analytics to more sophisticated diagnostic, predictive, and prescriptive analytics that offers an understanding of past

Table 1.1 Contrasting Traditional Business Analytics and AI-Driven Analytics

Dimension	*Traditional Analytics*	*AI-Driven Decision Intelligence*
Primary focus	What happened and why	What will happen and what to do
Data type	Structured data	Structured and unstructured data (e.g., text, images, audio)
Analytical methods	Descriptive and diagnostic	Predictive and prescriptive
Speed and frequency	Periodic, batch-based analysis	Real-time, continuous, and adaptive learning
Scalability	Limited to internal data and fixed models	Highly scalable across diverse sources, departments, and use cases
Automation	Minimal; relies heavily on human intervention	High; includes automated and autonomous decision cycles
Human role	Central to insight generation and decision-making	Primarily oversight and strategic validation of AI-driven insights
Technology foundation	Data warehouses, relational databases, rule-based systems	AI/ML algorithms, cloud infrastructure, big data platforms
Intelligence type	Rule-based, logic-driven, static	Learning-based, context-aware, dynamic

performance and actionable recommendations for future outcomes. AI-driven analytics tools can detect patterns and anomalies in real time, enabling proactive decision-making and faster response to market changes, customer behavior, and operational inefficiencies. For example, AI algorithms can forecast demand, personalize marketing strategies, identify supply chain bottlenecks, and even anticipate financial risks with greater accuracy. Furthermore, by automating repetitive analytical tasks, AI frees human analysts from focusing on strategic thinking and problem-solving. However, successful integration requires coordination of technology utilization, promotion of a data-driven culture to ensure data quality and governance, management of ethical and privacy concerns, and investment in employee training and organizational readiness. As businesses continue to embrace digital transformation, the fusion of AI and BA stands as a cornerstone of sustainable competitive advantage in the data-driven economy.

The integration between AI and BA highlights the growing collaboration between humans and machines, alongside the integration of technology with BA. The collaboration between AI and BA is transforming the way organizations interpret data, evaluate performance, and make strategic decisions. By combining the predictive power of AI with the insights generated through BA, organizations can uncover deeper patterns, forecast future trends, and automate complex decision-making processes. AI enhances traditional DA by enabling real-time analysis, NLP, and advanced ML algorithms that continuously improve over time. This integration enables businesses to move beyond descriptive analytics toward predictive and prescriptive insights, offering more proactive and personalized solutions. All business functions, from optimizing marketing campaigns to streamlining operations, detecting fraud, or improving customer experience, can benefit from this integration and the synergy between AI and BA by empowering businesses to reach new levels of efficiency, agility, and innovation across industries. The integration of AI and BA is evolving rapidly, driven by advances in technology, data availability, and changing business demands.

The rapid adoption of AI and BA across industries has created a demand for skilled professionals who can merge technical expertise with business acumen. With the rapid evolution of BA and AI, there is a demand for a comprehensive resource that covers these fields in an accessible, unified approach. BA can be integrated with AI to leverage data-driven insights and AI technologies to enhance strategic decision-making, optimize operations, and foster innovation in a dynamic global business environment by harnessing data for strategic advantage. This section attempts to bridge the gap between theoretical concepts and practical applications of AI in BA by (1) introducing the foundational principles of BA and AI; (2) demonstrating the integration of advanced AI techniques into BA processes; (3) presenting the demands for effective interactions of AI and HI; (4) exploring the ethical, legal, and social implications of using AI in business contexts; and (5) providing case studies and real-world applications from diverse industries to highlight best practices. Emerging trends in AI and BA integration could occur in embedding AI into Customer Relationship Management (CRM), Enterprise Resource Planning (ERP), and BI tools to improve usability and real-time insights across departments, using Responsible and Explainable AI (XAI) to increase emphasis on transparency, bias mitigation, fairness, and explainability, moving from centralized data lakes to distributed, domain-oriented data platforms, combining RPA with AI to create Intelligent Automation (IA), and customizing AI solutions tailored for finance, healthcare, retail, and manufacturing.

1.6 Interaction between AI and HI in Promoting Business Analytics

The interaction between AI and HI in promoting BA creates a powerful synergy that enhances performance assessment, decision-making, and strategic planning. While AI excels at processing large volumes of data, identifying hidden patterns, and delivering rapid, data-driven predictions, HI brings professional judgment, contextual understanding, and ethical considerations to ensure proper decision-making processes. Together, AI and HI enable organizations to make more nuanced and effective business decisions by combining machine efficiency with human creativity, judgment, and critical thinking. This collaborative approach allows businesses to automate routine analytics tasks as well as interpret complex insights in a way that aligns with organizational goals and values. As AI systems become more sophisticated, the human role shifts toward higher-level interpretation, oversight, and strategic application by fostering a data-informed culture that supports innovation, resilience, and sustainable growth. This interaction combines two business processes of doing and reviewing to ensure proper decision-making. The integration of AI capabilities with human skills creates a collaborative intelligence ecosystem where AI handles complexity and scale, and HI provides meaning, empathy, and ethics. Table 1.2 presents AI and HI and their combined impact.

The interaction between AI and HI can promote BA in many ways through:

- **Business Analysis and Automation**: AI-powered tools process vast amounts of data, recognizing patterns, automating repetitive tasks, and delivering predictive and prescriptive analytics at a scale and speed beyond human capacity.
- **Strategic Application**: HI ensures that AI-driven strategies are applied creatively and ethically in dynamic environments, leveraging strategic thinking to maximize AI's potential.
- **Hybrid Approach**: A combined approach allows AI to handle computational complexity while humans focus on innovation, decision-making, judgment considerations, and adapting to complex scenarios.
- **Data-Driven Decision Support**: AI generates insights, forecasts, and recommendations, while HI evaluates these outputs in context, ensuring decisions align with business goals. For example, AI may predict customer preferences, while human managers design personalized campaigns based on these predictions.

Table 1.2 Artificial Intelligence (AI) and Human Intelligence (HI) and Their Combined Impact

AI Role	*Human Intelligence Role*	*Combined Impact*
Pattern detection	Contextual understanding	Insightful decisions
Predictive analytics	Judgment & intuition	Smarter forecasting
Automated reporting	Narrative creation	Persuasive communication
Model output	Ethical filtering & strategic reasoning	Responsible business actions
Continuous learning	Continuous feedback	Adaptive, evolving analytics strategies
Automates repetitive tasks	Handles complex, nuanced, or interpersonal challenges	Productivity increases
Operates 24/7	Brings creativity, empathy, and moral judgment	Continuous service that remains human-centered
Integrates knowledge from multiple sources	Prioritizes relevant knowledge	Better synthesis of information for decision-making
Provides initial analysis	Detects ethical issues and unintended consequences	Reduces bias while preserving moral integrity

- **Real-Time Business Analysis and Intervention**: AI-powered platforms facilitate real-time data collection and analysis, enabling businesses to respond promptly to market changes. HI interprets anomalies flagged by AI and addresses risks or opportunities requiring strategic action, such as optimizing supply chain responses to disruptions.
- **Nuanced Interpretation**: AI tools like NLP analyze unstructured data, such as customer feedback or ESG reports. HI adds depth by interpreting language nuances, context, and sentiment, improving insights into investor needs, customer behavior, market trends, and stakeholder expectations.
- **Ethical Oversight**: HI ensures the ethical, transparent, and unbiased application of AI tools, aligning their use with regulatory frameworks and organizational values.
- **Collaborative Decision-Making**: AI-powered platforms, such as dashboards, virtual assistants, and decision-support systems, serve as "co-pilots" that enhance human decision-making, amplifying human efforts rather than replacing them.
- **Learning and Supervision**: AI systems improve over time through data-driven learning, while HI supervises this evolution to ensure alignment with business strategies and objectives.
- **Bridging Data and Practicality**: HI bridges the gap between AI-generated data and real-world applicability. For instance, AI might analyze trends and predict outcomes, but human experts provide domain-specific insights to refine strategies in finance, marketing, and sustainability.
- **Fraud Detection and Beyond**: Practical examples include AI identifying suspicious transactions while human analysts confirm fraud, AI suggesting upselling opportunities while sales teams tailor approaches, and AI monitoring ESG metrics while professionals strategize improvements.

1.7 The Role of AI and BA in Transforming Industries

The integration of AI and BA is playing a transformative role across industries by enabling smarter, faster, and more data-driven decision-making. AI enhances the capabilities of BA by automating data processing, uncovering complex patterns, and providing predictive and prescriptive insights that were previously unattainable through traditional methods. Together, AI and BA empower organizations to optimize operations, personalize customer experiences, manage risks, and drive innovation. In sectors such as healthcare, finance, manufacturing, and retail, this synergy is revolutionizing how businesses forecast trends, allocate resources, and respond to dynamic market conditions. By combining machine efficiency with human judgment, AI and BA are reshaping business models and creating a competitive edge in the era of digital transformation. The role of AI and BA in transforming industries is vital in reshaping how organizations operate, compete, and deliver shared value for all their stakeholders, from shareholders to employees, customers, suppliers, communities, and the environment. AI and BA empower industries of all sizes and types to move from reactive to proactive strategies by enabling real-time data processing, predictive modeling, and automated decision-making. For example, in sectors such as healthcare, finance, manufacturing, retail, and logistics, combined AI and BA technologies are streamlining operations, enhancing customer experiences, reducing costs, and uncovering new market opportunities. AI-driven analytics can forecast consumer demand, detect fraud, optimize supply chains, and personalize marketing at scale. By harnessing the power of AI and BA technologies, businesses gain deeper insights into performance metrics and customer behavior, leading to smarter, faster, and more agile responses to market dynamics. This transformation is not only improving efficiency but also driving innovation and sustainable growth across industries worldwide.

The role of AI and BA is transforming industries worldwide by driving significant technological advances across various sectors and enabling organizations to optimize operations, enhance customer experiences, make data-driven decisions, and support innovation and growth. Integration of AI and BA are transforming industries in many ways including (1) improving decision-making as the integration of AI and BA enables organizations to process vast amounts of data to uncover patterns, trends, and insights that were previously inaccessible, leverage ML algorithms to predict future outcomes, such as customer behavior, market trends, and potential risks, and provide real-time analytics, allowing businesses to respond quickly to changing conditions; (2) enhancing operational efficiency as AI automates repetitive and time-consuming tasks, reducing human error and freeing up employees to focus on higher-value activities, and advanced BA can identify inefficiencies in workflows, supply chains, and production processes, enabling businesses to streamline operations, and optimize resource allocation, ensuring that assets, personnel, and budgets are used effectively; (3) meeting customer expectations by analyzing customer data to deliver personalized recommendations, marketing messages, and product offerings, providing 24/7 customer support, improving response times and satisfaction, and analyzing customer feedback and social media interactions to understand customer sentiment and improve services; (4) supporting innovation and product development by identifying emerging trends and unmet customer needs, guiding the development of new products and services, enabling simulations and data analysis speed up research and development processes in industries like pharmaceuticals, manufacturing, and technology and creating highly customized products and services tailored to individual customer preferences; (5) enabling risk assessment and management to mitigate risks, such as credit risk, operational risk, and market volatility; (6) detecting anomalies and patterns indicative of fraudulent and responding to threats such as cybersecurity in real time; (7) supporting supply chain and logistics transformation by improving demand forecasting accuracy, reducing overstocking and stockouts, optimizing inventory levels, ensuring the right products are available at the right time, optimizing delivery routes, reducing costs and improving efficiency in logistics; and (8) achieving sustainability and environmental impact by optimizing energy consumption, reducing costs and environmental impact, and identifying areas where waste can be minimized in manufacturing and supply chains. Overall, AI and BA tools and techniques enable businesses to operate more efficiently, innovate faster, and deliver superior customer experiences, and these technologies are evolving, reshaping industries, and creating new opportunities for growth, innovation, and competitiveness.

1.8 Summary

AI is no longer confined to research labs or science fiction; it is driving real-world outcomes in industries as diverse as finance, healthcare, retail, logistics, and energy. To fully appreciate its impact, this chapter introduces AI foundations by addressing key questions: What is AI? How did it evolve? And why is it central to the future of business? It explores the fundamental concepts underpinning AI and BA, setting the stage for deeper technical and strategic discussions in later chapters.

This chapter provides a foundational overview of BA and AI, explaining how data-driven technologies are reshaping modern business environments. It defines key terms and concepts; distinguishes between descriptive, predictive, and prescriptive analytics; and explains how these methods support decision-making across business functions. The chapter traces the evolution of BA from traditional statistical techniques to AI-driven tools, highlighting the growing role of big data, ML, and NLP. It also examines how organizations leverage AI to automate processes, enhance customer experiences, optimize operations, and gain strategic insights.

The chapter further introduces key components of the analytics process, including data collection, preprocessing, model building, and interpretation, while outlining types of AI (narrow AI, general AI, and superintelligence) and noting the dominance of narrow AI in current business applications. Emphasis is placed on real-world applications across sectors such as finance, marketing, supply chain management, and human resources. Case examples illustrate the impact of integrating AI with BA, from fraud detection to customer segmentation and demand forecasting. The chapter concludes by addressing ethical considerations, data privacy concerns, and the importance of responsible AI use, setting the stage for more advanced discussions on AI techniques, implementation strategies, and ethical implications.

Notes

1 Davenport, T. H. (2006). Competing on analytics. *Harvard Business Review*, 84(1), 98–107.
2 Hillier, F. S., & Lieberman, G. J. (2021). *Introduction to Operations Research* (11th ed.). McGraw-Hill.
3 Bertsimas, D., & Kallus, N. (2020). From predictive to prescriptive analytics. *Management Science*, 66(3), 1025–1044.
4 Liberatore, M. J., & Luo, W. (2013). The analytics movement: Implications for operations research. *Interfaces*, 43(6), 543–554.
5 Wang, Y., Kung, L., & Byrd, T. A. (2018). Big data analytics: Understanding its capabilities and potential benefits for healthcare organizations. *Technological Forecasting and Social Change*, 126, 3–13.
6 Popovič, A., Hackney, R., Tassabehji, R., & Castelli, M. (2018). The impact of big data analytics on firms' high value business performance. *Information Systems Frontiers*, 20(2), 209–222.
7 Shmueli, G., & Koppius, O. R. (2011). Predictive analytics in information systems research. *MIS Quarterly*, 35(3), 553–572.

8 Korteling, J. H., van de Boer-Visschedijk, G. C., Blankendaal, R. A., Boonekamp, R. C., & Eikelboom, A. R. (2021). Human-versus artificial intelligence. *Frontiers in Artificial Intelligence*, 4, 622364. https://doi.org/10.3389/frai.2021.622364. Available at https://www.frontiersin.org/journals/artificial-intelligence/articles/10.3389/frai.2021.622364/full

9 Korteling, J. H., van de Boer-Visschedijk, G. C., Blankendaal, R. A., Boonekamp, R. C., & Eikelboom, A. R. (2021). Human-versus artificial intelligence. *Frontiers in Artificial Intelligence*, 4, 622364. https://doi.org/10.3389/frai.2021.622364. Available at https://www.frontiersin.org/journals/artificial-intelligence/articles/10.3389/frai.2021.622364/full

10 Oracle License Management Service, R//C. (2024). AI Algorithms Demystified: Applications and Best Practices. August 2, 2024. Available at https://redresscompliance.com/ai-algorithms-demystified-applications-and-best-practices/

11 Oracle License Management Service, R//C. (2024). AI Algorithms Demystified: Applications and Best Practices. August 2, 2024. Available at https://redresscompliance.com/ai-algorithms-demystified-applications-and-best-practices/

12 Saghiri, A. M., Vahidipour, S. M., Jabbarpour, M. R., Sookhak, M., & Forestiero, A. (2022). A survey of artificial intelligence challenges: Analyzing the definitions, relationships, and evolutions. *Applied Sciences*, 12(8), 4054. https://doi.org/10.3390/app12084054. Available at https://www.mdpi.com/2076-3417/12/8/4054

2 Data Science Fundamentals

Learning Objectives

- Understand the definition of data and its attributes
- Learn structured, semi-structured, and unstructured data
- Understand data preparation, management, and utilization
- Conduct data cleaning and preprocessing
- Explore feature engineering and dimensionality reduction techniques
- Learn data identification, collection, cleaning, analysis, visualization, and interpretation to support decision-making

2.1 Introduction

Data is the fuel of AI and BA that can take many forms, including numbers, text, images, audio, video, or sensor readings. Data can become information relevant to decision-making when it is cleaned, processed, organized, and given meaning. This chapter is intended to provide a solid foundation for better understanding and application of the principles of data science (DS) by introducing the core concepts, tools, and techniques that form the backbone of DS, from data collection and cleaning to advanced ML algorithms. It covers the entire DS lifecycle in a clear and accessible manner with popular programming languages like Python and R, as well as essential libraries and frameworks such as Pandas, NumPy, and Scikit-learn. The key topics covered in this chapter include data visualization, statistical analysis, predictive modeling, and the ethical considerations of working with data that enable organizations to address data challenges, make data-informed decisions, and contribute to data-driven innovation. This chapter presents students with the knowledge and tools to turn raw data into information relevant to decision-making and actionable insights, exploring the critical stages of data handling: from acquisition and preparation to ethical governance, empowering students to thrive in an increasingly data-centric world.

2.2 Definition and Types of Data

Conceptually, data refers to raw, unprocessed facts, insights, figures, and statistics that are collected through observation, measurement, events, conditions, or experimentation, which can serve as the foundational input for information and knowledge creation. Data can exist in

DOI: 10.4324/9781003664550-2

various forms, including numbers, text, images, audio, and video, and on its own may lack context or meaning. However, when data is processed, analyzed, and interpreted, it becomes information that supports decision-making. Thus, data is the lifeblood of AI and BA, which empowers organizations to make informed, strategic, and forward-looking decisions by transforming data into information and actionable insights through analytical and AI-driven tools. Data enables AI systems to identify patterns, predict outcomes, and automate decision-making processes, and with continuous data input, AI models can evolve and improve over time through learning. Particularly, AI systems that use ML and deep learning rely heavily on large volumes of high-quality data to train algorithms and improve accuracy. Data is also the core of BA, especially in descriptive analytics, which uses historical data to understand what happened in the past, in predictive analytics, which utilizes statistical models and ML to forecast future events based on historical data, and in prescriptive analytics, which recommends actions by evaluating data-driven scenarios and optimizing outcomes. Data can enhance decision-making by reducing reliance on intuition and providing empirical evidence for strategic choices.

Data can be categorized based on its nature, structure, and usage. Understanding the different types of data is important for data preparation, management, and utilization aspects presented in the previous section and for effective data analysis, decision-making, and technological applications such as AI, ML, and BI. Data can be classified by nature (qualitative vs. quantitative), measurement scale (nominal, ordinal, interval, ratio), source (primary vs. secondary), time dimension (cross-sectional, time series, panel), structure (structured, semi-structured, unstructured), and analytical role in research as summarized in the following section.

2.2.1 Structured Data

Structured data is highly organized data that fits neatly into rows and columns and is typically prepared based on a predefined format. It is usually stored in relational databases (SQL-based systems, customer transaction records, spreadsheets). It adheres to a strict schema, making it easily searchable and analyzable using traditional tools like SQL. Key attributes and characteristics of structured data are as follows: (1) easily searchable with query languages (e.g., SQL); (2) typically stored in relational databases or data warehouses; (3) follows a fixed schema (i.e., data types, field lengths, constraints); and (4) often includes numerical and categorical data. Structured data is easy to search for, analyze, and process using data analytics and ML models by storing tables with rows and columns, and using schemas and relational databases (e.g., MySQL, PostgreSQL). Examples of structured data are (1) financial data such as revenue, expenses, assets, liabilities, stock prices, and transaction records; (2) sustainability and environmental, social, and governance data; (3) customer data, including names, contact information, and purchase history; and (4) inventory records and supply chain transactions. The advantages of structured data are that it is easy to input, search, and analyze; has high data integrity and consistency; and is well-suited for BI and reporting tools. Disadvantages of structured data include limited flexibility (data must fit the schema) and its unsuitability for complex, dynamic, or multimedia data.

2.2.2 Unstructured Data

Unstructured data is not based on a predefined format, which makes it more complex to store, process, and analyze, and usually requires AI-powered tools and techniques (e.g., NLP, computer vision) for analysis. Key attributes and characteristics of unstructured data are as follows: (1) does not follow a consistent structure or schema; (2) often text-heavy or multimedia content; (3) requires advanced tools (e.g., NLP, computer vision, ML) for analysis; and (4) stored in data lakes or non-relational databases. Examples of unstructured data include (1) text data such as emails, reports, ESG disclosures, audit reports; (2) multimedia data of images, videos, audio recordings; (3) legal, regulatory and compliance documents such as contracts, policies, financial reports; (4) sustainability data of global warming, climate change, satellite images, climate models, environmental reports; and (5) social media data of tweets, posts, comments, customer reviews. Unstructured data is typically stored in various formats (PDFs, videos, images, text, cloud storage), requires AI/ML models (NLP, deep learning) for processing, and is harder to analyze using traditional methods. Advantages of unstructured data are that it is rich in information and insights (especially AI and sentiment analysis), and has high potential for innovation in analytics. Disadvantages are that it is difficult to store, process, and analyze; requires significant preprocessing and computing power; and has lower reliability and structure for traditional analytics.

2.2.3 Semi-Structured Data (A Hybrid Type)

Semi-structured data has elements of both structured and unstructured data, which do not strictly follow relational database formats but still have some organizational properties (e.g., tags, hierarchies). Semi-structured data, however, includes some metadata or tags that help in organizing it. Attributes and characteristics of semi-structured data are as follows: (1) does not reside in traditional databases but still contains elements (e.g., tags, delimiters) that distinguish fields and records; (2) can be stored in non-relational (NoSQL) databases; and (3) supports variability in data formats and structures. Examples of semi-structured data are web data, emails, and financial and ESG sustainability reports. The advantages of semi-structured data are that it is more flexible than structured data, easier to adapt to changes in data requirements, and widely used in web and mobile applications, IoT, and application programming interfaces (APIs). The disadvantages are that they require more complex processing than structured data and may not support complex queries without transformation.

Table 2.1 presents attributes of data according to its structure.

Table 2.1 Data Attributes

Feature	*Structured Data*	*Semi-Structured Data*	*Unstructured Data*
Schema	Fixed, predefined schema	Flexible or partial schema	No formal schema
Storage	Relational databases (e.g., MySQL, PostgreSQL)	NoSQL databases, XML/JSON files	Data lakes, distributed file systems (e.g., HDFS, S3)
Format examples	Tables (SQL, Excel), CSV	XML, JSON, YAML, Avro	Text documents, images, audio, video, social media posts
Ease of analysis	High—standardized structure simplifies processing	Moderate—requires custom parsing and mapping	Low—complex formats, requires specialized tools
Processing tools	SQL, BI tools (e.g., Tableau, Power BI)	NoSQL queries, custom parsers, ETL pipelines	NLP, computer vision, speech recognition, AI/ML frameworks
Examples	Sales transactions, employee records, financial data	Web logs, sensor data, API responses	Emails, customer reviews, satellite images, call center recordings
Use cases	Operational reporting, dashboards, compliance	Web analytics, IoT monitoring, metadata management	Sentiment analysis, image classification, voice assistants

2.3 The Role of Data in Modern Business

The role of data in modern business is essential in serving as a foundational asset that drives decision-making, innovation, and competitive advantage (CA). In today's technological advances and global digital economy, businesses collect vast amounts of data from various sources, including customers, operations, markets, and digital interactions, and use advanced BA-assisted AI-powered tools and techniques to extract valuable insights. Data is the lifeblood of business organizations by enabling them to understand customer behavior, personalize services, optimize supply chains, forecast trends, and improve overall efficiency. It also supports evidence-based strategies, enabling leaders to make informed decisions rather than relying solely on intuition. Moreover, data plays a critical role in risk assessment and management, regulatory compliance, oversight functions, and performance measurement. As businesses increasingly embrace digital transformation and globalization, the ability to harness and protect data effectively has become a key determinant of success in the modern landscape. Data plays a vital role in modern business, shaping business strategies, driving innovation, and enhancing decision-making in the emerging digital economy. The ability to collect, analyze, and utilize data effectively has become a key CA for organizations worldwide. In today's data-driven decision-making (DDDM) process, proper collection, management, and analysis of data enables organizations to uncover valuable Insignts into market demand, customer behavior, preferences, and market dynamics, allowing them to personalize products and services, optimize pricing strategies, and enhance customer experience. Data-driven approaches also support predictive analytics, allowing businesses to forecast demand, detect fraud, manage risks, and make informed investments. Furthermore, data empowers process automation and operational improvements through technologies like AI, ML, and robotic process automation. Modern business models, especially in e-commerce, finance, healthcare, and logistics, are increasingly built around data-centric platforms that monetize insights and foster agile, real-time decision-making. The effective use of data demands robust data governance mechanisms, ensuring data quality, privacy, security, and compliance with all applicable laws, rules, and regulations (e.g., GDPR and CCPA). As organizations embrace AI-assisted technologies along with digital transformation, cultivating a data-driven culture becomes vital in decision-making. The emergence of rapid technological change and global competition necessitates the strategic use of data as a fundamental pillar of sustainable business success.

2.3.1 Informed and Data-Driven Decision-Making

Data plays an essential role in decision-making by providing objective, verifiable, and quantifiable insights that enable individuals and businesses to make informed decisions. Decision-makers can analyze historical and real-time data to identify trends, evaluate alternatives, forecast future outcomes, and reduce uncertainty. In today's data-driven environment, leveraging data enhances reliability and accuracy, supports strategic planning, and promotes efficiency across business functions. DDDM enables organizations to respond proactively to challenges, seize new opportunities, and maintain a competitive edge in many sectors, such as finance, marketing, operations, or human resources. Thus, data transforms intuition-based decisions into evidence-based actions. Businesses use data to analyze market demands and trends, customer behavior, and market conditions, and rely on data analytics to make informed decisions, reduce uncertainty, and improve strategic planning. DDDM is a fundamental and strategic approach for organizations to leverage data analysis and interpretation to guide business decisions. The DDDM enables businesses to make data-driven and rational decisions rather than relying solely on intuition, experience, or guesswork. Businesses can uncover patterns, trends, and correlations that may not be immediately obvious by integrating quantitative evidence into the decision-making process, allowing for more accurate forecasting, risk assessment, and resource allocation. DDDM encompasses the use of tools such as BI platforms, statistical models, dashboards, and advanced analytics that are powered by AI and ML to transform raw data into actionable insights. For example, organizations can analyze customer data to personalize marketing campaigns, assess operational data to streamline supply chains, or monitor financial metrics to enhance budgeting and investment strategies. Data-driven decisions can foster innovation by identifying unmet market needs or testing new product features through A/B testing and simulations beyond improving efficiency and profitability. However, successful implementation of DDDM demands a data-literate workforce, a culture that values evidence-based thinking, and strong data governance practices to ensure accuracy, privacy, and ethical use of information beyond the mere use of technology. The effective and proper use of DDDM can reduce uncertainty and bias and enhance agility, accountability, and strategic alignment, allowing organizations to thrive in an increasingly complex and data-saturated business environment.

2.3.2 Enhancing Customer Understanding and Experience

Data plays a pivotal role in enhancing customer understanding and experience by enabling business organizations to gain insight into customer preferences, behaviors, expectations, and needs. Organizations can create personalized experiences, tailor products and services, and deliver targeted marketing messages by analyzing customer data such as purchase history, browsing patterns, feedback, and engagement metrics. This level of personalization fosters stronger customer relationships, increases satisfaction, and builds brand loyalty. Furthermore, real-time data enables organizations to respond promptly to customer concerns and improve service delivery, creating a seamless and positive customer journey. Indeed, data empowers businesses to move from a one-size-fits-all approach to a customer-centric strategy that drives long-term value. The use of data to enhance customer experience has become a fundamental part of modern business strategy, allowing organizations to deliver highly personalized, seamless, and engaging interactions across all customer aspects. Organizations can gain deep insights into customer preferences, needs, pain points, and expectations by collecting and analyzing data from various sources, including website behavior, purchase history, social media activity, customer feedback, and support interactions. These insights enable organizations to tailor products, services, and communications in real time, creating more meaningful and relevant experiences that drive customer satisfaction and loyalty. For example, e-commerce platforms use browsing and purchase data to recommend personalized products, whereas financial institutions analyze transaction patterns to offer customized financial advice. In the case of customer support, data analysis provides predictive service by identifying potential issues before they arise and routing inquiries to the most suitable agents. Furthermore, customer journey analytics allows companies to map and optimize the end-to-end experience, identifying friction points and opportunities for improvement. Advanced technologies such as AI-powered tools and ML further enhance this process by enabling real-time decision-making, sentiment analysis, and automated personalization at scale. Thus, the proper and effective use of data empowers businesses to meet anticipated customer needs and build stronger relationships, increase retention, and gain a competitive edge in today's experience-driven environment.

2.3.3 *Operational Efficiency and Process Optimization*

Data plays a vital role in driving operational efficiency and process optimization by providing insights that assist business organizations in streamlining workflows, reducing waste, improving resource allocation, and collecting and analyzing data from various operational activities such as production output, supply chain logistics, inventory levels, and employee performance. Organizations can identify inefficiencies, uncover bottlenecks, and implement data-informed improvements by collecting and analyzing data from various operational activities such as production output, supply chain logistics, inventory levels, and employee performance. Predictive analytics further enhances efficiency by anticipating maintenance needs, optimizing schedules, and minimizing downtime. Furthermore, real-time monitoring enables organizations to make quick adjustments to changing conditions, ensuring smooth and responsive operations. Ultimately, leveraging data for process optimization leads to cost savings, higher productivity, and enhanced overall performance. Data enables organizations to identify inefficiencies in operations, supply chains, and workflows that may result in streamlining operations, automating processes, and optimizing supply chain management to minimize cost, improve productivity analytics, and use real-time data to monitor performance and minimize waste. For instance, real-time monitoring and predictive analytics can help manufacturers anticipate equipment failures and schedule maintenance proactively, reducing downtime and repair costs. In logistics, data helps optimize delivery routes, inventory levels, and warehouse operations, leading to faster turnaround times and lower transportation expenses. Data-driven workforce management empowers businesses to align staffing levels with demand, minimizing labor costs while maintaining service quality. Furthermore, automation and AI, powered by data, can replace repetitive manual tasks, significantly improve productivity, and reduce human error. Organizations can reallocate resources to higher-value activities by using financial data analysis that supports more accurate budgeting and cost control. Data also empowers decision-makers to implement strategies that reduce overhead, increase agility, and ultimately drive sustainable growth by fostering a culture of continuous improvement based on measurable outcomes. The strategic use of data for operational efficiency and cost reduction is vital in a competitive landscape where margins are tight and customer expectations are high.

2.3.4 *Achieving Competitive Advantage*

Data plays a crucial role in achieving CA by enabling organizations with the insights needed to make smarter, faster, and strategically more innovative decisions than their competitors. Organizations can better understand market trends, customer demands, and emerging opportunities by harnessing data analytics that allow them to adapt quickly and stay ahead in a rapidly changing environment. Data-driven strategies enable businesses to personalize offerings, optimize pricing, improve product development, and enhance customer engagement to differentiate themselves from competitors in crowded markets. Furthermore, predictive and prescriptive analytics help anticipate competitors' moves and mitigate risks proactively. Indeed, data transforms into a powerful asset that drives innovation, agility, and sustained market leadership. Data allows us to identify high-performing products, customer segments, and sales channels to optimize pricing models based on demand and competition, driving revenue growth. Data can provide insights into competitors, market trends, and emerging opportunities for business in determining their marketing strategies and developing innovative products or services. Data can also enable organizations to measure the success of marketing campaigns and adjust pricing and marketing strategies in real time. Data-driven innovation enables organizations to develop new products, improve services, and effectively compete globally. One study investigates the effect of data strategy on CA, focusing on how defensive data strategy (DDS), which prioritizes regulatory compliance, risk mitigation, and operational efficiency, and offensive data strategy (ODS), which emphasizes innovation, market responsiveness, and revenue growth, can influence organizational performance. The study concludes that both DDS and ODS directly and positively impact CA, with ODS playing a mediating role in strengthening the relationship between DDS and CA, suggesting that organizations must align their data strategy with their strategic positioning and analytical capabilities to unlock the full value of their data.[1]

2.3.5 Risk Assessment, Management, and Compliance

Data plays an important role in risk management and fraud detection by identifying, assessing, and managing risks and turning challenges into opportunities for growth and innovation. Data empowers organizations to identify, evaluate, mitigate, and monitor potential threats to their operations, finances, reputation, and legal standing. Businesses can develop a comprehensive understanding of their risk exposure across multiple dimensions, including operational, financial, strategic, cybersecurity, and regulatory risks, by collecting and analyzing historical and real-time data from internal systems, market trends, financial transactions, cyber activity, and regulatory sources. Advanced BA, AI-assisted technologies, and ML models can predict the likelihood and potential impact of specific risk events, including fraud, supply chain disruptions, credit defaults, or compliance violations, enabling organizations to proactively implement controls and contingency plans. For example, financial institutions use data to assess credit risk and detect money laundering, whereas healthcare providers leverage data to ensure patient privacy and regulatory compliance with HIPAA. In highly regulated industries, data supports compliance by tracking audit trails, maintaining records, and automating reporting to meet the requirements of laws such as GDPR, SOX, and CCPA. Furthermore, real-time data monitoring systems can flag anomalies and generate alerts, enabling swift response to emerging risks before they escalate. Organizations can protect themselves from costly penalties and reputational damage and foster greater transparency, accountability, and resilience by embedding data-driven risk assessment and compliance frameworks into daily operations. In an increasingly complex and regulated business landscape, the strategic use of data for risk management and compliance is vital for long-term sustainability and stakeholder trust.

2.3.6 Strategic Planning and Business Sustainability

Data plays a pivotal role in strategic planning and business sustainability by providing the evidence-based insights needed to make long-term, informed decisions that align with both organizational financial goals and environmental, social, and governance (ESG) considerations. Business organizations can evaluate their current position, anticipate future challenges, and identify opportunities for sustainable growth through the collection and analysis of diverse datasets ranging from financial performance and market trends to resource usage, stakeholder feedback, and regulatory requirements. Data enables organizations to set measurable objectives, monitor progress toward sustainability targets, and adjust strategies in real time based on evolving internal and external conditions. For example, sustainability data can reveal inefficiencies in energy consumption, waste management, or supply chain operations, prompting strategic investments in cleaner technologies or more ethical sourcing practices. Predictive analytics can help organizations forecast the long-term impacts of strategic decisions on profitability, reputation, and compliance, fostering resilience in an increasingly volatile and socially conscious global market. Business organizations are better equipped to balance short-term performance with long-term strategic goals by integrating data into strategic planning processes to ensure they remain competitive, innovative, and accountable in a rapidly changing world. Data-driven strategic planning is a tool for business growth and thus a cornerstone of sustainable value creation and ethical leadership.

2.3.7 Regulatory Compliance and Data Governance

Data plays an important and transformative role in regulatory compliance and data governance by serving as the foundation upon which organizations ensure adherence to all applicable laws, rules, regulations, as well as legal, ethical, and operational standards. In an increasingly data-driven world, regulatory bodies across industries mandate strict requirements for how data is collected, stored, accessed, processed, and protected. Compliance with applicable laws, rules, and regulations requires organizations to maintain accurate, complete, and timely data that can be audited and verified. Effective data governance frameworks are vital in this context, as they define the policies, procedures, roles, and responsibilities necessary for managing data assets throughout their lifecycle.

Data governance ensures consistency, accountability, and transparency in data management, which in turn facilitates compliance by creating structured processes for data quality assurance, risk mitigation, and reporting. Furthermore, real-time data monitoring and analytics empower organizations to identify anomalies, prevent breaches, and demonstrate compliance proactively rather than reactively. Organizations can minimize legal and financial risks, build trust with stakeholders, and enhance decision-making capabilities by integrating compliance requirements directly into data governance strategies. In essence, data is not just a compliance burden but also a strategic asset that, when governed effectively, can drive operational efficiency, innovation, and long-term sustainability. Data is the lifeblood of businesses and invaluable to their success and sustainability. However, as businesses collect vast amounts of data, they should ensure compliance with applicable data protection regulations and data accuracy, completeness, and consistency. Effective and robust data governance measures help maintain data integrity, security, integration, and ethical use of data from multiple sources.

2.3.8 Innovation, Growth, and Competitive Advantage

Data can serve as a powerful catalyst for innovation, growth, and CA by providing organizations with the insights and agility needed to identify new opportunities, develop innovative products and services, and differentiate themselves in crowded markets. Organizations can uncover unmet needs, emerging consumer behaviors, and technological advancements that drive innovation by harnessing vast amounts of structured and unstructured data from customers, competitors, market trends, and operational processes. Data-driven innovation enables companies to experiment rapidly with product features, pricing models, and marketing strategies through techniques such as A/B testing, predictive analytics, and customer segmentation, minimizing risk while maximizing impact. Furthermore, data supports scalable growth by optimizing customer acquisition and retention efforts, streamlining supply chains, and improving decision-making across all levels of the organization. In highly competitive industries, the ability to leverage data effectively becomes a critical differentiator, allowing organizations to anticipate market shifts, personalize experiences, and deliver superior value faster than competitors. Businesses that integrate data into their strategic planning and culture are better equipped to adapt to changing conditions, identify blue ocean markets, and foster a continuous cycle of learning and improvement. Thus, the strategic use of data empowers businesses to transform raw information into actionable insights, fueling sustained innovation, accelerating growth trajectories, and securing a durable competitive edge in an increasingly data-driven global economy.

2.4 Data Preparation, Management, and Utilization

The convergence of DDDM technology capabilities has given rise to a new paradigm in which AI and BA have emerged as a transformative force, fundamentally reshaping how data is curated, processed, and utilized. Data plays an essential role in decision-making in today's digital and data-driven world. Data preparation, management, and utilization form the backbone of effective AI-driven and BA-enabled decision-making. Data preparation involves collecting, cleaning, integrating, and transforming raw data from diverse sources to ensure accuracy, completeness, consistency, and relevance for analysis. Data management focuses on governing data throughout its lifecycle, covering storage, security, quality control, metadata management, privacy, and regulatory compliance to ensure that data remains reliable, accessible, and trustworthy over time. Data utilization then converts well-prepared and well-managed data into actionable insights by applying analytics, ML, and visualization techniques to support operational efficiency, strategic planning, risk management, and innovation. Together, these interconnected processes, which are thoroughly described in the following subsections, ensure that organizations move beyond simply possessing data to systematically extracting value from it, enabling evidence-based decisions, robust governance, sustainable performance, and CA in a knowledge-based and data-driven economy.

2.4.1 Data Preparation

Data preparation, as a foundational step in DS, is the process of collecting, cleaning, transforming, and organizing raw data into processed information in a usable format to ensure that data is accurate, consistent, complete, and ready for analysis. The conventional manual and time-consuming data preparation process has been significantly improved by AI technologies. AI-driven tools help improve data quality, reduce processing time, and increase analytical efficiency by automating and optimizing various stages of data handling. The key steps in data preparation are (1) data collection, which is gathering data from various sources such as databases, APIs, surveys, or web scraping; (2) data cleaning, which includes reviewing, editing to identify and correct errors, duplicates, and inconsistencies while handling missing values; (3) data transformation, including standardizing formats, normalizing data, and encoding categorical variables for analysis; (4) data integration, that is, merging data from multiple sources to create a comprehensive dataset; (5) data enrichment, which means enhancing data with additional information from external sources; (6) data analysis, which is creating new features or variables that can be used in improving predictive modeling and analysis; (7) data validation, which includes ensuring accuracy and integrity of the data; and (8) data splitting, that is dividing data into training, validation, and test sets. Some AI-powered tools and technologies for data preparation are as follows.[2]

2.4.1.1 Automated Data Cleaning and Preprocessing

Automated data cleaning and preprocessing is the process of leveraging algorithms, rules engines, and AI-driven techniques to systematically detect, correct, and standardize data with minimal human intervention. This process automatically handles common data quality issues such as missing values, outliers, duplicates, inconsistencies, and noise, while transforming raw data through normalization, encoding, feature scaling, and feature engineering to make it suitable for analytics and ML models. Organizations improve data accuracy, consistency, and timeliness; reduce manual effort and human bias; and enable scalable, real-time data processing across large and complex datasets by embedding automation into data pipelines. Ultimately, automated data cleaning and preprocessing empower organizations to enhance model reliability, accelerate analytics workflows, and support more robust, repeatable, and trustworthy data-driven insights. Specifically, AI technologies (ML, NLP) can detect anomalies, outliers, and missing values using pattern recognition and statistical modeling. ML algorithms can learn common data entry errors and suggest corrections, whereas NLP can interpret and standardize textual data, such as cleaning unstructured customer feedback. For example, OpenRefine (with AI plugins) can clean and transform messy data, Trifacta Wrangler (AI-driven data wrangling) uses ML to suggest transformations, DataRobot Paxata is an AI-powered self-service data preparation, and Tamr uses ML for entity resolution and data unification.

2.4.1.2 AI-Assisted Feature Engineering

AI-assisted feature engineering employs ML and automated algorithms to identify, create, transform, and select the most informative features from raw data, which reduces reliance on manual and trial-and-error processes. AI-powered tools and BA-assisted techniques can automatically generate new features, optimize transformations, and rank feature importance to improve model performance and interpretability by analyzing patterns, relationships, and nonlinear interactions within large and complex datasets. These techniques adapt dynamically as new data becomes available, supporting continuous learning and model refinement across structured and unstructured data such as text, images, and sensor data. Ultimately, AI-assisted feature engineering enhances predictive accuracy, accelerates model development, and enables organizations to scale advanced analytics while maintaining consistency, efficiency, and analytical rigor. Specifically, AI-powered tools can match and merge data from disparate sources using entity recognition and semantic analysis to identify relationships between different data schemas, even when naming conventions or formats differ. FeatureTools automates feature engineering using deep feature synthesis. AutoFeat (Python library) automatically generates meaningful features. H2O.ai's Driverless AI enables AI-driven feature engineering and selection.

2.4.1.3 Synthetic Data and Missing Value Imputation

Synthetic data generation and missing value imputation use statistical methods, BA-driven methods, and AI-assisted models to address data gaps, sparsity, and privacy constraints while preserving the underlying structure and relationships of the original data. Synthetic data techniques create artificial yet realistic datasets that mimic real-world distributions by enabling model training, testing, and validation when access to sensitive, incomplete, or imbalanced data is limited. Missing value imputation applies ML, probabilistic modeling, or deep learning approaches to estimate absent observations based on patterns in existing data to reduce bias and information loss compared to simple deletion or mean substitution. Ultimately, these approaches enhance data completeness, improve model robustness and generalizability, and support ethical, scalable, and reliable analytics in data-intensive and regulated environments. Specifically, Generative AI models such as Generative Adversarial Networks (GANs) or LLMs can create realistic synthetic data to augment training datasets, address data imbalance issues, and preserve privacy while enabling analysis on sensitive data. For example, Synthetic Data Vault (SDV) generates synthetic datasets using AI, whereas DataWig (Amazon's library) uses deep learning for missing value imputation, and MissForest (Python/R) enables random forest-based imputation.

2.4.1.4 *Data Labeling and Annotation*

Data labeling and annotation are essential processes for creating ML-ready datasets by assigning accurate, consistent, and meaningful labels to raw data to assist ML models in learning from them effectively. This process may involve human experts, crowd-sourced contributors, automated labeling tools, or hybrid human-in-the-loop approaches to tag text, images, audio, video, or structured records with predefined classes, attributes, or relationships. High-quality labeling emphasizes clear annotation guidelines, inter-annotator agreement, and continuous quality checks to minimize bias, noise, and subjectivity. Well-labeled and annotated datasets improve model training, validation, and testing, which leads to higher predictive accuracy, better generalization, and more trustworthy AI systems suitable for deployment in real-world applications. Specifically, supervised learning models require labeled data, which is often difficult and expensive to produce manually. However, AI-assisted labeling uses active learning to identify the most informative data points to label. Semi-supervised learning can propagate labels from a small, labeled cluster to a larger, unlabeled set. For example, Label Studio (AI-assisted labeling) can speed up annotation with ML predictions. Snorkel AI allows programmatic labeling using weak supervision, whereas Prodigy (by Explosion AI) can actively learn-based annotation.

2.4.1.5 *Intelligent Data Transformation*

Intelligent data transformation applies AI- and rule-based techniques to automatically convert raw data into structured, standardized, and analytics-ready formats that align with business and modeling objectives. These transformations include normalization, aggregation, encoding, feature scaling, dimensionality reduction, and semantic mapping across heterogeneous data sources such as transactional systems, text, images, and sensor streams. Ultimately, intelligent data transformation reduces manual intervention, improves consistency, and enhances scalability across enterprise data pipelines by leveraging ML to learn transformation rules and adapt to evolving data patterns. Thus, organizations can ensure data interoperability, improve model performance, and accelerate the delivery of reliable insights to support advanced analytics and AI-driven decision-making. ML algorithms can automatically suggest or perform data transformations such as feature engineering (e.g., creating new variables from existing ones), dimensionality reduction (e.g., PCA or t-SNE) to reduce complexity, and encoding categorical data or scaling numerical data as per model requirements.

Several AI-powered tools for data preparation that can integrate AI capabilities for seamless data preparation are (1) Trifacta (now part of Google Cloud Dataprep), which uses ML to recommend transformations and data wrangling steps; (2) Tableau Prep with Einstein Discovery, which leverages predictive modeling to assist in data shaping;

(3) DataRobot Paxata, which provides AI-driven data profiling and enrichment; (4) AutoML Platforms that have built-in data preparation tools (e.g., Google AutoML, H2O. ai, Amazon SageMaker); and (5) Azure Data Factory, which offers AI capabilities for smart data flows and transformation. The potential benefits of these AI technologies in data preparation are efficiency of automating repetitive and manual tasks; reducing preparation time; accuracy of reducing human error by using consistent, data-driven methods; scalability of handling large-scale and diverse datasets across industries; and adaptability of continuously improving through learning from feedback and new data. The perceived challenges are biased propagation of poor-quality or biased data that can lead to biased AI models, data privacy of handling sensitive data ethically, with proper anonymization or differential privacy techniques, over-reliance on automation that demands human oversight to validate AI-driven processes and ensure contextual relevance, and model transparency that requires AI decisions in data preparation to be interpretable, especially in regulated industries.

2.4.2 Data Management

Data management phase involves assessing, storing, securing, retrieving, maintaining, and organizing data to ensure its accessibility, integrity, transparency, and usability for decision-making. The important components of this phase are (1) Database Management Systems (DBMS) for organizing structured data in relational databases (SQL) or unstructured data in NoSQL systems; (2) data assessment and governance for establishing policies for data quality, security, and compliance with all applicable laws, rules, regulations standards (e.g., GDPR, CCPA, FASB, IASB, ISSB); (3) data mining and warehousing for storing large datasets in centralized repositories for analysis, use, and reporting; (4) cloud storage and big data solutions for using platforms like AWS, Google Cloud, and Azure for scalable storage and computing; and (5) metadata management for documenting data elements, attributes, definitions, and lineage to maintain transparency. AI-powered tools and technologies that can be used in this phase of data management are SQL, NoSQL (MongoDB, Cassandra), Hadoop, Apache Spark, and cloud-based platforms, among others. There are some challenges of managing heterogeneous data in data lakes, where enterprises often store unstructured, semi-structured, and structured data without effective organization, leading to data silos or data swamps. Java Annotation for Manipulating Data Lakes (JAMDL) can be integrated with AI techniques, such as Long Short-Term Memory (LSTM) and GRU neural networks, to automate Data Manipulation Language (DML) operations to enhance data governance and significantly improve the efficiency of data manipulation in data lakes by providing a unified object model for diverse data structures, dynamic JSON generation, and advanced table-join methods.[3]

The integration of AI technologies into data management systems is revolutionizing how organizations store, process, and utilize data. AI enhances both the efficiency and value of data management by automating routine tasks, improving data quality, and enabling intelligent decision-making. As AI technologies continue to evolve, they will play an increasingly vital role in helping organizations become more agile, data-driven, and competitive in the digital era. AI platforms are transforming data management by enabling organizations to handle vast volumes of data more efficiently, accurately, securely, and in a timely manner. Traditional data management systems are often inadequate in managing big data of high volume, velocity, and variety. AI technologies can provide automation, intelligence, and scalability to key data management functions, including data integration, quality, governance, security, and analytics. Examples of AI-powered tools and technologies for data management are as follows.[4]

2.4.2.1 AI-Enhanced Database Systems

AI-enhanced database systems can integrate AI and ML capabilities directly into database architectures to improve data storage, retrieval, management, and analytics. These systems can automatically optimize query execution, indexing, and resource allocation based on usage patterns and workload dynamics by embedding intelligent algorithms within traditional relational and non-relational databases. AI-driven databases also support automated data classification, anomaly detection, and data quality monitoring by enabling real-time identification of errors, inconsistencies, and potential security threats. Advanced features such as natural language querying, semantic search, and predictive caching allow users to interact with data more intuitively while improving performance and scalability. Ultimately, AI-enhanced database systems are essential in data management to transform databases from passive data repositories into adaptive, self-tuning platforms that support advanced analytics, AI applications, and DDDM on scale.

2.4.2.2 Vector Databases

Vector databases play a pivotal role in modern data management by enabling the storage, indexing, and retrieval of high-dimensional vector representations generated by ML and AI models. Unlike traditional relational databases that rely on exact matches and structured queries, vector databases support similarity search using distance metrics such as cosine similarity or Euclidean distance, which makes them well-suited for unstructured data, including text, images, audio, and video. In data management pipelines, vector databases facilitate semantic search, recommendation systems, anomaly detection, and retrieval-augmented generation (RAG) by efficiently matching embeddings at scale. These vector databases also support real-time updates, metadata filtering, and hybrid search that combines vector similarity with structured attributes. As organizations increasingly deploy AI-driven analytics and generative AI applications, vector databases have become a foundational infrastructure for managing intelligent, context-aware, and continuously evolving data assets.

AI systems enable real-time data analysis and predictive insights by leveraging ML algorithms on large datasets to identify trends, patterns, and correlations that are not apparent through traditional analysis. AI-driven analytics tools empower businesses to make faster, data-driven decisions and improve operational efficiency. AI can help manage the entire data lifecycle in predicting which data should be archived, what needs to be retained for compliance, and which datasets are most relevant to ongoing business processes, which could result in optimized storage and reduced data redundancy. Examples are Pinecone, which is a managed vector database for AI embeddings; Weaviate, which is an open-source vector search with ML models; Milvus, a scalable vector database for similarity search; and Qdrant, a high-performance vector similarity engine.

2.4.2.3 AI-Optimized Data Lakes and Warehouses

AI-optimized data lakes and data warehouses enhance traditional data management and storage architecture by embedding AI and ML capabilities to improve data ingestion, organization, governance, and analytics. These systems automatically classify and tag structured and unstructured data, detect anomalies, and optimize storage formats and partitioning strategies based on usage patterns. AI-driven query optimization and workload management improve performance and reduce costs by dynamically allocating computing resources and recommending efficient data access paths. In addition, AI-enabled data lakes and warehouses support advanced analytics, real-time reporting, and predictive insights by seamlessly integrating with ML pipelines and generative AI applications. AI-optimized data lakes and warehouses enable organizations to scale analytics, improve data quality, and accelerate DDDM across the enterprise by transforming passive repositories into intelligent, self-managing platforms. Maintaining and optimizing data quality is a major challenge for organizations. AI platforms can continuously monitor data for errors, duplicates, missing values, and outliers. AI tools can proactively detect and resolve data quality issues by learning from past corrections to ensure that decision-makers have access to accurate and reliable information.

2.4.2.4 AI-Driven Data Governance and Metadata Management

AI-driven data governance and metadata management use AI-powered technologies and ML to automate and strengthen the oversight, quality, and usability of enterprise data assets. These systems intelligently discover, classify, and catalog data across diverse sources, generating dynamic metadata that captures data lineage, ownership, sensitivity, and usage patterns in real time. AI-assisted techniques enable automated policy enforcement, privacy compliance, and risk detection by continuously monitoring data access and identifying anomalies or violations. In addition, ML-based metadata enrichment improves data discoverability through semantic tagging and contextual relationships, supporting self-service analytics and AI applications. AI-driven data governance and metadata management enhance trust, transparency, regulatory compliance, and the strategic value of data across the organization by shifting governance from manual, rule-based processes to adaptive and intelligent frameworks.

AI facilitates data governance by automatically enforcing policies related to data access, usage, and retention by detecting anomalies; ensuring compliance with all applicable laws, rules, and regulations (such as GDPR or HIPAA); and providing audit trails. AI-assisted systems can also identify sensitive data and recommend appropriate protection measures. AI also enables automating the creation of data catalogs by using NLP and ML to classify, tag, and organize data assets. This enhances discoverability and supports better data governance. AI can also recommend metadata based on usage patterns and relationships between datasets. AI enhances data security by detecting unusual data access patterns, potential breaches, and vulnerabilities in real time to support advanced threat detection and response mechanisms, including behavioral analytics and automated remediation. AI can also assist in anonymizing or masking data to ensure privacy and compliance. Examples are Collibra (AI Governance), an automated metadata tagging and lineage; Alation (with behavioral analysis) of AI-powered data catalog; and IBM Watson Knowledge Catalog of AI-curated metadata and compliance.

2.4.3 Data Utilization

Data utilization refers to the process of transforming raw data into actionable insights and usable information that support decision-making, innovation, and strategic growth. AI plays an essential role in this transformation by enabling faster, smarter, and more accurate analysis and interpretation of data. This final phase determines how data can be leveraged for various applications, including BA, BI, research, and AI-driven insights, once data is prepared and managed in the previous two phases. Primary applications of data utilization are (1) descriptive analytics of summarizing historical data using dashboards and reports; (2) predictive analytics of using ML to forecast trends, customer behavior, or financial and nonfinancial key performance indicators (KPIs); (3) prescriptive analytics of providing data-driven recommendations for decision-making; (4) AI and ML applications of training models for NLP, image recognition, or automation; and (5) BA and strategic decision-making of using data insights to optimize operations, marketing, innovation, growth, and investments. AI-powered tools and technologies that can be used in this final phase are Power BI, Tableau, Python (scikit-learn, TensorFlow), R, AI/ML platforms, among others. The effective utilization of data in the context of Industry 4.0 technologies can transform traditional organizations into smart, data-driven enterprises by enabling organizations to optimize processes, improve decision-making, and enhance competitiveness through data-driven strategies.[5] Some of the AI-powered and BA-assisted technologies for data utilization are as follows.[6]

2.4.3.1 AI-Augmented Business Intelligence (BI) and Visualization

AI-augmented business intelligence (BI) and visualization enhance traditional reporting and dashboarding by embedding AI-powered technologies and ML capabilities that automate insight generation, pattern recognition, and decision support. These systems move beyond descriptive analytics by applying predictive and prescriptive models to identify trends, forecast outcomes, and recommend actions directly within BI platforms. AI-driven visualization tools dynamically select appropriate charts, highlight anomalies, and surface key drivers using XAI techniques, reducing cognitive overload for decision-makers. Natural language querying and automated narrative generation further democratize data access by allowing users to interact with dashboards conversationally and receive context-aware explanations. Organizations transform static reports into intelligent, interactive, and real-time decision environments that improve data utilization, managerial judgment, and strategic responsiveness across the enterprise by integrating AI with BI and visualization. AI systems can analyze vast and complex datasets far beyond the capabilities of traditional tools. AI uncovers hidden patterns, correlations, and trends, turning data into meaningful insights without requiring manual effort using ML algorithms. This automation empowers businesses to make informed decisions in real time, increasing responsiveness and competitiveness. Examples of these tools are Microsoft Fabric (with Copilot AI), which provides AI-driven insights in Power BI; Tableau GPT (Einstein Analytics) of NLP-powered analytics; ThoughtSpot (Search & AI Analytics), which provides natural language queries; Qlik Sense (AI-Assisted Insights), which auto-generates visualizations; and Looker (Google's ML-Powered BI) of predictive analytics integration.

2.4.3.2 AutoML and AI Model Deployment

AutoML and AI model deployment streamline the development, validation, and operationalization of ML models by automating complex and resource-intensive stages of the analytics lifecycle. AutoML platforms automatically handle data preprocessing, feature selection, model selection, hyperparameter tuning, and performance evaluation by enabling organizations to develop robust models with greater speed, consistency, and scalability. Once models are built, AI deployment frameworks support seamless integration into production environments through APIs, cloud platforms, and edge systems, while enabling continuous monitoring, version control, and performance retraining. These capabilities ensure that models remain accurate, explainable, and aligned with changing business conditions. Ultimately, these systems of AutoML and AI model deployment lower technical barriers, accelerate time to value, and enable organizations to operationalize AI responsibly and effectively across data-driven decision processes.

2.4.3.3 AI-Powered Statistical and Advanced Analytics

AI-powered statistical and advanced analytics integrate traditional statistical methods with ML and AI to enhance the depth, speed, and scalability of data analysis. These systems automate model selection, hypothesis testing, and parameter estimation while incorporating advanced techniques such as deep learning, ensemble models, and probabilistic reasoning to uncover complex, nonlinear relationships in large and high-dimensional datasets. AI-driven analytics also support real-time analysis, scenario simulation, and predictive and prescriptive insights, enabling organizations to move beyond retrospective reporting toward forward-looking decision-making. AI-powered statistical and advanced analytics improve analytical rigor, reduce human bias, and enable more accurate, explainable, and actionable insights across business, finance, and sustainability applications by augmenting classical statistical analysis with adaptive learning and automation.

AI systems facilitate real-time data analysis, which is vital in dynamic environments such as finance, healthcare, supply chains, and e-commerce. These systems can support immediate decisions of adjusting prices, detecting fraud, or rerouting logistics based on current conditions. AI facilitates real-time data analysis, which is critical in dynamic environments such as finance, healthcare, supply chains, and e-commerce. AI systems can support immediate decisions of adjusting prices, detecting fraud, or rerouting logistics based on current conditions by continuously monitoring data streams and adapting to new information. AI platforms enable the utilization of user data to deliver personalized experiences and recommendations. In sectors like retail, entertainment, and education, AI analyzes user behavior to tailor content, products, or services to individual preferences to enhance customer satisfaction and engagement.

2.4.3.4 Explainable AI (XAI) and Model Interpretability

XAI and model interpretability enable making AI and ML models transparent, understandable, and trustworthy for users, regulators, and stakeholders. XAI techniques provide insights into how models generate predictions by identifying key features, decision rules, and causal relationships, using methods such as feature attribution, surrogate models, and visualization tools. These capabilities are especially essential in high-stakes domains such as finance, auditing, healthcare, and sustainability reporting, where accountability, fairness, and regulatory compliance are essential. Ultimately, XAI supports better validation, bias detection, and risk management while increasing user confidence in AI-driven decisions by enhancing transparency and enabling human oversight. Overall, explainable and interpretable AI bridges the gap between model complexity and human judgment, enabling responsible and ethical deployment of advanced analytics.

AI technologies, particularly XAI, can identify inefficiencies, bottlenecks, and opportunities for improvement in a responsible manner by analyzing operational data, optimizing workflows, reducing waste, and enhancing allocation across departments. For instance, in manufacturing, AI can use data to optimize production schedules and reduce downtime. AI unlocks the potential of data to drive innovation. AI helps organizations develop new products, services, and business models by analyzing market trends, consumer feedback, and competitor actions. It supports strategic planning and scenario analysis by simulating the impact of different decisions under various conditions. Examples are SHAP (SHapley Additive exPlanations) of model explainability; LIME (Local Interpretable Model-agnostic Explanations), which is black-box model insight; IBM Watson OpenScale of monitoring AI fairness and bias; and TensorFlow Explainability (TFX), which is built with interpretability tools.

2.5 Data Engineering and Data Management

Data engineering and data management provide the foundational infrastructure that enables effective analytics, BI, and AI applications by ensuring that data is reliable, accessible, and fit for purposes.[7] Data engineering focuses on the design, construction, and maintenance of scalable data pipelines that ingest, transform, and integrate structured and unstructured data from diverse sources, while data management emphasizes governance, quality control, security, and lifecycle management of organizational data assets. Together, they support efficient data utilization by enabling timely access to high-quality data, enforcing standards and metadata, and aligning data architectures with analytical and strategic objectives. Thus, the effectiveness and robust data engineering and management capabilities are crucial for transforming raw data into actionable insights and sustaining DDDM and AI-enabled innovation across organizations.

2.6 Data Collection, Cleaning, and Preprocessing Techniques

Data collection, cleaning, and preprocessing techniques are essential stages in the BA and AI lifecycle, as the quality of analytical outcomes is highly dependent on the quality of input data. Data collection involves systematically acquiring structured and unstructured data from internal and external sources, while data cleaning addresses errors, inconsistencies, duplicates, and missing values that can bias analytical results.[8] Preprocessing techniques such as normalization, transformation, feature scaling, and encoding prepare raw data for statistical analysis and ML by improving consistency, comparability, and computational efficiency. Thus, effective data preparation can account for a substantial portion of the overall analytics effort and significantly enhances model accuracy, robustness, and interpretability. Ultimately, rigorous data collection and preprocessing practices form the foundation of reliable, scalable, and trustworthy DDDM.

Data collection, cleaning, and preprocessing are vital steps in the DS and analytics landscape by establishing the foundation for accurate and reliable analysis. Data collection involves gathering raw data from various sources such as databases, APIs, web scraping, sensors, surveys, and transactional systems. This data collection process is essential to ensure data relevance, consistency, and security while considering ethical standards and compliance with data privacy regulations like GDPR. Raw data gathered through the data collection process often contains noise, inconsistencies, duplicates, missing values, and outliers, which must be addressed through data cleaning techniques. The data cleaning process involves tasks such as handling null values (through imputation or removal), correcting data entry errors, standardizing formats, removing duplicates, and ensuring consistent encoding for categorical variables. The next step after cleaning is the data preprocessing process that transforms the cleaned data into a suitable format for analysis or ML models. This process involves normalization or standardization of numerical features, encoding categorical variables using methods like one-hot encoding or label encoding, feature scaling, dimensionality reduction (e.g., PCA), and data transformation through techniques like log transformation or binning. Preprocessing may encompass data partitioning into training, validation, and test sets to support robust model evaluation. Tools like Python's Pandas, NumPy, Scikit-learn, and data integration platforms such as Talend and Apache NiFi are frequently used to automate and streamline these tasks. Together, the data collection, cleaning, and preprocessing processes ensure that data is clean, consistent, and correctly formatted. Ultimately, these processes enhance the quality and predictive power of analytics and ML outcomes, ultimately driving more informed and impactful decision-making.

2.7 Data Visualization and Exploratory Data Analysis (EDA)

Data visualization and exploratory data analysis (EDA) are integral components of the DS process by serving as the bridge between raw data, processed information, and meaningful insights. EDA is an essential technique for understanding data structure, identifying patterns, detecting anomalies, and generating analytical insights prior to formal modeling.[9] Visualization transforms complex datasets into graphical representations, such as charts, plots, and dashboards, that support intuitive interpretation and comparative analysis, while EDA employs summary statistics, visual diagnostics, and interactive exploration to assess distributions, relationships, and data quality issues. These techniques enable analysts to uncover underlying trends, validate assumptions, and inform model selection and feature engineering. Effective visualization and EDA enhance analytical reasoning, reduce cognitive bias, and improve the reliability of statistical and ML outcomes by fostering deeper engagement with the data. Thus, data visualization and EDA serve as foundational practices for robust, transparent, and insightful DDDM. EDA is the initial investigative approach to analyzing data sets by summarizing their main characteristics through visual and quantitative methods, without making any prior assumptions. EDA uses statistical graphics, plots, and information tables to identify patterns, spot anomalies, test hypotheses, and check assumptions. Data visualization, as a complementary and often overlapping practice, provides intuitive and interactive representations of data through tools such as histograms, scatter plots, box plots, heatmaps, and dashboards, making complex data more accessible and understandable for both technical and non-technical audiences. The integration of EDA and visualization empowers organizations and their analysts to uncover relationships between variables, detect outliers, recognize trends over time, and inform the selection of appropriate statistical or ML models. Tools like Python's Matplotlib, Seaborn, and Plotly, as well as platforms like Tableau and Power BI, have become indispensable for creating dynamic visualizations that support storytelling and DDDM. Together, EDA and visualization enhance analytical accuracy and foster transparency, insight, and collaboration across teams in diverse fields such as business, healthcare, finance, and environmental science by enabling a deeper understanding of the data before any formal modeling begins.

2.8 Data Governance and Ethics in AI-Driven Decision-Making

Data governance and ethics are central to responsible AI-driven and BA-assisted decision-making, as they establish the policies, controls, and ethical principles that guide how data are collected, managed, and used in algorithmic systems.[10] Effective data governance frameworks ensure data quality, privacy, security, accountability, and regulatory compliance, while ethical AI principles address issues such as fairness, transparency, explainability, and bias mitigation in automated decisions. In AI-driven contexts, weak governance and ethical oversight can lead to discriminatory outcomes, loss of stakeholder trust, and regulatory risk. Thus, integrating ethical considerations and governance mechanisms into AI systems enhances decision legitimacy, supports human oversight, and aligns AI applications with organizational values and societal expectations. Accordingly, robust data governance and ethical frameworks are crucial for ensuring that AI-enabled decisions are trustworthy, accountable, and sustainable.

2.9 Data Wrangling, Feature Engineering, and Dimensionality Reduction

Data wrangling, feature engineering, and dimensionality reduction are essential processes in the data preparation phase that significantly impact the performance and interpretability of ML models. Data wrangling, feature engineering, and dimensionality reduction are foundational stages in AI-driven analytics that transform raw, heterogeneous data into structured, informative inputs suitable for robust modeling and decision-making.[11] Data wrangling encompasses processes such as data integration, cleaning, normalization, and transformation to address missing values, noise, inconsistencies, and scale differences across diverse data sources, thereby improving data quality and model reliability. Feature engineering builds on this foundation by constructing, selecting, and encoding variables that capture domain-relevant patterns, interactions, and nonlinear relationships, often leveraging automated and AI-assisted techniques to enhance predictive power and interpretability. Data wrangling, also known as data munging, encompasses transforming and mapping raw, often messy or unstructured data into a more organized and usable format. This process involves merging datasets, handling missing values, filtering or reshaping data, and correcting inconsistencies to ensure that the data is clean and aligned with analytical objectives. Once the data is wrangled, feature engineering becomes vital in creating new input variables or modifying existing ones to enhance the model's ability to learn underlying patterns by encoding categorical variables, extracting date-time components, creating interaction terms, normalizing or scaling values, or incorporating domain knowledge to generate meaningful features.

Robust engineered features usually have a more significant impact on model performance than the choice of algorithm itself by addressing issues like overfitting, increased computational cost, and reduced interpretability. Dimensionality reduction techniques such as PCA, t-Distributed Stochastic Neighbor Embedding (t-SNE), and feature selection methods can be employed to reduce the number of input variables while preserving essential information.[12] These techniques help simplify models, highlight the most informative features, and enhance the visualization and understanding of high-dimensional data. A combination of data wrangling, feature engineering, and dimensionality reduction ensures that ML models are built on a strong, efficient, and insightful data foundation, leading to more accurate, generalizable, and explainable outcomes. Together, these interrelated processes enable scalable, efficient, and XAI models by aligning data preparation with analytical objectives and downstream business or policy decisions.

2.10 Summary

Data is the fuel of AI and BA. Without clean, well-structured, and relevant data, even the most sophisticated algorithms will perform poorly. This chapter explores the critical stages of data handling: from acquisition and preparation to ethical governance. Whether you're working with customer transactions, social media streams, or sensor data, understanding how to manage data effectively is essential for successful AI integration. This chapter focuses on preparing raw data for analysis. Readers will learn about structured versus unstructured data, preprocessing steps, data cleaning techniques, and the importance of high-quality data. The quality of data directly influences the accuracy of AI models. This chapter delves into managing raw data through various preparation stages, emphasizing structure, preprocessing, and cleanliness for reliable outcomes. This chapter provides a comprehensive introduction to the field of DS as an interdisciplinary domain that combines methods from statistics, ML, and computer science to extract meaningful knowledge and actionable insights from large volumes of both structured and unstructured data. It explores the foundational concepts, methodologies, and tools that underpin modern data-driven discovery and decision-making.

The chapter begins by defining DS and positioning it at the intersection of various disciplines, highlighting its importance in the age of big data. It discusses the types of data encountered, such as structured, semi-structured, and unstructured, and the challenges and opportunities associated with each. Key concepts such as data wrangling, EDA, and data visualization are introduced as essential steps in the DS workflow. A significant portion of the chapter is dedicated to statistical techniques and ML algorithms commonly used in DS, including regression, classification, clustering, and dimensionality reduction. The importance of model evaluation, validation techniques, and avoidance of bias and overfitting is emphasized. The chapter also examines the computational tools and programming languages (such as Python and R) that are widely used in DS projects, along with an overview of data storage and processing frameworks like SQL, Hadoop, and Spark. Finally, the chapter concludes with a discussion on the ethical considerations and real-world applications of DS across sectors such as business, healthcare, finance, and environmental monitoring. By grounding theoretical concepts in practical use cases, the chapter equips readers with a solid foundation for understanding and engaging in DS practices.

Notes

1 Medeiros, M. M. D., Maçada, A. C. G., & Freitas Junior, J. C. D. S. (2020). The effect of data strategy on competitive advantage. *The Bottom Line*, 33(2), 201–216. https://doi.org/10.1108/BL-12-2019-0131. Available at https://www.emerald.com/insight/content/doi/10.1108/bl-12-2019-0131/full/html
2 Jordan, M. I., & Mitchell, T. M. (2015). Machine learning: Trends, perspectives, and prospects. *Science*, 349(6245), 255–260. https://doi.org/10.1126/science.aaa8415
3 Hoi, L. M., Ke, W., & Im, S. K. (2024). Manipulating data lakes intelligently with Java annotations. *IEEE Access*. https://doi.org/10.1109/ACCESS.2024.3372618. Available at https://ieeexplore.ieee.org/abstract/document/10458132
4 Alaskar, T. H. (2025). Integrated artificial intelligence and business analytics for sustaining data management. *Sustainability*, 17(19), 8749. https://doi.org/10.3390/su17198749
5 Janík, S., Szabó, P., Mĺkva, M., & Mareček-Kolibiský, M. (2022). Effective data utilization in the context of industry 4.0 technology integration. *Applied Sciences*, 12(20), 10517. https://doi.org/10.3390/app122010517. Available at https://www.mdpi.com/2076-3417/12/20/10517
6 Chen, H., Chiang, R. H. L., & Storey, V. C. (2012). Business intelligence and analytics: From big data to big impact. *MIS Quarterly*, 36(4), 1165–1188.
7 Chen, H., Chiang, R. H. L., & Storey, V. C. (2012). Business intelligence and analytics: From big data to big impact. *MIS Quarterly*, 36(4), 1165–1188.
8 Rahm, E., & Do, H. H. (2000). Data cleaning: Problems and current approaches. *IEEE Data Engineering Bulletin*, 23(4), 3–13.
9 Cleveland, W. S. (1993). *Visualizing Data*. Hobart Press.

10 Khatri, V., & Brown, C. V. (2010). Designing data governance. *Communications of the ACM*, 53(1), 148–152. https://doi.org/10.1145/1629175.1629210
11 Jolliffe, I. T., & Cadima, J. (2016). Principal component analysis: A review and recent developments. *Philosophical Transactions of the Royal Society A*, 374(2065), 20150202.
12 Jolliffe, I. T., & Cadima, J. (2016). Principal component analysis: A review and recent developments. *Philosophical Transactions of the Royal Society A*, 374(2065), 20150202.

3 Business Statistics and Analytics

Learning Objectives

- Understand probability, distributions, and statistical inference
- Learn statistical techniques using powerful machine learning algorithms in AI applications
- Become familiar with hypothesis testing and statistical modeling
- Explore Bayesian statistics and its applications in machine learning
- Explain key statistical terms and concepts relevant to AI and data analytics
- Apply probability and distributions to business scenarios
- Conduct hypothesis tests and interpret statistical results
- Differentiate between descriptive, predictive, and prescriptive analytics

3.1 Introduction

Robust and solid foundations in statistics are vital for leveraging AI and BA effectively in decision-making. This chapter provides sufficient understanding and application of statistical concepts, tools, and techniques necessary to extract meaningful insights from data to make data-driven decisions, improve performance, optimize operations, gain a competitive edge in the market, and maintain business sustainability. Some essential statistical foundations that are crucial for organizations are descriptive statistics, probability theory, inferential statistics, regression analysis, univariate and multivariate statistical analyses, Bayesian statistics, experimental design, big data analytics, software and tools, and ML- and AI-powered tools and techniques. These statistical foundations and their applications in BA and AI, including optimization, risk assessment and management, and predictive analytics, are presented in this chapter. Readers are introduced to the statistical tools that power modern analytics. Topics include probability, distributions, hypothesis testing, Bayesian statistics, and how these support descriptive, predictive, and prescriptive analytics in business.

3.2 Probability, Distributions, and Statistical Inference

Probability, distributions, and statistical inference provide the theoretical foundation for BA, ML, and AI-driven decision-making by formalizing uncertainty, variability, and evidence-based reasoning. Probability theory quantifies uncertainty and underpins stochastic

DOI: 10.4324/9781003664550-3

modeling by enabling analysts to represent real-world phenomena through random variables and probability laws. Common probability distributions such as the normal, binomial, Poisson, and exponential serve as analytical tools for modeling data-generating processes, error structures, and risk profiles across business, finance, and scientific applications. Building on these concepts, statistical inference uses sample data to draw conclusions about underlying populations through estimation, hypothesis testing, confidence intervals, and Bayesian updating, allowing decision-makers to assess significance, reliability, and robustness under uncertainty. In modern AI and analytics contexts, inference principles remain essential for model validation, uncertainty quantification, explainability, and responsible decision-making, ensuring that predictive insights are statistically sound and aligned with real-world uncertainty rather than purely algorithmic optimization. Probability theory, distribution models, and statistical inference form the essential toolkit for data-driven decision-making in modern business environments. These methodologies enable organizations to quantify uncertainty, identify patterns in operational data, and draw reliable conclusions from limited information. Three fundamental components work together to transform raw data into actionable BI.

3.2.1 Probability: Measuring Uncertainty in a Quantitative World

As mentioned in the above paragraph, probability is a fundamental concept in mathematics and statistics that provides a systematic way to measure and analyze uncertainty in a quantitative world. It enables assigning numerical values to the likelihood of different outcomes, allowing informed decision-making in the face of incomplete or unpredictable information. Probability offers a structured framework for drawing conclusions, making predictions, and understanding complex systems by modeling random phenomena and quantifying uncertainty governed by chance.

3.2.1.1 Foundations of Probability

Probability fundamentals play a crucial role in business decision-making as they allow firms to quantify uncertainty and derive meaningful inferences from data. A foundational understanding of probability begins with several core definitions. Probability itself is defined as a measure quantifying the likelihood that a particular event will occur, expressed as a value between 0 (impossible) and 1 (certain).[1] A basic component related to probability is an outcome, which refers to a possible result of an experiment, while an event is a set of outcomes that share a common characteristic.[2] Collectively, these elements form the building blocks of probability theory.

Key rules of probability include the addition rules, multiplication rules, and conditional probability. The addition rule states that the probability of the occurrence of at least one of two mutually exclusive events is the sum of their individual probabilities. For example, if event A has a probability of 0.4 and event B has a probability of 0.6, the combined probability of either A or B occurring is $0.4 + 0.6 = 1$ (assuming they cannot happen simultaneously). The multiplication rule, on the other hand, applies to independent events, indicating that the joint probability of both events occurring is the product of their individual probabilities.[3] This is critical in business contexts where multiple independent actions may influence outcomes. Additionally, conditional probability presents a framework to evaluate the probability of an event, given that another event has already occurred. This is essential in business environments where decisions must be adjusted based on prior outcomes or established conditions.[4] For example, a business may ascertain the likelihood of customer purchase after a marketing campaign based on historical data.

3.2.1.2 Conditional Probability

Conditional probability is a fundamental concept in probability theory that enables the evaluation of the likelihood of an event given that another event has already occurred. This concept is particularly valuable in various fields, including statistics, finance, and ML, where understanding dependencies between events can lead to better decision-making. Conditional probability is used in many aspects of business statistics and analysis. Conditional probability is defined as the probability of an event A occurring given that another event B has already happened. Mathematically, it is represented as:

$$P(A|B) = \frac{P(A \cap B)}{P(B)}, \quad \text{provided that } P(B) > 0$$

where:

$P(A|B)$ = Probability of event A occurring given that event B has already occurred.
$P(A \cap B)$ = Probability of both A and B occurring (joint probability).
$P(B)$ = Probability of event B occurring.

3.2.2 *Distributions: Modeling the Patterns in Business Data*

Distributions are pivotal tools in statistics that model the patterns and variability observed in business data by helping organizations understand and anticipate behavior across a range of scenarios. Distributions enable us to identify trends, detect anomalies, and make data-driven decisions by describing how data points are spread out, whether symmetrically, skewed, or concentrated. Common distributions, such as the normal, binomial, and Poisson, as explained in the following subsection, provide mathematical models for real-world phenomena like customer demand, sales performance, and service wait times. Understanding distributions empowers organizations to assess and manage risks, improve forecasting accuracy, and optimize operations by revealing the underlying structure of the data.

3.2.2.1 Discrete Probability Distributions

Discrete probability distributions are crucial tools in business statistics and analysis, enabling organizations to model and analyze data that consists of countable outcomes. Two prevalent discrete probability distributions are the Binomial distribution and the Poisson distribution, both of which serve specific functions in handling various business-related scenarios. Discrete probability distributions model random variables that take on countable values and play a central role in statistical analysis, decision theory, and AI-driven modeling of event-based and categorical phenomena. These distributions describe the probability mass function governing the likelihood of each possible outcome by enabling analysts to quantify uncertainty in processes involving counts, occurrences, or binary events. Common discrete distributions include the Bernoulli and binomial distributions for modeling binary outcomes and repeated trials, the geometric and negative binomial distributions for waiting-time and success-failure processes, and the Poisson distribution for modeling the frequency of rare or independent events over fixed intervals. In applied analytics and ML, discrete probability distributions are widely used in classification tasks, risk modeling, quality control, text mining, and network analysis, where outcomes naturally occur in discrete forms. A sound understanding of discrete distributions is therefore essential for constructing probabilistic models, interpreting likelihood-based results, and supporting statistically grounded inference and decision-making under uncertainty, as discussed in this section.

The Binomial distribution is applicable in situations where there are a fixed number of trials with two possible outcomes for each trial—typically labeled as "success" and "failure." Specifically, it models the probability of achieving a certain number of successes in a given number of trials, assuming that each trial is independent and has the same probability of success. The key characteristics of the binomial distribution, namely the number of trials (n) and the probability of success (p), allow businesses to analyze various operational decisions. For example, a marketing manager may use the Binomial distribution to predict the likelihood of achieving a certain number of sales from a targeted advertising campaign, based on the known conversion rate from similar past campaigns.[5] Mathematically, it is represented as:

$$P(X=k)=\binom{n}{k}p^k(1-p)^{n-k}$$

where:

$P(X=k)$ = Probability of exactly k successes in n trials
n = Number of trials
k = Number of successes
p = Probability of success in a single trial

Conversely, the Poisson distribution models the count of events occurring within a fixed interval of time or space, particularly when these events happen independently. It is characterized by a parameter (λ), which represents the average rate of occurrence of the event in that interval. This distribution is particularly useful for businesses in scenarios where events are rare but can accumulate over time. For instance, a logistics company may use Poisson distribution to estimate the average number of delivery truck arrivals at a distribution center within an hour, assisting in resource allocation and workforce management.[6] Mathematically, it is represented as:

$$P(X=k)=\frac{\lambda^k e^{-\lambda}}{k!}$$

where:

$P(X=k)$ = Probability of observing k events in a fixed interval
λ = The average number of events (mean rate) in that interval
e = Euler's number, approximately 2.718
$k!$ = Factorial of kk

Furthermore, both distributions can be leveraged with sophisticated statistical techniques to model and analyze more complex datasets. For example, the discrete nature of these distributions can help in assessing customer behaviors, managing inventory, and forecasting demand—all essential aspects of effective business operations.[7]

3.2.2.2 Continuous Probability Distributions

Continuous probability distributions are essential tools in business statistics and analysis, providing a framework for modeling random variables that can take any value within a given range. Unlike discrete probability distributions, which deal with countable outcomes, continuous distributions handle uncountable outcomes, making them suitable for various business applications where data is measured, rather than counted. A fundamental characteristic of continuous distributions is that the probability of a specific value is always zero; instead, probabilities are calculated over intervals, which makes the concept of the PDF crucial.

One of the most used continuous probability distributions is the Normal distribution, often referred to as the Gaussian distribution. It is characterized by its bell-shaped curve, defined by its mean (μ) and standard deviation (σ). Normal distribution is important in business statistics as it often describes phenomena like product sales, customer satisfaction scores, and other metrics that exhibit variability around a central value. For instance, a company might analyze sales performance to determine how many units are likely to be sold given historical data; understanding this distribution allows for more accurate forecasting and inventory management. This assertion is well-supported in the literature about the normal distribution and its applications, particularly in understanding measures of central tendency and variability in statistical analysis.[8] Mathematically, it is represented as:

$$f(x) = \frac{1}{\sqrt{2\pi\sigma^2}} e^{-\frac{(x-\mu)^2}{2\sigma^2}}$$

where:

$f(x)$ = The value of the probability density function at the point x
μ = Mean of the distribution
σ = Standard deviation

Another significant continuous distribution is the Exponential distribution, which models the time until an event occurs, such as customer arrival times or the time until a machinery failure. Characterized by its rate parameter (λ), the exponential distribution is particularly useful for businesses in operations management and service delivery. For example, a retail store can use this distribution to model the time between customer arrivals, allowing managers to optimize staffing levels during peak and off-peak hours. Continuous probability distributions can be effectively employed in developing more advanced statistical models to solve complex business problems. Mathematically, it is represented as:

$$f(x) = \lambda e^{-\lambda x}, \quad x \geq 0$$

where:

$f(x)$ = Probability density function of the exponential distribution
λ = Rate parameter (inverse of the mean)
x = Time or space interval (non-negative)

3.2.3 Statistical Inference: Making Decisions under Uncertainty

Statistical inference is the process of drawing conclusions about a population based on sample data, enabling decision-making under uncertainty. This process combines probability theory with observed data to estimate parameters, test hypotheses, and assess the reliability of conclusions as explained in the following subsections. In a business context, statistical inference enables organizations to make informed choices, such as determining if a marketing strategy increased sales or whether a new product meets quality standards, without needing to measure the entire population. Statistical inference provides a rigorous framework for making sound, evidence-based decisions even when complete information is unavailable by accounting for variability and sampling error.

3.2.3.1 Sampling and the Central Limit Theorem (CLT)

Sampling and the Central Limit Theorem (CLT) are critical components of business statistics, equipping organizations with the tools needed to derive actionable insights from data. By implementing effective sampling strategies and understanding the implications of the CLT, businesses can enhance their analytical capabilities, leading to improved strategies and optimizing operational efficiency.

Sampling involves selecting a subset of individuals, items, or data points from a larger population to estimate characteristics or parameters of that population. Effective sampling is crucial because it allows businesses to gather insights without the need to analyze the entire population, which can be unfeasible or cost prohibitive. For instance, a company may want to assess customer satisfaction by surveying a few hundred customers instead of all its clients. This approach saves resources while still providing valuable information about customer attitudes and behaviors.[9] The key to successful sampling lies in its methodology, which can include random sampling, stratified sampling, or systematic sampling, among others. Each method aims to minimize bias and ensure that the sample accurately represents the population. Businesses that utilize proper sampling techniques can make reliable inferences and facilitate informed decision-making.[10] The CLT further enhances the reliability of conclusions drawn from samples. The CLT states that, given a sufficiently large sample size, the sampling distribution of the mean will be approximately normally distributed, regardless of the original distribution of the population, given that the samples are independent and identically distributed. This theorem serves as the backbone of inferential statistics; it allows businesses to make predictions and perform hypothesis testing based on sample data.

3.2.3.2 Estimation: Point and Interval

Estimation is a fundamental aspect of statistical analysis, particularly in business contexts, allowing decision-makers to make informed choices based on data. Two primary types of estimation are point estimation and interval estimation. Understanding these concepts is crucial for effectively analyzing business data. Point estimation provides a single value as an estimate of a population parameter. This estimate serves as the best guess of the true parameter based on sample data, such as the average revenue generated per month or the expected number of units sold. For example, a company may calculate the average purchase amount of customers in a given month using sample data, yielding a point estimate for the expected sales performance. However, while point estimates are straightforward and easy to interpret, they do not convey the uncertainty inherent in the estimate itself.

Interval estimation, on the other hand, extends the concept of estimation by providing a range of values, known as a confidence interval, within which the true population parameter is likely to fall. This method is particularly valuable because it incorporates uncertainty by acknowledging potential variability in the sample data. For instance, a marketing team might report that they are 95% confident that the average customer transaction value lies between $45 and $55. This interval gives a better understanding of the estimate's reliability and helps stakeholders make more informed business decisions based on their level of confidence.

3.3 Hypothesis Testing and Statistical Modeling

In the dynamic world of business, decisions are rarely made with absolute certainty. Whether evaluating the success of a marketing campaign or predicting next quarter's sales, managers are constantly faced with questions that require more than intuition as they demand evidence. Hypothesis testing and statistical modeling offer powerful tools to transform raw data into actionable insights. Hypothesis testing provides a structured method to assess assumptions and measure the strength of observed effects by helping businesses avoid decisions based on chance alone. Hypothesis testing provides a formal framework for assessing competing claims about population parameters by specifying null and alternative hypotheses and using test statistics, p-values, and confidence intervals to determine whether observed evidence is statistically significant. Statistical modeling extends this framework by representing complex relationships between dependent and independent variables through parametric and non-parametric models, including linear and generalized linear models, time series models, and hierarchical structures, allowing analysts to explain variation, generate predictions, and test theory-based assumptions.

3.3.1 Hypothesis Testing: Making Decisions under Uncertainty

Hypothesis testing is a fundamental statistical method used to make decisions under uncertainty by evaluating assumptions about a population based on sample data. It involves developing and stating a null hypothesis, which typically represents no effect or status quo, and an alternative hypothesis that reflects a potential change or difference. This process enables organizations to assess claims, validate strategies, and support evidence-based decisions, such as determining whether a process change increases efficiency or a new product improves customer satisfaction. Hypothesis testing provides an informed, structured, and objective approach to decision-making in uncertain environments.

3.3.1.1 Introduction to Hypothesis Testing

Hypothesis testing is a fundamental statistical method employed in business analysis to make inferences about populations based on sample data. The process involves formulating a hypothesis, collecting data, performing statistical tests, and drawing conclusions regarding the hypothesis. It maps out the journey from an initial assumption to a well-supported conclusion, enabling businesses to address various questions and uncertainties within operational and strategic contexts. A hypothesis is a statement or assertion that can be tested through data analysis. In business contexts, hypotheses often relate to parameters such as sales performance, customer satisfaction, or the effectiveness of marketing strategies. Typically, two competing hypotheses are formulated: the null hypothesis (H_0), which posits that there is no effect or no difference, and the alternative hypothesis (H_1 or H_2), which suggests that there is an effect or a difference. The goal of hypothesis testing is to determine which hypothesis is more supported by the sample data.[11]

The hypothesis testing process typically has six steps: (1) formulate hypotheses by defining the null and alternative hypotheses based on the business question at hand; (2) select significance level by deciding on a significance level (commonly set at 0.05), which indicates the probability of rejecting the null hypothesis when it is true (Type I error); (3) collect data by gathering sample data relevant to the hypotheses; (4) conduct statistical test by applying an appropriate statistical test (e.g., *t*-tests, ANOVA, chi-square tests) to analyze the data and calculate the test statistics; (5) make a decision by comparing the test statistics to critical values or compute a *p*-value—if the *p*-value is less than the significance level, reject the null hypothesis in favor of the alternative hypothesis; and (6) draw conclusions by interpreting the results in the context of the business question, providing actionable insights based on the findings.

3.3.1.2 Types of Hypothesis Tests

Hypothesis testing is a critical tool in statistical analysis, employed to determine whether there is enough evidence to reject a null hypothesis in favor of an alternative hypothesis. Various types of hypothesis tests are available to address different research questions and data types; each tailored to specific contexts within business statistics and analysis. Within this framework, hypothesis tests are bifurcated into two main categories: parametric tests and non-parametric tests. Each category includes different methodologies suitable for various data conditions and research designs.

3.3.1.2.1 PARAMETRIC TESTS

Parametric tests assume that the data follows a known distribution (typically normal) and involve hypotheses about population parameters (e.g., mean, variance).

3.3.1.2.1.1 *t*-Test

In the rhythm of everyday business, questions often arise that require us to compare two groups: Is the new product more effective than the old one? Do male and female customers spend differently? Does the new training program improve performance? When our goal is to compare means between two groups based on sample data, the *t*-test becomes our statistical compass.

The *t*-test is a family of hypothesis tests used to determine whether differences in sample means are statistically significant, or simply the result of random variation. It is especially valuable when the population standard deviation is unknown, and the sample size is relatively small—two conditions common in real-world business settings. There are various forms of the *t*-test:

Independent *t*-Test: Compares means between two independent groups (e.g., control vs. treatment). Mathematically, it is represented as:

$$t = \frac{\overline{X_1} - \overline{X_2}}{\sqrt{\frac{s_1^2}{n_1} + \frac{s_2^2}{n_2}}}$$

where:

$\overline{X_1}, \overline{X_2}$ = Sample means of groups 1 and 2
s_1^2, s_2^2 = Sample variances of groups 1 and 2
n_1, n_2 = Sample sizes of groups 1 and 2

Paired *t*-Test: Compares means from the same group at different times (e.g., before and after treatment).
One-Sample *t*-Test: Tests the mean of a single group against a known value.[12]

For example, a two-sample *t*-test assesses whether the means of two independent groups are significantly different from each other. This test is particularly useful in BA when comparing the effectiveness of two marketing strategies or product versions. The *t*-test also extends to paired samples (paired *t*-tests), where the same subjects are measured under two different conditions. This can be applied in situations like evaluating the impact of a training program on employee performance.

Example: One-Sample *t*-Test

Business Question:
A retail manager wants to know whether the store's average daily sales differ from the company's benchmark of $500 per day.

Step 1. Formulate Hypotheses
Null hypothesis (H_0): $\mu = 500$
Alternative hypothesis (H_1): $\mu \neq 500$
This sets up a two-tailed test.
Step 2. Select Significance Level
Choose $\alpha = 0.05$, meaning we accept a 5% chance of a Type I error (rejecting a true null).
Step 3. Collect Data
A random sample of $n = 10$ days of sales (in dollars) is taken:
{520, 495, 510, 505, 490, 530, 515, 500, 525, 480}
Step 4. Conduct Statistical Test
Sample mean: $\overline{x} = 507$
Sample standard deviation: $s = 16.43$
Test statistic:

$$t = \frac{\overline{x} - \mu_0}{s / \sqrt{n}} = \frac{507 - 500}{16.43 / \sqrt{10}} = \frac{7}{5.20} = 1.35$$

Step 5. Make a Decision

Degrees of freedom: $df = 9$

Critical value for two-tailed test at $\alpha = 0.05: \pm 2.262$

Since $-2.262 < 1.35 < 2.262$, we fail to reject H_0.

Step 6. Draw Conclusions

There is no statistically significant evidence at the 5% level that average daily sales differ from \$500. The observed \$7 difference is likely due to random variation, not a meaningful deviation.

3.3.1.2.1.2 Analysis of Variance (ANOVA)

Analysis of Variance (ANOVA) compares means across three or more groups to determine if at least one differs significantly.

ANOVA is employed when comparing means across multiple groups. It tests the null hypothesis that all group means are equal against the alternative that at least one group mean differs. This method is frequently used in business settings when assessing performance across different categories, such as sales across different regional offices. For instance, one-way ANOVA can be used to determine if sales performance is significantly different across various product lines. It is important to ensure that the assumptions of ANOVA (normality and homogeneity of variance) hold true for valid results. Mathematically, it is represented as:

$$y_{ij} = \mu + \tau_i + \varepsilon_{ij}$$

where:

y_{ij} = Observed value of the response variable for group i and subject j

μ = Overall mean (grand mean) of all groups

τ_i = Effect of treatment (or group) i (i.e., the deviation from the grand mean)

ε_{ij} = Random error term for observation j in group i

3.3.1.2.1.3 z-Test

A z-test compares sample means to a population mean when the population standard deviation is known (or for large samples, $n > 30$). A z-test evaluates whether there is a significant difference between sample and population means, or across sample means. It is broadly applicable in business contexts, such as quality control processes, where a company may want to determine if the output of a manufacturing process meets specifications. Mathematically, it is represented as:

$$z = \frac{\bar{X} - \mu_0}{\frac{\sigma}{\sqrt{n}}}$$

where:

$\bar{X}$ = Sample mean

μ_0 = Population mean

σ = Population standard deviation

3.3.1.2.2 NON-PARAMETRIC TESTS

Non-parametric tests do not assume a specific data distribution, making them useful for ordinal, skewed, or small-sample data.

3.3.1.2.2.1 Mann-Whitney *U* Test

In many real-world business settings, the data we collect may not meet the assumptions required for traditional parametric tests like the independent two-sample *t*-test—especially the assumption of normal distribution. When faced with skewed data, small sample sizes, or ordinal outcomes, the Mann-Whitney *U* test offers a robust, non-parametric alternative for comparing two independent groups.

Rather than comparing means, the Mann-Whitney *U* test evaluates whether one group tends to have larger values than the other by analyzing the ranks of the data points. It is especially useful when dealing with customer satisfaction scores, performance ratings, or sales data that exhibit outliers or non-normal patterns. Mathematically, it is represented as:

$$U = n_1 n_2 + \frac{n_1 (n_1 + 1)}{2} - R_1$$

where:

R_1 = Sum of ranks in the first sample

3.3.1.2.2.2 Kruskal-Wallis Test

This non-parametric method extends the Mann-Whitney *U* test to compare three or more independent groups. The Kruskal-Wallis test evaluates whether there are statistically significant differences between the medians of the groups. In BA, we often want to compare more than two groups—whether it is assessing regional sales performance, customer satisfaction across product lines, or engagement rates across marketing channels. When the assumptions of normality or equal variance required for traditional ANOVA are violated, the Kruskal-Wallis test steps in as a powerful non-parametric alternative.

The Kruskal-Wallis test extends the logic of the Mann-Whitney *U* test to three or more independent groups. It works by ranking all data points across groups and analyzing whether the rank distributions differ significantly. Rather than comparing means, it tests for differences in central tendencies (usually medians), making it suitable for ordinal data, skewed distributions, or datasets with outliers. Mathematically, it is represented as:

$$H = \frac{12}{N(N+1)} \sum_{i=1}^{k} \frac{R_i^2}{n_i} - 3(N+1)$$

where:

R_i = Sum of ranks in group *i*
N = Total sample size

3.3.1.2.2.3 Chi-Square Test

Tests relationships between categorical variables or goodness-of-fit to a distribution. Not all business data comes in numbers we can average or regress. Often, the most telling insights hide in categories—Did the customer churn or stay? Was the product purchased or ignored? Was the respondent from the North, South, East, or West? To explore the relationship between such categorical variables, the Chi-Square Test of Independence is an essential statistical tool.

The Chi-Square test evaluates whether two categorical variables are statistically independent—in other words, whether knowing one variable gives you any information about the other. It compares the observed frequencies in a contingency table (the actual data) to the expected frequencies (what we'd expect if the variables were unrelated). Mathematically, it is represented as:

$$\chi^2 = \Sigma \frac{(O_i - E_i)^2}{E_i}$$

where:

O = Observed frequency
E = Expected frequency

Both parametric and non-parametric tests play crucial roles in statistical analysis, enabling researchers to derive insights from empirical data. The choice between these tests hinges upon data characteristics, sample size, and the specific hypotheses being tested. Understanding these foundational test types enhances research design and data interpretation skills, providing a robust framework for making informed decisions in analytics and business strategy formulation.[13]

3.3.1.3 *Practical Business Applications of Hypothesis Tests*

Hypothesis testing is extensively applied across various business scenarios. For instance, a company may want to evaluate whether a new advertising campaign has significantly increased sales compared to a previous period. The null hypothesis (H_0) could be that the new campaign has no effect on sales, while the alternative hypothesis (H_1) posits an increase in sales due to the campaign. By collecting sales data and applying a relevant statistical test, the company can determine if there is sufficient evidence to reject the null, guiding subsequent marketing strategies.[14]

Another relevant example can be found in product quality control. A manufacturer may test whether a production process meets specified quality standards. Here, the null hypothesis would state that the proportion of defective items produced is within acceptable limits, while the alternative hypothesis would assert that the defect rate exceeds those limits. Statistical testing allows the organization to make informed decisions about whether to accept or reject batches of their products based on the data collected during sample inspections.[15]

3.3.2 *Statistical Modeling: Understanding and Predicting Business Outcomes*

Statistical modeling, as explained in detail in the following subsections, is a powerful and objective technique for understanding relationships within data and predicting future business outcomes. Statistical models empower organizations to identify key factors that influence performance, such as sales trends, operational efficiency, and/or customer behavior, by using mathematical equations to represent real-world processes. These models range from simple linear regressions to complex multivariate or time series models, offering insights that drive informed strategic decision-making. In a competitive business environment, statistical modeling allows organizations to forecast demand, optimize pricing, assess risk, and improve resource allocation. Ultimately, it transforms raw data into insights and actionable intelligence that enhances both understanding and predictive accuracy in business operations.

3.3.2.1 Introduction to Statistical Modeling

Statistical modeling represents an essential aspect of business statistics and analysis, enabling organizations to make informed decisions based on data-driven insights. It involves the formulation of mathematical equations that represent real-world processes or phenomena, allowing analysts to describe, analyze, and predict behaviors within business contexts. At its core, statistical modeling provides a structured way to investigate relationships among variables, make predictions, and evaluate the possible outcomes of various decisions. Statistical modeling is defined as the process of creating models to represent data and draw inferences about the underlying population from which the data is drawn. These models help in simplifying complex phenomena by capturing the essential features of data while ignoring noise and irrelevant details. By providing a simplified representation, businesses can understand trends, forecast future outcomes, and facilitate decision-making processes.[16]

3.3.2.2 Types of Statistical Models

Statistical models can be categorized broadly into descriptive and predictive models, each serving distinct purposes in business statistical analysis.

3.3.2.2.1 DESCRIPTIVE MODELS

Descriptive models focus on summarizing and understanding historical data. These models include the following.

3.3.2.2.1.1 Linear Regression
This approach is used to model the relationship between a dependent variable and one or more independent variables. In business applications, linear regression finds use in predicting sales based on various marketing expenditures.[17] Linear regression stands as a fundamental technique for quantifying relationships between business variables. The standard linear regression model takes the form: $Y = \beta_0 + \beta_1 X_1 + \ldots + \beta_n X_n + \varepsilon$, where Y represents the outcome variable (such as sales revenue), X's denote predictor variables (like marketing expenditures), β's are coefficients quantifying each variable's impact, and ε accounts for random error. This model finds extensive application in marketing effectiveness analysis, pricing strategy development, and operational performance evaluation. Normally, simple linear regression is often used. Mathematically, it is represented as:

$$\hat{y} = \beta_0 + \beta_1 x$$

where:

$\hat{y}$ = Predicted value of the dependent variable
β_0 = Intercept
β_1 = Slope (regression coefficient)
x = Independent variable

3.3.2.2.1.2 Logistic Regression

Particularly useful for modeling binary outcomes, logistic regression helps businesses understand the factors influencing outcomes that can be categorized into two groups (e.g., purchase or no purchase) based on predictor variables.[18] Organizations routinely employ this technique for customer churn prediction, credit risk assessment, and campaign response modeling. The model's ability to provide interpretable odds ratios makes it particularly valuable for understanding the relative importance of different business factors in dichotomous outcomes. Both linear and logistic regression models benefit from diagnostic measures like R^2, adjusted R^2, and pseudo R^2 that help analysts assess model fit and predictive power in business applications. Mathematically, it is represented as:

$$\Pr\left(y_i = 1 \middle| x_i\right) = \frac{1}{1 + e^{-\left(\beta_0 + \beta_1 x_{i1} + \beta_2 x_{i2} + \cdots + \beta_p x_{ip}\right)}}$$

where:

y_i = Binary outcome variable for observation i (typically 0 or 1)
x_i = Vector of predictors for observation iii
β_0 = Intercept
β_j = Coefficients for predictors

3.3.2.2.2 PREDICTIVE MODELS

Predictive models aim to forecast future events and outcomes based on historical data. They include:

3.3.2.2.2.1 Time Series Models

These models analyze data points collected or recorded at specific time intervals. Time series analysis is crucial for businesses to forecast sales, inventory levels, or resource planning, allowing executives to make timely decisions.[19] Time series analysis, particularly through ARIMA (AutoRegressive Integrated Moving Average) models, provides businesses with robust tools for forecasting. These models prove indispensable for demand forecasting, inventory optimization, and financial market analysis, allowing businesses to account for seasonality, trends, and cyclical patterns in their planning processes. Mathematically, it is represented as:

$$\phi(B)(1-B)^d y_t = \theta(B)\varepsilon_t$$

where:

y_t = Observed time series value at time t
B = Backshift operator, such that $By_t = y_{t-1}$
d = Order of differencing (the "I" part in ARIMA)
ε_t = White noise error term (residual)
$\phi(B)$ = Autoregressive (AR) polynomial of order p
$\theta(B)$ = Moving average (MA) polynomial of order q

3.3.2.2.2.2 Multivariate Analysis

This refers to the analysis of multiple variables to determine patterns and relationships among them. Techniques such as MANOVA (Multivariate Analysis of Variance) help in assessing the impact of several factors simultaneously, particularly valuable in marketing and operational strategies. This proves particularly valuable in comprehensive marketing campaign evaluation, where businesses need to assess impact across various customer behavior metrics concurrently. Advanced applications include portfolio optimization in finance and product feature optimization in consumer goods, where multiple performance indicators must be considered simultaneously. Mathematically, it is represented as:

$$Y = XB + E$$

where:

Y = All observed outcomes (multiple dependent variables for each subject)
X = Design matrix that encodes group membership or experimental conditions
B = Parameters showing how group membership influences dependent variables
E = Unexplained variation (leftover error after accounting for the model)

3.3.2.2.3 STRUCTURAL EQUATION MODELING (SEM)

Structural Equation Modeling (SEM) is a complex statistical technique that allows for the analysis of relationships between multiple variables, accommodating latent variables that are not directly observed. SEM offers businesses a sophisticated framework for analyzing complex, interconnected relationships that traditional regression cannot adequately capture. SEM comprises two key components: the measurement model linking observed indicators to latent constructs, and the structural model specifying relationships between these constructs. This dual approach allows businesses to model abstract concepts like customer satisfaction, brand loyalty, and organizational culture that cannot be measured directly but significantly impact performance outcomes.

In practice, SEM enables comprehensive testing of theoretical business models through path analysis and confirmatory factor analysis. SEM is widely used in business research for validating theoretical models by assessing construct validity and analyzing causal relationships between constructs.[20] This approach provides a comprehensive method to understand business phenomena, such as customer satisfaction and loyalty. The model fit is assessed using indices like CFI (Comparative Fit Index), RMSEA (Root Mean Square Error of Approximation), and SRMR (Standardized Root Mean Square Residual), with typical thresholds of CFI > 0.90, RMSEA < 0.08 indicating acceptable fit. Businesses apply SEM to diverse areas, including customer experience mapping, employee engagement analysis, and supply chain relationship modeling, where understanding complex, mediated relationships is crucial for strategic decision-making. Mathematically, the measurement model is represented as:

$$X = \Lambda_x \xi + \delta$$

where:

X = Vector of observed exogenous variables
Λ_x = Matrix of factor loadings for x
ξ = Vector of latent exogenous variables
δ = Measurement error in X

The structural model is represented as:

$$\eta = B\eta + \Gamma\xi + \zeta$$

where:

η = Vector of latent endogenous variables (factors)
B = Matrix of coefficients among latent endogenous variables
Γ = Matrix of coefficients from exogenous to endogenous latent variables
ξ = Vector of latent exogenous variables
ζ = Structural disturbances (errors in equations)

3.3.2.2.4 ML MODELS

Recent advancements have integrated ML approaches in statistical modeling for business analysis. These models learn from data patterns and can make decisions without being explicitly programmed for specific tasks. For instance, businesses can employ algorithms for customer segmentation or predictive analytics, leveraging vast amounts of customer data to enhance marketing strategies.[21]

Statistical modeling is a key tool in today's data-driven business world. It helps organizations analyze past trends, identify important relationships between different factors, and make informed predictions about the future. As businesses rely more on data analytics, understanding these techniques has become essential for uncovering meaningful insights and staying competitive.

From basic linear regression to more complex methods like SEM and ML, these approaches offer valuable ways to tackle different business challenges. By choosing the right model for each situation, companies can make better, data-backed decisions that drive success.

3.3.2.3 Resampling Methods

Resampling methods are powerful statistical techniques that enable analysts to reuse observed data to evaluate uncertainty, assess model performance, and strengthen inference. By generating repeated samples from the original dataset, these methods bypass many of the restrictive assumptions of traditional parametric models, offering robust, data-driven approaches that are widely applicable in contemporary research. Among the most influential resampling techniques are bootstraps and cross-validation, both of which play central roles in modern statistics and ML.

The bootstrap method, originally introduced by Efron, is a non-parametric resampling approach that estimates the sampling distribution of a statistic by repeatedly sampling with replacement from the observed data. Each bootstrap sample is the same size as the original dataset, but because some observations may be drawn multiple times while others are omitted, variability across resamples naturally emerges. By calculating statistics such as means, regression coefficients, or prediction errors across thousands of bootstrap samples, analysts can derive confidence intervals and standard errors without relying on strict distributional assumptions. This flexibility makes the bootstrap particularly valuable in situations where data are limited, distributions are unknown, or models are complex.

Cross-validation is primarily employed to evaluate how well statistical models and ML algorithms generalize to independent data. By partitioning the dataset into subsets for training and testing, cross-validation helps select optimal model parameters while guarding against overfitting. Among its variations, k-fold cross-validation is most common: the data are divided into k folds, the model is trained on $k-1$ folds, and validated on the remaining fold, with the process repeated until each fold serves as a test set. Averaging the performance across folds yields a robust measure of predictive accuracy.

3.4 Bayesian Statistics and Its Applications in ML

In business, decisions are rarely made under perfect certainty. Markets fluctuate, customer preferences evolve, and data often arrives incomplete or ambiguous. Traditional statistics, grounded in fixed models and long-run frequencies, can struggle to adapt to these dynamic conditions. Bayesian statistics offer an alternative perspective. It views knowledge as something that evolves, shaped continuously by new information. This approach does not fear uncertainty, which incorporates it, quantifies it, and uses it as a foundation for reasoning. In the world of ML, Bayesian methods have become essential for building systems that learn, adapt, and make predictions in real time. For business analysts, understanding Bayesian thinking means gaining a powerful tool for navigating complexity with clarity and flexibility.

3.4.1 Foundations of Bayesian Statistics

Bayesian statistics is an area of statistical inference that combines prior beliefs with new evidence to update the probability of a hypothesis. It is founded on Bayes' theorem, which formalizes how probabilities can be updated as more data becomes available. In business statistics and analysis, Bayesian methods allow analysts to incorporate insights and expert opinions, leading to more robust data-informed strategies. Key concepts in Bayesian statistics are essential for understanding its application and effectiveness:

Prior Probability: Prior probability represents the initial belief about a parameter or hypothesis before observing any data, denoted as $P(\theta)$. This can be subjective, based on prior experience or expert opinion, or objective, determined through predetermined criteria. The choice of prior can influence the posterior results significantly, making it a crucial aspect of Bayesian analysis.

Likelihood: Likelihood refers to the probability of observing the data given a specific parameter (θ), expressed as $P(D|\theta)$. It quantifies how well the parameter explains the observed data, serving as a fundamental building block in Bayesian inference.[22]

Posterior Probability: The posterior probability $P(\theta|D)$ reflects the updated belief about the parameter after integrating the prior information with the likelihood of the observed data. It is computed using Bayes' theorem, which combines the prior and the likelihood to yield an updated inference.[23]

Bayes' Theorem: Bayes' theorem mathematically formalizes the relationship among the prior, likelihood, and posterior probabilities, articulated as follows:

$$P(\theta|D) = \frac{P(D|\theta) \cdot P(\theta)}{P(D)}$$

where:

θ = The parameter or hypothesis we want to estimate.
D = The observed data.
$P(\theta|D)$ = The posterior distribution — our updated belief about the parameter after seeing the data.
$P(D|\theta)$ = The likelihood — the probability of the data given the parameter.
$P(\theta)$ = The prior distribution — our belief about the parameter before seeing the data.
$P(D)$ = The evidence or marginal likelihood — the total probability of the data across all possible parameter values.

Understanding these key components is fundamental to effectively implementing Bayesian methods, particularly in business contexts where uncertainty is prevalent and decision-making relies heavily on integrating both prior knowledge and new evidence.

In summary, while Bayesian statistics is centered around updating beliefs with continuous information, it significantly contrasts with frequentist approaches, which focus solely on the data at hand without incorporating prior probabilities. Therefore, Bayesian methods offer flexible, robust frameworks that are particularly valuable in BA and decision-making.[24]

3.4.2 Applications in BA

Bayesian statistics has emerged as a crucial methodology within BA, offering various applications that enhance decision-making processes. Its ability to incorporate prior knowledge and continuously update beliefs based on new data presents a significant advantage in environments characterized by uncertainty and evolving information. One key application of Bayesian statistics in business is predictive modeling, where it aids in estimating uncertain outcomes based on prior distributions and observational data. Businesses can leverage Bayesian methods for customer behavior prediction, thereby making informed marketing decisions. For example, the integration of Bayesian techniques in customer segmentation allows companies to refine their targeting strategies by continuously updating their understanding of customer preferences as new data comes in.[25] Another vital area of application is risk assessment and management. Bayesian frameworks enable organizations to quantify risks by combining prior knowledge with new evidence. This is particularly beneficial in finance and insurance sectors, where uncertainty is prevalent. By utilizing Bayesian models, firms can calculate the probability distributions of potential losses and adjust their risk management strategies accordingly, thereby improving their financial robustness.[26]

Bayesian statistics also finds application in resource allocation. Businesses often need to allocate resources under uncertainty, a task facilitated by Bayesian decision theory. By updating beliefs based on new information, companies can optimize their investment strategies and operational resources effectively. This iterative process allows for better forecasting of outcomes and enhances overall decision-making in project management and operational planning.[27] Moreover, Bayesian methods are increasingly used in clinical trials and healthcare analytics, where they assist in evaluating treatment efficacy and safety. By analyzing historical clinical data along with ongoing trial results, Bayesian frameworks help researchers adapt and refine trial designs dynamically. This application is particularly relevant in the pharmaceutical industry, where timely adjustments based on Bayesian analysis can accelerate the development of new therapies and improve patient outcomes.[28]

Finally, the growing prevalence of ML in BA has ushered in the application of Bayesian methods in algorithm development. Bayesian methods are foundational to various ML algorithms, enhancing model performance and interpretability.[29] Their ability to incorporate prior distributions makes them ideal for environments with limited data where traditional frequentist methods may falter.[30] In conclusion, the applications of Bayesian statistics in BA encompass predictive modeling, risk assessment, resource allocation, and healthcare analytics, alongside their foundational role in ML. This versatility highlights their value in modern business practices, enabling organizations to navigate complex data landscapes more effectively.

3.4.3 From Bayesian Statistics to ML

In recent years, Bayesian thinking has gained increasing traction in the field of ML. As models become more complex and are deployed in environments with noisy, evolving, or limited data, the ability to quantify uncertainty is no longer a luxury but a necessity. Unlike traditional ML approaches that produce single-point estimates, Bayesian methods return entire distributions over parameters and predictions. This allows models not only to make forecasts but also to express how confident they are in those forecasts. In high-stakes applications, such as fraud detection, medical diagnostics, or dynamic pricing, this capability becomes invaluable. Bayesian models are also more robust to overfitting, particularly when data is scarce, by allowing prior knowledge or domain expertise to shape the learning process using priors.

One of the foundational tools in Bayesian ML is Bayesian linear regression. While classical linear regression estimates fixed coefficients based solely on observed data, Bayesian regression treats these coefficients as random variables with associated probability distributions. This means that instead of producing a single "best" model, Bayesian regression acknowledges multiple plausible models and weighs them according to their probability. In business settings, this leads to more cautious and calibrated decision-making. For example, a firm predicting sales based on marketing spend might use Bayesian regression to not only estimate the likely effect of ad campaigns but also to quantify the uncertainty of those estimates given recent market volatility. Another powerful framework is the Bayesian network, a graphical model that represents probabilistic relationships among variables. These networks are especially useful in situations involving complex dependencies, such as supply chain logistics, financial risk assessment, or consumer behavior modeling. By combining data with domain knowledge, Bayesian networks can infer hidden causes, forecast future events, and update beliefs in real time as new evidence becomes available. Their transparent structure also makes them particularly valuable for business users who require both performance and interpretability in predictive analytics.

A more recent and rapidly growing application of Bayesian methods is Bayesian optimization, particularly in tuning the hyperparameters of ML models. In contrast to grid search or random search, Bayesian optimization builds a probabilistic model of the objective function and uses it to decide where to evaluate next. This strategy significantly improves efficiency, especially in scenarios where model training is expensive or data is limited. Companies use Bayesian optimization to fine-tune marketing strategies, maximize return on investment in ad placement, or optimize user interface experiments. In advanced applications, Bayesian inference is also used in recommendation systems to model user preferences under uncertainty, continually refining predictions as new user interactions occur. This results in systems that are not only more personalized but also more adaptive and trustworthy. Table 3.1 presents a comparison of key Bayesian methods in ML.

3.5 Descriptive, Predictive, and Prescriptive Analytics

Descriptive, predictive, and prescriptive analytics represent a progression of analytical maturity that transforms data into insight, foresight, and actionable decision support. Broadly speaking, analytics can be understood in three layers: descriptive, predictive, and prescriptive. Each type answers a different question. Descriptive analytics ask what has happened, providing a factual summary of past events by focusing on summarizing and visualizing historical data to explain what has happened through techniques such as aggregation, reporting, dashboards, and exploratory data analysis, thereby establishing a factual baseline for understanding organizational performance. Predictive analytics move forward, estimating what is likely to occur based on historical patterns by applying statistical models, ML, and probabilistic methods to forecast future outcomes, estimate risks, and identify patterns in data, addressing the question of what is likely to happen next. Prescriptive analytics goes a step further by recommending decisions to achieve optimal outcomes by representing the most advanced stage by integrating predictive models with optimization, simulation, and decision rules to recommend optimal actions under constraints and uncertainty, effectively answering what should be done to achieve desired objectives.[31] Together, these forms of analytics empower organizations to move from hindsight to foresight to actionable strategies by providing evidence-based management and AI-driven decision-making, linking historical insight to forward-looking predictions and optimal strategic choices. Understanding their distinctions and how they work together is essential for anyone seeking to make evidence-based decisions in a data-rich business environment.

3.5.1 Descriptive Analytics: Understanding the Past and Present

Descriptive analytics serves as a foundational component of business statistics and analytics, focusing primarily on the interpretation of historical data to enhance decision-making processes. This analytic style is principally concerned with summarizing past events and trends to offer insights into organizational performance and behavior without making predictions or recommendations about future actions.[32] The insights gained from descriptive analytics help businesses understand their current state, which is a critical step before engaging in more complex predictive or prescriptive analytical processes.[33]

Table 3.1 Comparison of Key Bayesian Methods in Machine Learning

Method	*Definition*	*Primary Use*	*Typical Business Scenario*	*Main Advantage*
Bayesian linear regression	Model coefficients as probability distributions instead of fixed values	Predictive modeling under uncertainty	Forecasting sales based on ad spend or economic indicators	Captures uncertainty in predictions and model parameters
Bayesian networks	Graph-based model showing probabilistic relationships among variables	Inference and reasoning with dependent variables	Credit risk modeling, supply chain decision-making	Incorporates expert knowledge and updates with new observations
Bayesian optimization	Probabilistic method for optimizing complex functions	Hyperparameter tuning and decision optimization	Maximizing ad ROI, tuning ML models	Requires fewer evaluations, efficient for costly computations
Bayesian recommender systems	Learns and updates user preferences over time	Personalized content and product recommendation	Suggesting products in e-commerce, streaming content	Adapts in real time and accounts for preference uncertainty

Common tools and techniques utilized in descriptive analytics include data visualization methods such as dashboards, reports, and charts, which effectively communicate insights drawn from large datasets.[34] Tools like Google Analytics exemplify how organizations track user engagement and data patterns over time, relying on summary statistics and visual representations to guide operational strategies.[35] Furthermore, literature indicates that qualitative methods, alongside quantitative techniques, may also contribute to descriptive analytics by analyzing social phenomena in context.[36] Despite its utility, descriptive analytics is not without limitations. One of the primary constraints is its inability to predict future outcomes or prescribe action. It is purely retrospective, providing no guidance on how organizations should respond to identified trends.[37] Additionally, relying solely on descriptive analysis may lead stakeholders to overlook potential patterns that could be more fully explored using diagnostic or predictive analytics. There is also the challenge of data quality; if the underlying data utilized in descriptive analytics is flawed or insufficient, the resultant insights may mislead organizational decisions.

In summary, descriptive analytics plays a crucial role in the realm of business statistics and analytics by elucidating historical data trends and performance metrics essential for informed decision-making. Understanding its goals, common applications, and inherent limitations lays the groundwork for integrating more advanced analytics methodologies. Table 3.2 presents methods of descriptive analytics.

Table 3.2 Methods of Descriptive Analytics

Category	*Key Methods/ Techniques*	*Purpose/Function*	*Common Tools/ Platforms*
Summary statistics	Mean, median, mode, variance, standard deviation, range	Describe central tendency and dispersion	Excel, R, Python (pandas, NumPy), SPSS, SAS
Data aggregation	Grouping, subtotals, cross-tabulation, pivot tables	Summarize large datasets into digestible views	Excel PivotTables, SQL (GROUP BY), Tableau
Data visualization	Bar charts, histograms, pie charts, line graphs, boxplots	Reveal trends, distributions, and comparisons visually	Tableau, Power BI, Excel, Python (matplotlib, seaborn)
Exploratory data analysis	Scatterplots, correlation matrix, distribution plots	Identify patterns, anomalies, relationships	Python (pandas profiling, seaborn), R (ggplot2)
Frequency analysis	Counts, proportions, frequency tables	Examine how often values occur in a dataset	Excel, R, Python, SPSS
Data profiling	Data completeness, uniqueness, consistency checks	Understand data quality and readiness for analysis	Trifacta, Talend, Python (pandas), OpenRefine
Reporting and dashboards	Key performance indicators (KPIs), scorecards, automated reports	Communicate insights to stakeholders in real time	Power BI, Tableau, Google Data Studio, Looker
Comparative analysis	Year-over-year (YoY), month-over-month (MoM), benchmarking	Compare performance across time or against standards	Excel, SQL, Tableau, business intelligence tools

3.5.2 Predictive Analytics: Anticipating What Might Happen

Predictive analytics represents a critical advancement in the field of business statistics and analytics, focusing on making forecasts about future events based on historical data. This branch of analytics combines statistical techniques, data mining, ML, and AI to identify patterns and predict potential outcomes.[38] The core methods of predictive analytics include regression analysis, time series analysis, classification, and clustering, each serving specific needs and data types.

Predictive analytics applies statistical and ML techniques to historical data to forecast future events or trends. At its core, it relies on patterns hidden within data—patterns that can be modeled, quantified, and used to make informed predictions about what is likely to happen next. Regression and classification algorithms like linear regression and logistic regression form the foundational building blocks. Meanwhile, time series models provide a lens for forecasting temporal data, which is essential for financial markets, sales, and inventory planning. As the complexity of data grows, ensemble models like Random Forests and Gradient Boosting rise to prominence by combining multiple weak learners into powerful predictive engines. For non-tabular data or deep patterns, neural networks, especially deep learning architectures, open new frontiers in image, text, and sequence prediction.

Predictive analytics is not just a single tool, but it is an evolving ecosystem. The most powerful predictive models today are hybrid systems, combining statistical intuition, ML, and domain knowledge to transform uncertainty into probability and data into foresight. Table 3.3 presents methods of predictive analytics.

Table 3.3 Methods of Predictive Analytics

Category	*Key Methods/Algorithms*	*Purpose/Function*	*Common Tools/ Platforms*
Regression techniques	Linear regression, logistic regression, Ridge/Lasso regression	Predict continuous or binary outcomes	R, Python (scikit-learn, statsmodels), SPSS, SAS
Time series analysis	ARIMA, SARIMA, exponential smoothing, Prophet	Forecast trends, seasonality, and future values	R (forecast), Python (statsmodels, Prophet), Excel
Decision trees & ensembles	CART, random forests, gradient boosting (XGBoost, LightGBM)	Classification and regression with high interpretability	scikit-learn, XGBoost, LightGBM, R, Weka
Machine learning algorithms	k-nearest neighbors (kNN), Naïve Bayes, support vector machines (SVM)	Pattern recognition and classification	scikit-learn, Weka, KNIME, Orange
Neural networks	Multilayer perceptron, deep learning (CNNs, RNNs)	Capturing complex, nonlinear relationships in large datasets	TensorFlow, Keras, PyTorch, H2O.ai
Clustering (for prediction)	K-means, DBSCAN, hierarchical clustering	Grouping similar observations; used in segmentation	R, Python, Tableau, KNIME
Dimensionality reduction	Principal component analysis (PCA), t-SNE, UMAP	Reduce variables while preserving predictive signal	scikit-learn, MATLAB, Orange
Ensemble methods	Bagging, boosting, stacking	Combine multiple models to improve accuracy and robustness	XGBoost, CatBoost, scikit-learn, H2O.ai

3.5.3 Prescriptive Analytics: Guiding Decision-Making

Prescriptive analytics is an essential branch of analytics that focuses on providing actionable recommendations for decision-making processes within organizations. It builds on the foundations laid by descriptive and predictive analytics by identifying historical trends, predicting future outcomes, and suggesting optimal courses of action to leverage these insights effectively.[39] The primary aim of prescriptive analytics is to guide decision-makers toward achieving desired outcomes while considering various constraints and uncertainties present in business environments.[40]

3.5.3.1 Tools and Techniques of Prescriptive Analytics

A variety of tools and techniques are employed in prescriptive analytics, ranging from optimization algorithms to simulation models. Optimization techniques, such as linear programming and integer programming, enable organizations to identify the best possible solutions from a set of alternatives while adhering to specified constraints.[41] Additionally, simulation models allow businesses to analyze complex scenarios and assess the impact of different variables on outcomes, aiding in risk assessment and mitigation. ML methods also play a significant role in prescriptive analytics, as they help derive insights from large datasets that inform decision-making frameworks.[42] Human-augmented systems are gaining traction, integrating AI with human decision-making processes to enhance the quality and timeliness of prescriptions.[43] Each technique plays a distinct role. The optimization models offer mathematically optimal solutions, simulations navigate uncertainty, heuristics provide fast approximations, and decision analysis structures complex choices. Meanwhile, prescriptive ML introduces adaptive intelligence, and business rules inject domain expertise into automated systems. Table 3.4 presents tools and techniques of prescriptive analytics.

Table 3.4 Tools and Techniques of Prescriptive Analytics

Technique/Toolset	*Key Methods/Algorithms*	*Typical Applications*	*Popular Tools/Software*
Optimization models	Linear programming, integer programming, goal programming	Resource allocation, supply chain, workforce planning	Excel Solver, IBM CPLEX, Gurobi, PuLP, Pyomo (Python)
Simulation-based optimization	Monte Carlo simulation, discrete event simulation, simulated annealing	Risk analysis, logistics, finance, healthcare	AnyLogic, Arena, Simul8, SimPy, DEAP (Python)
Decision analysis	Decision trees, expected value/utility	Investment decisions, medical diagnostics	TreeAge, PrecisionTree, dtreeviz (Python)
Heuristics & metaheuristics	Genetic algorithms, tabu search, ant colony optimization	Routing, scheduling, complex planning problems	Google OR-Tools, mlrose, DEAP
Constraint programming	Variable-constraint satisfaction, backtracking, propagation	Timetabling, crew rostering, product configuration	IBM CP Optimizer, Google OR-Tools, MiniZinc
Prescriptive machine learning	Reinforcement learning, uplift modeling, contextual bandits	Pricing, personalization, ad targeting	TensorFlow, PyTorch, EconML, Vowpal Wabbit

(*Continued*)

Table 3.4 (Continued)

Technique/Toolset	*Key Methods/Algorithms*	*Typical Applications*	*Popular Tools/Software*
Business rules/ expert systems	IF-THEN logic rules, decision tables	Fraud detection, compliance, credit scoring	Drools, Jess, CLIPS
Scenario planning/ what-if	Scenario trees, sensitivity analysis, Monte Carlo simulation	Strategic forecasting, stress testing	Excel, @Risk, Crystal Ball

3.5.3.2 Challenges of Prescriptive Analytics

Despite its transformative potential, prescriptive analytics faces several challenges. One significant hurdle is the complexity of integrating various data sources and analytics tools into a cohesive decision support system.[44] Organizations often operate with multiple legacy systems, making it difficult to obtain a comprehensive view of the data landscape necessary for effective prescriptive analytics. Furthermore, the interpretability of prescriptive models can sometimes be a concern; decision-makers may find it challenging to understand the rationale behind recommendations generated by complex algorithms. The dependency on high-quality data is another critical issue, as incorrect or biased data inputs can significantly distort the recommendations provided, leading to potentially negative outcomes. Lastly, resistance to adopting new methodologies or analytics approaches within organizational cultures can impede the effective implementation of prescriptive analytics systems. In conclusion, prescriptive analytics enhances business decision-making by turning insights into actionable recommendations. By understanding the available tools, techniques, and associated challenges, organizations can better assess their ability to effectively implement prescriptive analytics in the context of business statistics and analytics.

3.6 Summary

This chapter provides the statistical underpinnings of data-driven decision-making in AI and analytics. Students will learn essential statistical concepts that form the basis for building predictive models and evaluating AI systems. Topics include probability distributions, statistical inference, hypothesis testing, Bayesian statistics, and the analytics continuum. This chapter introduces the core statistical tools necessary for data analytics and AI applications by discussing probability theory, statistical inference, hypothesis testing, Bayesian statistics, and the analytics continuum. These foundations are critical for model development and interpretation in business environments. This chapter provides a comprehensive introduction to business statistics and analytics, laying the mathematical and conceptual foundation for building predictive models, extracting valuable insights, and supporting data-driven decision-making in modern organizations. It explores the critical role that statistical concepts, tools, and techniques play in understanding and interpreting data to improve performance, optimize operations, and maintain a competitive edge.

The chapter begins by defining key terms in statistics and analytics and explaining their relevance in business contexts. It highlights how descriptive statistics, inferential statistics, and predictive analytics work together to turn raw data into actionable knowledge. Emphasis is placed on data collection methods, data visualization, probability distributions, hypothesis testing, regression analysis, and forecasting techniques. Each concept is linked to practical applications in areas such as customer behavior analysis, market segmentation, risk assessment, and operational efficiency. By integrating real-world examples and case studies, the chapter illustrates how businesses use statistical tools to uncover patterns, test assumptions, reduce uncertainty, and support strategic decision-making. It also emphasizes the importance of data quality, ethical data use, and critical thinking in interpreting statistical results. Finally, this chapter underscores the strategic value of statistics and analytics in driving innovation, sustaining long-term growth, and fostering resilience in an increasingly data-driven and competitive business environment.

Notes

1 Durica, M., Valaskova, K., & Janoskova, K. (2019). Logit business failure prediction in V4 countries. *Engineering Management in Production and Services*, 11(4), 54–64. https://doi.org/10.2478/emj-2019-0033. Available at https://reference-global.com/2/v2/download/pdf/10.2478/emj-2019-0033
2 Hatos, R., Cioban, S., Bea, G., Dodescu, A., & Hatos, A. (2022). Assessing the impact of entrepreneurial education on entrepreneurial intentions among Romanian doctoral students and postdoctoral researchers. *Sustainability*, 14(14), 8369. https://doi.org/10.3390/su14148369. Available at https://www.mdpi.com/2071-1050/14/14/8369
3 Feng, C., Yu, J., Fan, Y., & Chen, H. (2025). Performance implications of match between social media–enabled interactions and contracts in interfirm governance. *Internet Research*, 35(1), 264–293. https://doi.org/10.1108/INTR-10-2022-0844. Available at https://www.emerald.com/intr/article-abstract/35/1/264/1241719/Performance-implications-of-match-between-social?redirectedFrom=fulltext
4 Julio, B., & Yook, Y. (2012). Political uncertainty and corporate investment cycles. *The Journal of Finance*, 67(1), 45–83. https://doi.org/10.1111/j.1540-6261.2011.01707.x. Available at https://onlinelibrary.wiley.com/doi/full/10.1111/j.1540-6261.2011.01707.x
5 Yağın, F. H., Güldoğan, E., & Çolak, C. (2021). A web-based software for the calculation of theoretical probability distributions. *The Journal of Cognitive Systems*, 6(1), 44–50. https://doi.org/10.52876/jcs.878742. Available at https://dergipark.org.tr/en/pub/jcs/article/878742
6 Betsch, S., Ebner, B., & Nestmann, F. (2022). Characterizations of non-normalized discrete probability distributions and their application in statistics. *Electronic Journal of Statistics*, 16(1), 1303–1329. https://doi.org/10.1214/22-EJS1983. Available at https://projecteuclid.org/journals/electronic-journal-of-statistics/volume-16/issue-1/Characterizations-of-non-normalized-discrete-probability-distributions-and-their-application/10.1214/22-EJS1983.full
7 Eliwa, M. S., Ahsan-ul-Haq, M., Almohaimeed, A., Al-Bossly, A., & El-Morshedy, M. (2023). Discrete extension of Poisson distribution for over dispersed count data: Theory and applications. *Journal of Mathematics*, 2023(1), 2779120. https://doi.org/10.1155/2023/2779120. Available at https://onlinelibrary.wiley.com/doi/full/10.1155/2023/2779120
8 Onyancha, B. N., & Ogbonnaya, U. I. (2022). Undergraduate students' proficiencies in solving bivariate normal distribution problems. *Journal of Pedagogical Sociology and Psychology*, 4(1), 20–34. https://doi.org/10.33902/JPSP.202212259. Available at https://www.j-psp.com/article/undergraduate-students-proficiencies-in-solving-bivariate-normal-distribution-problems-12090
9 Dewangga, M. A. K. W., & Layman, C. V. (2023). The cost leadership, entrepreneurship orientation, and differentiation strategies of Bali's MSME in tourism sector. *APMBA (Asia Pacific Management and Business Application)*, 12(1), 101–114. https://doi.org/10.21776/ub.apmba.2023.012.01.7. Available at https://apmba.ub.ac.id/index.php/apmba/article/view/681
10 Bhandari, H. P. (2024). Content dimensions in academic decision-making: Exploring threats and opportunities among Oxford College Undergraduates. *The OCEM Journal of Management, Technology, and Social Sciences*, 3(1), 117–126. https://doi.org/10.3126/ocemjmtss.v3i1.62231. Available at https://journal.oxfordcollege.edu.np/index.php/ojmts/article/view/40
11 Emmert-Streib, F., & Dehmer, M. (2019). Understanding statistical hypothesis testing: The logic of statistical inference. *Machine Learning and Knowledge Extraction*, 1(3), 945–962. https://doi.org/10.3390/make1030054. Available at https://www.mdpi.com/2504-4990/1/3/54
12 Kim, T. K. (2015). T test as a parametric statistic. *Korean Journal of Anesthesiology*, 68(6), 540–546. https://doi.org/10.4097/kjae.2015.68.6.540. Available at https://synapse.koreamed.org/articles/1156170

13 Dash, B., & Ali, A. (2019). Importance of hypothesis testing, type i, and type ii errors – A study of statistical power. December 5, 2019. https://doi.org/10.2139/ssrn.4575635. Available at https://papers.ssrn.com/sol3/papers.cfm?abstract_id=4575635

14 Fachri, H. (2023). The effect of reputation and partnership strategy on business performance of internet service provider company. *Journal of Asian Multicultural Research for Social Sciences Study*, 4(3), 26–34. https://doi.org/10.47616/jamrsss.v4i3.463. Available at http://amrsjournals.com/index.php/jamrsss/article/view/463

15 Naibei, I. K. (2021). Demystifying hypothesis testing in business and social sciences studies. https://doi.org/10.29322/IJSRP.11.12.2021.p12047. Available at https://www.researchgate.net/profile/Isaac-Naibei/publication/357448650_Demystifying_Hypothesis_Testing_in_Business_and_Social_Sciences_Studies/links/61ceb857b6b5667157b95f37/Demystifying-Hypothesis-Testing-in-Business-and-Social-Sciences-Studies.pdf

16 Muerza, V., Gargallo, P., Salvador, M., & Turón, A. (2024). Impact of problem-based learning on the perception, understanding, and application of statistical concepts in business administration and management students. *Sustainability*, 16(4), 1591. https://doi.org/10.3390/su16041591. Available at https://www.mdpi.com/2071-1050/16/4/1591

17 Hsu, J. L., Jones, A., Lin, J. H., & Chen, Y. R. (2022). Data visualization in introductory business statistics to strengthen students' practical skills. *Teaching Statistics*, 44(1), 21–28. https://doi.org/10.1111/test.12291. Available at https://onlinelibrary.wiley.com/doi/abs/10.1111/test.12291?casa_token=ZsVZWZnYY2YAAAAA:tFcSvwA_UvqRiWNNLNwqFQgEVKxsIdtHKV6hu-kclmLxnUpSUxTsdVEOD8kg0NaCRl2cJ69ZBA7iAYxa

18 Levine, D. M., & Stephan, D. F. (2011). Teaching introductory business statistics using the DCOVA framework. *Decision Sciences Journal of Innovative Education*, 9(3), 395–400. https://doi.org/10.1111/j.1540-4609.2011.00316.x. Available at https://onlinelibrary.wiley.com/doi/abs/10.1111/j.1540-4609.2011.00316.x?casa_token=yuyZboCE68kAAAAA:cZ1KKiaqn1kjMwjn5RbV-pANWslzZfPjZzyiElq4AgCacFMmTQVglplDW4WVe_tNc9wsgPwAUOm31GAW

19 Hartmann, P. M., Zaki, M., Feldmann, N., & Neely, A. (2016). Capturing value from big data–a taxonomy of data-driven business models used by start-up firms. *International Journal of Operations & Production Management*, 36(10), 1382–1406. https://doi.org/10.1108/IJOPM-02-2014-0098. Available at https://www.emerald.com/ijopm/article-abstract/36/10/1382/303563/Capturing-value-from-big-data-a-taxonomy-of-data?redirectedFrom=fulltext

20 Prabhu, S. L. N. (2025). Examining the factors affecting the success of the biotechnology firms in the Kingdom of Saudi Arabia. *SBS Journal of Applied Business Research*, 1(1). https://doi.org/10.70301/. Available at https://jabr.sbs.edu/article/view/59

21 Pimenowa, O., Pimenov, S., Fyliuk, H., Sitnicki, M. W., Kolosha, V., & Kurinskyi, D. (2023). Sustainable business model of modern enterprises in conditions of uncertainty and turbulence. Sustainability, 15(3), 2654. https://doi.org/10.3390/su15032654. Available at https://www.mdpi.com/2071-1050/15/3/2654

22 Diciccio, T. J., Kuffner, T. A., & Young, G. A. (2012). Objective Bayes, conditional inference and the signed root likelihood ratio statistic. *Biometrika*, 99(3), 675–686. https://doi.org/10.1093/biomet/ass028. Available at https://academic.oup.com/biomet/article-abstract/99/3/675/360079

23 Toni, T., Ozaki, Y. I., Kirk, P., Kuroda, S., & Stumpf, M. P. (2012). Elucidating the in vivo phosphorylation dynamics of the ERK MAP kinase using quantitative proteomics data and Bayesian model selection. *Molecular BioSystems*, 8(7), 1921–1929. https://doi.org/10.1039/C2MB05493K. Available at https://pubs.rsc.org/en/content/articlelanding/2012/mb/c2mb05493k/unauth

24 Ratmann, O., Andrieu, C., Wiuf, C., & Richardson, S. (2009). Model criticism based on likelihood-free inference, with an application to protein network evolution. *Proceedings of the National Academy of Sciences*, 106(26), 10576–10581. https://doi.org/10.1073/pnas.0807882106. Available at https://www.pnas.org/doi/abs/10.1073/pnas.0807882106

25 Polmear, M., Vasilopoulos, T., O'Hara, N., & Krupko, T. (2022). Death of the P value? Bayesian statistics for orthopaedic surgeons. *JAAOS-Journal of the American Academy of Orthopaedic Surgeons*, 10, 5435. https://doi.org/10.5435/JAAOS-D-24-00813. Available at https://journals.lww.com/jaaos/fulltext/2025/03150/death_of_the_p_value__bayesian_statistics_for.2.aspx

26 Ospel, J. M., Brown, S., Holodinsky, J. K., Rinkel, L., Ganesh, A., Coutts, S. B., … & Goyal, M. (2024). An introduction to Bayesian approaches to trial design and statistics for stroke researchers. *Stroke*, 55(11), 2742–2753. https://doi.org/10.1161/STROKEAHA.123.044144. Available at https://www.ahajournals.org/doi/full/10.1161/STROKEAHA.123.044144

27 Jackson, M. L., Ferdinands, J., Nowalk, M. P., Zimmerman, R. K., Kieke, B., Gaglani, M., … & Jackson, L. A. (2021). Differences between Frequentist and Bayesian inference in routine surveillance for influenza vaccine effectiveness: A test-negative case-control study. *BMC Public Health*, 21, 1–8. https://doi.org/10.1186/s12889-021-10543-z. Available at https://link.springer.com/article/10.1186/s12889-021-10543-z#citeas

28 Al Amer, F. M., Thompson, C. G., & Lin, L. (2021). Bayesian methods for meta-analyses of binary outcomes: implementations, examples, and impact of priors. *International Journal of Environmental Research and Public Health*, 18(7), 3492. https://doi.org/10.3390/ijerph18073492. Available at https://www.mdpi.com/1660-4601/18/7/3492

29 Hackenberger, B. K. (2019). Bayes or not Bayes, is this the question?. *Croatian Medical Journal*, 60(1), 50.

30 Oluwale, F. V. (2023). Inferring the allometric growth coefficient of juvenile African mud catfish, Clarias gariepinus (Burchell, 1822), using Bayesian and Frequentist regression models. *Zoologist (The)*, 23(1), 1–7. https://doi.org/10.4314/tzool.v23i1.1. Available at https://www.ajol.info/index.php/tzool/article/view/268071

31 Bertsimas, D., & Kallus, N. (2020). From predictive to prescriptive analytics. *Management Science*, 66(3), 1025–1044. https://doi.org/10.1287/mnsc.2018.3253. Available at https://pubsonline.informs.org/doi/abs/10.1287/mnsc.2018.3253

32 Lunsford, D. L., & Phillips, P. P. (2018). Tools used by organizations to support human capital analytics. *Performance Improvement*, 57(3), 6–15. https://doi.org/10.1002/pfi.21767. Available at https://onlinelibrary.wiley.com/doi/abs/10.1002/pfi.21767?casa_token=nnhtNz0f2uUAAAAA:8oiPpdmw8Cji5vFaRHk991HFRMXf_p07Na_-9W9eExefO4KTXgK9hs9n6aPegZrLtIZW4FQNFoo_KdlU

33 Marzouk, M., & Enaba, M. (2019). Analyzing project data in BIM with descriptive analytics to improve project performance. Built environment project and asset management, 9(4), 476–488. https://doi.org/10.1108/BEPAM-04-2018-0069. Available at https://www.emerald.com/bepam/article-abstract/9/4/476/63590/Analyzing-project-data-in-BIM-with-descriptive?redirectedFrom=fulltext

34 Goforth, E., El-Dakhakhni, W., & Wiebe, L. (2022). Network analytics for infrastructure asset management systemic risk assessment. *Journal of Infrastructure Systems*, 28(2), 04022006. https://doi.org/10.1061/(ASCE)IS.1943-555X.0000667. Available at https://ascelibrary.org/doi/full/10.1061/%28ASCE%29IS.1943-555X.0000667

35 Chotiyarnwong, P., Harvey, N. C., Johansson, H., Liu, E., Lorentzen, M., Kanis, J. A., & McCloskey, E. V. (2019). Temporal changes in access to FRAX® in Thailand between 2010 and 2018. *Archives of Osteoporosis*, 14, 1–7. https://doi.org/10.1007/s11657-019-0613-2. Available at https://link.springer.com/article/10.1007/s11657-019-0613-2#citeas

36 Nakasholol0, T., & Iyamu, T. (2019). Understanding big data analytics and the Interpretive approach for analysis purposes. *Journal of Contemporary Management*, 16(1), 272–289. https://doi.org/10.35683/jcm18096.0014. Available at https://journals.co.za/doi/pdf/10.35683/jcm18096.0014

37 Reier Forradellas, R. F., & Garay Gallastegui, L. M. (2021). Digital transformation and artificial intelligence applied to business: Legal regulations, economic impact and perspective. *Laws*, 10(3), 70. https://doi.org/10.3390/laws10030070. Available at https://www.mdpi.com/2075-471X/10/3/70

38 Joel, O. T., & Oguanobi, V. U. (2024). Data-driven strategies for business expansion: Utilizing predictive analytics for enhanced profitability and opportunity identification. *International Journal of Frontiers in Engineering and Technology Research*, 6(02), 071–081. https://doi.org/10.53294/ijfetr.2024.6.2.0035. Available at https://pdfs.semanticscholar.org/91f6/eae8c85629f950d39beac7a18519e42ac674.pdf

39 Brandt, T., Dlugosch, O., Abdelwahed, A., van den Berg, P. L., & Neumann, D. (2022). Prescriptive analytics in urban policing operations. *Manufacturing & Service Operations Management*, 24(5), 2463–2480. https://doi.org/10.1287/msom.2021.1022. Available at https://pubsonline.informs.org/doi/abs/10.1287/msom.2021.1022

40 Hirvonen, M., Kauppi, K., & Liesiö, J. (2025). Identifying enablers for the successful deployment of prescriptive analytics – A multiple case study. *European Business Review*, 37(2), 245–277. https://doi.org/10.1108/EBR-08-2023-0253. Available at https://www.emerald.com/ebr/article/37/2/245/1242724/Identifying-enablers-for-the-successful-deployment

41 Lepenioti, K., Bousdekis, A., Apostolou, D., & Mentzas, G. (2021). Human-augmented prescriptive analytics with interactive multi-objective reinforcement learning. *IEEE Access*, 9, 100677–100693. https://doi.org/10.1109/ACCESS.2021.3096662. Available at https://ieeexplore.ieee.org/abstract/document/9481230

42 Bertsimas, D., & Kallus, N. (2020). From predictive to prescriptive analytics. *Management Science*, 66(3), 1025–1044. https://doi.org/10.1287/mnsc.2018.3253. Available at https://pubsonline.informs.org/doi/abs/10.1287/mnsc.2018.3253

43 Lo, V. S., & Pachamanova, D. A. (2023). From meaningful data science to impactful decisions: The importance of being causally prescriptive. *Data Science Journal*, 22(1). https://doi.org/10.5334/dsj-2023-008. Available at https://datascience.codata.org/articles/10.5334/dsj-2023-008?_rsc=lzqcu

44 Olaleye, I., Mokogwu, V., Olufemi-Phillips, A. Q., & Adewale, T. T. (2024). Unlocking competitive advantage in emerging markets through advanced business analytics frameworks. *GSC Advanced Research and Reviews*, 21(02), 419-426. https://doi.org/10.30574/gscarr.2024.21.2.0455. Available at https://www.researchgate.net/profile/Titilope-Adewale-4/publication/386278741_Unlocking_competitive_advantage_in_emerging_markets_through_advanced_business_analytics_frameworks/links/679e5a2c645ef274a45ae11e/Unlocking-competitive-advantage-in-emerging-markets-through-advanced-business-analytics-frameworks.pdf

4 Machine Learning Essentials

Learning Objectives

- Understand machine learning (ML), its definition, types, and main components
- Learn supervised, unsupervised, and reinforcement learning
- Understand machine learning and AI technologies
- Learn key algorithms: linear regression, decision trees (supervised), clustering (unsupervised)
- Understand model evaluation and performance metrics
- Understand AI algorithms and their use for business
- Understand different types of machine learning
- Recognize popular ML algorithms and their applications
- Evaluate model performance using standard metrics
- Identify the bias-variance trade-off

4.1 Introduction

Machine Learning (ML), as an essential component and a cornerstone of AI, is revolutionizing the way organizations employ technologies to make decisions, address business issues, and solve complex problems. ML is a subset of AI that focuses on building systems capable of learning from data, identifying patterns, and making decisions with minimal human intervention.[1] This chapter is designed to provide a clear and comprehensive understanding of the evolving field of ML by addressing the core concepts of ML, explaining what it is, how it works, why it matters, and how it contributes to advancing AI. This chapter (1) examines the three main types of ML, namely, supervised, unsupervised, and reinforcement learning (RL), and their applications for organizations of all sizes and types; (2) provides students an understanding of fundamental algorithms, such as linear regression, decision trees, clustering, and neural networks; (3) guides students through the process of building, training, and evaluating ML models using popular tools and techniques like Python, TensorFlow, and Scikit-learn, as hands-on examples, coding exercises, and real-world case studies help reinforce learning; and (4) provides a tangible understanding of how ML can be applied to solve real-world problems. Ethical considerations, including bias in algorithms and data privacy, are presented to ensure students are equipped to approach ML responsibly and

DOI: 10.4324/9781003664550-4

thoughtfully. Ultimately, this chapter is intended to present key concepts in ML in a highly structured and pedagogical manner, making it accessible even to readers with limited knowledge of the field, while still offering value to more experienced readers by providing an excellent overview.

4.2 Machine Learning

ML is a core branch of AI that focuses on developing algorithms and models capable of learning patterns from data and improving performance on tasks without being explicitly programmed. Rooted in statistics, optimization, and computer science, ML enables systems to infer relationships, detect structure, and generate predictions or decisions based on empirical evidence rather than fixed rules.[2] ML methods are commonly categorized into supervised learning, unsupervised learning, and RL, as described in detail in the next section. Supervised learning uses labeled data to train models for prediction and classification tasks, such as linear and logistic regression, decision trees, SVMs, and neural networks. Unsupervised learning focuses on discovering latent structures in unlabeled data through techniques such as clustering, dimensionality reduction, and topic modeling, while RL enables agents to learn optimal actions through interaction with an environment and feedback in the form of rewards.[3]

A defining feature of modern ML is its ability to scale large, complex, and high-dimensional datasets, making it particularly well-suited for applications involving text, images, sensor data, and transactional records. Advances in computational power, big data infrastructure, and algorithmic design, especially deep learning architectures such as convolutional and RNNs, have significantly expanded the scope and performance of ML systems across domains, including finance, healthcare, manufacturing, marketing, and sustainability analytics. In business and policy contexts, ML supports predictive analytics, risk assessment, anomaly detection, personalization, and automation, often outperforming traditional rule-based or purely statistical approaches when relationships are nonlinear or data are unstructured. Ultimately, ML has become a foundational technology for AI-driven analytics, enabling organizations to convert data into predictive insight and strategic value while underscoring the need for sound methodological, ethical, and governance frameworks.

4.3 Supervised, Unsupervised, and Reinforcement Learning

ML encompasses a set of computational methods that enable systems to learn patterns from data and improve performance without being explicitly programmed. The three foundational paradigms of ML are supervised learning, unsupervised learning, and reinforcement learning, which differ primarily in how learning signals are provided and how models interact with data and environments, as thoroughly explained in the following subsections.[4]

4.3.1 Supervised Learning

Supervised learning is the main aspect of ML where the algorithm is trained on a labeled dataset, where training examples are paired with an output label. The primary objective of supervised learning is to learn a mapping function from inputs to outputs by enabling the model to predict outcomes for unseen data with high accuracy. Supervised learning is the most widely used ML paradigm and operates on labeled datasets, where input variables are paired with known output labels. Supervised learning tasks are typically categorized into classification, where outputs are discrete categories (e.g., fraud detection, credit risk classification), and regression, where outputs are continuous values (e.g., earnings forecasts, demand prediction). Supervised learning is commonly used in both classification tasks, where the goal is to assign inputs to discrete categories (e.g., fraud vs. no fraud), and regression tasks, where the objective is to predict continuous values (e.g., forecasting sales or stock prices). The learning process involves feeding the algorithm a large set of input–output pairs by allowing it to iteratively adjust internal parameters to minimize the error between predicted and actual outputs. Common algorithms used in supervised learning include linear regression, logistic regression, decision trees, SVMs, *k*-nearest neighbors (KNN), and neural networks.

Common supervised algorithms include linear and logistic regression, SVMs, decision trees, random forests, gradient boosting models, and neural networks.[5] Supervised learning is particularly effective in structured decision-making contexts such as finance, healthcare, and auditing, where labeled historical data are available and predictive accuracy is paramount. However, its performance is highly dependent on data quality, labeling accuracy, and the stability of underlying relationships. The performance of a supervised learning model is often assessed using metrics such as accuracy, precision, recall, *F*1-score, and mean squared error, depending on the task type. One of the key strengths of supervised learning is its ability to generalize from historical data, but this also depends heavily on the quality, quantity, and representativeness of the labeled data used during training.

4.3.2 Unsupervised Learning

Unsupervised learning is a type of ML that can handle data that has no labeled responses, meaning the algorithm is given input data without corresponding output labels. It operates on unlabeled data and seeks to uncover hidden structures, patterns, or relationships without predefined outcome variables. Rather than prediction, the primary goals are exploration, pattern discovery, and dimensionality reduction. The primary objective of unsupervised learning is to explore the underlying structure or distribution of data to learn more about it without prior guidance. This is commonly achieved by identifying patterns, groupings, or features within the data, making it especially useful for tasks such as clustering, dimensionality reduction, and anomaly detection. Core unsupervised techniques include clustering algorithms (e.g., *k*-means, hierarchical clustering, density-based spatial clustering (DBSCAN)), association rule learning, and dimensionality reduction methods such as PCA, *t*-Distributed Stochastic Neighbor Embedding (*t*-SNE), and autoencoders.[6] Clustering algorithms, such as *K*-means, DBSCAN, and hierarchical clustering, group data points based on similarity, enabling organizations to segment customers, detect fraud, or identify hidden structures in complex datasets. Dimensionality reduction techniques, such as PCA and *t*-SNE, simplify data by reducing the number of features while preserving important information, which is valuable for visualization and preprocessing. Unlike supervised learning, which learns from known outcomes, unsupervised learning must rely solely on the inherent properties of the data, making it more challenging but also more flexible in uncovering previously unknown insights. Evaluation of the performance of unsupervised learning models can often be difficult and typically requires domain expertise or the use of metrics like silhouette score, Davies-Bouldin index, or visual assessment because there are no predefined labels.

4.3.3 Reinforcement Learning

RL is a type of ML where an algorithm learns to make decisions by performing certain actions and evaluating outcomes by interacting with an environment to achieve a specific goal. It represents a distinct paradigm in which an intelligent agent learns optimal behavior through interaction with a dynamic environment. Unlike supervised learning, where the model learns from labeled data, RL is based on a system of rewards and penalties that guide the learning process. The agent/algorithm observes the current state of the environment, acts, and receives feedback in the form of a reward or punishment by learning the best actions to take over time to maximize cumulative rewards. This trial-and-error approach mimics how humans and animals learn from their surroundings and is particularly effective for sequential decision-making problems. The agent seeks to maximize cumulative rewards by balancing exploration (trying new actions) and exploitation (leveraging known successful actions). Key RL concepts include states, actions, policies, rewards, and value functions, with foundational algorithms such as *Q*-learning, policy gradients, and deep reinforcement learning (DRL).[7] RL has demonstrated strong performance in complex sequential decision problems, including robotics, autonomous systems, dynamic pricing, portfolio optimization, and supply chain management. However, RL models often require substantial computational resources, careful reward design, and robust governance to mitigate risks associated with instability, bias, and unintended behavior.

Key components of RL include the agent (learner or decision-maker), the environment (everything the agent interacts with), the policy (the strategy the agent follows), the reward signal (feedback from the environment), and the value function (a prediction of future rewards). RL algorithms, such as *Q*-learning, Deep *Q*-Networks (DQNs), and policy gradient methods, are used in a wide range of applications, from robotics and game playing (e.g., AlphaGo and reinforcement-learned agents in video games) to resource management, autonomous vehicles, and customized recommendations. One of the key challenges in RL is the exploration–exploitation trade-off, where the agent must balance trying new actions to discover better rewards (exploration) with using known actions that yield high rewards (exploitation). Furthermore, RL can become computationally expensive and complex in high-dimensional environments, requiring advanced techniques like DRL and model-based RL. Despite these challenges, RL represents a powerful and dynamic approach to building intelligent systems capable of autonomous learning and adaptation in uncertain and evolving environments. It is modeled as a reward system, where positive outcomes increase the likelihood of the action being taken in the future. This method is particularly useful for sequential decision-making problems like robotics and game playing. There are main RL algorithms of model-free and model-based approaches, as well as DRL techniques that leverage neural networks for function approximation, and both RL and DRL can have remarkable success in complex, high-dimensional environments, surpassing human performance in tasks such as game playing and robotics.[8]

4.4 ML Technologies

ML technologies represent a transformative frontier in the digital era by enabling machines to simulate human intelligence and learn from data to make decisions, solve problems, and adapt over time to new environments and challenges. ML, a core subset of AI, focuses on developing algorithms that allow systems to learn patterns and make predictions or decisions without being explicitly programmed for each task. AI technologies extend beyond ML to include NLP, computer vision, robotics, expert systems, and knowledge representation.

Together, these tools are revolutionizing industries by automating complex processes, enhancing decision-making, and enabling innovative applications such as autonomous vehicles, virtual assistants, fraud detection, personalized healthcare, and predictive maintenance. At the heart of these advancements is the ability to process vast amounts of data at high speed, uncover insights, and continuously improve system performance. The integration of ML and AI technologies also raises important considerations around ethics, transparency, data privacy, and responsible use, prompting ongoing research and policy development. As AI technologies evolve, they are becoming increasingly accessible through platforms, cloud services, and open-source tools, empowering businesses, researchers, and developers to create intelligent systems that perform specific tasks and adapt to dynamic environments, anticipate needs, and drive innovation in ways previously thought impossible.

4.4.1 ML Algorithms

ML algorithms are computational procedures that enable systems to learn patterns, relationships, and decision rules from data to make predictions, classifications, or decisions without explicit programming. These algorithms can be broadly categorized into linear models (e.g., linear and logistic regression), tree-based methods (e.g., decision trees, random forests, and gradient boosting), kernel-based models (e.g., SVMs), instance-based learners (e.g., KNN), probabilistic models (e.g., naïve Bayes and hidden Markov models), and neural network architectures, including deep learning models, as thoroughly explained in the following subsections.[9] With the help of ML, computers may learn from data and use that knowledge to make well-informed predictions or judgments. Each of these algorithms has a certain function and is categorized according to the type of learning. Every algorithm has distinct advantages and works well for different tasks. We describe each algorithm and its business-related uses below, classifying them according to their learning kinds. This taxonomy offers a useful foundation for comprehending their many functionalities and real-world uses.

4.4.1.1 Supervised Learning Algorithms

Algorithm selection involves trade-offs among predictive accuracy, interpretability, computational complexity, and data requirements, with ensemble methods often achieving superior performance by aggregating multiple learners to reduce bias and variance.[10] Recent advances in deep learning have further expanded algorithmic capabilities, particularly for high-dimensional, unstructured data such as text, images, and time series, while raising important considerations related to transparency, robustness, and governance in real-world applications. Thus, effective deployment of ML algorithms requires technical optimization and careful alignment with domain knowledge, ethical standards, and decision-making objectives.

Linear Regression: Linear regression is a statistical method that models the relationship between a dependent variable (what you want to predict) and one or more independent variables (your input). It identifies the best-fitting straight line through your data points that minimizes overall prediction error. This algorithm captures the relationship between variables by fitting a linear equation to the observed data. Its goal is to find the best-fitting straight line (or hyperplane in higher dimensions) that reduces the difference between predicted and actual values.[11]

Logistic Regression: Despite its name, logistic regression is primarily used for classification problems rather than regression. It predicts the probability that an observation belongs to a particular category (e.g., "yes" or "no," "high risk," or "low risk"). The algorithm transforms a linear equation using the logistic function (also known as the sigmoid function), predicting the likelihood of an instance belonging to a specific class, which maps any real-valued number to a value between 0 and 1. Logistic regression can identify employees at risk of burnout or attrition based on workload, work–life balance, and survey responses. This allows for proactive interventions to enhance employee well-being and reduce turnover.[12]

Decision Trees: Decision trees are hierarchical models that make decisions by following a tree-like structure of conditions, resembling a flowchart. Starting from a root node, they split the data based on feature values, creating branches until they reach leaf nodes that provide predictions. These algorithms construct a tree-like model of decisions, where the leaf nodes represent the final classification for the problem statement. Each internal node represents a test on an attribute, each branch reflects the test's outcome, and each leaf node indicates a class label or predicted value. Decision trees are interpretable and can handle both categorical and numerical data. Decision trees can be used to classify waste streams for optimal recycling pathways based on material composition, contamination levels, and the availability of recycling infrastructure.[13]

Random Forests: Random forests are ensemble learning methods that construct multiple decision trees during training and output the mode of classes (for classification) or the mean prediction (for regression) from the individual trees. This method leverages the power of multiple decision trees (weak classifiers) to create a strong classifier, improving accuracy and generalization by combining their predictions. This ensemble learning method builds on decision trees by creating various trees, each trained on a random subset of the data and features.[14] The final prediction is made by aggregating the predictions of all individual trees, often through majority voting for classification or averaging for regression. Random Forests are robust, reduce overfitting, and typically offer high accuracy. Random Forests can be used to predict renewable energy generation (solar, wind) based on weather data, time of day, and seasonal variations, thereby improving grid management and energy planning.[15]

Support Vector Machines (SVMs): SVMs are powerful algorithms for both linear and nonlinear classification and regression. They aim to find an optimal hyperplane that separates different classes, maximizing the margin (distance) between the boundary and the closest points from each class, known as support vectors. For nonlinear problems, SVMs can utilize kernel functions to map data into higher-dimensional spaces where linear separation becomes feasible.[16]

K-Nearest Neighbors (KNN): KNN is a non-parametric, instance-based learning algorithm used for classification and regression. Given N training vectors, the KNN algorithm identifies the KNN. It classifies a new data point by considering the classes of its "k" nearest neighbors in the training dataset. The class that appears most frequently among the "k" neighbors is assigned to the new data point. KNN is simple to implement and effective for datasets with complex decision boundaries. For example, KNN can identify financial transactions that share similar risk profiles with past fraudulent activities by comparing features such as amount, location, and time against historical data on fraudulent transactions.

4.4.1.2 Unsupervised Learning Algorithms

Unsupervised learning algorithms are designed to identify latent structures, patterns, and relationships in unlabeled data without predefined outcome variables, making them particularly valuable for exploratory analysis and knowledge discovery. These algorithms are commonly classified into several types, including clustering methods, dimensionality reduction techniques, density estimation models, and association rule learning. Clustering algorithms such as *k*-means, hierarchical clustering, and DBSCAN group observations based on similarity or distance metrics, enabling applications such as customer segmentation and anomaly detection, as thoroughly explained in the following subsections. Dimensionality reduction techniques, including PCA, factor analysis, and autoencoders, transform high-dimensional data into lower-dimensional representations while preserving essential variance or structure, thereby improving interpretability and computational efficiency.[17] Density-based and probabilistic models, such as Gaussian mixture models and latent Dirichlet allocation (LDA), estimate the underlying data-generating process and are widely used in topic modeling and pattern recognition.[18] Together, unsupervised learning algorithms provide powerful tools for extracting insights from complex, high-dimensional datasets, although their effectiveness often depends on careful model selection, parameter tuning, and expert interpretation.

_K_-means Clustering: This algorithm divides data points into "*k*" distinct clusters. It iteratively assigns each data point to the nearest cluster centroid and updates the centroids based on the mean of the points assigned to each cluster. Points are assigned to the nearest centroid, indicating similarity, and the algorithm iteratively recalculates centroids by averaging the points assigned to each one. This process continues until data point assignments stabilize and no longer change. The goal is to minimize the within-cluster sum of squared distances.

Hierarchical Clustering: This method builds a hierarchy of clusters. It can be agglomerative (bottom-up), starting with each data point as a separate cluster and iteratively merging the closest clusters, or divisive (top-down), starting with a single cluster containing all data points and recursively splitting clusters.[19] Hierarchical clustering generates a tree-like structure (dendrogram) representing the clustering process. For example, hierarchical clustering can identify employee engagement patterns across various departments or divisions using employee survey data and engagement metrics, revealing organizational units with particularly high or low levels of engagement.

Principal Component Analysis (PCA): PCA is a dimensionality reduction technique that transforms high-dimensional data into a lower-dimensional space while preserving maximum variance. It identifies principal components, which are orthogonal linear combinations of the original features, ordered by the amount of variance they explain. PCA also serves as a unifying concept across various perspectives in representation learning, like a simple form of linear manifold learning, characterizing lower-dimensional regions in the input space where the data density is significant.[20] By reducing dimensionality, PCA simplifies analysis and highlights the most significant drivers of business performance.

Anomaly Detection: These techniques aim to identify data points that deviate significantly from normal patterns in a dataset.[21] They help in detecting unusual patterns in data without relying on labeled examples. Anomalies can represent errors, outliers, or significant events that require attention. Various methods exist, including statistical methods, ML models, and proximity-based techniques. For example, Isolation Forests are specialized ensemble ML algorithms designed specifically for anomaly detection that work by explicitly isolating outliers in the data. For example, anomaly detection can flag suspicious financial transactions or unusual trading activities that might indicate fraud or insider trading.

4.4.1.3 Semi-supervised Learning Algorithms

Semi-supervised learning algorithms integrate a small set of labeled observations with a larger pool of unlabeled data to improve learning efficiency and predictive performance, particularly in settings where labeling is costly, time-consuming, or subject to expert judgment. These algorithms are commonly categorized into several types, including self-training and pseudo-labeling methods, co-training approaches, graph-based models, and generative and consistency-based techniques, as thoroughly examined in the following subsections. Collectively, semi-supervised learning is increasingly applied in domains involving large volumes of unstructured data, such as text analytics, image recognition, and ESG disclosure analysis, where it balances predictive accuracy with practical constraints on labeled data availability.

Self-Training: Self-training methods iteratively assign predicted labels to unlabeled instances and retrain the model using high-confidence predictions, while co-training leverages multiple conditionally independent feature views to enhance label propagation.[22] This is an iterative approach in which a supervised learning model is initially trained on a small, labeled data set. The trained model is then used to predict labels (pseudo-labels) for the unlabeled data. High-confidence pseudo-labeled instances are then added to the labeled dataset, and the model is retrained. This process is repeated iteratively, gradually expanding the labeled dataset.[23] For example, self-training can be applied to classify satellite imagery for deforestation detection. Initially, a model is trained by a small set of labeled images (deforested vs. non-deforested). This model then predicts the likelihood of deforestation on a larger set of unlabeled images. High-confidence predictions are added to the training set, and the model is retrained, enhancing its ability to identify deforestation patterns over time with limited labeled data.

Generative and Co-Training: Generative models, such as semi-supervised Gaussian mixture models and variational autoencoders (VAEs), incorporate unlabeled data into probabilistic frameworks, while modern consistency-based methods enforce prediction stability under data perturbations, particularly in deep learning contexts.[24] Co-training extends self-training by employing multiple supervised classifiers. In this approach, two or more classifiers are trained iteratively on labeled data, where each classifier adds its most confident predictions of unlabeled data to the other's labeled dataset during each iteration. A critical requirement for successful co-training is that the classifiers should not be highly correlated in their predictions; this condition is known as the diversity criterion. For example, for governance risk assessment, co-training could involve two classifiers: one trained on financial data and another on textual data from news articles and reports, to predict corporate business risk. Each classifier can leverage its strengths in its respective data domain and collaboratively enhance the overall risk prediction by utilizing high-confidence predictions from the other classifier on unlabeled data. This method can also combine financial reports to improve business risk classification.

Graph-Based Learning: Graph-based algorithms construct similarity graphs to propagate label information across connected data points, exploiting the manifold structure of the data space.[25] Graph-based methods utilize graph structures to model relationships between data points for label propagation and classification. Consisting of three main steps: graph creation, graph weighting, and inference, they typically use a local similarity measure to create a graph of all data points. These methods represent data points as nodes in a graph, with edges connecting nodes that exhibit some level of similarity based on predefined measures. The overarching idea is to leverage the connections between labeled and unlabeled data points to propagate information and make predictions.

4.4.1.4 Reinforcement Learning Algorithms

RL algorithms are types of ML methods in which an autonomous agent learns optimal behavior through repeated interaction with an environment by maximizing cumulative reward over time. Unlike supervised learning, RL does not rely on labeled input–output pairs; instead, it is formulated as a sequential decision-making problem, commonly modeled using Markov Decision Processes (MDPs), where the agent observes states, takes actions, receives rewards, and updates its policy accordingly.[26] Classical RL algorithms include value-based methods such as *Q*-learning and SARSA, which estimate action–value functions, as well as policy-based methods that directly optimize decision policies using gradient-based techniques. More recent advances integrate deep neural networks with RL, giving rise to DRL, exemplified by DQNs and actor–critic architectures, which enable RL to scale to high-dimensional and complex environments as thoroughly explained in the following subsections. RL algorithms have been widely applied in robotics, game playing, resource allocation, finance, and autonomous systems, where long-term optimization and adaptive decision-making under uncertainty are critical.[27] RL is particularly well-suited for problems involving sequential decision-making, where optimal action relies on the environment's current state and previous actions.

Q-Learning: *Q*-Learning is an RL algorithm that learns the value (quality) of taking specific actions in particular states to maximize cumulative rewards over time. *Q*-learning iteratively updates the *Q*-function based on observed rewards and transitions in the environment. This algorithm is ideal when an agent must learn optimal decision-making through trial and error, without requiring a model of the environment. *Q*-Learning equips agents with the capability to learn optimal strategies over time by interacting with and adapting to their environment based on received rewards and penalties, making it applicable in various fields such as robotics, game playing, and resource management in smart grids.[28] For example, *Q*-learning can optimize energy usage in smart buildings by learning control policies for HVAC systems, lighting, and appliances based on real-time occupancy, weather conditions, and energy prices.

Deep Q-Networks (DQNs): DQN extends *Q*-Learning by employing deep neural networks to approximate the *Q*-value function, enabling handling large and high-dimensional state spaces. DQNs combine *Q*-learning with deep neural networks to approximate the *Q*-function, enabling RL to handle high-dimensional state spaces, such as images or complex sensor data. Deep neural networks provide the function approximation capability to generalize from limited experiences to unseen states. DQNs are suitable for complex decision-making problems where the state space is too large for traditional *Q*-Learning.[29] For example, DQNs can manage dynamic supply chain logistics to minimize their carbon footprint.

Policy Gradient Methods: Policy Gradient Methods aim to maximize the cumulative reward directly and readily integrate with nonlinear function approximators like neural networks. These RL algorithms optimize the policy itself, a mapping from states to actions, without explicitly learning a value function like *Q*-learning. Instead of relying on a value function to derive the policy, these methods parameterize the policy (often using neural networks) and adjust its parameters by estimating the gradient of expected returns with respect to those parameters. Policy gradient methods adjust the policy parameters iteratively to increase the probability of actions that lead to higher rewards. They are effective in continuous or complex action spaces and useful when smooth policy updates are desired, especially in systems with many possible actions.[30]

Proximal Policy Optimization (PPO): PPO is a policy gradient method that enhances training stability and sample efficiency compared to basic policy gradient algorithms. PPO introduces constraints on the policy update process to ensure that policy changes are not overly drastic in each iteration, resulting in more robust and reliable learning. This method aims to improve the efficiency and simplicity of existing approaches in RL. It is recommended for training RL agents in environments that require stable learning with continuous actions.[31] For example, PPO can optimize logistics routes for transportation companies to minimize emissions and fuel consumption. The state space may encompass traffic conditions, road networks, vehicle characteristics, and delivery schedules. The actions would involve route selections, and the reward function would seek to minimize fuel consumption and emissions while meeting delivery deadlines.

4.4.2 Neural Networks

Neural networks are ML techniques inspired by the structure and function of the human brain.[32] They use a system of interconnected nodes called artificial neurons (or nodes). They consist of interconnected layers of neurons, including an input layer, one or more hidden layers, and an output layer, as depicted in Figure 4.1. Each neuron receives input, processes it, and produces an output. The processing typically involves applying a weighted sum of the inputs, followed by a nonlinear activation function. They are designed to recognize patterns and make decisions based on input data. Neural networks are powerful tools for modeling complex relationships in data and are particularly effective for tasks such as image recognition, NLP, and speech recognition. Their ability to learn from large data sets, model complex relationships, and generalize new data makes them a cornerstone of advanced ML and AI models, particularly deep learning applications.

4.4.3 Deep Learning Algorithms

Deep learning utilizes various types of neural networks to perform specific tasks. Many different types of deep learning models are available, each employing different types of learning.

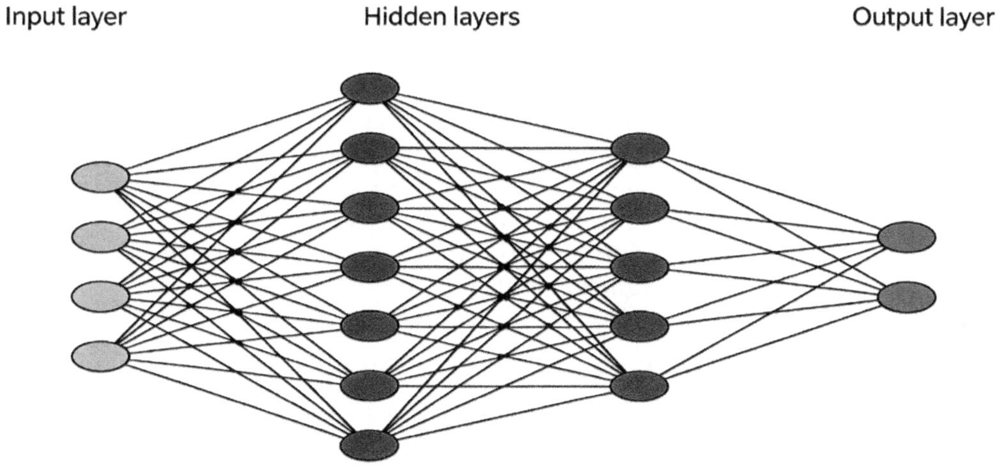

Figure 4.1 An Example of a Neural Network with Two Hidden Layers.

Some models are generative, meaning they can create new data like their training data. In the following sections, we present some of the most common types of deep learning algorithms.

Neural networks use basis functions that follow the same form as equation (4.1) so that each basis function is itself a nonlinear function of a linear combination of the inputs, where the coefficients in the linear combination are adaptive parameters.

$$y(x,w) = f\left(\sum_{j=1}^{m} w_j \phi_j(x)\right) \tag{4.1}$$

This leads (equation (4.1)) to the basic neural network model, which can be described as a series of functional transformations. First, we construct m linear combinations of the input variables $x_1,\ldots,x_n$ in the form:

$$a_j = \sum_{i=1}^{n} w_{ji}^{(1)} x_i + w_{j0}^{(1)} \tag{4.2}$$

where $j = 1,\ldots,m$, and the superscript (1) indicates that the corresponding parameters are in the first "layer" of the network. We refer to the parameters $w_{ji}^{(1)}$ as weights and the parameters $w_{j0}^{(1)}$ as biases.

The quantities a_j are known as activations. Each of them is then transformed using a differentiable, nonlinear activation function $h(\bullet)$ to give

$$z_j = h(a_j) \tag{4.3}$$

These quantities correspond to the outputs of the basic functions in equation (4.1) that, in the context of neural networks, are called hidden layers. The nonlinear functions $h(\bullet)$ are generally chosen as sigmoidal functions, such as the logistic sigmoid function. Following equation (4.1), these values are again linearly combined to produce the output unit activations

$$a_k = \sum_{j=1}^{m} w_{kj}^{(2)} z_j + w_{k0}^{(2)} \tag{4.4}$$

where $k = 1,\ldots,k$, and k is the total number of outputs. This transformation corresponds to the second layer of the network, and the $w_{k0}^{(2)}$ are bias parameters. Finally, the output unit activations are transformed using an appropriate activation function to give a set of network outputs y_k. The choice of activation function is determined by the nature of the data and the assumed distribution of target variables. Each output layer activation is transformed using a logistic sigmoid function so that

$$y_k = \sigma(a_k) \tag{4.5}$$

where

$$\sigma(a) = \frac{1}{1+e^{-a}} \tag{4.6}$$

This development corresponds to a neural network with an input layer, two hidden layers, and an output layer, as presented in Figure 4.1.[33]

4.4.3.1 Feedforward Neural Networks (FNN)

Feedforward Neural Networks (FNNs) are one of the most important and widely used architectures in the field of artificial neural networks and ML. Information in FNNs flows in one direction from input nodes, through one or more hidden layers, and finally to the output layer without any feedback loops or cycles. Each layer in an FNN is composed of interconnected nodes (also called neurons), where each node performs a weighted sum of its inputs followed by the application of a nonlinear activation function, such as ReLU (Rectified Linear Unit), sigmoid, or tanh. This structure enables FNNs to learn complex patterns and relationships in data, making them suitable for a wide range of supervised learning tasks, including classification, regression, and function approximation. Training a feedforward neural network commonly involves the backpropagation algorithm combined with an optimization method like stochastic gradient descent, where the network's weights are iteratively updated to minimize a loss function based on the difference between the predicted and actual outputs. FNNs are powerful universal function approximators, meaning that they can approximate any continuous function given enough neurons and layers, and their effectiveness heavily depends on the quality and quantity of training data, network architecture, and proper tuning of hyperparameters. FNNs remain a critical building block in the development of more complex neural models and continue to be used in various applications such as medical diagnosis, financial forecasting, and customer behavior prediction. However, they do not inherently handle spatial or sequential data as efficiently as specialized networks. FNNs main attributes and characteristics are that they (1) are the simplest type of deep learning model; (2) consist of input, hidden, and output layers; (3) are used for basic classification and regression tasks; (4) require information flows in one direction, from input to output; and (5) focuses on learning algorithms designed to enhance generalization performance and convergence rates in ML applications.[34]

4.4.3.2 Convolutional Neural Networks (CNN)

Convolutional Neural Networks (CNNs) are deep learning algorithms that are well-suited for processing data with a grid-like topology, such as images. Inspired by the structure and function of the visual cortex in animals. CNNs have revolutionized the field of computer vision by enabling machines to automatically learn hierarchical patterns and features from raw pixel data. CNNs often consist of several layers, including convolutional layers, pooling layers, and fully connected layers. The convolutional layers apply a set of learnable filters to the input, detecting local patterns such as edges, textures, and shapes, which become increasingly complex and abstract at deeper layers. Pooling layers then reduce the spatial dimensions of the data, improving computational efficiency and helping to control overfitting. Fully connected layers at the end of the network serve to interpret the learned features and make predictions, such as classifying objects within an image. CNNs excel in tasks like image recognition, object detection, and facial recognition, and even extend to areas such as NLP and time series analysis. CNNs' success is mainly due to their ability to exploit spatial hierarchies and reduce the need for manual feature extraction. Recent advancements in powerful GPUs and large datasets have made CNNs a cornerstone of modern AI applications, continually pushing the boundaries of what machines can perceive and understand from visual data. Key attributes and characteristics of CNNs are that they (1) are specialized for image and video processing; (2) use convolutional layers to extract features from images; (3) are commonly used in computer vision tasks like image recognition, object detection, and facial recognition; (4) employ architectures, including classic and advanced models, as well as experimental evaluations of activation functions, loss functions, optimizers, and hyperparameters and their applications of CNNs in 1-D, 2-D, and multidimensional scenarios, such as time series prediction, image classification, object detection, and human action recognition; and (5) are capable of driving advancements in AI with challenges, such as model compression for deployment on resource-constrained devices and vulnerabilities to adversarial attacks.[35]

4.4.3.3 *Recurrent Neural Networks (RNN)*

RNNs are types of artificial neural networks that are designed for processing sequential data, where the order of inputs plays a critical role, such as in time series, natural language, audio, or video data. Unlike traditional FNNs, RNNs have loops that allow information to persist by enabling them to maintain a form of memory about previous inputs in the sequence. This is achieved through hidden states that are passed from one step to the next by allowing the network to learn temporal dependencies and contextual relationships within the data. RNNs are effective in tasks like language modeling, speech recognition, translation, and sentiment analysis, where understanding the flow and structure of sequences is essential. However, they may suffer from limitations such as vanishing and exploding gradients, which hinder their ability to capture long-range dependencies. To overcome these challenges, advanced variants like Long Short-Term Memory (LSTM) networks and Gated Recurrent Units (GRUs) have been developed. These architectures incorporate gating mechanisms that regulate the flow of information and enable the network to retain relevant information over longer sequences. Despite their power, RNNs are recently being complemented or even replaced in some applications by newer models like Transformers, which use attention mechanisms to capture relationships in sequences more efficiently. Nevertheless, RNNs remain a foundational concept in deep learning for sequence modeling and have significantly contributed to the evolution of neural network architectures for temporal and sequential data. Key attributes and characteristics of RNNs are that they are (1) designed for sequential data processing; (2) have memory (hidden states) that allows it to retain information from previous steps; (3) used in NLP, speech recognition, and time series forecasting; (4) advanced variants like LSTM and GRU, which have significantly improved performance in tasks requiring temporal dependencies, such as financial forecasting and healthcare diagnostics; and (5) advancements in RNNs, which include LSTM networks, GRUs, and hybrid models integrating attention mechanisms and transformers, and they are effective in processing sequential data with challenges like vanishing gradients, and their applications in NLP, speech recognition, time series forecasting, autonomous vehicles, and anomaly detection.[36]

4.4.3.4 *Long Short-Term Memory (LSTM) Networks*

LSTM networks are a classic and specialized type of RNN that are designed to overcome the limitations of traditional RNNs in learning long-term dependencies in sequential data. Standard RNNs tend to struggle with capturing long-range relationships due to the vanishing or exploding gradient problem, which makes learning across long sequences difficult. LSTM networks address this issue by incorporating a more complex memory cell structure and gating mechanisms that regulate the flow of information over time. Each LSTM cell contains three gates: the input gate, the forget gate, and the output gate. These gates control what information is added to or removed from the cell state, the internal memory of the network, which enables the LSTM to retain or discard information as needed. This structure allows LSTMs to effectively "remember" important features in the data for long periods while discarding irrelevant details. In essence, LSTM networks are highly effective for tasks involving long sequences, such as language modeling, machine translation, speech recognition, time series forecasting, and video analysis. Their ability to maintain context over time has made them a foundational architecture in deep learning for sequential data, particularly in applications where understanding past information is crucial for accurate prediction or classification. LSTMs will continue to be widely used and remain a crucial concept in the study and application of deep learning for sequence modeling. Key attributes and characteristics of LSTMs are that they (1) are designed to handle long-term dependencies; (2) address the vanishing gradient problem of standard RNNs; (3) are used in machine translation, speech synthesis, and financial forecasting; (4) can address the vanishing/exploding gradient problem that make them a state-of-the-art solution for recurrent and deep neural networks; (6) excel in time series prediction, NLP, sentiment analysis, image/video captioning, computer vision, and text recognition; and (7) can be hybrid architecture, such as CNN-LSTM and bidirectional LSTM (BLSTM), often outperforming vanilla LSTM in tasks requiring spatial or temporal context.[37]

4.4.3.5 Gated Recurrent Units (GRU)

GRUs are a specialized and efficient variant of RNNs that were introduced as an alternative to LSTM networks. They are intended to capture long-term dependencies in sequential data while maintaining a simpler architecture. Like LSTMs, GRUs are designed to mitigate the vanishing gradient problem that plagues traditional RNNs, which hinders learning across long sequences. GRUs achieve this by introducing two gating mechanisms of the update gate and the reset gate, which regulate the flow of information within the unit without relying on separate memory cells as in LSTMs. The update gate determines how much of the past information needs to be passed along to the future, while the reset gate decides how much of the past information to forget. This gating mechanism enables GRUs to maintain relevant context over time and discard irrelevant details while making them highly effective for tasks like time series prediction, NLP, speech recognition, and video sequence modeling. GRUs often outperform standard RNNs and can match the performance of LSTMs on many tasks, despite having fewer parameters and requiring less computational overhead. This makes them particularly appealing in scenarios where computational efficiency is critical, such as mobile or embedded systems. Ultimately, their relatively simpler structure makes it easier to implement and train. While newer architectures like Transformers have gained prominence for handling long-range dependencies more efficiently and in parallel, GRUs remain an important tool in the deep learning toolkit, especially when working with sequential data where model simplicity and performance must be balanced. Key attributes and characteristics of GRUs are that they (1) are a simplified version of LSTMs with fewer parameters; (2) retain memory efficiently while requiring less computational power; (3) can be applied in NLP, speech recognition, and time series analysis; (4) are simplified architecture that often yield faster training times and lower errors, though LSTM remains popular due to its robustness in handling complex temporal patterns; and (5) struggle with challenges including LSTM's declining accuracy over extended periods and GRU's limitations with very long sequences.[38]

4.4.3.6 Generative Adversarial Networks (GANs)

Generative Adversarial Networks (GANs) are a class of deep learning models designed for generative tasks, where the goal is to produce new data samples that resemble a given dataset. Introduced by Ian Goodfellow in 2014, GANs consist of two neural networks, the generator and the discriminator, that are trained simultaneously in a game-theoretic framework. The generator creates synthetic data instances (e.g., images), while the discriminator evaluates them against real data, attempting to distinguish between the two. Through this adversarial process, the generator improves its ability to produce realistic data, while the discriminator becomes better at detecting fakes. Over time, the generator learns to produce outputs that are nearly indistinguishable from real data. GANs have been widely used in applications such as image generation, style transfer, data augmentation, and deepfake creation. Despite their success, they can be challenging to train due to issues like mode collapse and instability, prompting ongoing research into more robust GAN architectures and training techniques. Their main characteristics are that they (1) consist of two neural networks: a generator and a discriminator; (2) are used for generating synthetic data, including images, text, and videos; and (3) are applied in deepfake generation, art creation, and data augmentation.

4.4.3.7 Autoencoders

Autoencoders are a type of artificial neural network used primarily for unsupervised learning, particularly for dimensionality reduction, feature learning, and data compression. They consist of two main components: an encoder, which transforms the input data into a compressed, lower-dimensional representation (often called a latent space or bottleneck), and a decoder, which reconstructs the original input from this compressed representation. The goal of training an autoencoder is to minimize the difference between the original input and the reconstructed output, typically measured by a loss function such as mean squared error. Autoencoders are useful in applications like image denoising, anomaly detection, and pretraining for deep learning models. Variants such as sparse autoencoders, denoising autoencoders, and VAEs extend the basic architecture to enhance performance and interpretability for specific tasks. Key attributes and characteristics of autoencoders are that they (1) are used for unsupervised learning and feature extraction; (2) consist of an encoder (compresses data) and a decoder (reconstructs data); (3) are applied in anomaly detection, data denoising, and dimensionality reduction; and (4) can be categorized into basic and regularized types, discussing their structures, training methods, and loss functions, while also examining their relationships with shallow and deep learning models and they are versatile tools for unsupervised learning and nonlinear feature extraction, with applications in computer vision, recommender systems, pattern recognition, and data generation.[39]

4.4.3.8 Transformer

Transformer Networks are a groundbreaking architecture in deep learning, particularly well-suited for processing sequential data such as text, time series, and even images. Introduced in the landmark 2017 paper "Attention is All You Need" by Vaswani et al., transformers departed from traditional RNNs by eliminating recurrence altogether and instead relying entirely on a mechanism known as *self-attention* to process input data in parallel. This innovation allows the model to weigh the importance of different elements in a sequence relative to one another, enabling it to capture long-range dependencies and complex contextual relationships more effectively than previous models. A transformer consists of an encoder–decoder architecture: the encoder reads and encodes the input data into a set of continuous representations, and the decoder generates the output sequence by attending to both its previous outputs and the encoder's representations. The key components of a transformer include multi-head attention layers, feedforward neural networks, layer normalization, and positional encoding to preserve the order of the input sequence. Transformers have become the foundation for many state-of-the-art models in NLP, such as BERT, GPT, and T5, and have also been successfully adapted to other domains like computer vision (e.g., Vision Transformers or ViTs) and speech processing. Their scalability and ability to handle massive datasets have revolutionized AI research and applications, making them central to modern advancements in ML. Their main characteristics are that they (1) are a type of deep learning model for processing sequential data; (2) use self-attention mechanisms to capture long-range dependencies; (3) power NLP models like GPT, BERT, and T5; and (4) are transformer models that can be adapted for graph-structured data, focusing on their architectural innovations and performance in graph-related tasks in modeling complex graph data, making it a valuable resource for researchers in ML and graph analysis.[40]

4.4.3.9 Graph Neural Networks (GNN)

Graph Neural Networks (GNNs) are a type of deep learning model specifically designed to work with graph-structured data, where relationships between entities (nodes) are as important as the entities themselves. Unlike traditional neural networks that assume data lies in a Euclidean space (like grids or sequences), GNNs can learn from data represented as nodes and edges, such as social networks, molecular structures, knowledge graphs, and transportation systems. GNNs operate by iteratively aggregating and transforming feature information from a node's local neighborhood through a process often referred to as *message passing*. At each layer, a node updates its representation by combining its current state with messages received from its neighbors, allowing the network to capture both local and global patterns in the graph. This approach enables GNNs to model complex dependencies and topological information that traditional models cannot handle effectively. Popular variants include Graph Convolutional Networks (GCNs), Graph Attention Networks (GATs), and GraphSAGE, each introducing different strategies for aggregation and weighting neighbor information. GNNs have shown remarkable performance across various applications, such as node classification, link prediction, graph classification, and recommendation systems. Despite their success, GNNs face challenges, including scalability to large graphs, over-smoothing in deep architectures, and handling dynamic or heterogeneous graphs, all of which are active areas of research. However, GNNs represent a powerful and flexible tool for learning from non-Euclidean data structures, opening new possibilities in many domains where relational data is key. Their main characteristics are they (1) are designed to process graph-structured data; (2) are used in applications like social network analysis, fraud detection, and molecular property prediction; (3) have shown remarkable success in generating realistic data, but their training remains unstable and requires innovative solutions to improve performance and reliability; (4) have potential to revolutionize areas like image generation, domain adaptation, and unsupervised learning, making it a valuable resource for researchers in AI and ML. However, advancements like conditional

GANs, Wasserstein GANs, and memory networks are promising approaches to mitigate these issues.[41] GNNs, while powerful for modeling graph-structured data, present unique computational challenges due to their dependence on input graphs, alternating dense and sparse operations, and scalability requirements.[42]

4.4.3.10 Self-Supervised Learning Models

Self-supervised learning models represent a powerful and increasingly influential approach in ML, enabling models to learn useful representations from unlabeled data by generating their own supervision signals. Unlike traditional supervised learning, which relies heavily on large amounts of labeled data, self-supervised learning leverages the inherent structure or context within the data itself to create pretext tasks of artificial learning objectives that do not require human-annotated labels. For example, in NLP, models like BERT use self-supervised techniques such as masked language modeling, where certain words in a sentence are masked, and the model is trained to predict them based on context. In computer vision, self-supervised models may involve tasks like predicting image rotations, solving jigsaw puzzles, or contrasting different views of the same image to learn meaningful visual features. A particularly popular framework in this field is contrastive learning, where models learn to distinguish between similar (positive) and dissimilar (negative) data pairs, encouraging the network to learn discriminative representations. These representations can then be fine-tuned on downstream tasks such as classification, object detection, or sentiment analysis with much less labeled data.

4.5 Model Evaluation and Performance Metrics

Model evaluation and performance metrics are pivotal components of ML and statistical modeling by providing systematic ways to assess how well a model generalizes to unseen data and supports reliable decision-making. This evaluation typically involves partitioning data into training, validation, and test sets or using resampling techniques such as cross-validation to mitigate overfitting and selection bias.[43] Model evaluation is an essential step in the ML process because it helps in measuring how well the models perform and finding areas to improve. The purpose of model evaluation is not just to see how well a model does on a particular task but also to understand its strengths and weaknesses.

4.5.1 The Relevance and Importance of Model Evaluations

Performance metrics vary by task. For example, classification models with commonly used measures include accuracy, precision, recall, $F1$-score, and the area under the receiver operating characteristic curve (AUC-ROC), each capturing different aspects of predictive effectiveness, particularly under class imbalance.[44] For regression models, evaluation often relies on metrics such as mean squared error (MSE), root mean squared error (RMSE), and mean absolute error (MAE), which quantify prediction error magnitude and robustness to outliers.[45] In more advanced applications, model evaluation also emphasizes interpretability, stability, and fairness, incorporating tools such as confusion matrices, calibration curves, and explainability techniques to ensure transparency and ethical use of predictive models.[46] Together, rigorous evaluation frameworks and appropriately chosen performance metrics are critical for validating model effectiveness and ensuring trustworthy deployment in real-world applications.

The importance and relevance of model evaluation and performance metrics lie in their central role in ensuring that analytical and ML models are accurate, reliable, and fit for their intended purpose. Rigorous evaluation allows researchers, analysts, and practitioners to assess a model's generalizability, detect overfitting, and compare alternative modeling approaches in a principled and transparent manner. Performance metrics provide quantitative evidence of predictive quality and decision usefulness, enabling stakeholders to understand trade-offs between competing objectives such as accuracy versus interpretability or precision versus recall, particularly in high-stakes and imbalanced settings, as thoroughly explained in the following subsections. Beyond predictive accuracy, evaluation metrics are increasingly used to assess robustness, stability, fairness, and bias, which are critical for responsible and ethical deployment of domains such as finance, healthcare, and public policy. Ultimately, well-chosen evaluation frameworks and performance metrics not only support methodological rigor and reproducibility in academic research but also enhance trust, accountability, and informed decision-making in real-world AI and analytics applications.

4.5.1.1 Improving Model Accuracy

Enhancing the accuracy of a predictive or analytical model involves improving data quality, choosing robust models, and systematically tuning performance. The key is to work with clean, relevant, and representative data, removing duplicates, fixing errors, and balancing across categories to reduce bias and variance. Feature engineering plays a crucial role: creating meaningful variables, transforming skewed data, and removing irrelevant or redundant features help the model focus on important patterns. Choosing the right algorithm is just as important. Simpler models like linear regression or decision trees may perform well on straightforward datasets, while more complex architectures such as ensemble methods (Random Forest, Gradient Boosting) or deep learning models are better suited for high-dimensional or nonlinear problems. Hyperparameter optimization, through techniques like grid search, random search, or Bayesian optimization, fine-tunes the model's internal settings for the best performance.

Regularization techniques like Lasso and Ridge ($L1, L2$) help prevent overfitting, while cross-validation ensures the model generalizes well beyond the training data.[47] Monitoring feature importance and periodically retraining with new data keeps the model relevant as conditions change. Finally, using model ensemble methods—combining predictions from multiple models—can improve accuracy by balancing out individual weaknesses. Improving model accuracy is an ongoing process that involves domain expertise, statistical rigor, and computational testing to produce reliable and actionable results.

4.5.1.2 Reducing Overfitting

Overfitting happens when a model learns patterns that are too closely tied to the training data, capturing noise, anomalies, or random fluctuations instead of the true underlying relationships. As a result, the model performs well on training data but poorly on new, unseen data. To reduce overfitting, start by simplifying the model: use fewer parameters, select only the most relevant features, and avoid overly complex architectures, which helps prevent memorization of the training data. Regularization techniques like $L1$ and $L2$ penalize large weights, helping the model focus on important patterns.[48] For decision trees and similar models, limiting depth, pruning branches, or setting minimum sample requirements can enhance generalization. Cross-validation is essential for detecting overfitting early and confirming performance across multiple data splits.

Another effective approach is data augmentation—artificially expanding the training set by adding slight variations—common in image, audio, and text domains. When more data is available, increasing the dataset size naturally helps the model learn more representative patterns. For neural networks, dropouts randomly disable neurons during training, encouraging the model to distribute learning and avoid reliance on specific nodes. Ultimately, reducing overfitting is about balancing underfitting and excessive complexity. It requires careful tuning, validation, and continuous monitoring, so the model not only fits the training data but also adapts effectively to real-world situations.

4.5.1.3 Selecting the Best Model

Selecting the best model is a crucial step in the ML workflow because it directly affects accuracy, efficiency, and long-term sustainability. The process starts by understanding the problem type-classification, regression, clustering, or recommendation, since each one needs different algorithm families. For instance, logistic regression or random forests may work well for classification, while linear regression, gradient boosting, or neural networks might be suitable for regression tasks. Once candidate algorithms are identified, it is important to establish evaluation criteria. These can include accuracy, precision, recall, $F1$-score, RMSE, or domain-specific metrics. Often, trade-offs must be made; for example, a fraud detection model might prioritize recall over accuracy to minimize false negatives. Cross-validation is used to compare models fairly, ensuring results are not dependent on a single train-test split.

Computational efficiency also matters—especially in production environments where prediction speed, memory usage, and scalability affect decisions. Simpler models are often easier to interpret and maintain, making them preferable in regulated industries where explainability is crucial. Conversely, if the accuracy improvements from complex models like deep neural networks outweigh interpretability concerns, they may be justified. The final selection should be based on both quantitative performance and practical constraints, including data availability, computational resources, and deployment requirements. Often, the "best" model is not the one with the highest raw score but the one that finds the right balance between performance, interpretability, and operational feasibility.

4.6 Summary

This chapter presents ML as a core branch of AI that focuses on developing algorithms and models capable of learning patterns from data and improving performance on tasks without being explicitly programmed. Then it dives into supervised, unsupervised, and RL, along with key algorithms such as decision trees, regression, and clustering. This chapter also explores ML in business contexts such as customer analytics, risk modeling, and financial forecasting. Students learn to apply ML algorithms to real-world business problems. This chapter introduces the foundational concepts of ML, a subfield of AI that enables systems to learn from data and improve their performance over time without being explicitly programmed. It explores ML's definition, core types, essential components, and wide-ranging practical applications across industries. The chapter begins with a clear definition of ML, emphasizing its role in developing algorithms that can identify patterns, make decisions, and adapt to new data autonomously. It then outlines the three main types of ML: (1) supervised learning, where the model learns from labeled data to make predictions or classifications; (2) unsupervised learning, where the model discovers patterns and structures in unlabeled data; and (3) RL, where agents learn to make decisions by interacting with an environment to maximize cumulative rewards. This chapter also discusses the key components of an ML system, including datasets (input features and target labels); models (such as decision trees, neural networks, or SVMs); algorithms (used to train models); loss functions and optimization (to evaluate and improve model performance); and evaluation metrics (like accuracy, precision, recall, and *F*1-score). The chapter also explores the practical applications of ML across various sectors. In healthcare, ML supports diagnostics and personalized treatment plans. In finance, it's used for fraud detection and algorithmic trading. In marketing, ML enables customer segmentation and recommendation systems. In transportation, ML powers autonomous vehicles and route optimization. The chapter concludes by addressing challenges and considerations in implementing ML, including data quality, interpretability, overfitting, and ethical concerns such as bias and transparency. By the end, readers gain a solid grounding in the concepts, workflows, and real-world relevance of ML, preparing them for more advanced study or application in data-driven environments.

Notes

1 Mitchell, T. M. (2006). *The Discipline of Machine Learning* (Vol. 9, p. 3). Carnegie Mellon University, School of Computer Science, Machine Learning Department.
2 Murphy, K. P. (2012). *Machine Learning: A Probabilistic Perspective*. MIT Press.
3 James, G., Witten, D., Hastie, T., & Tibshirani, R. (2021). *An Introduction to Statistical Learning* (2nd ed.). Springer.
4 Bishop, C. M. (2006). *Pattern Recognition and Machine Learning*. Springer.
5 Hastie, T., Tibshirani, R., & Friedman, J. (2009). *The Elements of Statistical Learning: Data Mining, Inference, and Prediction* (2nd ed.). Springer.
6 Jolliffe, I. T., & Cadima, J. (2016). Principal component analysis: A review and recent developments. *Philosophical Transactions of the Royal Society A*, 374(2065), 20150202.
7 Sutton, R. S., & Barto, A. G. (2018). *Reinforcement Learning: An Introduction* (2nd ed.). MIT Press.
8 Shakya, A. K., Pillai, G., & Chakrabarty, S. (2023). Reinforcement learning algorithms: A brief survey. *Expert Systems with Applications*, 231, 120495. https://doi.org/10.1016/j.eswa.2023.120495
9 Bishop, C. M. (2006). *Pattern Recognition and Machine Learning*. Springer.
10 Dietterich, T. G. (2000). Ensemble methods in machine learning. *Multiple Classifier Systems*, 1857, 1–15.
11 Hastie, T., Tibshirani, R., & Friedman, J. H. (2009). *The Elements of Statistical Learning: Data Mining, Inference, and Prediction*. Springer.
12 Hastie, T., Tibshirani, R., & Friedman, J. H. (2009). *The Elements of Statistical Learning: Data Mining, Inference, and Prediction*. Springer.
13 Hastie, T., Tibshirani, R., & Friedman, J. H. (2009). *The Elements of Statistical Learning: Data Mining, Inference, and Prediction*. Springer.
14 Reinders, C., Ackermann, H., Yang, M. Y., & Rosenhahn, B. (2019). Learning convolutional neural networks for object detection with very little training data. In: Yang, M. Y., Rosenhahn, B., & Murino, V (eds.) *Multimodal Scene Understanding* (pp. 65–100). Academic Press.
15 Bishop, C. M. (2006). *Pattern Recognition and Machine Learning*. Springer.
16 Bishop, C. M. (2006). *Pattern Recognition and Machine Learning*. Springer.
17 Jolliffe, I. T., & Cadima, J. (2016). Principal component analysis: A review and recent developments. *Philosophical Transactions of the Royal Society A*, 374(2065), 20150202.
18 Blei, D. M., Ng, A. Y., & Jordan, M. I. (2003). Latent Dirichlet allocation. *Journal of Machine Learning Research*, 3, 993–1022.
19 Ghosal, A., Nandy, A., Das, A. K., Goswami, S., & Panday, M. (2020). A short review on different clustering techniques and their applications. In *Emerging Technology in Modelling and Graphics: Proceedings of IEM Graph 2018* (pp. 69–83).
20 Bengio, Y., Courville, A., & Vincent, P. (2013). Representation learning: A review and new perspectives. *IEEE Transactions on Pattern Analysis and Machine Intelligence*, 35(8), 1798–1828.

21 Braei, M., & Wagner, S. (2020). Anomaly detection in univariate time-series: A survey on the state-of-the-art. arXiv preprint arXiv:2004.00433
22 Zhu, X., & Goldberg, A. B. (2009). Introduction to semi-supervised learning. *Synthesis Lectures on Artificial Intelligence and Machine Learning*, 3(1), 1–130.
23 Van Engelen, J. E., & Hoos, H. H. (2020). A survey on semi-supervised learning. *Machine Learning*, 109(2), 373–440.
24 Chapelle, O., Schölkopf, B., & Zien, A. (2006). *Semi-Supervised Learning*. MIT Press.
25 Belkin, M., Niyogi, P., & Sindhwani, V. (2006). Manifold regularization: A geometric framework for learning from labeled and unlabeled examples. *Journal of Machine Learning Research*, 7, 2399–2434.
26 Sutton, R. S., & Barto, A. G. (2018). *Reinforcement Learning: An Introduction* (2nd ed.). MIT Press.
27 Li, Y. (2018). Deep reinforcement learning: An overview. arXiv preprint arXiv:1701.07274.
28 Yadav, K. (2023). Design, optimization and performance analysis of microgrids using multi-agent Q-learning. In: Sharma, D. K., Sharma, R., Jeon, G., & Kumar, R. (eds.) *Data Analytics for Smart Grids Applications—A Key to Smart City Development* (pp. 15–24). Springer Nature Switzerland.
29 Yadav, K. (2023). Design, optimization and performance analysis of microgrids using multi-agent Q-learning. In: Sharma, D. K., Sharma, R., Jeon, G., & Kumar, R. (eds.) *Data Analytics for Smart Grids Applications—A Key to Smart City Development* (pp. 15–24). Springer Nature Switzerland.
30 Schulman, J., Moritz, P., Levine, S., Jordan, M., & Abbeel, P. (2015). High-dimensional continuous control using generalized advantage estimation. arXiv preprint arXiv:1506.02438
31 Schulman, J., Wolski, F., Dhariwal, P., Radford, A., & Klimov, O. (2017). Proximal policy optimization algorithms. arXiv preprint arXiv:1707.06347
32 O'shea, K., & Nash, R. (2015). An introduction to convolutional neural networks. arXiv preprint arXiv:1511.08458
33 O'shea, K., & Nash, R. (2015). An introduction to. arXiv preprint arXiv:1511.08458, 13.
34 Khan, W. A., Chung, S. H., Awan, M. U., & Wen, X. (2020). Machine learning facilitated business intelligence (Part I) Neural networks learning algorithms and applications. *Industrial Management & Data Systems*, 120(1), 164–195.
35 Li, Z., Liu, F., Yang, W., Peng, S., & Zhou, J. (2021). A survey of convolutional neural networks: analysis, applications, and prospects. *IEEE Transactions on Neural Networks and Learning Systems*, 33(12), 6999–7019. https://doi.org/10.1109/TNNLS.2021.3084827
36 Mienye, I. D., Swart, T. G., & Obaido, G. (2024). Recurrent neural networks: A comprehensive review of architectures, variants, and applications. *Information*, 15(9), 517. https://doi.org/10.3390/info15090517
37 Van Houdt, G., Mosquera, C., & Nápoles, G. (2020). A review on the long short-term memory model. *Artificial Intelligence Review*, 53(8), 5929–5955. https://doi.org/10.1007/s10462-020-09838-1
38 Furizal, F., Fawait, A. B., Maghfiroh, H., Ma'arif, A., Firdaus, A. A., & Suwarno, I. (2024). Long short-term memory vs gated recurrent unit: A literature review on the performance of deep learning methods in temperature time series forecasting. *International Journal of Robotics and Control Systems*, 4(3), 1506–1526. https://doi.org/10.31763/ijrcs.v4i3.1546
39 Chen, S., & Guo, W. (2023). Auto-encoders in deep learning – A review with new perspectives. *Mathematics*, 11(8), 1777. https://www.mdpi.com/2227-7390/11/8/1777
40 Min, E., Chen, R., Bian, Y., Xu, T., Zhao, K., Huang, W., … & Rong, Y. (2022). Transformer for graphs: An overview from architecture perspective. arXiv preprint arXiv:2202.08455. https://doi.org/10.48550/arXiv.2202.08455
41 Saxena, D., & Cao, J. (2021). Generative adversarial networks (GANs) challenges, solutions, and future directions. *ACM Computing Surveys (CSUR)*, 54(3), 1–42. https://doi.org/10.1145/3446374
42 Abadal, S., Jain, A., Guirado, R., López-Alonso, J., & Alarcón, E. (2021). Computing graph neural networks: A survey from algorithms to accelerators. *ACM Computing Surveys (CSUR)*, 54(9), 1–38. https://doi.org/10.1145/3477141
43 Hastie, T., Tibshirani, R., & Friedman, J. (2017). *The Elements of Statistical Learning: Data Mining, Inference, and Prediction* (2nd ed.). Springer.
44 Powers, D. M. W. (2011). Evaluation: From precision, recall and F-measure to ROC, informedness, markedness and correlation. *Journal of Machine Learning Technologies*, 2(1), 37–63.

45 James, G., Witten, D., Hastie, T., & Tibshirani, R. (2021). *An Introduction to Statistical Learning: With Applications in R* (2nd ed.). Springer.
46 Molnar, C. (2022). *Interpretable Machine Learning* (2nd ed.). Leanpub.
47 Owen, A. B. (2007). A robust hybrid of lasso and ridge regression. *Contemporary Mathematics*, 443(7), 59–72. https://web.archive.org/web/20070824060436id_/http://www-stat.stanford.edu/~owen/reports/hhu.pdf
48 Owen, A. B. (2007). A robust hybrid of lasso and ridge regression. *Contemporary Mathematics*, 443(7), 59–72. https://web.archive.org/web/20070824060436id_/http://www-stat.stanford.edu/~owen/reports/hhu.pdf

5 Business Analytics Tools and Techniques

Learning Objectives

- Learn essential tools and techniques of business analytics
- Understand Python, R, and data analytics
- Obtain an understanding of the use of business analytics tools in accounting
- Learn the applications of business analytics tools in fraud detection and risk analysis
- Understand data visualization and communication
- Understand the importance of programming languages in AI and analytics
- Become familiar with key data analytics and ML libraries
- Set up and use integrated development environments (IDEs)

5.1 Introduction

BA tools and techniques enable organizations to transform raw data into processed information for decision-making and actionable insights to improve performance, optimize operations, and gain a competitive advantage in the marketplace. The choice of BA tools and techniques depends on the specific goals and needs of the organization, and the nature of the data being analyzed. This chapter presents the essential BA tools and techniques of data collection and management, data cleaning and preparation, descriptive, predictive and prescriptive analytics, text and sentiment analysis, risk analytics, marketing analytics, supply chain analytics, geospatial analytics, cloud-based analytics, real-time analytics, social media analytics, collaborative analytics, and ethical and responsible analytics. The types of essential BA and their tools and techniques are presented in this chapter.

5.2 Essentials of Business Analytics (BA) Tools and Techniques

BA tools and techniques form the backbone of modern data-driven decision-making in organizations across industries, encompassing a broad array of methodologies and technologies that enable organizations to collect, process, analyze, and interpret data to drive informed decision-making. Descriptive analytics uses tools such as dashboards, reports, and data visualization software (e.g., Tableau, Power BI) to summarize historical data and

DOI: 10.4324/9781003664550-5

reveal patterns, whereas predictive analytics employs statistical models and machine learning algorithms, including regression analysis, decision trees, and neural networks, to anticipate future events based on current and historical data. Finally, prescriptive analytics employs optimization and simulation techniques to suggest the best course of action under specific constraints.

Essential BA techniques can be employed to analyze business data for better decision-making. Examples of these techniques are (1) descriptive analytics of answering what happened by summarizing historical data (Excel, Tableau, Power BI, KPI dashboards, financial reporting, sales trends; (2) diagnostic analytics of answering "Why did it happen?" by identifying patterns and causes of past performance (SQL, R, Python, Power BI, root cause analysis, churn analysis); (3) predictive analytics of answering "What is likely to happen?" by using historical data and machine learning to forecast future trends such as sales forecasting, risk assessment, demand prediction (Python (Scikit-Learn, TensorFlow), R, SAS, AutoML; (4) prescriptive analytics of "What should be done?" by suggests optimal actions based on data-driven insights such as dynamic pricing, supply chain optimization, personalized marketing (AI, optimization algorithms, decision trees); (5) real-time and streaming analytics of processes live data streams for instant insights for fraud detection, stock market analysis (Apache Kafka, Spark Streaming, Google BigQuery); (6) text and sentiment analysis like NLP for extracting insights from unstructured text data such as customer feedback analysis, ESG disclosures sentiment analysis (NLP libraries, NLTK, SpaCy, Transformers); and (7) AI and automation in BA for automated data analysis and decision-making, AI-driven financial analysis, automated reporting (AI-powered chatbots, RPA, UiPath, Automation Anywhere).

For example, a specific type of predictive analytic tool called a decision tree involves determining the plausibility of a certain event happening or forecasting future trends by utilizing the on-hand data within a corporation, and can be applied in numerous different settings, such as image processing, machine learning, and data mining.[1] Data visualization has certainly become a key BA tool in the modern business landscape by translating real-time data into visualizations that make it easier to understand and identify different trends and metrics that help to enhance the business decision-making process.[2] Some of these BA tools and techniques, including machine learning, predictive analytics, data visualization, and even robotics automation processing, are being used in the accounting and audit field to enhance the accounting and auditing services provided by accountants and auditors.[3] Table 5.1 summarizes BA tools and techniques, whereas Figure 5.1 provides an analytics lifecycle flowchart and tools guide.

5.3 Machine Learning for Business Insights

In today's data-abundant economy, the complexity of business decision-making often outpaces the limits of human intuition. Patterns once too subtle to detect now shimmer beneath the surface of transactional histories, customer behaviors, and operational flows, awaiting discovery. This is where machine learning enters as both a lens and a lever: a computational lens that reveals hidden regularities and a strategic lever that drives intelligent action. Machine learning algorithms learn from data itself, adapting and evolving to capture the dynamics of real-world business systems. Whether predicting customer churn, optimizing pricing strategies, or segmenting markets, machine learning empowers organizations to move beyond hindsight and embrace foresight, transforming data not just into knowledge but into insights that compel action.

Table 5.1 Business Analytics Tools and Techniques

Type of Analytics	*Representative Tools*	*Core Techniques*
Descriptive analytics	Excel, Tableau, Power BI, Google Data Studio, Qlik Sense	Data aggregation, summary statistics, trend analysis, data visualization
Diagnostic analytics	SQL, R, Python, Power BI	Root cause analysis, pattern identification, drill-down analysis, correlation analysis
Predictive analytics	Python (scikit-learn, TensorFlow), R, SAS, AutoML (Google Cloud AutoML, H2O.ai, DataRobot)	Regression modeling, time series forecasting, decision trees, neural networks, machine learning
Prescriptive analytics	AI, optimization algorithms, IBM CPLEX, simulation models	Optimization modeling, simulation, scenario analysis, decision analysis
Real-time & streaming analytics	Apache Kafka, Spark Streaming, Google BigQuery	Stream processing, event-driven analysis, real-time computation
Text & sentiment analysis	NLP libraries (NLTK, SpaCy, Transformers)	Natural Language Processing (NLP), sentiment analysis, topic modeling, text mining
Machine learning & AI-powered analytics	TensorFlow, PyTorch, IBM Watson Analytics, AutoML tools	Supervised learning, unsupervised learning, reinforcement learning, deep learning
Data management & processing	SQL (MySQL, PostgreSQL, SQL Server, Oracle, BigQuery), NoSQL (MongoDB, Cassandra, Firebase), Apache Hadoop, Spark	Data extraction, data cleaning, data transformation, data integration
Data visualization & business intelligence (BI)	Tableau, Microsoft Power BI, Google Data Studio, Qlik Sense	Dashboard creation, interactive visualization, data storytelling
Data analysis & statistical computing	Excel, R, Python (Pandas, NumPy, SciPy, Matplotlib, Seaborn), SPSS, SAS	Statistical modeling, hypothesis testing, exploratory data analysis, variance analysis
Cloud-based analytics platforms	AWS (Redshift, S3, QuickSight), Google Cloud (BigQuery, Looker, Vertex AI), Microsoft Azure (Synapse Analytics, Power BI, Azure ML)	Cloud-based data warehousing, distributed computing, scalable analytics
AI & automation in business analytics	AI-powered chatbots, Robotic Process Automation (RPA) tools (UiPath, Automation Anywhere)	Automated analytics, robotic process automation, AI-driven optimization

5.3.1 Supervised Learning

Supervised learning is characterized by its reliance on labeled datasets, where each training example is paired with a corresponding output label. The objective is to learn a mapping from inputs to outputs that can be used to make predictions on unseen data. Common algorithms used in supervised learning include regression analyses, decision trees, and support vector machines. This learning approach is widely applied in business applications such as credit scoring, where historical customer behavior and their credit data can be modeled to predict future financial risks and opportunities.

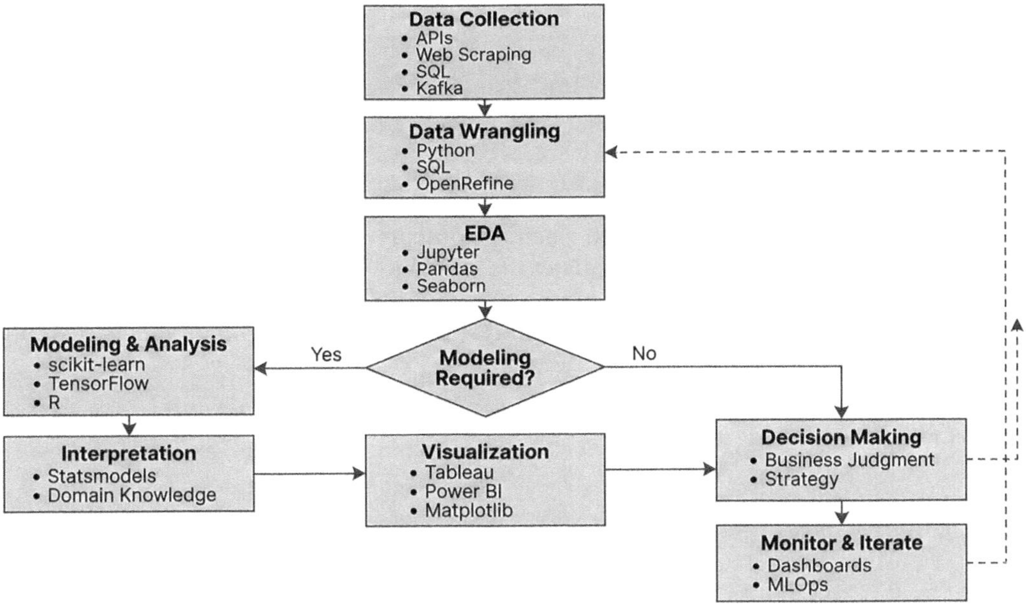

Figure 5.1 Analytics Lifecycle Flowchart and Tools Guide.

5.3.1.1 Linear and Logistic Regression

Linear regression is one of the most fundamental and widely used techniques in predictive analytics, ideal for estimating a continuous outcome based on one or more explanatory variables. In its most basic form, simple linear regression models the relationship between a single independent variable and a dependent variable, using the equation:

$$y = \beta_0 + \beta_1 x + \varepsilon$$

where:

β_0 = The intercept, the expected value of y when $x = 0$.
β_1 = The slope coefficient, the change in y for a one-unit change in x.
ε = The error term captures the variability in y not explained by the model.

However, in real-world business scenarios, outcomes are rarely determined by a single factor. Here, multivariate (or multiple) linear regression becomes essential, as it extends the model to incorporate several input variables. Multivariate regression estimates the simultaneous effects of multiple variables, allowing analysts to assess each feature's marginal contribution while controlling for others. Mathematically, it is represented as:

$$y = \beta_0 + \beta_1 x_1 + \beta_2 x_2 + \cdots + \beta_p x_p + \varepsilon$$

where:

β_0 = The intercept, expected y when all $x_i = 0$.
β_i = The regression coefficient for each x_i; represents the marginal effect of x_i on y, holding other variables constant.
ε = The error term, as before.

In contrast, logistic regression is used when the outcome is binary or categorical. Instead of predicting a numerical value, it estimates the probability that a given observation belongs to a particular category. The model outputs probabilities through a logistic (sigmoid) function, mapping predictions to the [0, 1] range. Its power lies in its ability to model odds and log odds. Mathematically, it is represented as:

$$P(y=1 \mid x) = \frac{1}{1+e^{-(\beta_0+\beta_1 x_1+\beta_2 x_2+\cdots+\beta_p x_p)}}$$

Alternatively, expressed in log-odds (logit) form:

$$\log\left(\frac{P(y=1)}{1-P(y=1)}\right) = \beta_0 + \beta_1 x_1 + \beta_2 x_2 + \cdots + \beta_p x_p$$

where:

$x_1, x_2, \ldots, x_p$ = The independent variables, as in linear regression.
β_0 = The intercept of the logistic function.
β_i = The log-odds coefficient, a one-unit increase in x_i multiplies the odds of $y=1$ by e^{β_i}.

A related technique is Poisson regression, designed for predicting count-based outcomes. Poisson regression models the number of times an event occurs within a fixed interval, which assumes that the variance of the outcome is equal to its mean. Mathematically, it is represented as:

$$\log(\lambda) = \beta_0 + \beta_1 x_1 + \beta_2 x_2 + \cdots + \beta_p x_p$$

where:

λ = The expected count or event rate (e.g., number of website clicks, complaints).
$x_1, x_2, \ldots, x_p$ = The independent variables.
β_0 = The intercept.
β_i = The regression coefficients, a one-unit increase in x_i changes the log of the expected count.

5.3.1.2 Decision Trees and Random Forests

5.3.1.2.1 DECISION TREES

Decision trees are one of the most interpretable and intuitive algorithms in machine learning. A decision tree models decisions in the form of a flowchart-like structure, where each internal node represents a test on a feature, each branch represents an outcome of the test, and each leaf node represents a predicted class label or a value. At its core, a decision tree operates by recursively partitioning the dataset into subsets that become increasingly homogeneous. The goal is to maximize information gain or minimize impurity at each split. Splitting Criterion—Gini Impurity:

$$\text{Gini}(t) = 1 - \sum_{i=1}^{C} p_i^2$$

where:

t = Denotes a node in the decision tree.
C = Total number of classes.
p_i = Represents the proportion of samples in class i at node t.

5.3.1.2.2 RANDOM FORESTS

A random forest builds multiple decision trees on bootstrapped samples and averages their predictions. Each of these samples is drawn with replacement, meaning some observations may appear more than once while others may be left out. For each of these datasets, a decision tree is built. However, unlike traditional trees, random forests introduce additional randomness at each split: instead of considering all features when determining the best split, only a random subset of features is evaluated.

5.3.1.3 Gradient Boosting Machines

Among the most powerful techniques in the modern machine learning toolbox, GBMs are celebrated for their exceptional predictive performance on structured data. Each new tree is trained to correct the prediction errors made by the ensemble of all previous trees. Tools like XGBoost and LightGBM have become industry standards for structured data problems due to their high predictive performance and speed. In business contexts, GBMs are often used for complex classification and ranking tasks such as lead scoring, churn prediction, or targeted marketing response modeling. Mathematically, a GBM builds the predictive function $F(x)$ in an additive manner:

$$F_m(x) = F_{m-1}(x) + \gamma h_m(x)$$

where:

$F_m(x)$ = The prediction after the mth iteration
$F_{m-1}(x)$ = The prediction from the previous iteration
$h_m(x)$ = The new base learner (typically a decision tree)
γ = The learning rate

5.3.1.4 Neural Networks

Multilayer Perceptrons (MLPs), a type of feedforward neural network consisting of an input layer, one or more hidden layers, and an output layer, can capture complex nonlinear relationships in structured datasets. Each layer contains neurons, which perform a weighted sum of the inputs followed by a nonlinear activation function. MLPs can outperform simpler models in tasks like revenue forecasting, customer behavior modeling, and pricing optimization.

The basic operation within each neuron is:

$$a^{(l)} = \sigma\left(W^{(l)}a^{(l-1)} + b^{(l)}\right)$$

where:

$a^{(l)}$ = Activation output at layer l
$W^{(l)}$ = Weight matrix for layer l
$b^{(l)}$ = Bias vector
$\sigma(\cdot)$ = Activation function (e.g., ReLU, sigmoid, tanh)

5.3.2 *Unsupervised Learning*

Unsupervised learning involves training algorithms on data that does not have predefined labels. The main goal is to identify inherent structures or patterns within the data. Techniques such as clustering, dimensionality reduction, and anomaly detection are prevalent in unsupervised learning. This learning is especially effective in high-dimensional data environments, providing strategic advantages through enhanced data analysis capabilities.

5.3.2.1 *Clustering Algorithms*

Clustering is the process of grouping data points into distinct clusters based on similarity, such that items within the same cluster are more alike than those in different clusters. It is one of the most widely used unsupervised techniques in BA.

5.3.2.1.1 *K*-MEANS CLUSTERING

K-means clustering is one of the most widely used and conceptually straightforward unsupervised learning algorithms. It partitions a dataset into k distinct clusters based on feature similarity, intending to minimize intra-cluster variance and maximize inter-cluster separation. Each cluster is represented by its centroid, which is the mean of all points assigned to that cluster. The algorithm iteratively updates cluster assignments and centroids until convergence. *K*-means aims to minimize the within-cluster sum of squared distances (WCSS), also called inertia:

$$\arg\min_{S} \sum_{i=1}^{k} \sum_{x \in S_i} |x - \mu_i|^2$$

where:

k = Number of clusters
S_i = Data points in cluster i
μ_i = Centroid of cluster i
$|x - \mu_i|^2$ = Squared Euclidean distance between point x and centroid μ_i

5.3.2.1.2 DBSCAN (DENSITY-BASED SPATIAL CLUSTERING OF APPLICATIONS WITH NOISE)

DBSCAN is a density-based clustering algorithm that groups data points by identifying regions of high density separated by areas of low density, making it highly effective for discovering clusters of arbitrary shapes and detecting noise points. DBSCAN does not require the number of clusters to be predefined, instead relying on two key parameters: ε (eps), which defines the neighborhood radius around each point, and min_samples, which specifies the minimum number of points required to form a dense region. The algorithm classifies points into three categories: core points (those with at least min_samples neighbors within ε), border points (points within ε of a core point but lacking sufficient neighbors themselves), and noise points (outliers that do not belong to any cluster).

5.3.2.2 Dimensionality Reduction

Business datasets often contain dozens or even hundreds of features. Dimensionality reduction simplifies data by reducing the number of variables while preserving essential patterns and structure. Feature importance refers to a suite of analytical techniques designed to quantify how much each input variable contributes to the prediction or explanation of patterns in data. In supervised learning scenarios, such as regression or decision trees, it highlights the most influential features in driving model outcomes. In unsupervised contexts, such as clustering or dimensionality reduction, feature importance helps identify variables that shape the underlying data structure. Feature importance serves as a bridge between complex predictive models and human interpretability by enabling researchers, analysts, and decision-makers to discern which variables truly matter, offering transparency in fields where opaque algorithms can have critical consequences.[4]

5.3.2.2.1 PRINCIPAL COMPONENT ANALYSIS (PCA)

PCA is a fundamental technique for dimensionality reduction, widely used in BA to simplify complex datasets while retaining their most informative patterns. At its core, PCA transforms the original, possibly correlated variables into a new set of uncorrelated variables called principal components, which are ordered by the amount of variance they capture from the data. The first principal component captures the greatest variance, the second captures the next highest variance orthogonal to the first, and so on. Mathematically, PCA performs an eigen decomposition of the covariance matrix of the data, projecting it onto directions (eigenvectors) that maximize variance. This results in a compact representation:

$$Z = XW$$

where:

X = Data matrix.
W = Matrix of eigenvectors of the covariance matrix of X.
Z = Projection of the data into the lower-dimensional space.

5.3.2.2.2 *t*-SNE AND UMAP: NONLINEAR DIMENSIONALITY REDUCTION FOR VISUALIZATION

t-Distributed Stochastic Neighbor Embedding (t-SNE) and Uniform Manifold Approximation and Projection (UMAP) are powerful nonlinear dimensionality reduction methods specifically designed to visualize complex high-dimensional data in two or three dimensions while preserving meaningful topological relationships. Both techniques excel at maintaining local structures, making them particularly valuable for exploration data analysis, cluster validation, and pattern recognition. *t*-SNE achieves this through a probabilistic approach that models pairwise similarities in high-dimensional space and optimizes a low-dimensional embedding using Student's *t*-distributions to mitigate crowding effects, though it tends to be computationally intensive and focuses primarily on local structures. In contrast, UMAP employs principles from algebraic topology and Riemannian geometry to construct a more scalable framework that better preserves both local and global structures while offering significantly faster performance on larger datasets.

5.3.2.3 Association Rule Learning

Association rule learning is a powerful data mining technique that identifies meaningful relationships and co-occurrence patterns between variables in large datasets. This method is particularly renowned for its application in market basket analysis, where it helps retailers understand product purchasing patterns by revealing which items are frequently bought together. The insights gained from this analysis enable businesses to optimize product placement, design targeted promotions, and improve cross-selling strategies.

At the core of association rule learning lies the Apriori algorithm, which efficiently discovers frequent item sets and generates meaningful association rules from transactional data. The algorithm operates on the principle that if an itemset is frequent, then all its subsets must also be frequent, allowing for systematic pruning of the search space. The quality and significance of discovered rules are typically evaluated using three key metrics:

Support measures how frequently an itemset appears in the dataset, calculated as the proportion of transactions containing both items A and B. A high support value indicates that the item combination occurs often in the dataset.

Confidence assesses the reliability of the inference made by the rule, representing the conditional probability that item B is purchased given that item A has been purchased. While useful, confidence alone can be misleading as it does not account for the baseline frequency of item B.

Lift provides a more nuanced measure by comparing the observed frequency of co-occurrence to what would be expected if the items were statistically independent. A lift value greater than 1 indicates a positive association between the items, while values below 1 suggest a negative relationship.

5.3.3 Reinforcement Learning

RL is a paradigm of machine learning that focuses on sequential decision-making, in which an autonomous agent learns to select actions through trial-and-error interactions with an environment in order to maximize cumulative long-term rewards. The learning process is commonly formalized using a Markov Decision Process (MDP), where the agent observes states, takes actions, receives scalar rewards, and updates its behavior through a policy that balances exploration and exploitation. Advances in deep RL integrate neural networks with RL algorithms, enabling successful applications in complex domains such as robotics, autonomous systems, finance, and strategic game playing.

RL architecture comprises four essential components: environmental states (system representations), possible actions (decision options), reward signals (performance feedback), and policy frameworks (action-selection strategies). These four components interact through the agent-environment feedback loop, forming a continuous cycle of learning and adaptation.

5.4 Introduction to Python, R, and Data Analytics Libraries

In the evolving landscape of BA, Python and R stand as the two most influential programming languages, each offering distinct advantages shaped by their origins and design philosophies. Python is celebrated for its versatility, scalability, and integration capabilities, making it ideal for end-to-end data workflows and business applications. R, by contrast, excels in statistical rigor and visualization, providing researchers and analysts with unparalleled tools for in-depth data exploration and modeling. Understanding the comparative strengths, limitations, and underlying philosophies of these languages helps professionals choose the one that best aligns with their analytical goals and organizational needs.

5.4.1 Python for BA

5.4.1.1 Key Libraries and Tools

Python's extensive ecosystem of libraries and tools is a critical asset that enhances its applicability in BA.

5.4.1.1.1 PANDAS

Built upon the computational foundation of NumPy, Pandas introduces high-level data structures such as the DataFrame and Series, which emulate tabular and spreadsheet-like formats while offering superior flexibility and control. These structures enable efficient handling of diverse data types, including transactional records, time series, and customer profiles, making Pandas particularly suited for real-world data challenges. The library excels in data wrangling, providing robust functionalities for merging, filtering, reshaping, and imputing datasets, as well as performing advanced aggregations and summaries. Its intuitive syntax and optimized performance streamline EDA and automate reporting workflows, thereby enhancing productivity in business and research contexts. Moreover, Pandas is essential in preparing datasets for downstream analytical tasks, ensuring data quality and facilitating the discovery of actionable insights that support strategic decision-making.

5.4.1.1.2 NUMPY

NumPy (Numerical Python) serves as the fundamental library for numerical computation in Python, providing robust support for multi-dimensional arrays (ndarrays) and a comprehensive suite of mathematical functions to operate on these structures. Its architecture is optimized for performance, leveraging low-level C implementations to execute computationally intensive operations, such as matrix multiplication, linear algebra, and statistical calculations. This makes NumPy indispensable for processing large datasets that demand high-speed numerical computations. Beyond its core functionality, NumPy's memory-efficient design and vectorized operations eliminate the overhead of Python loops, enabling seamless integration with other scientific computing libraries. Its versatility extends to diverse domains, including signal processing, image analysis, and simulations, where efficient array operations are critical.

5.4.1.1.3 MATPLOTLIB AND SEABORN

The Python data visualization ecosystem is built upon Matplotlib, a foundational library offering unparalleled customization for creating static, animated, and interactive visualizations, enabling precise control over every graphical element for publication-quality outputs. Complementing this, Seaborn provides a higher-level interface optimized for statistical visualization, featuring elegant themes and color palettes that produce professional-quality plots with minimal code. Together, they form a comprehensive toolkit that excels at revealing complex data relationships through intuitive graphics, from Seaborn's sophisticated statistical visualizations like distribution plots and correlation matrices to Matplotlib's versatile support for everything from basic charts to advanced 3D representations. These libraries empower analysts across business and research domains to transform raw data into compelling visual narratives, uncovering hidden patterns and trends, while recent advancements in interactivity and web integration further enhance their utility for data storytelling and decision-making as integral components of Python's data science stack.

5.4.1.1.4 SCIKIT-LEARN

Scikit-learn has established itself as the gold standard for machine learning implementation in Python, offering a comprehensive suite of algorithms for classification, regression, clustering, and dimensionality reduction. Built on NumPy and SciPy, its carefully designed API provides a consistent interface across all machine learning tasks, making it exceptionally accessible for both beginners and experienced practitioners. The library's true strength lies in its seamless integration with Python's data science stack, allowing analysts to effortlessly transition from data manipulation with pandas to sophisticated predictive modeling. Beyond its core algorithms, scikit-learn includes essential utilities for model evaluation (cross-validation, metrics), preprocessing (scaling, encoding), and workflow automation (pipelines), forming a complete ecosystem for machine learning development. This combination of breadth and usability has made it the go-to choice for business applications ranging from customer segmentation to sales forecasting and risk assessment.

5.4.1.1.5 STATSMODELS

Statsmodels serves as a powerful Python library dedicated to statistical modeling and inference, offering comprehensive tools for regression analysis, hypothesis testing, and EDA. Statsmodels emphasizes interpretability and rigorous statistical validation, making it indispensable for deriving actionable insights from data. It supports a wide range of models, including linear and generalized linear models, time series analysis, and non-parametric methods, each accompanied by detailed statistical summaries. These outputs, such as coefficients, p-values, confidence intervals, and diagnostic tests.

5.4.1.1.6 JUPYTER NOTEBOOKS

Jupyter Notebooks have transformed analytical workflows by combining executable code, visual outputs, and rich documentation in interactive documents that support literate programming—enabling seamless data storytelling, concept demonstration, and reproducible research. This versatile platform serves as both an analytical sandbox and a communication tool, allowing businesses to bridge the gap between technical analysis and stakeholder understanding through shareable notebooks that foster collaboration across multidisciplinary teams while maintaining transparency in methodology and results.

Table 5.2 Python Data Analytics Libraries

Library/Tool	*Primary Function*	*Common Business Use Cases*
Pandas	Data manipulation and wrangling	Cleaning data, time series analysis, reporting
NumPy	Fast numerical computation and array processing	Matrix ops, simulations, feeding ML models
Matplotlib	Customizable visualizations	Line charts, bar plots, dashboards
Seaborn	Statistical visualization	Heatmaps, pair plots, distribution analysis
Scikit-learn	Machine learning algorithms and model tools	Forecasting, segmentation, classification
Statsmodels	Statistical inference and regression analysis	A/B testing, econometrics, causal modeling
Jupyter Notebooks	Interactive analysis and documentation	Prototyping, presentations, knowledge sharing
Streamlit	App development for interactive analytics	Dashboards, model apps, user-driven simulations

5.4.1.1.7 STREAMLIT

Streamlit has emerged as a transformative library for building interactive web applications that bring data analytics to life. Designed with simplicity and accessibility in mind, it enables analysts to convert Python scripts into dynamic dashboards with minimal code—eliminating the need for front-end development skills in JavaScript, HTML, or CSS. Organizations are increasingly adopting Streamlit to create real-time, user-friendly interfaces that enable stakeholders to visually explore data, adjust parameters, and uncover insights on the fly. From financial forecasting models to customer behavior dashboards, Streamlit's intuitive framework supports rapid prototyping and deployment, bridging the gap between analytical workflows and business decision-making. Table 5.2 summarizes these Python data analytics libraries.

5.4.2 R for Business Analytics

5.4.2.1 Key Libraries and Tools

The R programming language offers a comprehensive array of libraries and tools that are essential for effective BA.

5.4.2.1.1 TIDYVERSE

At the heart of R's data analytics revolution lies the Tidyverse, which is a coherent collection of packages that share a common design philosophy and data structure. Spearheaded by Hadley Wickham, the Tidyverse includes foundational tools such as ggplot2 (for elegant graphics), dplyr (for data manipulation), tidyr (for reshaping messy data), and readr (for fast data import). These packages follow a "grammar of data science," allowing analysts to write clean, readable code using intuitive verbs like filter, mutate, and summarize. In business contexts, Tidyverse is invaluable for wrangling survey data, visualizing KPIs, and performing EDA with clarity and composability.

5.4.2.1.2 CARET

Short for Classification and Regression Training, caret is one of R's most powerful and accessible tools for machine learning. It provides a unified interface to over 200 algorithms from data preprocessing and model training to resampling, tuning, and validation. With caret, analysts can switch between models with minimal code changes, making it ideal for benchmarking multiple algorithms or quickly iterating on predictive tasks. Whether it's churn prediction, credit risk scoring, or sales forecasting, caret offers the flexibility and structure to translate business problems into scalable predictive models.

5.4.2.1.3 FORECAST

The forecast package, developed by Rob J Hyndman, is a cornerstone of time series analysis in R. It provides implementations of classical methods like ARIMA, Exponential Smoothing (ETS), and Seasonal Decomposition, as well as more advanced techniques like auto.arima for automated model selection. The package emphasizes interpretability and accuracy, producing forecasts that are statistically sound and easy to visualize. In BA, forecast plays a crucial role in demand planning, sales prediction, financial time series modeling, and capacity management, as any scenario where temporal patterns shape decisions.

5.4.2.1.4 SHINY

shiny transforms R from a scripting language into an interactive application framework, empowering analysts to build dynamic web apps directly from their code, without the need for front-end development skills. With just a few lines of code, users can build dashboards with sliders, dropdowns, and real-time plots, making complex analyses accessible to decision-makers. Shiny apps are increasingly used in industries like finance and marketing to create live reports, scenario simulators, and data exploration portals.

5.4.2.1.5 RSTUDIO

RStudio is the de facto integrated development environment (IDE) for R, purpose-built for data science workflows. It provides a seamless interface to script writing, visualization, version control, and package management. Features like built-in markdown rendering, project management, and integration with Shiny and R Markdown make RStudio an indispensable hub for reproducible analytics. For business users, it creates a productive space to develop, document, and deploy insights, making the analytical process not only efficient but narratively rich and transparent. Table 5.3 summarizes R data analytics libraries and tools.

5.4.3 Comparison of Python and R

5.4.3.1 Strengths and Limitations: Python versus R

Python has gained widespread popularity in the BA domain due to its versatility and ease of use. Its strength lies in its comprehensive set of libraries.[5]

R, on the other hand, excels in statistical modeling and graphical representation. It offers a wealth of packages designed specifically for statistical analysis. Nonetheless, R's limitations emerge in its programming paradigm, which can be less flexible than that of

Table 5.3 R Data Analytics Libraries and Tools

Library/Tool	*Primary Function*	*Common Business Use Cases*
Tidyverse	Data wrangling and visualization using a unified syntax	Cleaning datasets, visualizing KPIs, and exploratory analysis
caret	Unified interface for machine learning models	Churn prediction, credit scoring, sales forecasting
forecast	Classical and automated time series modeling	Demand planning, inventory forecasting, and financial trends
shiny	Interactive web apps and dashboards	Live reporting tools, business simulations, stakeholder engagement
RStudio	Integrated development environment for R	Script writing, reproducible analysis, Shiny/RMarkdown projects

Python. This can hinder the integration of R with other programming languages or technologies, making Python the preferred choice for projects that require extensive data handling or integration with web applications.[6]

5.4.3.2 Philosophical Divide: Flexibility versus Rigor

The philosophical distinction between Python and R reflects a fundamental tension between flexibility and specialization in data analysis. Python embodies versatility as a general-purpose language capable of handling diverse tasks—from web development to machine learning—within a unified ecosystem. This "do-anything" approach enables analysts to fluidly move between data cleaning, model building, and application deployment using a single language, making it ideal for cross-functional teams requiring broad computational capabilities. In contrast, R was purpose-built for statistical analysis, prioritizing methodological rigor and reproducibility through its specialized packages and frameworks. Its domain-specific design offers unparalleled depth for advanced statistics, featuring robust implementations of time series analysis, Bayesian modeling, and experimental design that meet the exacting standards of academic researchers and professional statisticians.

This divergence manifests in their analytical philosophies: Python encourages exploratory problem-solving with multiple valid approaches, while R promotes structured best practices through curated ecosystems, such as the Tidyverse. The Tidyverse's opinionated grammar for data manipulation and visualization enforces consistency and readability, embodying R's commitment to statistical elegance and literate programming. Where Python empowers users with flexibility—asking "How should we solve this?"—R responds with domain expertise, asserting "Here's the statistically optimal approach." For projects demanding strict adherence to statistical protocols or specialized analytical techniques, R's rigor proves indispensable, whereas Python's adaptability shines in end-to-end workflows requiring integration with other systems or disciplines.

Overall, the decision between Python and R ultimately depends on the specific journey an organization is pursuing in the realm of data analytics. If the focus is on EDA, statistical modeling, and generating detailed visualizations, R may provide a more robust and user-friendly environment.[7] This is particularly true in industries such as academic research or healthcare, where nuanced statistical interpretation is paramount. Conversely, if the goal encompasses broader data science applications, such as integrating machine learning, developing applications, or automating data pipelines, Python emerges as the more suitable

Table 5.4 Python vs. R: Choosing the Right Tool for Business Analytics

Feature	*Python*	*R*
Primary focus	General-purpose programming, AI, automation	Statistical analysis, visualization
Learning curve	Easier syntax, great for beginners	Steeper curve, but strong for data manipulation
Libraries	pandas, scikit-learn, TensorFlow	ggplot2, dplyr, forecast
Use case	Business, tech, production systems	Research, academia, data exploration
Strength	Scalability & integration	Statistical depth & visualization

choice. Its flexibility allows professionals to conduct end-to-end data workflows effectively. Organizations may also adopt a hybrid approach, utilizing both languages to leverage the strengths of each, depending on specific project requirements. Ultimately, the choice should align with the team's familiarity with the language, the specific needs of the project, and long-term organizational goals in data analytics.

5.5 Data Wrangling and Feature Engineering

In the world of BA, the spotlight often falls on algorithms and models, but behind every successful analysis lies a quieter, more foundational effort. Before predictions can be made, before dashboards light up with insight, raw data must be cleansed, transformed, and shaped into something meaningful. Data wrangling, feature engineering, and dimensionality reduction are the unglamorous but indispensable groundwork. It is alchemy that turns disorder into structure, noise into signal, and mere numbers into strategic advantage.

5.5.1 Data Wrangling: From Chaos to Clarity

5.5.1.1 Key Activities of Data Wrangling

5.5.1.1.1 HANDLING MISSING DATA

Missing data is a significant challenge in real-world analytics, often overlooked yet capable of distorting statistical insights and undermining model performance. It can stem from various sources, including system failures, human errors, or incomplete data collection. Analysts must carefully assess the nature of the missingness and the business context before selecting an appropriate handling strategy.

When missing values are few and randomly distributed (MCAR), simple deletion may be acceptable, though it risks reducing dataset size and introducing bias. A more refined approach is imputation, such as mean or median substitution, preserving the data structure, but may underestimate variability. For greater accuracy, model-based imputation leverages machine learning or statistical techniques to predict missing values based on observed patterns, making it particularly valuable for complex datasets.

5.5.1.1.2 DATA TYPE CONVERSION

Data often requires transformation to meet the requirements of analytical models. Variables may be stored in formats that misrepresent their true nature, such as categorical data coded as text or numerical identifiers treated as continuous values. Proper data type conversion ensures variables align with their intended statistical and semantic roles. This includes parsing string-based dates into datetime objects, encoding categorical responses numerically, or converting binary indicators (e.g., "yes"/"no") into Boolean values. These conversions are not just technical steps but conceptual clarifications that dictate how variables function within an analysis.

Tools like Python's pandas and R's dplyr provide efficient methods for inspecting and converting data types, enabling consistent and accurate data preparation. For example, predictive modeling often requires categorical variables to be numerically encoded, and these libraries streamline such transformations. Through structured management of data types, analysts maintain alignment with analytical methods and enhance the trustworthiness of their outcomes.

5.5.1.1.3 STANDARDIZATION AND CONSISTENCY

Inconsistent data entry can undermine analytical accuracy and reliability, such as mixed date formats, irregular capitalization, or varying measurement units. Standardization addresses these issues by enforcing uniformity across datasets, ensuring consistency in text (e.g., converting "NY" and "New York" into a single category), date formats (e.g., using ISO 8601 for all timestamps), and numerical units (e.g., converting all currencies to USD). It also involves maintaining coherent column naming conventions, missing value indicators, and encoding schemes, particularly when integrating multiple data sources.

Tools like OpenRefine are highly effective for detecting and correcting inconsistencies, while scripting languages such as Python and R enable automated and reproducible cleaning workflows. Though these steps may seem tedious, they are critical for data integrity, analytical results risk being flawed or misleading without them. For instance, inconsistent text casing can create false duplicates, while mismatched date formats disrupt time-based analysis.

5.5.1.2 Application in Business

5.5.1.2.1 APPLICATIONS OF DATA WRANGLING IN BA

Data wrangling facilitates the detection and correction of common data issues such as missing values, inconsistencies, and erroneous entries, which can significantly impact the quality of insights. Moreover, businesses that leverage dynamic data context can automate certain data wrangling processes, boosting efficiency and minimizing the need for manual data preparation.

The utilization of data wrangling tools like Pandas (for Python) and dplyr (for R) has transformed the way analysts handle data. These libraries offer robust functionalities for transforming, cleaning, and structuring data, allowing business analysts to enhance data quality effectively. Organizations engaged in computational journalism and similar fields have also acknowledged the value of interactive wrangling applications, which streamlines the transformation of multi-table datasets into actionable insights for visual presentation and analysis.

5.5.1.2.2 TECHNIQUES FOR EFFECTIVE DATA WRANGLING

Advanced automation techniques have emerged that utilize machine learning to further enhance data wrangling capabilities. For instance, tools that leverage neural-backed program synthesis can efficiently manage and manipulate large volumes of data, translating spreadsheet data into formats suitable for machine learning applications. Such advancements

Table 5.5 Categories of Tools for Data Wrangling

Category	*Purpose*	*Examples*
Programming libraries	Code-based manipulation of data structure, missing values, and formatting	Python: pandas, numpy R: dplyr, tidyr, data.table
Visual wrangling platforms	GUI-based interactive cleaning and transformation	OpenRefine, Trifacta (now part of Google Cloud Dataprep), Excel Power Query
Integrated notebook tools	Interactive scripting environments that support wrangling and exploration	Jupyter Notebook (Python), RStudio (R), Google Colab

demonstrate how integrating machine learning within the data wrangling process can significantly boost productivity for business analysts. Table 5.5 presents categories of tools for data wrangling, including purpose and examples.

5.5.2 Feature Engineering

Feature engineering, also known as creating analytical gold, refers to the process of transforming raw data into meaningful, informative variables that enhance the predictive power and interpretability of analytical and machine learning models. Feature engineering enables models to better capture underlying patterns, relationships, and signals embedded in complex datasets by incorporating domain knowledge, statistical transformations, and data-driven techniques.

5.5.2.1 Core Techniques and Tools

5.5.2.1.1 CORE TECHNIQUES IN FEATURE ENGINEERING

5.5.2.1.1.1 Feature Selection

As datasets grow larger and more complex, not all features contribute equally to model accuracy or interpretability. Feature selection involves identifying and retaining the most informative variables while eliminating redundant, irrelevant, or noisy ones. This step is crucial for reducing overfitting, improving computational efficiency, and enhancing model clarity, especially when dealing with high-dimensional data. Methods range from statistical approaches, such as correlation filtering and variance thresholds, to algorithmic techniques, including recursive feature elimination and embedded methods like LASSO regression.

5.5.2.1.1.2 Data Transformation

Data transformation reshapes variables to meet the mathematical and structural requirements of different analytical models. This includes scaling techniques like normalization and standardization, which adjust values for compatibility with distance-based algorithms or assumptions of linearity. Transformation also encompasses categorical data into numerical forms, such as one-hot, ordinal, or target encoding. For variables with skewed distributions, log, square root, and reciprocal transformations can reduce outliers' influence and improve model stability. In addition, binning continuous variables into categories can reveal underlying trends, particularly useful in segmentation or decision-tree-based models.

5.5.2.1.1.3 Feature Creation

Feature creation is the imaginative and strategic act of designing new variables that capture hidden patterns or meaningful relationships within the data. Rather than relying solely on raw attributes, analysts often craft composite features, such as customer lifetime value, average purchase frequency, or interaction terms like "age multiplied by income." Time-based features are also powerful, as extracting elements such as the day of the week, month, quarter, or proximity to holidays can significantly enhance models that involve consumer behavior or seasonality.

5.5.2.1.2 TOOLS FOR FEATURE ENGINEERING

5.5.2.1.2.1 Core Programming Libraries for Feature Engineering

In Python, the scikit-learn library is a fundamental toolkit that includes preprocessing utilities for encoding categorical variables, scaling numerical data, and selecting informative features. For more advanced automation, feature tools provide deep feature synthesis, enabling the creation of hierarchical or relational features across multiple data tables. The category encoders package further extends feature engineering capabilities by offering a range of encoding schemes, including ordinal, binary, and target encoding, which go beyond the basic one-hot approach. On the R side, caret and recipes form a powerful duo, allowing analysts to define step-by-step preprocessing plans that include imputation, normalization, dummy variable creation, and more.

5.5.2.1.2.2 Automated Feature Engineering Platforms

While manual feature engineering remains foundational, automated machine learning platforms are increasingly used to streamline and accelerate the process. Tools such as DataRobot, H2O.ai, Google AutoML, and Azure Machine Learning Studio incorporate automated feature generation, transformation, and selection as part of their end-to-end modeling pipelines. These platforms often analyze data types, infer variable importance, and construct engineered features. This is especially useful for non-technical users or in environments where rapid prototyping is critical.

5.5.2.1.2.3 Visualization as a Guide to Feature Engineering

Data visualization platforms play a pivotal role in the discovery and refinement of useful features. Tools like Tableau and Power BI allow analysts to quickly identify trends, seasonality, outliers, and nonlinear relationships through interactive charts and dashboards. In scripting environments, Python's Seaborn and Plotly, or R's ggplot2, enable detailed visual exploration that can inspire the creation of new variables. Visualization can also guide binning strategies, such as identifying natural groupings in income or age, or revealing the presence of skewness that may warrant a log transformation. Table 5.6 presents categories of tools for feature engineering, including their purposes and examples.

5.6 Portfolio Management and Predictive Financial Modeling

In the symphony of modern finance, where markets pulse with the rhythm of global sentiment and data flows like a ceaseless tide, portfolio management stands as both an art and a science. Once guided solely by instinct and experience, the architecture of investment portfolios has evolved into a domain increasingly governed by the precision of analytics

Table 5.6 Categories of Tools for Feature Engineering

Category	*Purpose*	*Examples*
Core programming libraries	Manual, customizable feature creation, transformation, and selection	Python: scikit-learn, featuretools, category_encoders R: caret, recipes, vtreat
Automated feature engineering	Automatically generate and select features within end-to-end ML workflows	DataRobot, H2O.ai, Google AutoML, Azure ML Studio
Visualization tools for insight	Support feature discovery through pattern recognition and data exploration	Tableau, Power BI, Seaborn (Python), ggplot2 (R), Plotly

and the foresight of algorithms. Predictive financial modeling, armed with statistical acumen and machine learning intelligence, now breathes life into the decision-making process, enabling investors to peer into probable futures, estimate returns, and calibrate risk with granular finesse. This fusion of classical financial theory and cutting-edge analytical tools signals not merely a methodological shift but a paradigmatic transformation. In this chapter, we examine how BA enables portfolio managers to shift from reactive strategies to anticipatory insights, thereby reshaping the construction, preservation, and growth of value in a world of uncertainty.

5.6.1 Fundamentals of Portfolio Management

Portfolio management focuses on the systematic construction and ongoing oversight of a collection of financial assets to achieve an investor's objectives of desired returns on investment while managing risk. Portfolio management is grounded in modern portfolio theory (MPT), which emphasizes diversification as a means of reducing unsystematic risk without proportionally sacrificing expected return.[8] The process typically involves defining investment objectives and constraints, asset allocation across major asset classes, security selection within those classes, and continuous monitoring and rebalancing to maintain the desired risk–return profile.

5.6.1.1 Key Concepts

5.6.1.1.1 RISK VERSUS RETURN

In the language of finance, risk and return are inseparable partners. Return represents the gain (or loss) an investor expects from an investment, typically measured by average returns or compound annual growth. Risk is the uncertainty surrounding that return—the possibility that the actual outcome deviates from expectations. It is often quantified through standard deviation, variance, or Value at Risk (VaR). High-return investments typically carry higher levels of uncertainty, forming what is known as the risk–return trade-off.

5.6.1.1.2 DIVERSIFICATION AND THE EFFICIENT FRONTIER

Diversification is the financial world's answer to the proverb "Don't put all your eggs in one basket." By spreading investments across a range of assets, stocks, bonds, commodities, sectors, or geographies, investors reduce the impact of any single asset's poor performance.

The statistical basis lies in correlation: if asset returns are imperfectly correlated, then negative movements in some can be offset by positive movements in others. The mathematical elegance of this idea is captured in the concept of the Efficient Frontier. It is a curve that shows the set of optimal portfolios, those offering the maximum expected return for a given level of risk, or the minimum risk for a given level of expected return.

5.6.1.1.3 CAPITAL ASSET PRICING MODEL (CAPM)

CAPM asserts that the expected return on security is proportional to its systematic risk, represented by beta (β). This model articulates that higher levels of systematic risk yield higher expected returns as compensation. It effectively outlines the Security Market Line (SML), which visually represents the expected returns of assets relative to their betas. Traditional interpretations of CAPM show an upward-sloping SML, indicating a positive correlation between risk and return. Under ideal conditions, securities conforming to SML are generally mean-variance efficient. The core formula is:

$$\text{Expected Return} = R_f + \beta \cdot \left(R_m - R_f\right)$$

where:

R_f = Risk-free rate
R_m = Expected return of the market
β = Sensitivity of the asset to market movements (beta)

5.6.1.1.4 MODERN PORTFOLIO THEORY (MPT)

MPT represents a paradigm shift in investment management by establishing a quantitative framework for portfolio construction. The theoretical foundational insight is that an investment's risk and return characteristics should be evaluated in the context of its contribution to an overall portfolio rather than in isolation. Through mean-variance optimization, MPT identifies efficient portfolios that maximize expected return for a given level of risk. The theory further introduces the concept of the tangency portfolio, which, when combined with a risk-free asset, defines the Capital Market Line (CML), representing the optimal risk–return trade-off available to investors.

5.6.1.2 Traditional versus Analytics-Driven Approaches

5.6.1.2.1 HEURISTIC METHODS VERSUS DATA-DRIVEN OPTIMIZATION

For much of financial history, investment decisions have been steered by heuristics. These methods, while intuitive and often elegantly simple, rest on assumptions about the world that may not always hold true. The 60/40 portfolio split between equities and bonds, the equal-weighted allocation across a basket of blue-chip stocks, or the age-based glide paths in retirement investing are all examples of heuristic strategies. Heuristics thrive in conditions where information is scarce or computation is costly. But today's financial markets are neither: they are information-rich, dynamic, and computationally intensive. Here is where data-driven optimization emerges—not as a rejection of intuition but as a refinement of it. These methods rely on historical data, probabilistic models, and mathematical optimization to allocate assets in a way that explicitly accounts for risk, return, and correlation structures. Through mean-variance optimization, investors can systematically construct portfolios on the efficient frontier. With Monte Carlo simulations, they can project thousands of possible futures. With machine learning algorithms, they can uncover subtle, nonlinear relationships that heuristics could never intuit. In this data-driven realm, decisions are no longer guided by instinct alone but by quantifiable trade-offs, simulations, and constraints. This transformation represents a move away from simplicity for its own sake toward a more precise, adaptive, and evidence-based approach to portfolio design.

5.6.1.2.2 TRANSITION FROM QUALITATIVE JUDGMENT TO QUANTITATIVE MODELING

In the traditional investment landscape, much of a portfolio manager's role resembled that of a storyteller—reading financial statements like novels, interpreting macroeconomic events as narrative arcs, and drawing conclusions through analogies, metaphors, and mental models. Investment committees would gather around forecasts, intuit trends, and build strategies informed by experience, intuition, and consensus. While such approaches brought the richness of human perception and contextual awareness, they were often opaque, subjective, and difficult to scale. The rise of quantitative modeling does not erase this artistry. Models such as CAPM, Fama-French multi-factor models, GARCH volatility models, and Bayesian estimators allow for the structuring of financial questions into testable hypotheses. The analyst becomes not merely a forecaster but a designer of experiments, evaluating performance under uncertainty, and stress-testing assumptions against empirical data. These models can process vast amounts of information and transform it into structured forecasts and optimization strategies.

5.6.2 Predictive Modeling in Finance

Beyond traditional methods, machine learning models offer flexibility and predictive power, especially when relationships between variables are complex and nonlinear. Random Forests and GBM ensemble decision trees to improve accuracy and reduce variance, while XGBoost, known for its speed and precision, has become a favorite in financial competitions and fintech applications. SVMs draw clear boundaries between asset classes, predicting credit risk, price movement direction, or volatility regimes with remarkable clarity in high-dimensional spaces. Models such as RNNs and their more sophisticated cousin, the LSTM networks, are designed specifically to handle sequential, temporal data.

Taken together, these techniques do not represent a hierarchy but rather a toolbox. Each is suited to different types of data, different market environments, and different investment questions. The skilled financial analyst is not just a technician but a strategist, choosing models not for their complexity but for their alignment with the problem at hand. In a domain where the future is unknowable, but patterns can be estimated, these predictive techniques form the scaffolding of insight. Table 5.7 summarizes a comparison of predictive modeling techniques in finance.

5.6.3 Portfolio Optimization Techniques

5.6.3.1 Mean–Variance Optimization (Markowitz Model)

At the foundation of MPT lies mean-variance optimization, a framework introduced that revolutionized the way investors approach asset allocation. The model assumes that rational

Table 5.7 Comparison of Predictive Modeling Techniques in Finance

Technique	*Strengths*	*Limitations*	*Typical Use Cases*
ARIMA	Interpretable, good for stationary series	Assumes linearity, sensitive to parameter tuning	Forecasting asset prices, interest rates
GARCH	Model volatility clustering; widely used in risk management	Complex estimation; assumes symmetric volatility	Volatility forecasting, Value-at-Risk (VaR), options pricing
Linear regression	Simple, interpretable; good for baseline modeling	Limited to linear relationships; sensitive to multicollinearity	Predicting returns from macro variables, factor analysis
Logistic regression	Probabilistic output; interpretable for binary classification	Assumes linear decision boundary	Credit risk prediction, bankruptcy forecasting
LASSO/ridge regression	Handles multicollinearity; useful for feature selection	Can underfit if penalty is too strong	High-dimensional predictive modeling (e.g., many macro or firm-level factors)
Random forest	Nonlinear modeling; robust to overfitting; handles missing values	Slower; less interpretable than linear models	Asset classification, credit scoring, sentiment analysis
Gradient boosting/ XGBoost	High accuracy; handles interactions well	Computationally expensive; prone to overfitting without tuning	Price movement prediction, portfolio ranking
Support vector machine (SVM)	Works well with high-dimensional data; robust decision boundaries	Requires careful kernel choice; hard to interpret	Binary classification (up/ down market), default prediction
RNN/LSTM	Captures time dependencies; ideal for sequential data	Requires large data; risk of vanishing gradients	Stock price prediction, financial sentiment from text, sequence forecasting

investors seek to maximize expected return for a given level of risk, or conversely, minimize risk for a given level of expected return. Assets are selected not in isolation, but in combination, considering their covariances with one another, rather than just individual variances. Despite its elegance, the Markowitz model is not without flaws: it is highly sensitive to the accuracy of inputs like expected returns and covariances, and it assumes that these parameters are stable over time. Still, its core insight endures risk that is not merely the sum of its parts but a function of how assets interact, a principle that continues to guide portfolio construction in both academic and professional practice.

5.6.3.2 Black-Litterman model

To address some of the practical limitations of mean-variance optimization, the Black-Litterman model offers a more robust and flexible framework. Developed by Fischer Black and Robert Litterman at Goldman Sachs, this model allows investors to combine market equilibrium returns with their own subjective views on asset performance. It begins with the implied returns from a market-capitalization-weighted portfolio, and then adjusts those returns based on the investor's confidence-weighted opinions. The result is a posterior distribution of expected returns that balances market wisdom with informed discretion, tempering often unstable results of traditional optimization. This model is particularly useful in institutional contexts where forward-looking views. The Black-Litterman model maintains diversification while preventing extreme portfolio weights, making it a favorite among quantitatively inclined portfolio managers seeking both structure and flexibility in their investment strategies.

5.6.3.3 Risk Parity Strategies

Risk parity represents a departure from traditional allocation methods that distribute capital. Rather than investing, for example, 60% in equities and 40% in bonds, a risk parity portfolio aims to equalize the volatility contribution of each asset class. The rationale is elegant: assets with lower volatility (like bonds) receive higher weights. In contrast, riskier assets (like equities or commodities) receive smaller allocations, such that each contributes equally to total portfolio risk. This strategy tends to produce more balanced performance across different market regimes and is particularly resilient during times of economic stress. However, risk parity strategies are sensitive to accurate estimation of volatilities and correlations and may underperform in equity bull markets where leverage is constrained. Popularized by firms such as Bridgewater Associates, risk parity is being increasingly adopted in institutional asset allocation and target-risk funds, offering a disciplined, volatility-aware approach to portfolio construction.

5.6.3.4 Monte Carlo Simulation for Portfolio Stress Testing

Financial markets are fraught with uncertainty, and few tools embrace this uncertainty as boldly as Monte Carlo simulation. This technique uses random sampling and probability distributions to simulate thousands or even millions of possible future portfolio outcomes. It is particularly valuable for stress testing, where portfolios are exposed to extreme market conditions, fat-tailed events, and unexpected correlations. Investors can analyze downside risks, calculate metrics like Value at Risk (VaR) or Conditional VaR, and test the resilience of strategies under historical or hypothetical scenarios, such as interest rate shocks, recessions, or pandemics. Monte Carlo methods allow decision-makers to move beyond static point estimates and embrace the stochastic nature of markets. Though computationally intensive and reliant on the quality of input distributions, this method fosters a more probabilistic mindset in investment management, reminding investors that the future is not a single path but a branching set of possibilities shaped by randomness.

5.6.3.5 Reinforcement Learning and Adaptive Strategies

In the era of AI, portfolio optimization has begun to shift toward more dynamic, self-improving algorithms, most notably through RL. Inspired by behavioral psychology and game theory, RL models treat portfolio management as a sequential decision-making problem, where an agent learns optimal strategies by interacting with a simulated market environment. These algorithms receive feedback through rewards (returns) and punishments (loses or volatility), adjusting their allocation policies over time. RL can adapt to changing regimes, detect evolving patterns, and even anticipate shifts in market behavior.

5.7 Data Visualization and Communication

Data visualization enables users to identify patterns, trends, and anomalies more efficiently than through numerical tables alone by leveraging graphical representations. Effective data communication extends beyond visual design to include narrative structure, contextual framing, and audience awareness, ensuring that analytical results are interpreted accurately and acted upon appropriately. In business and financial contexts, well-designed data visualization enhances transparency, reduces information overload, and bridges the gap between technical analysis and managerial judgment in improving the quality and impact of data-driven decisions. This section explores the principles, tools, and ethics of visual analytics, showing how design and narrative work hand in hand to turn analysis into action.

5.7.1 Principles of Effective Data Visualization

At its essence, effective data visualization is not merely a technical craft; it is a disciplined art of storytelling, where clarity, accuracy, and ethical integrity converge to reveal the truth embedded within data. Far from being a passive display, a powerful visualization distills complexity into lucid insight, allowing decision-makers to grasp nuance without distortion or distraction. This is the spirit of Edward Tufte's data-ink ratio: to maximize the ink that conveys actual information and to minimize what he famously called "chartjunk." A chart should be enlightening, not entertaining; it must be elegant, not decorative.

Clarity lies at the heart of this transformation. Visuals must be intelligible, accessible, and purposeful. Tools like heatmaps offer elegant simplicity by emphasizing critical metrics and drawing the eye toward salient variations. The deliberate use of color, guided by both aesthetic judgment and perceptual psychology, shapes how data is perceived: red may signal danger, green prosperity, but hues must also be chosen with sensitivity to accessibility, including color blindness. Visual hierarchy, purposefully guiding attention through layout, proportion, and labeling, allows insights to emerge naturally.[9]

Interactivity further deepens engagement. Interactive dashboards empower users to explore, filter, and drill down into the data, tailoring the analytical lens to their needs. This dynamic capability transforms static observation into analytical inquiry, fostering hypothesis testing, scenario modeling, and real-time decision support. When layered with predictive algorithms and trend analyses, visualization becomes not just a lens to view the past but a compass to navigate the future.[10]

5.7.2 Visualizing Financial and Business Data

5.7.2.1 Time Series Data: Returns, Prices, Trends, and Volatility

Whether tracking stock returns, commodity prices, interest rates, or volatility indices, financial analysts rely on time-based visualization to uncover patterns that tables alone cannot reveal. Line graphs, candlestick charts, and rolling averages allow viewers to detect momentum, reversals, and seasonal shifts. Volatility plots, especially when aligned with historical events, expose the emotional undercurrents of the market. These visual tools highlight the spikes that signal crisis and the periods of calm that suggest market complacency. The power of time series visualizations lies in their ability not only to show what happened but also how markets behave over time. For portfolio managers and financial decision-makers, these visuals transform numeric histories into unfolding narratives that inform both present understanding and future expectations.

5.7.2.2 Comparative Analysis: Portfolio Performance across Sectors, Geographies, and Risk Levels

Evaluating portfolio performance often requires comparing outcomes across various sectors, regions, and risk categories. Visualization provides a dynamic and intuitive way to observe these differences. Grouped bar charts, faceted line plots, and multi-axis radar graphs can show how technology portfolios thrive during growth phases while defensive sectors hold steady during downturns. These visual comparisons are not just descriptive but strategic. They help investors assess whether diversification efforts are working, where hidden concentrations might exist, and how different parts of the portfolio contribute to overall return and volatility. Stacked area charts can reveal how asset weights have shifted over time, while bubble plots illustrate the balance between performance and risk. Through comparative visualization, analysts can elevate static data into a meaningful performance dialogue that encourages deeper questioning and more informed decision-making.

5.7.2.3 Risk and Return Mapping: Scatter Plots and Efficient Frontier Visualizations

The scatter plot of risk and return is one of the most iconic visualizations in finance. Each plotted point represents a portfolio, fund, or asset class, placed according to its historical volatility and average return. In a single image, the trade-off between risk and reward becomes visually explicit. Some assets offer high returns but come with high volatility, while others cluster in lower-risk zones with modest gains. When an efficient frontier is added to this plot, a new layer of insight emerges. This curve shows the portfolios that achieve the highest return for a given level of risk, or the lowest risk for a given level of return. Assets or strategies that fall below the curve are considered suboptimal. This visual framework enables analysts to assess portfolio quality in relation to theoretical efficiency, providing a benchmark for evaluating investment performance within a broader context rather than in isolation.

5.7.2.4 Interactive Dashboards for Portfolio Analysis, Forecasting, and Decision Support

Static charts are often inadequate in fast-moving financial environments where conditions change rapidly, and questions evolve in real time. Interactive dashboards provide a flexible and user-driven interface for exploring portfolio performance, economic indicators, forecast scenarios, and risk assessments. Built with tools such as Tableau, Power BI, Shiny, or Dash, these dashboards allow users to filter, drill down, and dynamically adjust parameters to generate custom insights. A well-designed dashboard does more than display data; it creates a workspace for decision-making. Users can examine sector performance, adjust time frames, test rebalancing strategies, and explore model forecasts all within a single interface. This level of interactivity transforms analysis from a passive report into an active conversation, where insights are discovered through engagement rather than delivered as conclusions.

5.7.2.5 Visualizing Key Performance Indicators (KPIs) in Executive Reporting

Key performance indicators, such as return on assets, Sharpe ratio, drawdown percentages, and benchmark comparisons, must be presented in a way that is both concise and informative. Visual elements, such as bullet charts, scorecards, gauges, and small multiples, help present these metrics with precision and visual balance. Effective KPI dashboards do not

Table 5.8 Summary of Visualization Techniques for Financial and Business Data

Aspect	*Purpose*	*Common Visual Tools*	*Typical Applications*
Time series data	Track changes in values over time	Line graphs, candlestick charts, and moving averages	Stock price trends, return volatility, and interest rate paths
Comparative analysis	Compare performance across categories or time frames	Grouped bar charts, faceted plots, stacked area charts	Sector or geographic portfolio breakdown, asset class performance
Risk and return mapping	Visualize trade-offs between risk and expected return	Scatter plots, efficient frontier curves, bubble charts	Portfolio optimization, asset screening, and Sharpe ratio visualization
Interactive dashboards	Enable dynamic exploration and real-time decision support	Tableau, Power BI, Shiny, Dash	Multi-asset portfolio analysis, forecasting, scenario simulation
KPI visualization	Communicate high-level performance metrics with clarity	Scorecards, bullet charts, gauges, sparklines	Executive dashboards, fund manager reporting, and performance monitoring

overwhelm the viewer with excess detail. In financial reporting, well-crafted KPI visuals elevate conversations from numeric reporting to strategic assessment. They help ensure that decisions are anchored in evidence and that attention is directed where it matters most. Table 5.8 provides a summary of visualization techniques for financial and business data.

5.7.3 *Communication Ethics and Bias*

5.7.3.1 *Visual Bias and Framing Effects in Chart Design*

Visual bias arises when certain elements in a chart inadvertently lead to misinterpretation or skew audience understanding. For instance, the choice of color, scale, and design can create misleading impressions about the data's significance, as documented in research on visual framing in various contexts. In financial analytics, such biases may stem from the strategic use of visuals to emphasize trends or performance metrics while obscuring others, contributing to distorted perceptions of an organization's financial health.

Framing effects influence how data is perceived by audiences, thereby shaping interpretations and decision-making processes in significant ways. This importance is particularly evident in the financial sector, where the representation of data through visual tools can substantially impact resource allocation, investment decisions, and market perceptions.

5.7.3.2 *Avoiding Cherry-Picking, Color Manipulation, and False Comparisons*

Cherry-picking refers to the selective presentation of data to support a particular viewpoint while ignoring data that may contradict that viewpoint. This practice can skew an audience's understanding and lead to poorly informed decisions. Misleading visualizations, which focus on favorable data points while neglecting broader context, can significantly affect stakeholders' perceptions and actions in financial markets. Visualization tools must be designed to present comprehensive data sets, ensuring that users are informed of the complete picture rather than a one-sided narrative.[11]

Color manipulation in financial charts can introduce bias. Colors can evoke emotions and influence perceptions in ways that are not directly related to the data presented. For example, using red to denote losses and green for gains is common; however, manipulating saturation or using contrasting colors can create misleading implications about the severity of certain performance metrics.[12] Clear standards for color usage in financial visualizations can promote consistency and enhance interpretive clarity, thereby fostering more reliable decision-making. Furthermore, false comparisons can emerge from improperly designed charts that lack clear context, such as axes that are not scaled uniformly or statistics represented out of context.

5.7.3.3 Communicating Uncertainty with Confidence and Clarity

Effective communication of uncertainty is crucial for fostering trust among stakeholders, enabling investors, analysts, and decision-makers to comprehend the potential risks and implications inherent in financial data. One of the primary challenges in communicating uncertainty is the tendency to present information that oversimplifies or misrepresents risk. It is crucial to include confidence intervals, error bars, or ranges in visualizations, which can provide a clearer picture of the variability and reliability of the data presented. Providing such context can help stakeholders grasp not only the central estimates but also the uncertainties surrounding these estimates, thereby enabling a more informed understanding of potential outcomes.

Additionally, the choice of language and the clarity of visual elements play significant roles in conveying uncertainty effectively. Precise terminology is vital in financial contexts, where ambiguous language can lead to misinterpretation. Similarly, visual representations must be designed to convey uncertainty clearly.

5.8 Summary

This chapter provides a comprehensive overview of the foundational programming languages, tools, and techniques that drive modern AI, data analytics, and BA. It highlights how these technological components interact to support data-driven decision-making and innovation across industries including an in-depth discussion of the primary programming languages used in AI and data analytics of (1) Python as the dominant language in AI and data science due to its simplicity, extensive libraries (e.g., TensorFlow, scikit-learn, Pandas, NumPy), and active community support; (2) R as a popular tool in statistical analysis and visualization, especially among academics and researchers; (3) SQL as an essential tool for querying, managing, and manipulating structured data in relational databases; (4) Java and C++, which are often used in production-level AI systems and performance-intensive applications; (5) Julia and Scala as emerging languages gaining traction for high-performance analytics and big data processing. This chapter also presents data analytics and visualization tools for data manipulation, analysis, and visualization including (1) Excel and Power BI, which are common in business environments for dashboarding, reporting, and quick insights; (2) Tableau, a leader in interactive data visualization for exploring trends and patterns; (3) Apache Spark as a powerful engine for big data processing and real-time analytics; and (4) Jupyter Notebooks as a popular environment for EDA and model development.

BA tools and techniques of descriptive analytics, prescriptive analytics, simulation and scenario analysis, and diagnostic analytics, which are widely used techniques in BA, emphasizing their applications and strategic value, are presented in this chapter. These tools and languages integrate into broader ecosystems such as Cloud Platforms (AWS, Azure, Google Cloud): Offering scalable AI and analytics services, Data Warehouses and Lakes (Snowflake, BigQuery, Databricks): Supporting large-scale data storage and querying, Enterprise Systems (ERP, CRM): Providing the data foundation for BA solutions.

Notes

1 Lee, C. S., Cheang, P. Y. S., & Moslehpour, M. (2022). Predictive analytics in business analytics: Decision tree. *Advances in Decision Sciences*, 26(1), 1–29. Available at https://www.proquest.com/docview/2674049708?pq-origsite=gscholar&fromopenview=true&sourcetype=Scholarly%20Journals
2 Ajax, R., Joseph, O., & Own, J. (2025). Enhancing Business Intelligence with Data Visualization Tools. Available at Enhancing-Business-Intelligence-with-Data-Visualization-Tools.pdf
3 Chu, M. K., & Yong, K. O. (2021). Big data analytics for business intelligence in accounting and audit. *Open Journal of Social Sciences*, 9(9), 42–52. Available at BigDataAnalyticsforBusinessIntelligenceinAccountingandAudit
4 Mehari, T., Sundar, A., Bosnjakovic, A., Harris, P., Williams, S. E., Loewe, A., … & Aston, P. J. (2024). ECG feature importance rankings: Cardiologists vs. algorithms. *IEEE Journal of Biomedical and Health Informatics*, 28(4), 2014–2024. https://doi.org/10.1109/JBHI.2024.3354301. Available at https://ieeexplore.ieee.org/abstract/document/10400809
5 Lall, R., & Robinson, T. (2023). Efficient multiple imputation for diverse data in Python and R: Midaspy and Rmidas. *Journal of Statistical Software*, 107, 1–38. https://doi.org/10.18637/jss.v107.i09. Available at https://www.jstatsoft.org/article/view/v107i09
6 Jia, H., Bian, Y., Yuan, J., Zhang, Y., & Zhang, S. (2025). The potential role of C4 MYH11+ fibroblasts and the MDK-SDC2 ligand-receptor pair in lung adenocarcinoma: Implications for prognosis and therapeutic strategies. *Translational Oncology*, 55, 102364. https://doi.org/10.1016/j.tranon.2025.102364. Available at https://www.sciencedirect.com/science/article/pii/S1936523325000956
7 Odell, D., Brune, C. R., Phillips, D. R., deBoer, R. J., & Paneru, S. N. (2022). Performing Bayesian analyses with AZURE2 using BRICK: An application to the 7Be system. *Frontiers in Physics*, 10, 888476. https://doi.org/10.3389/fphy.2022.888476. Available at https://www.frontiersin.org/journals/physics/articles/10.3389/fphy.2022.888476/full
8 Sharpe, W. F. (1964). Capital asset prices: A theory of market equilibrium under conditions of risk. *The Journal of Finance*, 19(3), 425–442. https://doi.org/10.1111/j.1540-6261.1964.tb02865.x. Available at https://onlinelibrary.wiley.com/doi/full/10.1111/j.1540-6261.1964.tb02865.x
9 Tiwari, V. (2024). Role of data analytics in business decision making. *Knowledgeable Research: A Multidisciplinary Peer-Reviewed Refereed Journal*, 3(01), 18–27. Available at https://knowledgeableresearch.com/index.php/1/article/view/282
10 Ochuba, N. A., Amoo, O. O., Okafor, E. S., Akinrinola, O., & Usman, F. O. (2024). Strategies for leveraging big data and analytics for business development: A comprehensive review across sectors. *Computer Science & IT Research Journal*, 5(3), 562–575. https://doi.org/10.51594/csitrj.v5i3.861. Available at https://www.researchgate.net/profile/Olukunle-Amoo/publication/378825033_STRATEGIES_FOR_LEVERAGING_BIG_DATA_AND_ANALYTICS_FOR_BUSINESS_DEVELOPMENT_A_COMPREHENSIVE_REVIEW_ACROSS_SECTORS/links/65eb52709ab2af0ef897ffd0/STRATEGIES-FOR-LEVERAGING-BIG-DATA-AND-ANALYTICS-FOR-BUSINESS-DEVELOPMENT-A-COMPREHENSIVE-REVIEW-ACROSS-SECTORS.pdf
11 Ko, S., Cho, I., Afzal, S., Yau, C., Chae, J., Malik, A., … & Ebert, D. S. (2016). A survey on visual analysis approaches for financial data. *Computer Graphics Forum*, 35(3), 599–617. https://doi.org/10.1111/cgf.12931. Available at https://onlinelibrary.wiley.com/doi/abs/10.1111/cgf.12931?casa_token=nOpHiDUPwfoAAAAA:S-PgfcoBAvQ4QZhnH7D-_u2av16muXg54lhu_3heEJh5HkVlaZgkj2nH98XjN7yxrv9DFY0QbRQchnQx
12 Sarlin, P., & Eklund, T. (2013). Financial performance analysis of European banks using a fuzzified self-organizing map. *International Journal of Knowledge-Based and Intelligent Engineering Systems*, 17(3), 223–234. https://doi.org/10.3233/KES-130261. Available at https://journals.sagepub.com/doi/abs/10.3233/KES-130261?casa_token=eC3arJRGQb4AAAAA:UufRAwubPdT7gic8BsbqJsymRlcdjceUJVGt9wIPQ2wrMBdZDak4csbxnDpN9Bp0eHpxd2XaDYYrOg

6 AI-Driven Business Strategies

Learning Objectives

- Learn the role of AI in decision-making
- Learn the use of AI in operations and supply chain optimization
- Understand AI deployment risks and challenges
- Learn data privacy, model bias, and security risks
- Recognize the impact of ML on business decisions
- AI in risk assessment, management, and auditing
- AI-enabled innovation and competitive advantage
- Learn effective AI strategies that require collaboration across departments, aligning IT, data science, marketing, finance, and HR
- Understand the role of AI in decision-making through predictive analytics, pattern recognition, and real-time insights, improving accuracy and speed

6.1 Introduction

Technological advances and the ever-growing digital landscape in recent years have promoted AI as a transformative force in reshaping industries and redefining the way businesses operate and establish their business strategies. This chapter presents AI-driven business strategies from automating routine tasks to establishing business strategic plans and enabling data-driven decision-making. AI has become an integral component of corporate culture and business environment, enabling organizations to harness the power of AI to gain a competitive edge and explore new opportunities for innovation, efficiency, and growth. AI-driven business strategies address how organizations can leverage AI-powered technologies to create value, optimize operations, and stay ahead in an increasingly competitive global market. This chapter presents the practical applications of AI across various business functions, including strategic planning, finance, marketing, supply chain management, and customer service, by examining the opportunities, ethical considerations, challenges, and risks associated with AI adoption and providing a balanced perspective for leaders and decision-makers. By understanding the potential of AI and its implications, students can learn about the development of intelligent automation, data-driven innovation, and strategic planning.

DOI: 10.4324/9781003664550-6

6.2 The Role of AI in Decision-Making

Decision-making is a fundamental aspect of strategic planning to achieve organizational and individual success. Traditionally, decision-making relies on human intuition, skills, experience, and data analysis. However, with the advent of AI, decision-making has transformed into a more data-driven, digital, automated, and predictive process. AI-powered tools and techniques play an essential role in decision-making in organizations of all types and sizes. The integration of AI in decision-making processes has revolutionized many industries, from education and finance to healthcare and government. AI-driven decision-making is expected to improve efficiency, reduce human errors and biases, and process vast amounts of data in real-time. Nonetheless, challenges such as ethical considerations, transparency, and accountability should be addressed when using AI in decision-making. This section examines the role of AI in decision-making, its benefits, challenges, potential risks, limitations, and the future trajectory of AI-enhanced decision systems. However, business organizations may face some challenges in leveraging AI in the decision-making process, including understanding the determinants of human and AI complementarity, (2) understanding human mental models of AI, and (3) developing effective methods of interaction with AI.[1]

The role of AI in decision-making involves the use of algorithms, ML, and deep learning models to collect and analyze complex datasets and generate insights that inform decisions. AI systems in decision-making are classified into (1) rule-based AI, which utilizes systems that follow predefined rules and logic; (2) ML-based AI, which employs systems that learn from data and improve over time; and (3) deep learning-based AI, which uses systems that mimic human neural networks to process unstructured data for decision-making. These AI-driven systems individually and collectively provide many benefits by enhancing decision-making in many ways, including (1) enabling speed and efficiency in making real-time decisions by processing vast datasets at high speeds; (2) presenting data-driven insights by extracting patterns and trends that may be overlooked by human analysts; (3) reducing human bias and errors by minimizing cognitive biases and human errors that may influence decision-making; (4) enabling predictive capabilities of forecasting trends and outcomes that allow proactive decision-making; and (5) achieving automation and cost reduction by reducing reliance on manual processes, optimizing resources and costs.

6.3 Data Preprocessing and Feature Engineering in Business Applications

In today's data-driven business environment, organizations generate vast amounts of data from sources such as customer transactions, digital platforms, sensors, and operational systems. However, raw data is rarely suitable for direct analysis or ML. Transforming this data into a form that supports reliable analytics requires two closely related processes: data preprocessing and feature engineering. Data preprocessing and feature engineering are foundational stages in BA and AI applications, as the quality of input data largely determines the reliability, interpretability, and predictive power of analytical models. Data preprocessing involves cleaning, transforming, and structuring raw data by addressing missing values, outliers, noise, and inconsistencies, as well as standardizing and normalizing variables to ensure comparability across diverse data sources common in business environments, including financial disclosures, earnings and market data, transactional logs, and customer data. Feature engineering builds on this process by creating informative variables that capture underlying business phenomena, such as profitability trends, customer behavior patterns, risk indicators, or sustainability signals, often through aggregation, interaction terms, text vectorization, and domain-driven transformations. Thus, well-designed features can significantly outperform algorithmic sophistication alone, improving model accuracy, robustness, and managerial relevance.

6.3.1 The Foundation of Data Quality

The foundation of data quality entails the systematic assurance that data is fit for its intended use in decision-making, BA, and AI applications. High-quality data is commonly defined by core attributes such as accuracy, completeness, consistency, timeliness, validity, and relevance, all of which jointly determine whether data can reliably support organizational objectives.[2] Establishing strong data quality foundations requires robust data governance frameworks, standardized data definitions, well-designed data collection processes, and continuous monitoring mechanisms that detect and correct errors throughout the data lifecycle. In modern BA and AI environments, data quality has become even more critical due to the growing reliance on large, heterogeneous, and often unstructured datasets used in ML and AI systems, where poor data quality can propagate bias, reduce model performance, and undermine trust in automated decisions. Consequently, organizations increasingly view data quality as both a technical afterthought and a strategic asset that underpins effective analytics, regulatory compliance, and sustainable value creation.

Data preprocessing serves as the foundation of all successful BA. Business data is often incomplete, inconsistent, and affected by errors arising from decentralized collection systems, evolving operational processes, and human input. If these issues are not addressed systematically, analytical results may be misleading or unreliable. Common data quality challenges include inconsistent data formats, missing values, outliers, and integration problems across multiple systems.[3] For example, customer information may be recorded differently across platforms, or historical datasets may reflect changes in data standards over time. Missing data can arise from system failures, privacy constraints, or user behavior, while outliers may reflect either genuine extreme events or data errors. Addressing these issues requires careful preprocessing informed by both statistical methods and domain knowledge.

6.3.2 Core Preprocessing Techniques for Business Data

Core preprocessing techniques for business data consist of a set of systematic BA-assisted and AI-driven methods used to transform raw, heterogeneous datasets into reliable, analysis-ready inputs for statistical modeling, BA, and AI applications. These techniques typically include data cleaning (e.g., handling missing values, outlier detection, and noise reduction), data integration from multiple internal and external sources, data transformation through normalization, standardization, and encoding, and data reduction methods such as feature selection and dimensionality reduction. In business contexts, effective preprocessing is essential for ensuring data consistency across operational systems, enhancing comparability across time and entities, and mitigating biases that may distort predictive or prescriptive insights.[4] Ultimately, preprocessing decisions often have a greater impact on model performance than the choice of algorithms themselves, particularly in large-scale analytics and ML environments where data quality issues can propagate rapidly. Thus, preprocessing is widely recognized as a foundational step in data-driven decision-making, directly influencing the reliability, interpretability, and governance of BA outcomes.

Effective preprocessing applies targeted techniques to address data quality challenges identified earlier. Data cleaning involves correcting errors, resolving inconsistencies, and standardizing representations. Missing data handling must be tailored to the business context, using deletion, imputation, or indicator variables depending on the nature and impact of the missingness.

Data transformation prepares variables for analysis by scaling numerical values, encoding categorical data, or restructuring inputs to highlight meaningful patterns. Outlier detection requires distinguishing between legitimate extreme observations and erroneous values, a decision that often depends on business context rather than statistical thresholds alone. When datasets originate from multiple systems, data integration techniques align schemas, reconcile conflicts, and create unified analytical views. For time-dependent data, preprocessing must also account for irregular intervals, seasonality, and structural changes to ensure comparability over time.

6.3.3 Feature Engineering for Creating Analytical Value

Feature engineering for creating analytical value refers to the process of transforming raw data into informative, task-relevant variables that enhance the predictive power, interpretability, and robustness of AI-powered and BA-driven models. Feature engineering is intended to enable models to capture underlying patterns that are otherwise inaccessible in raw datasets by leveraging domain knowledge, statistical transformations, and algorithmic techniques such as interaction terms, aggregation, scaling, encoding of categorical variables, and feature extraction from unstructured data.[5] In BA, effective feature engineering is often a primary driver of model performance, frequently outweighing the marginal gains achieved through more complex algorithms. Ultimately, well-designed features improve generalization, reduce overfitting, and enhance model interpretability, which is particularly critical for managerial decision-making, regulatory compliance, and explainable AI applications.

Consequently, feature engineering represents a strategic analytical capability that links data, business context, and modeling objectives to generate actionable insights and sustainable competitive advantage. Feature engineering extends preprocessing by transforming cleaned data into variables that better represent the drivers of business outcomes. This process requires a clear understanding of the analytical objective and the underlying business processes. Many of the most predictive features, such as behavioral trends, ratios, or interaction effects, are not present in raw data and must be derived.

Temporal features play a central role in BA, capturing trends, volatility, and seasonality that static snapshots cannot reflect. Interaction features reveal relationships between variables, while aggregation features summarize granular transactions into stable, interpretable patterns. In domains that rely on unstructured data, text-based feature engineering enables sentiment analysis, topic extraction, and semantic interpretation. Across all cases, effective feature engineering depends on close collaboration between domain experts and analytical specialists to ensure that engineered features reflect meaningful business relationships rather than spurious correlations.

6.3.4 Advanced Feature Engineering Strategies

Advanced feature engineering strategies play a fundamental role in enhancing the predictive power, interpretability, and robustness of AI, BA, and ML models by transforming raw data into meaningful representations aligned with underlying economic, behavioral, or operational processes. These strategies extend beyond basic transformations to include interaction terms, polynomial and nonlinear feature construction, domain-driven aggregation, temporal and lagged features, embedding techniques, and automated representation learning. In structured data, techniques such as target encoding, feature crosses, and entity embedding help capture complex relationships while reducing dimensionality and sparsity. Advanced feature engineering techniques aim to capture complex, nonlinear relationships and contextual dependencies within business data. Polynomial and interaction features model nonlinear effects, while lagged and cyclical variables account for delayed or seasonal impacts. Cross-entity features incorporate information about related customers, products, or regions, adding contextual depth to analytical models. Behavioral pattern features track changes over time, often providing stronger predictive signals than static attributes.

For time series and panel data, rolling statistics, seasonality indicators, and event-based features improve forecasting accuracy by embedding temporal dynamics. In unstructured data contexts, advanced feature engineering leverages natural language processing (NLP) methods such as TF–IDF weighting, word and sentence embeddings (e.g., Word2Vec, BERT), and topic modeling to extract semantic and contextual information from text.[6] External data integration further enhances analytical insight by incorporating economic indicators, weather data, or competitive signals. As feature sets grow, feature selection and dimensionality reduction become essential to prevent overfitting and maintain interpretability. Recent advances in automated feature engineering and representation learning, including deep learning and AutoML frameworks, further reduce human bias and improve scalability by systematically discovering high-value features.[7] Ultimately, these advanced strategies bridge domain expertise and algorithmic learning, enabling more accurate, stable, and explainable models in complex business and financial applications.

6.3.5 Business Applications and Industry Examples for Feature Engineering

The application of preprocessing and feature engineering varies across industries but consistently underpins analytical success. Feature engineering is a vital enabler of value creation across business functions and industries, as domain-specific feature design allows AI and BA models to capture economically meaningful patterns embedded in complex data environments. In financial services, these processes support credit risk modeling, fraud detection, and regulatory compliance. Retail and e-commerce rely on engineered behavioral and product features for pricing, recommendation systems, and inventory optimization. In finance and accounting, engineered features such as financial ratios, accruals, cash-flow volatility, text-based risk indicators, and lagged performance measures significantly improve credit scoring, fraud detection, earnings prediction, and audit risk assessment.

In marketing and customer analytics, behavioral features derived from clickstream data, customer lifetime value, recency-frequency-monetary (RFM) metrics, and sentiment scores extracted from social media enhance demand forecasting, churn prediction, and personalized recommendation systems.[8] In operations and supply chain management, feature engineering incorporates lead-time variability, capacity utilization, seasonal indicators, and sensor-based features from Internet of Things (IoT) data to optimize inventory control, predictive maintenance, and logistics performance.[9] Across industries, the integration of domain knowledge with automated feature extraction techniques such as NLP-based textual features and machine-learned embeddings enables more accurate, interpretable, and actionable analytics, reinforcing the strategic role of feature engineering in business decision-making.

6.3.6 Tools and Technologies for Implementation

The effective implementation of data preprocessing and feature engineering relies on a strong and robust ecosystem of analytical tools and technologies that support data cleaning, transformation, integration, and scalable feature construction across structured and unstructured data environments. A wide range of tools supports preprocessing and feature engineering in business environments. Programming languages such as Python and R provide foundational libraries for preprocessing and feature engineering, including pandas, NumPy, scikit-learn, and caret, which enable tasks such as missing value imputation, normalization, encoding, and feature selection within reproducible analytical pipelines.[10]

For large-scale or real-time data, distributed systems and cloud platforms enable scalable processing and integration. Automated feature engineering and AutoML tools help accelerate development but remain most effective when guided by domain knowledge. Data quality, governance, and workflow automation tools ensure reliability, transparency, and operational integration. Frameworks such as Apache Spark and Hadoop facilitate parallelized feature generation and transformation using tools like Spark MLlib and Spark SQL, which are suitable for high-volume business and IoT datasets.[11] Automated feature engineering and model development are increasingly supported by AutoML platforms, including H2O.ai, Auto-sklearn, and Google AutoML, which systematically generate, evaluate, and select high-value features while reducing manual effort and human bias.[12] In text- and image-based applications, natural language processing and deep learning frameworks such as spaCy, Hugging Face Transformers, TensorFlow, and PyTorch enable embedding-based feature extraction and representation learning from unstructured data. Together, these tools and technologies form an integrated implementation stack that enhances scalability, consistency, and interpretability in preprocessing and feature engineering, supporting robust AI-driven and BA-assisted decision-making in modern business applications.

6.4 Supervised and Unsupervised Learning for Business Applications

Supervised learning involves learning from examples, where both input data and desired outputs are known. This approach mirrors human learning from experience, using historical data to predict future outcomes. Supervised learning relies on labeled data to model relationships between inputs and known outcomes, making it well-suited for prediction and classification tasks such as credit risk assessment, fraud detection, demand forecasting, customer churn prediction, and financial distress modeling. Unsupervised learning uncovers hidden patterns within data without predefined outcomes. It is especially useful for understanding data structures, segmenting customers, or detecting anomalies like fraud or operational issues. Like supervised learning, unsupervised methods explore data to uncover insights that might not be obvious to human analysts.

6.4.1 Business Applications and Use Cases

The practical use of supervised and unsupervised learning techniques across various business sectors shows the transformative potential of ML in solving complex organizational problems. These applications cover multiple industries and areas, from CRM to operational efficiency, each requiring customized approaches aligned with specific business goals and constraints. Customer churn prediction is one of the most successful and widely used applications of supervised learning in business. Organizations in telecommunications, subscription services, financial services, online gaming, and software industries use these techniques to identify customers at risk of leaving. The impact of effective churn prediction goes beyond just customer retention, including revenue preservation, cost reduction, and strategic resource allocation. Customer churn prediction using ML methods shows that organizations implementing ML-based churn prediction systems saw significant improvements in customer retention and profitability. These systems help businesses predict customer churn more accurately by analyzing behavioral, demographic, and social interaction data. As a result, companies can customize their retention strategies more effectively, leading to higher customer loyalty and major financial gains, such as increased net present value and lower marketing costs. The study highlighted the importance of feature engineering in building effective churn prediction models, especially the value of behavioral indicators like usage patterns, service interactions, and engagement metrics.[13]

Unsupervised learning is used for managing complexity in business operations. It does this mainly by learning compressed representations of production process data to measure and analyze the inherent complexity without needing labeled data.[14] Fraud detection is another essential application area where both supervised and unsupervised learning techniques offer significant business benefits. Financial institutions, e-commerce platforms, insurance providers, and payment processors depend on ML systems to spot suspicious activities and stop fraudulent transactions. The ever-changing nature of fraud patterns demands adaptive learning systems that can evolve with shifting threat landscapes. Various ML algorithms have been used to classify companies as fraudulent or legitimate. These include Logistic Regression (LR), Random Forest (RF), Gradient Boosting Decision Tree (GBDT), Extreme Gradient Boosting (XGBOOST), Support Vector Machine (SVM), and Decision Trees (DT). Among these, ensemble methods that combine models, such as voting classifiers using LR and XGBOOST, demonstrated superior performance, achieving accuracy rates higher than 99% and strong predictive capability for detecting financial fraud.[15]

6.4.2 Real-World Implementation Strategies

Pilot project approaches allow organizations to test ML ideas and develop internal skills while reducing initial risks. Small-scale efforts let teams try different algorithms, data sources, and integration methods without needing full-scale enterprise deployment. Successful pilots serve as proof-of-concept and help build momentum for wider organizational adoption. Choosing the right pilot projects greatly affects the chances of success, with ideal options having clear business problems, accessible data, measurable success criteria, and supportive stakeholders. Common pilot projects include customer churn prediction, demand forecasting, and fraud detection because they offer clear business value and are relatively easy to implement.

Data strategy development includes the policies, procedures, and infrastructure needed to support ML efforts across the organization. This strategy should cover data collection, storage, quality management, privacy protection, and accessibility requirements, while ensuring compliance with relevant regulations and industry standards. Organizations must establish data governance frameworks that balance accessibility with security and privacy concerns. Investments in data infrastructure often constitute significant parts of ML project budgets, requiring careful assessment of storage technologies, processing capabilities, and integration needs. Cloud-based solutions provide scalability and flexibility benefits while lowering infrastructure management efforts, though organizations should carefully consider costs and security issues. Hybrid approaches combining on-premises and cloud resources may offer optimal solutions for organizations with specific security or performance needs.

Team composition and skill development are vital for successful ML implementation, requiring a mix of technical expertise, domain knowledge, and project management skills. Data scientists bring algorithmic expertise and analytical abilities, while domain experts offer business context and validation insights. Software engineers ensure reliable implementation and integration with existing systems, and project managers coordinate activities and keep stakeholders aligned. Since qualified ML professionals are scarce, organizations need to develop comprehensive talent strategies, including recruitment, training, consulting partnerships, or technological solutions that lower skill requirements. Internal training programs can also help current employees build ML skills, enhance organizational knowledge, and reduce reliance on external resources.

Agile development methodologies are especially effective for ML projects because of their iterative nature and focus on stakeholder feedback. Agile methods support rapid prototyping, frequent stakeholder reviews, and adaptive planning that handle evolving requirements and discoveries. User training and change management become essential when integrating ML solutions into business processes and decision workflows. End users need to learn how to interpret and act on ML insights while understanding the limitations and suitable use cases for automated recommendations. Training programs should cover both technical system operation and conceptual knowledge of ML capabilities. Quality assurance and validation processes ensure that ML models perform reliably in production and continue meeting business needs over time.

Model monitoring systems track performance, detect data drift, and trigger alerts for updates. They monitor technical metrics like accuracy and business metrics like conversion rates and customer satisfaction. Automated monitoring minimizes performance decline and supports proactive maintenance.

Risk management tackles challenges and uncertainties such as technical, organizational, and business risks. Contingency plans cover model performance drops, data issues, regulations, or resource limits, with strategies like backup algorithms, manual overrides, or phased rollouts. Regulatory compliance must be integrated early, affecting algorithm choice, documentation, audit trails, and validation. Legal teams should be involved from the start to ensure compliance. Performance measurement and continuous improvement help optimize ML over time, aligning KPIs with business goals. Regular reviews identify areas for enhancement, ensuring ongoing benefits. Collectively, success in ML implementation requires patience, persistence, and commitment to continuous learning and improvement. Organizations that approach ML as a long-term capability development initiative rather than a short-term technology deployment are more likely to achieve sustainable success and competitive advantage through data-driven decision-making capabilities.

6.5 AI-Powered Business Applications: Transforming Modern Enterprise Operations

AI has progressed from a theoretical idea to a practical necessity for businesses, fundamentally changing how organizations operate, compete, and deliver value to customers. At its core, AI is a collection of technologies that enable machines to perform tasks usually requiring human intelligence, such as learning from data, recognizing patterns, making decisions, and solving complex problems. In the business world, AI-powered applications use these capabilities to automate processes, improve decision-making, and open new opportunities for innovation and growth.

6.5.1 AI-Powered Customer Relationship Management

CRM systems enhanced with AI capabilities represent one of the most impactful applications of AI in business operations. These systems transform how organizations understand, engage with, and serve their customers by leveraging advanced analytics, ML, and automation technologies to create more personalized and effective customer experiences. Traditional CRM systems primarily served as repositories for customer data, tracking interactions, purchases, and basic demographic information. AI-powered CRM systems extend these capabilities significantly by analyzing customer behavior patterns, predicting future actions, and recommending optimal engagement strategies. These intelligent systems can identify which customers are most likely to make purchases, who might be considering switching to competitors, and who would be most receptive to specific marketing messages or product offerings. Predictive customer analytics forms the cornerstone of AI-enhanced CRM systems. By analyzing historical customer data, purchase patterns, interaction histories, and external factors such as market trends or seasonal influences, AI algorithms can forecast customer lifetime value, predict churn probability, and identify upselling and cross-selling opportunities. For example, an AI system might analyze a customer's purchase history, website browsing behavior, and response to previous marketing campaigns to predict their likelihood of purchasing a specific product within the next month.

Personalization at scale represents another significant advantage of AI-powered CRM systems. While human sales representatives might personalize their approach for a limited number of high-value customers, AI systems can create individualized experiences for thousands or millions of customers simultaneously. This personalization extends beyond simple demographic segmentation to include behavioral preferences, communication channel preferences, optimal timing for outreach, and personalized product recommendations. AI-powered CRM systems enable organizations to shift from reactive to proactive customer engagement. These systems can identify customers who might be facing issues before they contact support, automatically generate solutions for common problems, and direct complex issues to the most suitable human agents. This proactive approach not only boosts customer satisfaction but also reduces support expenses and improves operational efficiency. Automated lead scoring and qualification are practical ways AI is used in sales. Traditional methods use simple rules to assign points based on criteria like company size, industry, or job title. AI-powered systems analyze hundreds of variables at once, including online behavior, social media activity, email engagement, and company news, to give more accurate estimates of lead quality and chances of conversion. Using ML, automated lead scoring helps predict how likely a potential customer (lead) is to buy. Unlike manual methods that are often subjective, slow, and lack statistical basis, automated scoring leverages past behavioral data (such as browsing habits and email interactions) to train models that assign a purchase probability score to each lead.[16]

Customer segmentation through AI technologies allows for more advanced and flexible approaches to market targeting. Instead of depending on fixed demographic groups, AI systems can identify behavioral segments that evolve over time based on customer actions, preferences, and life circumstances. These dynamic segments enable more precise marketing campaigns, personalized product development, and tailored service offerings. Chatbots and virtual assistants powered by natural language processing and ML provide 24/7 customer support while continuously learning from interactions to enhance their responses. These AI-driven customer service tools can handle routine inquiries, guide customers through self-service options, and gather information for human agents when more complex assistance is needed. Advanced chatbots can even detect customer emotions and modify their responses accordingly, offering more empathetic and effective support. Sentiment analysis features allow AI-powered CRM systems to monitor customer feedback across multiple channels, including social media, review sites, email communications, and survey responses. By examining the emotional tone and content of customer interactions, these systems can identify satisfaction patterns, potential issues, and opportunities for improvement. This comprehensive sentiment monitoring provides organizations with real-time insights into customer perceptions and allows for quick responses to emerging concerns.

6.5.2 Applied AI for Business Operations

The application of AI to business operations encompasses a broad spectrum of activities designed to improve efficiency, reduce costs, enhance quality, and enable more informed decision-making across organizational functions. Applied AI transforms routine operational processes through intelligent automation while providing analytical capabilities that support strategic planning and continuous improvement initiatives.

Process automation through AI technologies extends far beyond simple rule-based automation to include intelligent systems that can adapt to changing conditions, learn from experience, and handle exceptions that would typically require human intervention. These systems can manage complex workflows, coordinate activities across multiple departments, and optimize resource allocation in real-time. For instance, AI-powered scheduling systems can automatically adjust production schedules based on demand fluctuations, equipment availability, and resource constraints while considering multiple optimization criteria simultaneously. Quality control and assurance represent critical areas where AI applications demonstrate significant value. Computer vision systems can inspect products with greater accuracy and consistency than human inspectors, identifying defects, inconsistencies, or deviations from specifications that might be missed by traditional quality control methods. These systems can operate continuously without fatigue, maintain consistent standards across shifts and locations, and provide detailed documentation of quality metrics for compliance and improvement purposes. AI applications in business operations enable organizations to achieve higher levels of operational excellence through data-driven insights and automated decision-making. AI systems can identify inefficiencies in operational processes, recommend improvements, and automatically implement optimizations that result in measurable performance gains. AI-powered Human–Robot Collaboration (HRC) is transforming customer service by combining mechanical, analytical, intuitive, and empathetic intelligence. These types of intelligence in HRC lead to multiple benefits: operational costs are reduced due to increased efficiency; productivity rises as robots handle routine tasks while humans focus on complex issues; decision-making is improved with AI-driven insights; and ultimately, the customer experience is enhanced through more timely, personalized, and emotionally sensitive service.[17]

Financial operations benefit greatly from AI applications that automate accounting tasks, spot anomalies in financial data, and offer predictive insights for budgeting and financial planning. AI-powered expense management systems can automatically categorize expenses, detect policy violations, and flag unusual spending patterns for review. Likewise, AI in accounts receivable can forecast payment delays, suggest collection strategies, and automatically send payment reminders based on customer payment histories and preferences. Human resources operations use AI technologies for talent acquisition, employee engagement, and performance management. AI-driven recruitment systems can screen resumes, evaluate candidate qualifications, and even conduct initial interviews using natural language processing and video analysis tools. These systems help identify top candidates, reduce bias in hiring, and make recruitment more efficient.

Inventory management is another area where AI provides substantial operational benefits.

Traditional inventory management depends on historical data and simple forecasting models that may overlook complex factors influencing demand. AI-powered systems analyze multiple data sources, including sales patterns, seasonal trends, marketing campaigns, economic indicators, and weather forecasts, to optimize inventory levels, lower carrying costs, and minimize stockouts. Document processing and data extraction through AI enable organizations to handle large volumes of unstructured data more efficiently. Natural language processing systems extract key information from contracts, invoices, reports, and other documents, automatically update databases, and trigger workflows. This reduces manual data entry, improves accuracy, and speeds up processing. Maintenance operations also benefit from AI by predicting equipment failures, optimizing maintenance schedules, and suggesting preventive actions based on equipment condition monitoring and historical maintenance data. Predictive maintenance detects subtle performance changes, enabling proactive interventions that cut downtime and extend equipment lifespan. Compliance monitoring and regulatory reporting are increasingly critical AI applications. Automated systems continuously oversee business activities for compliance issues, generate regulatory reports, and ensure practices align with laws and regulations. These systems adapt to evolving regulatory requirements and provide early warnings for potential compliance problems that arise.

6.5.3 AI in Operations and Supply Chain Optimization

Supply chain management represents one of the most complex and critical areas of business operations, involving the coordination of multiple suppliers, manufacturers, distributors, and retailers across global networks. AI technologies provide unprecedented capabilities to optimize these complex systems, improve visibility across supply chain networks, and enhance responsiveness to disruptions and changing market conditions. Demand forecasting through AI systems significantly improves accuracy compared to traditional forecasting methods by analyzing multiple data sources and identifying complex patterns that influence customer demand. These systems can incorporate factors such as seasonal variations, economic indicators, marketing campaigns, competitive activities, weather patterns, and social trends to generate more accurate demand predictions. Improved demand forecasting enables better inventory planning, production scheduling, and resource allocation throughout the supply chain.

Logistics optimization is a crucial area where AI technologies can greatly cut transportation costs and improve delivery performance. AI-driven route optimization systems can analyze multiple factors at once, such as traffic, vehicle capacity, delivery time windows, driver schedules, and fuel expenses, to find the best routes and schedules. These systems can adapt in real time and automatically reroute when disruptions happen. Supplier selection and management also gain from AI tools that evaluate supplier performance across various aspects like quality, delivery consistency, cost, and financial health. AI systems can continuously track suppliers, spot potential risks, and suggest alternatives when issues arise. This is especially useful for organizations with large supplier networks, where manual monitoring would be impractical. Warehouse operations utilize AI for inventory management, picking route optimization, and automated material handling. AI-powered warehouse systems can optimize storage based on product traits and picking frequency, create efficient picking routes that reduce travel time, and coordinate automated equipment like robots and conveyors. These improvements can lower operational costs while speeding up and increasing the accuracy of order fulfillment.[18]

Risk management in supply chains greatly benefits from AI applications that can detect potential disruptions before they happen and suggest mitigation strategies. AI systems can track multiple risk indicators, such as supplier financial stability, geopolitical factors, weather conditions, and transportation network status, to provide early warning signals of possible supply chain issues. This proactive approach allows organizations to implement contingency plans and reduce the impact of disruptions. Additionally, quality management across supply chains can be improved through AI applications that monitor product quality at various stages of production and distribution. AI-powered quality systems analyze data from suppliers, manufacturing processes, and customer feedback to spot quality trends and potential problems. These systems can automatically modify quality control settings and recommend corrective actions to ensure consistent product quality throughout the supply chain. AI technologies enable supply chain optimization through advanced analytics and ML algorithms that can identify inefficiencies and suggest improvements across complex supply networks. AI automates the transformation of natural language into executable simulation models for logistics systems, facilitating faster, more efficient, and collaborative modeling processes that combine human expertise with evolving AI capabilities.[19]

6.5.4 AI and Internet of Things Integration

The convergence of AI and Internet of Things (IoT) technologies creates powerful synergies that enable smart business applications capable of autonomous decision-making, real-time optimization, and predictive capabilities across various operational domains. This integration transforms traditional business processes by connecting physical assets, sensors, and devices to intelligent systems that can analyze data, identify patterns, and take automated actions to improve efficiency and performance. Smart manufacturing represents one of the most impactful applications of AI–IoT integration, where connected sensors throughout production facilities generate continuous streams of data about equipment performance, product quality, environmental conditions, and operational efficiency. AI systems analyze this real-time data to optimize production parameters, predict equipment failures, and automatically adjust manufacturing processes to maintain optimal performance. This integration enables manufacturers to achieve higher quality standards, reduce waste, and minimize downtime while improving overall equipment effectiveness. AI–IoT integration enables predictive maintenance strategies that greatly lower operational costs and enhance asset reliability. Connected sensors can monitor equipment vibration, temperature, pressure, and other performance indicators, while AI algorithms analyze these data streams to predict when maintenance is needed. This predictive approach allows organizations to schedule maintenance during planned downtime, reduce emergency repairs, and extend equipment lifespan.[20] Smart building management systems utilize AI–IoT integration to optimize energy consumption, improve occupant comfort, and lower operational expenses. Sensors installed throughout buildings track temperature, humidity, lighting, occupancy, and energy consumption, while AI systems analyze this data to automatically adjust heating, ventilation, air conditioning, and lighting. These smart building solutions can significantly reduce energy consumption while maintaining ideal environmental conditions for occupants. The use of IoT in smart buildings primarily involves connecting and controlling various appliances and systems through networked sensors and actuators to boost efficiency, safety, and comfort. IoT allows for real-time monitoring and control of building aspects like heating, cooling, lighting, air quality, and water management via wireless protocols, providing cost-effective and energy-efficient options.[21]

Supply chain visibility and tracking benefit substantially from AI–IoT integration, where connected sensors and devices provide real-time information about product location, condition, and environmental exposure throughout the supply chain. AI systems can analyze this tracking data to optimize logistics routes, predict delivery times, and identify potential quality issues before products reach customers. This integration enables organizations to provide customers with accurate delivery information while ensuring product quality and reducing supply chain risks. AI–IoT integration enables smart agriculture applications that monitor soil conditions, weather patterns, crop health, and irrigation needs to optimize productivity while reducing resource consumption. Connected sensors in fields gather data about soil moisture, nutrient levels, temperature, and plant growth, while AI systems analyze this information to recommend the best planting schedules, irrigation times, and fertilizer amounts. IoT in agriculture results in better farm management, higher crop yields, less environmental impact, and economic benefits for farmers by providing accurate, real-time, actionable data.[22] Fleet management and logistics operations utilize AI–IoT integration to monitor vehicle performance, optimize routes, and enhance driver safety. Connected vehicles produce data about location, speed, fuel consumption, engine performance, and driver behavior, while AI systems analyze this data to improve delivery routes, predict maintenance needs, and identify opportunities for fuel savings. This integration helps logistics companies lower operational costs while boosting service quality and safety. Smart retail applications use AI–IoT integration to enhance customer experiences, manage inventory more efficiently, and improve store operations. Sensors and cameras in retail locations track customer traffic patterns, product availability, and environmental conditions, while AI analyzes this data to optimize store layouts, adjust pricing strategies, and automatically reorder products when inventory runs low. Energy management systems benefit from AI–IoT combined with smart grid technologies that monitor energy use, predict demand changes, and adjust energy distribution automatically to improve efficiency and cut costs. Connected smart meters and sensors across electrical grids deliver real-time data on energy consumption and system performance, while AI algorithms analyze this data to balance supply and demand, prevent outages, and effectively integrate renewable energy sources.

6.6 Anomaly Detection and Clustering Algorithms

In the fast-changing world of data-driven decision-making, being able to spot unusual patterns and group similar observations is essential for understanding complex systems and detecting potential problems early. Anomaly detection and clustering algorithms are two key pillars of modern data analysis that help organizations extract meaningful insights from large amounts of data while maintaining operations efficiently and securely. Anomaly detection identifies data points, patterns, or behaviors deviating from what is normal, indicating phenomena like fraud, system failures, or market trends. The challenge is distinguishing meaningful anomalies from natural variation. Clustering groups similar data based on shared traits, helping analysts understand structures and segment customers, products, or processes. Data points that don't fit well into any cluster often signify potential anomalies needing investigation.

6.6.1 Fundamental Concepts and Theoretical Foundations

Anomaly detection relies on establishing baselines for normal behavior, which can be statistical (e.g., mean and standard deviations) or more complex, capturing temporal or interdependent patterns. The challenge is defining normal behavior in dynamic environments where customer preferences, market conditions, and operations change. Statistical methods often use measures like z-scores to identify data points that deviate from the mean, such as unusual customer spending or transactions outside expected ranges. However, these assume known data distributions, which may not fit complex datasets with multiple modes or seasonal patterns. Distance-based methods identify normal points that cluster together, while anomalies are far from these clusters. They measure distances like Euclidean or Manhattan, useful in customer segmentation to find behavior that differs from normal groups. Density-based approaches find low-density regions where anomalies often occur, such as in fraud detection, where legitimate transactions cluster and fraudulent ones are in sparse areas.

Clustering algorithms operate on different principles, focusing on finding natural groupings based on similarity measures, which vary depending on data and goals. Similarity can include numerical distances, shared categories, temporal patterns, or complex factors. Partitioning methods like k-means divide data into a set number of clusters by iteratively assigning points and updating centers, ideal when the number of clusters is known or estimated, and clusters are similar in size. In business, they segment customers by behavior, demographics, or engagement. Hierarchical clustering builds tree-like structures showing relationships at multiple levels, revealing nested groups like broad categories and subcategories. Useful when the number of clusters is unknown or for exploring data structures. Density-based algorithms identify high-density regions separated by low-density areas, detecting clusters of various shapes and sizes and determining the number of clusters automatically. This suits complex datasets where groups don't follow simple geometric forms or densities.

6.6.1.1 Types and Categories of Anomaly Detection Algorithms

Supervised anomaly detection algorithms require labeled training data that explicitly marks normal and abnormal observations. These methods treat anomaly detection as a classification problem, using ML techniques to learn patterns that differentiate between normal and unusual behavior. However, supervised methods face difficulties in environments where anomalies are rare, labeling is costly or time-consuming, and the nature of anomalies changes over time as fraud strategies evolve.

Unsupervised anomaly detection algorithms operate without labels, instead identifying anomalies based on the idea that they are a small minority that differs significantly from normal data points. These methods are especially useful in cases where anomalies are unknown, unlabeled, or constantly changing. Unsupervised techniques include statistical methods that find data points beyond certain limits, distance-based methods that flag points far from their neighbors, and density-based methods that detect data in sparse regions. The adaptability of unsupervised methods makes them suitable for exploratory analysis and monitoring tasks where the goal is to spot any unusual patterns that may need further checking.

Semi-supervised anomaly detection algorithms combine features of both supervised and unsupervised methods. They typically only use normal examples during training and detect anomalies as data points that differ from the learned normal model. This approach is especially practical when normal behavior examples are plentiful, but abnormal examples are rare or hard to get. One-class classification methods are part of the semi-supervised group. They learn a boundary around normal data points and label anything outside this boundary as a potential anomaly. These are useful for monitoring systems, where normal operation data is easy to acquire, but failures or attacks are rare and may have unknown forms.

Time series anomaly detection algorithms focus on spotting strange patterns in data over time, which depend on previous values and show trends, seasonal effects, and other temporal features. Business uses include monitoring website traffic for sudden spikes that might suggest attacks or viral content, detecting unusual patterns in sales data indicating market shifts or data problems, and spotting equipment issues that could signal upcoming failure.

Deep learning methods for anomaly detection have become popular because they can automatically learn complex patterns and representations from large datasets. These techniques can recognize nonlinear relationships and hierarchical patterns that traditional algorithms might overlook. For instance, autoencoders learn to reconstruct normal data patterns and identify anomalies as observations that cannot be reconstructed accurately. Recurrent neural networks can model temporal dependencies in time series data to detect unusual sequences or patterns.

Choosing the right anomaly detection algorithms depends on several factors, including the availability of labeled data, the application domain, computational needs, and interpretability. Business organizations should carefully evaluate these factors because selecting the wrong algorithm can lead to poor performance, many false positives, or missed anomalies that could significantly impact the business.

6.6.2 Clustering Algorithms and Their Applications

Clustering algorithms are a core part of unsupervised learning methods that organize data into meaningful groups based on similarity metrics. They help organizations uncover natural patterns within their datasets and craft targeted strategies for different segments. The wide range of clustering algorithms reflects the variety of data types, business goals, and analytical challenges faced when analyzing complex datasets.

Partitioning clustering algorithms split datasets into a fixed number of clusters by optimizing criteria like minimizing within-cluster variation or maximizing separation between clusters. The k-means algorithm is the most common partitioning method, repeatedly assigning data points to cluster centers and updating these centers until they stabilize. In customer segmentation, k-means might group customers based on purchasing habits, demographics, or engagement levels to support targeted marketing. The success of partitioning algorithms depends heavily on choosing the right number of clusters, often requiring domain knowledge or methods like the elbow technique or silhouette analysis.

Hierarchical clustering algorithms create tree-like structures that display relationships at multiple levels of detail, allowing exploration of data structures without fixing the number of clusters in advance. Agglomerative hierarchical clustering starts with individual data points and merges the closest clusters step-by-step until all points are joined into one cluster. Divisive clustering begins with all data points in one cluster and recursively splits them until each point stands alone. This structure helps analysts examine data relationships across different levels, from broad market segments to niche customer groups. It's especially useful in product portfolio management, revealing connections between products from broad categories to specific variants that directly compete.

Density-based clustering algorithms find clusters defined as high-density regions separated by low-density areas, are effective in discovering clusters of various shapes and sizes, and automatically determine their number. The DBSCAN method groups densely packed points together and marks sparse points as outliers, making it particularly useful for detecting anomalies along with clusters. Density-based methods are flexible and well-suited for complex business datasets where natural groups might not follow simple geometric patterns.

Distribution-based clustering assumes data points within each cluster follow specific probability distributions, usually Gaussian. Gaussian mixture models are advanced tools that can find overlapping clusters and assign points to clusters probabilistically rather than definitively. This approach is especially useful when customers or products belong partially to multiple segments. Because of their probabilistic nature, distribution-based clustering enables more detailed analysis of customer behavior, recognizing that individuals may display traits of several segments with different probabilities. This supports sophisticated marketing strategies that consider the likelihood of customer response based on their probabilistic cluster membership.

Clustering-based approaches can enhance anomaly detection capabilities by leveraging the inherent grouping structure in data to distinguish normal patterns from anomalies better. The natural groupings identified through clustering can provide context for anomaly detection, enabling more accurate identification of unusual patterns by considering the specific characteristics of different data segments. This integration is particularly valuable in business applications where normal behavior varies significantly across different customer segments or operational contexts.

Choosing the right clustering algorithm depends on several factors, including the type of data, business goals, computational limits, and how easily the results can be understood. Organizations need to decide if they require hard or soft cluster assignments, whether the number of clusters is known ahead of time or needs to be determined automatically, and if the clusters are expected to be spherical or could have more complex shapes. Assessing clustering results can be challenging because there is often no single correct way to group data. Businesses usually evaluate clustering solutions based on how useful they are for specific purposes, like improving targeted marketing or optimizing inventory for different product categories. Quantitative measures such as silhouette scores, Davies-Bouldin indices, and within-cluster sum of squares help assess the quality of clustering, but these should be interpreted in light of business goals and practical constraints.

6.6.3 Integration of Clustering and Anomaly Detection

The integration of clustering and anomaly detection techniques creates powerful analytical frameworks that utilize the complementary strengths of both methods to deliver more accurate and contextually relevant insights than either approach alone. This combination recognizes that anomalies often depend on specific contexts or segments rather than the entire dataset, allowing for more advanced and nuanced approaches to outlier identification. Clustering-based anomaly detection methods work on the idea that data points that do not fit well into any identified cluster are likely anomalies worth further investigation. This method addresses a key limitation of traditional anomaly detection, which considers the whole dataset as a single, uniform group, potentially missing anomalies that are normal within certain segments but unusual when viewed globally, or mistakenly flagging normal variations within segments as anomalies. The process usually starts with applying clustering algorithms to find natural groupings within the data, then assessing how well each data point matches its assigned cluster or the overall cluster structure. Data points that are distant from all cluster centers, belong to very small clusters, or show characteristics that differ significantly from their cluster mates are flagged as potential anomalies. This approach provides context for anomaly detection by considering local neighborhood behavior and segment-specific normal patterns.

One common method involves measuring the distance from each data point to its nearest cluster center or calculating the probability that a point belongs to its cluster. Points that are far from the center or have low probability scores are considered outliers. This technique is especially useful in business scenarios where customer behavior varies greatly across segments, such as retail environments with differing purchasing trends among demographic groups or regions. Another technique involves spotting clusters that are much smaller than expected or contain data points with unusual features compared to most clusters. These small or unusual clusters could indicate emerging market segments, fraud activities, or system anomalies needing attention. For example, in credit card fraud detection, small clusters of transactions might reveal new fraud patterns that haven't yet become widespread fraudsters.

Unified frameworks that combine clustering and anomaly detection can enhance the accuracy and interpretability of identifying outliers. Research indicates that clustering-based anomaly detection methods can lower false positive rates while better capturing subtle anomalies that traditional methods might overlook. This benefit is especially important in business settings where false alarms are costly and missed anomalies can lead to serious issues. In the automotive industry, integrating clustering with anomaly detection improves outlier identification by utilizing various clustering algorithms to group similar automotive components effectively. This grouping helps identify anomalies such as pricing inconsistencies and specification errors that might otherwise go unnoticed in large, complex datasets. The study shows that techniques like hierarchical clustering and K-Medoids can detect distortions in manufacturing costs and uncover data quality problems, which, once addressed, produce more accurate clusters and more reliable anomaly detection. Additionally, combining multiple clustering metrics and hybrid approaches (e.g., PSO-K) can overcome the limitations of individual algorithms, enhancing both detection performance and the practical applicability of the models in real industrial environments.

Integration also enables dynamic anomaly detection, where cluster structures are continuously updated as new data becomes available, allowing the system to adapt to evolving normal behavior patterns. This flexibility is essential in business environments where customer preferences, market conditions, and operational parameters shift over time. Traditional static anomaly detection models may become less effective as they age, but clustering-based approaches can stay effective by continuously learning new normal patterns.

Multi-level anomaly detection is another approach, identifying anomalies at different levels of the cluster hierarchy. Global anomalies affect the overall data distribution, local anomalies are unusual within specific clusters, and contextual anomalies break expected relationships between variables within contexts. This multi-level approach provides business analysts different perspectives on unusual patterns, enabling a more comprehensive understanding of potential issues or opportunities.

6.7 AutoML and No-Code AI—Democratizing AI for Non-Technical Users

The democratization of AI marks a major technological shift in the twenty-first century, transforming how organizations and individuals access advanced analytical tools once limited to experts. Automated Machine Learning (AutoML) and No-Code AI platforms are key in this shift, providing non-technical users with accessible ways to use ML without extensive programming or statistical knowledge. AutoML automates complex tasks like data preprocessing, algorithm selection, hyperparameter tuning, training, and evaluation, allowing users to focus on business problems and results. It encodes the expertise of data scientists into automated systems for smart model building. No-Code AI platforms go even further by providing easy-to-use graphical interfaces that let users create, deploy, and manage AI applications without writing any code. These platforms often feature drag-and-drop tools, visual workflow designers, and pre-built components that can be combined to develop advanced analytical solutions. The no-code approach removes traditional barriers to AI adoption by doing away with the need for programming skills while preserving the power and flexibility of ML technologies.

6.7.1 Historical Evolution and Current State of AutoML

The development of AutoML technologies marks a natural progression in the ML field, driven by the understanding that many aspects of model creation follow predictable patterns that can be automated. It also meets the rising demand for AI capabilities across organizations that lack extensive data science expertise. The shift from manual ML processes to fully automated systems reflects both technological progress and changing business needs for more accessible analytical tools. Initially, ML implementations required considerable manual effort at every stage, from data collection and preprocessing to algorithm selection, hyperparameter tuning, and model evaluation. Data scientists and ML engineers spent significant time on routine tasks such as cleaning datasets, testing different algorithms, and fine-tuning model parameters through trial-and-error. This manual process was not only time-consuming but also required specialized knowledge, limiting AI adoption to organizations with substantial technical resources. Recognizing these limitations led to the development of automated methods capable of managing routine parts of ML while preserving the flexibility and effectiveness of manual techniques. Early AutoML efforts targeted specific components of the ML pipeline, like automated hyperparameter tuning or feature selection, eventually evolving into comprehensive platforms that can handle entire model development workflows with minimal human intervention.

The current state of AutoML includes multiple approaches and methodologies, each designed to address different facets of automation. Neural Architecture Search (NAS) techniques automatically design and optimize neural network structures for specific tasks, removing the need for manual architecture design and allowing non-experts to harness deep learning capabilities. Integrating AutoML with cloud computing platforms has further accelerated adoption by providing scalable, accessible infrastructure capable of handling the computational demands of automated model development. Cloud-based AutoML services allow organizations to access advanced ML capabilities without investing in specialized hardware or maintaining complex software environments. These platforms often offer pay-as-you-go pricing models, making sophisticated AI accessible to small organizations and individual users who can't justify the costs of traditional ML infrastructure.

Modern AutoML platforms have evolved to address not only technical automation but also user experience, which is crucial for non-technical adoption. Intuitive interfaces, clear explanations of automated decisions, and comprehensive reporting enable users to understand and trust automated systems while maintaining control over key business decisions. The focus on explainability and interpretability highlights that successful AI democratization requires both technical accessibility and user confidence. The competitive landscape of AutoML solutions includes both specialized vendors focusing solely on automated ML and big tech companies integrating AutoML features into broader AI and analytics platforms. This competition has fueled rapid innovation in automation, user experience, and integration, while also reducing costs and boosting accessibility for potential users. Adoption of AutoML by enterprises has gained momentum as organizations realize its potential to scale AI capabilities across multiple departments and use cases without proportionally expanding their data science teams. Democratizing ML helps organizations apply AI to a wider array of problems, freeing expert data scientists to concentrate on more complex, strategic challenges that require human creativity and domain knowledge.

6.7.2 Core Components and Technologies

AutoML and No-Code AI platforms rely on advanced algorithms that automate decision-making traditionally done by experts. Understanding these components helps organizations choose and implement platforms effectively while understanding what automated ML can do. Automated data preprocessing is vital because input data quality affects model performance, regardless of subsequent steps. Modern AutoML uses intelligent algorithms to identify data types, detect missing values, recognize outliers, and apply transformations to prepare data for analysis. These platforms support various data formats, sources, and time-dependent data. The level of sophistication in automated feature engineering varies widely among AutoML platforms. Some offer basic transformations, while others use cutting-edge techniques like genetic algorithms, reinforcement learning, or deep learning to improve feature creation and selection. The success of these approaches often depends on the dataset and business challenge, making the choice of platform based on specific needs very important.

Algorithm selection and hyperparameter tuning are essential automation features that help users avoid needing deep knowledge of different algorithms or the complicated process of fine-tuning parameters. AutoML systems test multiple algorithms, experiment with various parameter combinations, and select the best approach based on automated validation. They often use advanced optimization techniques such as Bayesian optimization, genetic algorithms, or grid search to efficiently explore options. Model ensemble techniques automatically combine predictions from multiple algorithms to achieve better results than any single model. They leverage the idea that diverse models can complement each other's strengths and weaknesses. Automated ensemble methods find the best combinations, assign appropriate weights, and manage the complexity without requiring users to understand ensemble design.

Hyperparameter tuning algorithms are essential in AutoML, automatically adjusting many parameters that impact model performance. They typically utilize advanced search techniques to efficiently explore large parameter spaces and avoid lengthy, exhaustive searches. Automating hyperparameter tuning eliminates a time-consuming and expertise-dependent aspect of traditional ML and often produces better results than manual tuning. Integrating these vital components into a smooth AutoML platform requires careful coordination of multiple automated processes to ensure system reliability, performance, and user-friendliness. Successful platforms must strike a balance between automation and user control, providing enough automation for non-technical users while also allowing them to customize or override automated decisions when needed.

6.7.3 No-Code AI Platforms and User Experience Design

The evolution of No-Code AI platforms marks a major shift in how AI technologies are packaged and delivered to end users. These platforms focus on accessibility, ease of use, and business benefits rather than technical complexity. They understand that the main obstacle to adopting AI is not the lack of powerful algorithms but the difficulty of implementing and managing them in business settings where technical skills may be limited. User experience design in No-Code AI platforms emphasizes creating intuitive interfaces that let users perform complex analytical tasks through simple, familiar actions like drag-and-drop, form filling, and point-and-click navigation. The challenge is to hide the complex workings of ML while still offering full access to the power and flexibility of these tools. Successful platforms strike this balance by offering multiple interaction levels, ranging from basic automated workflows for casual users to in-depth settings for advanced users seeking more control.

Visual workflow designers are a key part of No-Code AI platforms, allowing users to build ML pipelines by connecting graphical components that represent different processing steps, such as data input, preprocessing, model training, and result visualization. These visual methods use familiar metaphors from other business software, offering clear visuals of data flow and processing logic that help users understand and modify their analytical workflows. Designing visual interfaces for ML requires careful thought on how to represent complex ideas like algorithm selection and model evaluation in ways that are meaningful to non-technical users. Successful platforms often use progressive disclosure techniques that show simple options first, while offering more detailed settings for users who need them. This approach helps platforms serve both beginners who want fully automated solutions and experienced users seeking more control over the process. Template-based solutions democratize AI by providing pre-configured tools for issues like customer churn, fraud detection, demand forecasting, and sentiment analysis. These templates incorporate best practices for specific use cases and can be customized with user data and needs. High-quality templates reduce development time and expertise, enabling effective AI solutions based on proven methods.

Adaptive user-centered design approaches for AutoML toolkits focus on making ML accessible to non-experts and HCI researchers. Key features include a user-friendly graphical interface that eliminates complex coding, enabling users from diverse fields to manage ML pipelines without deep AI knowledge. The toolkit incorporates incremental learning and model adaptation, allowing continuous updates to models based on new data and user-specific behaviors, thereby enhancing personalization and relevance. Platforms can automatically adjust their interfaces and recommendations according to user expertise levels and specific use case requirements. Personalization in No-Code AI platforms is essential because it allows adaptive interfaces to customize the user experience based on individual needs and abilities. This customization improves usability by simplifying interactions and offering relevant options aligned with users' expertise levels, reducing cognitive load, and making learning and remembering easier. Furthermore, adaptive interfaces boost effectiveness by supporting models to continuously update and personalize through incremental learning, which considers user-specific behaviors and changing data. Such personalization ensures the AI tools stay relevant, accurate, and practical over time for diverse users, especially non-AI experts.[23] These platforms typically provide multiple types of explanations, from high-level summaries of model behavior to detailed analyses of individual predictions. The challenge lies in presenting this information in ways that are meaningful to business users who may not understand statistical concepts but need to make decisions based on model outputs.

6.8 Summary

This chapter examines the transformative role of AI in shaping modern business strategies. It begins by outlining the foundational principles of AI and its integration into strategic decision-making across industries. The chapter addresses how AI technologies, including ML, natural language processing, and predictive analytics, are enabling organizations to improve financial viability, enhance operational efficiency, personalize customer experiences, optimize supply chains, and uncover new revenue opportunities and innovations.

Key strategic frameworks for AI adoption are discussed, emphasizing data-driven culture, leadership alignment, and ethical considerations. The chapter highlights real-world case studies demonstrating successful AI implementation in areas such as marketing, finance, human resources, and innovation management. It also addresses the challenges businesses face in AI adoption, including data quality, talent gaps, governance, and regulatory compliance.

Notes

1 Steyvers, M., & Kumar, A. (2024). Three challenges for AI-assisted decision-making. *Perspectives on Psychological Science*, 19(5), 722–734. https://doi.org/10.1177/17456916231181102. Available at https://journals.sagepub.com/doi/full/10.1177/17456916231181102

2 Wang, R. Y., & Strong, D. M. (1996). Beyond accuracy: What data quality means to data consumers. *Journal of Management Information Systems*, 12(4), 5–33. https://doi.org/10.1080/07421222.1996.11518099. Available at https://www.tandfonline.com/doi/abs/10.1080/07421222.1996.11518099

3 Mumuni, A.G., & Mumuni, F. (2024). Automated data processing and feature engineering for deep learning and big data applications: A survey. *Journal of Information & Intelligence*, 2(3). https://doi.org/10.1016/j.jiixd.2024.01.002. Available at https://www.sciencedirect.com/science/article/pii/S2949715924000027

4 Rahm, E., & Do, H. H. (2000). Data cleaning: Problems and current approaches. *IEEE Data Engineering Bulletin*, 23(4), 3–13. Available at https://cs.brown.edu/courses/cs227/archives/2017/papers/data-cleaning-IEEE.pdf#page=5

5 Guyon, I., & Elisseeff, A. (2003). An introduction to variable and feature selection. *Journal of Machine Learning Research*, 3, 1157–1182. Available at https://www.jmlr.org/papers/volume3/guyon03a/guyon03a.pdf

6 Mikolov, T., Sutskever, I., Chen, K., Corrado, G., & Dean, J. (2013). Distributed representations of words and phrases and their compositionality. In *Advances in Neural Information Processing Systems*. Available at https://proceedings.neurips.cc/paper/2013/hash/9aa42b31882ec039965f3c4923ce901b-Abstract.html

7 Heaton, J., Polson, N., & Witte, J. (2017). Deep learning for finance: Deep portfolios. *Applied Stochastic Models in Business and Industry*, 33(1), 3–12. https://doi.org/10.1002/asmb.2209. Available at https://onlinelibrary.wiley.com/doi/abs/10.1002/asmb.2209?casa_token=5N0hzznFka0AAAAA%3Asn6ocIeA9gkG4Wk_N3wqkzA2jsxsWr-RAYZTyOyBT6PrzJ1gf8pvC3P5-lmfEgFM4cWqFE8WRTbk95ks

8 Wedel, M., & Kannan, P. K. (2016). Marketing analytics for data-rich environments. *Journal of Marketing*, 80(6), 97–121. https://doi.org/10.1509/jm.15.0413. Available at https://journals.sagepub.com/doi/full/10.1509/jm.15.0413?casa_token=v7t0ljLvBAoAAAAA%3AYmezm1TEVPig3DUdOj4JTyMzbWhqzteYFixCjnnuQTtfSasWzdMAO7y-a4uCv_Dafh_6a1QCwxB-9Q

9 Waller, M. A., & Fawcett, S. E. (2013). Data science, predictive analytics, and big data: A revolution that will transform supply chain design and management. *Journal of Business Logistics*, 34(2), 77–84. https://doi.org/10.1111/jbl.12010. Available at https://onlinelibrary.wiley.com/doi/full/10.1111/jbl.12010

10 Pedregosa, F., Varoquaux, G., Gramfort, A., et al. (2011). Scikit-learn: Machine learning in Python. *Journal of Machine Learning Research*, 12, 2825–2830.

11 Zaharia, M., Xin, R. S., Wendell, P., et al. (2016). Apache Spark: A unified engine for big data processing. *Communications of the ACM*, 59(11), 56–65. https://doi.org/10.1145/2934664. Available at https://dl.acm.org/doi/fullHtml/10.1145/2934664

12 He, X., Zhao, K., & Chu, X. (2021). AutoML: A survey of the state-of-the-art. *Knowledge-Based Systems*, 212, 106622. https://doi.org/10.1016/j.knosys.2020.106622. Available at https://www.sciencedirect.com/science/article/abs/pii/S0950705120307516

13 Manzoor, A., Qureshi, M. A., Kidney, E., & Longo, L. (2024). A review on machine learning methods for customer churn prediction and recommendations for business practitioners. *IEEE Access*, 12, 70434–70463. https://doi.org/10.1109/ACCESS.2024.3402092. Available at https://ieeexplore.ieee.org/abstract/document/10531735

14 Hollenstein, L., Lichtensteiger, L., Stadelmann, T., Amirian, M., Budde, L., Meierhofer, J., Füchslin, R.M. and Friedli, T., 2019. Unsupervised learning and simulation for complexity management in business operations. In: Braschler, M., Stadelmann, T., & Stockinger, K. (eds.) *Applied Data Science: Lessons Learned for the Data-Driven Business* (pp. 313–331). Springer International Publishing. https://doi.org/10.1007/978-3-030-11821-1_17. Available at https://link.springer.com/chapter/10.1007/978-3-030-11821-1_17

15 Zhao, Z., & Bai, T. (2022). Financial fraud detection and prediction in listed companies using SMOTE and machine learning algorithms. *Entropy*, 24(8), 1157. https://doi.org/10.3390/e24081157. Available at https://www.mdpi.com/1099-4300/24/8/1157

16 Nygård, R., & Mezei, J. (2020). Automating lead scoring with machine learning: An experimental study. In *Proceedings of the 53rd Hawaii International Conference on System Sciences* (pp. 1439–1448). Available at https://scholarspace.manoa.hawaii.edu/server/api/core/bitstreams/1d4e8c2d-4096-4628-b4f8-4f6086aa6b53/content

17 Leocádio, D., Guedes, L., Oliveira, J., Reis, J., & Melão, N. (2024). Customer service with AI-powered human-robot collaboration (HRC): A literature review. *Procedia Computer Science*, 232, 1222–1232. https://doi.org/10.1016/j.procs.2024.01.120. Available at https://www.sciencedirect.com/science/article/pii/S1877050924001200

18 Goswami, S. S., Mondal, S., Sarkar, S., Gupta, K. K., Sahoo, S. K., & Halder, R. (2025). Artificial intelligence-enabled supply chain management: Unlocking new opportunities and challenges. *Artificial Intelligence and Applications*, 3(1), 110–121. https://doi.org/10.47852/bonview AIA42021814. Available at https://ojs.bonviewpress.com/index.php/AIA/article/view/1814

19 Jackson, I., Jesus Saenz, M., & Ivanov, D. (2024). From natural language to simulations: Applying AI to automate simulation modelling of logistics systems. *International Journal of Production Research*, 62(4), 1434–1457. https://doi.org/10.1080/00207543.2023.2276811. Available at https://www.tandfonline.com/doi/full/10.1080/00207543.2023.2276811

20 Zoha, A., Qadir, J., & Abbasi, Q. H. (2022). AI-powered IoT for intelligent systems and smart applications. *Frontiers in Communications and Networks*, 3, 959303. https://doi.org/10.3389/frcmn.2022.959303. Available at https://www.frontiersin.org/journals/communications-and-networks/articles/10.3389/frcmn.2022.959303/full

21 Verma, A., Prakash, S., Srivastava, V., Kumar, A., & Mukhopadhyay, S. C. (2019). Sensing, controlling, and IoT infrastructure in smart building: A review. *IEEE Sensors Journal*, 19(20), 9036–9046. https://doi.org/10.1109/JSEN.2019.2922409. Available at https://ieeexplore.ieee.org/abstract/document/8735760?casa_token=GW6FAQS-QWcAAAAA:9ESR8NlnjZXBMc8NSsvL4QPu5Ej-mCWAra3P58by_BuAvuEbOZx2QdZcX8cho2U1zLixyOSBT0s

22 Marcu, I. M., Suciu, G., Balaceanu, C. M., & Banaru, A. (2019, June). IoT based system for smart agriculture. In *2019 11th International Conference on Electronics, Computers and Artificial Intelligence (ECAI)* (pp. 1–4). IEEE. https://doi.org/10.1109/ECAI46879.2019.9041952. Available at https://ieeexplore.ieee.org/abstract/document/9041952

23 Gomaa, A., Sargious, M., & Krüger, A. (2024). AdaptoML-UX: An adaptive user-centered GUI-based autoML toolkit for non-AI experts and HCI researchers. arXiv preprint arXiv:2410.17469. https://doi.org/10.48550/arXiv.2410.17469. Available at https://arxiv.org/abs/2410.17469

7 Natural Language Processing (NLP)

Learning Objectives

- Learn natural language processing (NLP) for business insights
- Understand sentiment analysis, topic modeling, and sequence-to-sequence models
- Learn text preprocessing, tokenization, and word embeddings
- Understand the relation between AI, machine learning, and deep learning
- Learn supply chain optimization with machine learning
- Understand the basics of NLP and its relevance
- Learn about text preprocessing and vectorization
- Apply NLP models to real-world scenarios
- Explore business applications of NLP

7.1 Introduction

NLP is a rapidly growing and evolving field that integrates of integrating computer science, AI, and linguistics by enabling machines to understand, interpret, and generate human language in a way that is meaningful, relevant, and useful. This chapter examines NLP as an integral part of modern technology and business analytics, from the simple task of powering virtual assistants like Siri and Alexa to more sophisticated aspects of enabling real-time language translation, sentiment analysis, and content summarization. NLP algorithms can bridge the gap between human communication and computer understanding by transforming complex and often ambiguous human language into simple, processed, and analyzed text and speech data by using techniques from ML, deep learning, and computational linguistics. The NLP applications are relevant, useful, and transformative for a vast majority of organizations and industries, from education to healthcare, finance, customer service, and banking, in transforming unstructured text, automating customer support through chatbots to structured data for decision-making. NLP algorithms enable humans to interact with machines, and machines assist humans by improving accessibility with voice-to-text technologies. This chapter explores the fundamental concepts, main tools, key techniques, and real-world applications of NLP in business analytics and AI. This chapter also explains NLP techniques such as text preprocessing, sentiment analysis, topic modeling, and sequence modeling. Applications include social media analysis, customer feedback processing, and automated reporting.

DOI: 10.4324/9781003664550-7

7.2 Relationship between Natural Language Processing and Machine Learning

NLP is a subfield of AI concerned with enabling computer systems to understand, interpret, and generate human language. ML, also a subfield of AI, focuses on developing algorithms that learn patterns and make predictions from data rather than relying on explicitly programmed rules. Consequently, NLP and ML are deeply interrelated, with modern NLP systems relying heavily on ML techniques to model, interpret, and generate human language at scale. Traditionally, NLP depended on rule-based and statistical methods grounded in linguistics. However, the availability of large text corpora and advances in supervised, unsupervised, and deep learning have shifted the field toward data-driven approaches.

Recent breakthroughs in deep learning, particularly word embeddings, recurrent neural networks, and attention-based transformer architectures, have further strengthened this relationship by allowing models to capture contextual meaning and long-range dependencies in text.[1] LLMs exemplify the convergence of NLP and ML by integrating representation learning, probabilistic modeling, and optimization techniques to perform tasks such as text classification, information extraction, question answering (QA), and text generation.[2] Ultimately, ML serves as the computational foundation that enables NLP systems to scale, adapt, and continuously improve, while NLP provides rich, unstructured data that drives innovation in ML methodologies across business, social, and scientific applications. In contemporary applications, however, ML, particularly deep learning, forms the foundation of most NLP systems. Tasks such as text classification, sentiment analysis, machine translation, speech recognition, and large language modeling are now predominantly implemented using supervised, unsupervised, or self-supervised learning techniques. Modern NLP models, including transformer-based architectures, learn linguistic representations directly from large text corpora. As a result of this methodological shift, NLP is a domain-specific field within AI that, in modern practice, is primarily implemented using ML techniques. Figure 7.1 illustrates the conceptual and practical relationships among AI, ML, and NLP.

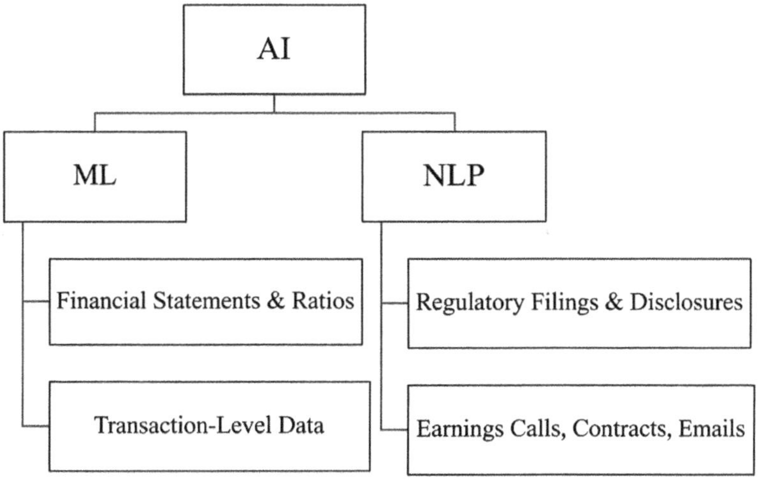

Figure 7.1 Evolution of Business Analytics

7.3 Fundamentals of NLP

NLP is a multidisciplinary field at the intersection of linguistics, computer science, and AI that focuses on enabling machines to understand, interpret, and generate human language in a meaningful and scalable way. The fundamentals of NLP involve the use of computers to understand, interpret, and generate human language in a way that is both meaningful and useful and are commonly organized into core linguistic levels, including lexical analysis (tokenization and morphology), syntactic analysis (part-of-speech tagging and parsing), semantic analysis (meaning representation and word sense disambiguation), and pragmatic and discourse analysis (context, intent, and coherence across texts). In essence, NLP combines computational linguistics, including rules-based modeling of human language, with statistical, ML, and deep learning models to process natural language data.

The NLP process encompasses several steps of (1) tokenization, which breaks down text into smaller units like words or phrases; (2) normalization techniques like stemming and lemmatization that reduce words to their base or root forms to handle variations; (3) part-of-speech tagging, which identifies the grammatical role of each word; (4) and syntactic parsing analyzes sentence structure to understand relationships between words. Furthermore, semantic analysis aims to grasp the meaning behind words and sentences, addressing challenges such as ambiguity and context-dependence. Named entity recognition (NER) extracts specific information such as names, dates, and locations from text, crucial for applications like information retrieval and QA. Ultimately, advanced NLP leverages ML models, including transformer-based architectures like BERT and GPT, which capture contextual nuances and long-range dependencies in language, enabling tasks such as text classification, sentiment analysis, language translation, summarization, and conversational AI. NLP systems must also handle challenges related to idiomatic expressions, sarcasm, and domain-specific jargon, making continual learning and adaptation essential. The integration of NLP into applications ranges from virtual assistants and chatbots to automated content generation and customer feedback analysis, fundamentally transforming how humans interact with technology by bridging the gap between natural language and machine understanding. Collectively, these fundamentals provide the conceptual and technical foundation for applying NLP to real-world business, scientific, and policy-oriented problems.

7.4 Attributes and Techniques of NLP

NLP relies on a set of core attributes and techniques that transform unstructured text into structured representations suitable for computational analysis and modeling. These attributes are explained thoroughly in the following paragraphs. For example, text preprocessing is the foundational step and typically includes tasks such as normalization, lowercasing, stop-word removal, punctuation handling, and noise reduction, all of which improve data quality and downstream model performance. Tokenization then segments text into meaningful units such as words, subwords, or sentences to establish the basis for syntactic and semantic analysis. Stemming and lemmatization further refine tokens by reducing words to their root or canonical forms, thereby reducing vocabulary size and improving generalization in text models.[3] Vectorization techniques convert textual data into numerical features that ML algorithms can process; traditional approaches include bag-of-words and term frequency–inverse document frequency (TF–IDF), which capture word occurrence and importance across documents.[4] More advanced representation methods, known as word embeddings, map words into dense, low-dimensional vector spaces that encode semantic and syntactic relationships based on contextual usage, enabling models to capture similarity, analogy, and meaning more effectively than sparse representations. Collectively, these attributes form the technical backbone of NLP pipelines and are essential for applications ranging from text classification and sentiment analysis to information extraction and large language model development.

Preprocessing is a key step in the NLP pipeline, essential for improving the quality and effectiveness of downstream tasks such as classification, information retrieval, and sentiment analysis. NLP combines various computational techniques to analyze, understand, and generate human language in a form that machines can process, where the text must undergo systematic preprocessing to convert unstructured data into a structured form. Preprocessing primarily involves a series of transformations on raw text input to convert it into a clean, structured format amenable to computational analysis. This process includes cleaning and standardizing raw text by removing irrelevant characters, handling missing values, correcting spelling errors, and converting text to lowercase, which guarantees word representation consistency and prevents inconsistencies between uppercase and lowercase versions.[5] Techniques like tokenization and stemming are used to enhance the quality and usability of the text data.

Tokenization marks the initial phase of this process and refers to splitting the continuous text into elementary units known as tokens, which typically correspond to words, subwords, or symbols, depending on the granularity adopted. Modern frameworks like Byte Pair Encoding (BPE) and WordPiece handle compound words and multilingual contexts effectively.[6] For example, tokenizing the sentence "Text preprocessing is a key step in NLP" yields eight individual tokens:

"Text"	*"preprocessing"*	*"is"*	*"a"*	*"key"*	*"step"*	*"in"*	*"NLP"*
1	2	3	4	5	6	7	8

This segmentation is particularly beneficial in multilingual models, where overlapping subword units across languages allow for parameter sharing and improved cross-lingual transfer learning. It is essential as it facilitates the manipulation and interpretation of text by isolating discrete linguistic units, thus serving as a foundation for all subsequent processing stages. After tokenization, another common step is stop-word removal, which eliminates frequent but semantically insignificant words such as "the" and "is," thereby reducing noise in the dataset and enhancing the model's focus on informative terms.[7] Stemming and lemmatization reduce words to their root forms, enabling better generalization during analysis. For example, "running," "runs," and "ran" are all reduced to "run," which helps consolidate different morphological variants to a single representation.[8]

Beyond character and tokens, tokenization frameworks also incorporate special tokens representing sentence boundaries, padding, unknown words, and task-specific markers. For instance, transformers like BERT use tokens such as "[CLS]" to denote the start of a sentence and "[SEP]" to separate segments, ensuring that models receive consistent and structured input representations.[9] Effective tokenization thus creates a robust foundation for subsequent stages of the NLP pipeline, including embedding generation, syntactic parsing, and semantic understanding. By converting raw text into well-defined atomic units, tokenization enhances the model's ability to capture the linguistic and contextual nuances essential for tasks such as classification, NER, and machine translation.

Following the normalization of tokens, vectorization translates textual data into a numerical space, enabling algorithmic manipulation. Classic vectorization methods, including Bag-of-Words (BoW) and Term Frequency-Inverse Document Frequency (TF-IDF), consider documents as unordered collections of tokens and assign weights based on token frequency or significance across a corpus. Although these approaches provide simplicity and efficiency, their inability to capture semantic relationships or word order limits their descriptive power. To overcome these shortcomings, the introduction of word embeddings, such as Word2Vec and GloVe, revolutionized NLP by mapping words into dense vector spaces where semantic similarities are preserved.[10] More recently, contextual embeddings from transformer models like BERT dynamically adjust representations based on surrounding text, producing dynamic word vectors that adapt according to the context of neighboring words. This capability greatly enhances performance on downstream tasks by capturing complex meanings and relationships within language.[11] Proper tokenization also affects the overall performance and expressiveness of NLP models in various tasks like NER, sentiment analysis, machine translation, and QA. Proper tokenization also affects the overall performance and expressiveness of NLP models across various tasks like NER, sentiment analysis, machine translation, and QA. For example, in NER, incorrect tokenization can improperly split named entities, resulting in a loss of semantic integrity and reduced recognition accuracy. Similarly, machine translation models require precise token boundaries to translate words or subwords accurately while maintaining fluency and grammatical correctness. Moreover, tokenization affects the handling of noisy data, such as typos, informal language, and neologisms common in social media and conversational AI applications, semantic integrity, and degraded recognition performance. Similarly, machine translation models need precise token boundaries to translate words or subwords accurately while maintaining fluency and grammaticality. Furthermore, tokenization impacts the handling of noisy data, such as typos, informal language, and neologisms typical in social media and conversational AI applications.

7.5 NLP for Business Insights: Sentiment Analysis and Topic Modeling

NLP has become a powerful tool for generating business insights by extracting actionable information from large volumes of unstructured textual data, such as customer reviews, earnings calls, social media posts, and corporate disclosures. NLP has become a key technology for extracting business insights from unstructured text data, with sentiment analysis and topic modeling as two of its most common techniques. Sentiment analysis, also called opinion mining, is one of the most widely used NLP applications in business by enabling organizations to assess opinions, emotions, and attitudes expressed in text and to link stakeholder sentiment to outcomes such as brand reputation, customer satisfaction, stock returns, and risk perceptions.[12] Sentiment analysis involves the computational detection and classification of sentiments in text, usually categorizing opinions as positive, negative, or neutral.[13] This approach allows businesses to understand customer attitudes toward products, services, or brands by analyzing data sources like social media posts, customer reviews, and survey responses. Automated sentiment processing offers real-time feedback, supporting strategic decisions in marketing, product development, and customer relations. Modern sentiment analysis methods have progressed from basic lexicon-based approaches that depend on predefined lists of positive and negative words to advanced ML and deep learning models that use context-aware embeddings and transformers, improving accuracy and managing linguistic complexities such as sarcasm or irony, and negation, making sentiment detection more accurate. For example, transformer-based sentiment models can differentiate between "I can't believe how fast the delivery was" and "I can't believe how slow the delivery was," correctly capturing opposite sentiments despite similar phrasing.

Advances in ML and deep learning have significantly improved sentiment classification accuracy by capturing contextual meaning and polarity beyond simple word counts. Topic modeling, another key NLP technique, is used to uncover latent themes and patterns within large document collections, allowing organizations to identify emerging trends, strategic issues, and areas of concern without prior labeling.[14] Furthermore, topic modeling has been applied to analyze management discussion and analysis (MD&A), sustainability reports, and analyst communications to assess disclosure strategies, risk narratives, and corporate priorities. Alongside sentiment analysis, topic modeling functions as an unsupervised learning method designed to uncover hidden themes within large text collections. By automatically identifying topics or themes, this approach helps categorize and summarize extensive documents, improving information retrieval, customer feedback analysis, and competitive intelligence. Techniques like Latent Dirichlet Allocation (LDA) and Non-negative Matrix Factorization (NMF) identify hidden themes within large corpora.[15] These methods segment documents into topics based on word co-occurrence patterns, while modern approaches use neural embeddings for better coherence and interpretability. These techniques enable organizations to spot emerging trends, monitor brand perceptions, and assess customer concerns without manual effort. Businesses use these insights to detect new market trends, evaluate campaign success, and refine customer segmentation. When combined with sentiment analysis, topic modeling offers a multidimensional view of consumer opinions, supporting data-driven strategic decision-making.

The integration of sentiment analysis and topic modeling within NLP pipelines provides organizations with a multidimensional understanding of customer opinions segmented by thematic content. For example, applying sentiment analysis to review data annotated by topics enables businesses to not only identify overall customer satisfaction but also identify specific features or services that trigger positive or negative reactions. This granular approach facilitates targeted actions such as product changes or marketing campaigns aligned with customer needs. Moreover, these techniques are used across various sectors, including finance, healthcare, and legal fields, where extracting relevant information from financial reports, clinical notes, or legal documents can drive operational efficiency and support strategic decision-making. Together, sentiment analysis and topic modeling enable data-driven decision-making by transforming qualitative text into structured insights that support strategic planning, market intelligence, risk management, and performance evaluation across industries.

7.6 Sequence-to-Sequence Models and Their Applications

Sequence-to-sequence (Seq2Seq) models have fundamentally changed the field of NLP by allowing flexible, end-to-end mapping of input sequences to output sequences. Seq2Seq models are integral components of neural architectures in NLP designed to map an input sequence to an output sequence of variable length, making them well-suited for tasks involving transformation or generation of sequential data. Originally developed for machine translation, these models have been successfully adapted to a wide range of applications, including social media, where generating and transforming text is crucial. The Seq2Seq architecture generally includes an encoder and a decoder, often implemented with RNNs or, more recently, transformer-based architectures that encode an input sequence into a fixed or contextual representation and then decode it into a target sequence, enabling applications such as machine translation, text summarization, speech recognition, and dialogue systems.[16] Traditionally based on encoder-decoder structures using RNNs, Seq2Seq models saw significant improvements with the addition of attention mechanisms.[17] These enhancements enabled models to concentrate on relevant parts of the input when producing outputs. The advent of the transformer architecture further transformed Seq2Seq tasks by introducing self-attention, which allows for parallel processing and better contextual understanding. More recently, transformer-based architectures have extended the Seq2Seq paradigm by replacing recurrence with self-attention, leading to substantial gains in efficiency and accuracy across large-scale language tasks. Today, these models support applications like social media analytics, where the need for efficient summarization, translation, and response generation arises from large, multilingual, and dynamic datasets.

7.7 Applications of NLP in Business

NLP has emerged as an essential tool across various business sectors, especially in legal, financial, and customer service areas, leading to notable improvements in efficiency and decision-making. Particularly, NLP has become a critical enabler of data-driven decision-making in business by transforming large volumes of unstructured text into actionable insights across legal, financial, and customer service domains. In the legal field, NLP is widely used for contract analytics, legal document review, e-discovery, and compliance monitoring, significantly reducing manual effort and improving accuracy in identifying risks, obligations, and relevant precedents. Its techniques facilitate the automation of tasks such as document analysis, extracting important information, and summarizing long documents to support faster and more accurate decisions. Advanced NLP models have shown success in predicting court decisions by analyzing legal texts, thus supporting lawyers and judges in managing large volumes of complex legal information effectively.[18] Automated text classification and semantic analysis assist in extracting relevant legal entities and understanding the context of statutes and precedents, enabling faster and more accurate legal research while reducing human error and labor costs. Moreover, by leveraging ML and neural network architectures, legal NLP applications can facilitate contract analysis, compliance monitoring, and risk assessment, which are vital in a heavily regulated environment.

In the financial sector, NLP plays an equally transformative role, especially in processing and interpreting large volumes of unstructured financial texts, including earnings reports, financial statements, and news articles. Its applications include sentiment analysis of earnings calls and news, automated analysis of financial disclosures, fraud detection, and risk assessment, helping investors, auditors, and regulators interpret qualitative information that complements quantitative financial data.[19] The use of sentiment analysis on text, combined with domain-specific dictionaries designed for financial contexts, enables the extraction of sentiment and risk-related insights that support investment decisions and market analysis.[20] Integrating NLP models into financial workflows allows for the automated parsing of complex documents such as 10-K filings, increasing the speed and accuracy of assessing financial disclosures. Furthermore, the adoption of pre-trained models and transfer learning techniques improves the ability of systems to generalize across various financial instruments and use cases, leading to better predictive analytics for market movements and credit risk. These applications have important implications for portfolio management, fraud detection, and regulatory reporting, helping financial institutions operate with enhanced agility and compliance. Sentiment analysis of financial texts further aids investment decisions by gauging market sentiment.

Customer service is another important area where NLP applications greatly enhance user experience and operational efficiency, as NLP, through chatbots, virtual assistants, and automated ticket classification systems, can enhance customer experience by providing real-time, personalized, and scalable support. The rise of dialogue systems powered by seq2seq and end-to-end neural network architectures has transformed how companies communicate with customers. These systems enable automated, real-time responses to customer questions, using hybrid methods that combine symbolic approaches with neural models to leverage the strengths of both.[21] Especially, question-answering agents that can query large knowledge bases simplify customer interactions by eliminating the need for manual query formulation, thus making information more accessible. Neural machine reading comprehension (MRC) models further improve answer accuracy, surpassing traditional keyword-based search engines in providing concise and contextually relevant responses. Additionally, reinforcement learning and deep learning techniques have been explored to optimize dialogue strategies, allowing systems to adapt quickly to different customer behaviors and complex conversation flows with minimal human input. These advancements have elevated conversational agents from basic chatbots to practical tools such as personalized recommendations, complaint resolution, and transactional support. Overall, advances in deep learning and large language models have further expanded these applications by enabling contextual understanding, natural language generation, and conversational intelligence across industries. Collectively, NLP applications in legal, financial, and customer service functions improve operational efficiency, decision quality, and stakeholder engagement, underscoring NLP's strategic importance in modern business analytics.

7.8 Deep Learning and Neural Networks

As discussed in previous chapters, deep learning is a subfield of ML that focuses on training artificial neural networks with multiple hidden layers to automatically learn hierarchical representations from large and complex datasets, whereas neural networks consist of interconnected neurons that transform inputs through weighted connections and nonlinear activation functions, enabling models to capture intricate patterns in data such as images, text, speech, and time series. Deep learning and neural networks represent a major shift in the field of NLP and AI, characterized by their ability to learn hierarchical feature representations from raw data through layered architectures. Originating from the basic perceptron model, which was limited in solving simple functions like the logical XOR, advances in neural network design introduced hidden layers, leading to multi-layer perceptrons and deep neural networks capable of modeling complex, nonlinear data relationships. These deep structures facilitate automatic feature extraction, eliminating the need for manual feature engineering, and have proven highly effective across various NLP tasks, from text classification to machine translation.

The strength of deep learning in NLP mainly stems from its capacity to represent words, phrases, and sentences as continuous, low-dimensional vectors. These vectors encode semantic and syntactic details that traditional discrete representations struggle to capture. This distributed representation underpins advanced neural architectures like RNNs, LSTMs, and the newer transformer models, which employ attention mechanisms to identify long-range dependencies in sequences. These innovations have resulted in models that significantly outperform traditional methods by better understanding context and managing the sequential nature of language. Transformers, specifically, have transformed the field by replacing recurrent structures with self-attention mechanisms that enable parallel processing of input sequences, solving issues related to long-range dependency modeling and the computational inefficiency of earlier recurrent models. The introduction of bidirectional training, as seen in models like BERT, allows for a contextual understanding of language inputs by considering the full surrounding context in both directions, thereby improving semantic comprehension necessary for complex language tasks. Such models typically undergo pre-training on large datasets using unsupervised objectives and later fine-tune on task-specific data, facilitating transfer learning and reducing the need for extensive labeled datasets.

Deep learning architectures go beyond classification and sequence labeling to include generative tasks like dialogue systems, MRC, and text summarization, using encoder-decoder frameworks that convert inputs into structured outputs. These models learn complex input–output relationships without manual steps but face challenges in interpretability, data needs, and handling ambiguous inputs. External knowledge bases via memory-augmented networks and attention mechanisms have been explored to improve reasoning and factual accuracy. Despite significant progress in deep learning and neural networks, the field still faces challenges related to model efficiency, scalability, and fairness. Large models necessitate substantial computational resources and energy, leading to research focused on model compression and more efficient training methods. Furthermore, biases in training data can be unintentionally learned by these models, requiring ongoing efforts in debiasing and ethical AI development. Nevertheless, the transformative influence of deep learning on NLP is clear, offering unprecedented tools for understanding and generating human language and expanding the boundaries of machine intelligence.

7.9 Supply Chain Optimization with Machine Learning

ML has become a powerful and effective enabler of supply chain optimization by enhancing organizations' ability to forecast demand, assess risk, manage inventory, optimize logistics, and improve end-to-end operational efficiency in complex and uncertain environments. Unlike conventional optimization models that mainly rely on static assumptions, ML techniques leverage large volumes of historical and real-time data to identify nonlinear patterns and adapt dynamically to changing market conditions.[22] While supply chains are often associated with logistics, inventory, and transportation data, a significant portion of critical information exists in unstructured text emails, supplier updates, shipping logs, customs forms, and risk reports. ML and NLP are increasingly used to extract insights from this text, enabling smarter, more responsive supply chain decisions.

Traditional supply chain analytics rely on structured data like delivery times or stock levels. However, delays are often announced in emails with phrases like "port congestion," "customs hold," or "weather disruption." ML models, enhanced with NLP, can scan these communications to predict delays, assess risks, and trigger early warnings. Supervised learning models are widely used for demand forecasting and lead-time prediction, while unsupervised learning supports supplier segmentation, anomaly detection, and risk identification across supply networks.[23] For example, an ML system can flag a supplier email stating "production halted due to equipment failure" and automatically adjust inventory forecasts or reroute orders. Such applications benefit significantly from advances in transformer-based models and deep learning techniques (BERT, GPT) that improve the capacity to process and summarize large volumes of textual data accurately and efficiently. Integrating ML into supply chain optimization has transformed traditional methods by providing more accurate predictions, flexible decision-making, and greater operational efficiency. ML models analyze large amounts of data generated throughout the supply chain, from procurement and production to distribution and inventory management, to recognize patterns and support informed decisions. Their ability to learn from historical data and adapt dynamically allows for more agile and resilient supply chains that can better handle uncertainties in demand forecasting, capacity planning, and logistics.[24]

ML greatly improves demand forecasting by modeling complex, nonlinear relationships and integrating diverse data sources like sales history, promotional activities, economic indicators, and social media sentiment. Unlike traditional linear models, deep learning architectures such as recurrent neural networks and transformers effectively capture temporal dependencies and external market influences. This improves forecasting accuracy, enabling optimized inventory management that balances stock levels to prevent overstocking and stockouts, thus reducing costs and improving service. In logistics, ML algorithms, including reinforcement learning, optimize routing and vehicle scheduling by adapting to real-time factors like traffic and vehicle availability. This flexible adjustment helps reduce delivery times and operational costs. Also, predictive maintenance models use ML to track equipment health and predict failures in warehouses, manufacturing tools, and transport fleets, cutting down downtime and maintenance costs. ML also improves supplier selection and risk management by analyzing both structured and unstructured data to evaluate supplier reliability and geopolitical threats, strengthening supply chain resilience. Additionally, production scheduling benefits from ML's capacity to manage complex dependencies among variables, optimizing lead times, changeover costs, and quality.

Emphasizing AI-driven risk management is becoming essential in global supply chains, where disruptions from pandemics to geopolitical events are increasingly common.[25] By applying NLP to news feeds, social media, and regulatory updates, companies can detect emerging risks in real time. A manufacturer might learn of a factory shutdown in Asia through a local news article before official notifications arrive, allowing proactive adjustments. This reflects the growing importance of NLP in extracting timely and relevant information from diverse unstructured sources, which improves decision-making and operational responsiveness. Moreover, contract analysis using NLP helps procurement teams monitor supplier obligations, delivery terms, and penalties. ML models can classify contracts by risk level or highlight deviations from standard clauses, reducing compliance issues.

Predictive analytics also benefits from NLP. By combining text data (e.g., supplier communication sentiment) with historical performance, ML models can forecast supplier reliability. For instance, repeated use of phrases like "possible delay" or "under review" in emails might correlate with future late shipments, enabling preemptive action. This dual use of sentiment analysis and predictive modeling highlights NLP's role in sentiment detection and enhanced forecasting within supply chain management.[26] When integrated with NLP, these systems gain a deeper understanding of the "why" behind data patterns, not just the "what." This reflects the evolving trend toward hybrid models that combine extractive and abstractive NLP techniques to generate balanced and contextually accurate insights from complex datasets. Reinforcement learning has further advanced supply chain decision-making by enabling continuous optimization of inventory policies, transportation routing, and production scheduling through trial-and-error learning in simulated environments.[27] Furthermore, deep learning models have improved forecasting accuracy and resilience planning by capturing complex temporal and spatial dependencies across multi-tier supply chains.[28] Overall, ML-driven supply chain optimization enhances responsiveness, cost efficiency, and robustness, making it a critical capability for organizations facing increasing volatility, regulatory, globalization, and sustainability pressures.

7.10 NLP in Business Use Cases

NLP has become a powerful enabling technology for business applications that relies on understanding and generating human language at scale through chatbots, social media analytics, and voice assistants. In customer service and sales, NLP-powered chatbots and virtual agents use intent classification, dialogue management, and retrieval/generation methods to handle routine inquiries, triage support tickets, and personalize recommendations, reducing response times while freeing human agents for complex cases.[29] In marketing and risk/intelligence functions, social media analytics applies sentiment analysis, topic modeling, and stance/emotion detection to monitor brand perception, identify emerging issues, and support competitive and crisis surveillance; however, managers must account for domain shift, sarcasm/irony, and demographic or platform-driven biases that can distort inference from online text. Voice assistants extend NLP into speech-driven workflows by combining automatic speech recognition with natural language understanding and natural language generation to enable hands-free task execution (e.g., scheduling, order status, knowledge lookup) and to support accessibility and frontline operations (e.g., retail, logistics, healthcare). With the introduction of chatbots, social media analytics, and voice assistants, NLP has become more important in changing various business applications. NLP-powered chatbots have transformed customer service by delivering context-aware, personalized interactions.[30] They offer businesses an automated yet interactive channel that significantly enhances customer engagement and service efficiency. These conversational agents leverage advanced NLP models, such as transformer-based architectures, to comprehend and respond to diverse user queries effectively, thereby reducing the reliance on human customer support while maintaining a high level of user satisfaction.

Unlike traditional rule-based systems, modern chatbots use transformer models to understand intent and generate natural responses. Chatbots are virtual agents that interact with customers via text or voice. Powered by NLP, they understand user queries, determine intent, and generate appropriate responses. In customer service, chatbots handle routine inquiries such as checking order status, resetting passwords, or booking appointments, freeing human agents for complex issues. The evolution from rule-based systems to neural network approaches, including models like BERT and GPT, has been instrumental in improving the contextual understanding and generation capabilities of chatbots, enabling more natural and meaningful interactions. NLP-driven chatbots reduce response times and operational costs while maintaining high satisfaction rates. Advanced chatbots use Seq2Seq models and transformer architectures (like BERT or GPT) to deliver more natural, context-aware conversations. For example, a banking chatbot can remember earlier parts of a conversation ("I was asking about my mortgage") and provide coherent follow-up answers. NLP-driven chatbots and virtual assistants improve customer support by efficiently understanding and responding to queries, leading to better service quality and customer satisfaction, which positively impacts brand reputation. Modern chatbots, including commercial personal assistants like Amazon Alexa, Google Assistant, Facebook M, and Microsoft Cortana, function as hybrid systems using statistical methods such as intent classification along with hand-crafted rules. This approach enhances robustness and allows handling of tasks like personal assistance and casual chitchat, for example, telling jokes or answering common queries. These systems exemplify the integration of data-driven AI with domain-specific engineered components to balance flexibility and reliability.

Chatbots broadly fall into two categories: task-oriented bots and social (chitchat) bots. Task-oriented chatbots focus on helping users achieve specific goals, such as making restaurant reservations or scheduling meetings. These bots typically use modular architectures with access to external databases for retrieving and managing relevant information, enabling them to handle structured dialogues efficiently. In contrast, social chatbots prioritize human-like conversational abilities to provide companionship and entertainment. They rely heavily on deep neural network models trained on large datasets of human conversations, generating responses designed to mimic natural interaction. Recently, there has been progress in grounding these chats with contextual information like world knowledge and images to enrich the conversation and make it more engaging. Microsoft's development of a chitchat chatbot highlights the trend of building chatbots that sustain engaging and fluid conversations. While early chatbots relied primarily on data-driven response generation, incorporating additional contextual elements such as real-world knowledge has increasingly become a focus. This evolution helps make chatbot interactions more meaningful and interesting for users, moving beyond simple scripted dialogues.

Furthermore, the integration of conversational AI into QA systems has advanced significantly. Leading technology companies like Google, Microsoft, and Baidu have embedded multi-turn QA capabilities into their search engines, enhancing the conversational user experience, particularly on mobile devices. Publicly known examples, such as Bing QA and Satori QA, demonstrate how architectures combining natural language understanding with information retrieval facilitate accurate and context-aware responses. This convergence of chatbots and QA systems highlights the broad utility and impact of conversational AI across different domains. For example, in customer service, chatbots provide instant support by answering common questions and resolving issues without human intervention. In healthcare, conversational agents assist patients by answering medical queries, scheduling appointments, and offering personalized health advice. The finance sector utilizes chatbots to help users manage accounts, process transactions, and access financial data securely. E-commerce platforms employ AI chatbots for product recommendations, order tracking, and customer engagement. Additionally, educational technologies leverage conversational AI to offer tutoring, language learning, and interactive study assistance. These examples demonstrate how conversational AI enhances user experience and operational efficiency across diverse real-world applications.

Similarly, social media analytics use NLP to extract actionable insights from large amounts of unstructured text data generated across platforms, to monitor brand health, detect trends, and engage audiences at scale. It involves systematic collection, measurement, and analysis of data generated from social media platforms to extract actionable insights regarding user behavior, opinions, trends, and influence. By understanding user preferences through NLP, platforms like Amazon, YouTube, and Netflix tailor recommendations that enhance customer engagement with their brand, fostering loyalty and personalized experiences.[31] The proliferation of social media has provided unprecedented volumes of real-time, user-generated content rich in demographic, sentiment, and relational information, which organizations and researchers leverage to understand and predict social dynamics, market patterns, and public sentiment. Sentiment analysis, topic modeling, and trend detection are common techniques used to measure public opinion, monitor brand reputation, guide marketing strategies, and track consumer trends in real time. By processing language that considers semantics and syntactic structures, these models can detect subtle nuances in consumer feedback, helping businesses make data-driven decisions quickly and accurately. Current research highlights the importance of pre-trained language models in improving the robustness and flexibility of these analytical tools, especially when dealing with the informal and changing language typical of social media contexts. During a public relations incident, companies can use NLP to track the spread of misinformation, identify influential voices, and prioritize engagement strategies. Companies use sentiment analysis and topic modeling to analyze millions of posts on platforms like Twitter, Facebook, and Reddit. During a product launch, a brand can track sentiment in real time, identifying praise, complaints, or viral memes. Highlighting how social media analytics transforms unstructured chatter into strategic insights, helping marketers refine messaging and respond to crises quickly. Social media has transformed the marketing landscape, requiring organizations to adopt real-time monitoring and agile response mechanisms. Tools like Brandwatch or Hootsuite use NLP to categorize mentions, identify influencers, and measure campaign impact. NLP-powered dashboards enable marketing and PR teams to visualize sentiment trends, detect emerging issues, and measure campaign effectiveness, turning unstructured chatter into strategic intelligence.

Multimodal recommendation engines leverage NLP to analyze and understand textual data alongside other modalities such as images, voice, and video. NLP processes various forms of user-generated text, including reviews, queries, product descriptions, and voice commands, extracting meaningful insights that enhance the recommendation system's comprehension of user intent and product attributes. For example, voice-activated platforms like Amazon Alexa and Google Assistant use NLP to interpret spoken queries and provide personalized recommendations based on natural language input.[32] Additionally, NLP can work together with computer vision by analyzing captions, metadata, or spoken content within videos, enabling the system to offer more contextually relevant product suggestions. NLP enables multimodal recommendation engines to comprehend and utilize textual and spoken inputs harmoniously with other data modalities. It facilitates conversational interfaces via voice or chatbots, making it easier and more engaging for users to interact with recommendation systems. This results in highly accurate, personalized, and user-friendly recommendations, transforming how users discover products and engage with digital platforms. NLP expands the types of data the system can interpret, going beyond visual or numeric data, thus improving the robustness and flexibility of the recommendation engine and contributing to a richer and more nuanced user profile, enabling hyper-personalized product discovery experiences.

Voice assistants like Amazon Alexa, Google Assistant, Microsoft Cortana, and Apple's Siri use NLP to understand spoken commands, enabling smooth interactions and improving accessibility. NLP fosters business innovation by allowing human-like voice interactions. These assistants enable users to interact with devices naturally through voice commands, understanding spoken language, processing the intent, and providing relevant responses or performing tasks. These systems rely on speech recognition combined with advanced language understanding to interpret and perform commands, providing hands-free experiences across many devices. Progress in transfer learning and unified text-to-text transformers has increased the scalability and language coverage of voice assistants, making them more accessible and effective in various commercial environments. Companies incorporate voice technology into customer support and smart settings to improve user experiences. Despite these advances, issues with domain-specific understanding and resolving ambiguity still exist, indicating ongoing chances for research and development to refine further NLP-driven business applications. Voice assistants typically rely on wake words (e.g., "OK Google") to activate the system, after which NLP components interpret the user's input, manage dialogue state, and determine appropriate actions. Advances in NLP have significantly improved the accuracy and fluency of voice assistants, making them essential tools for hands-free information retrieval, task automation, and enhanced user experiences. Furthermore, platforms such as Microsoft's Task Completion Platform, Amazon's Alexa Skills Kit, and IBM's Watson Assistant provide developers with robust tools to create and customize multi-domain dialogue systems, further expanding the capabilities and applications of voice assistants in both consumer and enterprise settings. When a user says, "Order more paper towels," the system converts speech to text, extracts intent, and triggers an action. These assistants are increasingly used in smart offices and homes, but also in business settings, for example, retrieving sales reports or scheduling meetings via voice. Voice interfaces improve accessibility and efficiency, especially in hands-free environments like warehouses or call centers. Together, these use cases show how NLP connects human communication with digital systems. They enable 24/7 customer engagement, real-time decision-making, and scalable insights, transforming how businesses interact with customers and internal teams. Collectively, across these use cases, modern transformer-based language models have substantially improved accuracy and fluency, but responsible deployment still requires governance around privacy, security, explainability, and performance monitoring to avoid harmful or noncompliant outcomes.

7.11 Summary

This chapter introduces text analytics and NLP techniques for extracting business insights from unstructured data. Applications include social media analysis, chatbots, and sentiment detection. This chapter also shows how businesses can analyze unstructured text data using NLP. This chapter provides a comprehensive overview of NLP, a subfield of AI that enables machines to understand, interpret, and generate human language. It begins by introducing the core objectives of NLP, including language recognition, sentiment analysis, machine translation, and conversational AI. The chapter explores foundational concepts such as syntax, semantics, tokenization, stemming, lemmatization, and part-of-speech tagging. Key NLP techniques are discussed, including rule-based methods, statistical approaches, and modern ML models such as word embeddings, transformers, and LLMs. Practical applications of NLP are examined in business contexts such as customer service (chatbots), market intelligence (text mining), compliance (document classification), and accessibility (speech-to-text and text-to-speech systems). The chapter also addresses the challenges of NLP, including ambiguity, cultural context, sarcasm, and ethical concerns such as bias in language models. It concludes with an exploration of emerging trends and future directions in NLP, highlighting its growing importance in building more intelligent, human-centric AI systems that can process and respond to natural language with increasing sophistication and accuracy. Students explore key concepts and technologies powering chatbots, sentiment analysis, and text mining.

Notes

1 Vaswani, A., Shazeer, N., Parmar, N., Uszkoreit, J., Jones, L., Gomez, A. N., … Polosukhin, I. (2017). Attention is all you need. *Advances in Neural Information Processing Systems*, 30, 5998–6008. Available at https://proceedings.neurips.cc/paper/2017/hash/3f5ee243547dee91fbd053c1c4a845aa-Abstract.html

2 Brown, T. B., Mann, B., Ryder, N., Subbiah, M., Kaplan, J., Dhariwal, P., … Amodei, D. (2020). Language models are few-shot learners. *Advances in Neural Information Processing Systems*, 33, 1877–1901. Available at https://proceedings.neurips.cc/paper_files/paper/2020/hash/1457c0d6bfcb4967418bfb8ac142f64a-Abstract.html?utm_source=transaction&utm_medium=email&utm_campaign=linkedin_newsletter

3 Porter, M. F. (1980). An algorithm for suffix stripping. *Program*, 14(3), 130–137. https://doi.org/10.1108/eb046814. Available at https://www.emerald.com/dta/article-abstract/14/3/130/328346/An-algorithm-for-suffix-stripping?redirectedFrom=fulltext

4 Salton, G., & Buckley, C. (1988). Term-weighting approaches in automatic text retrieval. *Information Processing & Management*, 24(5), 513–523. https://doi.org/10.1016/0306-4573(88)90021-0. Available at https://www.sciencedirect.com/science/article/abs/pii/0306457388900210

5 Kowsari, K., Jafari Meimandi, K., Heidarysafa, M., Mendu, S., Barnes, L., & Brown, D. (2019). Text classification algorithms: A survey. *Information*, 10(4), 150. https://doi.org/10.3390/info10040150. Available at https://www.mdpi.com/2078-2489/10/4/150?source=post_page

6 Sennrich, R., Haddow, B., & Birch, A. (2016). Neural machine translation of rare words with subword units. In *Proceedings of the 54th Annual Meeting of the Association for Computational Linguistics* (Volume 1: Long Papers, pp. 1715–1725). Association for Computational Linguistics. Available at https://aclanthology.org/P16-1162.pdf

7 Sawicki, J., Ganzha, M., & Paprzycki, M. (2023). The state of the art of natural language processing – A systematic automated review of NLP literature using NLP techniques. *Data Intelligence*, 5(3), 707–749. https://doi.org/10.1162/dint_a_00213. Available at https://direct.mit.edu/dint/article/5/3/707/115133/The-State-of-the-Art-of-Natural-Language

8 Siino, M., Tinnirello, I., & La Cascia, M. (2025). From foundations to GPT in text classification: A comprehensive survey on current approaches and future trends. *Foundations and Trends® in Information Retrieval*, 19(5), 557–711. https://doi.org/10.1561/1500000107. Available at https://www.emerald.com/ftinr/article-abstract/19/5/557/1331515/From-Foundations-to-GPT-in-Text-Classification-A?redirectedFrom=fulltext

9 Devlin, J., Chang, M. W., Lee, K., & Toutanova, K. (2019). BERT: Pre-training of deep bidirectional transformers for language understanding. NAACL-HLT. https://doi.org/10.18653/v1/N19-1423. Available at https://aclanthology.org/N19-1423/?utm_campaign=The+Batch&utm_source=hs_email&utm_medium=email&_hsenc=p2ANqtz-_m9bbH_7ECE1h3lZ3D61TYg52rKpifVNjL4fvJ85uqggrXsWDBTB7YooFLJeNXHWqhvOyC

10 Pennington, J., Socher, R., & Manning, C. D. (2014). GloVe: Global vectors for word representation. In *Proceedings of the 2014 Conference on Empirical Methods in Natural Language Processing (EMNLP)* (Vol. 14, pp. 1532–1543). Association for Computational Linguistics. Available at https://aclanthology.org/D14-1162.pdf

11 Mikolov, T., Chen, K., Corrado, G., & Dean, J. (2013). Efficient estimation of word representations in vector space. arXiv preprint arXiv:1301.3781. https://doi.org/10.48550/arXiv.1301.3781. Available at https://arxiv.org/abs/1301.3781

12 Pang, B., & Lee, L. (2008). Opinion mining and sentiment analysis. *Foundations and Trends in Information Retrieval*, 2(1–2), 1–135. Available at https://aclanthology.org/anthology-files/anthology-files/pdf/J/J09/J09-2007.pdf

13 Cambria, E., Schuller, B., Xia, Y., & Havasi, C. (2017). New avenues in opinion mining and sentiment analysis. *IEEE Intelligent Systems*, 28(2), 15–21. https://doi.org/10.1109/MIS.2013.30. Available at https://ieeexplore.ieee.org/abstract/document/6468032?casa_token=3AfQPrGpOIEAAAAA:KiYoZH-j52DDdi4sZFOL5Z-iSv_Y9tolOTQffcwjjotr8hiqGIthQVRruVfgl_RgPQmKjAC7CV4

14 Blei, D. M., Ng, A. Y., & Jordan, M. I. (2003). Latent Dirichlet allocation. *Journal of Machine Learning Research*, 3, 993–1022. Available at https://www.jmlr.org/papers/volume3/blei03a/blei03a.pdf

15 Blei, D. M., Ng, A. Y., & Jordan, M. I. (2003). Latent Dirichlet allocation. *Journal of Machine Learning Research*, 3, 993–1022. Available at https://www.jmlr.org/papers/volume3/blei03a/blei03a.pdf

16 Sutskever, I., Vinyals, O., & Le, Q. V. (2014). Sequence to sequence learning with neural networks. *Advances in Neural Information Processing Systems*, 27, 3104–3112. Available at https://proceedings.neurips.cc/paper_files/paper/2014/hash/5a18e133cbf9f257297f410bb7eca942-Abstract.html

17 Bahdanau, D., Cho, K., & Bengio, Y. (2015). Neural machine translation by jointly learning to align and translate. arXiv preprint arXiv:1409.0473. Available at https://abaj.ai/doc/papers/1409.0473v7.pdf

18 Aletras, N., Stergiou, S., & Jurafsky, D. (2016). Predicting judicial decisions of the European Court of Human Rights: A natural language processing perspective. *PeerJ Computer Science*, 2, e93. Available at https://peerj.com/articles/cs-93.pdf

19 Kearney, C., & Liu, S. (2014). Textual sentiment in finance: A survey of methods and models. *International Review of Financial Analysis*, 33, 171–185. https://doi.org/10.1016/j.irfa.2014.02.006. Available at https://www.sciencedirect.com/science/article/pii/S1057521914000295?casa_token=RhILhsLrUIkAAAAA:tbpJZFSLrK6_GxpovpYpnDsJcgiAZ3Lm1lQf-xte8psYI8wF2kChVX1maKq0u2za5AUpK48Rzps

20 Loughran, T., & Mcdonald, B. (2011). When is a liability not a liability? Textual analysis, dictionaries, and 10-Ks. *The Journal of Finance*, 66, 35–65. https://doi.org/10.1111/j.1540-6261.2010.01625.x. Available at https://onlinelibrary.wiley.com/doi/abs/10.1111/j.1540-6261.2010.01625.x?casa_token=yOtdRmUJUlgAAAAA%3AZxq-RxbL42jiXez4Z2-xvts70EbBhq7qICw7EIlVoVjDTrGCiFlIvTk-nkj1PyWBEl_4LLHpz1xpdKYh

21 Gao, J., Galley, M., & Li, L. (2019). Neural approaches to conversational AI: Question answering, task-oriented dialogues and social chatbots, now foundations and trends. In *SIGIR'18: The 41st International ACM SIGIR Conference on Research & Development in Information Retrieval* (pp. 1371–1374). https://doi.org/10.1145/3209978.3210183. Available at https://dl.acm.org/doi/abs/10.1145/3209978.3210183

22 Choi, T. M., Wallace, S. W., & Wang, Y. (2018). Big data analytics in operations management. *Production and Operations Management*, 27(10), 1868–1883. https://doi.org/10.1111/poms.12838. Available at https://journals.sagepub.com/doi/full/10.1111/poms.12838?casa_token=Kzv8ClZSq04AAAAA%3AUJ1IEieNft02WS2j31FybWdoyncqv8eahGzPlvR-jswyVLICBLXHIz3bbsVhly0EuoPfBv_rbaRLYA

23 Carbonneau, R., Laframboise, K., & Vahidov, R. (2008). Application of machine learning techniques for supply chain demand forecasting. *European Journal of Operational Research*, 184(3), 1140–1154. https://doi.org/10.1016/j.ejor.2006.12.004. Available at https://www.sciencedirect.com/science/article/pii/S0377221706012057?casa_token=8oYPvmT2DdsAAAAA:3w6os8EI7JeLwtTUNw-KAnzTLyA6YRpo3xAsJZgnsQgSi50WXHA6ThmR_PdJXB8G4ZqA1VYmiBY

24 Wang, G., Gunasekaran, A., Ngai, E. W., & Papadopoulos, T. (2020). Big data analytics in logistics and supply chain management. *International Journal of Production Economics*, 176, 98–110. https://doi.org/10.1016/j.ijpe.2016.03.014. Available at https://www.sciencedirect.com/science/article/abs/pii/S0925527316300056

25 Sadeek, S. N., & Hanaoka, S. (2023). Assessment of text-generated supply chain risks considering news and social media during disruptive events. *Social Network Analysis and Mining*, 13(1), 96. https://doi.org/10.1007/s13278-023-01100-0. Available at https://link.springer.com/article/10.1007/s13278-023-01100-0

26 Deiva Ganesh, A., & Kalpana, P. (2022). Supply chain risk identification: A real-time data-mining approach. *Industrial Management & Data Systems*, 122(5), 1333–1354. https://doi.org/10.1108/IMDS-11-2021-0719. Available at https://www.emerald.com/imds/article-abstract/122/5/1333/180050/Supply-chain-risk-identification-a-real-time-data?redirectedFrom=fulltext

27 Ivanov, D., Dolgui, A., & Sokolov, B. (2019). The impact of digital technology and Industry 4.0 on the ripple effect and supply chain risk analytics. *International Journal of Production Research*, 57(3), 829–846. https://doi.org/10.1080/00207543.2018.1488086. Available at https://www.tandfonline.com/doi/abs/10.1080/00207543.2018.1488086

28 Min, H., Zacharia, Z. G., & Smith, C. D. (2019). Defining supply chain management: In the past, present, and future. *Journal of Business Logistics*, 40(1), 44–55. https://doi.org/10.1111/jbl.12201. Available at https://onlinelibrary.wiley.com/doi/abs/10.1111/jbl.12201?casa_token=92iU51YVcQgAAAAA:cSiK9pJjHmdUsmLiISSG65HzJYiXNuRCpqTT2zTh9SjrDavVTwEB67oV3c1568GB_BDS_eykryHvFWvI

29 Huang, M., Zhou, L., & Yang, D. (2007). Extracting chatbot knowledge from online discussion forums. In *Proceedings of IJCAI* (pp. 423–428). Available at https://www.researchgate.net/profile/Jizhou-Huang-5/publication/220813357_Extracting_Chatbot_Knowledge_from_Online_Discussion_Forums/links/5eaa6a8f92851cb2676665ba/Extracting-Chatbot-Knowledge-from-Online-Discussion-Forums.pdf

30 Fadhil, A., & Gabrielli, S. (2017). Addressing challenges in promoting healthy lifestyles: The AI chatbot approach. In *Proceedings of the 11th EAI International Conference on Pervasive Computing Technologies*. https://doi.org/10.1145/3154862.3154914. Available at https://dl.acm.org/doi/abs/10.1145/3154862.3154914

31 Abishek, M. N., & Keren Judi, E. (2025). A study on exploring consumer engagement with AI-driven experiences on Netflix streaming platform. In *International Conference on Artificial Intelligence in Commerce and Management* (pp. 93–100). Available at https://www.shanlaxpublications.com/p/ICAICM-2025/ch013.pdf

32 SuperAGI. (2025). The Future of Product Discovery: Trends and Innovations in AI Recommendation Engines for 2025 and Beyond. Available at https://superagi.com/the-future-of-product-discovery-trends-and-innovations-in-ai-recommendation-engines-for-2025-and-beyond/

8 Prescriptive Analytics and Optimization

Learning Objectives

- Learn linear optimization models
- Understand integer linear optimization models
- Learn nonlinear optimization models
- Understand simulation modeling techniques
- Differentiate between linear, nonlinear, and integer programming
- Apply ML in optimization scenarios
- Learn the use of prescriptive analytics in supply chain optimization, pricing strategies, scheduling, logistics, marketing, and operations management

8.1 Introduction

Prescriptive analytics and optimization play an important role in today's data-driven world, enabling organizations to understand past performance and predict future outcomes in making informed decisions that drive optimal results. This chapter presents prescriptive analytics and optimization that go beyond descriptive and predictive analytics by (1) providing actionable recommendations and decision options to achieve specific objectives; (2) combining data, mathematical models, and business rules to suggest the best course of action in complex scenarios; and (3) finding the most efficient and effective solution to a problem, often under constraints. Optimization techniques presented in this chapter enable organizations to improve resource allocation, enhance operational efficiency and effectiveness, maximize profits, and minimize costs by making data-driven decisions that align with their strategic plans and stated goals. This chapter also provides (1) integrated tools from operations research, ML, simulation, and AI to address real-world issues and challenges across all industries of supply chain management, healthcare, finance, marketing, and logistics; and (2) prescriptive analytics and optimization techniques that assist organizations to transform raw data into actionable insights in maintaining their sustainability performance and staying competitive in an increasingly complex and dynamic environment.

DOI: 10.4324/9781003664550-8

8.2 Essentials of Prescriptive Analytics and Optimization

Essential prescriptive analytics and optimization refer to the advanced frontier of AI and BA in providing organizations with powerful tools to predict future outcomes and to recommend the best possible actions to achieve strategic plans and desired objectives. While predictive analytics models, presented in Chapter 9, focus on forecasting what might happen, prescriptive analytics go a step further by analyzing various decision scenarios and their potential impacts, thus enabling organizations to identify optimal strategies and solutions with available resources under given constraints. This involves the use of mathematical optimization techniques such as linear programming (LP), integer programming, and nonlinear optimization that systematically evaluate multiple alternatives to determine the most efficient allocation of resources, whether in production scheduling, pricing strategies, supply chain management, or workforce planning. Prescriptive analytics can simulate different scenarios, assess trade-offs, and quantify risks, empowering decision-makers to choose actions that maximize profits, minimize costs, improve customer satisfaction, or achieve sustainability goals by integrating predictive insights with optimization models with the use of AI tools. Furthermore, prescriptive analytics often incorporate simulation and heuristic methods to solve complex, real-world problems that may be too large or dynamic for exact optimization. The rise of AI and ML has further expanded prescriptive analytics capabilities by enabling organizations to utilize adaptive, data-driven decision systems that learn from outcomes and continuously refine recommendations. This integration of AI-powered tools and techniques and advanced analytics and optimization facilitates not only smarter decision-making but also agility and resilience in an increasingly competitive and uncertain business environment. Ultimately, essential prescriptive analytics and optimization transform raw data and predictive forecasts into strategic insights, actionable plans that drive efficiency, innovation, and long-term value creation for organizations across industries and worldwide.

8.3 Business Statistics and Analytical Foundations

In a world increasingly driven by data, the power to understand what has happened and predict what might happen is no longer sufficient. Businesses face the pressing need to determine what should be done. This imperative marks the domain of prescriptive analytics, where statistics and optimization converge not merely to interpret the world but to shape it. At the heart of this analytical frontier lies a foundation built on rigorous statistical reasoning, guiding decisions under uncertainty and informing models that recommend optimal courses of action. Prescriptive analytics transforms data into directives, patterns into policies, and forecasts into finely tuned strategies.

8.3.1 Transition from Predictive to Prescriptive Analytics

Specifically, it reflects a shift from forecasting what is likely to happen (e.g., demand, default risk) to recommending what decision to take to achieve specific objectives under constraints (e.g., maximize profit, minimize risk, satisfy service-level targets, achieve forecasted earnings). Predictive analytics employs historical data and statistical algorithms to forecast potential future events and trends by analyzing patterns and relationships within the data. Prescriptive analytics builds on these forecasts by integrating them with optimization, simulation, and decision-analysis methods to identify actions that improve outcomes, which are often formalized as "predict-then-optimize" pipelines or integrated decision-focused learning approaches.[1] Prescriptive analytics can significantly outperform predictive analytics in terms of its influence on firm performance, particularly regarding financial outcomes.[2] For instance, ML is employed within prescriptive analytics to conduct scenario analyses and simulations, ultimately enabling firms to ascertain optimal decision paths amid uncertainty.

8.3.2 Types of Prescriptive Analytics Models

8.3.2.1 Rule-Based Systems

Rule-based systems rely on a set of predefined rules or heuristics to guide decision-making, codifying expert knowledge into deterministic "if-then" logic that triggers specific actions under defined conditions. These rules are established based on expert knowledge or historical data, facilitating automated reasoning processes that suggest actions under specific conditions. Often implemented in environments where clear guidelines are necessary, such as e-commerce (e.g., offering discounts for cart abandonment) or finance (e.g., flagging high-value transactions), rule-based systems offer the advantages of interpretability, reliability, and straightforward implementation.

8.3.2.2 Simulation-Based Optimization

Simulation-based optimization (SBO) integrates simulation techniques with optimization algorithms to assess the performance of various decision alternatives, particularly in complex, nonlinear, or stochastic systems, where traditional analytical solutions are insufficient. This approach allows organizations to replicate business processes under various conditions, observe outcomes across scenarios, and identify optimal input parameters for desired performance metrics. While computationally intensive, SBO provides a flexible framework for decision-making under uncertainty.

8.3.2.3 Mathematical Programming Approaches

Mathematical programming serves as the backbone of modern prescriptive analytics, offering structured and scalable methods for solving optimization problems. These models, including linear, integer, and nonlinear programming (NLP), define decision variables, an objective function (e.g., cost minimization or profit maximization), and constraints reflecting real-world limitations. In addition to these core techniques, prescriptive analytics benefits from integrating AI and ML, enhancing model adaptability and effectiveness.

8.3.2.4 AI-Driven Prescriptive Models

These emerging AI-driven prescriptive models, such as reinforcement learning and evolutionary algorithms, have gained prominence for their ability to learn optimal policies through interaction with the environment and adapt to changing business contexts. Collectively, these models form the analytical backbone of prescriptive analytics by transforming data-driven insights into actionable, value-maximizing decisions.

8.4 Linear Optimization Models

In the symphony of data-driven decision-making, linear optimization models serve as the disciplined conductor, directing limited resources, competing objectives, and complex constraints into harmonious efficiency. Where descriptive analytics recounts the past and predictive analytics ventures into the probable, prescriptive analytics recommend what action should be taken. At its core lies the mathematical precision of LP, a framework that translates real-world problems into systems of equations and inequalities, guiding us toward the best possible course of action within defined boundaries.

8.4.1 Key Components of a Linear Optimization Model

8.4.1.1 Objective Function

In linear optimization models, the objective function serves as the primary criterion for decision-making, directing the optimization process toward achieving valuable outcomes. This function mathematically encapsulates the model's goals, typically maximizing or minimizing a specific quantity, such as profit, cost, resource allocation, or other performance metrics. The nature of the objective function fundamentally shapes the structure and feasibility of any LP problem. The objective function in standard linear optimization is represented as a linear combination of decision variables, where each variable is assigned a coefficient that reflects its contribution to the overall objective. The linearity assumption simplifies mathematics and facilitates the application of efficient solution methodologies, such as the simplex algorithm or interior point methods (IPMs), which can handle large-scale problems effectively. This characteristic allows for straightforward optimization across feasible decision spaces, created by the constraints that define the limits within which these variables can operate.

8.4.1.2 Constraints

Constraints are critical components that define the feasibility of solutions and delineate the boundaries within which decision variables must operate. They are mathematical expressions, typically presented as linear inequalities or equations, that must be satisfied by the solution to accurately reflect the problem being modeled. The constraints can represent capacity limits, resource availability, budget restrictions, or various logical conditions relevant to the specific optimization scenario and often translate real-world limitations, such as resource availability, capacity, or policy restrictions, into linear equations or inequalities that bound feasible solutions.[3] Constraints in linear optimization can be categorized as either equality or inequality constraints. Equality constraints define precise relationships between variables; for example, the total production must equal the total demand. In contrast, inequality constraints limit the values of decision variables to be less than or equal to (≤) or greater than or equal to (≥) a particular threshold, reflecting situations like budget ceilings or minimum production requirements.[4]

8.4.1.3 Non-negativity Restrictions

Non-negativity restrictions are a pivotal consideration that ensures decision variables remain within the feasible and realistic bounds dictated by the nature of the problem.

Specifically, they stipulate that certain decision variables must take on values greater than or equal to zero. This requirement arises in various practical applications, including resource allocation, production planning, and financial modeling, where negative values of decision variables do not make logical sense. The primary purpose of imposing non-negativity restrictions is to reflect real-world constraints accurately. For example, in financial models, non-negativity constraints ensure that investment decisions or resource distributions are non-negative, aligning with real-world economic interpretations.

8.4.1.4 Decision Variables

In the context of linear optimization models, decision variables are fundamental components that represent the choices available to decision-makers to optimize a specific objective function under certain constraints. Typically, these decision variables can be continuous, integer, or binary types depending on the structure of the problem and the nature of the decisions being made and represent the controllable choices available to the decision-maker, such as production quantities or investment levels, and they form the basis of the model's solution space.

8.4.2 Solving Linear Optimization Problems

8.4.2.1 Graphical Methods

Graphical methods are essential tools in solving linear optimization problems, serving to visualize constraints, objective functions, and feasible regions, thereby facilitating understanding and analysis of complex decision spaces. In two-dimensional LP problems, graphical methods enable practitioners to plot constraints as lines in a Cartesian coordinate system. Each line corresponds to inequality, and the feasible region where all constraints overlap is visually clear and helps identify potential solutions. The objective function can similarly be plotted as a line, with the optimization goal being to move this line parallel to maximize or minimize the objective value until it meets the boundaries of the feasible region. The last point of contact, often at a vertex of the feasible region, represents the optimal solution.[5]

8.4.2.2 The Simplex Method

The Simplex Method, developed by George Dantzig in the 1940s, is a widely utilized algorithm for solving LP problems to systematically explore extreme points of the feasible region to locate the optimal solution with proven practical efficiency. This method addresses optimization problems involving multiple variables and constraints by iteratively moving along the edges of the feasible region defined by the constraints, ultimately aiming to find the optimal vertex that maximizes or minimizes the objective function. At the heart of the Simplex Method lies its ability to convert linear inequalities into equalities by introducing slack, surplus, and artificial variables. This transformation enables the construction of a tableau that summarizes the coefficients of the variables, the objective function, and the constraints in a structured format. The algorithm then uses pivot operations to iteratively adjust the tableau, maintaining optimality while exploring feasible solutions. Each iteration results in a new basic feasible solution, with the goal of improving the objective function value with respect to the defined constraints.

8.4.2.3 Interior Point Methods

IPMs have gained prominence as powerful techniques for solving linear optimization problems since their introduction by Karmarkar in 1984. These methods offer an alternative to the Simplex Method, approaching optimal solutions by traversing the interior of the feasible region rather than moving along its boundaries.[6] By doing so, IPMs can effectively exploit the structure of LP problems, particularly in high-dimensional spaces where traditional methods may struggle. The core of the IPMs is the concept of barrier functions, which prevent the iterates from approaching the boundaries of the feasible region too closely. These functions guide the optimization process by penalizing solutions that attempt to reach the boundary, thus ensuring that all searches remain in a feasible and practical domain. As a result, IPMs exhibit robust convergence properties, often requiring fewer iterations to reach optimal solutions compared to methods that rely on vertex traversals.[7]

8.4.2.4 Software and Tools

At the introductory level, Excel Solver provides a highly intuitive environment for formulating and solving small to medium-sized linear programs. It allows users to define decision variables, set objective functions, and impose constraints through a simple spreadsheet interface, making it ideal for business analysts, students, and professionals working with well-structured data. Despite its ease of use, Excel Solver includes powerful features such as sensitivity reports and linearity checks, offering a window into the mechanics of optimization. For more complex, dynamic, or large-scale problems, programming languages such as Python and R offer significantly greater flexibility and control over the modeling process. Libraries like PuLP and SciPy.optimize in Python, and lpSolve in R, enable users to define optimization problems through code, automate iterative scenarios, and integrate optimization routines into broader analytics pipelines.

When solving industrial-strength optimization problems that involve thousands of variables and constraints, commercial solvers such as Gurobi and CPLEX are the tools of choice. These solvers implement highly efficient versions of the Simplex Method, IPMs, and cutting-edge heuristics, optimized for speed, memory management, and numerical stability. Beyond finding optimal solutions, they also facilitate sensitivity analysis, provide dual values and shadow prices, and enable integration with predictive models, allowing for the kind of prescriptive insight that modern decision-support systems demand.

8.5 Importance of Statistics in AI and BA

In BA, statistical methods support descriptive and diagnostic analysis, causal inference, and performance evaluation, allowing managers to distinguish signal from noise and make evidence-based decisions. Many AI techniques, including regression, Bayesian networks, and probabilistic graphical models, are explicitly statistical in nature, while even data-intensive methods such as deep learning rely on statistical assumptions for optimization, validation, and generalization. Ultimately, statistics serve as the backbone of AI and BA by transforming raw data into reliable insights and actionable intelligence. It is vital for model evaluation and governance through metrics, experimental design, and robustness checks, which are critical for trustworthy and explainable AI systems in business contexts.

8.5.1 Why Statistics Matters: Foundations for AI and BA

Statistics matters as the foundational discipline for AI and BA because it provides the principles required to model uncertainty, extract reliable patterns from data, and support evidence-based decision-making. Fundamental statistical concepts such as probability theory, sampling, estimation, and hypothesis testing enable AI models to learn from data while assessing variability, bias, and generalizability, which are essential for robust model development. Ultimately, statistics support model evaluation, experimentation, and governance through performance metrics, experimental design, and uncertainty quantification, which are critical for building trustworthy, explainable, and ethically responsible AI systems in business applications.

8.5.2 Statistical Challenges in Modern AI and BA

Overfitting, bias, and the illusion of precision remain major statistical challenges in AI and BA. Overfitting occurs when models latch onto noise rather than true patterns, leading to strong training performance but weak generalization, especially in small or imbalanced datasets common in business. Bias further distorts predictions when data or model choices systematically favor certain groups or features, reducing fairness and reproducibility. The illusion of precision arises when metrics such as p-values or R-squared are interpreted too confidently, masking uncertainty and overstating model accuracy. Robust validation methods like cross-validation and bootstrapping are essential to counter these risks and produce more trustworthy results.

8.6 Statistical Inference and Hypothesis Testing

Statistical inference is the silent engine behind intelligent decision-making, quietly transforming uncertain data into actionable insight. In the realm of prescriptive analytics and optimization, where the goal is not just to understand but to act, statistical inference serves as the foundation upon which robust strategies are built. Confidence intervals, p-values, hypothesis tests, and related tools allow us to quantify uncertainty, test assumptions, and validate relationships before committing to high-stakes decisions.

8.6.1 Confidence Intervals: Estimating the Range for Decision-Making

Confidence intervals are a fundamental statistical tool for decision-making because they quantify the uncertainty surrounding point estimates by providing a plausible range of values for an unknown population parameter. Rather than relying on single estimates such as sample means or regression coefficients, confidence intervals incorporate sampling variability to indicate the degree of precision and reliability of empirical results. In BA and AI applications, confidence intervals support managerial judgment by enabling comparisons across alternatives, assessing risk, and evaluating whether estimated effects are economically and statistically meaningful. They are widely used in forecasting, quality control, and performance evaluation to determine whether observed outcomes differ significantly from benchmarks or targets. Additionally, confidence intervals play a critical role in model validation and explainable AI by communicating uncertainty to stakeholders, regulators, and decision-makers, thereby reducing overconfidence in automated predictions.

8.6.2 *p*-Values: The Compass of Statistical Significance

p-values serve as a central inferential tool in statistical analysis by quantifying the strength of evidence against a null hypothesis, thereby acting as a "compass" for assessing statistical significance. Statistically, a *p*-value represents the probability of observing data at least as extreme as the sample results, assuming the null hypothesis is true, and it provides a standardized metric for hypothesis testing across disciplines.[8] In BA and AI research, *p*-values are commonly used to evaluate model parameters, compare alternative strategies, and determine whether observed effects are unlikely to have occurred by random chance alone.[9]

8.6.3 *t*-Tests: Comparing Means for Decision Scenarios

t-tests are among the most widely used inferential statistical tools for comparing mean outcomes across decision scenarios and determining whether observed differences are statistically meaningful. Formally, *t*-tests allow analysts to assess whether changes in performance, treatment effects, or policy interventions are likely due to systematic factors rather than random sampling error by evaluating the difference between sample means relative to their variability. Common variants include the one-sample *t*-test, which compares a sample mean to a known benchmark; the independent-samples *t*-test, which evaluates differences between two distinct groups; and the paired-samples *t*-test, which analyzes before-and-after or matched observations. In BA and AI-supported decision environments, *t*-tests are frequently applied in A/B testing, quality improvement initiatives, and experimental validation of predictive models to guide managerial decisions.

8.6.4 ANOVA (Analysis of Variance): Beyond Two Groups

Analysis of Variance (ANOVA) is a fundamental statistical technique used to compare mean differences across three or more groups by extending hypothesis testing beyond simple two-group comparisons. ANOVA evaluates whether observed variations in group means are statistically significant by decomposing total variability into between-group and within-group components and assessing their relative magnitudes through an *F*-statistic. In BA and AI-enabled decision environments, ANOVA is widely applied in experimental design, marketing analysis, operations management, and quality improvement to assess the effects of different strategies, treatments, or process conditions on performance outcomes. Extensions such as one-way, two-way, and factorial ANOVA allow analysts to examine both main effects and interaction effects among multiple factors by providing richer insight into complex decision scenarios. When ANOVA results indicate significant differences, post hoc tests further identify which specific groups differ, supporting actionable managerial interpretations.

8.6.5 Chi-Square Tests: Categorical Clarity in Decisions

Chi-square tests play an essential role in BA and AI-driven decision-making by providing a rigorous statistical framework for analyzing relationships among categorical variables. Commonly applied in the form of the chi-square test of independence or goodness-of-fit, these tests assess whether observed frequencies differ significantly from expected frequencies under a specified null hypothesis.[10] Chi-square tests offer categorical clarity by enabling analysts to evaluate associations such as customer preferences across demographic groups, the effectiveness of marketing campaigns across regions, or differences in compliance outcomes across governance structures. Their non-parametric nature makes them especially valuable when data do not meet normality assumptions, a frequent condition in real-world business and sustainability datasets. In AI-enhanced analytics, chi-square statistics are often used for feature selection, model validation, and bias detection in classification tasks, ensuring that categorical predictors contribute meaningfully to predictive performance without introducing spurious relationships.

8.7 Bayesian Statistics and Business Applications

8.7.1 Core Principles of Bayesian Statistics

Bayesian statistics is grounded in a coherent probabilistic framework that treats uncertainty as a degree of belief and updates that belief systematically as new information becomes available. The core principle is Bayes' theorem, which combines prior beliefs about unknown parameters with evidence from observed data to produce a posterior distribution that reflects updated knowledge.[11] Bayesian inference directly quantifies uncertainty through probability distributions, enabling more intuitive interpretation of results such as credible intervals and posterior probabilities. Another fundamental principle is the explicit incorporation of prior information, which can be informative or weakly informative, allowing analysts to integrate domain expertise, historical data, or regulatory expectations into the inferential process.[12] Bayesian methods also emphasize model comparison and prediction using posterior predictive distributions, facilitating decision-making under uncertainty in BA, finance, and AI applications.

8.7.1.1 Bayes' Theorem

Bayesian statistics is a paradigm of statistical analysis that centers on Bayes' theorem to update the probability of a hypothesis as more evidence becomes available. This approach differs significantly from frequentist statistics, which relies on fixed parameters and sampling distributions. Bayes' theorem mathematically describes how to calculate the posterior probability $(P(H \mid E))$, given prior knowledge $(P(H))$ and the likelihood $(P(E \mid H))$, as follows:

$$P(H \mid E) = \frac{P(E \mid H) \cdot P(H)}{P(E)}$$

where:

$P(H \mid E)$ = Posterior probability — the probability that the hypothesis H is true given the observed evidence E.
$P(E \mid H)$ = Likelihood — the probability of observing E if H were true.
$P(H)$ = Prior probability — the probability of H before seeing the evidence.
$P(E)$ = Marginal likelihood (or evidence) — the total probability of observing E under all possible hypotheses.

This equation encapsulates the central mechanisms of Bayesian inference, which involves incorporating prior beliefs (the prior distribution) into the statistical analysis and refining these beliefs based on observed data (the likelihood) to produce updated beliefs (the posterior distribution). A key strength of Bayesian methods is their ability to formally incorporate uncertainty into statistical models, allowing for coherent decision-making even in complex scenarios with inherent uncertainties. Specifically, Bayesian frameworks not only handle data uncertainty but also enable the integration of diverse data sources for robust model building.

8.7.1.2 Priors and Posteriors

In Bayesian statistics, the prior encapsulates our beliefs about a parameter before observing the data. A subjective prior is rooted in expert judgment, market experience, or domain-specific intuition. For example, in launching a new product, a retail company might base its prior on sales patterns from similar past launches, adjusted by the intuition of product managers. While critics argue that subjectivity can bias results, in practice, it allows decision-makers to integrate valuable non-quantitative insights into the analytical process. In contrast, an objective prior (such as a non-informative or Jeffreys prior) minimizes subjective influence, aiming to let the data "speak for itself." This approach is particularly useful when there is little reliable domain knowledge or when neutrality is desired for transparency and defensibility in regulatory or high-stakes corporate contexts. The choice between subjective and objective priors often reflects the strategic trade-off between leveraging institutional memory and maintaining analytical impartiality. The defining strength of Bayesian inference lies in its ability to update beliefs dynamically as fresh data becomes available. The posterior distribution from one stage of analysis becomes the prior for the next, creating a living model that adapts to unfolding realities.

8.7.1.3 Decision-Theoretic Foundations

Bayesian decision theory links statistical inference directly to action. The framework defines an optimal decision as the one that minimizes expected loss or, equivalently, maximizes expected utility, given the posterior distribution of uncertain quantities. Loss functions can reflect a variety of business priorities: revenue shortfalls, inventory holding costs, or customer churn penalties. The explicit articulation of these functions ensures that statistical modeling is aligned with strategic objectives rather than abstract accuracy metrics. A Bayesian optimization (BO) model can embed this asymmetry directly into its decision rule, prescribing production levels that account for both probabilistic demand forecasts and the differing costs of error. This tight coupling between inference and payoff makes Bayesian methods particularly suited to prescriptive analytics. Optimization in the Bayesian framework is not simply about finding the most probable parameter values; it is about choosing the action that yields the best expected outcome under uncertainty. This shifts the optimization problem from a search for "truth" to a search for "consequence," where every action is evaluated considering both its expected benefit and the uncertainty surrounding it.

8.7.2 Bayesian Methods in Prescriptive Analytics

8.7.2.1 Bayesian Decision Analysis

Bayesian Decision Analysis (BDA) is an approach that incorporates uncertainty and complexity in decision-making processes by using Bayesian principles. BDA merges statistical modeling with decision theory, enabling informed choices based on subjective prior knowledge and observed data. The integration of Bayesian methods into prescriptive analytics allows decision-makers to systematically update their beliefs and make predictions based on new evidence. The foundational principle of BDA is the use of prior distributions, which represent initial beliefs about uncertain parameters before data is observed, and posterior distributions, which are updated beliefs that also consider the new evidence. A notable feature of BDA is its flexibility in incorporating expert knowledge into the prior, thus accommodating real-world uncertainty. This flexibility can also serve to monetize risks by evaluating the expected utility of different strategies under varying scenarios, making BDA especially relevant in sectors.

8.7.2.2 Bayesian Optimization

BO is a notable approach within Bayesian methods that is increasingly adopted in business to enhance decision-making processes, particularly in scenarios characterized by uncertainty and limited data. The primary goal of BO is to optimize complex, expensive, and noisy objective functions efficiently, which is especially relevant for applications like hyperparameter tuning in ML and resource allocation in operational strategies. At the heart of BO lies the construction of a surrogate model, typically a Gaussian Process (GP), which estimates the behavior of the objective function. This model integrates prior beliefs about the function's characteristics, which are updated progressively as new data points are available. A key advantage of this approach is its probabilistic nature, which captures uncertainty in function evaluations and guides the search for optimal solutions by balancing exploration (sampling uncertain areas) with exploitation (focusing on promising regions).

8.7.3 Applications in Business Domain

In marketing, Bayesian statistics enhances consumer insight, campaign evaluation, and strategic decision-making. Bayesian analysis of customer reviews transforms unstructured feedback into actionable intelligence while accounting for uncertainty in consumer sentiment. Bayesian structural time series models allow firms to estimate the true causal impact of advertising by comparing treated and control markets. Variable-selection methods such as spike-and-slab identify the most influential elements of user-generated content on purchase intent, helping marketers refine messaging. Bayesian approaches also guide decisions in dynamic B2B relationships, integrating prior knowledge with new evidence to evaluate the effects of marketing interactions and to predict customer responses to pricing and promotions.

Bayesian methods play a central role in finance by improving risk modeling, portfolio optimization, and investment decision processes under uncertainty. Bayesian dynamic financial networks incorporate time-varying predictors, allowing real-time updates of risk assessments as markets shift. In portfolio management, Bayesian updating blends prior beliefs with market data to produce more stable estimates of expected returns and to guide optimal asset allocation. Bayesian inference also strengthens expected-utility analysis and improves asset-pricing models by evaluating the quality of decision approximations. More broadly, Bayesian decision-theoretic frameworks support structured, multi-dimensional investment analysis, offering a systematic and adaptive foundation for pricing, risk evaluation, and strategic financial planning.

8.8 Integer Linear Optimization Models

Integer Linear Optimization (ILO) models stand at the heart of prescriptive analytics, transforming raw data and predictive insights into actionable, optimized decisions. ILO accommodates the reality that many business decisions are inherently discrete. By expressing both the objective function and constraints in linear form, while restricting decision variables to integer or binary values, these models capture the logical and combinatorial nature of real-world problems. In doing so, they bridge the gap between theoretical optimization and practical decision-making, enabling organizations to navigate complex trade-offs with clarity, discipline, and a mathematically grounded sense of direction. In the broader landscape of analytics, ILO serves as a precise compass, guiding enterprises not merely to plausible solutions but to the best solutions attainable within their operational and strategic limits.

8.8.1 Fundamental Concepts

8.8.1.1 Optimization Problem Structure

Integer Linear Programming (ILP) is a fundamental approach for modeling and solving optimization problems in which the objective function and constraints are linear, and some or all of the variables are restricted to take integer values. The essential components of an ILP include decision variables, an objective function, and a set of constraints. Decision variables, which may be integer or binary, define the feasible solution space. The objective function, designed to be minimized or maximized, specifies the optimization goal. Constraints impose limitations on the decision variables, ensuring that feasible solutions satisfy specified conditions. The structure of optimization problems in ILP is inherently multifaceted, requiring a deliberate arrangement of decision variables, objective functions, and constraints that collectively influence algorithmic performance. A thorough understanding of these structural elements and their adaptation to specific problem contexts can significantly enhance the effectiveness of ILP applications across various fields.

8.8.1.2 Linear and Integer Optimization

In the domain of optimization, distinguishing between LP and ILP is essential for understanding how the characteristics of optimization problems influence their solvability and efficiency. Although both LP and ILP are based on the same principle of optimizing a linear objective function subject to linear constraints, they differ significantly in their decision variables. LP permits decision variables to assume any values within specified bounds, typically real numbers, enabling efficient solutions through polynomial-time algorithms such as the Simplex Method or IPMs. In contrast, ILP imposes the restriction that some or all decision variables must be integers, a condition that introduces substantial complexity. Solving ILPs is generally classified as NP-hard, with no known polynomial-time algorithms capable of resolving all instances. The requirement for integer constraints fundamentally changes the problem landscape. Whereas the feasible region of an LP forms a convex polyhedron defined by linear constraints, the feasible region of an ILP often comprises discrete points dispersed within that polyhedron. This results in a combinatorial solution space, complicating the search for optimal solutions.

8.8.2 Formulating Integer Linear Optimization Models

Formulating ILO models involves systematically translating real-world decision problems with discrete choices into a structured mathematical framework that can be solved using optimization algorithms. The formulation process begins with clearly defining decision variables, the objective function, and the development of linear constraints and resource limitations, logical relationships, technological requirements, and policy rules. Careful attention is also given to constraint tightness and model scaling to improve computational tractability, as poorly formulated models can lead to excessive solution times or numerical instability. In business and industry applications, effective formulation is essential, as well-structured integer linear models enable accurate representation of complex planning, scheduling, and allocation problems while supporting robust and transparent prescriptive decision-making.

8.8.2.1 Common Modeling Patterns

The central strength of ILP lies in its adaptability to represent diverse decision-making scenarios through recurring modeling patterns. These patterns provide standardized frameworks that allow complex real-world systems to be translated into mathematical formulations suitable for optimization. By recognizing and employing these structures, practitioners can streamline model development, leverage established solution techniques, and ensure that formulations remain both interpretable and computationally tractable.

One of the most prevalent patterns is binary selection, where binary decision variables (0–1) indicate whether a specific option is chosen. Binary selection constraints elegantly capture the yes/no nature of these discrete decisions, ensuring feasibility and cost-effectiveness in implementation. Another widespread pattern is the assignment problem, which involves mapping elements of one set to those of another. Classic applications include assigning tasks to workers or machines to jobs, where the goal is to achieve efficiency while meeting operational or fairness requirements. Such models typically employ binary variables to represent whether a particular assignment is made, combined with constraints that enforce exclusivity or capacity restrictions.

Knapsack-type constraints represent a third common pattern and are central to modeling limited-resource allocation problems. These constraints arise when items, projects, or tasks compete for a scarce resource, such as budget, time, or capacity. By restricting the total "weight" or resource usage of selected options, knapsack-type formulations ensure that only feasible subsets are chosen while maximizing the return (e.g., profit, utility). Table 8.1 presents common modeling patterns in ILP, their description, applications, and decision variable type.

8.8.3 Solution Methods

8.8.3.1 Exact Methods

Exact methods for solving ILP problems are grounded in mathematical rigor, offering guarantees of global optimality. Mixed-Integer Linear Programming (MILP) techniques are the primary exact approach, systematically searching through the solution space while eliminating infeasible or suboptimal branches. The Branch-and-Bound algorithm remains a cornerstone of this category, efficiently partitioning the feasible region and applying bounding criteria to prune the search tree.

Table 8.1 Common Modeling Patterns in ILP

Modeling Pattern	*Description*	*Typical Applications*	*Decision Variable Type*
Binary selection	Selects or rejects options using binary variables (0 = no, 1 = yes).	Facility location, project selection, and capital budgeting	Binary (0/1)
Assignment problems	Assigns elements of one set to another under exclusivity or capacity rules.	Task-to-worker, machine-to-job, school-to-student matching	Binary
Knapsack constraints	Selects items subject to resource limitations while maximizing total benefit.	Budget allocation, marketing campaigns, portfolio design	Binary/integer
Scheduling formulations	Models task execution over time, often with precedence and resource constraints.	Production scheduling, workforce planning, transport routing	Binary/integer (time-indexed)
Network design	Determines the structure of nodes and arcs subject to flow and connectivity rules.	Supply chain design, telecommunication networks, routing	Binary (edge/node), integer (flow)

The strength of exact methods lies in their ability to provide decision-makers with certainty in high-stakes environments where suboptimal outcomes carry significant costs. For small to medium-sized ILP problems, these methods are computationally tractable and can exploit problem-specific structures such as sparsity, symmetry, or decomposability. By reformulating complex systems into MILP models, practitioners can leverage existing LP solvers to handle combinatorial challenges effectively.

8.8.3.2 Heuristics and Metaheuristics

Heuristic methods adopt a more pragmatic stance toward solving ILP problems, focusing on producing high-quality solutions within a limited computational timeframe rather than guaranteeing global optimality. These approaches rely on problem-specific rules or constructive algorithms that guide the search process, making them especially valuable when exact methods are computationally prohibitive. The appeal of heuristics lies in their simplicity, adaptability, and speed. They often exploit domain knowledge, enabling rapid problem decomposition and solution generation.

Metaheuristics extend beyond problem-specific heuristics by providing high-level frameworks that can be adapted to a wide range of ILP problems. These techniques aim to explore the solution space more comprehensively, balancing intensification (searching around good solutions) with diversification (exploring new regions). A distinguishing feature of metaheuristics is their ability to escape local optima, which often trap simpler heuristics. By incorporating stochastic elements and adaptive search strategies, metaheuristics can continue improving solutions over time.

8.8.3.3 Software and Solvers

Advances in optimization software have significantly broadened the accessibility and applicability of ILP. Commercial solvers such as IBM ILOG CPLEX and Gurobi, along with open-source alternatives such as SCIP, provide robust implementations of exact and heuristic algorithms, often incorporating advanced preprocessing, cutting planes, and parallelization. The importance of choosing an appropriate solver is underscored in benchmarking studies, which reveal substantial differences in speed, memory use, and robustness across tools. In genome-scale metabolic modeling, solver performance directly influences the feasibility of complex simulations, highlighting the critical role of computational efficiency in practical optimization.

8.9 Nonlinear Optimization Models

In the landscape of prescriptive analytics, decision-making rarely unfolds along straight, predictable paths. While linear optimization models have long provided a foundation for resource allocation, scheduling, and strategic planning, they often fall short when confronted with the complexities of real-world systems. Nonlinear optimization models rise to this challenge, allowing analysts and decision-makers to capture the curvature inherent in costs, revenues, risks, and operational constraints. By accommodating nonlinear relationships, these models offer a richer, more nuanced view of the decision space, enabling organizations to uncover optimal strategies that reflect the true dynamics of markets, technologies, and human behavior. In essence, nonlinear optimization transforms prescriptive analytics from a realm of simplified assumptions into a tool capable of navigating the intricate terrain of practical decision-making.

8.9.1 General Nonlinear Programming (NLP) Structure

In the field of nonlinear programming (NLP), a clearly defined mathematical formulation is essential for addressing optimization problems characterized by nonlinear objective functions and constraints. The general structure of NLP provides a framework that facilitates the understanding and solution of these complex problems. A generic NLP model can be expressed as:

Minimize or maximize: $f(x)$

subject to:

$$
\begin{aligned}
&g_i(x) \leq 0, \quad i = 1,\ldots,m \\
&h_j(x) = 0, \quad j = 1,\ldots,p, \\
&x \in R^n
\end{aligned}
$$

where:

$f(x)$ = The objective function (nonlinear in general)
$g_i(x)$ = Inequality constraints (possibly nonlinear)
$h_j(x)$ = Equality constraints (possibly nonlinear)
x = Decision variables to be determined

Considerable research has been devoted to solution techniques in NLP. Sequential Quadratic Programming (SQP) is recognized as a robust method for solving constrained optimization problems. SQP iteratively solves a series of quadratic approximations of the original nonlinear problem, effectively handling both equality and inequality constraints. Its iterative nature provides flexibility in managing diverse objective functions, making it applicable to a wide range of NLP problems.

Penalty methods are another notable approach in NLP. These techniques reformulate constrained problems as a sequence of unconstrained problems by incorporating penalty terms into the objective function. This transformation simplifies the optimization process while maintaining adherence to constraints. Furthermore, exact penalty functions have been developed to ensure that solutions to the penalized problems correspond to solutions of the original constrained problem under certain conditions.

8.9.2 Types of Nonlinear Optimization Models

8.9.2.1 Convex Nonlinear Programming Models

Convex NLP models are distinguished by their defining property: both the objective function and the feasible region are convex. This convexity ensures that any local minimum is also a global minimum, a powerful guarantee that significantly simplifies both analysis and computation. The mathematical structure allows for a range of efficient algorithms, including gradient-based methods, interior point methods, and cutting-plane techniques, all of which can converge to optimal solutions without the risk of being trapped in suboptimal local minima.

A typical convex nonlinear program can be expressed in the form:

$$\textit{Minimize} \quad f(x) \quad \text{subject to} \quad g_i(x) \leq 0, \quad h_j(x) = 0$$

where:

$f : R^n \to R$ = Convex.
g_i = Convex constraint functions.
h_j = Affine equality constraints.

The feasibility set defined by these constraints is convex, which is the core reason for the existence of global optimality guarantees. This theoretical clarity makes convex NLP not only mathematically elegant but also broadly applicable in economics, finance, and operations research.

8.9.2.2 Nonconvex Nonlinear Programming Models

Nonconvex NLP models encompass problems where either the objective function or the feasible region (or both) is nonconvex. This lack of convexity removes the guarantee that a local minimum is also a global minimum, thereby introducing multiple local minima, saddle points, and other complexities into the search landscape. As a result, solving nonconvex problems is generally more challenging, requiring advanced techniques to explore and evaluate multiple regions of the solution space.

These models are often formulated as:

$$\textit{Minimize} \quad f(x) \quad \text{subject to} \quad g_i(x) \leq 0, \quad h_j(x) = 0$$

With f or g_i exhibiting nonconvexity. The feasible set may be disconnected or have irregular boundaries, and standard convex optimization algorithms may fail to find the best possible solution. Instead, solution strategies often include global optimization methods such as branch-and-bound, cutting-plane methods adapted for nonconvex problems, or heuristic and metaheuristic techniques like simulated annealing (SA), genetic algorithms (GAs), and particle swarm optimization. Nonconvexity is often unavoidable due to nonlinear physics, combinatorial constraints, or complex cost functions. The emphasis in these cases shifts from guaranteeing global optimality to finding high-quality solutions efficiently, often using hybrid methods that blend exact optimization techniques with heuristics to balance precision and computational feasibility.

8.9.2.3 Unconstrained Nonlinear Models

Unconstrained nonlinear models describe optimization problems where the decision variables are not subject to explicit constraints. The only requirement is to find a point in the domain of the objective function where the function achieves its minimum or maximum value. Such problems focus entirely on the shape and properties of the objective function, making the analysis and algorithms primarily concerned with calculus-based optimality conditions.

The standard form for unconstrained optimization is simply:

$$\textit{Minimize} \quad f(x), \quad x \in R^n$$

with no g_i or h_j constraints. First-order optimality conditions require that the gradient of $f(x)$ vanishes at optimal points, while second-order conditions involve examining the Hessian to determine whether a stationary point is a minimum, maximum, or saddle point. Depending on the nature of $f(x)$, the problem may be convex or nonconvex, which in turn determines the complexity of finding the optimum.

8.9.2.4 Constrained Nonlinear Models

Constrained nonlinear models involve an objective function to be minimized or maximized subject to one or more constraints on the decision variables. These constraints can be equality constraints, inequality constraints, or a combination of both, and may be linear or nonlinear in form. The presence of constraints fundamentally changes the optimization landscape, as feasible solutions must lie within a restricted set, which may be convex or nonconvex depending on the problem structure.

The general formulation of a constrained nonlinear optimization problem is:

$$\textit{Minimize} \quad f(x) \quad \text{subject to} \quad g_i(x) \leq 0, \quad h_j(x) = 0$$

where the constraint functions g_i and h_j can introduce significant complexity. The solution process must account not only for optimality conditions—such as those expressed by the Karush–Kuhn–Tucker (KKT) framework—but also for feasibility. Computational methods for constrained problems include SQP, augmented Lagrangian methods, and penalty function approaches, each suited to different problem types and sizes.

8.10 Simulation Modeling Techniques

In the realm of prescriptive analytics, simulation modeling stands as both a laboratory of imagination and a crucible of rigor—a place where decision-makers can safely experiment with the future before committing scarce resources in the present. Simulation thrives in the messy, nonlinear, and uncertain realities of business systems. It allows us to mimic the complexity of supply chains buffeted by shifting demand, healthcare networks under unpredictable patient loads, or financial portfolios exposed to volatile markets. In doing so, simulation does not merely predict outcomes; it illuminates the intricate interplay of variables, constraints, and uncertainties, enabling decision-makers to craft strategies that are both optimal in theory and resilient in practice.

8.10.1 Foundations of Simulation Modeling

8.10.1.1 Key Simulation Paradigms

Simulation modeling is increasingly recognized as a critical technique in business decision-making, particularly for simulating complex environments and system dynamics. Two prominent paradigms in this context are Agent-Based Modeling and Simulation (ABMS) and Business Process Simulation (BPS). ABMS is especially valuable for enabling granular exploration of individual behaviors and interactions within a system, offering a greater capacity to manage complexity than traditional models. Agent-Based Modeling serves as an effective approach for simulating ecosystems and evaluating the interactions between agents, which represent individuals or entities within the system. ABM also facilitates the analysis of human behaviors across a variety of contexts. In contrast, BPS focuses on the representation and optimization of business processes. Using established frameworks such as Business Process Model and Notation (BPMN), organizations can simulate process flows to identify and evaluate opportunities for improvement. Methodologies for designing and implementing BPS effectively enable businesses to translate simulation results into operational efficiency gains.

8.10.1.2 Core Elements of Simulation Models

Simulation models are constructed around three fundamental components: inputs, process logic with state transitions, and outputs. These elements collectively define how a model represents reality, processes information, and generates insights for decision-making. Inputs form the foundational layer of any simulation model. They encompass decision variables alongside fixed parameters and probability distributions. Parameters define the static aspects of the system, while probability distributions capture uncertainty in factors such as demand fluctuations, processing times, or environmental conditions. The careful specification of inputs is critical, as they directly influence the model's fidelity and the validity of subsequent analysis.

Process logic and state transitions represent the dynamic mechanism of the simulation. Process logic governs how the system operates under varying conditions, dictating the rules, sequences, and interactions that occur within the modeled environment. State transitions capture how the system evolves over time or in response to specific events. This element allows the model to replicate the temporal and structural changes inherent in complex systems.

Outputs serve as the measurable results of the simulation, enabling the assessment of system performance and the comparison of alternative scenarios. Outputs typically include performance measures as well as cost-benefit outcomes that quantify the trade-offs between efficiency, quality, and resource utilization. These results provide decision-makers with actionable insights, guiding the selection of strategies that balance optimal performance with operational feasibility.

8.10.2 Integrating Simulation with Optimization

8.10.2.1 Simulation–Optimization Frameworks

Simulation–optimization frameworks combine the exploratory power of simulation with the prescriptive precision of optimization, enabling decision-makers to identify strategies that perform well under uncertainty and complexity. This integration is particularly relevant when systems are too intricate to be described by closed-form analytical models, yet strategic recommendations must still be generated. SBO treats the simulation model as a "black box" evaluator. The optimization algorithm proposes a set of variable decision values, and the simulation estimates the resulting performance metrics. The optimizer then uses these estimates to guide the search for better solutions.

Optimization via Simulation (OvS) embeds simulation within an iterative search process. Rather than solving an optimization problem directly, the algorithm explores the solution space by generating candidate solutions, simulating their performance, and refining the search based on observed results. OvS is particularly useful when the performance function is noisy or highly irregular. Metaheuristics with Simulation leverage population-based and neighborhood search techniques, such as GAs, tabu search (TS), particle swarm optimization, or SA, to efficiently navigate large and complex solution spaces.

8.10.2.2 Hybrid Modeling Approaches

Hybrid modeling approaches extend the flexibility of simulation–optimization frameworks by combining them with other analytical or computational techniques. One widely used strategy is integrating simulation with mathematical programming. In such models, the deterministic aspects of a system are formulated as mathematical programming models, while simulation captures stochastic elements. This dual structure allows decision-makers to simultaneously address uncertainty and enforce rigorous optimization constraints. Another increasingly relevant approach is embedding simulation within DSS for real-time analytics. In these systems, live operational data streams continuously update the simulation model, allowing decision-makers to evaluate "what-if" scenarios instantly and select actions adaptively. Hybrid approaches also facilitate multi-method simulation, where different paradigms, such as discrete-event simulation, agent-based modeling, and system dynamics, are combined within the same framework to capture multiple perspectives of a complex system.

8.10.2.3 Trade-Offs

While simulation–optimization frameworks and hybrid approaches are powerful, they involve balancing several trade-offs. The first is accuracy versus computational efficiency. High-fidelity models can capture intricate details of a system's behavior, making recommendations more reliable under realistic conditions. A second challenge is overfitting simulated scenarios versus producing generalizable prescriptions. When optimization is tuned too closely to specific simulated conditions, such as a narrow range of demand forecasts or fixed operating parameters, the resulting solution may fail under different real-world conditions. A third trade-off concerns the balance between model transparency and complexity. While hybrid and metaheuristic-based frameworks can deliver superior solutions, they may operate as "black boxes" that are difficult for stakeholders to interpret.

8.10.3 Simulation Modeling Techniques for Prescriptive Decision-Making

8.10.3.1 Scenario Analysis and What-If Exploration

Simulation modeling techniques, particularly those focused on scenario analysis and what-if exploration, play a significant role in prescriptive decision-making processes across various business contexts. These methods allow decision-makers to visualize potential outcomes based on different strategic choices and external variables, thereby enhancing their capacity to make informed and strategic decisions. The integration of scenario analysis in simulation modeling involves constructing multiple plausible futures to evaluate the potential impacts of business decisions. What-if analysis serves as another critical component that complements scenario analysis by enabling businesses to examine the effects of altering specific parameters on overall performance. Prescriptive analytics frameworks that incorporate simulation enhance decision-making in environments characterized by complexity and uncertainty. A simulation-supported prescriptive analytics approach has been shown to optimize maintenance decision-making by evaluating various actionable strategies through probabilistic cost-benefit analyses.

8.10.3.2 Robust Optimization Under Uncertainty

Robust optimization under uncertainty serves as a pivotal strategy in prescriptive decision-making, particularly within business contexts where organizations frequently encounter varying degrees of uncertainty regarding demand, supply, and operational constraints. The integration of simulation with robust optimization techniques enables decision-making that can withstand fluctuations and unforeseen events. One approach to robust optimization incorporates simulation to evaluate multiple uncertainty scenarios, producing more resilient decision strategies. The application of simulation-supported prescriptive analytics, combined with probabilistic cost-benefit analyses, has also proven valuable in optimizing maintenance decision-making.

8.10.3.3 Multi-objective Optimization

Multi-objective optimization (MOO) has become a critical tool in prescriptive decision-making within business contexts, enabling organizations to balance multiple competing goals effectively. These methods allow decision-makers to optimize several objectives simultaneously and navigate the complexities of operational environments through structured frameworks. At the core of MOO lies the concept of obtaining a Pareto optimal solution set, where no objective can be improved without worsening another.

8.10.3.4 Adaptive and Real-Time Simulation

Adaptive and real-time simulations are increasingly essential in the domain of prescriptive decision-making within businesses, enabling decision-makers to respond swiftly to changing conditions and thereby strengthening the resilience and adaptability of organizational strategies in complex environments. A fundamental advantage of adaptive simulation lies in its ability to incorporate real-time data into ongoing decision-making processes. Leveraging sensor-driven data analytics enhances the adaptability of decision models by updating time-dependent parameters, which results in more reliable outcomes in rapidly changing contexts. This integration is particularly significant for organizations seeking to optimize operational efficiency and improve responsiveness to unpredictable circumstances. The Optimal Agent Framework offers further insights into how adaptive simulation can be integrated with agent-based modeling (ABM) to improve decision-making in complex systems. By aligning decision-making processes with ABM, organizations can simulate interdependencies among agents more effectively, enabling better decision-making under uncertainty and enhancing strategic planning capabilities. Real-time simulation frameworks also support multi-objective decision-making by enabling continuous analysis of operational trade-offs.

8.11 Machine Learning Optimization Models

In the age of data abundance, the challenge for decision-makers is no longer the scarcity of information, but the ability to translate torrents of predictions into precise, impactful actions. Prescriptive analytics stands at this frontier, transforming foresight into strategy by answering the question, "Given what we know, what should we do?" ML optimization models emerge as a powerful synthesis. Rather than operating in isolation, these models form an integrated pipeline: ML anticipates outcomes, optimization prescribes the best possible choices under real-world constraints, and feedback loops refine decisions in a continuous cycle of learning. This convergence is reshaping how industries approach resource allocation, operational planning, and policy design, making prescriptive analytics not merely a tool for insight but a compass for action in complex, uncertain landscapes.

8.11.1 Conceptual Framework

8.11.1.1 Core Components

The architecture of ML optimization within prescriptive analytics can be understood through three essential components that collectively enable the transformation of raw data into informed action: prediction, optimization, and feedback.

Prediction Layer: At the front end of the system lies the predictive engine, powered by ML models. These models estimate uncertain parameters, anticipate future demands, and assign probabilities to potential scenarios. Without this layer, optimization would be operating in a vacuum, uninformed by the dynamic realities that shape decision outcomes.

Optimization Layer: The predictive outputs form the input data for the optimization component, where the focus shifts from describing "what might happen" to prescribing "what should be done." Here, mathematical optimization models—ranging from linear and integer programming to nonlinear or stochastic frameworks—determine the best set of actions under constraints such as cost, capacity, or regulatory compliance. The synergy of prediction and optimization ensures that decisions are both informed and practical.

Feedback Loop: Decisions, however, cannot be regarded as static one-time prescriptions. The environment evolves, markets shift, and unexpected disruptions occur. Thus, the feedback loop becomes indispensable. Outcomes from implemented decisions are collected, assessed, and reintegrated into the system. If a predicted demand level deviates significantly from reality, or if an optimization plan underperforms, the feedback loop triggers recalibration of both predictive and optimization models. Over time, this self-correcting mechanism strengthens the robustness of the system, creating a cycle of continuous improvement.

8.11.1.2 Data-to-Decision Pipeline

The data-to-decision pipeline describes how organizations turn raw information into actionable prescriptions through an iterative, learning-oriented process. It begins with preprocessing, where heterogeneous data is cleaned, integrated, and engineered to ensure quality. ML models then generate forecasts, demand, risk, and customer behavior, which serve as inputs to optimization models that convert predictions into decisions aimed at maximizing value or minimizing cost. These prescriptions are implemented through operational changes such as resource allocation or policy adjustments. Finally, performance is evaluated to determine whether forecasts and decisions were effective, and these insights feed back into the system. In essence, the cycle of Data → Prediction → Optimization → Action → Evaluation creates a continuously improving ecosystem that links evidence, decision-making, and adaptability.

8.11.2 Categories of ML-Integrated Optimization Models

8.11.2.1 ML for Parameter Estimation in Optimization

In contemporary business environments, the integration of ML techniques in optimization models has gained significant traction, particularly concerning parameter estimation. A critical aspect of this integration is the use of supervised learning methods to predict model parameters, which can substantially improve decision-making processes in various domains, including supply chain optimization. Gradient boosting techniques, such as XGBoost and LightGBM, have demonstrated remarkable performance in predicting outcomes and optimizing parameters within business processes. These models leverage the power of ensemble learning to improve accuracy, making them suitable for complex datasets typical in BA. Additionally, integrating automated machine learning (AutoML) allows organizations to streamline the process of selecting appropriate models for parameter estimation, facilitating quicker and more efficient adaptations to market changes.

Deep learning has also emerged as a powerful tool in predicting model parameters. This approach is particularly prevalent within contexts that involve unstructured data, such as customer interactions. By utilizing neural networks, businesses can glean insights from vast datasets, enabling more nuanced predictions. Furthermore, the interaction between ML and optimization strategies facilitates enhanced operational efficiency. Organizations employing ML-integrated optimization models can dynamically adjust strategies based on real-time data, enabling proactive decision-making.

8.11.2.2 End-to-End ML Optimization

The emergence of ML in the context of optimization has significantly impacted various business sectors, particularly through models that integrate optimization objectives directly into ML training. This approach, known as end-to-end ML optimization, leverages architectural innovations such as differentiable optimization layers and neural combinatorial optimization frameworks, facilitating a cohesive integration of predictive analytics with operational objectives.

Differentiable optimization layers enable direct optimization of parameters within the ML pipeline. These layers allow gradients to be computed through the optimization process, meaning that the optimization of ML algorithms can be aligned with business objectives in a unified framework. This method enhances the training of models by aligning loss functions directly with performance metrics relevant to the business. Furthermore, differentiable programming paradigms have been shown to facilitate automatic differentiation of optimization problems, leading to rapid convergence and improved solution quality across various applications.

Neural combinatorial optimization represents another significant advancement, particularly for complex decision-making and resource allocation problems often faced in business contexts. This approach uses neural networks to tackle combinatorial optimization tasks, enabling more efficient solution searches in high-dimensional spaces.

8.11.2.3 Reinforcement Learning (RL) for Sequential Decision-Making

Reinforcement Learning (RL) has emerged as a transformative approach in business, particularly for sequential decision-making in dynamic environments. By serving as a bridge between simulation and optimization, RL adeptly addresses complex decision processes that require real-time adaptability to evolving circumstances. Its methodology enables the formulation of intricate strategies that optimize long-term outcomes, a valuable characteristic for businesses operating in competitive or rapidly changing markets.

At the core of RL is the principle of learning through interaction with the environment. Agents receive feedback in the form of rewards or penalties, which inform future actions. This iterative feedback process is essential for developing optimal decision policies, especially in scenarios where business strategies need to adjust based on fluctuating market conditions or consumer behaviors. Additionally, the integration of RL with simulation enables businesses to test various decision-making strategies in controlled virtual environments before deploying them in real-world operations. This simulation–optimization synergy fosters an understanding of different scenarios and prepares organizations for potential market variations or operational challenges.

8.11.2.4 Black-Box Optimization with ML Surrogates

Black-box optimization with ML surrogates has become a crucial methodology in various business applications. This technique involves using ML models to approximate complex or expensive-to-evaluate objective functions, making it possible to explore and optimize systems more efficiently than traditional methods might allow. Surrogates can capture the essential relationships between input design variables and output performance measures, significantly reducing the number of expensive evaluations needed. This approach has been illustrated in applications such as the design optimization of noise filters, where models can utilize black-box optimization techniques to efficiently find optimal solutions while minimizing computational resources. The ML models used as surrogates in black-box optimization often belong to the category of black-box models themselves due to their inherent opacity. Techniques such as GPs, random forests, and deep neural networks can function effectively as surrogates, offering predictions that involve very few assumptions about the underlying systems they represent. These models benefit from their ability to learn complex patterns and make accurate predictions without requiring detailed domain knowledge. Additionally, in the context of dealing with multiple objectives, incorporating BO allows the model to make informed decisions based on prior evaluations, further streamlining the optimization process.

8.11.3 Optimization Techniques in ML-Driven Prescriptive Analytics

8.11.3.1 Classical Optimization

In the realm of ML-driven prescriptive analytics, classical optimization techniques such as LP, MILP, and Quadratic Programming (QP) are critical tools for businesses seeking to optimize decision-making processes. By incorporating ML inputs, these optimization techniques can be enhanced, allowing organizations to establish more refined constraints and objectives that reflect real-world complexities. LP is a common optimization approach deployed in various business applications where the relationships involved can be expressed through linear equations. The LP methodology facilitates the efficient allocation of limited resources among competing activities. ML outputs can refine the constraints used in the LP model, ensuring that decisions are based not only on historical data but also on predictive analytics.

MILP extends LP by allowing for both continuous and integer variables, which is particularly useful in scenarios that require decisions about discrete choices. QP pertains to optimization problems where the objective function is quadratic, and constraints are linear. Integrating insights from ML can enhance the accuracy of the optimization process. By adapting these predictive outputs into the QP framework, organizations can create investment strategies that are not only optimal mathematically but also aligned with expected market behavior.

8.11.3.2 Metaheuristics and Hybrid Approaches

Metaheuristics and hybrid approaches, particularly utilizing GAs, SA, and TS, enhanced by ML guidance, provide robust frameworks for solving complex optimization problems in business contexts. GAs are particularly useful in scenarios requiring optimization over large and complex search spaces. GAs mimic natural selection processes to evolve solutions iteratively. Integrating ML can enhance the performance of GAs by utilizing previous results to inform mutation and crossover operations.

SA, like GAs, is a probabilistic technique for approximating the global optimum of a given function. It is particularly suited for discrete optimization problems where traditional methods may falter. The methodology follows a cooling schedule analogous to physical annealing in metallurgy. When combined with ML, SA can utilize predictive analytics to adjust its cooling parameters dynamically.

TS is another metaheuristic that extends the capabilities of local search methods by maintaining a "tabu list" of previously explored solutions to avoid cycles and encourage exploration of new areas in the solution space. With the integration of ML, businesses can enhance TS by training models to predict which areas of the search space are likely to yield optimal solutions based on historical data.

8.11.3.3 Stochastic and Robust Optimization

In the domain of ML-driven prescriptive analytics, the ability to address prediction uncertainty is fundamental to ensuring effective decision-making. Since ML models often generate forecasts that are subject to noise, variability, or structural changes, decision-makers cannot rely on predictions alone without accounting for their inherent uncertainty. To address this challenge, two families of optimization methods have been widely applied: stochastic optimization and robust optimization. Both approaches provide frameworks that allow organizations to design strategies capable of withstanding variability in predictive outputs and external conditions, thereby enhancing the resilience of prescriptive decisions in dynamic business environments.

Stochastic optimization addresses uncertainty by embedding it directly into the optimization process. Instead of treating predictions as fixed values, stochastic models incorporate probabilities associated with different potential outcomes, thereby enabling strategies that are feasible across a range of scenarios. A common technique within this framework is the use of chance constraints, which guarantee that certain decision criteria will be satisfied with a specified level of probability. Robust optimization focuses on ensuring that strategies perform effectively under worst-case scenarios. This perspective is particularly important when the true probability distribution of uncertain parameters is unknown or subject to abrupt shifts. Distributionally robust optimization (DRO) extends this concept by constructing ambiguity sets that encompass a family of possible probability distributions, thereby allowing organizations to hedge against unexpected deviations in the data. By protecting against worst-case outcomes, DRO enables decision-makers to maximize operational performance even under adverse conditions.

8.12 AI-Powered Resource Planning

8.12.1 Defining Resource Planning in the Digital Era

Resource planning has long been at the heart of organizational management, serving as the process through which firms allocate scarce resources—capital, labor, materials, and technology—toward competing priorities. In its traditional form, resource allocation was primarily deterministic and rule-based, relying on historical averages, managerial intuition, and rigid scheduling systems. These methods, while effective in relatively stable environments, often struggled to adapt to fluctuations in demand, disruptions in supply, and the growing complexity of modern operations. The result was a planning paradigm characterized by efficiency under certainty, but brittleness under uncertainty.

In contrast, AI-driven resource planning reimagines this process as adaptive, data-rich, and continuously optimized. Rather than relying solely on static rules or linear projections, AI integrates real-time data streams, predictive modeling, and prescriptive optimization techniques to dynamically adjust resource allocation. ML algorithms can anticipate demand spikes, detect inefficiencies, and uncover hidden patterns, while optimization engines translate these insights into actionable strategies that balance cost, efficiency, and resilience. The digital era thus marks a fundamental shift: from resource planning as a one-time scheduling task to resource planning as a living, intelligent system that learns, adapts, and prescribes decisions in complex and uncertain environments.

8.12.2 AI-Powered Enhancements to Resource Planning

AI-powered enhancements to resource planning significantly improve organizations' ability to allocate, schedule, and optimize resources in complex and uncertain environments. AI-powered technologies enable more accurate demand forecasting, dynamic capacity planning, and real-time adjustment of resource allocation decisions by integrating ML, predictive analytics, and optimization algorithms into traditional resource planning systems.[13] AI-driven models can analyze large volumes of structured and unstructured data, such as historical transactions, sensor data, and market signals, to identify patterns and anticipate disruptions, thereby reducing inefficiencies and bottlenecks in supply chains, workforce scheduling, and capital utilization.

8.12.2.1 Dynamic Demand Forecasting

Dynamic demand forecasting, empowered by AI, represents a transformative approach to enhancing resource planning within supply chains. This capability addresses critical operational challenges by minimizing demand variability and improving overall efficiency in supply chain management. AI technologies improve forecasting accuracy by harnessing vast datasets and advanced algorithms, offering more reliable predictions compared to traditional methods. The adaptability of AI in forecasting supports dynamic resource allocation, particularly in environments characterized by demand uncertainty. Resource allocation methodologies based on dynamic frameworks, tailored to AI and ML applications, optimize workload attributes, resource availability, and real-time demand, thus reducing latency and enhancing performance.

8.12.2.2 Scenario Generation and Simulation

AI-driven scenario generation and simulation represent major advancements in resource planning, particularly within business contexts. These methodologies enable organizations to conduct "what-if" analyses and support continuous improvement through simulation-based optimization and reinforcement learning. The application of AI in scenario generation allows businesses to analyze large datasets and uncover patterns that inform strategic planning. AI-driven simulation extends beyond scenario generation to incorporate advanced optimization techniques, which enhance decision-making quality and operational efficiency. Simulation-based optimization integrates AI models to evaluate alternative scenarios, enabling firms to identify the most effective strategies in response to dynamic conditions. This process allows organizations to test operational strategies, assess resilience, and prepare for demand volatility or supply chain disruptions.

8.12.2.3 Resource Matching and Allocation

AI-powered enhancements to resource planning, particularly in intelligent matching and allocation of resources such as human capital, inventory, and assets, have become vital components of effective operational strategies in modern business contexts. Natural Language Processing (NLP) plays a central role in this transformation by enabling the analysis of unstructured data, which is highly relevant in workforce planning and decision-making.

Intelligent resource matching allows organizations to optimize the allocation of both human capital and physical assets according to operational needs. Forecasting methods that link workforce availability to expected service volumes ensure alignment between resource supply and demand, thereby reducing inefficiencies and enhancing productivity. Achieving this balance is critical for maintaining service quality while minimizing costs. NLP makes significant contributions by extracting insights from unstructured data sources commonly found in workforce planning.

Simulation-based approaches further enrich AI-driven resource planning. Dynamic modeling techniques can provide a comprehensive understanding of the supply–demand equilibrium, supporting more accurate predictions of resource needs and enabling the implementation of targeted strategies for workforce and asset allocation. The integration of AI with simulation fosters continuous improvement in operational efficiency while equipping organizations with the agility to adapt to shifting market conditions.

8.12.2.4 Multi-Objective Optimization

AI-powered enhancements in resource planning, particularly through MOO, are transforming business operations by enabling organizations to balance competing demands such as cost, time, quality, sustainability, and resilience. The application of AI-driven trade-off analysis supports the identification of Pareto-efficient solutions, thereby improving decision-making in complex resource allocation contexts. At the core of MOO lies the challenge of reconciling conflicting criteria.

Trade-off analysis within MOO operates through identifying Pareto-efficient solutions, where improving one objective necessarily entails concessions in another. This enables organizations to visualize decision pathways and evaluate the implications of their choices. Insights derived from such analyses allow firms to manage trade-offs proactively, improving resource utilization while strengthening competitive advantage.

8.12.3 Future Directions

RL combined with optimization offers a powerful path for more adaptive resource planning. RL learns policies through continuous interaction with dynamic environments, making it well-suited for conditions marked by uncertainty, fluctuating demand, and variable resource availability. When paired with optimization, RL yields not just reactive responses but forward-looking decisions that improve over time. As simulation capabilities expand, RL-enhanced optimization will enable more resilient planning in sectors such as energy and logistics, where real-time adjustments and long-horizon strategy are equally important.

Autonomous planning systems push prescriptive analytics toward self-correcting, real-time decision engines. These systems sense, analyze, and act in a closed loop, adjusting plans instantly as conditions shift—rerouting logistics, reallocating medical resources, or managing supply disruptions without human intervention. Future systems will likely blend optimization, forecasting, and RL to anticipate disruptions before they occur. As autonomy grows, organizations will need governance and transparency mechanisms to ensure these systems remain trustworthy and aligned with strategic objectives.

Human–AI collaboration will remain vital, especially when choices carry ethical trade-offs or demand contextual judgment. AI will function as a decision co-pilot—surfacing trade-offs, generating scenarios, and identifying efficient options—while humans retain authority over strategic direction. Effective collaboration requires interpretable and transparent systems that explain their recommendations. When done well, this partnership expands decision-making capacity and grounds data-driven insights in human experience and institutional values.

Sustainability-driven optimization brings environmental and social objectives into the core of resource planning. AI enables multi-objective models that balance cost, efficiency, carbon reduction, waste minimization, and workforce well-being. As ESG expectations intensify, firms will increasingly incorporate carbon accounting, circular economy principles, and life-cycle metrics directly into planning models. This shift reframes optimization as a long-term resilience strategy—ensuring organizations compete successfully while safeguarding environmental and social systems for future generations.

8.13 Summary

This chapter explores the field of prescriptive analytics, the third and most advanced stage of data analytics, following descriptive and predictive analytics. While descriptive analytics answers "What happened?" and predictive analytics answers "What might happen?", prescriptive analytics answers "What should we do?" by recommending actions that lead to optimal decision-making based on data, predictions, and constraints.

The chapter begins by defining prescriptive analytics and distinguishing it from other forms of analytics. It highlights its integration with optimization models, simulation, decision analysis, and ML, aiming to guide businesses toward the best possible outcomes. Key tools include LP, integer programming, stochastic optimization, and heuristics, which help solve complex problems in resource allocation, scheduling, supply chain management, pricing, and risk management. Various real-world applications are discussed, from supply chain optimization and workforce scheduling to dynamic pricing and logistics routing. The chapter also emphasizes the importance of aligning analytics with business objectives and constraints, ensuring that recommendations are both feasible and actionable. Finally, the chapter discusses emerging trends such as AI-powered prescriptive systems, real-time optimization, and automated decision-making, as well as the ethical considerations of deploying optimization algorithms that affect human lives and resource allocation. In summary, the chapter underscores those prescriptive analytics that empower organizations to move from insights to action, providing a competitive edge by enabling proactive and data-driven decision-making.

Notes

1 Bertsimas, D., & Kallus, N. (2020). From predictive to prescriptive analytics. *Management Science*, 66(3), 1025–1044. https://doi.org/10.1287/mnsc.2018.3253. Available at https://pubsonline.informs.org/doi/abs/10.1287/mnsc.2018.3253
2 Watson, H. J. (2014). Tutorial: Big data analytics—Concepts, technologies, and applications. *Communications of the Association for Information Systems*, 34, 1247–1268. https://doi.org/10.17705/1CAIS.03462. Available at https://aisel.aisnet.org/cais/vol34/iss1/65/
3 Piacentini, C., Castro, M., Cire, A., & Beck, J. C. (2018, April). Linear and integer programming-based heuristics for cost-optimal numeric planning. In *Proceedings of the AAAI Conference on Artificial Intelligence* (Vol. 32, No. 1). https://doi.org/10.1609/aaai.v32i1.12082. Available at https://ojs.aaai.org/index.php/AAAI/article/view/12082
4 Pedroso, J. P. (2002). An evolutionary solver for pure integer linear programming. *International Transactions in Operational Research*, 9(3), 337–352. https://doi.org/10.1111/1475-3995.00359. Available at https://onlinelibrary.wiley.com/doi/abs/10.1111/1475-3995.00359?casa_token=UQyrTklBKVYAAAAA%3AsI9PjMWEfiGd1N86UTZIExCiDk5fsa6xCwglzFuntyWXOpMOAz5RDV4TogUcda3khsF6D4dGLWve09VU
5 Charlton, J., Maddock, S., & Richmond, P. (2019). Two-dimensional batch linear programming on the GPU. *Journal of Parallel and Distributed Computing*, 126, 152–160. https://doi.org/10.1016/j.jpdc.2019.01.001. Available at https://www.sciencedirect.com/science/article/abs/pii/S074373151830399X
6 Jie, G. E. N. G., Zhang, M., & Dechun, Z. H. U. (2024). A full-Newton step feasible interior-point algorithm for the special weighted linear complementarity problems based on a kernel function. *Wuhan University Journal of Natural Sciences*, 29(1), 29–37. https://doi.org/10.1051/wujns/2024291029. Available at https://wujns.edpsciences.org/articles/wujns/abs/2024/01/wujns-1007-1202-2024-01-0029-09/wujns-1007-1202-2024-01-0029-09.html
7 Gondzio, J. (2013). Convergence analysis of an inexact feasible interior point method for convex quadratic programming. *SIAM Journal on Optimization*, 23(3), 1510–1527. https://doi.org/10.1137/120886017. Available at https://epubs.siam.org/doi/abs/10.1137/120886017
8 Wasserstein, R. L., & Lazar, N. A. (2016). The ASA's statement on p-values: Context, process, and purpose. *The American Statistician*, 70(2), 129–133. https://doi.org/10.1080/00031305.2016.1154108. Available at https://www.tandfonline.com/doi/full/10.1080/00031305.2016.1154108

9 Greenland, S., Senn, S. J., Rothman, K. J., Carlin, J. B., Poole, C., Goodman, S. N., & Altman, D. G. (2016). Statistical tests, p values, confidence intervals, and power: A guide to misinterpretations. *European Journal of Epidemiology*, 31(4), 337–350. https://doi.org/10.1007/s10654-016-0149-3. Available at https://link.springer.com/article/10.1007/s10654-016-0149-3

10 Pearson, K. (1900). On the criterion that a given system of deviations from the probable in the case of a correlated system of variables is such that it can be reasonably supposed to have arisen from random sampling. *Philosophical Magazine*, 50(302), 157–175. https://doi.org/10.1080/14786440009463897. Available at https://www.tandfonline.com/doi/pdf/10.1080/14786440009463897

11 Bayes, T. (1763). An essay towards solving a problem in the doctrine of chances. *Philosophical Transactions of the Royal Society of London*, 53, 370–418. https://doi.org/10.1098/rstl.1763.0053. Available at https://royalsocietypublishing.org/rstl/article/doi/10.1098/rstl.1763.0053/119736/LII-An-essay-towards-solving-a-problem-in-the

12 Gelman, A., Simpson, D., & Betancourt, M. (2020). The prior can often only be understood in the context of the likelihood. *Entropy*, 22(1), 1–13. https://doi.org/10.3390/e19100555. Available at https://www.mdpi.com/1099-4300/19/10/555

13 Choi, T. M., Wallace, S. W., & Wang, Y. (2018). Big data analytics in operations management. *Production and Operations Management*, 27(10), 1868–1883. https://doi.org/10.1111/poms.12838. Available at https://journals.sagepub.com/doi/full/10.1111/poms.12838?casa_token=nfhLAQE4tFEAAAAA%3AodNBaSl6Php3Phb-I38jnizlIpod64S8GqssdaaBMkACaejS85lh9SRrSdnuSTS8Ev_0i8tP6VVOFg

9 Predictive Analytics and Forecasting

Learning Objectives

- Learn time series analysis and forecasting methods
- Understand moving average, exponential smoothing, ARIMA, and state-space models
- Learn financial analytics and fraud detection
- Understand use cases in demand forecasting and financial modeling
- Engineer features for time series data
- Understand the modeling process of data cleaning, feature engineering, model selection, training, testing, and validation
- Learn forecasting techniques such as moving averages, exponential smoothing, and ARIMA, which are crucial for sequential data analysis
- Understand popular predictive models, including linear and logistic regression, decision trees, neural networks, support vector machines, and ensemble methods

9.1 Introduction

In today's digital world, organizations can utilize predictive analytics and forecasting techniques to anticipate future trends, behaviors, and outcomes to stay globally competitive. Predictive analytics and forecasting tools enable organizations to move beyond understanding what has happened (descriptive analytics) to predict what is likely to happen next. This forward-looking approach assists organizations in leveraging historical data, statistical algorithms, and ML techniques through predictive analytics to find actionable insights and be prepared for future opportunities and challenges. Predictive analytics and forecasting techniques presented in this chapter empower organizations to estimate future events or trends based on patterns and relationships identified in historical data in predicting customer demand, sales performance, market trends, assessing operational risks, and making proactive, data-driven decisions. The insights provided by utilizing predictive analytics and forecasting tools and techniques are invaluable for strategic planning, resource allocation, risk assessment and management, and decision-making to ensure a competitive edge in dynamic markets. This chapter presents predictive analytics and forecasting tools, methodologies to harness the power of predictive insights, unlock new opportunities, mitigate risks, and drive sustainable growth in today's data-centric world.

DOI: 10.4324/9781003664550-9

9.2 Essentials of Predictive Analytics and Forecasting

Predictive analytics and forecasting are integral components of modern business intelligence that enable organizations to anticipate future trends, behaviors, and outcomes based on analyzing historical and real-time data. Predictive analytics uses a combination of statistical techniques, AI-powered tools, ML algorithms, and data mining to build models that identify patterns and relationships within data, which can then be used to predict future events with a certain level of confidence. These models often incorporate variables from diverse sources, including customer demographics, transactional history, market conditions, and external factors like economic indicators, making predictions more accurate and relevant. Forecasting, a subset of predictive analytics, specifically focuses on estimating future values based on time series data and trend analysis, employing methods such as moving averages (MAs), time series analysis, regression models, decision trees, neural networks, ensemble methods, exponential smoothing, and ARIMA models to project sales, demand, stock prices, inventory needs, or financial performance. Together, predictive analytics and forecasting enable proactive decision-making by allowing businesses to optimize operations, tailor marketing strategies, manage risks, and allocate resources efficiently. These predictive analytics and forecasting techniques are extensively used in various sectors, from retail, where they help anticipate consumer buying patterns, to finance, where they assist in credit risk assessment and stock market prediction, to supply chain management, where they improve inventory control and logistics planning. Advances in AI, ML, and big data technologies have further enhanced the accuracy and scalability of these techniques, integrating real-time data streams and complex variable interactions to provide dynamic, continuously updated forecasts. As data availability, computational power, and AI-assisted technologies continue to grow, the integration of predictive models with real-time analytics and business intelligence systems has become increasingly essential for achieving operational excellence, enhancing customer experiences, and sustaining competitive advantage in today's dynamic and competitive business environment.

9.3 Time Series Foundations and Forecasting Approaches

Time flows forward, but data carries its echoes. Every stock price, every sales figure, every temperature reading is not merely a number; it is a point on a timeline, part of a story unfolding across days, months, or years. In predictive analytics, time series analysis stands as the art and science of listening to these stories, detecting the rhythms of seasonality, the steady hum of long-term trends, and the sudden disruptions of irregular shocks. Unlike cross-sectional snapshots, which freeze the world in a single instant, time series data reveals motion, continuity, and evolution. Forecasting, then, is not a matter of gazing into crystal balls but of using disciplined methods to harness the memory of the past to anticipate the shape of the future.

9.3.1 Key Components and Their Forecasting Approaches

9.3.1.1 Trend

Trends represent the long-term direction of a time series, capturing whether values are steadily rising, falling, or leveling off. In predictive analytics, identifying a trend is crucial because it shapes the baseline upon which seasonal or irregular fluctuations build. Forecasting methods like Holt's linear exponential smoothing explicitly model upward or downward trajectories, adapting to persistent growth or decline. Regression-based approaches can also be used to quantify and project these patterns, linking trends to explanatory variables such as population growth or economic expansion. By recognizing trends, forecasters can avoid mistaking steady structural movement for temporary noise.

9.3.1.2 Seasonality

Seasonality refers to repeating, predictable patterns that occur at fixed intervals, such as higher retail sales in December or increased electricity consumption in summer. For predictive analytics, seasonality is both a challenge and an opportunity: while it introduces variability, it also offers strong signals for future behavior. Forecasting methods like Holt-Winters exponential smoothing extend trend models to explicitly capture seasonal cycles, while SARIMA decomposes both autoregressive and MA dynamics with seasonal adjustments. Effective modeling of seasonality helps businesses anticipate recurring demands, aligning forecasts with the calendar's natural rhythms.

9.3.1.3 Stationarity

Stationarity is the bedrock assumption for many time series models, requiring that statistical properties such as mean and variance remain stable over time. Non-stationary series, which may drift or fluctuate unpredictably, can lead to unreliable forecasts if left unaddressed. Differencing—a process of subtracting each value from its predecessors is a common transformation used to achieve stationarity by removing persistent trends. ARIMA models rely heavily on this principle, combining differencing with autoregressive and MA components. Ensuring stationarity allows analysts to harness the underlying dependencies in data without being misled by shifting baselines.

9.3.1.4 Noise

Noise represents the irregular, unpredictable fluctuations that obscure underlying patterns in time series data. While noise can never be eliminated, effective forecasting requires separating the signal from randomness. Smoothing techniques, such as MAs or exponential smoothing, filter out short-term volatility to reveal the more stable structure beneath. Ensemble methods, which combine multiple models, can further mitigate the impact of noise by pooling diverse perspectives into more robust forecasts. For predictive analytics, managing noise is not about silencing uncertainty but about ensuring that random shocks do not dominate the story the data is trying to tell.

9.3.2 Applications in Predictive Analytics

A significant use case of predictive analytics is through established statistical models such as ARIMA, which has demonstrated high predictive accuracy for various types of time series data, including agricultural production forecasts. The autoregressive integrated moving average (ARIMA) model is favored due to its ability to analyze and forecast linear patterns in both stationary and non-stationary datasets. This versatility makes it particularly suitable for business environments where demand and supply fluctuations are inherent. Furthermore, advancements in ML have enriched the forecasting landscape. Techniques such as Generalized Regression Neural Networks have shown promise in utilizing information from multiple time series to improve individual forecasting. Furthermore, deep learning models are crucial in managing inherent noise in time series data, thereby improving predictive accuracy.

9.4 Probability Theory and Distributions

In the realm of prescriptive analytics, decisions are seldom made in the comfort of certainty. Whether optimizing supply chains, allocating resources, or managing risk, we often navigate environments shaped by chance and variability. This is where probability theory enters, not as a side note but as a fundamental language for encoding uncertainty and structuring decisions around it. Random variables serve as the building blocks of this language, allowing us to model and quantify uncertain events. From the number of late shipments to fluctuations in customer demand, probability distributions such as the binomial, Poisson, and normal distributions offer us tools to describe these phenomena with rigor. By understanding these distributions, analysts gain not just mathematical insight but the ability to craft optimization models that are more resilient, realistic, and responsive to the unpredictable nature of the real world.

9.4.1 Random Variables: The Bridge between Chance and Choice

9.4.1.1 Types of Random Variables

Discrete random variables take on a countable number of distinct values, often representing outcomes that can be enumerated. These variables are prevalent in scenarios where the underlying phenomena can be quantified into finite outcomes, such as the counting of occurrences (e.g., the number of heads in a series of coin flips). Discrete random variables might follow specific distributions, such as the binomial or Poisson distributions, which are widely used in areas like quality control and reliability engineering.

Continuous random variables can assume any value within a specified range and are used to model phenomena characterized by measurements, such as height, weight, or temperature. The distribution of a continuous random variable is described by a PDF, which outlines the likelihood of the variable falling within a certain range rather than taking distinct values. Notably, continuous variables can exhibit properties that differ markedly from their discrete counterparts, such as differences in entropy measures.

Mixed random variables, which contain both discrete and continuous components, exhibit characteristics of both types of variables. These variables appear frequently in complex real-world applications where an event can have both continual and discrete parameters, such as in financial models that account for both the continuous nature of asset prices and discrete events like defaults or bankruptcies.

9.4.1.2 Key Characteristics: Expectation and Variance

In the realm of probability and statistics, random variables serve as pivotal constructs that underline both theoretical analysis and practical decision-making. Key characteristics of random variables include expectation and variance, which provide essential insights into the behavior of these variables. Expectation refers to the average or mean value of a random variable, encapsulating the notion of central tendency. For discrete random variables, the expectation can be computed using the formula.

$$E[X] = \sum_i x_i \cdot P(X = x_i)$$

where:

x_i = Possible values that X can take.
$P(X = x_i)$ = Probability that X takes the value x_i.

In continuous cases, it is determined via the integral of the product of the variable's value and its PDF across its domain. For discrete random variables, the expectation can be computed using the formula.

$$E[X] = \int_{-\infty}^{\infty} x \cdot f(x) dx$$

where:

$f(x)$ = Probability density function (PDF) of X.

The concept of linearity of expectation is particularly noteworthy, as it holds irrespective of independence. That is, for any two random variables (X) and (Y), $E(X+Y) = E(X) + E(Y)$. This property simplifies complexity during analysis and applications across various domains.

Variance measures the dispersion or spread of a random variable's possible values around its expected value, providing crucial information about the variability inherent in the outcomes. For a discrete random variable, variance is calculated using the formula.

$$\text{Var}(X) = E\left[(X - E[X])^2\right] = \sum_i (x_i - \mu)^2 \cdot P(X = x_i)$$

where:

$\mu = E[X]$

In continuous cases, variance is derived using a similar approach but involves integration over the PDF.

$$\text{Var}(X) = E\left[(X - E[X])^2\right] = \int_{-\infty}^{\infty} (x - \mu)^2 \cdot f(x) dx$$

where:

$f(x)$ is the probability density function and $\mu = E[X]$.

Understanding variance is essential in fields such as finance, quality control, and risk assessment, where the degree of variability impacts strategic decision-making. The interplay between expectation and variance is pivotal in many analyses, influencing not only the theoretical frameworks but also the practical applications of random variable theory.

9.4.2 *Binomial Distribution: Modeling Discrete Successes*

9.4.2.1 *The Structure of a Binomial Process*

The binomial distribution is one of the foundational models in probability theory, particularly suited for analyzing outcomes that stem from repeated, discrete events. At its core lies a simple premise: an experiment or process is repeated a fixed number of times, each trial results in one of two mutually exclusive outcomes—success or failure—and the probability of success remains constant across trials. The trials must also be independent, meaning the outcome of one trial does not influence the outcome of another.

Mathematically, the probability of observing exactly k successes is given by the binomial probability mass function:

$$P(X = k) = \binom{n}{k} p^k (1-p)^{n-k}$$

where:

n = Number of independent trials
k = Number of observed successes (with $0 \le k \le n$)
p = Probability of success on a single trial
$1-p$ = Probability of failure on a single trial
$\binom{n}{k}$ = Represents the number of possible combinations of k successes out of n trials

This formula expresses the likelihood of achieving a specific number of successes across all possible arrangements. The mean of the distribution is np, and its variance is $np(1-p)$, which offers crucial insights for evaluating expected outcomes and their variability. These statistical summaries are especially valuable in prescriptive contexts where risk and uncertainty need to be quantitatively managed.

9.4.2.2 *Applications in Decision Models*

In quality control and operations management, the binomial distribution offers a principled way to assess the probability of producing a certain number of defective units in a batch. Consider a manufacturing line where 1% of items are defective on average. If 200 items are sampled, the binomial model allows managers to estimate the likelihood that more than a critical threshold (say, five items) is flawed—triggering preemptive maintenance or inspection protocols. In this way, binomial distribution becomes a risk assessment tool, helping organizations maintain high service quality with minimal waste.

Staffing and scheduling decisions can also benefit from binomial modeling. In healthcare, for example, hospital administrators may be concerned with the number of on-call nurses who report for duty during the flu season. Each nurse's availability might be uncertain, but with an estimated probability of attendance, the binomial model can predict the distribution of available staff. This information supports robust planning by allowing decision-makers to optimize shift assignments, backup resources, or patient load distributions.

9.4.3 Poisson Distribution: Modeling Rare Events over Time

9.4.3.1 Defining the Poisson Process

The Poisson process is defined as a stochastic process that counts the number of events occurring within a given time interval, if these events happen independently and with a constant average rate. Formally, a Poisson process $N(t)$ can be characterized by the following properties: (1) the number of events in non-overlapping intervals is independent, (2) the number of events in an interval of length (t) follows a Poisson distribution with parameter $\lambda(t)$ (where λ is the rate of events per time unit), and (3) the process has stationary increments, meaning that the probability of observing a certain number of events only depends on the length of the interval, not its location in time.

9.4.3.2 Use Cases in Prescriptive Settings

A critical application of Poisson distribution lies in service operations. Non-homogeneous Poisson processes, which allow the event rate to vary over time, have proven effective in modeling customer demand in environments such as call centers and healthcare facilities. This method allows organizations to forecast peak times and allocate personnel or resources more efficiently, thereby improving service quality through better alignment of capacity and fluctuations in demand. In the context of supply chain and logistics optimization, substantial benefits are derived from Poisson-based modeling. A process analytics framework was developed that leverages historical supply chain event data to anticipate demand fluctuations and support real-time decision-making. By applying the Poisson distribution to capture uncertainties in order arrivals, businesses can construct prescriptive models that reduce inventory costs while maintaining service continuity. This probabilistic insight supports agile and efficient logistics strategies in increasingly complex global supply networks.

9.4.4 Normal Distribution: Modeling Continuous Uncertainty

9.4.4.1 Properties and Importance of the Normal Curve

Normal distribution is a cornerstone of statistical analysis due to its distinctive properties and preeminence in various applications concerning continuous uncertainty. The normal curve, characterized by its symmetric, bell-shaped form, is defined by two parameters: the mean (μ), which denotes the center of the distribution, and the standard deviation (σ), which reflects the dispersion of data around the mean. One significant property of the normal distribution is its symmetry about the mean. This symmetric nature implies that the probability of obtaining a value below the mean is equal to the probability of obtaining a value above the mean. This characteristic allows for the application of simple statistical techniques and facilitates the interpretation of results in inferential statistics. The CLT further amplifies the importance of the normal distribution by asserting that the means of sufficiently large samples will approximate a normal distribution, regardless of the original distribution of the data.

9.5 Moving Average, Exponential Smoothing, ARIMA, and State-Space Models

9.5.1 Moving Average Models

9.5.1.1 Concept and Mechanics

MA models play a pivotal role in time series analysis by capturing the correlation of current observations with past random shocks or impulse responses. These models, first introduced by Slutsky, are foundational in fields like economics and finance, reflecting real-world processes where past errors influence current outcomes.[1] The quintessential framework emerges through the combination of MA and autoregressive processes, leading to the autoregressive moving average (ARMA) and its extension, the autoregressive integrated moving average (ARIMA) model, which is adept at handling non-stationary data by incorporating differencing.

The MA component of these models is significant as it encapsulates the notion that observations are influenced not solely by deterministic trends but also by stochastic elements. In a typical $\text{MA}(q)$ model, the current output is a linear combination of the past q error terms. This design acknowledges that any shock to the system has a finite impact on future values, thereby allowing analysts to forecast outcomes based on historical performance. Understanding the mechanics of MA models also extends to their order selection, which is crucial for model performance. Techniques such as Akaike Information Criterion (AIC) and Bayesian Information Criterion (BIC) aid in estimating both the autoregressive and MA components accurately, ensuring that models are appropriately fitted without overfitting.

9.5.1.2 Application in Prescriptive Analytics

One of the most prominent applications is in forecasting business trends. By smoothing out fluctuations in historical data, MAs help organizations anticipate future patterns in sales, demand, or market activity. This enables proactive decisions regarding inventory levels, pricing adjustments, and marketing campaigns, ensuring that resources are allocated effectively to meet anticipated demand. Performance analysis represents another critical domain where MAs prove useful. By monitoring KPIs, companies can identify emerging trends that warrant managerial intervention. For instance, a gradual decline in service quality metrics might prompt timely actions like retraining staff or reallocating resources, ensuring continuous improvement and sustained competitiveness.

9.5.2 Exponential Smoothing Models

9.5.2.1 Concept and Mechanics

Exponential smoothing is a family of forecasting techniques that places progressively decreasing weights on past observations, giving more influence to recent data while still retaining a memory of the longer history. The method's elegance lies in its recursive structure. Instead of recalculating averages across all past points, forecasts are updated dynamically as new observations arrive. This makes exponential smoothing computationally efficient and well-suited for real-time decision-making environments.

The most basic form is Single Exponential Smoothing (SES), appropriate for series without a clear trend or seasonality. The formula is:

$$F_{t+1} = \alpha Y_t + (1-\alpha) F_t$$

where:

F_{t+1} = Forecast for the next period
Y_t = Actual observation at time
F_t = Forecast made for period
α = Smoothing constant, $0 < \alpha < 1$, controlling responsiveness

When data exhibit a trend, SES proves inadequate, and Holt's Double Exponential Smoothing becomes more appropriate. Holt's method adds a trend component, updating both the level and the slope over time:

$$L_t = \alpha Y_t + (1-\alpha)(L_{t-1} + T_{t-1}) \backslash$$
$$T_t = \beta(L_t - L_{t-1}) + (1-\beta) T_{t-1} \backslash$$
$$F_{t+m} = L_t + mT_t$$

where:

L_t = Estimated level at time
T_t = Estimated trend at time
α, β = Smoothing parameters for level and trend
m = Forecast horizon

9.5.2.2 *Application in Prescriptive Analytics*

In dynamic pricing models, exponential smoothing helps firms adapt prices to evolving demand conditions. For example, in online retail or ride-sharing platforms, smoothed demand forecasts serve as inputs to optimization routines that determine optimal price points, balancing revenue maximization with customer satisfaction. Another application lies in supply chain safety stock optimization. Safety stock is often determined by balancing holding costs against the risk of stockouts, a problem highly sensitive to demand variability. By providing adaptive forecasts that adjust to trends and seasonality, exponential smoothing allows firms to set more accurate reorder points and optimize inventory buffers, thereby reducing both cost and risk.

Exponential smoothing also supports scenario-based optimization. For example, a retail chain may generate multiple forecasts using different smoothing parameters to represent optimistic, pessimistic, and baseline demand scenarios. These scenarios are then fed into optimization models that prescribe ordering and distribution strategies robust to demand uncertainty. Finally, exponential smoothing serves as a baseline forecasting method against which more complex models (ARIMA, state-space, or ML methods) are evaluated.

9.5.3 Autoregressive Integrated Moving Average (ARIMA) Models

9.5.3.1 Concept and Mechanics

The ARIMA model is one of the most widely used and versatile approaches to time series forecasting. It combines three fundamental ideas: autoregression (AR), differencing to induce stationarity (the "integrated" part), and MA of past forecast errors. By uniting these mechanisms, ARIMA models can capture both short-term dependencies and long-term patterns in data.

The autoregressive component (AR) expresses the current value of the series as a linear function of its past values. In a simple AR (p) process, the formula is:

$$Y_t = \phi_1 Y_{t-1} + \phi_2 Y_{t-2} + \cdots + \phi_p Y_{t-p} + \varepsilon_t$$

where:

Y_t = Value of the series at time
ϕ_i = Autoregressive coefficients
p = Order of autoregression
ε_t = Random error term

The MA component incorporates the effect of past shocks or errors, capturing autocorrelation through noise terms. An MA (q) model can be written as:

$$Y_t = \theta_1 \varepsilon_{t-1} + \theta_2 \varepsilon_{t-2} + \cdots + \theta_q \varepsilon_{t-q} + \varepsilon_t$$

where:

θ_j = Moving average coefficients
q = Order of the MA process.

The integrated component (I) refers to differencing the series to make it stationary. A first-order differencing is:

$$\nabla Y_t = Y_t - Y_{t-1}$$

Thus, a general $\text{ARIMA}(p,d,q)$ model incorporates autoregression of order p, differencing of order d, and an MA of order q.

When seasonality is present, the model can be extended to SARIMA, denoted $\text{ARIMA}(p,d,q)(P,D,Q)_s$, where s is the seasonal period. This extension allows the model to capture repeating seasonal structures common in retail sales, tourism, and energy demand.

9.5.3.2 Application in Prescriptive Analytics

In marketing and revenue management, ARIMA can forecast customer demand for promotional periods or product launches. For example, an e-commerce platform might predict how sales volumes respond to seasonal campaigns like Black Friday. These forecasts are then incorporated into pricing optimization models, enabling managers to set prices that maximize revenue while ensuring sufficient inventory availability.

In financial planning and risk management, ARIMA is frequently used to forecast cash flows, revenue streams, or even foreign exchange rates. A company planning capital investments can input ARIMA-based revenue forecasts into optimization models for budgeting and portfolio allocation. This integration allows firms to balance liquidity needs with investment opportunities, reducing the risk of overextension during downturns.

9.5.4 State-Space Models

9.5.4.1 Concept and Mechanics

The mechanics of a state-space model are built upon two fundamental equations: the state equation and the observation equation. These equations form the bedrock of the Kalman filter and broaden Bayesian state-space methodologies. The state equation (or transition equation) describes how the hidden state vector, typically denoted as α_t, evolves from one time period to the next. This evolution is often modeled as a linear process but includes a stochastic error term to account for unpredictable shocks. The observation equation (or measurement equation) defines how the actual observed data point, y_t, is generated from the current hidden state. This equation also includes a measurement error, representing the noise in the data collection process, such as short-term fluctuations or reporting inaccuracies.

A classic linear Gaussian state-space model can be represented by the following specific functions and formulas.

State Equation (System Evolution):

$$\alpha_t = T_t\alpha_{t-1} + R_t\eta_t$$

where:

α_t = Hidden state vector at time t (e.g., containing true demand, trend, and seasonality).
T_t = Transition matrix that defines how the state evolves from $t-1$ to t.
R_t = Matrix that selects which states are affected by the noise.
$\eta_t \sim N(0, Q_t)$ = Process noise, assumed to be normally distributed with mean zero and covariance matrix Q_t. This represents unexpected structural shifts.

Observation Equation (Measurement):

$$y_t = Z_t\alpha_t + \varepsilon_t$$

where:

y_t = Observed data point at time t (e.g., reported sales).
Z_t = Observation matrix that maps the hidden state to the observations.
$\varepsilon_t \sim N(0, H_t)$ = Observation noise, normally distributed with mean zero and variance H_t. This represents measurement error.

The Kalman filter is a celebrated algorithm for this framework. It operates recursively in two steps: prediction and update. The prediction step uses the state equation to project the current state and its uncertainty forward in time. The update step then incorporates the new observation y_t to refine this prediction, resulting in an optimal estimate of the true state. In a Bayesian formulation, the prediction step represents the prior belief about the state, and the update step yields the posterior belief after seeing new evidence. This recursive nature makes the model highly adaptive, as it continuously updates its understanding of the system with each new piece of data.

However, these strengths come with notable limitations. The most prominent is that SSMs can be computationally intensive, especially for high-dimensional states or nonlinear/non-Gaussian problems. While the basic Kalman filter is computationally efficient, more general cases requiring Markov Chain Monte Carlo (MCMC) methods for Bayesian estimation can be prohibitively slow for real-time applications with very large datasets. This computational demand can limit the frequency of model updates or require significant investment in computing infrastructure. Furthermore, state-space models require significant expertise to implement effectively. The modeler must make critical choices about the structure of the state vector (α_t), the transition matrix (T_t), and the various error distributions. Specifying an incorrect model can lead to poor forecasts and misguided decisions.

9.5.4.2 Application in Prescriptive Analytics

A key business application is in dynamic pricing and revenue management. Consider an airline or a hotel managing room rates. A state-space model can be used to represent the hidden, true level of price sensitivity and underlying demand. The observation is the number of bookings received. As new booking data arrives each day, the model updates its estimate of demand elasticity. This updated belief is then used as an input to a prescriptive pricing optimization model, which dynamically adjusts prices to maximize revenue, balancing the goal of selling inventory with the need to avoid selling too early at a low price. The model adapts prices in response to unobserved shifts in market conditions.

In financial trading and risk management, state-space models are used to estimate time-varying parameters, such as the volatility of an asset or the correlation between assets in a portfolio. The famous Stochastic Volatility model is a type of nonlinear state-space model where the log-volatility is a hidden state following an autoregressive process. These evolving risk estimates are then used prescriptively in portfolio optimization algorithms to dynamically adjust asset allocations, hedging against potential downturns and controlling risk exposure in a way that static models cannot. This allows for the creation of adaptive investment strategies that respond to changing market regimes.

9.6 Portfolio Management and Predictive Financial Modeling

9.6.1 Modern Portfolio Theory (MPT)

Introduced by Harry Markowitz in 1952, MPT revolutionized finance by quantitatively demonstrating that diversification can reduce portfolio risk without necessarily sacrificing returns. The core premise is that an investor should not evaluate an asset in isolation but based on its contribution to the portfolio's overall risk and return. MPT shifts the focus from seeking individual "winning" stocks to constructing an optimally balanced "portfolio" of assets. For a business like a mutual fund company, this provides a scientific framework to justify their product offerings, showing clients that the fund's diversified structure is designed to achieve a more favorable risk-return profile than holding any single security.

The mathematics of MPT involves calculating two key metrics for a portfolio: expected return and expected risk (variance or standard deviation). The expected return of a portfolio $E(R_p)$ is a weighted average of the expected returns of its constituent assets. For a two-asset portfolio, the formula is:

$$E(R_p) = w_A E(R_A) + w_B E(R_B)$$

where:

w_A and w_B = Portfolio weights invested in assets A and B (with $w_A + w_B = 1$).
$E(R_A)$ and $E(R_B)$ are the expected returns of assets A and B.

However, the portfolio risk σ_p is not a simple weighted average. It incorporates the covariance between the assets' returns, which measures how they move together:

$$\sigma_p^2 = w_A^2\sigma_A^2 + w_B^2\sigma_B^2 + 2w_A w_B \sigma_{A,B}$$

where:

σ_A^2 and σ_B^2 = Variances of assets A and B.
$\sigma_{A,B}$ = Covariance between A and B. Covariance can also be expressed as $\sigma_{A,B} = \rho_{A,B}\sigma_A\sigma_B$, where $\rho_{A,B}$ is the correlation coefficient.

The business application is profound. If two assets have low or negative correlation ($\rho_{A,B}$ is less than 1 or negative), the third term in the variance equation becomes smaller or negative, reducing the overall portfolio variance. This is mathematical proof of the benefits of diversification. A fund manager can combine volatile assets, but if they are uncorrelated, the overall portfolio volatility can be significantly lower.

The goal of MPT is to identify the Efficient Frontier. This is a set of optimal portfolios that offer the highest expected return for a given level of risk or the lowest risk for a given level of expected return. For an asset management business, any portfolio that lies below the efficient frontier is considered suboptimal because a higher return could be achieved for the same risk, or the same return could be achieved with lower risk. The practical business application involves using optimization software to input expected returns, variances, and covariances for a universe of assets to generate this frontier, which then serves as the guide for constructing client portfolios based on their specific risk tolerance.

9.6.2 *Predictive Financial Modeling*

9.6.2.1 *Overview of Predictive Models*

Time series models are fundamental for forecasting variables recorded over time, such as stock prices, exchange rates, or quarterly sales. The ARIMA model, for instance, is a workhorse for forecasting. Its structure, ARIMA (p,d,q), captures autocorrelations (AR), differencing the data to achieve stationarity (I), and models error terms (MA). A more advanced variant, GARCH, is indispensable in finance for modeling and forecasting volatility. GARCH recognizes that volatility clusters—periods of high volatility tend to be followed by more high volatility.

ML methods offer a different paradigm, often excelling at capturing complex, nonlinear relationships that traditional models might miss. Regression trees make predictions by splitting data into branches based on feature values, creating a set of decision rules. Random forests and Gradient Boosting Machines (like XGBoost) are ensemble techniques that combine hundreds or thousands of such trees to create a single, more accurate and robust model.

The most complex ML models, Neural Networks (NNs) and Deep Learning, are particularly effective for pattern recognition in high-dimensional data. In finance, RNNs and LSTM networks are specialized for sequential data like time series.

9.6.2.2 Feature Selection and Data Inputs

The accuracy of any predictive model is heavily dependent on the quality and relevance of the data fed into it. Macroeconomic indicators are foundational features for most financial models. Variables such as GDP growth rates, inflation (CPI), unemployment figures, and central bank interest rates provide a crucial backdrop for forecasting asset prices and corporate performance.

Beyond traditional metrics, microeconomic indicators offer granular insights. Company-specific data from financial statements are direct inputs for equity valuation models. For credit risk modeling, features like a firm's cash flow stability and interest coverage ratio are paramount.

The process of feature engineering—creating new, more predictive variables from raw data—is a critical step. For a time series model predicting stock returns, a raw price series is less useful than engineered features like MAs, momentum indicators (e.g., the rate of change over 12 months), or volatility measures. For an ML model, feature engineering might involve creating interaction terms (e.g., P/E ratio multiplied by sector growth rate) or reducing dimensionality using techniques like PCA to improve model performance and computational efficiency.

9.6.2.3 Model Evaluation

A model's performance on historical data is no guarantee of its future effectiveness; therefore, rigorous evaluation is a non-negotiable step in the business workflow. Predictive accuracy is quantified using specific metrics. The RMSE is a common metric that penalizes large errors more heavily than small ones, making it sensitive to outliers. It is calculated as the square root of the average squared differences between predicted and actual values. The MAE, which is the average of the absolute differences, provides a more intuitive measure of average error magnitude. For business contexts where relative error is more important, the Mean Absolute Percentage Error (MAPE) is used, expressing the error as a percentage of the actual value, which is easily communicable to management. The gold standard for evaluating financial models is backtesting. This involves running the model on historical data, simulating the decisions that would have been made, and calculating the resulting performance (e.g., portfolio returns, Sharpe ratio, maximum drawdown). A robust backtest must account for real-world constraints like transaction costs and slippage.

9.6.3 Integration with Prescriptive Analytics

9.6.3.1 From Prediction to Action

The first step in moving from prediction to action is the systematic translation of probabilistic forecasts into concrete portfolio decisions. A predictive model might output an expected return of 8% with a volatility of 15% for a particular stock. The prescriptive system must determine how this forecast, combined with forecasts for all other assets and their correlations, dictates a change in the portfolio's composition. This often involves creating a range of potential scenarios based on the predictive distribution. For instance, instead of relying on a single expected return, a portfolio manager might simulate 10,000 potential future paths for the market based on the model's parameters, creating a rich dataset of possible outcomes.

Scenario analysis and stress testing are crucial prescriptive tools that use predictive models to evaluate portfolio resilience. A scenario analysis might involve asking, "What is the optimal portfolio allocation if our model predicts a period of rising interest rates and slowing economic growth?" The predictive model generates asset return projections under this specific macroeconomic scenario, and the prescriptive optimizer then determines the best portfolio for that future state. Stress testing takes this further by examining the impact of extreme, but plausible, events—like a 2008-level financial crisis or a rapid spike in oil prices—on the portfolio. This allows risk managers to preemptively adjust positions to mitigate potential catastrophic losses.

A key business application is the use of predictive signals as inputs to decision rules. For example, a simple prescriptive rule might be: "IF the predicted 30-day return for Asset A is greater than 5% AND its predicted volatility is below its 6-month average, THEN increase its portfolio weight by 2%." More complex, ML-based rule engines can handle hundreds of such signals simultaneously, dynamically adjusting portfolio exposures based on the evolving predictive landscape. This systematizes the investment process, removing emotional bias and ensuring consistency in strategy execution.

Ultimately, the transition from prediction to action requires a robust decision framework that aligns the outputs of predictive models with the investor's objectives and constraints. This framework defines the utility function—what the investor truly cares about, whether it is maximizing absolute return, achieving a return target with minimal risk, or outperforming a benchmark. The predictive forecasts provide raw material, but the prescriptive engine is the architect that builds the optimal portfolio blueprint based on the investor's unique blueprint of goals and limitations.

9.6.3.2 Optimization Techniques

The core mathematical engine of prescriptive analytics is optimization. The most common approach in portfolio management is mean–variance optimization (MVO), a quadratic programming problem. The objective is to find the portfolio weights that either maximize expected return for a given level of risk or minimize risk for the given level of expected return.

In real-world business applications, constrained optimization is the norm. Portfolios must adhere to a host of legal, regulatory, and internal policy constraints. These can be linear constraints, such as sector exposure limits (e.g., "technology stocks ≤ 25% of the portfolio") or concentration limits on a single asset. They can also be more complex, non-linear constraints, such as a maximum portfolio tracking error against a benchmark. The optimization algorithm must efficiently navigate this complex feasible region to find the best possible solution.

For more realistic modeling, stochastic programming is a powerful technique that explicitly incorporates uncertainty. Instead of using single-point estimates for returns and variances, the optimization is performed over a tree of potential future scenarios generated by the predictive model. This is particularly useful for multi-period problems, such as pension fund liability matching, where the goal is to ensure that asset growth meets future payout obligations under a wide range of economic scenarios. The business value is a more robust portfolio that is prepared for multiple future states, not just a single, most likely forecast.

Multi-objective optimization addresses the reality that investors have several, often competing, goals. A typical formulation might seek to simultaneously maximize expected return, minimize risk (variance), and maximize liquidity (or minimize transaction costs). Since these objectives conflict, the solution is not a single optimal portfolio but a set of Pareto-optimal portfolios where you cannot improve one objective without worsening another. The investor or a senior management committee can then select the final portfolio from this efficient set based on their subjective trade-offs between the different goals.

9.6.3.3 Dynamic Portfolio Rebalancing

Portfolio management is not a one-time event but a continuous process. Dynamic rebalancing is the prescriptive strategy for maintaining the target portfolio allocation over time as market movements cause weights to drift. Rules-based rebalancing uses simple, predetermined triggers. The most common is a calendar-based rule (e.g., rebalance quarterly) or a tolerance-based rule (e.g., "rebalance an asset back to its target weight when its actual weight deviates by more than ±5%"). While simple to implement, this approach is suboptimal as it ignores the predictive signals about future asset performance and the costs of trading.[2]

Model-driven rebalancing is a more sophisticated prescriptive approach. It integrates continuous predictive forecasts into the rebalancing decision. The system constantly evaluates whether the benefits of rebalancing—capturing alpha from a new, more optimal allocation predicted by the model—outweigh the costs. This turns rebalancing from a mechanical maintenance task into an active, alpha-generating strategy. For example, if the model predicts a short-term continuation of a trend that has caused a deviation, it may prescribe delaying rebalancing to avoid trading against the momentum.

A critical aspect of realistic rebalancing is the incorporation of transaction costs and market impact. A naive optimizer might prescribe frequent, small trades to maintain perfect alignment with the target. A more sophisticated prescriptive model includes a cost term in the objective function:

$$\textit{Maximize}\left(\text{Expected return}\right) - \lambda\left(\text{Risk}\right) - \gamma\left(\text{Transaction costs}\right)$$

where γ is a parameter that represents the investor's sensitivity to costs, transaction costs can be modeled as a quadratic function to account for market impact: large trades tend to move prices adversely. By including this, the optimizer may prescribe a portfolio that is slightly suboptimal in terms of risk-return but is significantly cheaper to implement, leading to better net performance for the client.

Finally, tax-aware rebalancing is a crucial prescriptive application for wealth management. Instead of simply selling an overweight position, the system will scan the entire portfolio to identify lots with the most favorable tax status (e.g., harvesting losses to offset gains) or prescribe using new cash inflows to purchase underweight assets, thereby avoiding the tax liability of a sale altogether. This demonstrates how advanced prescriptive analytics moves beyond pure financial optimization to encompass the entire set of real-world constraints that impact the net, after-tax wealth of the investor, delivering truly superior business and client outcomes.

9.7 Forecasting Models

Forecasting models occupy a pivotal role in prescriptive analytics and optimization, serving as the bridge between understanding historical patterns and shaping actionable strategies for the future. While forecasting is traditionally classified as a predictive activity, its true value in business and policy contexts emerges when forecasts are embedded within optimization frameworks that guide decision-making under uncertainty. Accurate forecasts of demand, prices, resource availability, or customer behavior provide the raw inputs that prescriptive models translate into optimal inventory levels, pricing policies, investment allocations, and operational plans. In this sense, forecasting is not merely about predicting what is likely to happen but about equipping organizations with the foresight necessary to evaluate alternatives, anticipate risks, and prescribe actions that maximize value while mitigating uncertainty.

9.7.1 Categories of Forecasting Models

9.7.1.1 Machine Learning Models

ML models represent a paradigm shift from traditional statistical forecasting, leveraging algorithms that can learn complex patterns directly from data without being explicitly programmed with a specific equation. This category includes a diverse set of algorithms, such as Random Forests and Gradient Boosting Machines (e.g., XGBoost, LightGBM), which are powerful tree-based ensemble methods, and Neural Networks, including specialized architectures like LSTM networks designed for sequential data. These models are highly flexible and can be applied to both univariate time series forecasting and multivariate forecasting problems where numerous potential predictors are available.

The greatest strength of ML models is their ability to identify intricate nonlinear patterns and interactions among a high number of input features. Unlike traditional models, they can effortlessly incorporate dozens or even hundreds of potential explanatory variables, such as promotional calendars, weather data, or macroeconomic indicators, to improve forecast accuracy. They are particularly adept at handling large, high-dimensional datasets and can model complex relationships that would be impossible to specify manually in an econometric equation. Furthermore, models like tree-based ensembles are often robust to outliers and missing data, making them suitable for messy, real-world datasets.

A key weakness of ML models is their tendency to be "black boxes," offering limited interpretability compared to statistical models. Understanding why a specific forecast was generated can be difficult, which is a major drawback in business contexts where explaining the driver of a prediction is crucial. They also typically require very large volumes of clean, high-quality data to train effectively and avoid overfitting, where the model memorizes the noise in the training data rather than learning the underlying pattern. Additionally, without careful feature engineering for time series problems, ML models may ignore fundamental temporal structures like seasonality, assuming that data points are independent and identically distributed.

9.7.1.2 Causal and Econometric Models

Causal and econometric models form a category focused on understanding and quantifying the underlying relationships between variables.[3] The primary goal is not just to predict the future but to explain how changes in one or more driver variables (independent variables) cause changes in the outcome variable (dependent variable). This category includes standard regression models (linear and nonlinear), Vector Autoregression (VAR) models, which capture the linear interdependencies among multiple time series, and more complex Structural Models that are built on specific economic theories. These models are fundamentally designed for causal inference and "what-if" analysis.

The defining strength of this category is its explicit use for scenario planning and policy analysis. Because these models estimate the specific impact of each input variable, a forecaster can ask questions like, "What will happen to sales if we increase the advertising budget by 10%?" or "What is the projected impact of a 1% rise in interest rates on GDP?" This causal framework provides a deep level of interpretability, as the coefficients of the model have clear economic or business meanings. This makes the models highly valuable for strategic decision-making, where understanding the "why" behind a forecast is as important as the forecast itself.

The principal weakness of causal models is their strong reliance on correct model specification and the availability of valid, measurable explanatory variables. The modeler must have a strong theoretical understanding of the system to avoid omitted variable bias (leaving out an important cause) or including endogenous variables (where causation runs in both directions). Finding reliable, high-frequency data for all relevant drivers can be a major practical challenge. Furthermore, these models assume that the historical relationships between variables, which are used to estimate the parameters, will remain stable in the future, an assumption that can be broken during periods of structural economic change.

9.7.1.3 Hybrid and Ensemble Models

Hybrid and ensemble models are advanced approaches that seek to combine the strengths of different forecasting methodologies to achieve higher accuracy and robustness than any single model could provide.[4] Ensemble methods—such as combining forecasts from multiple ARIMA models or applying bagging/boosting with ML models—are based on the idea that a diverse collection of models can collectively reduce error and variance. Hybrid models extend this concept by integrating fundamentally different model types. For instance, a statistical time series model might capture linear trends and seasonality, while an ML model is then used to predict the remaining nonlinear residual patterns.

The main strength of this category is its ability to leverage the unique advantages of its constituent parts, often leading to a significant boost in forecasting accuracy. A hybrid model might use an ARIMA model to effectively model the strong seasonal pattern in electricity demand and then use a neural network to account for the nonlinear effects of temperature and humidity, which the ARIMA model would miss. Ensemble methods are particularly powerful because they mitigate the risk of relying on a single, potentially flawed model, as the errors of one model may be corrected by the others in the ensemble.

A major weakness of hybrid and ensemble models is their increased complexity in both implementation and maintenance. They require expertise in multiple modeling paradigms and can be computationally expensive to train and tune. This complexity also exacerbates the "black box" problem, making it even more challenging to interpret the final forecast and explain it to stakeholders. Furthermore, the development process can be time-consuming, as it involves training, validating, and combining multiple models, which may not be justified for simple forecasting problems where a single model performs adequately.

9.7.2 Integrating Forecasting with Optimization

The true value of a forecast is realized when it is used to inform and drive decision-making, and this is most formally achieved through integration with optimization models. Optimization provides a mathematical framework for selecting the best course of action from a set of alternatives, given specific constraints and objectives. The quality of these decisions is entirely dependent on the inputs, which are often forecasts of future demand, prices, or resource availability. The integration is not merely using a forecast number as a static input; it involves carefully aligning the nature of the forecast with the optimization methodology to account for uncertainty and risk. The primary approaches include deterministic optimization, which uses simple point forecasts; stochastic programming, which incorporates full probability distributions; robust optimization, which plans for worst-case scenarios; and multi-objective optimization, which balances forecast-driven trade-offs.

The simplest and most common integration method is deterministic optimization, which relies on a single, fixed-point forecast as a key input. In this approach, the future is treated as known with certainty, simplifying the optimization model significantly. For example, a supply chain model might use a demand forecast of 100 units to determine the optimal production quantity and inventory levels that minimize cost while meeting that specific predicted demand. While this method is computationally efficient and straightforward to implement, its critical weakness is its complete disregard for forecast uncertainty. If the actual demand turns out to be 120 or 80 units, the "optimal" plan derived from the point forecast may lead to severe stockouts or excessive inventory, proving to be highly suboptimal.

To directly address the limitation of deterministic models, stochastic programming explicitly incorporates forecast uncertainty by using the entire predicted probability distribution rather than a single point. This approach involves modeling multiple potential future scenarios, each with an assigned probability. The optimization model then seeks a solution that performs well on average across all these possible scenarios. For instance, a portfolio optimization model would not just use an expected return forecast but would use the distribution of returns to minimize risk (variance) while achieving a target return, ensuring the portfolio is resilient across different market conditions. Although this method is more realistic, it is also computationally intensive and requires accurate estimation of scenario probabilities, which can be complex.

Finally, robust optimization and multi-objective optimization provide sophisticated frameworks for managing uncertainty and conflicting goals. Robust optimization is a conservative approach that aims to find a solution that remains feasible and performs adequately under the worst-case realization of the forecast within a defined uncertainty set. This is crucial for high-stakes decisions in sectors like aerospace or healthcare, where system failure is unacceptable. Multi-objective optimization, meanwhile, uses forecasts to quantify and navigate trade-offs between competing objectives, such as using demand and cost forecasts to balance the goals of maximizing customer service levels and minimizing total supply chain cost. Together, these methodologies ensure that forecasts are not just passive predictions but active drivers of resilient, well-balanced, and truly optimal business strategies.

9.8 Predictive Analytics in Action

Predictive analytics, when set in motion within the framework of prescriptive analytics and optimization, transforms from a tool of foresight into a catalyst for action. By identifying patterns, estimating probabilities, and forecasting outcomes, predictive models provide the critical inputs that prescriptive systems use to determine the best course of action under given constraints. For instance, a predictive model might estimate the likelihood of customer churn, but only when this insight is coupled with optimization techniques can an organization determine how to allocate budgets across retention campaigns for maximum impact. In this sense, predictive analytics in action is not confined to anticipating the future; it is about embedding those predictions into decision models that prescribe strategies, optimize resources, and align organizational choices with long-term objectives.

9.8.1 Core Predictive Analytics Techniques

9.8.1.1 Classification Models

Classification models are used to predict a categorical outcome, assigning a data point to a specific class or category based on its features. In a prescriptive context, these models answer critical "what kind?" questions that drive decision rules. Key models in this category include logistic regression, which estimates the probability of class membership using a logistic function; decision trees, which create a hierarchical series of if-then rules to split data into homogeneous groups; and Random Forests, which are ensemble methods that aggregate the predictions of multiple decorrelated decision trees to improve accuracy and reduce overfitting.[5]

The primary strength of classification models in prescriptive analytics is their direct applicability to decision-making. For instance, a logistic regression model can predict the probability of customer churning, which can then be used to prescribe a targeted retention campaign. Decision trees are highly interpretable, providing a clear set of rules that can be directly translated into business logic, such as criteria for approving a loan. Random Forests and other ensemble methods build on this by offering high accuracy and robustness to noisy data, making them reliable for critical classification tasks.

A significant weakness of some classification models is their handling of complex, nonlinear relationships without significant tuning or assembling. Simple models like logistic regression assume a linear relationship between the input features and the log-odds of the outcome, which can be a limitation. While powerful, complex models like Random Forests can become "black boxes," losing the interpretability of a single decision tree and making it difficult to understand the exact reasoning behind a prescription, which can be a barrier in regulated industries.

9.8.1.2 Regression Models

Regression models are designed to predict a continuous numerical outcome, making them essential for forecasting quantities like demand, prices, or resource usage.[6] They form the quantitative backbone of many prescriptive optimization models. This category includes linear regression, which models a linear relationship between independent variables and the target; nonlinear regression, which captures more complex, curved relationships; and regularization methods (like Lasso and Ridge Regression), which penalize model complexity to prevent overfitting and improve generalizability.

The strength of regression models lies in their interpretability and well-understood statistical foundations. The coefficients in a linear regression provide a clear, quantitative measure of how much the target variable is expected to change for a one-unit change in a predictor. This direct causality is invaluable for prescriptive analytics, as it allows analysts to simulate the impact of changing an input variable (e.g., "What is the prescribed price if we want to achieve a demand of 10,000 units?"). Regularization methods enhance this by producing more robust and reliable models, especially when dealing with datasets containing many correlated variables.

The main weakness of traditional regression models is their reliance on the modeler correctly specifying the relationship between variables. If the true relationship is highly complex and nonlinear, a simple linear model will perform poorly. While nonlinear regression can help, it often requires prior knowledge of the specific nonlinear form. Furthermore, regression models can be sensitive to outliers and assume that errors are independent and normally distributed, assumptions that are often violated in real-world data, leading to unreliable predictions and prescriptions.

9.8.1.3 Machine Learning and AI Models

These models are particularly suited for problems where relationships are intricate and nonlinear. Prominent examples include Gradient Boosting Machines (e.g., XGBoost, LightGBM), which build decision trees sequentially, with each new tree correcting the errors of the previous ones; Neural Networks, composed of interconnected layers of nodes; and Deep Learning, which refers to large neural networks with many hidden layers that can automatically learn feature hierarchies.

The paramount strength of these models is their predictive power and ability to handle very complex, high-dimensional data, including unstructured data like images and text. They can capture subtle, nonlinear interactions between variables that simpler models would miss, often leading to superior forecast accuracy. This high accuracy is crucial for prescriptive models, as more accurate predictions lead to more effective prescriptions. For example, a deep learning model can forecast energy demand with high precision by analyzing historical load, weather data, and even calendar events, enabling highly efficient prescriptive grid management.

The primary weakness of these models is their lack of interpretability, often functioning as "black boxes." It can be extremely difficult to understand why a specific prediction was made, which hinders trust and makes it challenging to validate the model's logic for critical decisions. They are also notoriously data-hungry, requiring massive volumes of high-quality data to train effectively without overfitting. Furthermore, they are computationally intensive to train and require significant expertise to tune properly.

9.8.1.4 Probabilistic and Simulation Models

Probabilistic and simulation models focus on representing uncertainty explicitly rather than producing a single-point prediction. They are indispensable for prescriptive analytics under uncertainty, as they provide a full distribution of possible outcomes. Key techniques include Bayesian Networks, which model probabilistic relationships among a set of variables as a directed graph; and Monte Carlo Simulations, which use repeated random sampling to numerically estimate the distribution of potential outcomes for a complex, stochastic system.[7]

The greatest strength of these models is their ability to quantify uncertainty and answer "what-if" questions in a probabilistic framework. A Bayesian Network can model the chain of probabilistic events that lead to a system failure, allowing prescriptions for preventative maintenance that are based on the likelihood of component failures. Monte Carlo Simulation is the cornerstone of stochastic optimization; by simulating thousands of possible future scenarios (e.g., demand outcomes), it allows a prescriptive model to find a solution that is robust across this range of possibilities, such as a supply chain plan that minimizes expected total cost.

A key weakness is their computational cost and complexity. Monte Carlo Simulations can require thousands or millions of model evaluations, which is computationally expensive. Bayesian Networks require a well-defined structure, which often needs to be built with expert knowledge, and can become intractably complex for systems with a very large number of variables. The output, being probabilistic, can also be more difficult to communicate to stakeholders accustomed to deterministic answers.

9.8.2 Integration of Predictive and Prescriptive Analytics

The integration of predictive and prescriptive analytics represents a paradigm shift from passive insight generation to active, data-driven decision-making. This integration creates a powerful, systematic framework: Predict → Prescribe → Optimize. The process begins with predictive models forecasting future states or behaviors, such as customer demand or machine failure. These predictions are not the final output; instead, they become the foundational inputs for prescriptive models, which use optimization and simulation techniques to evaluate countless possible actions and prescribe the one that best achieves a specific business objective, such as maximizing profit or minimizing risk. This end-to-end pipeline ensures that decisions are not based on intuition alone but are quantitatively grounded in both foresight and strategic goals.

The operational backbone of this integration is the creation of decision pipelines, where predictive outputs are directly fed into optimization engines. In these pipelines, a predictive model's output, for example, a probability score for customer churn or a forecasted demand value—becomes a critical parameter or constraint within a mathematical optimization model. A prescriptive system for dynamic pricing might use a demand forecast as a key input to an optimization model that determines the profit-maximizing price, subject to constraints like inventory levels or competitive price caps. This seamless handoff from prediction to prescription allows organizations to automate complex decisions at scale, ensuring consistency and operational efficiency.

9.9 IoT, Edge Computing, and Real-Time AI

The fusion of the Internet of Things (IoT), edge computing, and real-time AI is reshaping how prescriptive analytics and optimization operate in dynamic environments. In contrast to traditional models that rely on static or batch data, this convergence enables organizations to harness continuous data streams, process them at the edge for speed, and apply adaptive AI to prescribe optimal actions in real time. From manufacturing floors and smart grids to healthcare systems and urban transportation networks, decisions can now be optimized not only with foresight but also with immediacy. This shift transforms prescriptive analytics from a planning-oriented tool into an always-on decision ecosystem, capable of sensing, predicting, and prescribing actions at the pace of events themselves.

9.9.1 Internet of Things (IoT) as the Data Foundation

9.9.1.1 IoT Devices and Sensors

IoT devices and sensors are the fundamental data-gathering endpoints in a connected ecosystem, acting as the digital senses of an organization. They are responsible for the initial capture of physical world phenomena, such as temperature, movement, pressure, or location, and converting them into digital signals. This process of data generation is continuous and automated, enabling a level of operational visibility that was previously unattainable.[8] In a business context, this translates to moving from periodic, manual checks to a state of constant, automated monitoring, forming the bedrock of data-driven decision-making.

A prime business example is in logistics and supply chain management. Fleet vehicles are equipped with a suite of sensors: GPS for real-time location, accelerometers for tracking harsh braking or acceleration, thermistors for monitoring refrigerated cargo temperature, and fuel-level sensors. These devices generate a constant stream of telemetry data, which is transmitted over cellular or satellite networks to a central platform. This allows a logistics manager to see not just where a truck is but how it is being driven and the condition of its perishable goods, enabling immediate intervention if anomalies are detected.

The primary function of these sensors is operational monitoring at an unprecedented granularity. For instance, a temperature sensor in a pharmaceutical shipment doesn't just report a single reading per hour; it may send data every minute or even second. This high-frequency monitoring creates a detailed historical record of the product's environment, which is crucial for compliance with safety regulations (e.g., FDA guidelines for cold chain logistics). It shifts the business posture from reactive problem-solving—discovering spoiled goods upon arrival—to proactive condition management, ensuring product integrity throughout the journey.

The reliability of the entire data-driven optimization chain is contingent on the quality and calibration of these physical sensors. A malfunctioning or poorly calibrated temperature sensor can generate false data, leading to incorrect decisions, wasted resources, and compliance failures. Therefore, businesses must invest not only in the deployment of IoT devices but also in robust sensor management protocols, including regular diagnostics and automated alerts for sensor failures, to ensure the data foundation is accurate and trustworthy.

9.9.1.2 Data Characteristics

IoT data is fundamentally characterized by the "3 Vs" of big data: Volume, Velocity, and Variety, which present both opportunities and significant challenges. The Volume is immense because a single asset, like a wind turbine, can have hundreds of sensors, each generating data points every few seconds. Across a fleet of thousands of such assets, this accumulates to terabytes of data daily. This scale necessitates robust, scalable cloud infrastructure for storage and processing, moving beyond traditional databases to data lakes and streaming platforms capable of handling such payloads.

The Velocity at which this data arrives is equally critical, as it is generated and transmitted in near real time. In a manufacturing context, sensors on an assembly line monitor machine vibration, throughput, and product dimensions continuously. This high-velocity data stream must be ingested, processed, and analyzed almost instantaneously to be useful for real-time quality control. A delay of even a few minutes in detecting a deviation could result in the production of thousands of defective units, leading to substantial scrap and rework costs.

Variety refers to the diverse range of data generated. IoT data is not just simple numerical readings. It includes structured data (e.g., timestamp, sensor ID, temperature value), semi-structured data (e.g., GPS coordinates with metadata), and unstructured data (e.g., images from a quality control camera or audio signatures from a malfunctioning engine). Correlating these different data types is essential for a holistic view. For example, a retail chain might combine structured foot-traffic sensor data with unstructured video feeds to optimize store layouts and product placements, requiring complex data integration pipelines.

The importance of data quality cannot be overstated amidst these three Vs. Raw IoT data is often noisy, incomplete, or erroneous due to sensor drift, transmission errors, or network latency. For business analytics to be effective, this data must be cleansed and contextualized. A simple but crucial function for assessing data quality at the point of ingestion is anomaly detection. A common statistical model used for this is the Z-score, which identifies how many standard deviations a data point is from the mean. The formula for the Z-score of a data point x is:

$$Z = \frac{(x - \mu)}{\sigma}$$

where:

x = Current sensor reading.
μ = Historical mean of the sensor readings.
σ = Historical standard deviation of the sensor readings.

Readings with a Z-score magnitude beyond a certain threshold (e.g., $|Z| > 3$) can be flagged for review, ensuring that only high-quality data feeds into downstream models.

9.9.1.3 IoT Data Streams in Optimization

IoT data streams are the vital link between the physical operational world and digital optimization models, transforming raw telemetry into actionable intelligence. By feeding near-real-time inputs into advanced analytical models, businesses can shift from descriptive analytics (what happened) to predictive (what will happen) and prescriptive (what should we do) analytics. This creates a closed-loop system where the physical state of assets continuously informs and refines digital decisions, which are then executed back in the physical world, leading to autonomous or semi-autonomous optimization.

A powerful business application is in predictive maintenance for industrial equipment. A stream of sensor data (vibration, temperature, acoustic emissions) from a critical pump in an oil refinery is fed into a predictive model. This model forecasts the remaining useful life (RUL) of the pump, allowing maintenance to be scheduled just before a predicted failure, thus avoiding costly unplanned downtime. This is far more efficient than traditional scheduled maintenance, which might replace parts too early, or reactive maintenance, which occurs after a failure has already caused disruption.

The predictive model itself often relies on ML algorithms. For example, a regression model can be used to estimate RUL based on the trend of a key sensor reading. A simple linear regression could be formulated as:

$$\text{RUL}(t) = \beta_0 + \beta_1 \cdot S(t) + \varepsilon$$

where:

$\text{RUL}(t)$ = Predicted Remaining Useful Life at time t.
$S(t)$ = Value of a key sensor (e.g., vibration amplitude) at time t.
β_0 (intercept) and β_1 (slope) = Model parameters learned from historical failure data.
ε = Error term.

As new sensor data $S(t)$ streams in, the model continuously updates the RUL prediction, providing a dynamic forecast.

The ultimate goal is to feed these predictions into a prescriptive model that recommends specific actions. This prescriptive model can be framed as an optimization problem. For instance, a manufacturing plant needs to minimize total maintenance costs while maximizing production output. The model would consider the predicted failure probabilities from all assets, along with constraints like crew availability and part inventories. The objective function might look like:

$$\text{Minimize } Z = \sum_{i=1}^{n}\left(C_{f,i} \cdot P_{f,i}(t) + C_{p,i} \cdot x_i\right) + C_d \cdot D$$

Subject to:

$\sum_{i=1}^{n} x_i \leq M$ (Maintenance crew capacity)

$D = f\left(x_i, P_{f,i}(t)\right)$ (Production delay function)

where:

$C_{f,i}$ = Cost of failure for asset i.
$P_{f,i}(t)$ = Probability of failure for asset i at time t (from the predictive model).
$C_{p,i}$ = Cost of preventive maintenance for asset i.
x_i = Binary decision variable (1 if maintain asset i, 0 otherwise).
C_d = Cost per unit of production delay.
D = Total production delay.
M = Maximum number of maintenance tasks possible.

By solving this optimization problem in near real time with streaming IoT data, the system can prescribe an optimal maintenance schedule, dynamically allocating resources to the most critical tasks and delivering significant business value.

9.9.2 Edge Computing for Real-Time Decision Support

9.9.2.1 Concept and Architecture of Edge Computing

Edge computing represents a significant evolution in computing paradigms, tailored to meet the growing demands of data processing driven by the proliferation of Internet of Things (IoT) devices and applications. At its core, edge computing is a distributed architecture that positions computational resources geographically closer to data sources rather than relying solely on centralized cloud infrastructures. By enabling computation at the "edge" of the network, this paradigm reduces latency, optimizes bandwidth usage, and enhances data privacy by decentralizing operations. The result is a hierarchical model in which time-sensitive decisions are executed locally, while less urgent tasks such as large-scale data aggregation and deep learning model training remain within the cloud. This dual structure is particularly critical for applications where milliseconds matter and continuous, high-volume transmission to the cloud is either impractical or prohibitively expensive.[9]

The architecture typically involves three tiers: the device edge, the local edge, and the cloud. The device edge consists of the sensors and actuators themselves, which may have limited processing capabilities. The local edge often involves an edge gateway, or a micro-data center located near the devices, such as in a factory or a retail store. This gateway aggregates data from multiple devices and hosts lightweight analytics and decision-making models. The cloud remains the repository for historical data and the platform for running complex, resource-intensive simulations and model training that are not time-critical.

9.9.2.2 Benefits for Prescriptive Analytics

The primary benefit of edge computing for prescriptive analytics is the radical acceleration of the optimization cycle, enabling true real-time decision-making. By processing data locally, the time between data acquisition (sensing an event) and executing a prescribed action (actuating a response) is minimized to milliseconds. This speed is crucial for closed-loop control systems where the environment is dynamic. It transforms analytics from a passive reporting tool into an active participant in operational processes, directly driving efficiency and preventing costly disruptions.

A powerful business benefit is reduced dependency on network connectivity. In many industrial settings, such as mining operations or offshore oil rigs, network connectivity can be unreliable, expensive, or completely absent. Edge computing allows critical prescriptive models to function independently of the cloud. For instance, an edge system on a drilling rig can continuously analyze sensor data from the drill bit and prescribe adjustments to the drilling speed and force to prevent equipment failure, all without needing a constant satellite link. This ensures operational continuity and safety even in remote locations.

Enhanced data privacy and security is another significant advantage. By processing sensitive data locally, businesses can avoid transmitting proprietary information or personally identifiable information (PII) over the network. In a retail setting, a smart camera using edge analytics can process video feeds locally to count customers and track in-store movement patterns. Instead of sending raw video to the cloud, which raises privacy concerns, the edge device only transmits anonymized, aggregated metadata (e.g., "15 people in aisle 3 at 2:05 PM"). This minimizes data exposure and helps comply with regulations like GDPR.

The models deployed at the edge are often simplified, deterministic versions of their cloud counterparts to ensure low-latency execution. For example, a cloud-based model might use a complex neural network to predict machine failure, while the edge uses a simpler, rule-based engine for immediate prescription. A common function for such real-time anomaly detection is the calculation of a simple moving average (SMA) and standard deviation against which current sensor readings are compared. The prescription is a direct if-then rule:

$$\text{If } \left|S(t) - \mu_t\right| > k \cdot \sigma_t, \text{then prescribe action } A$$

where:

$S(t)$ = Current sensor value.
μ_t = Moving average over a short, recent time window.
σ_t = Standard deviation over the same window.
k = Threshold multiplier (e.g., 3 for a "3-sigma" rule).
A = Prescribed action (e.g., "shut down conveyor belt").

9.9.2.3 *Edge versus Cloud in Optimization Workflows*

The choice between edge and cloud computing in optimization workflows involves navigating key trade-offs between computational power, latency, and scalability. The cloud offers virtually unlimited computational resources, making it ideal for tasks that are not time-sensitive but require massive processing power, such as training complex ML models on historical data or running large-scale simulations to redesign entire supply networks. The cloud's strength lies in its scalability and ability to perform "deep thinking" by correlating data from across the entire enterprise.

In contrast, the edge excels at "fast thinking." Its computational power is limited by the hardware constraints of local devices or gateways, but it provides ultra-low latency. This dichotomy creates a synergistic relationship rather than a pure replacement. A typical optimization workflow is hybrid: complex models are trained periodically in the cloud using aggregated historical data from all edge locations. The trained models are then deployed to the edge nodes, where they run inference on live data streams to generate immediate prescriptions. The edge nodes also send summarized data and performance results back to the cloud for continuous model retraining and improvement.

A business example of this hybrid workflow is in predictive maintenance for a chain of fast-food restaurants. Each restaurant's fryer is equipped with temperature and oil quality sensors connected to a local edge gateway. The cloud trains a model that predicts fryer failure based on years of data from all locations. This model is deployed to each restaurant's edge gateway. The edge model prescribes real-time actions, like alerting staff to filter the oil or preemptively ordering a replacement part. Simultaneously, the edge gateway sends a daily summary of the fryer's health metrics to the cloud, which uses this new data to retrain and improve the model for all locations, creating a continuous learning loop.

9.9.3 *Real-Time AI and Prescriptive Analytics*

9.9.3.1 *Real-Time Predictive Models*

Real-time predictive models are analytical engines designed to process live data streams and generate immediate forecasts, classifications, or anomaly scores. Unlike batch-oriented models that analyze historical data periodically, these models update their predictions continuously as new data arrives, enabling proactive responses to emerging situations. The core challenge is balancing accuracy with computational efficiency to meet strict latency requirements. In business, this capability transforms operations from reactive to anticipatory, allowing organizations to address issues before they escalate into significant problems.

A prime business application is in dynamic energy management for large commercial buildings. A real-time predictive model continuously analyzes streaming data from IoT sensors measuring temperature, humidity, occupancy levels, and external weather conditions.[10] Using techniques like online ML, the model forecasts the thermal load for each zone in the building for the next 15–30 minutes. This short-term forecasting allows the building management system to preemptively adjust HVAC settings, optimizing energy consumption while maintaining comfort, rather than reacting to temperature changes after they occur.

Anomaly detection is another critical function of real-time predictive models. For instance, in financial services, a credit card transaction monitoring system must classify each transaction as legitimate or fraudulent within milliseconds. The model analyzes features like transaction amount, merchant category, location, and the cardholder's typical spending patterns in real time. A common statistical approach for anomaly detection is to calculate a modified Z-score for each incoming transaction amount relative to the cardholder's recent spending history, flagging transactions that deviate significantly from their behavioral baseline.

The mathematical foundation for such real-time classification often involves probabilistic models. For example, a Naive Bayes classifier can be efficiently updated with new data and provides a probability score for each class (e.g., "fraudulent" or "legitimate"). The formula for the posterior probability that a transaction with features $f_1, f_2, \ldots, f_n$ is fraudulent (class C) is:

$$P\left(C \middle| f_1, f_2, \ldots, f_n\right) = \frac{P(C)\prod_{i=1}^{n} P\left(f_i \middle| C\right)}{P\left(f_1, f_2, \ldots, f_n\right)}$$

where:

$P\left(C \middle| f_1, f_2, \ldots, f_n\right)$ = Posterior probability of fraud given the transaction features.
$P(C)$ = Prior probability of fraud.
$P\left(f_i \middle| C\right)$ = Likelihood of observing feature f_i given fraud.

The denominator is the total probability of observing the set of features.

This model can be implemented efficiently at the edge, allowing for instantaneous classification of each transaction as it occurs.

9.9.3.2 Prescriptive Optimization in Real Time

Prescriptive optimization represents the pinnacle of automated decision-making, where AI not only predicts what will happen but also determines the best course of action to achieve desired outcomes. These systems take the predictions from real-time models and use them as inputs to optimization algorithms that solve for the best possible decision given current constraints and business objectives. The result is dynamic decision-making that can adapt to changing conditions instantaneously, moving beyond human reaction times and cognitive limitations for complex, multi-variable problems.

In logistics and delivery services, prescriptive optimization enables dynamic rerouting. A delivery fleet management system continuously monitors real-time traffic conditions, weather updates, vehicle locations, and package priorities. When the predictive model forecasts a delay on a planned route due to an accident, the prescriptive engine immediately solves a vehicle routing problem (VRP) to generate an optimal alternative route for each affected vehicle. This automated control system minimizes delivery delays, reduces fuel consumption, and improves customer satisfaction without requiring dispatcher intervention.

The core of such systems is often a mathematical optimization model that must be solved rapidly. For dynamic resource allocation in a cloud computing environment, an AI system might use a linear programming formulation to allocate computational resources (CPU, memory) to different applications in real-time based on predicted demand. The objective function could be to minimize total cost while meeting service-level agreements (SLAs). A simplified version of this optimization might look like:

$$\text{Minimize } Z = \sum_{j=1}^{m} c_j x_j$$

Subject to:

$$\sum_{j=1}^{m} a_{ij} x_j \geq d_i(t) \quad \text{for } i = 1, \ldots, n$$
$$x_j \geq 0 \quad \text{for } j = 1, \ldots, m$$

where:

x_j = Amount of resource type j to allocate.
c_j= Cost per unit of resource j.
a_{ij} = Capacity of resource j for application i.
$d_i(t)$ = Predicted demand for application i at time t (from the predictive model).

This model is solved continuously as demand predictions update, enabling adaptive resource allocation.

The business value of prescriptive optimization is profound in manufacturing quality control. Computer vision systems on production lines use real-time classification models to identify defective products. When a defect is detected, the prescriptive system does not just flag it—it automatically adjusts machine parameters (e.g., temperature, pressure, speed) to correct the root cause of the defect in real time. This creates a self-correcting manufacturing process that continuously improves quality and reduces waste, representing a significant competitive advantage through automated, intelligent control.

9.9.3.3 Integration with IoT and Edge

The integration of AI with IoT and edge computing creates powerful closed-loop systems where sensing, prediction, prescription, and action occur in a tightly coupled cycle at the network edge. This integration represents the operationalization of AI, moving it from dashboards and reports to direct control of physical processes. The IoT devices provide the real-world sensory input, edge computing provides the low-latency processing platform, and AI provides the intelligence to make optimal decisions. This synergy enables autonomous systems that can perceive their environment, make intelligent decisions, and implement those decisions immediately.

A compelling business example is in autonomous retail stores, such as Amazon Go. IoT sensors (cameras, weight sensors) continuously track customer movements and product selections throughout the store. Edge devices running computer vision and ML models process this data in real time to identify which products a customer has taken. The AI system maintains a virtual cart for each customer and prescribes the correct billing action when the customer leaves the store. This entire process—from sensing product removal to charging the customer's account—happens automatically without any checkout process, creating a frictionless shopping experience.

The mathematical representation of such a closed-loop system can be modeled as an MDP, which is fundamental to reinforcement learning and autonomous control. The system is defined by the tuple (S, A, P, R), where:

S represents the set of possible states (e.g., customer location, products in cart).
A represents the set of possible actions (e.g., add product to virtual cart, process payment).
$P(s'|s,a)$ is the transition probability from state s to state s' after taking action a.
$R(s,a)$ is the immediate reward received after taking action a in state s.

The AI's goal is to find a policy $\pi(s)$ that prescribes the best action for each state to maximize cumulative reward.

9.10 Customer Segmentation and Targeting

Customer segmentation and targeting lie at the heart of data-driven strategy, yet their true potential emerges when they are woven into the fabric of prescriptive analytics and optimization. Traditional segmentation identifies patterns among customers, classifying them into groups based on shared demographics, behaviors, or value profiles. Predictive models can then estimate which customers are most likely to buy, churn, or respond to an offer. But segmentation becomes genuinely powerful when prescriptive techniques transform these insights into optimized decisions—determining not only which customers to target but also how, when, and with what intensity to maximize returns under resource constraints. In this way, segmentation evolves from a descriptive exercise to a strategic engine for optimization, enabling organizations to allocate marketing budgets, personalize experiences, and design retention strategies with measurable precision.

9.10.1 Foundations of Customer Segmentation

9.10.1.1 Segmentation Approaches

Demographic and geographic segmentation represent the most traditional approaches, categorizing customers based on objective, observable criteria. Demographic segmentation uses variables such as age, income, education level, occupation, and family size. A financial services company, for example, might use demographic segmentation to target young professionals with student loan refinancing options, while marketing retirement planning services to older adults approaching retirement age. Geographic segmentation, meanwhile, groups customers by location—such as country, region, city, or climate zone—allowing a retail chain like Starbucks to customize its menu offerings to include iced beverages predominantly in warmer climates and hot specialty drinks in colder regions.

Psychographic and behavioral segmentation delve deeper into customer motivations and actions, providing a more nuanced understanding of why customers make purchases. Psychographic segmentation categorizes customers based on personality traits, values, attitudes, interests, and lifestyles. An outdoor apparel company like Patagonia uses psychographic segmentation to target environmentally conscious consumers who value sustainability and adventure. Behavioral segmentation, often considered the most actionable approach, groups customers based on their interactions with a brand, including purchase history, website engagement, product usage frequency, and brand loyalty. A streaming service like Netflix employs behavioral segmentation to identify "binge-watchers" who consume large volumes of content quickly versus casual viewers, offering each group different recommendations and retention incentives.

Value-based segmentation is arguably the most critical approach for direct revenue optimization, as it focuses on a customer's economic worth to the business. This method segments customers based on their current and potential lifetime value (LTV). A telecom company might segment its base into high-value (premium plan users with high data consumption), medium-value (standard plan users), and low-value (prepaid users) segments. The business objective function for prioritizing retention efforts can be modeled as maximizing the expected return from a retention campaign budget B*B*, allocated across segments. The optimization problem can be formulated as:

$$\text{Maximize } R = \sum_{s=1}^{S} LTV_s \cdot r_s\left(b_s\right)$$

subject to:

$$\sum_{s=1}^{S} b_s \leq B$$

where:

R = Total expected return.
S = Number of value-based segments.
LTV_s = Average lifetime value of the segment s.
$r_s\left(b_s\right)$ = Retention rate response function for segment s given budget allocation b_s.
B = Total retention budget.

This ensures marketing resources are invested where they generate the highest financial return.

9.10.1.2 Analytical Techniques for Segmentation

The evolution from simple rule-based segmentation to data-driven analytical techniques has dramatically increased the sophistication and effectiveness of customer grouping.[11] Modern segmentation relies heavily on statistical and ML methods that can identify complex, non-obvious patterns in large datasets. These techniques move beyond simplistic single-variable splits to create multidimensional segments based on numerous attributes simultaneously. The goal is to maximize homogeneity within segments and heterogeneity between segments, creating groups that are statistically distinct and managerially actionable for marketing strategies.

Clustering algorithms form the backbone of analytical segmentation, with *K*-means being one of the most widely used methods due to its simplicity and efficiency. *K*-means partitions customers into a predefined number of clusters (*K*) by iteratively minimizing the within-cluster variance. The algorithm's objective is to minimize the following function:

$$J = \sum_{j=1}^{k} \sum_{i=1}^{n} \left\| x_i^{(j)} - \mu_j \right\|^2$$

where:

J = Objective function to be minimized (total within-cluster variance).
K = Number of clusters.
n = Number of data points.
$x_i^{(j)}$ = i-th data point in cluster j.
μ_j = Centroid of cluster j.
$\| \|^2$ = Represents the squared Euclidean distance.

An e-commerce company might use K-means with features like purchase frequency, average order value, and product category affinity to identify distinct shopping behavior segments such as "bargain hunters," "premium loyalists," and "occasional gift shoppers."

Hierarchical clustering and DBSCAN offer alternatives to K-means, each with distinct advantages. Hierarchical clustering creates a tree-like structure (dendrogram) that shows how clusters merge at different similarity levels, allowing analysts to choose the appropriate segmentation granularity without pre-specifying the number of clusters. A luxury automobile manufacturer might use this to understand the natural hierarchy of customer preferences, from broad lifestyle groups to specific feature preferences. DBSCAN identifies clusters of arbitrary shapes and can detect outliers, making it valuable for fraud detection, where anomalous transaction patterns represent a critical segment of one.

Advanced ML techniques, including latent class analysis and neural networks, push segmentation further. Latent class models use probability distributions to identify unobserved (latent) segments based on observed customer behaviors and attributes. A mobile gaming company could use latent class analysis to identify player archetypes—such as "completionists," "social competitors," and "casual explorers"—based on their in-game behavior patterns, even when these patterns overlap. More recently, autoencoders (a type of neural network) are used for nonlinear dimensionality reduction before clustering, effectively handling the complex, high-dimensional data typical of digital customer interactions, thereby uncovering subtle but meaningful segments that traditional methods might miss.

9.10.1.3 Challenges in Segmentation

Customer segmentation faces significant challenges that can undermine its effectiveness if not properly addressed. The principle of "garbage in, garbage out" is particularly relevant, as the quality of segmentation models is entirely dependent on the quality of the underlying data. Common data issues include missing values, inconsistent formatting across systems, and temporal inconsistencies where customer attributes change over time. For instance, a retailer integrating online and offline purchase data might struggle with inconsistent customer identification, leading to fragmented views that prevent accurate segment assignment and personalization efforts.

Segment stability presents another major challenge, as customer behaviors and preferences are dynamic rather than static. A segment identified as "high-value loyalists" in one quarter may dissipate or change characteristics in the next due to market shifts, competitive actions, or changing consumer trends. This requires businesses to implement mechanisms for ongoing segment validation and refreshment. A subscription-based business like a software company (e.g., Adobe) must continuously monitor its segments because a customer's product usage and needs evolve significantly after major software updates or as their professional role changes, necessitating dynamic rather than fixed segment assignments.

Interpretability and actionability are critical challenges that determine whether segmentation insights translate into business value. Highly complex ML models might create statistically optimal segments that are nonetheless incomprehensible to marketing teams or impossible to target with existing channels. There is often a trade-off between statistical sophistication and practical usability. For example, a bank using a complex clustering algorithm might identify a segment characterized by subtle patterns in transaction timing and amount. However, if the segment cannot be clearly described ("customers who make small, frequent transactions between 7 and 9 PM") or reached through specific marketing channels, its business utility remains limited despite its statistical validity.

The final challenge lies in measuring segmentation ROI and avoiding over-segmentation. Creating too many segments can lead to operational complexity, diluted marketing messages, and insufficient sample sizes within each segment for statistically significant campaign analysis. A pragmatic approach involves validating segments against key business metrics. A common validation function assesses whether the mean values of KPIs differ significantly across segments using statistical tests like ANOVA. The F-statistic is calculated as:

$$F = \frac{\text{MSB}}{\text{MSW}} = \frac{\text{SSB}/(k-1)}{\text{SSW}/(n-k)}$$

where:

SSB = Sum of squares between groups.
SSW = Sum of squares within groups.
k = Number of segments.
n = Total number of customers.

A significant F-value indicates that the segments differ meaningfully on the target KPI (e.g., purchase frequency), justifying the segmentation scheme. Businesses must continuously balance segmentation granularity with operational feasibility to ensure sustainable implementation and measurable business impact.

9.10.2 From Segmentation to Prescriptive Targeting

9.10.2.1 Predictive versus Prescriptive Use of Segmentation

Customer segmentation traditionally serves a predictive function by identifying which customer groups are most likely to respond to specific marketing initiatives. This predictive approach answers questions such as "Which segment has the highest probability of purchasing a new product?" or "Which customers are most at risk of churning?" By analyzing historical data and behavioral patterns, businesses can forecast future actions with reasonable accuracy. For example, a retail bank might identify a segment of "digital-savvy young professionals," who are predicted to be highly receptive to a new mobile banking feature based on their past adoption of similar technologies. However, predictive segmentation alone leaves a critical gap between insight and action. It identifies opportunities but does not specify how to capitalize on them most effectively. This is where prescriptive segmentation provides transformative value by moving beyond prediction to specific recommendations.

Prescriptive analytics answers more complex questions: "Given a limited marketing budget, which specific actions should we take for each segment, and what level of investment will yield the optimal return?" It considers constraints, trade-offs, and business objectives to recommend precise interventions.

9.10.2.2 Optimization Frameworks for Targeting

Optimization frameworks provide the mathematical foundation for moving from descriptive segmentation to prescriptive targeting. These systems formalize business objectives—such as maximizing revenue, profit, or customer lifetime value—while incorporating real-world constraints like budget limitations, channel capacities, and operational capabilities. The core challenge they address is the efficient allocation of scarce marketing resources across multiple segments and touchpoints to achieve the best possible business outcomes given specific limitations.

Resource allocation represents the most fundamental optimization problem in targeting. Businesses must decide how to distribute limited marketing dollars across different customer segments to maximize overall returns. This involves not only identifying the most valuable segments but also determining the optimal investment level for each. A luxury automobile manufacturer, for instance, might use an optimization framework to allocate its marketing budget across segments like "current luxury sedan owners," "aspirational luxury buyers," and "high-net-worth professionals," with different investment levels and messaging strategies for each group based on their potential value and conversion probability.

Budget optimization takes resource allocation a step further by incorporating temporal and competitive dimensions. It answers questions about not just how much to spend on each segment, but when to spend it and how to adjust allocations based on performance feedback. A subscription-based streaming service like Netflix might use budget optimization to determine how much to spend on acquiring new subscribers in different geographic segments throughout the year, shifting allocations based on seasonal viewing patterns, competitive launches, and the performance of different acquisition channels to maximize subscriber growth within a fixed annual marketing budget.

9.10.2.3 Dynamic and Real-Time Targeting

Dynamic targeting represents the evolution of segmentation from static categorization to fluid, adaptive engagement based on real-time customer behaviors and contextual factors. Unlike traditional segmentation that groups customers based on historical patterns, dynamic targeting continuously updates marketing actions as new data becomes available. This approach recognizes that customer preferences and situations change rapidly, and marketing effectiveness depends on reaching the right person with the right message at the right moment through the right channel with unprecedented precision.

Adaptive offers exemplify dynamic targeting in action across numerous industries. In the hospitality sector, a hotel chain might monitor real-time booking patterns, local events, and competitor pricing to dynamically adjust offers for different customer segments. A business traveler searching for last-minute accommodation might receive an offer emphasizing convenience and premium amenities, while a family planning a vacation months in advance might receive value-oriented package deals. The system continuously refines these offers based on how similar customers have responded to previous communications, creating a self-optimizing target mechanism.

Recommendation engines represent perhaps the most widespread application of dynamic targeting, particularly in e-commerce and content streaming. Companies like Amazon and Netflix have perfected systems that prescribe personalized content and product suggestions based on real-time browsing behavior, purchase history, and similarities with other customers. These systems do not just recommend popular items broadly but dynamically adjust suggestions based on each individual's immediate context, what time of day it is, and what device they are using, creating a uniquely personalized experience that drives engagement and conversion through relevant prescription.

9.10.3 Applications of Segmentation and Targeting in Optimization

The logistics and supply chain industry leverages prescriptive analytics to transform traditional linear supply chains into responsive, adaptive networks. Fleet optimization systems utilize real-time GPS data, traffic patterns, weather conditions, and vehicle performance metrics to dynamically route shipments, minimizing fuel consumption and delivery times while maximizing asset utilization. Simultaneously, real-time inventory adjustment systems monitor sales data, warehouse levels, and incoming shipments to automatically recalibrate stock levels across distribution centers, preventing both stockouts and overstock situations. This creates a self-optimizing supply chain that can proactively respond to disruptions and fluctuating demand patterns, ensuring optimal service levels at minimal cost.

9.11 Summary

Predictive analytics leverage historical data, statistical algorithms, and ML techniques to anticipate future outcomes, identify patterns, and uncover trends. Forecasting, a specialized subset of predictive analytics, focuses on estimating future values based on time series data. The chapter begins by distinguishing between descriptive, predictive, and prescriptive analytics, emphasizing the forward-looking nature of predictive techniques. It explains how organizations use predictive models to forecast sales, manage inventory, assess credit risk, detect fraud, and personalize marketing strategies. Key components of predictive modeling, including data preparation, feature selection, model training, validation, and deployment, are presented in this chapter.

Popular modeling techniques, including regression analysis, decision trees, neural networks, support vector machines, and ensemble methods, are discussed, along with their use cases and advantages. The chapter also covers time series forecasting methods such as MAs, exponential smoothing, ARIMA models, and ML-based forecasting by focusing on time series analysis techniques used in demand forecasting, financial modeling, and operational planning. Furthermore, the chapter highlights best practices in model evaluation using metrics like MAE, RMSE, and R^2, and discusses the importance of cross-validation, overfitting prevention, and interpretability. Finally, ethical considerations, data quality issues, and the importance of human judgment in interpreting model outputs are also emphasized. In summary, this chapter provides students with an understanding of how predictive analytics and forecasting help organizations gain foresight, reduce uncertainty, and make proactive, informed decisions by applying traditional and ML-based forecasting models.

Notes

1 Li, D. (2012). A note on moving-average models with feedback. *Journal of Time Series Analysis*, 33(6), 873–879. https://doi.org/10.1111/j.1467-9892.2012.00802.x. Available at https://onlinelibrary.wiley.x?com/doi/abs/10.1111/j.1467-9892.2012.00802.x?x?casa_token=X9Wwm4V0MpgAAAAA%3A38CRf9xMUStMz0Fet0QNGmhuBQlysNkavRj6QzKN03tEMh2OXl9K4Tx?cyaPIx?c1PUnx4QgSjWx?cHd5O958

2 Moallemi, C. C., & Sağlam, M. (2017). Dynamic portfolio choice with linear rebalancing rules. *Journal of Financial and Quantitative Analysis*, 52(3), 1247–1278. https://doi.org/10.1017/S0022109017000345. Available at https://www.cambridge.org/core/journals/journal-of-financial-and-quantitative-analysis/article/abs/dynamic-portfolio-choice-with-linear-rebalancing-rules/745A5F645871D2A0E9AC2FA9F3D0F0E7

3 Wold, H. (1954). Causality and econometrics. *Econometrica: Journal of the Econometric Society*, 162–177. https://doi.org/10.2307/1907540. Available at https://www.jstor.org/stable/1907540?seq=1

4 Wu, H., & Levinson, D. (2021). The ensemble approach to forecasting: A review and synthesis. *Transportation Research Part C: Emerging Technologies*, 132, 103357. https://doi.org/10.1016/j.trc.2021.103357. Available at https://www.sciencedirect.com/science/article/pii/S0968090X21003594?casa_token=-fit_WAoC9AAAAAA:gjFgWEKUD072NnY04z-Kq-SnpyJjdFXHUUO-TvKcJ2BqRG7kdlpp5ciUWo03WxmH_6Hz-7e1EkM

5 Freitas, A. A. (2014). Comprehensible classification models: a position paper. *ACM SIGKDD Explorations Newsletter*, 15(1), 1–10. https://doi.org/10.1145/2594473.2594475. Available at https://dl.acm.org/doi/abs/10.1145/2594473.2594475

6 Fahrmeir, L., Kneib, T., Lang, S., & Marx, B. D. (2022). Regression models. In: Fahrmeir, L., Kneib, T., Lang, S., & Marx, B. D. (eds) *Regression: Models, Methods and Applications* (pp. 23–84). Springer Berlin Heidelberg. https://doi.org/10.1007/978-3-662-63882-8_2. Available at https://link.springer.com/chapter/10.1007/978-3-662-63882-8_2

7 Poole, D., & Raftery, A. E. (2000). Inference for deterministic simulation models: The Bayesian melding approach. *Journal of the American Statistical Association*, 95(452), 1244–1255. https://doi.org/10.1080/01621459.2000.10474324. Available at https://www.tandfonline.com/doi/abs/10.1080/01621459.2000.10474324?casa_token=LXRIIb_yQegAAAAA:hMAntPwJdO_zMwRl29FO6j069M3c_ftwWBaQvCzYD9Vd5ZoWCsYyrJy2LbMgTSR84p81gQyDdruA_Q

8 Tang, S., Shelden, D. R., Eastman, C. M., Pishdad-Bozorgi, P., & Gao, X. (2019). A review of building information modeling (BIM) and the internet of things (IoT) devices integration: Present status and future trends. *Automation in Construction*, 101, 127–139. https://doi.org/10.1016/j.autcon.2019.01.020. Available at https://www.sciencedirect.com/science/article/abs/pii/S0926580518305764

9 Sodiya, E. O., Umoga, U. J., Obaigbena, A., Jacks, B. S., Ugwuanyi, E. D., Daraojimba, A. I., & Lottu, O. A. (2024). Current state and prospects of edge computing within the Internet of Things (IoT) ecosystem. *International Journal of Science and Research Archive*, 11(1), 1863–1873.

10 Afroz, Z., Urmee, T., Shafiullah, G. M., & Higgins, G. (2018). Real-time prediction model for indoor temperature in a commercial building. *Applied Energy*, 231, 29–53. https://doi.org/10.1016/j.apenergy.2018.09.052. Available at https://www.sciencedirect.com/science/article/abs/pii/S030626191831362X

11 Akinrinoye, O. V., Kufile, O. T., Otokiti, B. O., Ejike, O. G., Umezurike, S. A., & Onifade, A. Y. (2020). Customer segmentation strategies in emerging markets: A review of tools, models, and applications. *International Journal of Scientific Research in Computer Science, Engineering and Information Technology*, 6(1), 194–217. https://doi.org/10.32628/IJSRCSEIT. Available at https://www.researchgate.net/profile/Omolola-Kufile/publication/394014688_Customer_Segmentation_Strategies_in_Emerging_Markets_A_Review_of_Tools_Models_and_Applications/links/688428c800a2407910a43f9a/Customer-Segmentation-Strategies-in-Emerging-Markets-A-Review-of-Tools-Models-and-Applications.pdf

10 Advanced Machine Learning Techniques

Learning Objectives

- Ensemble methods: Bagging, Boosting, and Random Forests
- Understand dimensionality reduction with PCA and t-SNE
- Learn dimensionality reduction with PCA and t-SNE
- Learn anomaly detection and clustering algorithms
- Understand generative and explainable AI technologies and their business applications
- Learn Hyperparameter Tuning Optimizes Model Performance (HTOMP) models
- Understand $L1$ (Lasso) and $L2$ (Ridge) regularization, which penalize large weights in models to enhance generalization on unseen data
- Learn how accuracy, precision, recall, $F1$-score, ROC-AUC, and confusion matrices can offer insights into model strengths and weaknesses
- Understand the role of k-fold and stratified cross-validation techniques to ensure model stability and reduce variance in performance evaluation

10.1 Introduction

Advanced machine learning (AML) techniques play an important role in extracting meaningful insights and solving intricate problems in today's data-driven and digital world. These techniques represent the cutting edge of AI by enabling systems to learn from data, identify patterns and norms, and make data-supported decisions with minimal human intervention. AML is transforming organizations and reshaping the future of businesses by empowering computer systems and autonomous vehicles and enabling natural language processing and predictive modeling. AML has advanced beyond basic algorithms like linear regression or decision trees to more sophisticated methods of deep learning, ensemble methods, reinforcement learning, and generative models. These advanced techniques are designed to handle high-dimensional data, unstructured data (like images, text, and audio), and complex problem domains. For example, deep learning, a subset of AML, has revolutionized fields like computer vision and speech recognition through neural networks with multiple layers to model intricate relationships in data. This chapter explores how AML can be applied to solve business problems such as customer segmentation, demand forecasting, fraud detection, and market trend analysis.

DOI: 10.4324/9781003664550-10

The applications of AML are significant and impactful in many sectors. For instance, in healthcare, AML assists in disease diagnosis and drug discovery; in accounting and finance, it enhances fraud prevention and detection and algorithmic forecasting and trading; and in marketing, it personalizes customer experiences and optimizes campaigns. However, the adoption of these AML techniques raises challenges and important considerations around ethics, fairness, interpretability, and the need for robust infrastructure and expertise. This chapter presents both opportunities and challenges of the use of AML tools and techniques, including their foundational concepts, cutting-edge methodologies, and real-world applications in providing students with sufficient knowledge and skills to understand and harness these powerful tools, drive innovation, and solve some of the most emerging challenging problems.

10.2 Ensemble Methods: Bagging, Boosting, and Random Forests

Ensemble methods improve predictive performance and robustness by combining multiple base learners to produce more accurate and stable models than any single estimator alone. Ensemble learning methods have become a cornerstone of modern AML and data analytics. They represent a class of algorithms that combine multiple models to produce more accurate, stable, and reliable predictions than those of any single constituent model. This section explores three of the most widely used ensemble techniques: Bagging, Boosting, and Random Forests. Each method provides a unique approach to model combination, addressing various challenges in AML such as bias, variance, and overfitting.

10.2.1 Overview of Ensemble Learning

Ensemble learning is based on the principle that combining multiple learners yields a more robust model than using a single learner. This principle is analogous to consulting multiple experts before deciding. By aggregating predictions from different models, ensemble methods often achieve improved generalization and resilience to data noise. The two main categories of ensemble methods are averaging methods, which reduce variance by averaging predictions (as in Bagging), and boosting methods, which reduce bias by sequentially correcting model errors.

10.2.2 Bagging (Bootstrap Aggregating)

Bagging, an abbreviation for Bootstrap Aggregating, is a fundamental ensemble learning technique.[1] It was designed to enhance the stability and accuracy of AML algorithms by reducing variance and mitigating overfitting. The main idea behind Bagging is to train multiple models—often of the same type—on different bootstrapped samples of the original dataset and then aggregate their predictions to form a final output. Each bootstrapped dataset is generated through random sampling with replacement, which ensures diversity among the individual learners. This randomness is crucial because it allows each model to capture different aspects of the underlying data distribution.[2]

The Bagging process begins by generating k bootstrapped datasets from the original data, each containing the same number of observations as the original dataset but drawn with replacement. A separate model is trained on each sample, and the ensemble's final prediction is obtained by averaging (for regression tasks) or majority voting (for classification tasks) the individual model outputs. Since each model is exposed to slightly different data, the ensemble tends to smooth out individual model fluctuations, thereby reducing variance without significantly increasing bias.

Bagging is especially effective when used with unstable learning algorithms, such as decision trees, where small variations in the data can lead to drastically different model outcomes. By averaging multiple trees, Bagging stabilizes predictions and improves generalization. One prominent extension of Bagging is the Random Forest algorithm,[3] which adds an extra layer of randomness by selecting random subsets of features at each split in the trees. This modification further decorrelates the models, leading to superior ensemble performance.

10.2.3 Boosting

Boosting is a powerful ensemble learning technique designed to convert a collection of weak learners into a strong learner capable of making highly accurate predictions. Introduced by Freund and Schapire in the 1990s, the concept behind Boosting is based on the sequential correction of errors made by earlier models.[4] Unlike Bagging, where models are trained independently on different bootstrapped samples, Boosting trains models in sequence; each model focuses on improving the mistakes of the previous ones. This iterative reweighting process allows the ensemble to concentrate its efforts on difficult or misclassified examples, thereby reducing both bias and variance in predictive modeling.[5]

The fundamental principle of Boosting can be understood through the Adaptive Boosting (AdaBoost) algorithm, which was among the first practical implementations of the method. In AdaBoost, each observation in the dataset is assigned a weight that reflects its importance in the learning process. Initially, all observations are given equal weight. After each iteration, the algorithm evaluates the model's performance and increases the weights of the misclassified samples while reducing the weights of correctly classified ones. A new model is then trained using these updated weights, ensuring that the subsequent learner focuses more on difficult cases. The final ensemble combines all the weak models into a weighted sum, where each model's influence depends on its individual accuracy. This mechanism allows the ensemble to produce a robust final prediction that outperforms any single weak learner.[6]

Beyond AdaBoost, Gradient Boosting represents a major evolution of the boosting framework. Gradient Boosting generalizes the idea by minimizing an arbitrary differentiable loss function through gradient descent. Each new model is trained to predict the residual errors (or gradients) of the previous ensemble, effectively learning to correct the ensemble's current shortcomings. This framework makes Gradient Boosting applicable to a wide range of problems, including regression, classification, and ranking tasks. One of the most influential implementations of this approach is the XGBoost algorithm.[7] XGBoost improves upon traditional Gradient Boosting by introducing regularization terms to control overfitting, parallelized computation for scalability, and efficient memory usage. Similarly, newer variants such as LightGBM and CatBoost have been developed to further enhance computational efficiency and handle categorical data more effectively.

Boosting offers several advantages over traditional ML algorithms. First, it is highly flexible and can be combined with a variety of weak learners, though decision trees are most commonly used due to their interpretability and adaptability to complex, nonlinear relationships. Second, boosting tends to achieve exceptional predictive accuracy, often outperforming Bagging-based methods like Random Forests in structured data problems. It is also robust against overfitting when proper regularization and early stopping techniques are applied. Furthermore, Boosting provides a systematic way to reduce both bias and variance simultaneously—bias by correcting earlier errors, and variance through model averaging.

In practice, Boosting has become a standard tool across many domains, including finance, healthcare, marketing, and cybersecurity. In finance, boosting algorithms are employed for credit scoring, fraud detection, and market forecasting. In healthcare, they are used for disease classification, patient outcome prediction, and biomarker identification. Boosting has also dominated AML competitions, such as those on Kaggle, due to its balance between predictive power and generalization performance. The continued development of more efficient and scalable boosting frameworks ensures that this method will remain at the forefront of predictive analytics and AI research for years to come.

10.2.4 Random Forests

Random Forests represent one of the most popular and effective learning methods in AML. Random Forests extend the concept of Bagging (Bootstrap Aggregating) by incorporating additional randomness into the model-building process. The algorithm constructs an ensemble of decision trees—each trained on a different bootstrapped sample of the data—and aggregates their predictions to form a final output. The key innovation of Random Forests lies in their method of random feature selection: at each split in a decision tree, the algorithm considers only a random subset of available features rather than all of them. This process reduces correlation among individual trees and enhances the overall predictive performance of the ensemble.

The construction of a Random Forest involves two main sources of randomness: data sampling and feature selection. First, the algorithm generates multiple bootstrapped datasets by sampling the original data with replacement. Each dataset is then used to train a separate decision tree. Second, during the tree-growing process, only a randomly selected subset of features is evaluated at each node for the best split. This technique ensures that no single predictor dominates the ensemble and that the trees capture diverse relationships in the data. Once all trees are trained, the Random Forest aggregates their predictions—using majority voting for classification tasks or averaging for regression tasks—to produce the result.

The use of random feature selection has several advantages. It decorrelates the individual trees, thereby reducing variance and improving generalization. Moreover, because each tree is trained on a different subset of features and samples, the ensemble becomes more resilient to overfitting, which is a common issue in single decision trees. Random Forests also handle high-dimensional data efficiently, making them suitable for complex real-world applications such as gene expression analysis, image classification, and financial modeling. Another important characteristic of Random Forests is their ability to estimate variable importance. By measuring how much each feature contributes to reducing impurity or prediction error, the algorithm provides insights into the relative influence of different predictors—an essential feature for applied research in disciplines like economics and medicine.[8]

10.2.5 Comparative Analysis of Bagging, Boosting, and Random Forests

Bagging, boosting, and random forests are closely related ensemble-learning strategies, but they differ in *how* they generate diversity among models and *what* they optimize.[9] Bagging (bootstrap aggregating) reduces variance by training many base learners (often deep decision trees) on bootstrap-resampled datasets and then averaging (regression) or majority voting (classification); because models are fit independently and symmetrically, bagging is especially effective for high-variance learners and is naturally parallelizable.[10] Boosting, by contrast, is sequential and adaptive: each new learner is trained to emphasize observations that prior learners handled poorly (e.g., via reweighting), and the final model is a weighted sum of weak learners; this tends to reduce bias (and can also reduce variance) and often yields state-of-the-art accuracy but can be more sensitive to noisy labels and requires careful regularization (e.g., shrinkage/early stopping).[11] Random forests can be viewed as an extension of bagging that injects additional *decorrelation* by randomly subsampling features at each split, which typically improves generalization beyond plain bagging while retaining robustness and strong out-of-the-box performance; they also provide useful internal diagnostics such as out-of-bag error estimates and variable-importance measures.[12] Thus, Bagging, Boosting, and Random Forests are three of the most influential ensemble learning methods in AML. The most fundamental difference between these methods lies in how individual learners are constructed and combined. Bagging, short for Bootstrap Aggregating, trains multiple base models independently on bootstrapped samples of the training data.

From a computational standpoint, Bagging and Random Forests are more straightforward to parallelize because each model can be trained independently. Boosting's sequential nature makes it more computationally intensive and less suited for parallel processing, although optimized implementations like XGBoost and LightGBM have mitigated this limitation through algorithmic improvements.[13] In terms of interpretability, single decision trees are inherently easy to understand but ensembles of hundreds or thousands of trees—whether produced by Bagging, Boosting, or Random Forests—are not. However, Random Forests offer the advantage of computing features that provide insights into the relative influence of predictors, which is particularly useful for applied fields such as economics, medicine, and marketing. Boosting models also provide similar importance metrics, but their output tends to be more complex and less transparent.

In practice, Bagging, Boosting, and Random Forests are all highly effective, but their suitability depends on the specific task. Bagging is most useful when dealing with high-variance, low-bias models like unpruned decision trees, and it performs well when the dataset contains little noise. Random Forests, as an extension of Bagging, have become a standard baseline model in both academia and industry due to their balance between accuracy, robustness, and ease of use. They are particularly effective in high-dimensional datasets where feature correlations can mislead simpler models. Boosting, by contrast, tends to outperform both Bagging and Random Forests when model accuracy is paramount and computational resources are available. Algorithms such as Gradient Boosting and XGBoost frequently dominate AML competitions because of their ability to achieve state-of-the-art accuracy through iterative error correction. However, they require careful hyperparameter tuning and regularization to avoid overfitting, particularly in noisy or small datasets.

10.2.6 Applications of Ensemble Methods

Ensemble methods—such as Bagging, Boosting, and Random Forests—have become indispensable in AML and data science because of their ability to improve predictive accuracy, reduce overfitting, and enhance model robustness. By combining multiple weak or strong learners, ensemble techniques can generalize better to unseen data than individual models. Over the past two decades, these methods have found extensive applications across numerous fields, including finance, healthcare, marketing, cybersecurity, and engineering. Their flexibility, scalability, and superior performance make them suitable for both academic research and industrial applications.

In the financial sector, ensemble methods are widely used for risk assessment, fraud detection, and algorithmic trading. Financial data often exhibits high dimensionality, nonlinearity, and volatility—conditions under which ensemble models excel. Random Forests and GBMs are commonly used for credit scoring because they can handle complex interactions among borrower characteristics and macroeconomic variables.[14] By aggregating predictions from multiple trees, these models minimize overfitting and provide interpretable measures of variable importance, helping financial institutions identify key risk drivers.

Boosting algorithms, such as XGBoost and LightGBM, have also proven effective for fraud detection by distinguishing subtle patterns in transaction data that may indicate fraudulent activity. Because Boosting focuses sequentially on misclassified instances, it can detect rare anomalies that traditional statistical models often overlook. Additionally, ensemble methods are applied in algorithmic trading and portfolio optimization, where Bagging and Random Forests improve return predictions by aggregating signals from diverse models trained on different market indicators.

In healthcare, ensemble methods play a crucial role in disease diagnosis, patient outcome prediction, and bioinformatics. Medical datasets are typically noisy, heterogeneous, and imbalanced, which makes ensemble approaches particularly useful. For example, Random Forests have been used for disease classification tasks such as cancer detection, diabetes diagnosis, and cardiovascular risk prediction.[15] Their robustness to noise and ability to capture nonlinear relationships among medical variables make them ideal for clinical decision-support systems. Boosting methods, particularly Gradient Boosting and XGBoost, have been widely adopted in genomics and medical imaging. In genomics, they identify gene expression patterns associated with specific diseases, while in radiology, they enhance the accuracy of image-based diagnostic systems by combining multiple weak image classifiers. Moreover, ensemble methods are often integrated with deep learning frameworks to improve interpretability and performance, such as combining neural networks with Random Forests for hybrid diagnostic models. These models aid clinicians in making more accurate and data-driven decisions.

In marketing analytics, ensemble models are essential for customer segmentation, churn prediction, and recommendation systems. Boosting algorithms help businesses identify customers most likely to respond to promotional campaigns or discontinue services, enabling proactive retention strategies. For instance, Gradient Boosting and Random Forests are used in telecommunications and e-commerce to predict customer churn with high precision by analyzing behavioral data, purchase histories, and engagement metrics. Bagging-based ensembles are also applied to market segmentation problems, where they group customers with similar purchasing behaviors, helping firms target marketing strategies more effectively. In recommendation systems, ensemble methods are often combined with collaborative filtering and deep learning models to enhance personalization. By aggregating outputs from multiple models, ensembles increase recommendation accuracy and adaptability, which improves user satisfaction and retention.

Cybersecurity has increasingly benefited from ensemble learning for intrusion detection, malware classification, and anomaly detection. Random Forests and Boosted Trees are particularly effective for detecting sophisticated attacks because they can learn from both structured network logs and unstructured text data. For example, Gradient Boosting algorithms are applied in spam filtering, phishing detection, and network intrusion systems to distinguish malicious behavior from normal patterns. Ensemble models' adaptability and ability to handle high-dimensional data make them suitable for dynamic cybersecurity environments.

In engineering, ensemble methods are used in predictive maintenance, fault detection, and quality control. Machine operators employ Random Forests to predict equipment failures by analyzing sensor data from industrial machines, thereby reducing downtime and maintenance costs. In civil engineering, ensemble methods are applied to structural health monitoring by integrating multiple sensor readings to detect early signs of stress or damage. These applications demonstrate the versatility of ensemble models in real-time and safety-critical systems.

10.3 Dimensionality Reduction with PCA and *t*-SNE

The exponential growth of data across industries has created challenges in storing, analyzing, and visualizing high-dimensional datasets. Dimensionality-reduction methods provide a solution by transforming large sets of correlated variables into a lower-dimensional space while retaining the essential structure and variability in the data. PCA and *t*-SNE are among the most popular dimensionality-reduction techniques in modern analytics and AML.[16] PCA is a linear method that identifies orthogonal axes maximizing variance, whereas *t*-SNE is a nonlinear approach designed to preserve local structure for visualization.

Dimensionality reduction simplifies datasets by reducing the number of variables under consideration. High-dimensional data often suffer from the "curse of dimensionality," where increased dimensionality can lead to sparse data, overfitting, and computational inefficiency.[17] By reducing dimensions, analysts can improve model performance, enhance interpretability, and facilitate data visualization. Two main types of dimensionality reduction exist: feature selection, which retains a subset of original variables, and feature extraction, which creates new variables representing the original data. PCA and *t*-SNE fall under feature extraction, generating new dimensions that capture the underlying patterns in the dataset.

10.3.1 Principal Component Analysis (PCA)

PCA is a statistical technique that transforms original correlated variables into a set of uncorrelated variables called principal components.[18] The first principal component accounts for the maximum variance in the data, and each subsequent component captures the maximum remaining variance orthogonal to previous components. PCA achieves dimensionality reduction while preserving as much variability as possible, making it a cornerstone in exploratory data analysis, predictive modeling, and feature engineering.

PCA is particularly useful in business and data science applications involving large datasets with multicollinearity. For example, in marketing analytics, PCA can reduce hundreds of customer behavioral features into a few components representing purchasing tendencies, website interaction, and engagement metrics. In finance, PCA is employed for risk modeling and portfolio optimization, where correlated asset returns are projected into a lower-dimensional space to identify latent risk factors. In research contexts, PCA helps in processing high-dimensional gene expression or survey datasets, enabling clearer insights and visualization.

The implementation of PCA typically involves centering and scaling the dataset, computing the covariance matrix, and performing eigen decomposition or singular value decomposition (SVD) to extract principal components. The selection of the number of components often relies on explained variance, commonly choosing enough components

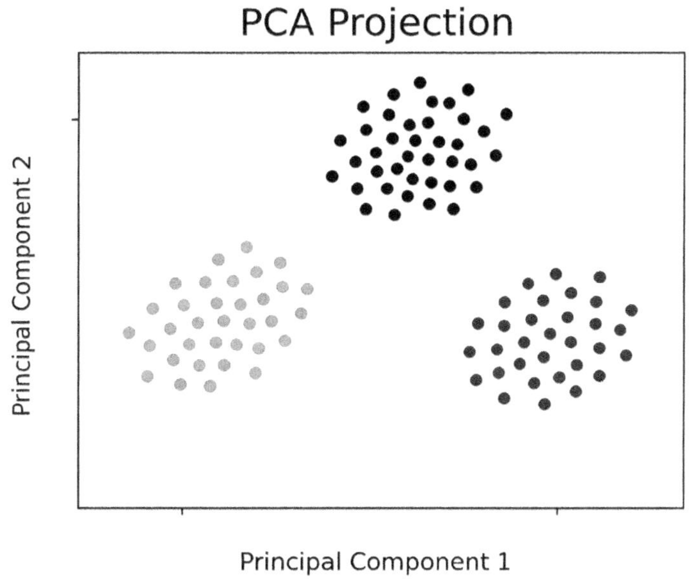

Figure 10.1 PCA Projection of High-Dimensional Data.

to capture 80–95% of the total variance. While PCA is computationally efficient and interpretable, its linear nature may limit its ability to capture complex, nonlinear relationships in the data.

Figure 10.1 illustrates an example of PCA applied to a high-dimensional dataset, showing how data points are projected onto the first two principal components to reveal underlying patterns and clusters.

10.3.1.1 t-Distributed Stochastic Neighbor Embedding (t-SNE)

t-SNE is a nonlinear dimensionality-reduction and visualization technique designed to preserve local neighborhood structures when projecting high-dimensional data into two or three dimensions. The method converts pairwise similarities in the original space into conditional probabilities using Gaussian kernels, while similarities in the low-dimensional embedding are modeled with a heavy-tailed Student-*t* distribution, which mitigates the "crowding problem" and enables better separation of clusters.[19] *t*-SNE excels at revealing complex manifolds and latent cluster structures in domains such as text embeddings, image features, genomics, and customer segmentation by minimizing the Kullback-Leibler divergence between high- and low-dimensional similarity distributions via gradient descent. However, *t*-SNE is primarily an exploratory and visualization tool rather than a general-purpose feature-reduction method with results that can vary across runs due to nonconvex optimization, and performance is sensitive to hyperparameters such as perplexity and learning rate.[20] As a result, best practice in analytics and ML research is to use *t*-SNE for qualitative insight and pattern discovery, often in conjunction with quantitative methods such as PCA or UMAP to validate structural interpretations. *t*-SNE is a nonlinear dimensionality-reduction technique. Unlike PCA, which maximizes global variance, *t*-SNE emphasizes preserving local structure and pairwise similarities in high-dimensional data. It converts Euclidean distances into conditional probabilities representing similarities and

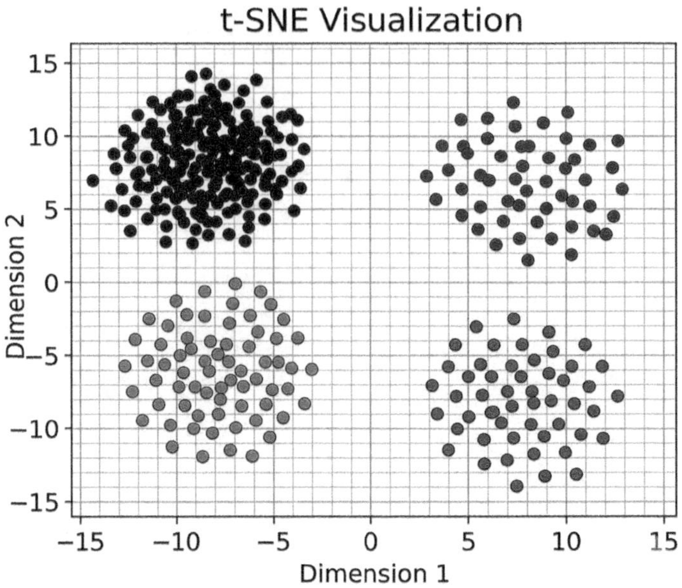

Figure 10.2 *t*-SNE Projection of High-Dimensional Data.

minimizes the Kullback-Leibler divergence between high-dimensional and low-dimensional probability distributions. This approach enables effective visualization of clusters and complex structures in two or three dimensions. Figure 10.2 provides an example of *t*-SNE visualization, demonstrating how high-dimensional data can be represented in two dimensions while preserving local relationships.

10.3.2 Comparative Analysis of PCA and t-SNE

PCA and *t*-SNE are two widely used dimensionality-reduction techniques that differ fundamentally in objectives, assumptions, and interpretability. PCA is a linear, variance-maximization method that projects data onto orthogonal components ranked by explained variance, making it well-suited for noise reduction, feature extraction, and downstream modeling where interpretability, stability, and preservation of global structure are essential.[21] In contrast, *t*-SNE is a nonlinear, probabilistic technique designed primarily for visualization; it preserves local neighborhood relationships by matching pairwise similarity distributions between high- and low-dimensional spaces, often revealing complex clusters and manifold structures that PCA cannot capture.[22] However, *t*-SNE does not preserve global distances or variance structure, is sensitive to hyperparameters (e.g., perplexity and learning rate), and produces embeddings that are not directly interpretable or suitable for predictive modeling. As a result, PCA is typically preferred for explainable dimensionality reduction and model preprocessing, whereas *t*-SNE is best used as an exploratory visualization tool to gain qualitative insights into high-dimensional data. Overall, PCA and *t*-SNE serve complementary purposes in dimensionality reduction. PCA is linear, interpretable, and computationally efficient, making it suitable for feature engineering, preprocessing, and predictive modeling. *t*-SNE, by contrast, excels at visualizing complex, nonlinear relationships and clustering patterns in high-dimensional data, but it is less suited for direct integration into predictive models. In business applications, PCA may be used for reducing features before building a regression or classification model, while *t*-SNE can provide visual insights into customer segments or product preferences.

Successful application of PCA and *t*-SNE requires careful consideration of preprocessing, scaling, and parameter selection. Both methods benefit from standardized data to ensure that variables contribute equally to the analysis. For PCA, selecting the appropriate number of components based on explained variance ensures that essential information is retained while reducing dimensionality. For *t*-SNE, hyperparameters such as perplexity, learning rate, and number of iterations strongly influence the resulting visualization. Additionally, using PCA for initial dimensionality reduction before applying *t*-SNE is a common strategy to improve computational efficiency and prevent overfitting in visualizations. Software implementations of PCA and *t*-SNE are widely available in Python (scikit-learn, TensorFlow) and R (stats, Rtsne). These libraries provide efficient routines for high-dimensional datasets and include options for scaling, normalization, and visualization. In business and research, integrating these tools into data pipelines enables scalable and interpretable dimensionality reduction, facilitating downstream predictive modeling, cluster analysis, and pattern discovery. Despite their utility, PCA and *t*-SNE have limitations. PCA is limited to capturing linear relationships and may overlook nonlinear structure in complex datasets. *t*-SNE, while effective for visualization, is computationally expensive and sensitive to hyperparameter selection. Both methods may be affected by outliers and require careful preprocessing. Interpretability is another concern: PCA components may be abstract combinations of original variables, while *t*-SNE embeddings are primarily visual tools and lack direct feature interpretation. Nevertheless, awareness of these limitations allows practitioners to apply these methods effectively and combine them to maximize insights in practical applications.

10.4 Anomaly Detection and Clustering Algorithms

Anomaly detection and clustering algorithms play an essential role in unsupervised and semi-supervised analytics by identifying hidden structures in data and detecting observations that deviate from normal patterns. Clustering algorithms such as k-means, hierarchical clustering, and density-based methods like DBSCAN group observations based on similarity or proximity, enabling the discovery of latent segments in applications ranging from customer analytics to bioinformatics and network analysis.[23] In contrast, anomaly detection algorithms focus on identifying rare, unexpected, or suspicious observations that may signal fraud, system failures, or emerging risks; widely used approaches include distance-based methods, density-based techniques (e.g., Local Outlier Factor), isolation-based models, and probabilistic methods.[24] While clustering seeks to model the dominant data structure, anomaly detection explicitly targets deviations from that structure, and the two are often complementary, as cluster boundaries can help define normal behavior against which anomalies are measured. Recent advances integrate ML and representation learning, such as autoencoders and hybrid clustering-outlier frameworks, to improve scalability and detection accuracy in high-dimensional and streaming data environments.

10.4.1 Clustering Algorithms

Clustering represents one of the most fundamental techniques in unsupervised learning. It aims to uncover the inherent grouping structures within a dataset by organizing objects into clusters so that those within the same group are more similar to each other than to those in different groups.[25] Unlike classification, clustering does not require predefined labels; instead, it discovers latent patterns directly from data. These algorithms are widely applied in data mining, pattern recognition, bioinformatics, marketing segmentation, and image analysis. Although there are many approaches, clustering methods can be broadly categorized into partitioning, hierarchical, density-based, and model-based techniques.

10.4.2 Partitioning Methods

Partitioning algorithms divide a dataset into k clusters, typically by optimizing an objective function such as minimizing within-cluster variance. The most well-known method is k-means, which iteratively assigns each data point to the nearest cluster centroid, then recalculates centroids until convergence.[26] Its simplicity, speed, and scalability make it suitable for large datasets. However, k-means assumes spherical clusters of similar sizes and is sensitive to outliers. K-medoids, an extension of k-means, mitigates sensitivity to extreme values by using actual data points (medoids) as cluster centers instead of arithmetic means. Despite their efficiency, partitioning methods require the number of clusters (k) to be specified in advance. Determining the optimal number of clusters often relies on evaluation metrics such as the Elbow method or Silhouette coefficient, which measure intra-cluster cohesion and inter-cluster separation.

10.4.3 Hierarchical Methods

Hierarchical clustering algorithms build a nested tree of clusters known as a dendrogram. They can be either agglomerative (bottom-up) or divisive (top-down). Agglomerative clustering begins with each data point as an individual cluster and successively merges the closest pairs based on a distance metric (e.g., Euclidean or Manhattan distance) and linkage criteria (e.g., single, complete, or average linkage). Divisive clustering starts with one large cluster and recursively divides it into smaller clusters. The main advantage of hierarchical methods is that they do not require specifying the number of clusters in advance. However, they are computationally expensive (often $O(n^2)$) and sensitive to noise and scaling.[27]

10.4.4 Density-Based Methods

Density-based clustering methods, such as DBSCAN, group data points that form dense regions separated by sparse areas.[28] DBSCAN is particularly effective for detecting clusters of arbitrary shapes and can automatically identify outliers as noise. It requires two parameters: & (neighborhood radius) and MinPts (minimum number of points in a dense region). A limitation of DBSCAN is its sensitivity to parameter selection and difficulty in handling datasets with varying density. OPTICS (Ordering Points to Identify the Clustering Structure) extends DBSCAN to address these issues by constructing an augmented cluster ordering based on reachability distances.

10.4.5 Model-Based Methods

Model-based clustering assumes that data are generated from a mixture of underlying probabilistic models. Gaussian Mixture Models (GMM), for example, represent each cluster as a Gaussian distribution characterized by a mean and covariance matrix. Using algorithms such as Expectation-Maximization (EM), GMM estimates parameters that best fit the observed data.[29] Unlike K-means, which assigns each point to a single cluster, GMM provides soft clustering, where each point has a probability of belonging to each cluster. Model-based approaches offer flexibility and a probabilistic interpretation but may struggle with high-dimensional data and overfitting if the number of mixture components is not properly chosen.

Clustering algorithms are designed to organize data into meaningful subgroups, revealing patterns and relationships that may not be immediately visible. They can be broadly categorized into partitioning, hierarchical, density-based, and model-based approaches. Partitioning methods such as k-means and k-medoids divide the dataset into k clusters by minimizing intra-cluster distance. Hierarchical clustering builds a tree-like structure (dendrogram) by successively merging or splitting clusters based on proximity measures. Density-based methods like DBSCAN and OPTICS detect clusters of arbitrary shape by identifying dense regions separated by low-density areas. Table 10.1 presents key clustering algorithms. Model-based approaches, such as GMM, assume data are generated by a mixture of underlying probability distributions.

Evaluating clustering results is inherently challenging because ground truth labels are often unavailable. Common internal metrics include Silhouette Coefficient, Davies-Bouldin Index, and Calinski-Harabasz Score, which assess cohesion and separation based solely on the data structure. External validation (when true labels exist) uses metrics like Adjusted Rand Index (ARI) or Mutual Information. Practical deployment of clustering algorithms requires attention to data preprocessing, such as feature scaling, dimensionality reduction (e.g., PCA), and handling noise. No single clustering algorithm performs best across all scenarios; hence, algorithm selection depends on data characteristics, desired cluster interpretability, and computational constraints.

Table 10.1 Key Clustering Algorithms

Algorithm	*Core Principle*	*Key Advantages/Limitations*
K-means	Partitions data into k clusters, minimizing distance to centroids.	Simple, efficient; assumes spherical clusters; sensitive to outliers.
DBSCAN	Groups of dense regions separated by sparse areas.	Detects arbitrary shapes; robust to noise; struggles with varying densities.
Hierarchical	Builds nested clusters using linkage criteria.	No need for preset k; computationally intensive on large data.
GMM	Models' data as mixtures of Gaussian distributions.	Probabilistic interpretation; may overfit if components are mis-specified.
Isolation forest	Isolates anomalies by random partitioning.	Efficient and scalable; assumes anomalies are few and different.
Local outlier factor (LOF)	Measures local deviation of density from neighbors.	Captures local anomalies; sensitive to parameter choice.
Autoencoder	Learns compressed representations and reconstructs inputs.	Captures complex nonlinear anomalies; requires large training data.

10.5 Explainable AI for Transparent Decision-Making

AI has become deeply embedded in decision-making across industries such as finance, healthcare, education, and public policy. While AI enables unprecedented levels of efficiency and prediction accuracy, the complexity of models like deep neural networks has created a "black-box" problem. Stakeholders, including end-users, policymakers, and regulators, often struggle to understand how AI systems reach their conclusions. This opacity threatens accountability and erodes trust, particularly when decisions have moral, legal, or social consequences. XAI addresses this gap by providing mechanisms to make AI systems interpretable and transparent. The goal is not merely to reveal how the algorithm works but to make its reasoning comprehensible to human users.[30] Thus, XAI provides the methodological foundation for making AI-driven decisions transparent, interpretable, and trustworthy by revealing how and why models generate specific outputs. As complex ML models such as deep neural networks and ensemble methods are increasingly used in high-stakes domains, including finance, healthcare, auditing, and public policy, concerns over opacity, bias, and accountability have intensified. XAI addresses these concerns through techniques such as feature importance measures, local and global surrogate models, counterfactual explanations, and visualization tools that translate model behavior into human-understandable insights. XAI supports regulatory compliance, ethical AI governance, and stakeholder trust, while enabling decision-makers to validate, challenge, and refine AI recommendations by enhancing interpretability. In prescriptive and decision-support contexts, explainability is particularly essential, as transparent reasoning allows users to assess trade-offs, understand risk implications, and justify actions taken based on AI outputs. As a result, XAI is widely recognized as a cornerstone of responsible and transparent decision-making in AI-enabled organizations, as explained in the following subsections.[31]

10.5.1 Foundations of Explainable AI

The growing integration of AI into decision-making systems across domains such as healthcare, finance, criminal justice, and education has amplified the need for transparency and interpretability. Complex AML models—particularly deep neural networks and ensemble methods—often operate as black boxes, producing highly accurate predictions without disclosing their internal logic.[32] This opacity challenges accountability, trust, and compliance with ethical and legal standards. The field of Explainable Artificial Intelligence (XAI) emerged in response to this challenge, aiming to design systems whose operations can be understood, trusted, and effectively managed by humans. The foundations of XAI combine technical, cognitive, and ethical dimensions, seeking to balance model performance with interpretability.

At its core, XAI seeks to answer a central question: "Why did the model make this decision?"[33] Two key but related notions underpin this field: interpretability and explainability. Interpretability refers to the degree to which a human can directly understand the internal mechanics of a model. For example, a linear regression's coefficients transparently indicate how each feature contributes to the prediction. Explainability, by contrast, emphasizes communication—providing human-understandable reasons for model behavior, even if the underlying model remains complex. Historically, interpretability has been intrinsic to early AI systems such as rule-based expert systems, where explicit "if-then" rules defined decision paths. However, the advent of data-driven learning, particularly deep learning, shifted the emphasis from symbolic logic to statistical inference, greatly improving accuracy but reducing transparency.[34] The performance-interpretability trade-off became a central concern: simple models are transparent but often less powerful, whereas complex models are accurate but inscrutable. Foundational research in XAI, therefore, focuses on bridging this divide through post-hoc interpretation and inherently interpretable architectures.

Explainability draws from multiple disciplines—computer science, philosophy of science, and cognitive psychology—to conceptualize how explanations should be generated and evaluated. From a computational standpoint, XAI encompasses both intrinsic and post-hoc approaches. Intrinsic approaches involve building models that are interpretable by design, such as decision trees, generalized additive models, or attention-based neural networks that visually reveal what the system "focuses" on. Post-hoc techniques, on the other hand, attempt to interpret existing black-box models after training through methods like feature attribution (e.g., SHAP, LIME) or visualization (e.g., Grad-CAM). Philosophically, explanations in AI align with principles of causality and contrastiveness. People understand decisions best when explanations reveal cause-and-effect relationships or contrast outcomes ("Why this rather than that?"). Cognitive theories suggest that humans prefer simple, selective, and context-relevant explanations. Consequently, effective XAI systems must balance fidelity, the accuracy of the explanation with respect to the model, and comprehensibility, the ease with which humans can grasp it. Methodologically, XAI integrates both quantitative and qualitative evaluation frameworks. Quantitative metrics assess the faithfulness or stability of explanations, while user-centered evaluations measure human trust, understanding, and satisfaction. This dual evaluation approach anchors XAI not only in computer science but also in the human factor domain.

Explainability techniques are generally categorized into model-agnostic and model-specific approaches. Model-agnostic methods can be applied to any model type, whereas model-specific methods are designed for particular architectures like neural networks. Common XAI techniques include feature importance analysis, visualization methods, surrogate models, and counterfactual explanations (see Table 10.2).

Explainability serves as a cornerstone of responsible AI governance. The ability to interpret algorithmic behavior directly supports regulatory compliance, such as the European Union's GDPR, which enshrines a "right to explanation." Moreover, XAI mitigates automation bias by allowing humans to critically assess machine recommendations rather than

Table 10.2 XAI Methods

Method	*Core Principle*	*Key Strengths/Limitations*
LIME (local interpretable model-agnostic explanations)	Builds simple interpretable models locally around predictions.	Flexible; intuitive for tabular and text data; unstable for high-dimensional data.
SHAP (SHapley Additive exPlanations)	Uses game theory to distribute credit for model predictions across features.	Theoretically sound; consistent explanations; computationally expensive.
Grad-CAM (gradient-weighted class activation mapping)	Highlights important image regions contributing to a neural network's output.	Effective for visual data; limited to CNN architectures.
Counterfactual explanations	Show how inputs could change to alter predictions.	Actionable and user-centered; depends on data plausibility.
Surrogate models	Approximate complex models with simpler interpretable ones.	Readable but may oversimplify underlying behavior.

accept them blindly. In safety-critical applications—autonomous driving, medical diagnostics, or credit scoring—such interpretability can be the difference between beneficial and harmful outcomes. The human-aligned foundation of XAI also extends to ethical accountability. By uncovering decision logic, explainable systems facilitate auditing, fairness assessments, and continuous monitoring. They make AI traceable, enabling organizations to justify their decisions to regulators and the public. This convergence of technical transparency and ethical governance represents a paradigm shift in AI, moving from systems that merely perform well to systems that are understandable, trustworthy, and socially aligned.

The foundations of XAI lie at the intersection of technical design, human cognition, and ethical responsibility. As AI becomes integral to societal decision processes, interpretability and transparency are no longer optional—they are prerequisites for legitimacy and trust. The conceptual core of XAI emphasizes interpretability, causality, and human-centered explanation, grounded in both computational rigor and psychological realism. Future developments will likely deepen these foundations by integrating causal inference, interactive explanation interfaces, and adaptive learning systems that adjust explanations to user needs. In sum, XAI represents not only a technical endeavor but also a commitment to making intelligent systems compatible with human understanding, values, and oversight.

10.5.2 Human-Centered Design in XAI

As AI systems increasingly influence critical decisions in finance, healthcare, criminal justice, and education, the demand for transparency, accountability, and user trust has become urgent. XAI offers a technical foundation for addressing these concerns by making model decisions interpretable to humans. However, achieving explainability is not merely a matter of technical clarity; it is fundamentally about communication and understanding. Traditional approaches to explainability often focus on algorithmic transparency, but explanations that are mathematically accurate may still be cognitively meaningless to end-users. This gap underscores the importance of human-centered design (HCD) in XAI: designing explanation systems that account for human cognition, usability, and context. Human-centered design in XAI emphasizes how people perceive, understand, and act upon explanations rather than merely how models generate them.[35] It integrates insights from psychology, HCI, cognitive science, and ethics to ensure that explanations are not only correct but also useful, relatable, and trustworthy. As a result, HCD transforms XAI from a purely technical exercise into a socio-technical discipline that bridges computational reasoning and human sense-making.

Historically, AI research viewed interpretability through a technical lens—how to expose internal mechanisms of AML models. This perspective, while essential, is often overlooked: the subjectivity of human interpretation. An explanation that satisfies a data scientist may not be meaningful to a physician or policymaker. Human-centered XAI reorients this focus from how algorithms explain themselves to how humans experience those explanations.[36] The shift toward human-centered design is grounded in cognitive realism, recognizing that people interpret explanations through mental models, prior knowledge, and goals. Explanations serve different purposes depending on the user's role: developers seek diagnostic insights to improve models, regulators demand transparency for compliance, and end-users desire reassurance and control. Therefore, a human-centered XAI system must adapt explanations to the user's cognitive level, context, and intent.[37] Cognitive psychology shows that humans prefer contrastive and selective explanations—those that clarify why an event happened instead of something else and that focus only on the most relevant features

(Miller, 2019). For example, in a credit decision system, an applicant does not need to know every factor considered by the model; rather, they want to understand which specific aspects caused their application to be rejected. Effective XAI systems thus provide contextualized explanations, highlighting actionable insights instead of overwhelming users with technical detail.

Human-centered XAI is inseparable from ethics. Explanations are not value-neutral—they shape how users perceive fairness, accountability, and legitimacy. By revealing the rationale behind AI decisions, XAI contributes to algorithmic accountability, but poorly designed explanations can create new biases or false impressions of transparency.[38] A human-centered ethical approach ensures that explanations are truthful, non-deceptive, and socially responsible. For example, simplifications made for accessibility should not distort the real functioning of the model. Additionally, explainability must respect privacy and autonomy; users have the right to understand decisions that affect them without exposing sensitive data or proprietary algorithms. Socially, HCD in XAI also emphasizes inclusivity and accessibility. Explanations should accommodate linguistic diversity and accessibility needs (e.g., visual impairments). The goal is not only to explain AI to experts but to democratize understanding so that AI systems remain accountable to society at large.

Future advancements in human-centered XAI will likely focus on personalized and adaptive explanation systems that adjust their communication style based on user behavior and preferences. For instance, novice users might receive simple analogies, while experts access detailed analytical justifications. Advances in affective computing may further allow AI systems to sense user emotions and adjust explanations dynamically. Moreover, human-centered XAI is evolving toward collaborative intelligence, where humans and AI systems learn from each other. Explanations will serve as feedback loops that enhance both model refinement and human understanding. As AI becomes more autonomous, ensuring human oversight through interpretable interfaces will remain a cornerstone of responsible AI design. Human-centered design transforms XAI from a technical mechanism into a human experience. It recognizes that the ultimate goal of explainability is not simply to expose algorithms but to empower people, to help them trust, question, and collaborate with AI systems. By integrating cognitive psychology, design thinking, and ethics, HCD ensures that explanations are contextual, comprehensible, and socially aligned. As AI continues to shape decision-making, the future of explainability depends on the ability to design systems that are not only powerful but also understandable, humane, and just. Human-centered XAI stands as the bridge between intelligent computation and meaningful human understanding, a necessary foundation for truly trustworthy AI.

10.5.3 Applications of Explainable AI in Transparent Decision-Making

AI increasingly influences decisions that shape human lives, ranging from credit scoring and medical diagnosis to hiring and criminal sentencing. While AI enables faster, data-driven decision-making, its growing opacity presents a challenge to accountability, fairness, and human oversight. The integration of XAI into decision processes seeks to make machine reasoning transparent and comprehensible, ensuring that automated decisions remain traceable, justifiable, and aligned with ethical norms. XAI bridges the gap between algorithmic precision and human understanding by clarifying how and why a system reaches specific conclusions. This transparency is vital for building trust among stakeholders, developers, regulators, and end-users, especially in sectors where decisions have legal, ethical, or financial consequences. The financial sector has been one of the earliest adopters of XAI due to its heavy reliance on risk-based decision models and regulatory oversight. Algorithms are now central to credit scoring, loan approvals, fraud detection, and investment strategies. However, the complexity of these models, especially deep learning and ensemble techniques, poses challenges to transparency and fairness. XAI addresses these challenges by providing interpretable insights into why certain financial decisions occur. For instance, local explanation methods such as LIME and SHAP can highlight key features influencing a loan rejection, such as income level, debt ratio, or credit history—thereby allowing applicants and regulators to understand the reasoning process.[39] Regulators such as the European Banking Authority (EBA) and US Federal Reserve have emphasized explainability as part of responsible AI governance. Transparency ensures compliance with fair lending laws like the Equal Credit Opportunity Act (ECOA) and reduces discrimination risks by allowing audits for bias in automated models.[40] Beyond compliance, explainability also strengthens customer trust. When clients understand why a model recommends an investment strategy or flags a transaction as fraudulent, they are more likely to engage confidently with digital financial platforms. Thus, XAI enables the financial sector to balance innovation with fairness, ensuring both algorithmic accountability and client transparency.

Healthcare represents one of the most promising yet sensitive domains for AI adoption. AML systems can outperform human clinicians in image classification, disease prediction, and drug discovery. However, the opacity of deep learning models in critical diagnostic applications raises profound ethical concerns: how can physicians trust an algorithm's recommendation if they cannot interpret its logic? XAI mitigates this problem by revealing model reasoning in clinical contexts, supporting physicians in evidence-based decision-making. For example, Grad-CAM (Gradient-weighted Class Activation Mapping) and Layer-wise Relevance Propagation (LRP) visualize which regions of an image influenced a diagnosis, such as identifying lesions in a chest X-ray or tumor regions in an MRI scan. These visual explanations enhance interpretability without compromising diagnostic accuracy. In patient-facing systems, natural language explanations can translate complex medical predictions into comprehensible terms, improving communication and patient trust. For instance, an AI tool predicting diabetes risk might explain: "Your risk is elevated because of high blood pressure, BMI, and glucose level trends." From a governance perspective, XAI is vital for meeting medical ethics principles: autonomy, beneficence, nonmaleficence, and justice. Transparent systems enable clinical accountability, allowing practitioners to justify AI-assisted decisions to patients and regulatory bodies. In short, XAI in healthcare ensures that automation supports rather than replaces human judgment, advancing both diagnostic accuracy and ethical transparency.

Public sector applications of AI, such as predictive policing, welfare allocation, and immigration screening, carry significant social implications. Decisions made by opaque algorithms can perpetuate bias or lead to unjust outcomes, eroding public trust. The inclusion of XAI techniques in government systems is therefore essential for democratic accountability and procedural fairness.[41] In predictive policing, for example, explainable models can help law enforcement agencies understand which variables drive risk assessments—such as location-based crime patterns—while ensuring that demographic factors are not improperly influencing outcomes. In welfare systems, explainability ensures that citizens can contest automated benefit determinations by understanding the rationale behind decisions. Legally, XAI supports the "right to explanation" under the GDPR, which mandates that individuals receive meaningful information about automated decisions that affect them. Explainable systems in governance make algorithmic processes auditable, enabling oversight bodies to detect and correct bias. Furthermore, human-centered XAI fosters citizen engagement, as people are more likely to accept and trust AI-driven public services when decisions are transparent and contestable.

In industrial automation, XAI improves safety, reliability, and operational efficiency. Smart factories increasingly rely on AI-driven predictive maintenance and quality control systems to monitor machinery performance and detect anomalies. However, opaque models can complicate troubleshooting when failures occur. XAI tools can provide root-cause analysis, identifying which sensor readings or process parameters led to an anomaly. For example, if an AI model predicts an impending equipment failure, SHAP-based explanations can pinpoint which temperature or vibration readings contributed most strongly to that prediction.[42] This interpretability allows engineers to verify model predictions, optimize system configurations, and intervene proactively before costly breakdowns. Additionally, XAI supports human-machine collaboration on production floors. When operators understand how AI systems make recommendations—such as adjusting machine speeds or quality thresholds—they can make informed decisions and maintain human oversight. By embedding explainability into industrial analytics, organizations enhance not only performance but also safety, transparency, and workforce trust.

Across domains, the integration of XAI offers three consistent benefits: trust, accountability, and compliance. Trust arises when users can verify that AI decisions align with logical and ethical expectations. Accountability emerges as organizations can trace decisions and assign responsibility for outcomes. Compliance is facilitated when explainable systems meet regulatory and ethical standards for fairness, privacy, and transparency. By making complex algorithms interpretable, XAI bridges the divide between technological sophistication and human understanding. The result is not only better decision outcomes but also stronger alignment between AI systems and societal values. Transparent decision-making thus becomes the foundation for sustainable, responsible AI adoption.

The applications of XAI in transparent decision-making extend across nearly every sector of modern society. In finance, it ensures fairness and compliance; in healthcare, it fosters clinical trust; in governance, it safeguards democratic accountability; in industry, it enhances safety and efficiency; and in education, it promotes fairness and agency. Ultimately, XAI is not merely a technical toolkit—it is a philosophy of responsible AI design that integrates transparency, ethics, and human-centered values. As machine intelligence continues to evolve, explainability will remain central to ensuring that automated decision-making serves humanity's best interests, not as an opaque authority but as a transparent collaborator in shaping informed, equitable, and trustworthy societies.

10.5.4 Ethical, Legal, and Governance Considerations

As AI systems increasingly influence critical decisions in society, ensuring their ethical integrity, legal compliance, and accountable governance has become paramount. XAI serves as a foundational mechanism for addressing these concerns by promoting transparency, fairness, and accountability in algorithmic decision-making. Ethical considerations in XAI focus on mitigating bias, preserving human autonomy, and ensuring that automated systems operate in ways consistent with societal values. When models are opaque, they risk perpetuating discrimination or unfair treatment, particularly in sensitive domains such as finance, employment, and criminal justice (Doshi-Velez & Kim, 2017). Explainability helps uncover potential biases, enabling developers and stakeholders to audit and correct unjust outcomes. From a legal perspective, explainable systems are essential for regulatory compliance and public accountability. Frameworks such as the European Union's GDPR establish a "right to explanation," granting individuals affected by automated decisions meaningful insight into how those decisions were reached.[43] Similar principles appear in emerging AI governance policies, including the EU AI Act and various US federal guidelines emphasizing algorithmic transparency. By making model behavior interpretable, XAI aligns with these legal requirements and supports organizations in documenting decision rationales—critical for both liability management and public trust.

Governance in XAI extends beyond individual systems to encompass institutional structures that ensure responsible AI lifecycle management. This includes clear accountability chains, ethics review boards, bias monitoring, and continuous auditing mechanisms. Effective governance frameworks promote human oversight, ensuring that AI remains a tool for augmentation rather than autonomous authority. Moreover, transparency fosters societal trust: when stakeholders can understand and challenge AI outcomes, they are more likely to accept automated systems as legitimate and fair.[44] In summary, the ethical, legal, and governance dimensions of XAI are inseparable from its technical foundations. Explainability operationalizes ethical principles, fulfills regulatory mandates, and enables responsible governance, ensuring that AI systems are not only powerful but also accountable, just, and aligned with human values.

10.6 Summary

This chapter explores sophisticated AML methods that go beyond foundational algorithms to tackle complex, real-world data problems. It begins by differentiating traditional models from advanced techniques and highlights the need for greater computational power, scalability, and interpretability in modern applications. The chapter examines ensemble learning methods like Random Forests, GBMs, and XGBoost, which combine multiple weak learners to achieve high accuracy and robustness. It also covers Support Vector Machines (SVMs), suitable for high-dimensional and nonlinear classification problems, and k-Nearest Neighbors (k-NN) for instance-based learning. This chapter discussed ethical AI considerations, the interpretability of complex models (e.g., SHAP and LIME), and real-world applications across industries such as finance, healthcare, marketing, and cybersecurity. In summary, students gain a strong understanding of cutting-edge AML techniques, their applications, advantages, limitations, and how they contribute to intelligent, data-driven decision-making.

Notes

1 Breiman, L. (1996). Bagging predictors. *Machine Learning*, 24(2), 123–140. https://doi.org/10.1007/BF00058655. Available at https://link.springer.com/article/10.1007/BF00058655

2 Hastie, T., Tibshirani, R., & Friedman, J. (2009). *The Elements of Statistical Learning* (2nd ed.). Springer. Available at https://d1wqtxts1xzle7.cloudfront.net/31156736/10.1.1.158.8831.pdf?1738058570=&response-content-disposition=inline%3B+filename%3DThe_elements_of_statistical_learning_dat.pdf&Expires=1769639819&Signature=GhDt-m0pJE9eDOvC~2yCmVHJIZMOXMmNulgXygfnEZIDWohmE38TOKL7fWsr5lrv2jnPUKCB2jMvVapRQD5-OkB9qSmRmaeEIy~cOLymmCQrseUAJCkUnKV~7t6Vc-DjAUcBqZhHhNEP0PVLvkl2-5PIIO3MuXZUqzUhh5A2B8JcsxeyQoA-NMIt6VDSMJJ377-hWfFhlsoKXNC1fhJH2PSP~1.1-v3vV~dDpZwvXT2Apt4h061.1ignPv3rYiD9XqhQW0TCyD6DrSfn2SGtBNL0XYXRA7oDnjxmijcad4JwkEiGXWCvO0q8pPkJ8wviSUyfszToB7-I7UgNsRQ8GA__&Key-Pair-Id=APKAJLOHF5GGSLRBV4ZA

3 Breiman, L. (2001). Random forests. *Machine Learning*, 45(1), 5–32. https://doi.org/10.1023/A:1010933404324. Available at https://link.springer.com/article/10.1023/a:1010933404324

4 Schapire, R. E. (1990). The strength of weak learnability. *Machine Learning*, 5(2), 197–227. https://doi.org/10.1007/BF00116037. Available at https://link.springer.com/article/10.1007/bf00116037
5 Freund, Y., & Schapire, R. E. (1997). A decision-theoretic generalization of on-line learning and an application to boosting. *Journal of Computer and System Sciences*, 55(1), 119–139. https://doi.org/10.1006/jcss.1997.1504. Available at https://www.sciencedirect.com/science/article/pii/S002200009791504X
6 Friedman, J. H., Hastie, T., & Tibshirani, R. (2000). Additive logistic regression: A statistical view of boosting. *Annals of Statistics*, 28(2), 337–407. https://doi.org/10.1214/aos/1016218223. Available at https://projecteuclid.org/journals/annals-of-statistics/volume-28/issue-2/Additive-logistic-regression--a-statistical-view-of-boosting-With/10.1214/aos/1016218223.full
7 Chen, T., & Guestrin, C. (2016). XGBoost: A scalable tree boosting system. In *Proceedings of the 22nd ACM SIGKDD International Conference on Knowledge Discovery and Data Mining* (pp. 785–794). https://doi.org/10.1145/2939672.2939785. Available at https://dl.acm.org/doi/abs/10.1145/2939672.2939785
8 Cutler, D. R., Edwards Jr., T. C., Beard, K. H., Cutler, A., Hess, K. T., Gibson, J., & Lawler, J. J. (2007). Random forests for classification in ecology. *Ecology*, 88(11), 2783–2792. https://doi.org/10.1890/07-0539.1. Available at https://esajournals.onlinelibrary.wiley.com/doi/abs/10.1890/07-0539.1
9 Freund, Y., & Schapire, R. E. (1997). A decision-theoretic generalization of on-line learning and an application to boosting. *Journal of Computer and System Sciences*, 55(1), 119–139. https://doi.org/10.1006/jcss.1997.1504. Available at https://www.sciencedirect.com/science/article/pii/S002200009791504X
10 Breiman, L. (1996). Bagging predictors. *Machine Learning*, 24(2), 123–140. https://doi.org/10.1007/BF00058655. Available at https://link.springer.com/article/10.1007/BF00058655
11 Friedman, J. H. (2001). Greedy function approximation: A gradient boosting machine. *Annals of Statistics*, 29(5), 1189–1232. Available at https://www.jstor.org/stable/2699986?casa_token=r0N7mL6XZOoAAAAA%3AFM-M5Z0iPpGCkKxE6Bf_AZhdjzFpMxIrjHm5INP5yWnC4y0_RATGrq5kd3KBTFqaKJUIPm6-ZrI3rWDYpwDgoKkY8uYwxgn7nM6P2iznB3GUacKYTI3h&seq=1
12 Breiman, L. (2001). Random forests. *Machine Learning*, 45(1), 5–32. https://doi.org/10.1023/A:1010933404324. Available at https://link.springer.com/article/10.1023/a:1010933404324
13 Breiman, L. (2001). Random forests. *Machine Learning*, 45(1), 7. https://doi.org/10.1023/A:1010933404324. Available at https://link.springer.com/article/10.1023/a:1010933404324
14 Lessmann, S., Baesens, B., Seow, H. V., & Thomas, L. C. (2015). Benchmarking state-of-the-art classification algorithms for credit scoring: An update of research. *European Journal of Operational Research*, 247(1), 124–136. https://doi.org/10.1016/j.ejor.2015.05.030. Available at https://www.sciencedirect.com/science/article/pii/S0377221715004208?casa_token=ffkgQ1BE3CAAAAAA:IaBXfiQXXE7-T7qTG6oYUgTq5qrpBJmwIp-EPZcl-JjlULfI6_GnL6s1Upe5Bf5Q5Dh-TP0LTcA
15 Chen, J., Chen, J., Huang, H., & Zhao, Y. (2017). Random forest classification of tumor types based on gene expression data. *Computational and Structural Biotechnology Journal*, 15, 1–8.
16 Van der Maaten, L., & Hinton, G. (2008). Visualizing data using t-SNE. *Journal of Machine Learning Research*, 9(86), 2579–2605. Available at https://www.jmlr.org/papers/volume9/vandermaaten08a/vandermaaten08a.pdf
17 Bellman, R. (1961). *Adaptive Control Processes: A Guided Tour*. Princeton University Press.
18 Jolliffe, I. T. (2002). *Principal Component Analysis* (2nd ed.). Springer.
19 van der Maaten, L., & Hinton, G. (2008). Visualizing data using t-SNE. *Journal of Machine Learning Research*, 9, 2579–2605. Available at https://www.jmlr.org/papers/volume9/vandermaaten08a/vandermaaten08a.pdf
20 Kobak, D., & Berens, P. (2019). The art of using t-SNE for single-cell transcriptomics. *Nature Communications*, 10, 5416. https://doi.org/10.1038/s41467-019-13056-x. Available at https://www.nature.com/articles/s41467-019-13056-x
21 Jolliffe, I. T., & Cadima, J. (2016). Principal component analysis: A review and recent developments. *Philosophical Transactions of the Royal Society A*, 374(2065), 20150202. https://doi.org/10.1098/rsta.2015.0202. Available at https://royalsocietypublishing.org/rsta/article-abstract/374/2065/20150202/115142/Principal-component-analysis-a-review-and-recent?redirectedFrom=fulltext

22 van der Maaten, L., & Hinton, G. (2008). Visualizing data using t-SNE. *Journal of Machine Learning Research*, 9, 2579–2605. Available at https://www.jmlr.org/papers/volume9/vandermaaten08a/vandermaaten08a.pdf

23 Jain, A. K. (2010). Data clustering: 50 years beyond k-means. *Pattern Recognition Letters*, 31(8), 651–666. https://doi.org/10.1016/j.patrec.2009.09.011. Available at https://www.sciencedirect.com/science/article/pii/S0167865509002323?casa_token=lkGYlZ8eL9EAAAAA:fWLEUVPq0PKgZsYHf8_rlxGg6rzPNycJqir-GAkh4e7cp70N7TnjP2RwzSFbIUOIuui_RQ8AAFk

24 Chandola, V., Banerjee, A., & Kumar, V. (2009). Anomaly detection: A survey. *ACM Computing Surveys*, 41(3), 1–58.

25 Han, J., Pei, J., & Tong, H. (2023). *Data Mining: Concepts and Techniques* (4th ed.). Morgan Kaufmann.

26 Jain, A. K. (2010). Data clustering: 50 years beyond K-means. *Pattern Recognition Letters*, 31(8), 651–666. https://doi.org/10.1016/j.patrec.2009.09.011. Available at https://www.sciencedirect.com/science/article/pii/S0167865509002323?casa_token=jlGCFCfPycoAAAAA:Jz7p_YgBRwbXDYrq-igt_I_ZcoUaDcffXGdgz9D_h1F--I_qvDc_pO0c2EGG-QZo9jQjUAZPh1o

27 Kaufman, L., & Rousseeuw, P. J. (2009). *Finding Groups in Data: An Introduction to Cluster Analysis*. Wiley.

28 Ester, M., Kriegel, H. P., Sander, J., & Xu, X. (1996). A density-based algorithm for discovering clusters in large spatial databases with noise. In *Proceedings of the 2nd International Conference on Knowledge Discovery and Data Mining (KDD)* (pp. 226–231). Available at https://cdn.aaai.org/KDD/1996/KDD96-037.pdf?source=post_page

29 Aggarwal, C. C. (2017). *Outlier Analysis* (2nd ed.). Springer.

30 Gunning, D., & Aha, D. W. (2019). DARPA's explainable artificial intelligence (XAI) program. *AI Magazine*, 40(2), 44–58. https://doi.org/10.1609/aimag.v40i2.2850. Available at https://ojs.aaai.org/aimagazine/index.php/aimagazine/article/view/2850

31 Doshi-Velez, F., & Kim, B. (2017). Towards a rigorous science of interpretable machine learning. arXiv preprint arXiv:1702.08608. https://doi.org/10.48550/arXiv.1702.08608. Available at https://arxiv.org/abs/1702.08608

32 Lipton, Z. C. (2018). The mythos of model interpretability. *Communications of the ACM*, 61(10), 36–43. Available at https://spawn-queue.acm.org/doi/pdf/10.1145/3236386.3241340

33 Miller, T. (2019). Explanation in artificial intelligence: Insights from the social sciences. *Artificial Intelligence*, 267, 1–38. https://doi.org/10.1016/j.artint.2018.07.007. Available at https://www.sciencedirect.com/science/article/pii/S0004370218305988

34 Doshi-Velez, F., & Kim, B. (2017). Towards a rigorous science of interpretable machine learning, arxiv preprint arXiv: 1702.08608. https://doi.org/10.48550/arXiv.1702.08608. Available at https://arxiv.org/abs/1702.08608

35 Eiband, M., Schneider, H., Bilandzic, M., Fazekas-Con, J., Haug, M., Hussmann, H. (2018). Bringing transparency design into practice. In *Proceedings of the 23rd International Conference on Intelligent User Interfaces (IUI'18)* (pp. 211–223). Association for Computing Machinery. https://doi.org/10.1145/3172944.3172961.Availableathttps://dl.acm.org/doi/abs/10.1145/3172944.3172961

36 Eiband, M., Schneider, H., Bilandzic, M., Fazekas-Con, J., Haug, M., Hussmann, H. (2018). Bringing transparency design into practice. In *Proceedings of the 23rd International Conference on Intelligent User Interfaces (IUI'18)* (pp. 211–223). Association for Computing Machinery. https://doi.org/10.1145/3172944.3172961. Available at https://dl.acm.org/doi/abs/10.1145/3172944.3172961, 26.

37 Abdul, A., Vermeulen, J., Wang, D., Lim, B. Y., & Kankanhalli, M. (2018). Trends and trajectories for explainable, accountable, and intelligible systems: An HCI research agenda. In *Proceedings of the 2018 CHI Conference on Human Factors in Computing Systems* (pp. 1–18). https://doi.org/10.1145/3173574.3174156. Available at https://dl.acm.org/doi/abs/10.1145/3173574.3174156

38 Eiband, M., Schneider, H., Bilandzic, M., Fazekas-Con, M., Haug, M., & Butz, A. (2018). Bringing transparency design into practice. In *Proceedings of the 23rd International Conference on Intelligent User Interfaces* (pp. 211–223). https://doi.org/10.1145/3172944.3172961. Available at https://dl.acm.org/doi/abs/10.1145/3172944.3172961

39 Ribeiro, M. T., Singh, S., & Guestrin, C. (2016). Why should I trust you? Explaining the predictions of any classifier. In *Proceedings of the 22nd ACM SIGKDD International Conference on Knowledge Discovery and Data Mining* (pp. 1135–1144). https://doi.org/10.1145/2939672.2939778. Available at https://dl.acm.org/doi/abs/10.1145/2939672.2939778

40 Barredo Arrieta, A., Díaz-Rodríguez, N., Del Ser, J., Bennetot, A., Tabik, S., Barbado, A., Garcia, S., Gil-Lopez, S., Molina, D., Benjamins, R., Chatila, R., & Herrera, F. (2020). Explainable artificial intelligence (XAI): Concepts, taxonomies, opportunities and challenges toward responsible AI. *Information Fusion*, 58, 82–115. https://doi.org/10.1016/j.inffus.2019.12.012. Available at https://digibug.ugr.es/handle/10481/77982

41 Edwards, L., & Veale, M. (2018). Enslaving the algorithm: From a "right to explanation" to a "right to better decisions"? *IEEE Security & Privacy*, 16(3), 46–54. https://doi.org/10.1109/MSP.2018.2701152. Available at https://ieeexplore.ieee.org/abstract/document/8395080?casa_token=ppk7lu0_zpUAAAAA:CULWowohH1vq_jecGXkPnSZFGx4VL6VxTHxaYlVW5GiVh1uzNBs-fydLbilU-P5TE_BblYK_dNY

42 Samek, W., & Müller, K. R. (2019). Towards explainable artificial intelligence. In: Samek, W., Montavon, G., Vedaldi, A., Hansen, L. K., Müller, K.-R. (eds) *Explainable AI: Interpreting, Explaining and Visualizing Deep Learning*. Springer. https://doi.org/10.1007/978-3-030-28954-6_1. Available at https://link.springer.com/chapter/10.1007/978-3-030-28954-6_1

43 Samek, W., & Müller, K. R. (2019). Towards explainable artificial intelligence. In: Samek, W., Montavon, G., Vedaldi, A., Hansen, L. K., Müller, K.-R. (eds) *Explainable AI: Interpreting, Explaining and Visualizing Deep Learning*. Springer. https://doi.org/10.1007/978-3-030-28954-6_1. Available at https://link.springer.com/chapter/10.1007/978-3-030-28954-6_1, 34.

44 Samek, W., & Müller, K. R. (2019). Towards explainable artificial intelligence. In: Samek, W., Montavon, G., Vedaldi, A., Hansen, L. K., Müller, K.-R. (eds) *Explainable AI: Interpreting, Explaining and Visualizing Deep Learning* (pp. 5–22). Springer. https://doi.org/10.1007/978-3-030-28954-6_1. Available at https://link.springer.com/chapter/10.1007/978-3-030-28954-6_1, 24.

11 Deep Learning and Neural Networks

Learning Objectives

- Understand deep learning essentials
- Understand the structure and components of neural networks
- Learn neural networks: structure, activation functions, and backpropagation
- Understand convolutional neural networks (CNNs) and recurrent neural networks (RNNs)
- Distinguish between CNNs, RNNs, and GANs
- Learn to enhance transparency and accountability through AI-driven data analytics
- Use frameworks like TensorFlow and PyTorch
- Apply deep learning in business applications
- Understand the use of deep learning in sustainability performance and reporting

11.1 Introduction

DL, as a subset of machine learning, has emerged as one of the most transformative and advanced technologies in recent decades. DL uses artificial neural networks, structured based on the human brain, to model complex patterns and relationships in data. DL is the leading edge of AI innovation, which involves training multi-layered neural networks to perform tasks like speech synthesis, image recognition, and predictive analytics. DL models automatically learn hierarchical representations of data, enabling them to be exceptionally powerful for handling unstructured data such as audio, images, and text. This chapter is intended to provide a foundational understanding of the key concepts, architectures, tools, and techniques that underpin DL basics of neural networks, backpropagation, CNNs, and RNNs, among others.

11.2 Deep Learning Frameworks

DL frameworks have become the cornerstone of modern AI by providing the computational and software infrastructure necessary to design, train, and deploy complex neural network models at scale. These frameworks present low-level numerical operations while

DOI: 10.4324/9781003664550-11

offering high-level APIs for constructing architectures such as CNNs, RNNs, transformers, and graph neural networks, thereby accelerating research and real-world deployment. Prominent frameworks such as TensorFlow and PyTorch support automatic differentiation, GPU/TPU acceleration, distributed training, and seamless integration with production pipelines, which are critical for handling large datasets and deep architectures.[1] In recent years, the flexibility and dynamic computation graphs of modern frameworks, particularly PyTorch, have enhanced experimentation and reproducibility, while static-graph approaches such as early TensorFlow versions have historically offered advantages in optimization and deployment efficiency. Specifically, DL frameworks have democratized access to advanced AI by enabling rapid prototyping, reproducible experimentation, and scalable deployment across domains including computer vision, NLP, finance, healthcare, and risk analytics, making them foundational to contemporary AI-driven decision-making systems.[2]

These frameworks accelerate experimentation and real-world application by providing modular and optimized environments for neural network construction, training, and deployment. The development of open-source platforms such as TensorFlow, PyTorch, and Keras has democratized AI research, enabling scalable model development across academia and industry. TensorFlow, created by Google Brain, emphasizes scalability and production readiness; PyTorch, developed by Facebook AI Research, prioritizes flexibility and dynamic computation; and Keras, initiated by François Chollet, focuses on user-friendliness and abstraction.[3] Understanding their underlying architectures and comparative advantages is essential for selecting the right tool in both research and applied AI development.[4]

11.2.1 Foundations of Deep Learning Frameworks

The rapid advancement of AI in recent years owes much of its success to DL frameworks, which provide the essential computational backbone for building, training, and deploying neural networks. The foundations of DL frameworks build on advances in neural network theory, numerical optimization, and high-performance computing that enable the efficient training of multi-layer models on large-scale data. At their core, these frameworks operationalize backpropagation and gradient-based optimization by allowing complex neural architectures to learn hierarchical feature representations from raw inputs.[5] Automatic differentiation systems are a key architectural component, systematically computing gradients for arbitrarily complex computation graphs and thereby reducing implementation error while accelerating experimentation.[6] Modern frameworks further rely on tensor-based abstractions and linear algebra optimizations to exploit parallel hardware such as GPUs and TPUs, addressing the computational demands of deep networks. Furthermore, modular design principles support extensibility, reproducibility, and scalability across research and production environments. Collectively, these foundational elements have transformed DL from a theoretically motivated approach into a practical, general-purpose methodology underpinning state-of-the-art applications in computer vision, NLP, and AI-driven analytics.

A DL framework is a software library designed to facilitate the development and execution of machine learning algorithms, particularly deep neural networks. It provides tools to define mathematical models, perform backpropagation, and execute computations on hardware accelerators such as GPUs and TPUs. Conceptually, frameworks are built to satisfy three main goals:

1 **Abstraction**: They simplify complex linear algebra and calculus operations into high-level API functions.
2 **Optimization**: They exploit hardware parallelism to maximize computational efficiency.
3 **Scalability**: They support distributed training and deployment across large datasets and cloud environments.

The computational graph lies at the heart of all modern DL frameworks. It represents the flow of data and operations in a model as a directed acyclic graph (DAG), where nodes correspond to mathematical operations (e.g., matrix multiplication, convolution), and edges represent data (tensors) flowing between them. There are two main types of computational graphs. First, Static computation graphs define the entire structure before execution. TensorFlow originally used this approach, compiling the computation plan before running it. Second, dynamic computation graphs, popularized by PyTorch, build and modify the graph at runtime. This approach, often referred to as define-by-run, provides greater flexibility and intuitive debugging since developers can use standard control flow constructs (loops, conditionals) directly within model definitions.[7] The tensor abstraction, a generalization of matrices to multi-dimensional arrays, is another foundational element. Tensors store numerical data and support various transformations through GPU-optimized operations. Frameworks manage tensors through low-level libraries such as cuDNN and CUDA, which enable parallelized computations on GPUs. Automatic broadcasting and memory optimization mechanisms ensure that tensor operations remain efficient even at scale. In essence, the combination of computational graphs and tensor abstractions allows frameworks to translate high-level model code into optimized low-level instructions that exploit modern hardware's parallel architecture.

PyTorch's Autograd engine dynamically constructs the computation graph during execution, automatically tracking operations on tensors and freeing memory once gradients are computed. TensorFlow's GradientTape, introduced in version 2.x, mimics this behavior, merging the flexibility of dynamic graphs with TensorFlow's scalability advantages. Through automatic differentiation, DL frameworks not only enhance efficiency but also make complex architectures, such as recurrent networks, transformers, and GANs, tractable to train. This automation has been instrumental in enabling the explosion of DL applications across industries.

The exponential growth in data and model size has necessitated the use of specialized hardware accelerators. DL frameworks are designed to leverage this hardware through parallelization and hardware abstraction layers. Frameworks integrate with GPUs and TPUs to execute thousands of operations simultaneously. Libraries such as CUDA, cuDNN, and MKL-DNN enable frameworks to perform tensor operations efficiently across hardware. TensorFlow's XLA (Accelerated Linear Algebra) compiler further optimizes execution by fusing operations and minimizing memory transfers. Similarly, PyTorch uses the TorchScript JIT compiler and CUDA Graphs to optimize runtime performance. At the distributed computing level, frameworks implement data parallelism and model parallelism to train large-scale models across multiple devices or nodes. TensorFlow's Distributed Strategy API and PyTorch's Distributed Data Parallel allow synchronization of parameters across GPUs, ensuring consistent gradient updates during large-batch training. This deep integration with hardware not only accelerates computation but also enhances energy efficiency—a critical consideration as model training becomes increasingly resource-intensive. Efficient hardware utilization is one of the main factors distinguishing modern frameworks from early DL implementations, enabling practical scaling of models such as GPT-4 or AlphaFold.

Beyond computation, DL frameworks have evolved into full-fledged ecosystems encompassing data preprocessing, visualization, experiment tracking, and deployment. TensorFlow, for example, includes TensorBoard for visual monitoring, TFX for end-to-end machine learning pipelines, and TensorFlow Lite for edge deployment. PyTorch's ecosystem includes TorchVision, TorchText, and TorchAudio, offering domain-specific libraries for vision, language, and audio tasks. Extensibility is another defining characteristic. Frameworks are designed to be modular, allowing integration with third-party tools such as ONNX (Open Neural Network Exchange) for cross-framework model export and deployment. This modularity enables researchers to prototype new architectures quickly, test novel optimization algorithms, and collaborate across heterogeneous computational environments. Furthermore, community-driven contributions, through open-source collaboration, have accelerated framework evolution. Thousands of contributors continuously improve APIs, develop extensions, and share pretrained models, ensuring rapid dissemination of innovations. As a result, frameworks have become living ecosystems that evolve in parallel with academic research and industrial needs.

Modern frameworks offer multiple levels of abstraction to cater to different user expertise levels. For instance, TensorFlow provides low-level APIs for detailed control over computational graphs and high-level APIs such as Keras for fast prototyping. PyTorch similarly provides flexibility through its dynamic computation graph, which allows users to modify models during runtime and experiment more easily with complex architectures. This multilayered design democratizes AI development. Beginners can build models with minimal code using sequential APIs, while researchers and engineers can access fine-grained control for experimentation or optimization. These abstraction layers create a unified workflow for model design, training, evaluation, and deployment, ensuring that frameworks remain both powerful and accessible.

11.2.2 TensorFlow

TensorFlow is an open-source DL framework designed to support large-scale numerical computation and machine learning model development across research and production environments. TensorFlow, originally developed by the Google Brain team in 2015, has become one of the most dominant frameworks in the DL landscape. It is built around a flexible dataflow-graph architecture in which computations are represented as directed graphs of tensor operations, enabling efficient execution across heterogeneous hardware such as CPUs, GPUs, and TPUs.[8] Its support for automatic differentiation, distributed training, and hardware acceleration makes it particularly well-suited for training deep neural networks at scale. TensorFlow provides both low-level APIs for fine-grained control and high-level interfaces (e.g., Keras) that simplify model construction, experimentation, and deployment, thereby bridging the gap between academic research and industrial applications. Designed for both research and production, TensorFlow provides a scalable, flexible, and efficient platform for developing machine learning and AI systems. The name TensorFlow refers to the flow of multi-dimensional data arrays, or tensors, through computational graphs that represent mathematical operations. These graphs allow for efficient execution and optimization of complex machine learning tasks across various hardware configurations, including CPUs, GPUs, and TPUs. TensorFlow's design philosophy centers around modularity, portability, and scalability. It allows users to construct computational models in a high-level, Python-based API, while the backend handles performance optimization and distributed computation. Initially, TensorFlow's steep learning curve and static graph model made it challenging for newcomers, but subsequent updates, particularly TensorFlow 2.0, introduced eager execution, tighter Keras integration, and streamlined APIs, significantly improving usability. As of today, TensorFlow serves as both a research enabler and a production powerhouse, with applications ranging from NLP to medical imaging and autonomous systems. Consequently, TensorFlow has become a foundational platform for DL applications in computer vision, NLP, recommendation systems, and large-scale analytics.

TensorFlow's architecture is built upon the concept of computation graphs, DAGs that define how data moves through a series of mathematical operations. Each node in the graph represents an operation (such as addition, convolution, or activation), and each edge represents a tensor, or multi-dimensional data array. This design abstracts complex neural network computations into modular, reusable components that can be optimized and parallelized. In its early versions, TensorFlow employed static computation graphs, which required users to define the full computational structure before execution. This design allowed for global optimization of operations and easy deployment in distributed environments, but limited flexibility during debugging and prototyping. In response to these challenges, TensorFlow 2.0 introduced eager execution, enabling dynamic computation where operations are executed immediately, allowing for interactive model development similar to PyTorch's "define-by-run" paradigm. TensorFlow's hybrid design—supporting both static and dynamic execution modes—offers the best of both worlds: static graphs for large-scale, production-oriented optimization, and eager execution for intuitive experimentation. Under the hood, TensorFlow also incorporates an XLA compiler, which optimizes computation graphs by fusing operations, reducing memory overhead, and leveraging low-level libraries like cuDNN for GPUs and MKL for CPUs.

11.2.3 PyTorch

Among the many DL frameworks available today, PyTorch has emerged as the preferred platform for research, experimentation, and increasingly, industrial deployment. PyTorch is an open-source DL framework widely adopted in academic research and industry due to its flexibility, ease of use, and strong support for dynamic model development. Developed by Facebook's Artificial Intelligence Research (FAIR) lab and released in 2016, PyTorch was designed with a clear philosophy to provide flexibility, speed, and usability for DL researchers.[9] PyTorch is built around an imperative, define-by-run programming paradigm in which computation graphs are constructed dynamically during execution, allowing researchers to intuitively debug models and rapidly experiment with complex neural architectures.[10] Unlike its predecessors, PyTorch introduced a dynamic computation graph model that allows operations to be defined and executed on the fly. This paradigm, known as define-by-run, revolutionized DL experimentation by making the model-building process more intuitive and Pythonic. PyTorch rapidly gained popularity within academia due to its ease of debugging, integration with Python's scientific stack (NumPy, SciPy), and strong support for GPU acceleration.

Over time, PyTorch has matured from a research-oriented library into a comprehensive ecosystem for machine learning and production-scale AI. Its adoption by leading research institutions, universities, and technology companies underscores its pivotal role in advancing DL applications, from NLP and computer vision to reinforcement learning and GenAI. Its integrated automatic differentiation engine (Autograd) efficiently computes gradients for tensor operations, while native support for GPU acceleration and distributed training enables scalable DL across large datasets and compute clusters. Empirical comparisons indicate that PyTorch's dynamic computation graphs are particularly advantageous for research-oriented workflows and models with variable structure, such as recurrent networks and attention-based architectures.[11] With the introduction of tools such as TorchScript and seamless interoperability with production systems, PyTorch has increasingly bridged the gap between research prototyping and deployment, making it a foundational framework for state-of-the-art applications in computer vision, NLP, and AI-driven analytics.[12]

At the heart of PyTorch lies a tensor-based architecture that supports efficient numerical computation across CPUs and GPUs. Like TensorFlow, PyTorch uses tensors as its primary data structure, multi-dimensional arrays that enable high-performance linear algebra operations. However, the distinguishing feature of PyTorch is its dynamic computation graph, which allows the model structure to be modified during runtime. This makes PyTorch exceptionally suited for research that involves variable-length sequences or models with conditional operations, such as RNNs and attention-based architectures.[13] In PyTorch, the computation graph is built implicitly as operations are executed. Each operation records its inputs, outputs, and gradients, allowing PyTorch's Autograd engine to perform automatic differentiation during backpropagation. This dynamic behavior aligns naturally with Python's control flow, meaning developers can use native loops, conditionals, and functions without predefined constraints. This flexibility enhances readability, debugging, and experimental creativity—qualities that make PyTorch especially attractive to the research community.

11.2.4 Keras

The evolution of DL over the past decade has been marked by a tension between power and accessibility. While early frameworks such as TensorFlow and Theano offered tremendous computational capability, they demanded deep technical expertise and manual configuration, limiting their use among non-specialists. Keras, introduced in 2015 by François Chollet, emerged as a response to this challenge, providing an intuitive, high-level interface for building and training DL models.[14] Keras is a high-level DL framework designed to simplify the design, training, and evaluation of neural networks by providing an intuitive and modular API. Keras emphasizes user friendliness, rapid prototyping, and readability, enabling researchers and practitioners to build complex models with minimal code. Its modular architecture, based on reusable components such as layers, optimizers, loss functions, and callbacks, supports experimentation with a wide range of neural network architectures, including convolutional, recurrent, and transformer-based models. Empirical studies suggest that high-level frameworks like Keras reduce development time and lower the barrier to entry for DL without sacrificing performance, particularly when combined with optimized backends for automatic differentiation and hardware acceleration.[15] Consequently, Keras has become a widely used framework in education, applied research, and industry, serving as a bridge between theoretical DL concepts and scalable, production-ready AI systems.

Built originally as a front-end library for Theano and later integrated into TensorFlow as its official API, Keras is designed around three guiding principles: user-friendliness, modularity, and extensibility.[16] These principles make it accessible to beginners while remaining powerful enough for advanced practitioners. The core philosophy of Keras is to enable rapid experimentation without sacrificing flexibility—a crucial feature in the iterative, experimental nature of DL research. Today, Keras stands as one of the most widely adopted DL libraries globally, used extensively in academia, industry, and education. It bridges the gap between conceptual model design and efficient implementation, democratizing access to AI tools. Keras's integration with TensorFlow in version 2.x transformed it from a standalone API into a central pillar of the TensorFlow ecosystem, combining simplicity with large-scale production readiness.

11.2.5 Comparing TensorFlow, PyTorch, and Keras

The exponential growth of AI and DL has been propelled by the development of powerful software frameworks that simplify model design, training, and deployment. Among these, TensorFlow, PyTorch, and Keras have emerged as the three most prominent frameworks, shaping modern AI research and application. TensorFlow, PyTorch, and Keras represent three closely related yet distinct approaches to DL framework design, differing primarily in abstraction level, computational graph construction, and typical use cases. Each framework reflects a distinct philosophy of how humans interact with machine learning systems, balancing flexibility, scalability, and accessibility. TensorFlow, created by Google Brain in 2015, was designed to enable large-scale, production-oriented machine learning with an emphasis on distributed computing and deployment efficiency. It emphasizes scalability and production readiness through its dataflow-graph architecture, offering robust support for distributed training, hardware acceleration, and deployment across heterogeneous environments. PyTorch, released in 2016 by FAIR lab, introduced dynamic computation and intuitive experimentation, rapidly becoming the research community's favorite, enabling greater flexibility, intuitive debugging, and rapid experimentation of features that have driven its widespread adoption in academic research and advanced model development. Keras, first launched in 2015 by François Chollet, emphasized simplicity and user experience, providing a high-level API for fast prototyping and educational use. While each framework can perform the same fundamental tasks—defining, training, and deploying neural networks—their design philosophies, computational models, and ecosystems cater to different audiences and use cases. It operates at a higher level of abstraction, prioritizing simplicity and modularity by providing a user-friendly API that runs atop backends such as TensorFlow, thereby accelerating prototyping and reducing development complexity without sacrificing performance. Comparatively, while PyTorch excels in research-oriented workflows and TensorFlow dominates large-scale deployment scenarios, Keras serves as an effective bridge between theory and practice, particularly in educational and applied analytics settings. Together, these frameworks form a complementary ecosystem that supports the full DL lifecycle from experimentation and model design to scalable deployment and enterprise integration.

Table 11.1 summarizes key distinctions among TensorFlow, PyTorch, and Keras based on architecture, usability, ecosystem, and deployment capability.

Table 11.1 TensorFlow, PyTorch, and Keras Key Distinctions

Feature	*TensorFlow*	*PyTorch*	*Keras*
Developer	Google Brain (2015)	Facebook AI Research (2016)	François Chollet (2015; integrated with TensorFlow)
Computation graph	Static + Eager (Hybrid)	Dynamic (Define-by-Run)	Uses TensorFlow backend
Ease of use	Moderate (simplified in 2.x)	High (Pythonic)	Very High (Beginner-friendly)
Primary focus	Production & Enterprise	Research & Experimentation	Education & Rapid Prototyping
Ecosystem	Extensive (TFX, Lite, Hub, Serving)	Modular (Lightning, ONNX, TorchServe)	Integrated with TensorFlow tools
Hardware acceleration	GPU, TPU, Cloud AI	GPU, ROCm, ONNX runtime	GPU, TPU via TensorFlow
Visualization	TensorBoard	TensorBoard-compatible	TensorBoard via TensorFlow
Deployment	Enterprise-grade, cloud optimized	TorchServe, ONNX export	TensorFlow Lite, TF.js
Community	Enterprise + Research	Research-focused	Education + Applied AI
Use cases	Cloud AI, NLP, Robotics	Generative AI, NLP, Vision	Education, Prototyping, Mobile AI

11.3 Neural Networks

Neural networks are the cornerstone of modern AI and DL. Inspired by the structure and function of the human brain, they consist of interconnected processing units, or neurons, that work collectively to recognize patterns, approximate complex functions, and perform intelligent tasks. Neural networks have evolved from theoretical constructions in cognitive science into powerful computational systems, driving breakthroughs in NLP, computer vision, and autonomous systems. Neural networks are a class of machine learning models inspired by the structure and function of biological neurons, designed to learn complex, nonlinear relationships from data through layered compositions of weighted transformations and activation functions. At their core, neural networks consist of interconnected layers of input, hidden, and output, where learning occurs by iteratively adjusting weights using backpropagation and gradient-based optimization to minimize a specified loss function. Advances in computational power, large-scale datasets, and improved training techniques have enabled deep neural networks with many hidden layers to achieve state-of-the-art performance across tasks such as image recognition, NLP, speech recognition, and financial prediction.[17]

Variants such as CNNs, RNNs, and transformer architectures are tailored to exploit spatial, temporal, and contextual structures in data, respectively. Despite their predictive power, neural networks raise challenges related to interpretability, overfitting, and computational cost, motivating ongoing research in explainable AI, regularization, and efficient training methods. At the core of every neural network are three foundational components: network structure, activation functions, and the learning algorithm, typically implemented through backpropagation. The structure defines how neurons are organized and connected; activation functions introduce nonlinearity, enabling networks to model complex relationships;

and backpropagation provides the mathematical mechanism that adjusts the network's parameters to minimize error. Understanding these elements is crucial to appreciating how DL models learn from data, generalize to unseen examples, and perform intelligent behavior.

11.3.1 Neural Network Structure

A neural network is a computational model composed of layers of interconnected nodes or neurons, each representing a mathematical function. The structure of a neural network determines how information flows from input to output and how the model captures patterns in the data.

1 **Layers and Connectivity**: Neural networks are typically organized into three main types of layers:

- **Input Layer**: The first layer that receives raw data (e.g., pixels, features, or words). It passes this data to subsequent layers without transformation.
- **Hidden Layers**: Intermediate layers where computation occurs. Each neuron in a hidden layer applies a weighted transformation followed by an activation function. Deep neural networks may contain dozens or even hundreds of hidden layers, allowing them to learn hierarchical representations.
- **Output Layer**: The final layer that produces the model's predictions. Its design depends on the task, such as a single neuron with a sigmoid activation for binary classification, or multiple neurons with SoftMax activation for multi-class problems.

Each connection between neurons carries a weight, representing the strength of the signal between them. During training, these weights are adjusted to minimize the difference between predicted and actual outputs. Additionally, each neuron includes a bias term, which allows it to shift the activation function, improving flexibility.

2 **Feedforward and Recurrent Architectures**: The most common architecture is the FNN, where information flows in one direction, from input to output, without cycles. This structure underlies models such as MLPs and CNNs.

In contrast, RNNs introduce feedback connections, enabling the model to maintain information across time steps. This temporal memory makes RNNs well-suited for sequential data such as speech, text, or time series. Variants like LSTM and GRU address the vanishing gradient problem inherent in deep recurrence.[18] Recent architectures, such as transformers, further expand this structural paradigm by using self-attention mechanisms rather than sequential recurrence. Despite these innovations, the fundamental building blocks—layers, weights, biases, and activations—remain consistent across architectures.

11.3.2 Mathematical Representation

Mathematically, a neuron performs a weighted sum of its inputs followed by a nonlinear transformation:

$$y = f\left(\sum_{i=1}^{n} w_i x_i + b\right) \tag{11.1}$$

where:

x_i = Input values
w_i = Corresponding weights
b = Bias
f = Activation function.

In vectorized form, for a layer l with input vector $x^{(l-1)}$, weights $W^{(l)}$, and bias $b^{(l)}$:

$$z^{(l)} = W^{(l)}x^{(l-1)} + b^{(l)} \text{ and } x^{(l)} = f\left(z^{(l)}\right) \tag{11.2}$$

This transformation is applied repeatedly across layers, allowing the network to compose simple functions into highly nonlinear mappings capable of approximating complex phenomena. The Universal Approximation Theorem[19] formally established that a feedforward network with at least one hidden layer and nonlinear activation can approximate any continuous function to an arbitrary degree of accuracy. This result underpins the theoretical power of neural networks.

11.3.3 Activation Functions

The activation function is one of the most critical elements in a neural network. It introduces nonlinearity into the model, enabling it to learn complex relationships that cannot be captured by simple linear transformations. Without activation functions, a network, regardless of its depth, would behave as a single linear model.

1 **Linear vs. Nonlinear Activations**: Linear activations (e.g., $f(x) = x$) do not alter the input and thus fail to capture interactions among features. Nonlinear activations, however, allow the composition of layers to model intricate, nonlinear dependencies, enabling the network to represent virtually any function.
2 **Common Activation Functions**:

- **Sigmoid Function**: The sigmoid maps input values to the range (0, 1), making it suitable for probabilistic outputs. However, it suffers from vanishing gradients, where derivatives become extremely small for large input magnitudes, hindering deep network training.

$$f(x) = \frac{1}{1+e^{-x}} \tag{11.3}$$

- **Hyperbolic Tangent (tanh)**: The tanh function outputs values between −1 and 1, centering data and improving convergence over the sigmoid. Yet it also faces vanishing gradient issues for deep layers.

$$f(x) = \tanh(x) = \frac{e^{x} - e^{-x}}{e^{x} + e^{-x}} \tag{11.4}$$

- **Rectified Linear Unit (ReLU)**: ReLU has become the dominant activation in deep networks due to its simplicity and computational efficiency. It mitigates vanishing gradients by maintaining a derivative of 1 for positive inputs. However, it can cause "dead neurons" when negative inputs produce zero gradients.

$$f(x) = \max(0, x) \tag{11.5}$$

- **Leaky ReLU and Parametric ReLU**: These variants address ReLU's limitations by allowing a small, non-zero gradient for negative inputs, ensuring continued learning.
- **SoftMax Function**: Used primarily in output layers for classification, SoftMax converts raw scores into probabilities:

$$f(x_i) = \frac{e^{x_i}}{\sum_j e^{x_j}} \tag{11.6}$$

It ensures the network's output represents a valid probability distribution across multiple classes.

- **Swish and GELU (Gaussian Error Linear Unit)**: Modern activations such as Swish $f(x) = x \cdot \text{sigmoid}(x)$, and GELU improve learning stability and are often used in transformer architectures.[20]

11.3.4 Backpropagation and Learning

Backpropagation is the foundational learning algorithm underlying the training of artificial neural networks by enabling models to iteratively adjust their parameters to minimize prediction error. Introduced formally by Rumelhart, Hinton, and Williams (1986), backpropagation applies the chain rule of calculus to efficiently compute gradients of a loss function with respect to network weights by propagating error signals backward from the output layer through successive hidden layers.[21] This gradient-based learning process allows neural networks to capture complex nonlinear relationships in data and has become central to modern DL architectures. Further theoretical work has clarified the convergence properties and limitations of backpropagation, particularly in deep networks where issues such as vanishing and exploding gradients can impede effective learning.[22] Advances such as improved weight initialization, adaptive learning rates, normalization techniques, and alternative activation functions have significantly enhanced the stability and efficiency of backpropagation-based learning.[23] Consequently, backpropagation remains the dominant learning mechanism in supervised DL, supporting a wide range of applications in computer vision, NLP, and AI-driven business analytics. While the structure and activation functions define how data flows through a network, the backpropagation algorithm defines how the network learns. Backpropagation enables neural networks to learn from data through gradient-based optimization.[24]

1. **Core Concept**: Backpropagation operates by propagating the error between the predicted and actual outputs backward through the network to adjust the weights. It relies on the chain rule of calculus to compute partial derivatives of the loss function with respect to each weight efficiently. The learning process involves two main phases:

- **Forward Pass**: Input data passes through the network layer by layer, producing predictions.
- **Backward Pass**: The loss (difference between prediction and target) is propagated backward, and gradients are computed for each parameter. Formally, for a given loss function L and weight $w_{ij}^{(l)}$ connecting neuron j in layer $l-1$ to neuron i in layer l:

$$\frac{\delta L}{\delta w_{ij}^{(l)}} = \frac{\delta L}{\delta a_i^{(l)}} \cdot \frac{\delta a_i^{(l)}}{\delta z_i^{(l)}} \cdot \frac{\delta z_i^{(l)}}{\delta w_{ij}^{(l)}} \tag{11.7}$$

where $a_i^{(l)}$, is the activation and $z_i^{(l)}$ is the pre-activation output.

The gradients are then used by optimization algorithms such as stochastic gradient descent (SGD) or Adam to update weights:

$$w_{ij}^{(l)} \leftarrow w_{ij}^{(l)} - \eta \frac{\delta L}{\delta w_{ij}^{(l)}} \tag{11.8}$$

where η is the learning rate.

2. **Optimization and Regularization**: While backpropagation defines how gradients are computed, optimization algorithms define how they are applied. Techniques such as momentum, adaptive learning rates, and regularization methods (e.g., dropout, $L2$ weight decay) improve convergence stability and prevent overfitting. Despite its effectiveness, backpropagation faces challenges like exploding or vanishing gradients, especially in very deep networks. Solutions include using normalized weight initialization, batch normalization, and specialized architectures such as residual connections.

11.3.5 Interplay between Structure, Activation, and Backpropagation

The interplay between network structure, activation functions, and backpropagation determines the effectiveness of learning capacity, stability, and efficiency of artificial neural networks. Network structure, as defined by depth, width, and connectivity, shapes the representational power of the model, with deeper architectures enabling hierarchical feature extraction but also increasing susceptibility to optimization challenges during backpropagation.[25] Activation functions mediate the flow of information and gradients through these structures; while early nonlinearities, such as sigmoid and hyperbolic tangent, facilitated universal approximation, they often induced vanishing gradients that hindered effective error propagation in deep networks.[26] The adoption of piecewise-linear activations such as ReLU and its variants substantially improved gradient flow and accelerated convergence, enabling backpropagation to scale to very deep architectures.[27] As a result, effective learning emerges from the joint design of network architecture and activation functions that align with the mechanics of backpropagation to ensure stable gradient transmission and efficient parameter updates. This interdependence underscores why advances in DL have largely stemmed from coordinated innovations in structural design, activation choices, and optimization strategies. Neural network performance depends on the synergistic relationship among structure, activation, and backpropagation.

- The structure determines representational capacity,
- Activation functions define nonlinear transformations, and
- Backpropagation ensures efficient learning of parameters.

For example, convolutional architectures leverage local connectivity and weight sharing to process images efficiently, while recurrent architectures depend on gating mechanisms and activations like tanh or ReLU to capture temporal dependencies. Without nonlinear activations, backpropagation would propagate constant gradients, and the network would fail to learn complex patterns. Similarly, without structured connectivity, backpropagation would be computationally intractable. Modern advancements, such as deep residual networks, transformers, and attention mechanisms, extend these fundamental principles, optimizing how information flows and how gradients propagate through extremely deep models. Yet the underlying foundation remains rooted in the triad of structure, activation, and backpropagation.

Neural networks owe their power to the interplay of structural design, nonlinear activation functions, and the backpropagation learning algorithm. Together, these elements enable models to approximate highly complex relationships and generalize from data. The structure defines how information is represented and processed; activation functions inject nonlinearity and depth; and backpropagation allows networks to self-correct through iterative learning. Over the decades, refinements in these components—such as ReLU activations, normalization techniques, and adaptive optimizers—have transformed neural networks from theoretical constructs into the foundation of intelligent systems. As research continues, new architectures (e.g., transformers), alternative training methods (e.g., self-supervised and energy-based learning), and biologically inspired activation functions are expected to further enhance the efficiency and interpretability of neural networks. Nonetheless, the core principles of structure, activation, and backpropagation remain the mathematical and conceptual backbone of DL.

11.4 Convolutional Neural Networks (CNNs) and Recurrent Neural Networks (RNNs)

CNNs and RNNs are two foundational DL architectures designed to exploit distinct structural properties of data. Among the most influential architectures in modern AI, CNNs and RNNs stand as foundational models in DL. CNNs are effective for spatially structured inputs, such as images and videos, as they employ convolutional filters, local receptive fields, and weight sharing to automatically learn hierarchical feature representations while reducing parameter complexity and improving translation invariance.[28] In contrast, RNNs are tailored for sequential and temporal data, modeling dependencies across time by maintaining hidden states that capture information from prior inputs; this makes them well-suited for applications in NLP, speech recognition, and time series forecasting.[29] Both architectures were developed to address specific computational challenges of CNNs to process spatially correlated data, such as images, and RNNs to model temporally sequential data, such as speech and text. Their unique structures and learning mechanisms have transformed computer vision, NLP, and time series prediction, laying the groundwork for modern architectures like transformers and generative models. While both CNNs and RNNs share the basic principles of neural computation—layers of weighted connections, activation functions, and backpropagation—they differ in how they structure these computations to exploit the statistical regularities of their target data domains. Together, CNNs and RNNs have driven major advances in perception and sequence modeling, and hybrid architectures increasingly combine convolutional and recurrent components to handle multimodal and spatiotemporal learning tasks. The following subsections explore the conceptual foundations, architecture, and learning mechanisms of CNNs and RNNs, their respective strengths and limitations, and their integration in hybrid DL systems.

11.4.1 Convolutional Neural Networks (CNNs)

The conceptual foundation of CNNs can be traced back to biological vision systems and the seminal work of Hubel and Wiesel, who discovered receptive fields in the visual cortex—neurons that respond selectively to specific visual features. This biological insight inspired the convolutional architecture, which applies filters across spatial dimensions to detect local patterns.[30] These ideas were formalized in LeNet-5, one of the first CNNs to successfully recognize handwritten digits.[31] Subsequent architectures such as AlexNet, VGGNet, and ResNet catalyze the DL revolution by achieving unprecedented accuracy in image recognition competitions.

11.4.2 Recurrent Neural Networks (RNNs)

RNNs are a class of neural architectures specifically designed to model sequential and temporal data by maintaining internal hidden states that capture dependencies across time steps. While CNNs excel at spatial pattern recognition, they are not designed for data with temporal dependencies, where context from previous inputs influences future outputs. To address this, RNNs were developed to incorporate feedback loops, allowing information to persist across time steps. In RNNs, each output depends not only on the current input but also on the hidden state from previous steps, giving the network a form of memory. Unlike feedforward networks, RNNs incorporate feedback connections that allow information from previous inputs to influence current outputs, making them well-suited for applications such as time series forecasting, speech recognition, and NLP.[32] This structure makes RNNs particularly suitable for sequential data such as natural language, speech, and financial time series, as RNNs are an essential conceptual foundation for sequential learning and continue to be applied in domains where temporal structure and interpretability are essential.

11.4.2.1 Architecture and Computation

An RNN processes a sequence of inputs $x_1, x_2, .\ ...., x_T$ as follows:

$$h_t = f\left(W_{xh}x_t + W_{hh}h_{t-1} + b_h\right) \tag{11.9}$$

$$y_t = g\left(W_{hy}h_t + b_y\right) \tag{11.10}$$

where:

h_t = Represents the hidden state at time t, capturing both the current input and past context

The function f (often tanh or ReLU) defines how information flows between states, while g defines the output transformation. Through weight sharing across time steps, RNNs can generalize across sequence lengths, learning temporal dynamics efficiently. However, during training, backpropagation through time (BPTT) can cause vanishing or exploding gradients, limiting the ability of standard RNNs to learn long-term dependencies.[33]

11.4.2.2 LSTM and GRU Networks

To overcome these limitations, researchers introduced LSTM and GRU architectures.

- **LSTM**: Incorporates gating mechanisms—input, forget, and output gates—that regulate information flow and preserve gradients across time. The cell state acts as long-term memory, while gates determine what to retain or discard.
- **GRU**: A simplified version of LSTM with fewer gates, offering comparable performance with reduced computational overhead.

These gated architectures have enabled RNNs to handle complex sequential patterns, supporting applications like speech recognition, language translation, and music composition.

11.4.2.3 Applications and Evolution

RNNs have been widely adopted in:

- **Natural Language Processing (NLP)**: Sentiment analysis, machine translation, and speech-to-text systems.
- **Finance**: Forecasting stock prices and detecting anomalies in sequential transaction data.
- **Healthcare**: Modeling patient histories for disease prediction and clinical decision support.

However, RNNs' sequential nature limits parallelization, making them slower than feed-forward architectures. This bottleneck led to the emergence of transformers, which replace recurrence with self-attention mechanisms, allowing global context modeling with superior efficiency. Nevertheless, RNNs remain foundational for sequence modeling and time-dependent data.

While CNNs and RNNs both learn hierarchical representations, Table 11.2 presents their differences in how they model relationships within data.

Table 11.2 Comparison of CNNs and RNNs

Aspect	*Convolutional Neural Networks (CNNs)*	*Recurrent Neural Networks (RNNs)*
Primary domain	Spatial data (images, video, text embeddings)	Sequential data (time series, text, speech)
Core operation	Convolution (local receptive fields)	Recurrence (temporal dependencies)
Connectivity	Feedforward; local connections	Cyclic, feedback connections
Parameter sharing	Across spatial positions	Across time steps
Parallelization	Highly parallelizable	Sequential, limited parallelism
Memory	Implicit, short-term (local features)	Explicit, long-term (hidden states)
Training challenges	Overfitting in large networks	Vanishing/exploding gradients
Strengths	High spatial awareness; efficient on GPUs	Captures sequence and context information
Applications	Vision, medical imaging, 3D recognition	NLP, speech, financial modeling

11.5 Generative AI and Business Applications

The emergence of Generative Artificial Intelligence (GenAI) represents one of the most transformative developments in the evolution of machine learning and digital innovation. Commonly, GenAI refers to a class of AI systems capable of creating new content such as text, images, code, audio, and synthetic data by learning underlying patterns from large-scale datasets. Recent advances in DL, particularly LLMs and generative architectures such as transformers, variational autoencoders (VAEs), and GANs, have significantly expanded the scope of GenAI applications in business contexts.[34] Unlike traditional AI systems designed for classification or prediction, generative models create new data that mimics real-world patterns, images, text, audio, or even 3D structures. These models, powered by architectures such as GANs and Diffusion Models, are redefining creativity, productivity, and value creation across industries.

In practice, organizations typically deploy GenAI to enhance productivity, automate knowledge-intensive tasks, and support decision-making across functions, including marketing, customer service, finance, supply chain management, and human resources. For example, GenAI-powered chatbots and virtual assistants improve customer engagement and service efficiency, while generative models support scenario analysis, risk assessment, financial forecasting, and sustainability reporting by synthesizing insights from unstructured data.[35] From a strategic perspective, GenAI enables business model innovation by reducing information asymmetry, accelerating innovation cycles, and augmenting human expertise rather than merely automating routine tasks.[36] However, the adoption of GenAI also raises critical governance, ethical, and regulatory challenges related to data privacy, bias, transparency, intellectual property, and accountability, underscoring the need for responsible AI frameworks and robust corporate oversight.[37] Overall, GenAI can be viewed as a transformative general-purpose technology with significant implications for business performance, governance, and sustainability. GenAI's capabilities extend beyond automation by enabling co-creation, where machines act as creative partners in design, marketing, product development, and strategic decision-making. From producing realistic digital content to designing new pharmaceuticals, the applications are vast. As businesses increasingly adopt generative systems, understanding their underlying technologies and economic implications becomes essential.

11.5.1 Foundations of Generative AI

GenAI is based on unsupervised and self-supervised learning, where models learn data distributions and generate new samples that statistically resemble training data. Early generative models, such as VAEs, captured latent representations of data, while GANs introduced adversarial training to enhance realism.[38] More recently, diffusion models (Ho et al., 2020) have surpassed GANs in image generation quality, using probabilistic processes that iteratively refine noise into coherent data. These innovations collectively mark a shift from discriminative to generative paradigms in machine learning, models that not only recognize but also create.

All generative models share a similar goal: to learn a latent space, a compressed representation of data, through which new, plausible instances can be synthesized. This involves two critical components:

- **Encoding**: Mapping high-dimensional data into a compact, meaningful latent representation.
- **Decoding**: Transforming latent representations back into the data domain.

While autoencoders achieve this through reconstruction, GANs and diffusion models introduce sophisticated training mechanisms to improve realism and diversity.

11.5.2 Generative Adversarial Networks (GANs)

GANs are a class of GenAI models that learn to synthesize realistic data by framing the learning process as a two-player minimax game between a generator and a discriminator. GANs typically produce synthetic samples that resemble real data, while the discriminator attempts to distinguish between real and generated observations, with both networks being trained simultaneously via backpropagation.[39] This adversarial learning paradigm enables GANs to capture complex, high-dimensional data distributions and has led to state-of-the-art performance in image synthesis, super-resolution, data augmentation, and anomaly detection. Despite their success, GANs present notable training challenges, including mode collapse, instability, and sensitivity to hyperparameter choices, which have motivated numerous architectural and optimization improvements such as Deep Convolutional GANs (DCGANs), Wasserstein GANs, and StyleGAN variants.[40] GANs have been increasingly applied in business and analytics contexts, including synthetic data generation for privacy-preserving analytics, fraud detection, and scenario simulation, where realistic but non-identifiable data are required. Overall, GANs represent a powerful yet technically demanding generative framework whose adversarial structure has reshaped the landscape of generative modeling. GANs consist of two neural networks engaged in a minimax game:

- The Generator (G) creates synthetic samples from random noise.
- The Discriminator (D) distinguishes between real and generated samples.

The generator aims to fool the discriminator, while the discriminator strives to correctly classify inputs. Through this adversarial training, both networks improve iteratively—G becomes better at producing realistic data, and D becomes better at detecting fakes. The equilibrium of this game results in a generator capable of producing outputs indistinguishable from real data.

Mathematically, GANs optimize the following objective:

$$\min_{G}\max_{D} V(D,G) = E_{x \sim p_{\text{data}}}\left[\log D(x)\right] + E_{z \sim p_z}\left[\log\left(1 - D\left(G(Z)\right)\right)\right] \tag{11.11}$$

Several variants have extended the basic GAN framework:

- **Conditional GANs (cGANs)**: Incorporate labels to generate class-specific data.
- **StyleGAN**: Developed by NVIDIA, capable of producing photorealistic human faces with controllable attributes.
- **CycleGAN**: Enables image-to-image translation (e.g., converting paintings to photos or summer landscapes to winter scenes).
- **BigGAN and GauGAN**: Scale GANs for high-resolution image synthesis.

These variants have dramatically enhanced both quality and controllability, establishing GANs as a cornerstone of GenAI. GANs are now integral to creative industries and digital commerce:

- **Marketing and Design**: Automatic generation of visuals, product mockups, and branding materials. Companies like Coca-Cola and Nike have used GANs for ad creativity and visual storytelling.
- **Fashion and Retail**: Virtual try-ons, clothing synthesis, and texture generation for e-commerce platforms.
- **Entertainment**: GANs assist in movie special effects, gaming environment generation, and realistic avatar creation.
- **Healthcare**: Generation of synthetic medical images for training diagnostic systems without violating patient privacy.[41]
- **Manufacturing and Engineering**: GANs help simulate product designs, predict material properties, and accelerate prototyping.

In essence, GANs have bridged the gap between data-driven modeling and creative design, enabling businesses to scale innovation and personalization.

11.5.3 Diffusion Models and the Next Generation of Generative AI

Diffusion models have emerged as a powerful next-generation paradigm in GenAI by enabling the achievement of state-of-the-art performance across image, audio, and text generation by modeling data generation as a gradual denoising process. Diffusion models represent the latest breakthrough in GenAI, particularly for high-quality image synthesis. Inspired by statistical physics, these models learn to reverse a diffusion process, a gradual transformation of data into noise. Originating from non-equilibrium thermodynamics, diffusion probabilistic models learn to reverse a forward process that incrementally corrupts data with noise, enabling the generation of high-fidelity samples through iterative denoising steps.[42] Diffusion models reconstruct data from random noise samples, yielding unprecedented realism and diversity by learning how to denoise step by step.[43] In essence, diffusion models approximate the conditional probability of a clean image given a noisy input, progressively refining it over multiple iterations. Subsequent advancements, including Denoising Diffusion Probabilistic Models (DDPMs), have demonstrated superior sample quality and training stability compared to earlier generative approaches such as GANs, largely due to their likelihood-based formulation and reduced susceptibility to mode collapse.[44] This process contrasts sharply with GANs' adversarial learning, focusing instead on probabilistic modeling and iterative refinement. Consequently, diffusion models now underpin many cutting-edge GenAI systems used in creative industries, scientific discovery, and business applications, supporting tasks ranging from image synthesis and data augmentation to scenario simulation and design optimization. The growing dominance of diffusion-based architectures signals a broader shift toward more stable, controllable, and theoretically grounded generative models, positioning them at the forefront of the next wave of GenAI innovation.

Diffusion models address key limitations of GANs:

- **Stability**: Training is less prone to mode collapse (where GANs produce limited diversity).
- **Controllability**: They allow conditioning on text prompts, sketches, or other modalities (as seen in models like Stable Diffusion and DALL-E 2).
- **High Fidelity**: They produce more coherent and detailed results across various domains.

These qualities have made diffusion models the backbone of today's most popular AI tools, including Midjourney, DALL-E, and Stable Diffusion, which democratize access to high-quality creative generation. Diffusion-based systems have rapidly penetrated commercial workflows:

- **Advertising and Branding**: Agencies use diffusion models for automated ad generation and campaign visualization.
- **Architecture and Industrial Design**: Designers employ AI-generated imagery for rapid concept iteration.
- **Pharmaceuticals and Materials Science**: Generative diffusion models assist in molecular design and drug discovery by simulating molecular structures.
- **Entertainment and Media**: These models generate game assets, storyboards, and film concepts, drastically reducing pre-production costs.

The open-source release of Stable Diffusion has further catalyzed innovation by enabling startups and individuals to integrate generative capabilities into custom business solutions.

11.5.4 AI-Generated Content and Innovation

AI-generated content (AIGC) refers to any digital material created autonomously or semi-autonomously by AI models. This includes text (via LLMs), images, videos, and audio. AIGC has become a new economic force—empowering marketers, journalists, and artists to create at scale while reducing cost and time-to-market. In recent years, AIGC has become a significant driver of innovation by augmenting human creativity, accelerating knowledge production, and reshaping organizational processes across industries. Advances in generative models of LLMs, diffusion models, and GANs enable the automated creation of text, images, code, designs, and synthetic data that support ideation, prototyping, and experimentation at unprecedented scale.[45] In sectors such as product development, marketing, software engineering, and scientific research, AI-generated artifacts increasingly function as "co-creators," complementing human expertise rather than replacing it.[46] Consequently, the literature suggests that AIGC represents a general-purpose innovation technology whose value depends critically on organizational capabilities, human–AI collaboration, and responsible oversight.

The trajectory of GenAI points toward multi-modal and interactive systems capable of generating not only content but also ideas, strategies, and decisions. Future models will integrate text, image, sound, and video generation in unified frameworks, creating fully synthetic environments for simulation and innovation. Moreover, the convergence of GenAI and blockchain technologies may enable secure ownership and monetization of digital creations through verifiable provenance (e.g., NFTs). In enterprise contexts, generative design systems will continuously optimize product features, logistics, and customer experience using AI-driven simulations. As GenAI becomes embedded across industries, its role will shift from content generation to strategic augmentation-empowering businesses to explore new markets, innovate faster, and make creativity scalable.

GenAI marks a paradigm shift from predictive intelligence to creative intelligence. Through architectures such as GANs and diffusion models, AI systems can now generate authentic, diverse, and meaningful content that rivals human creativity. In business, these technologies have unlocked new frontiers in design, marketing, innovation, and customer experience. While challenges surrounding ethics, regulation, and trust persist, the potential of GenAI to transform industries is undeniable. By combining algorithmic creativity with human oversight, organizations can harness generative models not merely as tools but as strategic collaborators in the next wave of digital transformation.

11.6 Summary

This chapter explores the fundamentals and advanced concepts of DL, a powerful subset of machine learning that utilizes neural networks with multiple layers to model complex patterns in data. The chapter explains how these networks learn through forward propagation and backpropagation using gradient descent optimization by starting with the basic structure of artificial neural networks composed of interconnected neurons organized in input, hidden, and output layers. The chapter highlights the evolution from shallow to deep architectures, emphasizing how DNNs leverage multiple hidden layers to automatically learn hierarchical feature representations. It discusses key challenges in training deep networks, such as the vanishing and exploding gradient problems, and presents solutions like activation functions (ReLU, Leaky ReLU), batch normalization, and advanced optimizers.

Specialized neural network architectures such as CNNs and RNNs are examined for their applications in image processing, NLP, and sequence modeling. The chapter also covers regularization techniques such as dropout and early stopping to mitigate overfitting and improve generalization. This chapter introduces neural networks, CNNs, and RNNs. It covers architecture, activation functions, and backpropagation, along with frameworks like TensorFlow and PyTorch. DL offers revolutionary capabilities in AI. We introduce neural networks, their structures, and their application in solving complex problems involving images, sound, and natural language. Finally, the chapter touches on transfer learning, which reuses pre-trained deep models for new tasks, accelerating training and enhancing performance, especially in data-scarce scenarios. Practical considerations such as model evaluation, hyperparameter tuning, and computational requirements are also discussed. In summary, this chapter provides a comprehensive foundation for understanding how DL and neural networks enable state-of-the-art solutions in diverse domains, from computer vision to speech recognition and beyond.

Notes

1 Paszke, A., Gross, S., Massa, F., Lerer, A., Bradbury, J., Chanan, G., … & Chintala, S. (2019). PyTorch: An imperative style, high-performance deep learning library. In *Advances in Neural Information Processing Systems (NeurIPS)* (pp. 8026–8037). Available at https://proceedings.neurips.cc/paper_files/paper/2019/file/bdbca288fee7f92f2bfa9f7012727740-Paper.pdf

2 LeCun, Y., Bengio, Y., & Hinton, G. (2015). Deep learning. *Nature*, 521(7553), 436–444. https://doi.org/10.1038/nature14539. Available at https://www.nature.com/articles/nature14539

3 Chollet, F. (2021). *Deep Learning with Python* (2nd ed.). Manning Publications.

4 Abadi, M., Barham, P., Chen, J., Chen, Z., Davis, A., Dean, J., … & Zheng, X. (2016). TensorFlow: A system for Large-Scale machine learning. In *12th USENIX Symposium on Operating Systems Design and Implementation (OSDI 16)* (pp. 265–283). Available at https://www.usenix.org/system/files/conference/osdi16/osdi16-abadi.pdf

5 Rumelhart, D. E., Hinton, G. E., & Williams, R. J. (1986). Learning representations by back-propagating errors. *Nature*, 323(6088), 533–536. https://doi.org/10.1038/323533a0. Available at https://www.nature.com/articles/323533a0

6 Baydin, A. G., Pearlmutter, B. A., Radul, A. A., & Siskind, J. M. (2018). Automatic differentiation in machine learning: A survey. *Journal of Machine Learning Research*, 18(153), 1–43. Available at https://www.jmlr.org/papers/volume18/17-468/17-468.pdf

7 Paszke, A., Gross, S., Massa, F., Lerer, A., Bradbury, J., Chanan, G., … & Chintala, S. (2019). PyTorch: An imperative style, high-performance deep learning library. In *Proceedings of the 33rd International Conference on Neural Information Processing Systems* (Vol. 32, pp. 8026–8037). Available at https://proceedings.neurips.cc/paper_files/paper/2019/file/bdbca288fee7f92f2bfa9f7012727740-Paper.pdf

8 Abadi, M., Barham, P., Chen, J., Chen, Z., Davis, A., Dean, J., … & Zheng, X. (2016). TensorFlow: A system for large-scale machine learning. In *Proceedings of the 12th USENIX Symposium on Operating Systems Design and Implementation (OSDI)* (pp. 265–283). Available at https://www.usenix.org/system/files/conference/osdi16/osdi16-abadi.pdf
9 Abadi, M., Barham, P., Chen, J., Chen, Z., Davis, A., Dean, J., … & Zheng, X. (2016). TensorFlow: A system for large-scale machine learning. In *Proceedings of the 12th USENIX Symposium on Operating Systems Design and Implementation (OSDI)* (pp. 265–283). Available at https://www.usenix.org/system/files/conference/osdi16/osdi16-abadi.pdf, 4.
10 Paszke, A., Gross, S., Massa, F., Lerer, A., Bradbury, J., Chanan, G., … & Chintala, S. (2019). PyTorch: An imperative style, high-performance deep learning library. In *Advances in Neural Information Processing Systems (NeurIPS)* (pp. 8026–8037). Available at https://proceedings.neurips.cc/paper_files/paper/2019/file/bdbca288fee7f92f2bfa9f7012727740-Paper.pdf
11 Bahrampour, S., Ramakrishnan, N., Schott, L., & Shah, M. (2015). Comparative study of deep learning software frameworks. In *Proceedings of the IEEE Conference on Computer Vision and Pattern Recognition Workshops (CVPRW)* (pp. 1–8). https://doi.org/10.48550/arXiv.1511.06435. Available at https://arxiv.org/abs/1511.06435
12 LeCun, Y., Bengio, Y., & Hinton, G. (2015). Deep learning. *Nature*, 521(7553), 436–444. https://doi.org/10.1038/nature14539. Available at https://www.nature.com/articles/nature14539
13 LeCun, Y., Bengio, Y., & Hinton, G. (2015). Deep learning. *Nature*, 521(7553), 436–444. https://doi.org/10.1038/nature14539. Available at https://www.nature.com/articles/nature14539, 3.
14 Chollet, F. (2015, April). *Keras*. GitHub Repository.
15 Bahrampour, S., Ramakrishnan, N., Schott, L., & Shah, M. (2015). Comparative study of deep learning software frameworks. In *Proceedings of the IEEE Conference on Computer Vision and Pattern Recognition Workshops (CVPRW)* (pp. 1–8). https://doi.org/10.48550/arXiv.1511.06435. Available at https://arxiv.org/abs/1511.06435
16 Chollet, F. (2021). *Deep Learning with Python* (2nd ed., 504pp). Manning. Available at https://www.manning.com/books/deep-learning-with-python-second-edition
17 LeCun, Y., Bengio, Y., & Hinton, G. (2015). Deep learning. *Nature*, 521(7553), 436–444. https://doi.org/10.1038/nature14539. Available at https://www.nature.com/articles/nature14539
18 Hochreiter, S., & Schmidhuber, J. (1997). Long short-term memory. *Neural Computation*, 9(8), 1735–1780. https://doi.org/10.1162/neco.1997.9.8.1735. Available at https://ieeexplore.ieee.org/abstract/document/6795963
19 Hornik, K. (1991). Approximation capabilities of multilayer feedforward networks. *Neural Networks*, 4(2), 251–257. https://doi.org/10.1016/0893-6080(91)90009-T. Available at https://www.sciencedirect.com/science/article/abs/pii/089360809190009T
20 Hendrycks, D., & Gimpel, K. (2016). Bridging nonlinearities and stochastic regularizers with Gaussian error linear units. arXiv preprint arXiv:1606.08415
21 Rumelhart, D. E., Hinton, G. E., & Williams, R. J. (1986). Learning representations by back-propagating errors. *Nature*, 323(6088), 533. https://doi.org/10.1038/323533a0. Available at https://www.nature.com/articles/323533a0
22 Hochreiter, S. (1998). The vanishing gradient problem during learning recurrent neural networks. *International Journal of Uncertainty, Fuzziness and Knowledge-Based Systems*, 6(2), 107–116. https://doi.org/10.1142/S0218488598000094. Available at https://www.worldscientific.com/doi/abs/10.1142/s0218488598000094
23 LeCun, Y., Bengio, Y., & Hinton, G. (2015). Deep learning. *Nature*, 521(7553), 436–444. https://doi.org/10.1038/nature14539. Available at https://www.nature.com/articles/nature14539
24 Rumelhart, D. E., Hinton, G. E., & Williams, R. J. (1986). Learning representations by back-propagating errors. *Nature*, 323(6088), 533–536. https://doi.org/10.1038/323533a0. Available at https://www.nature.com/articles/323533a0
25 Bengio, Y., Simard, P., & Frasconi, P. (1994). Learning long-term dependencies with gradient descent is difficult. *IEEE Transactions on Neural Networks*, 5(2), 157–166. https://doi.org/10.1109/72.279181. Available at https://ieeexplore.ieee.org/abstract/document/279181
26 Hochreiter, S. (1998). The vanishing gradient problem during learning recurrent neural networks. *International Journal of Uncertainty, Fuzziness and Knowledge-Based Systems*, 6(2), 107–116. https://doi.org/10.1142/S0218488598000094. Available at https://www.worldscientific.com/doi/abs/10.1142/s0218488598000094

27 Goodfellow, I., Bengio, Y., & Courville, A. (2016). *Deep Learning*. MIT Press.

28 Krizhevsky, A., Sutskever, I., & Hinton, G. E. (2012). ImageNet classification with deep convolutional neural networks. In *Advances in Neural Information Processing Systems (NeurIPS)* (pp. 1097–1105). Available at https://proceedings.neurips.cc/paper/2012/file/c399862d3b9d6b76c8436e924a68c45b-Paper.pdf

29 Elman, J. L. (1990). Finding structure in time. *Cognitive Science*, 14(2), 179–211. https://doi.org/10.1207/s15516709cog1402_1. Available at https://onlinelibrary.wiley.com/doi/abs/10.1207/s15516709cog1402_1

30 Hubel, D. H., & Wiesel, T. N. (1962). Receptive fields, binocular interaction and functional architecture in the cat's visual cortex. *Journal of Physiology*, 160(1), 106–154. https://doi.org/10.1113/jphysiol.1962.sp006837. Available at https://pmc.ncbi.nlm.nih.gov/articles/PMC1359523/

31 LeCun, Y., Bottou, L., Bengio, Y., & Haffner, P. (1998). Gradient-based learning applied to document recognition. *Proceedings of the IEEE*, 86(11), 2278–2324. https://doi.org/10.1038/nature14539. Available at https://www.nature.com/articles/nature14539

32 Elman, J. L. (1990). Finding structure in time. *Cognitive Science*, 14(2), 179–211. https://doi.org/10.1207/s15516709cog1402_1. Available at https://onlinelibrary.wiley.com/doi/abs/10.1207/s15516709cog1402_1

33 Elman, J. L. (1990). Finding structure in time. *Cognitive Science*, 14(2), 179–211. https://doi.org/10.1207/s15516709cog1402_1. Available at https://onlinelibrary.wiley.com/doi/abs/10.1207/s15516709cog1402_1, 11.

34 Goodfellow, I., Pouget-Abadie, J., Mirza, M., Xu, B., Warde-Farley, D., Ozair, S., … & Bengio, Y. (2014). Generative adversarial nets. In *Advances in Neural Information Processing Systems* (Vol. 27, pp. 2672–2680). Available at https://proceedings.neurips.cc/paper_files/paper/2014/file/f033ed80deb0234979a61f95710dbe25-Paper.pdf

35 Dwivedi, Y. K., Kshetri, N., Hughes, L., Slade, E. L., Jeyaraj, A., Kar, A. K., … & Wright, R. (2023). "So what if ChatGPT wrote it?" Multidisciplinary perspectives on opportunities, challenges and implications of generative conversational AI for research, practice and policy. *International Journal of Information Management*, 71, 102642. https://doi.org/10.1016/j.ijinfomgt.2023.102642. Available at https://researchportal.beds.ac.uk/en/publications/so-what-if-chatgpt-wrote-it-multidisciplinary-perspectives-on-opp-5/

36 Brynjolfsson, E., Li, D., & Raymond, L. R. (2023). Generative AI at work. *Journal of Economic Perspectives*, 37(4), 139–164.

37 Rai, A., Constantinides, P., & Sarker, S. (2020). Next-generation digital platforms: Toward human–AI hybrids. *MIS Quarterly*, 44(1), iii–ix.

38 Kingma, D. P., & Welling, M. (2013). Auto-encoding variational Bayes. arXiv preprint arXiv:1312.6114. Available at https://indico.math.cnrs.fr/event/11377/attachments/4589/6915/18012024_Kingma-and-Welling-2022%20Auto-Encoding%20Variational%20Bayes.pdf

39 Goodfellow, I., Pouget-Abadie, J., Mirza, M., Xu, B., Warde-Farley, D., Ozair, S., … & Bengio, Y. (2014). Generative adversarial nets. In *Advances in Neural Information Processing Systems* (Vol. 27, pp. 2672–2680). Available at https://proceedings.neurips.cc/paper_files/paper/2014/file/f033ed80deb0234979a61f95710dbe25-Paper.pdf

40 Arjovsky, M., Chintala, S., & Bottou, L. (2017). Wasserstein generative adversarial networks. In *Proceedings of the 34th International Conference on Machine Learning* (pp. 214–223). Available at https://proceedings.mlr.press/v70/arjovsky17a/arjovsky17a.pdf

41 Frid-Adar, M., Diamant, I., Klang, E., Amitai, M., Goldberger, J., & Greenspan, H. (2018). GAN-based synthetic medical image augmentation for increased CNN performance in liver lesion classification. *Neurocomputing*, 321, 321–331. https://doi.org/10.1016/j.neucom.2018.09.013. Available at https://www.sciencedirect.com/science/article/abs/pii/S0925231218310749

42 Sohl-Dickstein, J., Weiss, E. A., Maheswaranathan, N., & Ganguli, S. (2015). Deep unsupervised learning using nonequilibrium thermodynamics. In *Proceedings of the 32nd International Conference on Machine Learning* (pp. 2256–2265). Available at https://proceedings.mlr.press/v37/sohl-dickstein15.pdf

43 Ho, J., Jain, A., & Abbeel, P. (2020). Denoising diffusion probabilistic models. In *NIPS 20: Proceedings of the 34th International Conference on Neural Information Processing Systems* (pp. 6840–6851). Available at https://proceedings.neurips.cc/paper/2020/file/4c5bcfec8584af0d967f1ab10179ca4b-Paper.pdf

44 Ho, J., Jain, A., & Abbeel, P. (2020). Denoising diffusion probabilistic models. In *Advances in Neural Information Processing Systems* (Vol. 33, pp. 6840–6851). Available at https://proceedings.neurips.cc/paper/2020/file/4c5bcfec8584af0d967f1ab10179ca4b-Paper.pdf
45 Brown, T. B., Mann, B., Ryder, N., Subbiah, M., Kaplan, J., Dhariwal, P., … & Amodei, D. (2020). Language models are few-shot learners. In *Advances in Neural Information Processing Systems* (Vol. 33, pp. 1877–1901). Available at https://proceedings.neurips.cc/paper_files/paper/2020/file/1457c0d6bfcb4967418bfb8ac142f64a-Paper.pdf
46 Amabile, T. M. (2020). Creativity, artificial intelligence, and a world of surprises. *Academy of Management Discoveries*, 6(3), 351–354. https://doi.org/10.5465/amd.2019.0075. Available at https://journals.aom.org/doi/abs/10.5465/amd.2019.0075

12 AI and Business Analytics in Business and Industry

Learning Objectives

- Understand applications of AI and BA in finance, fraud detection, and risk assessment
- Learn to manage bias, fairness, and transparency
- Be able to build ethical AI frameworks for responsible business practices
- Learn AI for small and medium enterprises (SMEs)
- Explore supply chain optimization and predictive maintenance in manufacturing
- Recognize AI applications in different industries
- Understand the value of AI for ESG and sustainability
- Analyze real-world case studies
- Learn the importance of effective policies and practices for data integrity, security, and compliance in analytics initiatives
- Learn about responsible AI in improving transparency, fairness, accountability, and mitigation of biases
- Understand the outlook for AI and BA in driving digital transformation by enabling smarter, faster, and more adaptive businesses

12.1 Introduction

The integration of AI and BA has revolutionized and transformed how organizations operate, innovate, and globally compete. Businesses across industries and worldwide employ powerful AI and BA tools and techniques to generate insights, prioritize allocation of scarce resources, optimize processes, and make data-informed decisions that drive growth and efficiency. AI-powered and BA-driven platforms have reshaped and continue to influence the landscape of modern business, from predicting customer behavior and expectations to improving strategic planning and automating supply chains. A combination of AI and BA enables organizations to analyze data to identify trends, patterns, and actionable insights to address complex challenges, improve decision-making, and stay ahead in an increasingly globalized marketplace. This chapter presents the transformative role of AI and BA tools and techniques in various sectors, including marketing, retail, finance, healthcare, manufacturing, and banking, among others. It also describes key concepts such as predictive analytics, ML models, NLP, and data visualization, along with their real-world applications and case studies.

DOI: 10.4324/9781003664550-12

12.2 Artificial Intelligence and Business Analytics Opportunity

Together, AI and BA systems create powerful opportunities for organizations to transform data into insights in creating sustained economic and strategic value. BA traditionally focuses on descriptive, predictive, and prescriptive methods to understand past performance, forecast future outcomes, and optimize decisions, while AI, particularly ML and DL, extends these capabilities by enabling systems to learn complex patterns from large, high-dimensional data with minimal human intervention.[1] The convergence of AI-powered and BA-driven tools expands the opportunity space from reporting and optimization toward continuous, automated decision-making embedded directly into business processes.

One major opportunity generated by data-driven decision-making at scale through advances in ML algorithms, cloud computing, and big data platforms that empower organizations to integrate structured data (transactions, financials) with unstructured data (text, images, audio) to create richer insights than traditional analytics alone. Organizations that adopt data-driven decision-making outperform peers in productivity, asset utilization, and profitability by highlighting analytics capability as a strategic asset rather than a support function. Consequently, AI-enhanced BA enables faster, more consistent, and more objective decisions across functions such as marketing, finance, operations, and human resources.

A second opportunity related to the use of BA-assisted predictive and prescriptive intelligence. Predictive analytics powered by ML improves accuracy in forecasting demand, credit risk, churn, fraud, and operational failures, while prescriptive analytics, using optimization, simulation, and reinforcement learning, recommends actions that balance objectives and constraints.[2] The integration of AI with prescriptive models allows organizations not only to predict what is likely to happen but also to determine what should be done, moving analytics from insight generation to value realization. This shift is especially important in dynamic environments where human decision-makers struggle to process information at machine speed.

A third opportunity arises from automation and augmentation of knowledge work. NLP, computer vision, and generative AI enable BA systems to analyze documents, contracts, customer interactions, and regulatory disclosures that were previously inaccessible to large-scale analysis. These technologies augment professionals by reducing routine analytical tasks, improving consistency, and freeing human expertise for judgment-intensive activities.[3] AI-driven and BA-assisted technologies increasingly support a "human-in-the-loop" model in which algorithms provide recommendations and humans retain oversight and accountability rather than replacing decision-makers.

Fourth, AI-powered and BA-driven tools also present significant opportunities for innovation and new business models. Data and analytics capabilities enable personalization, platform-based services, outcome-based pricing, and real-time experimentation. Organizations can monetize data assets, create analytics-enabled products, and embed intelligence into offerings by shifting from product-centric to solution-centric value propositions.[4] At the same time, analytics-driven insights support strategic agility by allowing organizations to test ideas rapidly and adapt to market feedback.

Finally, the opportunity of AI and BA is inseparable from governance, ethics, and trust. As analytics increasingly influences high-stakes decisions, organizations must invest in explainability, fairness, data governance, and model risk management to ensure responsible use and regulatory compliance.[5] Organizations that successfully align the technical capabilities of AI and BA with ethical and organizational readiness are more likely to capture long-term value from AI-enabled analytics. Overall, the opportunity of AI and BA lies not merely in advanced algorithms but in building an integrated decision infrastructure that links data, models, people, and processes. Organizations that strategically combine AI and BA can enhance decision quality, operational efficiency, innovation capacity, and competitive advantage in an increasingly data-intensive economy.

12.3 Artificial Intelligence and Business Analytics Risk

As discussed in the previous section, AI and BA platforms can create tremendous opportunities for businesses in making data-driven decisions. With these opportunities and benefits, the potential threat to humanity should be considered as a societal risk as stated in the open letter that was signed by more than 350 technology executives, engineers, and researchers from the leading AI companies (e.g., OpenAI, Google DeepMind, Anthropic).[6] The concerns are that AI LLMs could soon be advanced to the level that enables misinformation and propaganda to spread, or that they could eliminate millions of white-collar workers. These concerns are viewed by many of these signatures as an existential threat to humanity that demands government intervention in regulating AI systems by requiring makers of large, cutting-edge AI models to register for a government-issued license.[7] AI and BA have become integral to modern business decision-making, offering powerful tools for forecasting, optimization, and strategic planning. These risks span technical, organizational, ethical, legal, and strategic dimensions and can undermine decision quality, stakeholder trust, and long-term firm performance if left unaddressed. As AI-driven analytics systems become embedded in high-stakes business processes such as credit approval, hiring, healthcare diagnostics, pricing, and regulatory compliance, the consequences of error, bias, or misuse are amplified. Overall, the integration of AI into BA introduces a range of risks that organizations must proactively identify, assess, and manage to ensure ethical, secure, and effective outcomes, as explained in the following subsections.

12.3.1 Risks

AI and BA risks are numerous and cover a lot of ground, from bias, privacy, and misinformation to loss of human jobs. The most severe risks are[8] (1) existential risks of advanced and superintelligent AI that could outthink and outperform humans and act in ways that are unpredictable or harmful, potentially posing a threat to humanity and society; (2) bias and discrimination caused by AI biases from their training data, leading to unfair outcomes; (3) privacy and security as AI handling massive datasets, which could raise concerns about how personal data is collected, stored, and potentially misused and security risks; (4) misinformation and deepfakes as AI can often generate unrealistic fake content (deepfakes, synthetic voices, fake news) that can detrimental to businesses and society; (5) job loss and displacement as AI automation could replace millions of jobs; (6) autonomy and loss of control as AI systems become more advanced and autonomous there will be of a risk humans might lose direct control, leading to unintended consequences; (7) concentration of power given to emerging AI platforms could lead to major inequalities in the job markets and even economic or political dominance for those with high-level AI capabilities; and (8) ethical and moral issues as AI systems continue to reshape many industries including healthcare, finance to ensure AI is aligned with human values.

These risks are further explained in the following subsections.[9]

12.3.1.1 Data Risk

One major category of risk is data-related risk. AI and BA systems are only as reliable as the data on which they are trained. Poor data quality, missing values, measurement error, and non-representative samples can lead to biased or unstable models that generate misleading insights. AI systems are heavily reliant on large volumes of structured and unstructured data. If the data used for training models is inaccurate, incomplete, biased, or unethically sourced, it can compromise the integrity of business insights generated by decision intelligence models. Data privacy concerns, especially regarding personal and consumer information, further compound this risk, with non-compliance potentially leading to regulatory penalties under laws such as GDPR and CCPA. Furthermore, data privacy and security risks increase as organizations collect, integrate, and analyze large volumes of sensitive personal and proprietary information using AI models, particularly when such information reflects past inequalities and discrimination in areas such as lending, hiring, and insurance.

12.3.1.2 Model Risk and Algorithmic Uncertainty

Model risk arises when AI-driven analytics models produce unreliable, inaccurate, incomplete, or unintended outputs. This can be due to incorrect assumptions, overfitting, lack of transparency (black-box models), or improper model validation.[10] Such risks can lead to flawed decision-making, especially in critical domains like credit scoring, fraud detection, or operational forecasting. ML models, especially complex "black-box" approaches such as deep neural networks, can be difficult to interpret, validate, and explain. This opacity complicates error detection, accountability, and regulatory compliance, particularly in highly regulated industries like finance and healthcare. AI and BA models may also degrade over time due to data drift, concept drift, or changes in the underlying business environment, leading to systematic performance deterioration if monitoring and retraining are inadequate. Furthermore, overreliance on automated predictions without sufficient human oversight further increases the risk of large-scale decision failures.

12.3.1.3 Ethical, Bias, and Societal Risk

AI-driven analytics systems can unintentionally reinforce existing biases in data, leading to discriminatory outcomes in areas such as hiring, lending, and customer segmentation. Ethical risks include the misuse of AI for manipulation, surveillance, or exclusionary practices.[11] Failing to address fairness and accountability can damage reputations and erode stakeholder trust. AI-driven analytics can affect fairness, transparency, and legitimacy in organizational decision-making. Issues such as algorithmic bias, lack of explainability, surveillance, and exclusion raise ethical questions about the appropriate boundaries of data use and automation. Public backlash, reputational damage, and loss of stakeholder trust may arise when firms deploy AI systems perceived as opaque or unjust, even if they are technically effective. Consequently, ethical AI principles of fairness, accountability, transparency, and human oversight are increasingly viewed as risk management tools rather than purely normative ideals.

12.3.1.4 Cybersecurity and Systemic Risk

As AI and BA systems become more interconnected and embedded within organizational infrastructure, they increase the attack surface for cyber threats. Adversarial attacks, data poisoning, and model manipulation are emerging threats that can compromise AI-driven analytics outputs and operations. A breach in one system can cascade across an entire ecosystem, leading to systemic failures.

12.3.1.5 Governance and Compliance Risk

The fast pace of AI-BA development has outstripped many existing governance frameworks. Businesses face risks from unclear regulatory environments, lack of internal controls over AI and BA applications, and insufficient regulatory oversight. Without robust AI governance, firms may struggle to demonstrate transparency, accountability, and alignment with ethical standards.

12.3.1.6 Operational and Strategic Risk

Overreliance on AI-driven analytics can lead to automation bias, where human judgment is undervalued or ignored.[12] Additionally, deploying AI tools without proper alignment with business strategy, employee training, or change management can result in failed implementations or unintended strategic shifts. There are strategic and competitive risks associated with AI and BA investments as large-scale analytics initiatives require substantial financial, human, and organizational resources, and returns are uncertain. Organizations may overinvest in advanced AI-driven analytics without a clear value proposition, underestimate implementation complexity, or fail to develop complementary capabilities such as data governance and talent management. In fast-moving environments, AI and BA models can quickly be imitated or rendered obsolete, limiting sustainable competitive advantage.

12.3.2 Managing AI and Business Analytics Risks

As discussed in the previous section, AI and BA risks are multidimensional and interrelated, and thus effective risk management requires a holistic approach that combines robust data governance, model validation and monitoring, ethical oversight, organizational alignment, and strategic discipline. Organizations that acknowledge and address these risks systematically are better positioned to harness AI and BA responsibly while safeguarding decision quality, compliance, and long-term value creation. As AI and BA become deeply embedded in organizational decision-making, mitigating their associated risks has become a strategic and governance imperative rather than a purely technical concern. Effective risk mitigation requires an integrated approach that spans data governance, model design and monitoring, organizational processes, ethical oversight, and regulatory compliance. Organizations that proactively address these dimensions are better positioned to realize the benefits of AI-enabled analytics while safeguarding decision quality, stakeholder trust, and long-term value creation.

Effectively assessing and managing these multiple risks is essential for ensuring that AI and BA technologies enable businesses to achieve financial viability and have social and environmental impacts. Integrating and balancing innovation with responsibility enables businesses to build public trust and encourages the responsible adoption of AI and BA. AI and BA risks must be assessed and managed to ensure intelligent decision outcomes. To manage these risks effectively, organizations should:[13]

- Implement robust data governance and ensure ethical data sourcing. Since analytics outcomes depend critically on input data, organizations must establish clear standards for data accuracy, completeness, consistency, and timeliness across the data lifecycle. This includes formal data ownership, metadata management, audit trails, and continuous data quality monitoring.

- Perform regular model audits, stress testing, and explainability analysis. AI and BA models should be treated as dynamic assets that require validation, documentation, and ongoing supervision. Best practices include separating model development from independent validation, stress-testing models under alternative scenarios, and benchmarking performance against simpler or interpretable baselines. Piloting models, scaling incrementally, and learning from failures enable organizations to adapt to governance and technical controls as technologies and regulations evolve. Overall, risk mitigation is not a one-time compliance exercise but also an ongoing capability that co-evolves with AI maturity.
- Develop AI ethics frameworks with principles of fairness, accountability, and transparency. To address bias and representativeness risks, organizations should evaluate training data for historical distortions and systematically test models across demographic and contextual subgroups. Privacy-preserving techniques such as data minimization, anonymization, and secure access controls are also essential to reduce legal and reputational exposure associated with sensitive data use.
- Establish cybersecurity protocols tailored to AI vulnerabilities. Mitigating AI and BA risk demands a holistic, enterprise-wide approach that integrates technical safeguards, human judgment, ethical principles, and strategic governance. Organizations that successfully institutionalize these practices can harness AI-driven analytics responsibly while protecting decision integrity, regulatory compliance, and long-term organizational resilience.
- Strengthening AI governance structures, including oversight committees and impact assessments. Continuous monitoring for model drift, both data drift and concept drift, is particularly important in volatile environments, as declining model performance can otherwise go unnoticed. Where possible, incorporating XAI techniques helps decision-makers understand drivers of predictions, facilitating error detection, accountability, and regulatory compliance. Many organizations establish cross-functional AI ethics boards or review panels to assess high-impact use cases, evaluate trade-offs, and oversee compliance with internal standards and external regulations. Organizations can reduce reputational risk and enhance stakeholder legitimacy, particularly in sensitive domains such as finance, healthcare, and human resources, by proactively addressing ethical concerns.
- Promote human–AI collaboration, ensuring that humans remain in the loop for critical decisions. Human oversight and organizational alignment are essential in mitigating analytics risk. Rather than fully automating high-stakes decisions, organizations increasingly adopt a human-in-the-loop or human-on-the-loop approach, in which AI systems provide recommendations while humans retain final authority and responsibility.

12.4 Transformative Role of AI and BA in Business

This section presents the transformative role of AI and BA tools and techniques in various sectors, including marketing, retail, finance, healthcare, manufacturing, and banking, among others. Theoretically, AI-powered and BA-driven tools are reshaping how organizations sense opportunities, make decisions, and execute operations across industries by converting large, heterogeneous data (transactions, text, images, sensor streams) into predictions and prescriptive actions. At the core of this transformation is a "data-to-decision" stack that typically combines (1) descriptive analytics and visualization to understand performance, (2) predictive modeling (ML and DL) to forecast outcomes, and (3) prescriptive analytics (optimization, simulation, and reinforcement learning) to recommend actions under constraints.[14] Recent advances in DL and foundation-model architectures, especially transformer-based NLP, have expanded BA from structured data analysis to scalable understanding and generation of unstructured language, enabling automated extraction of insights from customer conversations, clinical notes, and regulatory documents.

12.4.1 Application in Marketing

In marketing, AI and BA platforms enable granular customer understanding and real-time personalization. Modern marketing analytics blends experimentation tests, uplift modeling, and causal inference with predictive models for churn, next-best-offer, CLV, and attribution. As digital channels multiply, organizations increasingly rely on algorithmic targeting and measurement systems to allocate spending efficiently, while recommender systems tailor content and product suggestions at scale.[15] This shift moves marketing from broad segmentation to dynamic, individual-level decision-making, where models continuously learn from behavioral data and update campaigns in near real time. Marketing has been fundamentally reshaped through the integration of AI-powered and BA-assisted systems that shift the marketing function from intuition-driven decision-making toward data-driven, predictive, and prescriptive marketing. Furthermore, advances in digital platforms, customer data availability, and computational power have enabled marketers to analyze large volumes of structured and unstructured data ranging from transaction histories and clickstreams to social media text and images and translate them into actionable insights. Consequently, *t* AI-powered and BA-assisted marketing now plays a central role in customer acquisition, engagement, retention, and value creation. In recent years, the application of BA in marketing has become increasingly significant as organizations strive to derive actionable insights from vast data sources. BA employs analytical tools and techniques that enable informed decision-making, improve strategic planning, and enhance marketing performance across various channels.

12.4.1.1 Enhancing Customer Engagement and Relationship Management

BA strengthens customer engagement by providing deeper insights into consumer behavior. Through data analysis, organizations can identify trends, preferences, and purchasing patterns that guide personalized marketing strategies. Customer segmentation, based on these insights, allows marketers to deliver targeted campaigns that resonate with specific audiences. This data-driven approach enhances customer experiences, increases conversion rates, and fosters long-term loyalty. Applications of AI in marketing, along with customer analytics, enable organizations to engage in segmentation, targeting, and personalization. ML algorithms enable micro-segmentation by identifying fine-grained customer groups based on behavioral, contextual, and psychographic data. Compared with traditional rule-based segmentation, AI-driven approaches improve targeting precision and campaign effectiveness.[16] Predictive models of CLV, churn, and purchase propensity allow firms to allocate marketing resources more efficiently and tailor offers to customers with the highest long-term value potential.

12.4.1.2 Optimizing Marketing Investments

Analytics enables organizations to evaluate the effectiveness of marketing initiatives by linking expenditures to measurable outcomes such as sales growth or Return on Investment (ROI). By continuously analyzing performance metrics, marketers can allocate budgets more efficiently and refine campaigns for greater impact. Insights into CLV and campaign performance ensure that marketing resources are invested in strategies that generate the highest returns. AI-powered and BA-assisted marketing systems support automation and optimization across the marketing funnel as predictive models guide decisions on channel selection, timing, message design, and budget allocation, whereas reinforcement learning and experimentation frameworks continuously refine campaigns based on observed outcomes. From a BA perspective, these systems represent a shift toward closed-loop marketing, where insights, actions, and performance feedback are tightly integrated. These AI analytics in decision support and marketing science improve consistency, scalability, and return on marketing investment.[17]

12.4.1.3 Supporting Market Research and Demand Forecasting

AI-powered marketing transforms the role of marketers from campaign executors to orchestrators of customer experience by encouraging management to emphasize value creation that depends on coordinating interactions across channels and touchpoints over time rather than optimizing isolated transactions.[18] Organizations that successfully deploy AI and BA in marketing typically complement advanced technology with a strong analytics culture, cross-functional integration, and managerial judgment. Without these organizational capabilities, the potential benefits of AI-driven marketing remain underrealized. BA also plays a critical role in understanding market dynamics and predicting consumer demand. Using historical data and predictive modeling, organizations can forecast trends and anticipate shifts in customer preferences. This forward-looking approach allows for timely strategy adjustments, giving firms a competitive advantage in fast-changing markets. Additionally, analytics supports the identification of emerging opportunities, helping businesses respond swiftly to evolving consumer needs.

12.4.1.4 Strengthening Digital Marketing through Web Analytics

The rise of digital transformation has elevated the importance of web analytics within marketing strategies. Organizations gain valuable insights into digital customer behavior by analyzing online traffic, user interactions, and conversion patterns. These insights help refine content strategies, enhance engagement, and ensure that digital marketing efforts align with customer expectations and market trends. AI and BA systems are deeply embedded in digital marketing and social media analytics, where real-time data streams and unstructured content dominate. NLP and sentiment analysis extract insights from online reviews, social media posts, and customer feedback, enabling marketers to monitor brand perception and respond rapidly to emerging issues. Image and video analytics further support brand analysis and advertising effectiveness measurement. Thus, the integration of social media analytics into marketing strategy enhances market sensing and improves campaign agility in fast-moving digital environments.[19]

12.4.1.5 Personalization and Recommendation Systems

Personalization is further enhanced through recommender systems that dynamically adjust content, product suggestions, and pricing. AI-powered and BA-assisted personalization can significantly increase customer engagement and conversion rates when aligned with customer expectations and perceived value.[20] However, excessive personalization may trigger privacy concerns or perceptions of manipulation, underscoring the importance of responsible data use. Personalization has become the hallmark of modern digital marketing. Recommendation engines, using collaborative filtering or DL architectures, deliver individualized product or content suggestions in real time. Companies such as Amazon, Spotify, and Netflix exemplify how AI-based personalization enhances engagement and loyalty. Beyond e-commerce, dynamic personalization extends to email marketing, website interfaces, and advertising copy. AI platforms analyze behavioral signals, click paths, dwell time, and contextual intent to generate messages uniquely tailored to each user. This "segment of one" approach maximizes relevance and conversion rates while reinforcing brand attachment.

12.4.1.6 Content Creation and Generative AI

Generative AI technologies, including LLMs and diffusion models, have introduced a new frontier in content marketing. Tools like ChatGPT, Jasper, and DALL-E can generate product descriptions, advertisements, blog articles, social posts, and even visuals aligned with brand identity. While generative AI accelerates production, it also allows creative augmentation—helping marketers ideate, refine tone, and localize content across markets. When used responsibly, these systems increase efficiency while maintaining creativity and consistency.

12.4.1.7 Conversational Marketing and Chatbots

AI-powered chatbots and voice assistants facilitate instant, personalized communication across platforms. NLP enables these systems to understand intent, manage context, and deliver relevant responses. For instance, an AI chatbot on a retail website can recommend products, process payments, or handle post-purchase support, effectively functioning as a 24/7 digital salesperson. Voice interfaces like Alexa or Google Assistant extend conversational marketing to the auditory domain, creating seamless omnichannel experiences.

12.4.1.8 Sentiment and Social Listening

AI enhances social listening by mining public conversations across social media, reviews, and forums. Sentiment analysis algorithms classify emotions (positive, neutral, negative) and detect emerging trends or crises in real time. Marketers use these insights to gauge brand health, refine messaging, and adjust campaign tone. By combining sentiment data with predictive analytics, organizations can forecast the impact of communication strategies or detect potential reputational risks before escalation.

12.4.1.9 Ethical, Privacy, and Governance Considerations

AI-powered and BA-assisted marketing represents a paradigm shift toward intelligent, adaptive, and customer-centric marketing. Organizations can enhance marketing effectiveness and deepen customer relationships by leveraging predictive analytics, automation, and personalization. However, realizing these benefits requires more than advanced algorithms that demand robust data governance, ethical safeguards, and strategic alignment between analytics capabilities and marketing objectives. The growing reliance on AI in marketing raises important ethical and governance issues. Data privacy, consent, algorithmic bias, and transparency are central concerns, particularly as personalization and targeting become more sophisticated and as customers are more willing to share data and accept AI-driven personalization.[21] As a result, ethical AI principles and regulatory compliance are not peripheral constraints but essential enablers of sustainable, analytics-driven marketing.

12.4.2 Application in Retail

In retail, AI-powered and BA-driven tools drive demand forecasting, inventory optimization, pricing, and frictionless customer experiences. Predictive analytics improves replenishment and reduces stockouts, while prescriptive methods (e.g., mixed-integer optimization) recommend assortment and allocation decisions across stores and channels. Computer vision supports shelf monitoring and automated checkout, and recommender systems enhance cross-selling and basket expansion.[22] These technologies transform the retail industry in making better forecasts and integrating forecasts into operational decisions by linking demand signals to ordering, logistics, and promotions so the system "acts" on analytics rather than merely reporting it.

12.4.2.1 Customer Relationship Management

CRM has evolved far beyond traditional databases and contact-tracking systems into an intelligence-driven ecosystem that integrates AI and BA to drive strategic, data-driven customer engagement. The synergy between AI and BA allows organizations to understand customer behavior, anticipate needs, personalize experiences, and optimize decision-making across the customer lifecycle. In today's digital economy, where interactions span multiple platforms and generate massive data volumes, AI-powered and BA-assisted CRM systems serve as a cornerstone for sustainable competitive advantage by empowering organizations to sense customer needs, predict behaviors, personalize interactions, and optimize relationship value at scale. This shift reflects broader digital transformation trends in which data is generated through omnichannel interactions, digital platforms, and connected products is continuously converted into actionable customer insight.

12.4.2.2 Data Insights and Customer Understanding

AI-powered CRM systems rely on a portfolio of analytics techniques. Predictive analytics models forecast customer behaviors such as churn, purchase propensity, cross-selling opportunities, and CLV. BA allows organizations to analyze customer data to better understand needs and expectations. Insights from interactions and feedback enable firms to personalize products and marketing strategies, leading to improved satisfaction, loyalty, and retention. Overall, ML models can significantly outperform traditional statistical methods in predicting customer retention and profitability when rich behavioral data are available.[23]

12.4.2.3 Measuring and Improving CRM Performance

Analytics supports the evaluation of CRM initiatives through performance metrics such as satisfaction scores and conversion rates. Predictive models help anticipate customer behaviors, allowing proactive engagement that enhances experiences and prevents issues before they arise. Customer segmentation has similarly advanced from rule-based clustering to AI-driven micro-segmentation using unsupervised learning, enabling more granular and dynamic targeting strategies.[24]

12.4.2.4 Boosting Efficiency through Automation and Virtual Agents

Integrating analytics into CRM also drives operational efficiency. Automated data processes reduce routine work, allowing staff to focus on high-value activities. This improves productivity, lowers costs, and strengthens customer trust through faster and more reliable service. AI-driven chatbots and virtual agents streamline customer support, handle routine inquiries, and free human agents to focus on complex or value-added interactions. Reinforcement learning allows these bots to improve over time as they encounter new scenarios, leading to continuously enhanced service quality.

12.4.2.5 Data Mining for Strategic Advantage

Advanced data mining reveals hidden trends and customer patterns that guide strategic decisions in marketing, product development, and service delivery. These insights help organizations stay agile and responsive in competitive markets. AI-powered CRM presents a strategic advantage by embedding predictive and prescriptive intelligence directly into customer-facing and managerial processes, allowing organizations to move from descriptive insights ("what happened") to predictive ("what will happen") and prescriptive ("what should we do") actions.

12.4.2.6 Natural Language Processing (NLP) and Sentiment Analysis

NLP and sentiment analysis play a pivotal role in CRM by extracting insight from unstructured data such as emails, call-center transcripts, online reviews, and social media posts. These techniques enable organizations to monitor customer sentiment in real time, identify service failures, and tailor responses across channels. Collectively, NLP-driven CRM enables organizations to integrate structured and unstructured data, enhance understanding of customer experience, and manage relationships proactively.[25] NLP algorithms enable the system to interpret text and speech, extracting sentiment and meaning from customer communications. CRM systems can detect dissatisfaction early, trigger escalation workflows, or personalize responses that align with the customer's emotional state by analyzing tone and context.

12.4.2.7 Image and Voice Recognition

In industries such as retail and telecommunications, AI can interpret customer emotions through facial recognition or voice tone analysis. This data can inform customers of satisfaction metrics, enabling real-time intervention in service delivery or complaint resolution. The use of AI and BA in CRM enables organizations to integrate intelligent automation, including chatbots, virtual assistants, and recommendation engines. AI-driven conversational agents handle routine service requests, reduce response times, and free human agents to focus on complex or high-empathy interactions. Such integration improves engagement and conversion when aligned with customer expectations and privacy norms.[26]

12.4.2.8 Enhancing Customer Experience through Personalization

Historically, marketing evolved from mass communication—broadcasting uniform messages to undifferentiated audiences—to segmented marketing, where demographic and behavioral data enabled targeted campaigns. The next stage, made possible by AI and BA, is hyper-personalization, in which each interaction is informed by real-time analytics, predictive modeling, and contextual awareness. This evolution parallels advances in data infrastructure and computing power. Cloud-based Customer Data Platforms (CDPs) consolidate structured and unstructured data from sales, service, social, and sensor sources, while AI algorithms process this data instantaneously to determine what content, product, or action best suits each customer. AI technologies enable predictive, prescriptive, and adaptive personalization by continuously learning from customer interactions and feedback.

12.4.2.9 Challenges, Ethics, and Governance

AI-powered and BA-assisted CRM represents a paradigm shift from relationship management as recordkeeping to relationship management as continuous, analytics-driven value creation. Organizations can deepen customer relationships and improve performance by embedding predictive insight, automation, and personalization into CRM processes. However, realizing this potential requires advanced analytics and strong governance, ethical safeguards, and organizational alignment between technology, strategy, and customer-centric culture. Despite its benefits, AI-powered CRM raises important challenges. Data quality, system integration across silos, and model interpretability remain persistent concerns. From an ethical and governance perspective, issues of customer privacy, algorithmic bias, transparency, and trust are central. Ultimately, excessive automation or opaque personalization can erode customer trust if customers perceive CRM systems as intrusive or unfair. As a result, responsible AI practices of clear consent mechanisms, explainable models, and human oversight are critical components of sustainable CRM strategies.

12.4.3 Application in Finance and Banking

In finance and banking, AI-powered and BA-driven platforms have become central to credit-risk assessment, fraud detection, anti–money laundering (AML), trading, and customer service. Credit scoring and default prediction increasingly use high-dimensional behavioral and transactional features, improving risk discrimination and pricing.[27] Fraud detection systems combine anomaly detection, graph analytics, and supervised learning to identify rare, evolving patterns across large payment networks.[28] Meanwhile, NLP supports compliance by extracting obligations and risks from policies and regulations, and conversational AI scales service delivery through intelligent virtual agents. Finance plays a critical role in the economy and is highly regulated. Model governance and thereby validation, explainability, drift monitoring, and fairness have become as important as raw predictive power, pushing banks to institutionalize "responsible analytics" as a capability rather than a one-off control.[29]

In retail and commercial banking, AI-based credit underwriting and early-warning systems improve risk differentiation by capturing nonlinear patterns, interactions, and high-dimensional signals that traditional scorecards can miss. For example, ML credit-risk models that combine bureau variables with granular transaction data can materially improve delinquency/default prediction by exploiting behavioral indicators embedded in cash flows and spending patterns.[30] More broadly, benchmarking evidence from credit scoring shows that ensembles and modern classifiers often outperform older baselines, particularly when model selection and validation are done rigorously across multiple datasets and evaluation metrics.[31]

Advanced technologies form the backbone of modern financial data ecosystems. Big data analytics, AI, and blockchain have become integral tools that enhance the speed, accuracy, and reliability of financial insights. AI and ML enable predictive analytics by uncovering patterns in massive datasets and supporting data-driven decision-making. Blockchain contributes by ensuring the integrity and security of financial records, providing tamper-proof systems that reinforce trust within transactional processes. The integration of these technologies allows financial institutions to operate with both efficiency and confidence in increasingly complex markets. The effectiveness of a financial data ecosystem also depends on the collaboration among diverse stakeholders. Financial institutions, regulators, technology providers, and data aggregators must work together to ensure that data flows are seamless, reliable, and actionable. FinTech firms exemplify this collaborative spirit by developing solutions that bridge traditional banking practices with emerging market needs, such as microfinance and digital lending platforms. Such collaboration fosters innovation, expands market reach, and strengthens the resilience of the financial ecosystem.

Data ecosystems empower dynamic decision-making processes by providing timely, actionable insights. Real-time analytics enable organizations to detect anomalies, such as fraudulent activity, or assess credit risk based on behavioral patterns. Sophisticated modeling and algorithmic tools transform raw data into strategic intelligence, allowing decision-makers to respond quickly to market changes. This agility ensures that financial institutions can remain competitive while mitigating risks in volatile environments. Sustainability and resilience are critical considerations for financial data ecosystems. Markets are subject to economic downturns, regulatory shifts, and global crises, and an effective ecosystem must adapt to these challenges without compromising operational efficiency. Continuous innovation and strategic data management support the long-term stability of these systems, ensuring that institutions can navigate uncertainty while continuing to deliver meaningful insights.

12.4.4 Application in Healthcare

In healthcare, AI and BA technologies enable organizations to shift from reactive care to proactive, evidence-driven interventions by leveraging electronic health records (EHRs), imaging, and wearable data. DL models have demonstrated strong performance in image-based diagnostics (e.g., dermatology) and in learning risk representations from EHR data for predicting hospitalization, complications, and readmissions.[32] At the system level, analytics supports capacity planning, clinical pathway optimization, and population health management. Yet healthcare also highlights the limits of "accuracy-only" thinking: models must generalize across sites, avoid bias, preserve privacy, and integrate into clinical workflows to improve outcomes by emphasizing the sociotechnical nature of AI transformation.[33]

Rising costs, aging populations, chronic disease prevalence, and data complexity have encouraged healthcare organizations worldwide to be more cost efficient and performance effective by moving beyond descriptive reporting toward predictive, prescriptive, and intelligence-driven decision-making. In recent years, healthcare systems have undergone a profound transformation driven by AI and BA. AI-powered and BA-assisted healthcare integrates clinical, operational, and patient-generated data to improve care quality, efficiency, and outcomes while supporting more personalized and value-based care delivery. BA is playing an increasingly vital role in the healthcare sector by improving operational efficiency, enhancing patient outcomes, and supporting long-term sustainability. Through data-driven insights, healthcare organizations can analyze vast amounts of clinical and operational data to make more informed decisions, optimize resources, and improve the quality of care.

Healthcare has long been data intensive, with EHRs, medical imaging, genomics, wearable devices, and administrative systems generating massive volumes of structured and unstructured data. Traditional analytics focused on retrospective performance measurement and utilization review. However, the real value of healthcare data emerges when advanced analytics and AI are embedded directly into clinical and operational workflows, enabling timely and actionable insights.[34] AI extends BA by automating pattern recognition in complex, high-dimensional datasets and continuously learning as new data becomes available. AI has emerged as one of the most transformative technologies in modern healthcare and sustainability efforts. Its ability to process massive datasets, detect patterns, and generate predictive insights is reshaping how societies approach medical diagnostics, disease prevention, environmental health, and resource efficiency. In healthcare, AI bridges the gap between clinical data and actionable intelligence—supporting physicians, administrators, and patients in making faster and more accurate decisions. AI's predictive, analytical, and automation capacities position it as a cornerstone of future-ready systems that are both medically effective and environmentally responsible, as explained in the following subsections.

12.4.4.1 Enhancing Operational Efficiency

A key application of BA in healthcare lies in optimizing workflows and resource utilization. By analyzing data on patient admissions, staffing levels, and inventory use, healthcare institutions can predict peak demand periods and allocate resources more effectively. This reduces waiting times, minimizes operational bottlenecks, and enhances service delivery. The result is improved patient satisfaction and more sustainable healthcare operations through better cost control and reduced waste. Beyond clinical applications, AI streamlines hospital operations. NLP automates medical transcription, while robotic process automation (RPA) handles billing, scheduling, and claims management. These efficiencies free medical staff from repetitive administrative tasks, enabling greater focus on patient care. Moreover, AI chatbots assist patients with appointment scheduling, follow-up reminders, and preliminary symptom triage, enhancing accessibility and reducing healthcare system bottlenecks.

12.4.4.2 Improving Patient Outcomes through Predictive Analytics

AI and BA are increasingly used to enhance patient engagement and experience, aligning healthcare with service-oriented perspectives. Chatbots, virtual health assistants, and remote monitoring systems provide continuous support, improve access to care, and encourage adherence to treatment plans. Ultimately, AI-enabled healthcare services can improve responsiveness and personalization when designed around patient needs and trust. Wearables and mobile health applications further expand the data ecosystem, enabling real-time analytics and preventive care interventions. Predictive analytics enables healthcare providers to forecast patient outcomes and disease trends based on historical and demographic data. These insights allow clinicians to identify at-risk patients early and design preventive interventions that reduce hospital readmissions and improve overall health outcomes. By integrating predictive models into patient care, healthcare organizations shift from reactive to proactive treatment approaches, enhancing both efficiency and quality of care. Wearable devices and IoT health sensors further expand the predictive ecosystem by continuously monitoring vital signs—heart rate, sleep cycles, oxygen levels—and transmitting data to AI platforms that alert healthcare providers to abnormalities in real time. This shift from reactive to proactive care represents one of AI's most profound contributions to public health.

12.4.4.3 Optimizing Clinical Decisions with Electronic Health Records

One of the most significant applications of AI in healthcare is clinical decision support (CDS). ML and DL models are increasingly used for disease detection, diagnosis, and risk stratification across domains such as radiology, pathology, cardiology, and oncology. For example, AI-driven image analysis has demonstrated performance comparable to human experts in detecting abnormalities in medical imaging by supporting earlier and more accurate diagnoses. Predictive analytics models also identify patients at high risk of readmission, deterioration, or adverse events, enabling proactive interventions and improved care coordination. The integration of BA with EHR systems allows healthcare organizations to uncover valuable insights from clinical data. Analytics helps identify variations in treatment effectiveness, supports evidence-based clinical decisions, and improves adherence to best practices. By providing real-time access to accurate patient information, analytics-enhanced EHR systems strengthen patient safety and facilitate consistent, high-quality care delivery.

12.4.4.4 Strengthening Patient Engagement and Personalized Care

AI-powered analytics are central to the advancement of personalized and precision medicine, which tailors treatment to individual patient characteristics, behaviors, and genetic profiles. AI models can support treatment selection, dosage optimization, and therapy response prediction by integrating clinical data with genomics and real-world evidence. BA also supports personalized care by analyzing patient feedback, satisfaction scores, and interaction data. Healthcare providers can use these insights to tailor communication and treatment plans to individual patient needs. This personalization enhances the patient's experience, fosters engagement, and encourages adherence to medical advice in improving long-term health outcomes.

12.4.4.5 Personalized and Precision Medicine

AI facilitates precision medicine by integrating genetic, clinical, and lifestyle data to tailor treatments to individual patients. ML algorithms analyze vast genomic datasets to identify how specific genetic variations influence drug response or disease progression. In oncology, AI models guide clinicians in selecting targeted therapies based on a patient's molecular profile, improving efficacy while reducing adverse effects. AI also supports drug discovery and development, drastically reducing the time and cost traditionally associated with pharmaceutical innovation. AI accelerates the identification of viable candidates for clinical trials by simulating molecular interactions and predicting compound efficacy. AI and BA are increasingly used to enhance patient engagement and experience by aligning healthcare with service-oriented perspectives. Chatbots, virtual health assistants, and remote monitoring systems provide continuous support, improve access to care, and encourage adherence to treatment plans. Wearables and mobile health applications further expand the data ecosystem, enabling real-time analytics and preventive care interventions.

12.4.4.6 Ethical, Regulatory, and Governance Considerations

AI-powered and BA-assisted healthcare represents a paradigm shift from volume-based, reactive care to intelligent, predictive, and patient-centered healthcare systems. Healthcare organizations can improve outcomes, enhance efficiency, and support personalized care on a scale by embedding advanced analytics into clinical, operational, and service processes. However, realizing these benefits requires technological capability and strong governance, ethical safeguards, and close integration between analytics, clinicians, and healthcare leaders. Despite its promise, AI-powered healthcare raises significant ethical, legal, and governance challenges. Issues of data privacy, cybersecurity, algorithmic bias, transparency, and explainability are especially critical given the sensitivity of health data and the consequences of clinical errors. Responsible AI governance frameworks are therefore integral to sustainable adoption of AI and BA in healthcare.

12.4.5 Application in Manufacturing

In manufacturing, AI and BA technologies accelerate Industry 4.0 by enabling PdM, quality inspection, yield optimization, and adaptive process control. ML on sensor data forecasts equipment failures and schedules maintenance to reduce downtime, while computer vision automates defect detection on production lines.[35] Digital twin concepts of virtual representations of physical assets and processes support simulation-based optimization, allowing firms to test scenarios and improve throughput, energy use, and reliability before implementing changes in the real system.[36] As manufacturing becomes more connected, analytics also improves supply chain resilience through demand-supply synchronization, risk sensing, and multi-echelon inventory optimization.

Supply chain optimization uses mathematical programming and operations research (OR) to design and run manufacturing networks (facility location, capacity planning, production planning, transportation, and inventory control). Practically, strategic and tactical supply chain planning problems are naturally formulated as optimization models subject to capacity, lead-time, and service constraints, with objective functions that trade off cost, responsiveness, and robustness.[37] AI-powered and BA-driven systems can increasingly augment these OR models in demand forecasting and dynamic decision-making under uncertainty. Furthermore, ML and DL are now widely applied to supply chain tasks such as demand estimation, supplier selection, production and inventory control, and transport planning, largely because they can learn nonlinear patterns from large, noisy datasets.

AI-driven supply chain management involves using ML and BA technologies to enhance efficiency, predict disruptions, and optimize logistics by[38] (1) using AI and BA technologies to forecast demand for product and services through analyzing historical data, market trends, and external factors (e.g., weather, economic conditions) to improve demand predictions; (2) enabling effective inventory management by using smart inventory systems to minimize stockouts and overstock by adjusting orders in real time based on demand forecasts; (3) conducting supply risk assessments and management by considering geopolitical issues, financial stability, and past disruptions; (4) analyzing transportation route optimization and logistics by selecting the most cost-effective and timely transportation routes, considering traffic, fuel costs, and carrier reliability; and (5) using automation and robotics to streamline warehouse management and fulfillment centers, reducing human errors and inefficiencies.

12.4.6 Application in Human Resources (HR)

Human Resources (HR) and talent management have undergone a fundamental transformation as organizations increasingly rely on AI and BA to manage workforce planning, talent acquisition, development, and retention. Traditionally viewed as an administrative function, HR is now a strategic partner that leverages data-driven insights to enhance human capital outcomes, align workforce capabilities with organizational strategy, and create sustainable competitive advantage. AI-powered and BA-assisted HR systems enable evidence-based decision-making across the employee lifecycle, from recruitment to performance management and succession planning. AI is transforming nearly every domain of organizational management, and HR is no exception. Traditionally associated with administrative processes such as payroll, recruitment, and recordkeeping, HR has evolved into a strategic partner focused on workforce analytics, employee engagement, and organizational agility. Within this evolution, AI has become a pivotal enabler, enhancing how organizations attract, select, develop, and retain talent. AI's integration into HR and Talent Management leverages large volumes of employee data and advanced analytics to automate processes, reduce bias, and improve decision-making. From resume screening and predictive turnover modeling to performance analytics and career-pathing, AI applications extend throughout the employee lifecycle. The convergence of AI and human capital management systems (HCMS) has given rise to "intelligent HR ecosystems" that enable continuous learning, adaptive workforce planning, and data-driven strategic alignment.

Early HR information systems focused on recordkeeping and compliance reporting. Over time, the emergence of HR analytics provides the opportunity for the systematic analysis of workforce data to inform managerial decisions, shifting HR toward a more strategic role. In recent years, analytics-driven HR has improved organizational performance by linking human capital metrics (skills, engagement, turnover) to business outcomes (productivity, innovation, financial performance).[39] AI-driven models further extend HR analytics by automating pattern recognition, enabling prediction, and supporting prescriptive actions in many ways, as described in the following subsections.

12.4.6.1 Enhancing Performance Management

In performance management, AI-enabled analytics establish performance metrics and integrate performance evaluations, goal attainment, collaboration data, and learning outcomes to provide more continuous and objective feedback. Learning and development (L&D) functions often use recommender systems to personalize training pathways, matching employees with courses and experiences that align with their roles, aspirations, and skill gaps. This personalization improves learning effectiveness and supports long-term talent development.[40] BA strengthens performance appraisal systems by combining quantitative metrics with qualitative insights. This data-driven approach promotes objectivity and alignment between individual and organizational goals. Through analytics-based performance frameworks, HR professionals can identify high performers, support underperforming employees, and cultivate a culture of accountability and continuous improvement.

12.4.6.2 Predicting and Reducing Employee Turnover

Analytics plays a vital role in understanding and mitigating employee attrition. Predictive models can reveal patterns and risk factors associated with turnover, allowing HR departments to design targeted retention strategies such as engagement programs, career development paths, and improved workplace policies. Anticipating turnover through data insights helps minimize its negative impact on productivity and morale.

12.4.6.3 Optimizing Recruitment and Talent Acquisition

One of the most advanced applications of AI in HR is talent acquisition. ML models are widely used to screen résumés, rank candidates, and predict job performance and retention probabilities. These systems analyze structured data (education, experience, skills) and unstructured data (résumé text, video interviews) to improve hiring efficiency and quality. AI automates candidate sourcing, screening, and ranking through NLP and ML algorithms. Systems such as LinkedIn Recruiter or HireVue analyze resumes, social profiles, and video interviews to assess both technical and soft skills. Chatbots handle initial communication, answer candidate questions, and schedule interviews—reducing administrative workload for recruiters. Beyond efficiency, AI enhances the quality of hire through predictive analytics. Models trained on past hiring success can identify characteristics correlated with long-term performance or cultural fit. However, responsible implementation is critical to prevent perpetuating bias—models must be regularly audited to ensure fairness and compliance with equal employment opportunity standards. BA-assisted systems enable organizations to refine their recruitment strategies by analyzing historical hiring data and performance outcomes. This analytical approach helps identify candidates who fit both job requirements and organizational culture, leading to stronger hires, higher retention, and better overall team performance. AI-powered and BA-assisted predictive models can outperform traditional selection methods when trained on high-quality historical hiring and performance data.[41] Furthermore, NLP enables automated parsing of résumés and job descriptions, improving skill matching and reducing time-to-hire.

12.4.6.4 Onboarding and Training

AI-powered onboarding platforms personalize the experience for each new hire. Intelligent assistants guide employees through compliance modules, introduce team members, and tailor learning paths based on the individual's background. In training and development, adaptive learning systems use reinforcement learning and behavioral data to adjust course difficulty and content in real time. Learning management systems (LMS) such as Coursera for Business or Degreed integrate AI to recommend courses aligned with career goals, performance gaps, and industry trends. This ensures that professional development is continuous, personalized, and aligned with organizational needs. However, AI-based recruitment tools must be carefully designed to avoid reinforcing historical biases embedded in training data. Consequently, fairness-aware algorithms, transparency, and human oversight are increasingly emphasized as essential governance mechanisms in AI-assisted hiring.

12.4.6.5 Performance Management

Traditional annual reviews are increasingly being replaced by data-driven continuous performance management systems. AI analyzes project data, communication patterns, and feedback to provide real-time performance insights. Sentiment analysis applied to peer feedback or collaboration tools can identify engagement trends and leadership potential. Moreover,

AI-assisted evaluation reduces subjectivity in performance ratings. By correlating employee outcomes with objective key performance indicators (KPIs), AI systems help managers make evidence-based appraisal decisions, supporting meritocracy and fairness.

12.4.6.6 Measuring Employee Engagement and Satisfaction

BA supports the continuous monitoring of employee engagement through surveys and feedback analysis. Insights from these data sources guide HR in adjusting policies, enhancing workplace culture, and proactively addressing issues that could affect morale or productivity. A data-informed approach allows organizations to sustain a positive and motivating work environment. AI and BA are essential in managing employee engagement and well-being. Sentiment analysis of employee surveys, internal communications, and feedback platforms allows organizations to detect morale issues and cultural risks in near real time as engaged employees are less likely to leave and more likely to contribute discretionary effort, making engagement analytics a key lever in retention strategies. When combined with predictive turnover models, engagement insights enable HR leaders to design targeted retention initiatives and improve workforce stability.

12.4.6.7 Workforce Planning and Talent Analytics

AI-powered BA supports workforce planning by forecasting labor demand, identifying skill gaps, and optimizing workforce composition under different strategic scenarios. Predictive analytics helps organizations anticipate turnover, absenteeism, and internal mobility by enabling proactive interventions. In recent years, predictive models of employee turnover have significantly enhanced retention strategies when combined with targeted HR policies.[42] AI extends HR's role to strategic workforce forecasting. Predictive models project future skill needs, assess internal talent pipelines, and simulate the impact of business changes on staffing levels. These insights support evidence-based decisions about hiring, reskilling, or redeployment. In a global context, AI can integrate labor market data, industry trends, and macroeconomic indicators to forecast talent availability and compensation benchmarks. As organizations face rapid technological disruption, such analytics ensure that workforce strategies remain adaptive and resilient.

12.4.6.8 Ethical, Legal, and Governance Considerations

AI-powered and BA-assisted HR and talent management represent a paradigm shift from intuition-driven practices to evidence-based, strategic workforce decision-making. Organizations can better leverage human capital as a source of sustainable value by embedding predictive and prescriptive analytics across recruitment, development, performance, and retention. However, realizing these benefits requires advanced analytics capabilities, ethical safeguards, transparent governance, and strong alignment between technology, people, and organizational strategy. Despite its promise, AI-assisted HR raises significant ethical and governance challenges, including data privacy, algorithmic bias, transparency, and compliance with employment law. Typically, HR decisions directly affect individuals' livelihoods, making explainability and fairness especially critical in HR analytics applications.[43] Responsible AI in HR therefore requires robust governance frameworks, clear accountability, continuous monitoring for bias and drift, and alignment with organizational values and regulatory expectations.

12.4.7 Application in Other Sectors

Across other sectors, including logistics, energy, and the public sector, the pattern is similar as AI and BA algorithms that translate data abundance into smarter decisions and automated execution. The most transformative impact emerges when organizations couple technical advances (NLP, vision, optimization) with operating-model changes: data governance, platform integration, human-in-the-loop design, and continuous monitoring for drift, bias, and security. In practice, AI and BA are less a single technology than a decision infrastructure, one that redefines how organizations compete, comply, and create value by embedding learning and optimization into everyday processes.

12.5 Predictive Maintenance

PdM is a data-driven approach used in many industries, including manufacturing, by utilizing condition-monitoring data, statistical modeling, and AI and BA platforms to anticipate equipment failures before they occur, enabling maintenance to be performed at the optimal time.[44] Unlike reactive maintenance (fix after failure) or preventive maintenance (service at fixed intervals), PdM aims to minimize unplanned downtime, reduce maintenance costs, extend asset life, and stabilize production performance by empowering organizations to monitor the real-time condition of machinery and schedule maintenance when needed by leveraging technologies such as the Internet of Things (IoT), ML, and advanced analytics. PdM is also a cornerstone of prognostics and health management (PHM), which assists in detecting degradation early, diagnosing likely failure modes, and estimating remaining useful life (RUL) so maintenance can be scheduled with minimal disruption. A PHM review highlights the evolution from reactive and scheduled maintenance to condition-based and predictive strategies supported by continuous monitoring data and prognostic models. In manufacturing, PdM typically relies on vibration, acoustic, temperature, current, and process signals. A highly cited systematic review of PdM using digital twins identifies key design considerations (data variety, model complexity, computational burden) and stresses that successful implementations integrate physics/engineering knowledge with data-driven learning and lifecycle governance.[45] A comprehensive review of the AI and BA applications in PdM indicates the growing importance of AI techniques such as ML, DL, and reinforcement learning used for enhancing PdM accuracy, autonomy, and cost-efficiency across industries by classifying AI-based PdM systems into six core components: sensors, data preprocessing, AI algorithms, decision-making modules, communication/integration, and user interfaces.[46] Thus, this section is devoted to PdM systems, their applications across many industries, their benefits and challenges as presented in the following subsections because of their broad implications.

12.5.1 AI-Powered Tools and BA-Assisted Techniques for Predictive Maintenance

PdM applies AI-powered and BA-driven tools and techniques to predict equipment failures before they occur that could reduce downtime and maintenance costs by (1) using sensors to collect real-time data on machine temperature, vibration, pressure, and operational efficiency; (2) analyzing historical failure patterns to predict when maintenance is required, preventing unexpected breakdowns; (3) reducing maintenance expenses by avoiding unnecessary preventive maintenance and minimizing costly downtime; (4) addressing minor issues before they escalate, thereby extending the lifespan of machinery; and

(5) continuously monitoring equipment performance and identifying deviations that may indicate early signs of failure. Both AI and BA capabilities should be integrated into manufacturing to enable real-time adjustments and predictive modeling, process data at the edge (closer to the manufacturing floor), reduce latency, and enable faster decision-making and utilize Enterprise Resource Planning (ERP) systems to improve coordination across procurement, production, and distribution.

12.6 Managing Bias, Fairness, and Transparency in AI and BA Applications

This section addresses bias, fairness, and transparency in AI and BA, which are essential for ensuring responsible AI and ethical BA implementations in businesses. As AI and BA become embedded in high-impact decisions, including credit underwriting, hiring, pricing, healthcare triage, and fraud detection, organizations must actively manage bias (systematic error and inequitable outcomes), fairness (normative criteria for equitable treatment), and transparency (the ability to understand, communicate, and audit how data and models produce outcomes). Bias can emerge at multiple points. For example, even if sensitive attributes (e.g., race, gender) are excluded, proxies (ZIP code, job history, school) can encode protected information and produce disparate outcomes as discrimination can arise without intent, via disparate impact mechanisms in data-driven decisioning.

12.6.1 Managing Bias

Managing bias recognizes the possibility of inherent biases in AI models and ensures the mitigation of such biases. For example, some algorithms favor certain groups, and biases in AI development teams can influence models. Diverse, representative datasets; regular audits; fairness-aware ML techniques; and diverse, interdisciplinary teams can assess, manage, and mitigate these biases. Ensuring fairness in using AI and BA platforms in decision-making requires defining fairness, aligning it with business goals, implementing it in predictive models to prevent discriminatory outcomes, and continuous monitoring of fairness through bias and fairness detection tools.

12.6.2 Fairness

Fairness is not a single metric as it reflects competing values and context-specific constraints. Common criteria include (1) demographic parity (equal positive decision rates across groups), (2) equalized odds/equal opportunity (equal error rates or equal true-positive rates across groups), and (3) calibration (predicted risks correspond to observed outcomes within each group). These criteria are often mathematically incompatible under realistic conditions, which require organizations to choose metrics aligned with the decision context and harm model.[47] Practically, this means fairness management should start with an explicit fairness objective statement (e.g., minimize false negatives for a protected class in safety screening) and a cost-of-errors analysis, not just metric reporting.

12.6.3 Transparency

Transparency in using AI-driven and BA-assisted models is crucial in ensuring AI and BA systems follow all applicable laws, rules, regulations, standards, and best practices. AI and BA decision-making processes are transparent to all stakeholders, including investors, regulators, employees, and customers, and they are free from biases. Transparency is essential for trust, governance, and effective oversight, especially when models are complex. The AI ethical considerations should be addressed to mitigate AI bias, ensure transparency and accountability, and gain trust and transparency that pose a threat at the organizational level and to society.[48] Managing bias, fairness, and transparency in AI and BA platforms is not a one-off debiasing exercise. It is a governance discipline that combines (1) clear normative choices about fairness goals, (2) rigorous measurement and mitigation across the lifecycle, and (3) transparency mechanisms that make systems auditable, explainable, and accountable.

12.7 AI and BA for Small and Medium Enterprises (SMEs)

Small and medium-sized enterprises (SMEs) are widely recognized as essential engines of economic growth, innovation, and employment worldwide. However, they often operate with tighter resource constraints compared to larger firms, which can limit their access to advanced technologies. Over the past decade, AI and BA have emerged as transformative capabilities that can help SMEs compete more effectively by turning data into insights, automating routine tasks, and enhancing decision-making. The combined deployment of AI and BA holds particularly significant promise for SMEs seeking to increase efficiency, deepen customer understanding, and achieve sustainable growth in volatile markets.[49] BA has become an essential tool for small and medium-sized enterprises (SMEs), enabling them to enhance operational efficiency, improve decision-making, and drive sustainable growth. As key contributors to global economic activity, SMEs can leverage analytics to navigate competitive markets, streamline operations, and strengthen profitability.

The integration of AI with BA enables SMEs to extract actionable insights from their data more efficiently than traditional analytics alone. AI-driven technologies, including ML, natural language processing, and predictive modeling, extend the capabilities of standard BA by identifying patterns, forecasting future trends, and deriving recommendations that support strategic decisions across business functions. These capabilities help SMEs in areas such as customer segmentation, inventory optimization, financial forecasting, marketing personalization, and risk management. AI-enhanced analytics can improve operational performance and free up human resources for higher-value activities by automating repetitive processes and flagging critical business signals, as explained in the following subsection.

12.7.1 Enhancing Performance Measurement and Improvement

BA allows SMEs to measure and improve performance by analyzing KPIs and operational metrics. Through data-driven assessment of financial results, customer satisfaction, and productivity, SMEs can identify strengths and weaknesses within their operations. This insight supports informed decision-making, efficient resource allocation, and continuous improvement, helping smaller firms maintain competitiveness in dynamic market environments. AI strengthens BA by processing large and heterogeneous datasets to generate insights that support evidence-based decisions. SMEs using AI-driven analytics can better understand market trends, customer behaviors, and internal processes that contribute to smarter strategic choices and more agile responses to change.

12.7.2 Strengthening Financial Management

Effective financial management is vital to SME sustainability, and BA provides valuable support in this area. By analyzing financial data, market trends, and sales patterns, SMEs can forecast revenues, manage cash flow, and optimize investment decisions. These insights improve budgeting accuracy, enhance working capital management, and enable better control over profitability—critical advantages for businesses operating with limited financial resources. For example, automation of routine tasks, such as data entry, reporting, and basic customer service, reduces operational costs and minimizes human errors, which are valuable for SMEs with limited labor resources.

12.7.3 Understanding Markets and Customers

BA empowers SMEs to analyze customer data and market trends to gain a deeper understanding of consumer preferences and purchasing behavior. Insights derived from sales performance and feedback help tailor products, services, and marketing strategies to better meet customer needs. This data-driven approach enhances satisfaction and loyalty while also uncovering new market opportunities and guiding competitive pricing strategies that boost revenue growth.

12.7.4 Supporting Digital Transformation

AI-based personalization and targeted marketing enable SMEs to deliver customized experiences at scale, enhancing customer loyalty and market differentiation. Analytics can help identify niche opportunities and optimize pricing strategies in competitive landscapes. As SMEs increasingly adopt digital technologies, BA plays a key role in guiding their digital transformation. By analyzing web traffic, social media engagement, and online sales data, SMEs can design targeted marketing campaigns and adapt strategies in real time. This agility enables businesses to improve customer engagement, expand their digital presence, and gain a competitive edge in fast-evolving markets.

12.7.5 Strengthening Risk Management and Compliance

Data insights can support product innovation by revealing unmet customer needs, productivity bottlenecks, emerging demand patterns, and minimizing risks. BA also enhances risk management and regulatory compliance within SMEs. By continuously monitoring operational and financial data, organizations can identify potential risks, detect irregularities, and ensure adherence to industry standards and legal requirements. This proactive use of analytics minimizes exposure to financial or reputational risks and supports long-term business stability.

In summary, AI and BA models offer transformative opportunities for SMEs to enhance operational efficiency, support strategic decision-making, and compete more effectively with larger firms. SMEs can unlock insights that drive innovation, personalize customer experiences, and optimize performance across functions by integrating AI-driven analytics into core business processes. However, realizing these benefits requires addressing resource limitations, building technical capabilities, and aligning AI initiatives with broader business goals. SMEs can harness AI and BA to secure sustainable growth in a rapidly evolving digital landscape with thoughtful adoption strategies and supportive ecosystems. Consequently,

SMEs can pursue several enabling strategies to realize the full potential of AI and BA by (1) incremental adoption of phased implementation of AI and BA platforms; (2) leveraging Cloud and Platform Solutions of using Cloud-based AI and analytics services that reduce upfront costs and infrastructure requirements, making advanced capabilities more accessible to smaller firms; (3) collaborating with technology providers, industry associations, or universities to provide SMEs with access to expertise and shared resources; and (4) utilizing government initiatives that subsidize training, provide AI adoption grants, or support infrastructure development to strengthen SME competitiveness in the digital economy.

12.8 Campaign Optimization and ROI Analysis

Campaign optimization and ROI analysis are central to data-driven marketing and strategic decision-making. As organizations deploy campaigns across multiple channels of digital advertising, social media, email, mobile, and traditional media, they must address the challenge of executing campaigns and continuously optimizing them to maximize value. Campaign optimization refers to the systematic use of data, analytics, and experimentation to improve campaign performance over time, while ROI analysis evaluates whether marketing investments generate sufficient financial and strategic returns relative to their costs.[50] Optimizing campaigns and analyzing ROI using AI and BA is an essential area for marketing and strategic decision-making in today's digital environment. AI and BA in campaign optimization involve the determination of the role of ML, predictive analytics, and automation in optimizing marketing campaigns, customer segmentation, and targeting using AI-driven insights, reinforcement learning, and adaptive content strategies. ROI measurement and attribution models require the determination of KPIs for measuring campaign success (e.g., CAC, CLV, ROAS), multi-touch attribution models of first-touch, last-touch, and AI-driven attribution, and real-time tracking and predictive analytics for ROI forecasting. Data privacy, bias, and transparency in campaign personalization, regulatory compliance, and ethical advertising guidelines should be considered.

Case studies and industry applications regarding AI-driven and BA-assisted campaign success stories from different industries, along with their challenges and solutions and ROI optimization, should be presented. Generative AI can revolutionize the retail marketing landscape through automated campaign creation, real-time optimization, and customer segmentation. A case study of grocery retailers like FreshMart, Walmart, and Tesco reveals a measurable increase in campaign efficiency, engagement, and ROI through a 30% improvement in campaign efficiency and ROI following AI implementation, as well as significant cost reductions averaging 26.7% across case studies.[51] These case studies demonstrate the value of AI-driven and BA-assisted tools and techniques in refining creative content, enhancing targeting precision, and real-time campaign adaptability. These cases demonstrate that (1) campaign optimization relies on high-quality data drawn from customer interactions, transactions, and contextual signals; (2) descriptive analytics helps marketers monitor KPIs such as impressions, click-through rates, cost per acquisition, and engagement levels; (3) predictive analytics builds on this foundation by estimating customer response probabilities, churn risks, and expected conversion outcomes; (4) ML models such as logistic regression, random forests, and gradient boosting are increasingly used to predict which customers are most likely to respond to specific offers, enabling more efficient targeting and budget allocation; (5) accurate ROI analysis depends on the ability to attribute outcomes to marketing actions. Traditional last-touch or first-touch attribution models are increasingly viewed as inadequate in multi-channel environments because they oversimplify customer journeys; (6) more advanced attribution approaches, including multi-touch attribution, marketing mix modeling, and causal inference techniques, aim to distribute credit across channels based on their incremental contributions to outcomes; and (7) campaign optimization and ROI analysis are essential capabilities in modern marketing analytics.

12.9 Summary

This chapter examines the transformative role of AI and BA in modern business and industry by emphasizing how these technologies enable data-driven decision-making, operational efficiency, and competitive advantage. It begins by defining AI and BA, highlighting their interrelated nature. AI leverages advanced algorithms and ML models to automate and enhance analysis, while BA focuses on extracting actionable insights from data.

The chapter discusses key AI technologies such as ML, natural language processing, and RPA and how they integrate with BA tools to analyze large volumes of structured and unstructured data. It illustrates their applications across various industries, including finance, retail, healthcare, manufacturing, and supply chain management, demonstrating how AI-powered analytics improve forecasting, customer segmentation, risk management, and process optimization.

Finally, the chapter addresses challenges in implementing AI and analytics, such as data quality, privacy concerns, ethical considerations, and the need for skilled personnel. It also covers strategies for successful adoption, including data governance, change management, and aligning AI initiatives with business goals. In summary, the chapter underscores the strategic importance of AI and BA as core drivers of innovation and digital transformation, enabling organizations to respond proactively to market changes, optimize resources, and deliver enhanced value to customers. AI has diverse applications across industries. This chapter provides a cross-sectoral look at how AI is transforming finance, healthcare, ESG reporting, HR, and manufacturing.

Notes

1 Jordan, M. I., & Mitchell, T. M. (2015). Machine learning: Trends, perspectives, and prospects. *Science*, 349(6245), 255–260. https://doi.org/10.1126/science.aaa8415. Available at https://www.science.org/doi/full/10.1126/science.aaa8415?casa_token=s7pYQ0IHWWsAAAAA%3A6DOjkxjihMJdLoZg1J8913QYkNaQj9c6MjawX4hEonh08u21YV5hgoaMmQIxNRXL11zhKY0rrMEs5k8

2 Shmueli, G., & Koppius, O. R. (2011). Predictive analytics in information systems research. *MIS Quarterly*, 35(3), 553–572. https://doi.org/10.2307/23042796. Available at https://www.jstor.org/stable/23042796?casa_token=_Q1iI8OecxsAAAAA%3AFBmmgHvyuRsH5Kf8ui0JhhGQ2y0vPQM2IeQGH67V7OPJxt1oiHLhJRJopOxCfsEk95GI-WMPJQ3unk_CdMYhaG53AzSkezHMiV1p1ggYN5853dPkxyPM&seq=1

3 Vaswani, A., Shazeer, N., Parmar, N., Uszkoreit, J., Jones, L., Gomez, A. N., Kaiser, Ł., & Polosukhin, I. (2017). Attention is all you need. In *Advances in Neural Information Processing Systems* (p. 30). Available at https://proceedings.neurips.cc/paper/2017/file/3f5ee243547dee91fbd053c1c4a845aa-Paper.pdf

4 Porter, M. E., & Heppelmann, J. E. (2014). How smart, connected products are transforming competition. *Harvard Business Review*, 92(11), 64–88.

5 Rai, A., Constantinides, P., & Sarker, S. (2020). Next-generation digital platforms: Toward human–AI hybrids. *MIS Quarterly*, 44(1), iii–ix.

6 Roose, K. (2023). A.I. poses "risk of extinction," industry leaders warn. *The New York Times*, May 30, 2023. Available at https://www.nytimes.com/2023/05/30/technology/ai-threat-warning.html

7 Roose, K. (2023). A.I. poses "risk of extinction," industry leaders warn. *The New York Times*, May 30, 2023. Available at https://www.nytimes.com/2023/05/30/technology/ai-threat-warning.html
8 Roose, K. (2023). A.I. poses "risk of extinction," industry leaders warn. *The New York Times*, May 30, 2023. Available at https://www.nytimes.com/2023/05/30/technology/ai-threat-warning.html
9 Rai, A., Constantinides, P., & Sarker, S. (2020). Next-generation digital platforms: Toward human–AI hybrids. *MIS Quarterly*, 44(1), iii–ix.
10 Boudt, K., & Peterson, B. G. (2015). Model risk in financial analytics. *Journal of Financial Econometrics*, 13(4), 798–831. https://doi.org/10.1093/jjfinec/nbu025
11 Mehrabi, N., Morstatter, F., Saxena, N., Lerman, K., & Galstyan, A. (2021). A survey on bias and fairness in machine learning. *ACM Computing Surveys*, 54(6), 1–35. https://doi.org/10.1145/3457607
12 Davenport, T. H., & Ronanki, R. (2018). Artificial intelligence for the real world. *Harvard Business Review*, 96(1), 108–116.
13 Wamba-Taguimdje, S. L., Fosso Wamba, S., Kala Kamdjoug, J. R., & Tchatchouang Wanko, C. E. (2020). Influence of artificial intelligence (AI) on firm performance: The business value of AI-based transformation projects. *Business Process Management Journal*, 26(7), 1893–1924. https://doi.org/10.1108/BPMJ-10-2019-0411
14 Jordan, M. I., & Mitchell, T. M. (2015). Machine learning: Trends, perspectives, and prospects. *Science*, 349(6245), 255–260.
15 Wedel, M., & Kannan, P. K. (2016). Marketing analytics for data-rich environments. *Journal of Marketing*, 80(6), 97–121.
16 Huang, M.-H., & Rust, R. T. (2021). Artificial intelligence in service. *Journal of Service Research*, 24(1), 3–19.
17 Akter, S., Wamba, S. F., Gunasekaran, A., Dubey, R., & Childe, S. J. (2016). How to improve firm performance using big data analytics capability and business strategy alignment? *International Journal of Production Economics*, 182, 113–131.
18 Verhoef, P. C., Lemon, K. N., Parasuraman, A., Roggeveen, A., Tsiros, M., & Schlesinger, L. A. (2010). Customer experience creation: Determinants, dynamics and management strategies. *Journal of Retailing*, 86(3), 247–266.
19 Lemon, K. N., & Verhoef, P. C. (2016). Understanding customer experience throughout the customer journey. *Journal of Marketing*, 80(6), 69–96.
20 Davenport, T. H., Guha, A., Grewal, D., & Bressgott, T. (2020). How artificial intelligence will change the future of marketing. *Journal of the Academy of Marketing Science*, 48(1), 24–42.
21 Martin, K. D., & Murphy, P. E. (2017). The role of data privacy in marketing. *Journal of the Academy of Marketing Science*, 45(2), 135–155.
22 Wuest, T., Weimer, D., Irgens, C., & Thoben, K.-D. (2016). Machine learning in manufacturing: Advantages, challenges, and applications. *Production & Manufacturing Research*, 4(1), 23–45.
23 Huang, Y., Lu, X., & Wang, X. (2017). Customer churn prediction in telecommunications. *Decision Support Systems*, 95, 66–79.
24 Wedel, M., & Kannan, P. K. (2016). Marketing analytics for data-rich environments. *Journal of Marketing*, 80(6), 97–121.
25 Lemon, K. N., & Verhoef, P. C. (2016). Understanding customer experience throughout the customer journey. *Journal of Marketing*, 80(6), 69–96.
26 Davenport, T. H., Guha, A., Grewal, D., & Bressgott, T. (2020). How artificial intelligence will change the future of marketing. *Journal of the Academy of Marketing Science*, 48(1), 24–42.
27 Khandani, A. E., Kim, A. J., & Lo, A. W. (2010). Consumer credit-risk models via machine-learning algorithms. *Journal of Banking & Finance*, 34(11), 2767–2787.
28 Ngai, E. W. T., Hu, Y., Wong, Y. H., Chen, Y., & Sun, X. (2011). The application of data mining techniques in financial fraud detection: A classification framework and an academic review of literature. *Decision Support Systems*, 50(3), 559–569.
29 Jordan, M. I., & Mitchell, T. M. (2015). Machine learning: Trends, perspectives, and prospects. *Science*, 349(6245), 255–260.
30 Hand, D. J., & Henley, W. E. (1997). Statistical classification methods in consumer credit scoring: A review. *Journal of the Royal Statistical Society: Series A*, 160(3), 523–541.
31 Khandani, A. E., Kim, A. J., & Lo, A. W. (2010). Consumer credit-risk models via machine-learning algorithms. *Journal of Banking & Finance*, 34(11), 2767–2787.
32 Miotto, R., Li, L., Kidd, B. A., & Dudley, J. T. (2016). Deep patient: An unsupervised representation to predict the future of patients from the electronic health records. *Scientific Reports*, 6, 26094.

33 Rajkomar, A., Dean, J., & Kohane, I. (2019). Machine learning in medicine. *The New England Journal of Medicine*, 380(14), 1347–1358.

34 Raghupathi, W., & Raghupathi, V. (2014). Big data analytics in healthcare: Promise and potential. *Health Information Science and Systems*, 2(1), 3.

35 Wuest, T., Weimer, D., Irgens, C., & Thoben, K.-D. (2016). Machine learning in manufacturing: Advantages, challenges, and applications. *Production & Manufacturing Research*, 4(1), 23–45.

36 Tao, F., Zhang, H., Liu, A., & Nee, A. Y. C. (2018). Digital twin in industry: State-of-the-art. *IEEE Transactions on Industrial Informatics*, 15(4), 2405–2415.

37 Feizabadi, J. (2022). Machine learning demand forecasting and supply chain performance. *International Journal of Production Research*, 25(4), 1–24.

38 van Dinter, R., Tekinerdogan, B., & Catal, C. (2022). Predictive maintenance using digital twins: A systematic literature review. *Information and Software Technology*, 151, 107008.

39 Boudreau, J. W., & Ramstad, P. M. (2007). *Beyond HR: The New Science of Human Capital*. Harvard Business School Press.

40 Marler, J. H., & Boudreau, J. W. (2017). An evidence-based review of HR analytics. *International Journal of Human Resource Management*, 28(1), 3–26.

41 Kuncel, N. R., Klieger, D. M., Connelly, B. S., & Ones, D. S. (2013). Mechanical versus clinical data combination in selection and admission decisions: A meta-analysis. *Journal of Applied Psychology*, 98(6), 1060–1072.

42 Hausknecht, J. P., & Trevor, C. O. (2011). Collective turnover at the group, unit, and organizational levels: Evidence, issues, and implications. *Journal of Management*, 37(1), 352–388.

43 Leicht-Deobald, U., Busch, T., Schank, C., et al. (2019). The challenges of algorithm-based HR decision-making for personal integrity. *Journal of Business Ethics*, 160(2), 377–392.

44 Jardine, A. K. S., Lin, D., & Banjevic, D. (2006). A review on machinery diagnostics and prognostics implementing condition-based maintenance. *Mechanical Systems and Signal Processing*, 20(7), 1483–1510.

45 Benhanifia, A. et al (2025). Systematic review of predictive maintenance practices in the manufacturing sector. *Inteligent Systems with Applications*, 26, 200501. https://doi.org/10.1016/j.iswa.2025.200501

46 Ucar, A., Karakose, M., & Kırımça, N. (2024). Artificial intelligence for predictive maintenance applications: Key components, trustworthiness, and future trends. *Applied Sciences*, 14(2), 898. https://www.mdpi.com/2076-3417/14/2/898

47 Hardt, M., Price, E., & Srebro, N. (2016). Equality of opportunity in supervised learning. In *Advances in Neural Information Processing Systems (NeurIPS)*.

48 Mensah, G. B. (2023). Artificial intelligence and ethics: A comprehensive review of bias mitigation, transparency, and accountability in AI systems. Preprint, November, 10(1). https://www.researchgate.net/profile/George-Benneh-Mensah/publication/375744287_Artificial_Intelligence_and_Ethics_A_Comprehensive_Review_of_Bias_Mitigation_Transparency_and_Accountability_in_AI_Systems/links/656c8e46b86a1d521b2e2a16/Artificial-Intelligence-and-Ethics-A-Comprehensive-Review-of-Bias-Mitigation-Transparency-and-Accountability-in-AI-Systems.pdf

49 Yilmaz, C., & Hanisch-Blicharski, A. (2025). Navigating the challenges of AI integration into business analytics for SMEs. *Open Journal of Applied Sciences*, 15(07), 1970–1984.

50 Wedel, M., & Kannan, P. K. (2016). Marketing analytics for data-rich environments. *Journal of Marketing*, 80(6), 97–121.

51 Malikireddy, S. K. R. (2024). Generative AI for retail marketing: Automated campaign creation and optimization. *World Journal of Advanced Engineering Technology and Sciences*, 13(1), 1058–1068. https://www.researchgate.net/publication/387573659_Gen_AI_for_retail_marketing_Automated_campaign_creation_and_optimization

13 Responsible and Ethical AI and BA Frameworks

Learning Objectives

- Learn Responsible AI and ethical business practices
- Understand ethical considerations and potential biases in AI systems
- Explore legal and societal implications of AI deployment
- Learn strategies for building fair and transparent AI systems
- Understand data governance and privacy issues
- Identify ethical concerns in AI systems
- Understand explainable AI
- Explore frameworks for ethical AI governance
- Examine legal and societal implications
- Learn a step-by-step AI ethical approach that includes ethical design, stakeholder engagement, continuous monitoring, and adaptive governance
- Understand AI governance and regulation, including national and international frameworks (e.g., EU AI Act, OECD, UNESCO), which aim to guide ethical AI development and prevent misuse

13.1 Introduction

As AI platforms and BA methods are increasingly integrated into every facet of our society, from finance to healthcare and education, the ethical implications of their use have become a critical concern. AI-powered tools and BA-driven techniques have the potential to revolutionize businesses and industries, improve efficiency, and solve complex problems that result in economic growth and prosperity. However, their implementation and applications raise profound questions and serious concerns about their bias, fairness, accountability, transparency, and the potential for unintended consequences. This chapter on "ethics, bias, and responsible AI and BA" examines the intersection of technology and morality by addressing the challenges of developing and implementing AI systems that align with human values and societal norms and standards. It presents real-world implications for algorithmic bias, data privacy, and the potential for AI to perpetuate or exacerbate human capabilities. This chapter provides a deeper understanding of how organizations can harness the power of AI for the greater good while minimizing harm by examining the ethical frameworks, technical solutions, and policy considerations necessary to create responsible AI.

DOI: 10.4324/9781003664550-13

This chapter concludes that innovation and ethics are intertwined and will shape the future of AI and BA, their impact on humanity and suggests that policymakers, technologists, businesses, and society at large work together to prioritize ethical considerations and ensure that AI serves as a force for justice, innovation, and progress.

13.2 Responsible AI and Ethical Business Analytics

These two concepts of responsible AI and ethical BA are intertwined as AI has become an integral component and a cornerstone of modern businesses. Organizations should develop and use AI and BA technologies that are fair, transparent, and beneficial to society, while operating with integrity and accountability by creating the right balance between achieving innovation and profit and securing human welfare and trust. The continuous deployment of advanced AI and BA technologies brings privacy, bias, ethics, accountability, and governance issues that should be addressed to ensure effective, robust, and fair implications for businesses, society, and individuals. Effective assessment and management of potential AI and BA ethical concerns and considerations require a multidisciplinary approach involving technologists, policymakers, regulators, ethical philosophers, and the public to address these concerns and prevent their unintended consequences. The AI and BA ethical challenges should be addressed by (1) ensuring AI systems are trained on diverse, representative datasets and regularly audited for biases; (2) making AI algorithms and decision-making processes more understandable to users and stakeholders; (3) ensuring BA techniques are reliable, accurate, and transparent; (4) establishing legal frameworks delineating responsibilities and liabilities in AI deployment; (5) involving society in discussions about roles and impacts of AI and BA systems; (6) ensuring that technological advancements align with human values and ethics; and (7) encouraging international cooperation to establish and enforce global ethical standards for AI and BA development and use. These AI and BA challenges should be proactively and effectively addressed to achieve their potential benefits while minimizing their risks as described in this chapter.

Responsible AI refers to designing, building, and deploying AI technologies in a way that minimizes harm and maximizes good by making them work technically and ethically by addressing considerations of the potential issues that come with AI and how they should be mitigated once incorporated in operations.[1] Some of the key principles of responsible AI are (1) fairness, of avoiding bias and discrimination in the use of AI-powered tools and techniques; (2) transparency, of knowing how AI is making decisions of not considering AI as a black box; (3) accountability, of establishing clear lines of responsibility for all involved in AI decision-making from the manufacturer to the programmer and the AI itself; (4) privacy, of respecting private information and boundaries, (5) safety, by making AI robust and secure; (6) proper use of AI, to enhance efficiency while not eliminating human efforts and interventions; and (7) promotion of sustainability and stakeholder engagement and trust. Proper development and deployment, and robust regulation of AI platforms play vital roles in making AI responsible and ethical in practice. Responsible development of AI technologies requires accurate coding of the AI, feeding it data, setting its goals, building ethics into the foundation, and testing rigorously. Once AI is built, its deployment is crucial to ensure tailoring AI to its environment, monitoring how it adapts, modifying it as needed, and stopping it to prevent further damage and undesirable outcomes. Robust regulation in setting the rules of the game by enforcing standards, protecting people, and leveling the playing field. AI regulations should be proactive, effective, scalable, and adaptable. Development, deployment, and regulation are not standalone and should not be considered in isolation as proper AI development (bias-free, tested AI) makes deployment smoother and smart deployment (monitored, transparent) informs robust regulations and clear regulations (risk-based, proactive, enforceable) guide good development.

13.3 AI and BA Governance

The governance of AI and BA refers to corporate governance measures, the frameworks, regulations, policies, processes, and structures that guide the ethical, responsible, and effective use of AI-powered technologies and data-driven BA tools within organizations.[2] As organizations increasingly rely on AI-powered analytics and data-driven decision-making to achieve innovation, efficiency, and competitive advantage, strong governance becomes vital to mitigate risks, promote accountability, ensure compliance, and foster stakeholder trust. Several guiding principles of AI and BA governance are (1) transparency pertaining to clear documentation and implementation of algorithms, data sources, model decisions, and outcomes to promote interpretability, traceability, and auditability; (2) a functioning system of checks and balances to ensure accountability in defining roles and responsibilities for data scientists, AI engineers, managers, and executives to ensure accountability and ownership of outcomes; (3) fairness and bias mitigation of continuous assessment of algorithms to prevent discrimination and ensure fairness in decision-making; (4) privacy and security of safeguarding data from misuse, breaches, hacking, and unauthorized access through robust internal controls for cybersecurity and data governance practices; and (5) ethical and responsible AI and BA implementation strategies to ensure that AI and BA initiatives and efforts align with organizational values, human-centric principles, and societal norms.

Effective AI governance should consist of (1) implementing ethical principles of no harm to users, fairness to all stakeholders, public trust, and transparency; (2) investing in responsible development to monitor AI bias, employ diverse teams of technologists, and ensure accountability; (3) establishing AI systems with proper checks for proper oversight of AI systems, pilot testing of AI systems, closing the loops with proper feedback; (4) promoting transparency of what AI systems can do and can't do; (5) balancing jobs and automation by emphasizing human and machine integration and human–AI teamwork; (6) focusing on overall ethical ROI by measuring profit, monitoring trust, and maintaining sustainability; and (7) engaging stakeholders about AI-assisted performance and decision-making.[3] Overall, these AI governance measures and strategies, including standards, assessments, and certification, enable organizations to balance AI benefits with ethics by designing fair systems, deploying with care, and evaluating outcomes.

Effective AI governance encompasses both internal organizational governance mechanisms and external measures, including regulations and standards, that together ensure AI technologies align with human values, legal norms, and societal goals. AI governance measures consist of frameworks, regulations, policies, and practices that guide the development, deployment, and oversight of AI systems in a responsible, ethical, and transparent manner. Effective AI governance can mitigate the risks of perpetuation or exacerbation of bias and discrimination, threats to privacy and data protection, and economic disruption and inequality while promoting innovation and maximizing societal benefits. AI governance guiding principles are (1) transparency as AI systems should be explainable and their decision-making processes understandable to stakeholders; (2) fairness and non-discrimination as AI technologies should not reinforce existing biases or introduce new forms of inequality; (3) privacy and data protection as AI systems are expected to comply with data protection laws and regulations as well as respecting individual privacy; (4) accountability as AI systems should ensure responsibility AI-related decisions and outcomes; (5) human oversight of AI systems to ensure that they support rather than replace human agency and encourage human judgment in AI-related decisions; and (6) safety and robustness to ensure AI systems function reliably and securely under a wide range of conditions.

AI has become an integral component of corporate governance, business strategy, growth, product innovation, and operations that are refining the business environment, corporate models, workflows, and entire industries. Realizing the full power, potential, and opportunities of AI requires an understanding of its governance and risks. The board of directors plays an important role in overseeing managerial AI-related activities and advises on how AI may affect strategy, opportunities, and risks. Although the entire board has primary oversight of AI, the audit committee could have been given full responsibility for governance of AI and its strategic opportunities and risks, including overseeing the use of AI in financial reporting, internal control over financial reporting, risk management, governance, and compliance. The audit committee should evaluate which AI models they deem to present a higher risk to the organization so that their failure could substantially affect an organization's reputation, financial outcomes, or create potential legal issues. The audit committee should oversee and consider different factors to make the determination, including the types of data used, whether sensitive data is involved, whether the model is external facing, and even the volume of activity, security of data, and their utilization in decision-making. As organizations are using AI in financial reporting process, internal control assessment, and management, audit committees should understand where, why, and how AI systems are used and verify that appropriate controls and processes are in place to manage unique AI-related risks. As AI is used in financial reporting and internal control processes, audit committees should oversee how AI risks are managed by considering data quality, as this area can have a large bearing on the accuracy and reliability of financial reporting and how internal control over financial reporting is changing with the use of AI systems that perform reviews and approvals that were formerly done by humans. Audit committees should also consider how the internal audit is using AI to conduct its audits more effectively and efficiently.

The internal audit process can serve as a vital and effective governance tool to assess the development, deployment, and use of AI across the organization and provide important assurance to the audit committee. Internal audit should review the organization's responsible AI governance framework, which includes the inventory of AI agents, risk taxonomy, and the determination of higher-risk AI systems. Internal auditors can assist the audit committee, highlighting successes, risks, and challenges associated with AI model use. AI agents can be used in internal auditing to (1) enhance audit planning by performing planning activities, evaluating various inputs such as the risk assessment and applicable regulatory requirements, and drafting planning memoranda; (2) use advanced analytics in improving risk assessment and insights and incorporating quantitative analytics, pattern analysis, and complex data insights into audit plans to expand risk coverage, quickly detect anomalies, and perform continuous monitoring; (3) improve controls testing by drafting audit procedures based on requirements, identifying deficiencies in controls and summarizing issues to more quickly get to action and remediation; (4) prepare audit reports by writing initial draft audit reports, including audit background, executive summary, and observations and conclusions.

There are several internal and external mechanisms of AI governance, including (1) AI impact assessments that are usually conducted by AI developers evaluating the social, ethical, and legal implications of AI systems before deployment; (2) internal ethical AI guidelines and codes of conduct and rules established by organizations to guide developers and users in ensuring responsible AI; (3) algorithmic auditing and transparency reports prepared by organizations and their executives in reviewing AI performance and decision logic; (4) technical solutions of use of fairness-aware machine learning, XAI, privacy-preserving techniques (e.g., differential privacy); and (5) AI ethics boards or committees of multidisciplinary teams to review high-risk AI initiatives and practices.

Effective and robust AI and BA governance requires (1) vigilant oversight by the corporate board of directors and executives to ensure that strategic oversight of AI and analytics projects is aligned with business objectives; (2) adequate and effective risk assessment and management to properly respond to potential ethical, legal, and operational risks associated with the use of AI and BA technologies; (3) establishment and implementation of internal controls and accountability structures for decision-making, model development, and outcomes; and (4) compliance with all global applicable laws, rules, regulations, standards, and internal policies and external regulations such as GDPR, CCPA, and AI-specific guidelines (e.g., EU AI Act, US Executive Orders, China's AI governance framework). Business organizations should establish vigilant AI and BA governance boards and ethics committees composed of cross-functional teams of audit committee members, chief technology/AI/data officers, internal audit function, and legal teams to ensure ethical and responsible AI and BA activities, as well as risk management and regulatory compliance. This team should also address potential challenges of AI and BA governance, including the dynamic nature of AI and BA technologies, lack of expertise and resources, black-box models of some AI and BA platforms (e.g., deep learning, ensemble models), and lack of uniform and globally accepted regulations governing the use of AI and BA technologies. Effective and robust governance of AI and BA should address a safeguard against risk and a strategic enabler of innovation and sustainable performance. By establishing effective, ethical, legal, and operational controls to continuously assess and manage risks, organizations can leverage BA and AI's transformative potential while sustaining long-term value creation, maintaining stakeholder trust, and regulatory compliance. However, it is expected that AI and BA governance models will adapt to the emerging and evolving global legislative environment, employ AI and BA advanced auditing tools, and utilize collaboration between machine capabilities and human judgment.

13.4 AI Regulations, Policies, and Compliance

Regulators worldwide have established regulations and rules (e.g., the EU AI Act, US AI regulations) that set standards and requirements for the development and use of AI systems, including safety testing, data protection, and accountability. As more business organizations are leveraging complex AI technologies of generative AI and AI agents, there is an urgent need for regulations and standards to ensure transparency and fairness of AI applications. There are currently several AI standards, such as the European Union's AI Act, the Open Web Application Security Project Generative AI, LLM Security Guidance and Initiatives, and the National Institute of Standards and Technology AI Risk Management Framework. Compliance with these and other forthcoming AI rules and regulations ensures responsible AI governance through structural, relational, procedural, and effective governance measures. A widespread use of AI has necessitated several regulatory initiatives and developments in AI governance landscapes, including (1) the EU AI Act that classifies AI by risk level and imposes strict rules on high-risk applications; (2) US initiatives such as the AI Bill of Rights and the National AI Initiative Act emphasize human rights and innovation;

(3) China developments of focusing on state-driven governance with guidelines that balance control and competitiveness; (4) OECD in promoting international collaboration on AI policies and best practices. These regulations are thoroughly described in the following subsections. Despite all these AI governance initiatives and their promises, there are many challenges that need addressing including (1) rapid technological advancement causing governance to often lag behind the pace of innovation; (2) global fragmentation caused by differing legal and cultural approaches that create compliance complexity; (3) lack of enforcement mechanisms in some jurisdictions; (4) the use of voluntary AI governance principles that often lack legal teeth; and (5) the use of AI black-box models that result in complexity and opacity in AI algorithms that hinder explainability and accountability.

13.4.1 The EU Artificial Intelligence Act and Related Regulatory Initiatives

The European Union Artificial Intelligence Act (EU AI Act) represents the world's first comprehensive and horizontally structured regulatory framework governing AI and its implications. Adopted in 2024 and became effective in August 2024, the Act establishes a risk-based system designed to ensure that AI used within the European Union is safe, transparent, non-discriminatory, and aligned with fundamental rights.[4] The Act governs both AI *systems* and *general-purpose AI (GPAI) models*, including foundation models and generative AI systems developed outside the EU but deployed within EU markets.[5] The EU AI Act establishes a layered, risk-based regime that directly regulates both AI systems and general-purpose models, with particular focus on systemic-risk foundation models and high-risk use cases as explained below.

13.4.2 US AI Regulations

The regulatory landscape for AI in the United States has evolved significantly over the past decade. However, this regulatory development is often fragmented, sector-specific, and guided more by principles and agency enforcement than by comprehensive statutory mandates.[6] Unlike the European Union's AI Act, which introduces a unified, risk-based regulatory model, the US approach is pluralistic and decentralized, reflecting the federal structure, market-driven orientation, and longstanding reliance on sector-specific regulatory regimes.[7] The US AI regulatory frameworks can be categorized at the federal level and state-level AI regulations.

13.4.2.1 Federal AI Regulatory Approach

At the federal level, US AI governance relies primarily on existing laws, regulatory agency authority, executive directives, and voluntary frameworks rather than a single overarching AI statute and is often sector-specific and innovation-driven. This sectoral approach mirrors US data privacy governance, where domains such as healthcare, finance, and national security operate under distinct statutes and regulators. Federal agencies increasingly apply existing laws to AI-enabled systems including (1) consumer protection and unfair practices of the Federal Trade Commission (FTC) that has asserted authority under Section 5 of the FTC Act to investigate unfair, deceptive, or abusive AI practices, including biased algorithms and opaque automated decision systems[8]; (2) civil rights and employment discrimination of the Equal Employment Opportunity Commission (EEOC), which applies Title VII, ADA, and ADEA to algorithmic hiring and workplace monitoring tools, emphasizing that discrimination via AI constitutes discrimination under existing statutes[9]; (3) financial systems and credit of the Consumer Financial Protection Bureau (CFPB), which requires transparency and adverse-action explanations when AI affects credit decisions, interpreting the Equal Credit Opportunity Act (ECOA) to cover algorithmic models[10]; (4) healthcare and medical devices of the US Food and Drug Administration (FDA), which regulates AI-based medical devices under the 510(k) and De Novo pathways and is developing a total product lifecycle framework for continuously learning algorithms[11]; and (5) national security of the Department of Commerce and the Bureau of Industry and Security (BIS), which imposes export controls on advanced AI chips and large-scale computing systems, citing national security concerns.[12]

13.4.2.2 State AI Regulatory Approach

Several states, including Illinois, Colorado, New York, Maryland, and California, have adopted laws targeting algorithmic discrimination in hiring and employment screening tools, biometric and facial recognition technologies, personalized pricing and consumer profiling, and automated decision systems in public services. These AI regulations at the state level often create compliance complexity for firms operating nationally, heterogeneous protection for citizens, and pressures for federal preemption to ensure uniform standards.[13] There are also some non-binding but influential AI frameworks developed by the National Institute of Standards and Technology (NIST), which provide guidance for trustworthy AI, covering governance, mapping risks, measurement, and mitigation.[14] Overall, it is expected that (1) AI regulations in the United States continue to be leader-centric rather than regulation-centric by emphasizing international AI competitiveness and national security, even as individual states experiment with local solutions; and (2) debate over centralized federal standards versus state autonomy will continue into 2026 and beyond, potentially shaping future legislative frameworks or judicial outcomes.

13.4.3 Convergence Between the EU AI Act and US AI Regulation

Recent regulations in both EU and the United States relevant to AI are intended to ensure responsible, accountable, explainable, and provable AI platforms. However, there are some differences in terms of (1) regulatory philosophy, where EU AI Act emphasizes fundamental rights, human dignity, safety, and systemic-risk mitigation; adopts a precautionary and preventive approach, operationalized through ex ante obligations; and frames governance around public protection and ethical constraints, whereas US Act prioritizes innovation, economic competitiveness, and national security; favors an ex post, market-driven model relying on existing sectoral laws; and views overregulation as a threat to technological leadership; promotes voluntary standards. (2) In terms of legal architecture, the EU Act is a comprehensive, binding regulation with a unified risk-based structure, and it applies horizontally across sectors with harmonized obligations and strong enforcement powers, whereas there is no single federal AI law and governance is fragmented across agencies and states, often creating a regulatory mosaic rather than national harmonization in the United States. (3) Regarding risk framework, EU Act codifies four-tier risk taxonomy (unacceptable, high, limited, minimal), makes high-risk systems subject to mandatory requirements: conformity assessments, human oversight, data quality, documentation, robustness, and transparency, whereas the United States has no statutory risk tiers as risk is interpreted through sectoral laws and NIST guidance and foundation-model oversight relies on

Table 13.1 Comparative Analysis of EU versus US AI-Related Regulations

Dimension	*EU AI Act*	*US AI Governance*
Legal form	Binding, horizontal regulation (Regulation (EU) 2024/1689)	No comprehensive AI statute, sectoral laws + guidance
Core philosophy	Fundamental rights, safety, trustworthy AI	Innovation, competitiveness, national security
Risk management	Codified four-tier risk taxonomy with specific duties	Context- and sector-dependent, voluntary NIST AI RMF
Governance structure	AI Office, EU AI Board, national authorities	Multiple federal agencies, NIST for standards, state regulators
Enforcement	Administrative fines up to 7% global turnover	Enforcement under existing statutes, no unified AI fines
Territorial reach	Explicit extraterritorial scope	De facto via export controls, standards, and markets
Sub-national role	Minimal (harmonization objective)	Strong state-level AI and privacy laws

executive orders and voluntary safety testing rather than binding rules. (4) In terms of enforcement, the EU Act is centralized through the EU AI Office, national market-surveillance authorities, and notified bodies with strong enforcement mechanisms, including substantial fines, whereas US enforcement is dispersed across agencies using existing statutory powers (e.g., unfair practices, discrimination, safety violations) with no unified AI enforcement regime; no AI-specific fines. Even though mechanisms differ (hard law vs. soft law), as the EU AI Act is viewed as rules-based, ex ante, rights-centered, precautionary, whereas the US AI Act is considered market-centered, ex post, innovation-first, decentralized, their substantive goals are increasingly aligned as depicted in Table 13.1.

13.5 Best Practices of AI and BA Governance and Regulations

Effective governance and regulation of AI and BA require a comprehensive set of best practices that balance innovation, ethical integrity, organizational accountability, and robust regulations. Leading frameworks emphasize establishing a framework with defined roles, responsibilities, and oversight mechanisms that are supported by cross-functional AI ethics committees and model-risk management teams. There are two widely referenced governance anchors of (1) NIST AI RMF 1.0, which provides a risk management framework to incorporate trustworthiness considerations across the AI lifecycle[15]; and (2) ISO/IEC 42001:2023, an AI management system standard that specifies requirements and guidance for establishing and continually improving organizational AI governance.[16] Deployment and improvement strategies must be embedded within a broader governance framework to ensure accountability and alignment with organizational objectives. Governance mechanisms typically include clearly defined ownership, periodic reviews by cross-functional committees, and alignment with enterprise risk management and internal control systems. Frameworks such as the NIST AI Risk Management Framework and ISO/IEC 42001 emphasize that continuous monitoring, documentation, and corrective action are core governance responsibilities essential to agentic systems.[17] From an assurance perspective, continuous improvement generates evidence for internal and external stakeholders, including regulators, auditors, and boards of directors. Well-designed deployment pipelines produce artifacts such as monitoring reports, incident logs, retraining justifications, and post-implementation reviews. These artifacts support transparency and reinforce organizational learning by turning operational experience into institutional knowledge. Ultimately, AI governance, such as learning mechanisms, is essential for mitigating long-term ethical, operational, and strategic risks.[18]

Best practices include adopting risk-based approaches to AI deployment, ensuring that systems are designed effectively and trained properly, ensuring that AI systems are provable, explainable, and accountable, and monitoring them using high-quality, representative data to minimize bias and enhance fairness. Organizations should implement transparent documentation, including model cards, data lineage records, and audit trails, to support explainability, regulatory compliance, and stakeholder trust. Continuous monitoring and auditing of AI models, from pre-deployment to throughout their lifecycle, are essential to detect drift, ensure robustness, and maintain alignment with intended purposes. Additionally, organizations should incorporate human-in-the-loop oversight, especially for high-stakes applications such as healthcare, finance, and employment. Security and privacy protections must be integrated from the outset through privacy-by-design, secure model development pipelines, and safeguards against adversarial attacks. Finally, aligning internal governance with emerging regulatory frameworks, including the EU AI Act, NIST AI RMF in the United States, and sector-specific standards, as explained in the previous section, helps organizations ensure compliance while fostering responsible and trustworthy AI innovation. AI and BA's best governance attributes, regulations, and aspects are categorized and summarized as follows.

13.5.1 Ethical Principles

Organizations often adopt ethical guidelines for AI, including fairness, transparency, privacy, human oversight, and sustainability, to guide how AI should be built and deployed. However, there are urgent needs for establishing international AI governance frameworks and regulatory structures supporting the development of responsible AI by addressing ethical considerations and challenges.

13.5.2 Accountability and Liability

AI governance should foster a framework for focusing on extending current regulatory and liability approaches to ensure that if an AI system causes harm (e.g., a self-driving car crash), there are effective mechanisms and clear processes for investigating these incidents, preventing their further occurrences, assigning responsibility, and compensating victims.

13.5.3 Transparency, Provability, and Explainability

AI governance should provide transparency and expandability in addressing AI challenges and problems, offering options, and making recommendations to ensure ethical and responsible AI systems, and demand that AI systems be understandable to users and regulators in assisting in decision-making.

13.5.4 Risk Assessment, Management, and Monitoring

AI governance should require the establishment of adequate and effective AI internal control systems to assess, manage, and continuously monitor AI risks and behavior, and to implement internal audit models to prevent and detect bias or errors and correct them when needed.

13.5.5 International Coordination

The international theoretical and practical frameworks should be for AI governance and address the challenges in developing and enforcing such frameworks for countries to work together to handle global AI issues, such as AI arms races, cyberattacks, or unfair global advantages.

13.5.6 Stakeholder Engagement

An effective and robust AI governance demands involvement and engagement of all stakeholders from AI system developers to technology companies, businesses, governments, civil society groups, academics, researchers, and the public in determining and influencing how AI is governed.

13.6 AI Strategy and Implementation

In recent years, AI-powered tools and techniques have emerged as a transformative force that has significantly reshaped industries, business models, and decision-making processes and is expected to continue as essentials for businesses. However, successful adoption of AI-assisted systems requires more than just deploying technology as it demands a clear strategy and thoughtful implementation that aligns with organizational values, goals, and resources. Without a robust and coherent strategy, organizations risk fragmented initiatives, wasted investment, or ethical pitfalls. AI strategies are important in providing a roadmap for organizations to maximize the value of AI while managing its potential risks to ensure that AI initiatives are not isolated experiments but integrated into the broader business vision.[19] Some of the main benefits of an AI strategy include (1) alignment with business goals to ensure AI projects support organization goals, growth, efficiency, customer experience, or sustainability initiatives; (2) efficient resource allocation in effectively prioritizing initiatives with the highest potential ROI; (3) scalability of building a foundation that supports future AI expansion across departments; and (4) risk assessment and management of addressing issues such as data privacy, cybersecurity, and ethical use of AI.

Essential components of effective AI strategies are[20] (1) vision and objectives of defining how AI will create value, whether through cost savings, innovation, competitive differentiation, or sustainability outcomes; (2) data strategy of establishing policies for data collection, quality, governance, security, and compliance; (3) technology infrastructure of identifying the platforms, tools, and cloud solutions required for scalable AI deployment; (4) talent and skills development of creating cross-functional teams combining AI experts, domain specialists, and ethical advisors; (5) change management of providing employees and stakeholders with new workflows, decision-making processes, and cultural shifts; and (6) effective governance and ethics frameworks to ensure responsible AI through transparency, fairness, accountability, and bias mitigation. It is expected that AI strategy will intersect with broader corporate strategies, particularly in sustainability, resilience, and digital transformation as organizations utilize AI not only as a technological tool but also as a driver of cultural and organizational change.

Proper implementation of AI strategies requires a phased approach to reduce risks and accelerate learning by (1) assessment and readiness pilot test of evaluating existing digital maturity, data assets, and leadership commitment; (2) progressive implementation projects of starting small with high-impact, low-risk use cases (e.g., customer service chatbots, demand forecasting); (3) development of AI solutions by expanding successful pilots across functions while integrating with enterprise systems; (4) continuous monitoring and assessment of measuring outcomes (cost reduction, revenue growth, customer satisfaction) against desired KPIs; (5) adaptation of refining and improving AI models and strategies as technology evolves and business needs shift; (6) continuous education and training for employees at all levels; and (7) build trust by using transparent and XAI models to gain stakeholder confidence.

13.7 Business Analytics Strategy and Implementation

In today's data-driven environment, organizations utilize BA as a strategic resource for gaining insights, improving decision-making, and achieving competitive advantage. Business organizations are developing a clear strategy and effective implementation plans to benefit from the full potential of analytics.[21] A well-defined BA strategy ensures alignment with organizational objectives, resource optimization, and sustainable performance improvements. An effective and robust BA strategy can enable organizations to establish a roadmap that connects data initiatives to corporate goals by[22] (1) ensuring BA projects directly support organizational goals such as revenue growth, customer retention, or sustainability; (2) transforming raw data into actionable insights that generate measurable business impact; (3) assessing and managing risks relevant to data security, privacy, and compliance concerns; (4) establishing a foundation for analytics initiatives to expand across departments; and (5) empowering organizations to respond more quickly to market changes and customer needs. Essential components of a BA strategy are (1) vision and objectives of defining the role of analytics in driving innovation, efficiency, and value creation; (2) data strategy of ensuring data quality, governance, accessibility, integration, and security; (3) technology infrastructure of establishing platforms, tools, and cloud solutions that enable real-time analytics and scalability; (4) proper corporate culture of encouraging data-driven thinking across the organization by promoting trust, transparency, and adoption; and (5) effective governance and ethics of designing and implementing standards for data privacy, ethical analytics, and responsible AI use.

Effective implementation of BA strategies requires a proper approach in assessing organizational maturity, existing tools, and leadership support, selecting high-impact areas such as customer insights, operational efficiency, or financial forecasting, expanding successful projects enterprise-wide and integrating analytics into core processes, continuous monitoring of performance progress, and adapting the analytics strategy with emerging technologies, feedback loops, and market shifts. The integration of both AI and BA strategies empowers organizations to enhance efficiency and profitability and strengthen resilience, sustainability, and innovation. A robust AI strategy provides the essential roadmap for organizations to harness AI as a transformative force, moving beyond isolated experiments to achieve integrated, value-driven outcomes. This requires a clear vision aligned with core business objectives, supported by foundational investments in data governance, scalable technology, and cross-functional talent. Best practices emphasize starting with high-impact, low-risk use cases, adopting a phased implementation approach, and establishing strong governance frameworks for ethics, risk, and continuous adaptation. The tangible value of this strategic approach is evidenced in real-world applications across key industries. In retail, leaders like Amazon and Starbucks utilize AI for demand forecasting and personalized marketing, driving significant revenue growth and inventory efficiency. Within healthcare, institutions such as the Mayo Clinic deploy AI for rapid cardiac arrhythmia detection, dramatically improving diagnostic speed and accuracy. The financial sector relies on systems like JPMorgan Chase's COIN to automate complex document review, saving hundreds of thousands of work hours, while PayPal employs deep learning to drastically reduce false positives in fraud detection. For sustainability, pioneers like Google use DeepMind AI to cut data center cooling energy by 40%, turning environmental stewardship into operational excellence. In manufacturing, companies like Siemens and Bosch leverage predictive maintenance and AI-powered visual inspection to minimize downtime and enhance product quality. Ultimately, successful AI implementation is not merely a technological deployment but a strategic endeavor that fosters organizational learning, builds stakeholder trust, and embeds intelligent capabilities into the very fabric of business operations to secure a sustainable competitive edge.

13.8 Explainable AI and Ethical Decision-Making

The extensive use of AI-powered models across many industries including healthcare, finance, law enforcement, and business strategy demand assurance about ethical and accountable AI applications. AI models often operate as a "black box," producing outcomes that are difficult for humans to understand. This lack of transparency and accountability can pose significant risks to ethical decision-making, trust, and accountability. XAI has been suggested to address these challenges by making AI decisions more interpretable, transparent, and aligned with ethical principles, particularly with the growing use of Agentic AI systems. XAI refers to methods and techniques that enable humans to understand, interpret, and trust the outputs of AI systems.[23] XAI systems are essential to (1) promote transparency by clarifying how inputs are transformed into outputs; (2) build trust by assisting users and stakeholders gain confidence in AI recommendations; (3) ensure accountability by enabling organizations to justify decisions made with AI support; (4) support compliance with all applicable and emerging laws, rules, and regulations that demand explainability (e.g., EU AI Act, GDPR); and (5) encourage human–AI collaboration by enabling humans to effectively oversee and complement AI systems.

Ethical decision-making in AI is necessary to ensure fairness, justice, and respect for human rights.[24] Many things can go wrong, and ethical risks emerge when AI systems lack transparency and accountability, including (1) bias and discrimination when algorithms are trained on biased data, which may reinforce inequalities; (2) opacity and lack of responsibility when outcomes cannot be explained and accountability for errors or harm is blurred; (3) autonomy and consent if users are subject to decisions they do not understand or cannot contest; and (5) lack of trustworthiness with without clarity, stakeholders may distrust AI systems, limiting adoption. Several methods have been developed to enhance interpretability, including[25] (1) Model Transparency Approaches of using inherently interpretable models such as decision trees, linear regression, or rule-based systems; (2) Post-hoc Explanations of using tools such as LIME and SHapley provide insights into complex models like deep learning systems; (3) Visualization Methods of designing heatmaps in computer vision or feature importance graphs in structured data analysis; and (4) Counterfactual Explanations of showing "what-if" scenarios to illustrate how small input changes could alter the outcome.

XAI is becoming essential as emerging regulations, stakeholder expectations, and societal pressure are pushing organizations to move beyond performance metrics toward transparency and responsibility. Organizations should adopt best practices to balance XAI with ethical decision-making by ensuring fairness, transparency, and accountability principles from the outset; combining expertise from AI, law, ethics, and domain knowledge; improving AI literacy to enable meaningful engagement with explanations; performing review AI systems for ethical compliance; and modifying the level of detail based on the needs of different user groups.

13.9 Establishing Ethical AI and BA Frameworks

This section explores the development of a conceptual framework, analyzes existing ethical AI models, and proposes guidelines for responsible AI implementation in business with a keen focus on a specific industry and a broader approach across various sectors. As AI and BA systems increasingly influence high-stake organizational and societal decisions, ranging from credit approval and hiring to healthcare triage and public policy, there is a growing imperative to design, govern, and deploy these systems ethically. Ethical AI and BA frameworks provide structured guidance to ensure that analytics-driven decisions are lawful, fair, transparent, accountable, and aligned with human values. The conceptual AI and BA ethical framework is structured around principles of fairness, transparency, accountability, privacy, and social impact by incorporating regulatory perspectives, industry best practices, and case studies consisting of three components: (1) analysis of existing ethical AI models such as IEEE's ethically aligned design, EU's AI Act, OECD AI principles, and corporate AI ethics guidelines (e.g., Google, Microsoft); (2) conceptual framework for ethical AI and BA by integrating principles such as fairness, accountability, transparency, and sustainability into AI governance; and (3) guidelines for responsible AI and BA in business, including practical recommendations for companies to align AI and BA strategies with ethical considerations, addressing compliance, risk management, and stakeholder engagement. Academic research provides an extensive review of over 100 ethical AI frameworks, tools, and methodologies, highlighting the challenge of turning abstract ethical principles into actionable design practices; organizing these efforts into categories such as algorithms, software libraries, process models, checklists, and audits; and offering a robust taxonomy that maps ethical concerns to specific design interventions.[26]

AI is transforming business operations across industries, enhancing decision-making, automating workflows, and unlocking new productivity frontiers. Yet this expansion has raised profound ethical, legal, and societal concerns. Algorithms that lack transparency or fairness can amplify bias, erode trust, and create reputational and regulatory risk.[27] As firms increasingly rely on intelligent systems for hiring, lending, marketing, and customer engagement, ethical AI governance has become a strategic necessity rather than compliance afterthought. Building ethical AI frameworks provides the structure for responsible innovation. Such frameworks establish guiding principles, oversight mechanisms, and accountability processes that align technology deployment with organizational values, stakeholder expectations, and societal welfare.[28]

13.10 Summary

This chapter focuses on fairness, transparency, accountability, and bias mitigation in AI systems. Legal and ethical considerations of AI deployment in businesses are also discussed. This chapter examines the foundational principles, challenges, and frameworks related to the development and deployment of responsible and ethical AI. It begins by defining ethical AI as the alignment of AI systems with moral values, human rights, and societal norms. The concept of *responsible AI* is introduced as a broader approach that includes fairness, accountability, transparency, privacy, and safety throughout the AI lifecycle. Key ethical concerns are examined, including algorithmic bias, data privacy, lack of transparency (the "black box" problem), and potential harm from autonomous decision-making systems. The chapter highlights real-world cases where unethical AI use led to societal backlash, reinforcing the need for oversight and governance.

The chapter also presents global initiatives and regulatory efforts such as the EU AI Act, OECD AI Principles, and UNESCO's AI Ethics Guidelines aimed at standardizing ethical AI practices. Industry-led frameworks and tools for responsible AI development are discussed, such as impact assessments, bias audits, explainability tools, and ethical review boards. The role of interdisciplinary collaboration among technologists, ethicists, policymakers, and civil society is emphasized to ensure that AI serves the public good. The chapter concludes by offering practical guidelines and a proposed framework for organizations to embed ethical considerations into AI design, development, deployment, and monitoring.

Notes

1 Mensah, G. B. (2023). Artificial intelligence and ethics: A comprehensive review of bias mitigation, transparency, and accountability in AI systems. Preprint, November, 10(1). https://www.researchgate.net/profile/George-Benneh-Mensah/publication/375744287_Artificial_Intelligence_and_Ethics_A_Comprehensive_Review_of_Bias_Mitigation_Transparency_and_Accountability_in_AI_Systems/links/656c8e46b86a1d521b2e2a16/Artificial-Intelligence-and-Ethics-A-Comprehensive-Review-of-Bias-Mitigation-Transparency-and-Accountability-in-AI-Systems.pdf
2 Batool, A., Zowghi, D., & Bano, M. (2025). AI governance: A systematic literature review. *AI & Ethics*, 5, 3265–3279. https://doi.org/10.1007/s43681-024-00653-w
3 Agarwal, A., Nene, M. J. (2025). A five-layer framework for AI governance: Integrating regulation, standards, and certification. arXiv preprint. Published 14 September 2025.
4 European Commission. (2024). EU artificial intelligence act – High-risk AI obligations: Guidance documents. Publications Office of the EU.
5 European Commission. (2024). General-purpose AI: Obligations for model providers under the AI Act. Directorate-General for Communications Networks, Content and Technology.
6 Thierer, A. (2023). Permissionless innovation in the age of AI. Mercatus Center.
7 Cummings, C. (2024). Toward a U.S. model of AI governance: Lessons from sectoral regulation. *Yale Journal on Regulation*, 41(2), 315–367.
8 Federal Trade Commission. (2021). Aiming for truth, fairness, and equity in AI.
9 EEOC. (2023). Technical assistance document: Assessing AI hiring tools under federal civil rights laws.
10 CFPB. (2022). CFPB warns lenders using AI algorithms that they must comply with ECOA and adverse action requirements.
11 FDA. (2023). Artificial intelligence and machine learning in medical devices: Regulatory framework.
12 Bureau of Industry and Security. (2024). Export controls on advanced computing and semiconductors.
13 Calo, R., & Citron, D. (2023). The automated administrative state: A crisis of legitimacy. *Harvard Law Review*, 136(7), 1898–1962.
14 National Institute of Standards and Technology. (2023). AI Risk Management Framework 1.0.
15 NIST. (2023). Artificial Intelligence Risk Management Framework (AI RMF 1.0) (NIST AI 100-1). Available at https://www.nist.gov/itl/ai-risk-management-framework?utm_source=chatgpt.com
16 SO/IEC 42001:2023 – Artificial intelligence management system. ISO. Available at https://www.iso.org/standard/42001?utm_source=chatgpt.com
17 See NIST, 2023; ISO/IEC, 2023
18 Weidinger, L., Mellor, J., Rauh, M., Griffin, C., Uesato, J., Huang, P.-S., … Gabriel, I. (2021). Ethical and social risks of harm from language models. arXiv preprint arXiv:2112.04359
19 Iansiti, Marco, & Karim R. Lakhani. (2020). *Competing in the Age of AI: Strategy and Leadership when Algorithms and Networks Run the World.* Harvard Business Review Press.
20 Batool, A., Zowghi, D., & Bano, M. (2025). AI governance: A systematic literature review. *AI & Ethics*, 5, 3265–3279. https://doi.org/10.1007/s43681-024-00653-w
21 El-Adaileh, N. A., & Foster, S. (2019). Successful business intelligence implementation: A systematic literature review. *Journal of Work-Applied Management*, 11(2), 121–132. https://doi.org/10.1108/JWAM-09-2019-0027
22 Pacis, A., & dela Cruz, P. (2025). Business analytics implementation: A systematic literature review. *International Journal of Industrial Management*, 19(2). https://doi.org/10.15282/ijim.19.2.2025.11462

23 Albarracin, M., Hipólito, I., Essafi Tremblay, S., Fox, J. G., René, G., Friston, K., & Ramstead, M. J. D. (2023). Designing explainable artificial intelligence with active inference: A framework for transparent introspection and decision-making. arXiv preprint. https://arxiv.org/abs/2306.04025
24 Freyer, N., Groß, D., & Lipprandt, M. (2024). The ethical requirement of explainability for AI-DSS in healthcare: A systematic review of reasons. *BMC Medical Ethics*, 25, 104. https://doi.org/10.1186/s12910-024-01103-2
25 Fok, R., & Weld, D. S. (2023). In search of verifiability: Explanations rarely enable complementary performance in AI-advised decision making. arXiv preprint. https://arxiv.org/abs/2305.07722
26 Prem, E. (2023). From ethical AI frameworks to tools: A review of approaches. *AI and Ethics*, 3(3), 699–716. https://link.springer.com/article/10.1007/s43681-023-00258-9
27 Jobin, A., Ienca, M., & Vayena, E. (2019). The global landscape of AI ethics guidelines. *Nature Machine Intelligence*, 1(9), 389–399. https://doi.org/10.1038/s42256-019-0088-2
28 European Commission. (2024). *Artificial Intelligence Act: Regulation of the European Parliament and of the Council on Laying Down Harmonised Rules on Artificial Intelligence*. Publications Office of the European Union.

14 AI-Driven Analytics Strategies and Organizational Transformation

Learning Objectives

- Learn the AI-driven analytics framework
- Understand AI-driven strategy in business
- Implementing AI-driven business practice
- Learn measuring AI and BA business impact
- Align AI strategy with business goals
- Understand AI maturity models
- Prepare organizations for AI transformation
- Scale AI projects sustainably
- Learn strategies for fostering a data-driven culture
- Understand AI in decision-making and optimization techniques
- Explore AI and business process automation (RPA & intelligent automation)
- Understand regulatory and compliance aspects of AI

14.1 Introduction

In recent years, businesses have increasingly recognized the transformative potential of AI to drive innovation, improve performance, enhance decision-making, and create competitive advantages. Data analytics (DA) has supported business analytics (BA) and intelligence for a decade. However, the rise of AI represents a paradigm shift, enabling organizations to move beyond descriptive insights to predictive and prescriptive capabilities. This transition from traditional DA to AI-driven BA models requires a strategic rethinking and planning, cultural transformation, and business innovations, with a clear, robust, and transparent roadmap for implementation. This chapter is a comprehensive framework and guide to navigate this complex journey by exploring the critical steps organizations must take to successfully integrate AI into their corporate culture, business environment, operations, from identifying high-impact use cases and transparency to building robust data infrastructure to fostering a culture of innovation and addressing ethical considerations. It focuses on the importance of aligning AI initiatives with broader organization missions, business goals, and developing the talent and governance frameworks necessary to sustain long-term and sustainable success. This chapter (1) presents a roadmap for businesses to harness the full potential of AI by providing real-world examples,

DOI: 10.4324/9781003664550-14

practical frameworks, and actionable insights; (2) equips students with the knowledge and tools necessary to transform a traditional organization into an AI-driven enterprise; and (3) suggests new opportunities for growth, effectiveness, efficiency, and value creation in the age of intelligent automation.

14.2 Evolution of AI-Driven Analytics

Organizations have traditionally used operations research models, advanced toward using DA tools and techniques, and ultimately transformed to AI-driven BA systems in optimizing resource utilization, increasing operational efficiency, and improving decision-making. Moving from DA to ADA represents a transformative shift from retrospective, descriptive assessments of organizational performance to proactive, intelligent systems capable of learning, predicting, and autonomously optimizing decisions. Traditional DA focuses on summarizing historical patterns and supporting managerial judgment, whereas ADA leverages ML, NLP, and advanced optimization to uncover complex relationships, generate real-time insights, and enable automated decision-making at scale. Crucially, the predictive and prescriptive capabilities of AI are built upon the reliable outputs of core BA functions. For instance, accurate sales forecasting models (AI) depend entirely on clean, integrated historical sales data, trend analyses, and well-defined performance metrics (BA). The shift is not a replacement but an augmentation, where BA provides the verified "what happened" and "why," creating the trusted baseline from which AI can reliably project "what will happen" and "what should be done." The effective transition consists of a three-step progression of analytics-enabled insight, AI-enabled action, and AI-enabled learning at scale.[1] In the first step, organizations use analytics to understand "what happened" and "why. In the second step, organizations begin to automate or augment decisions starting with targeted use cases that align with existing analytical strengths rather than "moon shots," such as improving detection, classification, and forecasting in specific processes. In the final step, AI becomes a repeatable enterprise capability that empowers organizations with decision rights, controls, and accountability to support hybrid decision structures of delegation to AI, sequential human–AI collaboration, or aggregated human and AI judgments.

This transition requires restructuring the analytical workflow from manual data processing and static dashboards to dynamic, self-updating models embedded in business processes. This transformation also demands robust capabilities in data engineering, algorithmic design, and model governance. ADA also enhances strategic agility by allowing firms to simulate scenarios, anticipate risks, and personalize stakeholder engagement. These advanced use cases are preceded and validated by BA disciplines. Scenario simulation relies on robust financial and operational models built using spreadsheets or dedicated planning software. Risk anticipation is grounded in historical variance analysis and trend monitoring. Personalization begins with customer segmentation and lifetime value analysis derived from BA. Thus, BA provides the strategic questions and business context that guide where and how AI should be applied for maximum impact. As organizations progress along this continuum, they must address challenges related to data quality, workforce skill capabilities, ethical implications, and change management. For BA, these challenges manifest distinctly: ensuring data quality requires establishing master data management (MDA) and universal metric definitions; building workforce skills necessitates training in data literacy, statistical reasoning, and BI tools; addressing ethics involves upholding transparency in reporting methodologies and avoiding cherry-picking of data; and managing change focuses on shifting the organizational mindset from opinion-based to evidence-based decision-making at all levels. Ultimately, the shift to ADA is a strategic transformation from insight generation to decision automation/augmentation and continuous learning that hinges on building organizational capabilities of governance, talent, data/ML ops, and operating model redesign. It provides a foundation for intelligent enterprises where insights are reported and continuously generated, contextualized, and operationalized to create sustained competitive advantage.

14.3 Strategies for Fostering a Data-Driven Culture

Fostering a data-driven culture (DDC) is vital for organizations aiming to leverage BA and AI technologies for data-driven strategic decision-making. The DDC is multi-dimensions consisting of data-driven mindset, data-driven leadership, data literacy, data accessibility, and data governance, which require alignment across people, processes, and technology, with leadership playing a pivotal role in embedding data-centric values and practices to foster organizational success.[2] Specifically, a DDC refers to an organizational environment and business culture in which data are systematically collected, evaluated, analyzed, shared, and embedded into decision-making processes. at all levels of the organization. In a DDC, strategic, operational, and tactical decisions are guided primarily by solid evidence rather than intuition, hierarchy, or tradition. The emergence of big data, BA, AI, and BI systems has elevated DDC from a technical aspiration to a strategic imperative for organizational competitiveness and sustainability.

14.3.1 Conceptual Foundations of Data-Driven Culture

Fundamentally, a DDC integrates technology, DA, human capital, governance, and organizational norms to ensure that data are accurate, trusted, accessible, and actionable. The DDC strategy extends beyond the adoption of analytics tools and requires a substantial shift in organizational mindset, values, and behaviors toward evidence-based reasoning.[3] Organizations with a strong DDC encourage employees to question assumptions, test hypotheses using data, and continuously learn from analytical insights. DDC is closely linked to the resource-based view (RBV) of the firm, where data, analytics capabilities, and data-savvy human capital are viewed as strategic resources that are valuable, rare, inimitable, and non-substitutable.[4] From this perspective, culture acts as the connective tissue that transforms data assets into sustained competitive advantage. Several interrelated dimensions of a mature DDC are (1) leadership commitment and governance that play a critical role in shaping DDC by signaling the importance of data-based decision-making, allocating resources, and establishing accountability structures; (2) data accessibility and quality as an effective DDC depends on reliable, timely, and well-governed data and poor data quality or restricted access undermines confidence in analytics and discourages adoption; (3) analytical skills and data literacy for establishing analytical competencies and data literacy among employees, not only technical skills but also the ability to interpret results, communicate insights, and translate analytics into business action; and (4) decision rights and incentives to determine who can act on data insights and how performance is evaluated to ensure incentive systems are aligned with data-driven outcomes, reinforce desired behaviors, and reduce resistance to change.[5]

14.3.2 Data-Driven Culture, Organizational Performance, and Challenges

Organizations that adopt DDC can gain higher productivity, profitability, innovation, and market responsiveness compared to intuition-based organizations.[6] In accounting, finance, marketing, and governance contexts, DDC enhances forecasting accuracy, risk assessment, fraud detection, and sustainability reporting by enabling continuous monitoring and evidence-based evaluation. Furthermore, DDC is increasingly recognized as a foundational enabler of ADA business transformation, as discussed in this chapter. Advanced ADA systems rely on high-quality data, cross-functional collaboration, and organizational trust in algorithmic outputs as without a supportive culture, AI initiatives often fail to scale or deliver strategic value. Despite its benefits, cultivating a DDC presents challenges as cultural resistance, data silos, skill gaps, and overreliance on algorithms can undermine effectiveness. Thus, DDCs must be balanced with ethical judgment, transparency, and human oversight, particularly as AI and automated decision systems become more prevalent. Responsible data use, fairness, and explainability are vital to sustaining trust among stakeholders and ensuring effective adoption of DDC. Overall, DDC represents a strategic organizational capability that integrates data, analytics, and human judgment into coherent decision-making processes. DDC is not a purely technological phenomenon but a socio-technical transformation that requires leadership commitment, data governance, analytical competence, and ethical awareness. As organizations transition from descriptive analytics to ADA systems, DDC will remain a critical determinant of long-term performance, resilience, and sustainability.

14.3.3 Key Strategies

The key strategies to establish and sustain a DDC are (1) tone at the top of leadership commitment and vision to champion data-driven decision-making by integrating data strategies into business objectives, consistently using data to support decisions, and creating a Chief Data Officer (CDO) executive position or similar role to oversee data governance and analytics initiatives; (2) data literacy and training of Investing in upskilling employees with data literacy programs, ensuring they can interpret and utilize data effectively, fostering a mindset where data is considered as a strategic asset rather than a technical function, and providing training on BA tools, AI applications, and ethical data use; (3) accessible and integrated data infrastructure by utilizing AI-driven tools and techniques to automate data collection, processing, management, and visualization and establish self-service BA platforms to empower employees with real-time insights; (4) data governance and quality management of establishing governance measures and policies for data privacy, security, and compliance to ensure responsible AI and data usage, standardizing data collection and processing methods to maintain consistency and accuracy, and implement AI-driven data validation tools to detect and correct inconsistencies; (5) cross-functional collaboration of encouraging different departments/functions share insights and collaborate on data-driven projects and using AI-powered collaboration tools and techniques to enhance communication and knowledge-sharing; (6) AI and automation integration and adaptability of leverage AI to automate reporting, streamline data analysis, and provide intelligent recommendations, using NLP tools to analyze sustainability reports and other unstructured data, and continuously updating AI and analytics strategies to align with evolving technologies; and (7) ethical and responsible ADA of establishing ethical guidelines for AI and BA deployment to ensure fairness, transparency, and accountability. Through case studies, best practices, and actionable initiatives, these strategies can help organizations navigate the complexities of AI adoption and use data in decision-making. Establishing strategies for fostering a DDC enables businesses to create a resilient, adaptive, and innovative enterprise that is ready to thrive in the AI-powered future.

14.4 Data-Driven Decision-Making

Data-Driven Decision-Making (DDDM) refers to the systematic use of data, analytics, AI platforms, and robust evidence to inform, evaluate, and justify organizational decisions. DDDM emphasizes structured analysis, ADA, statistical inference, and algorithmic insights to improve decision quality, consistency, and accountability, rather than relying primarily on intuition, experience, or hierarchical authority. Advances in big data, BA, and AI-powered methods have significantly expanded the scope and impact of DDDM across strategic, operational, financial, and governance contexts. The DDDM process is suggested for integrating AI, BA, ADA, and human intelligence in enhancing organizational efficiency, innovation, and strategic planning, resulting in a shift from intuition-based to data-driven approaches, driven by advancements in AI and BA in fostering a DDC, investing in robust infrastructure, and ensuring ethical data use to overcome these barriers.[7]

The conceptual foundations of DDDM draw from multiple theoretical perspectives of rational decision-making, RBV, and dynamic capability theory.[8] From a rational decision-making viewpoint, data reduces uncertainty by providing objective inputs for evaluating alternatives and expected outcomes and by leveraging analytics and AI to extend human information-processing capabilities. From the RBV, data and analytics capabilities are considered strategic organizational resources that enable superior decision outcomes and sustained competitive advantage, whereas dynamic capability theory emphasizes the role of analytics in sensing environmental changes, seizing opportunities, and reconfiguring organizational resources in rapidly evolving markets.

Several interdependent components that enable effective DDDM are (1) data availability and quality, as high-quality, timely, and relevant data are prerequisites for reliable decisions, whereas poor data integrity undermines trust in analytics and can lead to systematically biased or erroneous decisions; (2) AI-powered systems and BA-assisted tools and techniques as DDDM relies on a range of analytical methods, including descriptive, diagnostic, predictive, and prescriptive analytics as well as ML and AI, which further enhance decision processes by identifying complex patterns and generating probabilistic forecasts beyond human cognitive capacity; (3) human judgment and interpretation as human expertise remains critical for contextual interpretation, ethical evaluation, and strategic alignment; and (4) organizational culture and governance to encourage evidence-based reasoning, transparency, and learning from analytical outcomes in ensuring that insights translate into action.[9]

Organizations that adopt DDDM outperform their peers in productivity, profitability, innovation, and operational efficiency as data-driven organizations (DDOs) exhibit significantly higher output and market value than intuition-based competitors. In accounting, marketing, and finance, DDDM improves forecasting accuracy, risk management, fraud detection, audit planning, marketing strategies, and capital allocation by enabling continuous, evidence-based evaluation. DDDM also plays a central role in ADA and AI-enabled decision systems, where algorithms support or automate decisions in areas such as credit scoring, supply chain optimization, sustainability assessment, and regulatory compliance. Despite its advantages, DDDM presents several risks of overreliance on quantitative metrics that may crowd out qualitative judgment, creativity, and ethical reflection. Algorithmic bias, data privacy concerns, and lack of transparency can compromise decision legitimacy and stakeholder trust. Overall, an effective DDDM reflects a fundamental shift in how organizations evaluate choices and allocate resources by integrating high-quality data, advanced analytics, and informed human judgment to enhance decision accuracy, consistency, and strategic alignment. As organizations move toward ADA systems, presented in Chapter 14, the effectiveness of DDDM will increasingly depend on governance, ethical safeguards, and the ability to balance algorithmic intelligence with human values and professional judgment.

14.5 Data-Driven Organization

A DDO is an organization in which data, analytics, AI-powered platforms, ADA, and evidence-based reasoning are systematically embedded into strategy formulation, operational processes, governance mechanisms, and organizational culture. In a DDO, data are treated as a strategic asset, and decisions across all organizational levels, including strategic, tactical, and operational, are guided primarily by AI-driven analytical insights rather than intuition, tradition, or hierarchical authority. The rapid growth of big data, cloud computing, advanced analytics, and ADA has made the transition toward DDOs a central objective of modern organizational transformation.

The five core DDO dimensions are data sourcing and sensemaking, data capabilities, DDC, data-driven decision-making, and data-driven value creation that combine both outside-in (data exploitation) and inside-out (data exploration) perspectives, which collectively underscore the importance of DDOs in the digital age, offering theoretical contributions by consolidating existing research and practical insights for organizations aiming to become data-driven.[10] However, the perceived conceptual ambiguity surrounding "data-driven culture" in organizational contexts prevents a unified framework for understanding its role in enhancing business performance because a DDC is a dynamic construct shaped by shared values, tools, and mechanisms like frames, stories, and categories.[11] Thus, the alignment of organizational culture with data-driven digital transformation (DDDT) goals is critical for successful transformation, as cultural values can either enable or hinder the adoption of data-driven initiatives and their integration enhances operational performance, contradicting the notion of a digitalization paradox, suggesting the interplay between organizational culture and DDDT, offering actionable insights for practitioners.[12]

The concept of the DDO is grounded in several complementary theoretical perspectives of RBV, dynamic capability theory, and organizational learning theory.[13] For example, from the RBV, data, analytics infrastructure, and analytical talent constitute valuable, rare, and difficult-to-imitate organizational resources that can generate sustained competitive advantage when effectively deployed. However, RBV alone is insufficient to explain how organizations continuously extract value from data in dynamic environments. The DDO is not defined merely by technology adoption but by its ability to continuously learn, adapt, and innovate using data by emphasizing the role of analytics in enabling organizations to sense market changes, seize opportunities, and reconfigure resources in response to technological and competitive disruptions. Furthermore, insights from organizational learning theory highlight how data-driven feedback loops, experimentation, and performance measurement foster continuous improvement and institutional learning.

Several defining characteristics that distinguish DDOs from traditional organizations are (1) strategic use of data to support long-term planning, competitive positioning, and value creation rather than serving only reporting or compliance functions; (2) integrated analytics infrastructure, including data warehouses, data lakes, and AI-enabled analytics platforms, to ensure timely access to high-quality data across organizational units; (3) DDC and leadership in legitimizing data-based decision-making and encouraging employees to challenge assumptions using evidence; (4) human capital and data literacy among managers and professionals to interpret analytics, ask the right questions, and translate insights into action; and (5) governance and ethical oversight to ensure data quality, security, privacy, and ethical use.

Ultimately, DDOs outperform less data-oriented peers in the sense that these organizations exhibit higher productivity, profitability, and market valuations by enhancing forecasting accuracy, risk management, audit planning, fraud detection, and sustainability performance measurement through continuous, evidence-based monitoring. Furthermore, DDOs provide the organizational foundation necessary for ADA, and AI-enabled and agentic, as advanced analytics require not only data availability but also organizational trust in algorithmic outputs and the capability to act on them effectively.[14] Despite their advantages, transitioning to a DDO presents significant challenges. Data silos, legacy systems, skill shortages, and resistance to change frequently impede transformation efforts and overreliance on quantitative metrics that can marginalize qualitative judgment and ethical considerations. Overall, a DDO represents a holistic socio-technical system in which data, analytics, human judgment, and governance are tightly integrated. As organizations increasingly adopt ADA and autonomous decision systems, the principles underlying DDOs will remain fundamental to achieving resilience, accountability, and long-term value creation.

14.6 AI-Driven Analytics Strategy in Business

As presented in the earlier chapters, AI-powered models and BA-assisted systems have created opportunities for organizations to build competitive advantage in today's data-driven economy. Organizations across industries are leveraging both AI and BA technologies to improve decision-making, optimize operations, enhance customer experiences, and drive innovation. Understanding ADA strategy in business requires examining its definitions, interplay, and strategic integration. AI was previously defined as technologies that enable machines to simulate human intelligence with capabilities of learning from data, recognizing patterns, making predictions, and automating decisions, whereas BA refers to the systematic use of data and statistical analysis to gain insights, predict future outcomes, and guide business decisions. Thus, while BA provides a foundation of data-driven insight, AI takes analytics to the next level by enabling adaptive, autonomous, and real-time decision-making. Thus, integration of AI and BA into ADA strategy is vital in ensuring planning and implementation of AI and BA systems to achieve organizational goals, improve efficiency, and drive competitive advantage. It requires aligning AI capabilities with BA to achieve responsible AI use and continuously adapting to BA technological advancements. Understanding ADA strategy means recognizing their complementary roles as BA provides insight into the past and present, whereas AI predicts and shapes the future. This creates a powerful continuum of intelligence from descriptive and diagnostic to predictive and prescriptive.

Ultimately, ADA empowers organizations to (1) foster decision-making by moving from intuition-based choices to data-driven and evidence-based strategies; (2) improve efficiency by automating repetitive processes, reducing time and cost; (3) gain competitive advantage by enabling insights faster and more effectively than competitors; (4) innovate new products and services through new business models such as AI-powered platforms and data-driven ecosystems; and (5) encourage customer engagement by tailoring offerings through predictive modeling and AI-driven recommendations. It is expected that as businesses evolve, ADA strategies will be increasingly integrated in empowering organizations to rely on real-time analytics, augmented decision-making, and autonomous systems to adapt quickly to market changes. This integration is steering toward the concept of "Augmented Intelligence," where human expertise is synergistically combined with machine intelligence for superior outcomes. This underscores that technological investment alone is insufficient as strategic value is unlocked through deliberate organizational design and leadership to avoid a narrow, purely technical focus and ensure the strategy is robust and sustainable. An effective ADA strategy can promote advanced business capabilities for predictive analytics, personalized customer experiences, automation, and decision-making enhancement that can enable organizations to improve efficiency, innovation, and competitive advantage.

Consequently, important components of ADA strategy in business consist of (1) defining AI and BA objectives and their alignment with corporate strategies of cost reduction, revenue growth, or innovation; (2) determining data strategy and infrastructure to ensure access to high-quality, structured, and unstructured data and invest in data governance, storage, and processing capabilities; (3) choosing AI model selection and BA development by using ML, deep learning, or generative AI based on business needs; (4) considering ethical AI and BA risk management by addressing AI and BA bias, fairness, and transparency; (5) integrating AI and BA with business processes by automating repetitive tasks, enhancing decision-making, and improving customer interactions; (5) developing skills and talent for employees to work alongside AI-driven and BA-assisted systems; and (6) establishing effective and robust governance and continuous monitoring of adopted AI and BA systems. Furthermore, a successful strategy must be iterative, incorporating feedback loops to learn from pilots and scale successes, thereby creating a culture of continuous innovation and data-driven refinement.

14.7 AI-Driven Analytics Adoption Framework

The successful adoption of integrated ADA systems requires more than technology investment as it demands a structured framework that aligns people, processes, data, and technology with organizational strategy. The ADA adoption framework provides a roadmap for guiding organizations through this transformation. The integrated AI and BA adoption framework provides a structured approach for organizations to transition effectively and digitally from traditional DA to ADA decision-making. From the perspective of BA, this transition also reflects an organizational shift from descriptive and diagnostic reporting toward predictive and prescriptive analytics that directly support managerial decision-making across functional areas. An effective ADA adoption framework explains why organizations decide to adopt AI analytics, how they implement and routinize it, and when adoption actually translates into measurable value. This process is shaped by perceived relative advantage, compatibility with existing processes, and complexity attributes that consistently predict diffusion outcomes as well as perceived usefulness and ease of use, performance expectancy, effort expectancy, social influence, and facilitating conditions. The robust ADA adoption framework should (1) guide strategy by aligning AI and BA initiatives with corporate objectives; (2) enhance value creation ensuring investments in AI and BA deliver measurable and desirable business outcomes; (3) reduce risks by assessing and managing challenges such as data quality, bias, and integration issues; and (4) build capabilities by enhancing organizational readiness in terms of skills, infrastructure, and governance. The AI and BA adoption framework should be dynamic in responding to technological advances and market demands. For BA adoption, this dynamism is particularly important as data sources, business processes, and performance metrics continuously evolve.

The adoption framework includes key components such as strategy, technology, data, people, governance, and ethical considerations. The AI adoption frameworks are categorized into four groups—regulatory, normative, applicative, and evaluative—with regulatory frameworks providing standardized guidelines for AI adoption, whereas normative frameworks emphasize ethics and human rights to build public trust, applicative frameworks help achieve responsible AI outcomes, and evaluative frameworks identify areas for improvement in public service delivery.[15] Ultimately, an effective ADA framework should explicitly separate adoption from value realization as organizations capture performance gains only when they develop ADA capabilities, including data assets, talent, processes, and learning routines.

Organizational adoption of ADA is no longer merely a technical decision; rather, it is a strategic transformation requiring integrated capabilities across people, technology, information, and governance. The ADA adoption framework should focus on four core interdependent pillars of talent, infrastructure, data, and leadership that collectively determine an organization's capacity to implement and scale intelligent technologies. Talent refers to technically skilled professionals in AI, ML, and data science, as well as analytically competent managers capable of interpreting insights and integrating them into strategic decisions. From a BA perspective, this expands to include critical roles such as BI analysts, data visualization specialists, and analytical translators who can bridge technical outputs with business needs. Ultimately, it requires cultivating data literacy across the entire organization, empowering employees in finance, marketing, and operations to independently interpret dashboards, perform self-service analysis, and make evidence-based decisions in their daily workflows.

Infrastructure refers to the technical backbone that enables ADA to operate efficiently and at scale and encompasses the digital architecture that includes cloud computing, high-performance hardware, platforms, and tools necessary to support model development, deployment, and continuous learning. The infrastructure priority is a modern BI and analytics stack. This includes scalable data warehouses and data lakes for integrated reporting, robust Extract, Transform, Load (ETL) pipelines to ensure data flow, and user-friendly visualization platforms (e.g., Tableau, Power BI) that enable secure, self-service access to insights. The infrastructure must support not only data storage but also the efficient processing and delivery of reports, dashboards, and KPIs to stakeholders at all levels. Consequently, infrastructure investments are linked to increased technology readiness and routinized analytics use, which position infrastructure as an indispensable organizational resource for competitive advantage. Thus, organizations that lack scalable infrastructure struggle to operationalize models beyond pilot stages and cannot sustain real-time analytical processes.

Data represents the foundational asset driving ADA systems, requiring organizations to establish robust data governance, quality assurance, integration, and security to ensure that analytics outputs are accurate, reliable, and ethically produced. The data imperative is to create a single source of truth. This involves implementing MDM for core entities like "customer" or "product," defining and standardizing key metrics across departments, and enforcing data quality rules to ensure consistency in reporting. The goal is to move from fragmented, siloed data to a trusted, well-documented, and accessible enterprise data asset that supports descriptive and diagnostic analytics with complete reliability. Thus, effective adoption frameworks articulate the need for robust data governance frameworks that define data ownership, lineage, privacy protection, and ethical oversight. Data governance aligns technical efforts with regulatory, compliance, and ethical norms to ensure AI analytics outputs are reliable and defensible. Data readiness, including maturity assessment, integration across silos, and metadata management, is considered a prerequisite for scalable AI analytics adoption, which enables organizations to extract actionable insights and embed analytics into core processes.

Leadership provides the vision, governance, and cultural support needed to align AI initiatives with business strategy, foster cross-functional collaboration, and promote responsible and ethical AI practices. In the context of BA, leadership must actively champion a DDC. This means leaders themselves using data in decision-making forums, investing in analytics capabilities as a core business function, and establishing clear governance for who owns data, reports, and analytical processes. Leaders can shape culture and governance by promoting experimentation, tolerance of failure, and iterative learning. Effective leadership breaks down silos by mandating cross-departmental data sharing and creating centers of excellence or steering committees to prioritize analytical projects that deliver the highest business value. Strategic leadership navigates adoption through long-term investment horizons, performance metrics that reward outcomes, and integration of AI/BA into decision-making at operational and strategic levels.

Together, these four pillars of ADA form a comprehensive framework that guides organizations in assessing readiness, designing implementation roadmaps, mitigating operational and ethical risks, and capturing long-term value from ADA investments, initiatives, and developments. Specifically, talent and leadership together cultivate a learning environment that sustains innovation and analytics literacy, whereas infrastructure and data together create the technical ecosystem necessary for reliable model deployment and AI analytics production.

The general understanding is that regulations often fall short in addressing AI's fair use, highlighting the need for governance strategies that balance risk and value and integration of AI and BA technologies into accounting and business curricula to align with industry and public demands. The adoption of robust BA supported by AI technologies can enhance product innovation and organizational performance through the mediating role of a DDC to enable business process performance, product innovation that ultimately improves overall organizational performance, and business value.[16] Specifically, ADA enables organizations to formalize DDC through dashboards, KPIs, variance analysis, and performance monitoring systems that embed analytics into everyday managerial routines. The key factors influencing ADA adoption are applicability, readiness, job-fit, complexity, perceived consequences, affect toward use, social factors, tangible benefits, leadership support, and facilitating conditions that collectively enhance efficiency, innovation, and decision-making across operations management components to improve product inspection and quality control in manufacturing, enable real-time core capability identification in product development, and optimize supply chain operations.

The ADA framework consists of (1) strategic alignment of defining business objectives, aligning AI and BA adoption with corporate goals, identify key areas where AI and BA can create value (e.g., accounting, finance, marketing, operations, sustainability); (2) data infrastructure and management by ensure high-quality, structured, and unstructured data availability, implementing robust data governance and security measures, and developing scalable data lakes and warehouses for ADA; (3) technology development and integration by assessing and implementing AI tools, ML models, and BI platforms and ensuring interoperability between AI systems and legacy applications; (4) development talent and organizational culture of training skilled employees in AI, ML, and data literacy, and fostering a culture of innovation and AI-driven experimentation; (5) governance, ethics, and compliance by establish ADA governance frameworks to mitigate risks (bias, transparency, accountability), ensuring compliance with all applicable laws, rules and regulatory and ethical AI standards, develop policies for responsible AI use in BA; (6) implementation and scaling by conducting pilot projects to test AI and analytics solutions, measuring success through KPIs, and scaling successful AI and BA initiatives across departments and business units; and (7) continuous improvement and innovation by leveraging ADA technologies for predictive and prescriptive analytics, monitoring AI models and BA systems for completeness and accuracy, and iterating on ADA strategies based on evolving business needs and technological advancements.

In practice, the adopted ADA framework shows several stages from readiness to adoption decision, implementation, assimilation/routinization, value capture, and continuous improvement, along with feedback loops of monitoring, model drift management, and governance updates that keep AI and BA aligned with strategy and risk tolerance over time. The ethical challenges and implications of ADA adoption frameworks should also be considered to address potential ethical issues, such as transparency, accountability, bias in AI algorithms, and the potential erosion of professional skepticism and judgment in adopting the ADA framework. In the context of BA, maintaining professional skepticism and managerial judgment is essential to prevent overreliance on quantitative outputs and to ensure analytics complements, rather than replaces, human expertise.

14.8 Implementing AI-Driven Analytics (ADA) Systems

Implementing ADA systems is a process of operationalizing a socio-technical system, which connects data-to-decision pipelines, embeds models into business processes, and continuously governs performance, risk, and learning. ADA technologies have made significant progress in recent years, and, thus, their proper implications create both opportunities and challenges for organizations. Proper and effective implementation of ADA systems requires a structured, strategic, and iterative approach that aligns technological capabilities with organizational priorities, business culture, and values. Effective implementation begins with identifying high-impact business problems and defining clear use cases where AI or analytics can deliver measurable value by prioritizing use cases based on strategic needs where data-driven clarity is urgently needed, such as improving the accuracy of financial forecasting, optimizing marketing campaign ROI through attribution modeling, or reducing operational costs via process mining and performance benchmarking. The focus is on questions that start with "why" and "how" to improve existing processes. Organizations must then assess their readiness across key dimensions, from data maturity, technological infrastructure, talent availability, and leadership commitment, to determine gaps that may inhibit adoption. Building on this assessment, organizations should establish a scalable data governance framework, integrate secure data pipelines, and adopt cloud-based or hybrid architectures to support model development and deployment. The cornerstone of ADA implementation is building this trusted data foundation. This involves deploying a modern data stack, including cloud data warehouses, ETL/ELT tools, and a semantic layer, to create centralized, cleansed data assets.

Implementation of an ADA strategy requires establishing a business-facing analytics catalog and data dictionary so users can find, understand, and trust the data they use for decision-making. Pilot testing, experimentation, and phased rollouts allow firms to refine algorithms, validate outcomes, and manage risks before full-scale implementation. Cross-functional collaboration among IT, data science teams, and business units is essential for ensuring that analytical insights are actionable and aligned with operational needs. This collaboration is institutionalized through the creation of an analytics center of excellence or the formal role of "business analysts" or "analytical translators." These professionals work within business units to translate needs into technical requirements and, conversely, to explain technical outputs in business terms, ensuring that every report and dashboard drives a specific action or decision. Finally, organizations must invest in training, change management, and ethical oversight to promote responsible AI use, safeguard stakeholder trust, and institutionalize analytics-driven decision-making. Through these practical steps, businesses can transform ADA from isolated technical projects into sustainable sources of strategic advantage.

Ultimately, ADA system implementation starts with selecting use cases where AI can change a decision or automate an action, such as risk scoring, exception routing, forecasting, and next-best action. Second, a robust integration program establishes an enterprise data governance model including roles, decision rights, standards, controls, and monitoring to ensure that data quality, lineage, access, and risk are managed systematically. Third, integration requires governance for fairness, transparency, privacy, and accountability, especially where models affect individuals' credit, hiring, pricing, healthcare, or regulated outcomes. Finally, ADA systems should achieve measurable performance when it builds repeatable organizational and DA capabilities that translate into dynamic and operational capabilities of faster sensing of opportunities, rapid experimentation, and process transformation.

14.9 Measuring AI-Driven Analytics Impact

The effectiveness of ADA systems depends on how accurately organizations implement and measure their success. Measuring ADA impact requires a multidimensional evaluation framework that captures both quantitative and qualitative value created across the organization. Traditional metrics such as cost savings, productivity gains, revenue growth, and process efficiencies remain essential, but AI-driven initiatives often generate broader strategic benefits that extend beyond immediate financial returns. These include improvements in decision accuracy, risk mitigation, customer engagement, innovation capacity, and operational resilience. Because AI systems learn and improve over time, organizations must adopt dynamic performance measures by tracking model accuracy, provability, scalability, explainability, transparency, and adaptability as part of ongoing ROI assessments, focusing on the health and utility of the analytics ecosystem itself. Key ADA metrics include data freshness (latency), system uptime for critical reports, user adoption rates of dashboards and self-service tools, and a reduction in "shadow analytics" (unapproved spreadsheets). Measuring ROI for ADA is challenging because the benefits are often indirect, distributed across processes, and delayed. Furthermore, the quality of insights is measured through user feedback on report clarity and actionability, and the speed at which analytical findings are incorporated into business processes. Additionally, organizations should account for intangible benefits such as enhanced DDC, strengthened governance, and improved compliance, while also evaluating potential risks, including bias, privacy concerns, and implementation costs.

The intangible ROI of ADA is particularly significant. It manifests as a cultural shift measured by the prevalence of data references in strategic meetings, the empowerment of frontline managers to make decisions based on dashboards, and the reduction in time spent debating "whose numbers are right." Strengthened governance is measured by adherence to data policies and the auditability of core metrics. A major risk for BA is insight inertia from the cost of decisions delayed or opportunities missed because analysts or leaders failed to act on available data. A balanced scorecard or value-realization framework that integrates financial, operational, strategic, and ethical indicators enables organizations to assess the business impact of ADA investments more holistically. This balanced scorecard should include dimensions such as financial (cost of manual reporting, ROI of campaigns guided by analytics); operational (process efficiency gains, reduction in data-related rework); strategic (improvement in strategic planning speed and quality, competitive response time); and cultural/governance (enterprise-wide data literacy scores, percentage of key decisions supported by formal analysis).[17] Ultimately, measuring AI ROI demands that organizations focus on short-term returns and long-term organizational transformation and sustainable competitive advantage. Meaningful ADA ROI components that should be measured are (1) financial value of using standard capital budgeting (incremental cash flows, NPV/IRR) and liking cash flows to measurable operating levers (e.g., fewer fraud losses, lower warranty claims, reduced working capital, higher margin via better pricing); (2) operational impact of measuring the operational mechanisms that ADA systems are intended to achieve (e.g., forecast error, fill rate, on-time delivery, call-handle time, churn rate, false-positive costs); (3) risk, quality, and governance impact of creating value by lowering downside risk (fraud, credit losses, safety incidents, compliance breaches) and improving governance; and (4) adoption and utilization of tracking decision adoption metrics such as override rate, acceptance rate, percent of eligible decisions touched by the model, and time-to-action. Ultimately, a strong ADA impact report should include a clear business objective and decision point the model influences, a theory of value (which process levers change and how that becomes cash flow), a measurement plan with leading indicators (process KPIs) and lagging indicators (financial results), and complete lifecycle maintenance.

14.10 Continuous Monitoring of AI-Driven Analytics

Organizations typically prioritize and balance the short-term and long-term success of their ADA systems, with a keen focus on their sustainability and growth of these systems. Continuous monitoring of ADA for long-term business growth requires organizations to move beyond isolated pilots toward an enterprise capability that repeatedly converts data into better decisions, redesigned processes, and sustained performance improvements by institutionalizing analytical capabilities, embedding intelligent systems into core operations and corporate environment, and fostering a culture of continuous learning. improvement and innovation. As organizations move beyond pilot projects, they must develop scalable architecture such as modular data platforms, cloud-native environments, and automated MLOps pipelines that support large-scale model deployment, monitoring, and lifecycle management. This process necessitates the evolution from departmental reporting tools to an enterprise-grade analytics platform. This includes centralizing data models to ensure consistency, implementing a governed self-service analytics environment where users can safely explore data, and establishing automated data pipelines that feed real-time dashboards and performance scorecards across the organization. The goal is to create a scalable "insights as a service" layer that is reliable, secure, and accessible. Sustainable scaling also depends on robust governance frameworks that ensure model reliability, ethical integrity, regulatory compliance, and risk management as AI systems expand across business functions. Continuous monitoring of ADA requires its own distinct governance to prevent fragmentation and ensure trust built on complementary organizational resources (process changes, governance, skills, and incentives) and on how digital capabilities are embedded across the organization.

Ultimately, continuous monitoring of ADA is less about deploying more models and more about building a repeatable operating system for analytics-driven value creation process of a centralized analytics governance body that owns the enterprise data dictionary, standardizes calculation methodologies for key metrics, manages access controls, and enforces version control for critical reports.[18] Consequently, continuous monitoring of ADA requires institutionalizing reusable data products, standardized feature pipelines, model governance, and cross-functional delivery teams, and thereby new use cases can be launched faster with lower marginal cost. This prevents the re-emergence of data silos and "report anarchy," ensuring that as analytics scales, it remains a single source of truth. Equally important is cultivating a workforce equipped with advanced analytical skills and cross-functional literacy, enabling collaboration between data scientists, domain experts, and decision-makers. Long-term ADA growth depends on democratizing data skills. This builds a hybrid workforce where every manager is analytically capable, and every analyst understands the business. Organizations should adopt portfolio-based strategies that prioritize high-value AI applications, reinvest analytics-generated gains into innovation, and continuously refine models using real-time feedback loops. Finally, organizations can transform isolated analytics successes into enterprise-wide capabilities that drive innovation, operational excellence, stakeholder value creation, and sustained competitive advantage by aligning continuous monitoring of ADA efforts with long-term strategic goals, which depend on reliability, maintainability, and adaptability as models meet changing markets and shifting data. Long-term business growth from ADA can be achieved when organizations pair technology investment with broader organizational change of new processes, new skill mixes, and new performance systems, which integrate ADA into decision structures and human–AI collaboration.

14.11 Summary

This chapter provides a roadmap for ADA adoption, from building business cases to integrating AI into processes. It explores change management and cultural transformation. This chapter examines how AI transforms traditional BA into a more dynamic, predictive, and automated decision-making process. It begins by introducing the foundations of BA, highlighting the shift from descriptive and diagnostic analytics to predictive and prescriptive analytics powered by AI. The chapter explores key ADA technologies, including ML, NLP, and computer vision, and their applications in various business functions, including marketing, finance, operations, and human resources.

The chapter also discusses the integration of AI with big data platforms and real-time analytics tools to uncover insights that drive competitive advantage. It covers the role of AI in improving forecasting accuracy, customer segmentation, risk assessment, fraud detection, and supply chain optimization. Additionally, it addresses challenges such as data quality, algorithmic bias, model interpretability, and the need for human oversight. Finally, case studies and industry examples are provided to illustrate how organizations leverage ADA to enhance performance, innovate processes, and make smarter strategic decisions. The chapter concludes with a forward-looking discussion on ethical considerations, workforce implications, and the future of analytics in an AI-enabled business environment.

Notes

1 Shrestha, Y. R., Ben-Menahem, S. M., & von Krogh, G. (2019). Organizational decision-making structures in the age of artificial intelligence. *California Management Review*, 61(4), 66–83. Available at https://cmr.berkeley.edu/2019/08/61-4-organizational-decision-making-structures-in-the-age-of-artificial-intelligence/?utm_source=chatgpt.com

2 Javed, B., & Akhlaq, A. (2024). A systematic review of exploring the multiple dimensions of data-driven culture. *International Journal of Trends and Innovations in Business & Social Sciences*, 2(4), 522–536. https://doi.org/10.48112/tibss.v2i4.953. Available at https://journals.irapa.org/index.php/TIBS/article/view/953

3 McAfee, A., & Brynjolfsson, E. (2012). Big data: The management revolution. *Harvard Business Review*, 90(10), 60–68.

4 Wamba, S. F., Gunasekaran, A., Akter, S., Ren, S. J. F., Dubey, R., & Childe, S. J. (2017). Big data analytics and firm performance. *Journal of Business Research*, 70, 356–365.

5 Brynjolfsson, E., & McElheran, K. (2016). The rapid adoption of data-driven decision-making. *American Economic Review*, 106(5), 133–139.

6 Gupta, M., & George, J. F. (2016). Toward the development of a big data analytics capability. *Information & Management*, 53(8), 1049–1064.

7 Adeyeye, O. J., & Akanbi, I. (2024). A review of data-driven decision making in engineering management. *Engineering Science and Technology Journal*, 5(4), 1303–1324. https://www.researchgate.net/publication/385378691_A_REVIEW_OF_DATA-DRIVEN_DECISION_MAKING_IN_ENGINEERING_MANAGEMENT

8 Wamba, S. F., Gunasekaran, A., Akter, S., Ren, S. J. F., Dubey, R., & Childe, S. J. (2017). Big data analytics and firm performance. *Journal of Business Research*, 70, 356–365.

9 Kiron, D., Prentice, P. K., & Ferguson, R. B. (2014). Raising the bar with analytics. *MIT Sloan Management Review*, 55(2), 29–33.

10 Fischer, H., Wiener, M., Strahringer, S., Kotlarsky, J., & Bley, K. (2023). Data-driven organizations: Review, conceptual framework, and empirical illustration. *Australasian Journal of Information Systems*, 27. https://doi.org/10.3127/ajis.v27i0.4425. Available at https://ajis.aaisnet.org/index.php/ajis.article/view/4425

11 Anton, E., Oesterreich, T. D., Aptyka, M., & Teuteberg, F. (2023). Beyond digital data and information technology: conceptualizing data-driven culture. *Pacific Asia Journal of the Association for Information Systems*, 15(3), 1. https://doi.org/10.17705/1pais.15301. Available at https://aisel.aisnet.org/pajais/vol15/iss3/1/

12 Ghafoori, A., Gupta, M., Merhi, M. I., Gupta, S., & Shore, A. P. (2024). Toward the role of organizational culture in data-driven digital transformation. *International Journal of Production Economics*, 271, 109205. https://doi.org/10.1016/j.ijpe.2024.109205. Available at https://www.sciencedirect.com/science/article/pii/S0925527324000628?casa_token=1eXcZGcdTT0AAAAA:-x_7iwM8RhLozhr2gSiOaoWsraP9sufj6FvqAbJjMRqCKI-ayxACqZaIpeoANkaTXXDqqTjyrt4

13 Ransbotham, S., Kiron, D., Gerbert, P., & Reeves, M. (2020). Expanding AI's impact with organizational learning. *MIT Sloan Management Review*, 61(4), 1–8.

14 Ransbotham, S., Kiron, D., Gerbert, P., & Reeves, M. (2020). Expanding AI's impact with organizational learning. *MIT Sloan Management Review*, 61(4), 1–8.

15 Alshehhi, K., Cheaitou, A., & Rashid, H. (2022). Adoption frameworks for artificial intelligence in the public sector: A systematic review of literature. In *Proceedings of the 3rd South American International Industrial Engineering and Operations Management* (pp. 919–929). https://ieomsociety.org/proceedings/2022paraguay/211.pdf

16 Chaudhuri, R., Chatterjee, S., Vrontis, D., & Thrassou, A. (2024). Adoption of robust business analytics for product innovation and organizational performance: The mediating role of organizational data-driven culture. *Annals of Operations Research*, 339(3), 1757–1791. https://doi.org/10.1007/s10479-021-04407-3. Available at https://link.springer.com/article/10.1007/s10479-021-04407-3

17 Kohli, R., & Devaraj, S. (2003). Measuring information technology payoff: A meta-analysis of structural variables in firm-level empirical research. *Information Systems Research*, 14(2), 127–145. Available at https://ideas.repec.org/a/inm/orisre/v14y2003i2p127-145.html?utm_source=chatgpt.com

18 Kohli, R., & Devaraj, S. (2003). Measuring information technology payoff: A meta-analysis of structural variables in firm-level empirical research. *Information Systems Research*, 14(2), 127–145. Available at https://ideas.repec.org/a/inm/orisre/v14y2003i2p127-145.html?utm_source=chatgpt.com

15 Emerging Issues of BA and AI in Business

Learning Objectives

- Explore the future of AI in business: trends and predictions
- Learn explainable AI (XAI) and interpretability
- Understand AI for sustainability
- Learn the role of AI in cybersecurity
- Understand the evolving landscape and future of data analytics in business
- Learn AutoML and no-code AI tools for business users
- Identify emerging AI trends
- Understand the future of work in an AI-driven economy
- Explore upcoming regulations and challenges
- Strategize for long-term AI adoption
- Understand AI as a strategic asset in driving competitive advantage and innovation
- Understand the role of AI in supply chains by making supply chains more agile, responsive, and resilient to disruptions
- Explain human–AI collaboration to promote synergistic human–AI collaboration rather than AI replacement
- Learn Agentic AI, Gemini AI, and prompt engineering applications

15.1 Introduction

The synergy between AI and BA is expected to reshape businesses and industries, redefine competitive landscapes, and present unprecedented opportunities for innovation in the ever-growing era of rapid technological advancements and data-driven decision-making. As organizations increasingly rely on AI and data-driven business analytics. BA to establish strategic plans, optimize operations, and enhance customer experiences, the intersection of AI and BA has emerged as a main theme of business in the twenty-first century and a cornerstone of modern enterprise success. The future of this synergy between AI and BA is expected to be transformative, with emerging trends such as GenAI, XAI, edge computing, and autonomous decision-making systems. This future integration of technology and business with the use of AI-driven analytics tools and techniques and advancements will

DOI: 10.4324/9781003664550-15

revolutionize how businesses harness data to enhance the accuracy and efficiency of BA and enable organizations to anticipate market movements, personalize customer interactions, and automate complex business processes.

This chapter examines the cutting-edge developments shaping the application of AI and BA by addressing their implications for businesses, offering insights into how organizations can prepare to thrive in an increasingly AI-driven analytics environment, and presenting the global perspectives on the future of AI and BA. Organizations can position themselves at the forefront of innovation, leveraging the power of AI and BA to unlock new levels of growth and resilience through understanding and embracing these trends. However, these opportunities and future global perspectives on AI and BA come with challenges, such as ethical considerations, data privacy concerns, and the need for skilled technology professionals, *Agentic AI*, Gemini AI, and *prompt engineering* as presented in this chapter.

15.2 The Integration of AI and Business Analytics

The integration of AI and BA into AI-driven analytics is expected to shape the future of corporate strategy planning, innovation, and competitiveness as businesses increasingly rely on data to drive decision-making. AI-powered systems and BA-driven tools play essential roles in offering unprecedented insights, automation, and decision-making capabilities. As businesses transition from traditional data analytics to AI-driven analytics, the landscape of BI continues to evolve. The convergence of AI-powered technologies and BA-assisted systems enables organizations to move from descriptive and diagnostic analytics toward predictive and prescriptive insights, fundamentally transforming how businesses operate and compete. It is expected that the application of AI-driven analytics in forecasting market trends and understanding consumer behavior by using AI techniques such as ML, deep learning, and NLP continues to advance in analyzing vast datasets, detecting patterns, and predicting future trends with high accuracy.[1] Key trends and advancements in AI and BA include the following.

15.2.1 AI-Driven Predictive and Prescriptive Analytics

AI systems are revolutionizing the role of BA by enabling real-time, predictive, and even prescriptive analytics. Traditional BI tools have focused on what happened and why it happened, whereas with AI, businesses can now anticipate what will happen next and decide the best course of action in several ways. First, AI-driven predictive analytics models that forecast future outcomes based on historical data. These models, such as those for demand forecasting or customer churn prediction, are built upon the time series analyses, regression studies, and statistical baselines first developed by business analysts. The BA function is critical for curating the relevant historical datasets, defining the forecast horizons, and validating the model's outputs against actual business outcomes to ensure they remain accurate and relevant. Second, AI-driven prescriptive analytics that recommends optimal actions by simulating various scenarios. Prescriptive analytics represents the convergence of predictive models with business constraints and objectives. This requires deep BA involvement in modeling the business environment by incorporating constraints like budget, capacity, and regulations, and defining the optimization goals (e.g., maximizing profit, minimizing risk). The prescriptive engine simulates scenarios, but it is the business analyst who interprets the recommendations, assesses their feasibility within the organizational context, and translates them into executable business plans. Third, AI autonomous decision-making agents that can take real-time actions without human intervention (e.g., in supply chain management or fraud detection). Even in autonomous systems, BA provides the governance and oversight framework. Analysts establish control parameters and guardrails for these agents, design the monitoring dashboards to track their performance and unintended consequences, and conduct periodic audits. The decision logic of these agents is often derived from and must align with business policies first documented and analyzed through business process modeling. Predictive analytics using ML models is intended to forecast future trends based on historical data. Prescriptive analytics is an advanced model of recommending actions based on the insights provided by predictive analytics models. Organizations are increasingly adopting AI-powered tools and techniques in conjunction with both predictive and prescriptive analytics models to optimize operations, manage risks, and enhance decision-making. Enhancing smart devices and systems with AI can create more intuitive, efficient, and personalized user experiences in smart homes, cities, and healthcare.

15.2.2 Enhanced Data Processing Capabilities and Interpretation

The future of BA tools empower organizations to process massive volumes of structured, semi-structured, and unstructured data from various sources (IoT devices, social media, sensors, transactional systems) by using (1) NLP to analyze text-based data such as customer reviews and ESG disclosures; (2) Computer Vision to analyze image and video data in retail, manufacturing, and healthcare; and (3) Deep Learning to uncover hidden patterns in large, complex datasets. NLP enables AI systems to process and analyze unstructured data, such as customer reviews, emails, and social media interactions, to improve sentiment analysis, customer service automation, and real-time BI. These AI capabilities are critical in dynamic markets where consumer behavior is influenced by factors like economic conditions and social media trends, while challenges in implementing AI-driven predictive analytics, including data quality issues, privacy concerns, improved data governance, workforce training, and the need for specialized skills, will be further addressed.[2] The AI-powered platforms enable organizations to gain insights faster and more accurately, leading to improved responsiveness and efficiency.

15.2.3 AI-Augmented Analytics

AI-assisted augmented analytics involves the use of AI and ML to automate data preparation, insight generation, and insight explanation by enabling organizations to interact with data through conversational analytics (e.g., chatbots, voice assistants), automated data storytelling, and self-service dashboards driven by AI recommendations. Advanced BA and AI models can now highlight key trends, detect anomalies, and suggest data-driven actions in real time, transforming data visualization and automatically generating insights, dashboards, and narratives. AI-powered technologies will continue to advance to enhance data visualization for real-time analytics by offering dynamic tools to interpret and visualize vast datasets, transforming raw information into actionable insights, and their applications span sectors like finance, healthcare, and marketing, where real-time dashboards and voice-based queries enhance decision-making.[3] As these tools become more advanced and prevalent, data literacy across organizations is expected to increase, leading to democratized access to powerful analytical capabilities.

15.2.4 Automated Machine Learning (AutoML)

AutoML refers to the process of automating the entire end-to-end tasks by applying ML to real-world problems to make it accessible to non-experts and streamlining the workflow for data scientists. The AutoML enables non-technical users to harness AI's power without requiring deep expertise in data science by simplifying the process of developing and deploying ML models through automating data preprocessing, feature selection, and hyperparameter tuning. AutoML systems are intended to automatically select the most appropriate algorithms, preprocess data, optimize model parameters (hyperparameter tuning), and even conduct model evaluation and deployment with minimal human intervention. AutoM models enable faster experimentation and enhance productivity while maintaining or even improving model performance by streamlining the complex and time-consuming steps involved in traditional ML pipelines. These models leverage techniques such as NAS, Bayesian optimization, ensemble learning, and meta-learning to intelligently explore the vast space of model configurations and feature transformations. AutoML is particularly useful in domains where large volumes of data must be processed quickly and accurately, such as finance, healthcare, marketing, and cybersecurity. Furthermore, AutoML systems are designed to enhance democratization of AI by allowing business analysts, domain experts, and other non-technical professionals to build powerful predictive models without deep knowledge of coding, programming, or statistics.

15.2.5 Real-Time Business Analytics and Edge AI

AI-driven analytics is advancing to more real-time and decentralized systems that enable businesses to process data closer to the source, allowing faster decision-making and reducing latency in critical operations such as supply chain management and fraud detection. This shift is fundamentally enabled by the evolution of BA from a periodic, batch-oriented function to a continuous, streaming discipline. Real-time analytics requires a new data architecture and governance model, which the BA function designs and maintains. Real-time BA and Edge AI (RTBA&EAI) represent a powerful convergence of BA for data processing capabilities and AI that is transforming how organizations utilize data in making decisions and responding to dynamic market conditions. Real-time business analytics (RTBA) involves the immediate processing and analysis of data as it is generated, allowing organizations to gain instant insights and take proactive actions based on current information rather than historical trends. Implementing RTBA demands that BA teams architect streaming data pipelines that can ingest, cleanse, and aggregate high-velocity data from sources like transaction logs, IoT sensors, and web clicks. It also requires designing new real-time dashboards and alerting systems that present these insights in an immediately actionable format for frontline operators and managers. This BA capability is vital in sectors such as finance, manufacturing, retail, logistics, and healthcare, where timely responses can lead to significant competitive advantages. Edge AI improves this process by bringing computation and ML algorithms directly to the edge of the network, closer to data sources like sensors, IoT devices, and mobile endpoints to minimize latency associated with sending data to centralized cloud servers. This integration enables faster decision-making, enhances data privacy and security, reduces bandwidth consumption, and ensures uninterrupted operation even in environments with limited connectivity by empowering organizations to monitor operations, detect anomalies, predict outcomes, and personalize customer experiences with remarkable speed and precision. Examples of applications are real-time fraud detection and predictive maintenance, personalized marketing, and adaptive supply chain management.

15.2.6 Explainable AI (XAI) and Ethical AI Practices

XAI and ethical AI practices are critical components in the development and deployment of trustworthy AI systems, especially as AI becomes increasingly embedded in high-stakes decision-making processes across industries such as healthcare, finance, law enforcement, and human resources. XAI refers to methods and techniques that make the decisions and predictions of AI models understandable to human users, offering transparency into how algorithms arrive at specific outcomes. XAI focuses on making AI models interpretable by addressing regulatory requirements and building trust in AI-driven analytics. XAI refers to a set of computer tools and techniques intended to make AI models more transparent, interpretable, and understandable to humans. This interpretability is vital for fostering trust, improving model performance, detecting biases, and enabling human oversight. Techniques such as SHAP, LIME, and model-agnostic visualizations are typically used to reveal the inner workings of opaque ML models, especially complex deep learning architectures. Ethical AI practices also encompass the design, development, and deployment of AI systems in ways that prioritize ethics, fairness, accountability, transparency, privacy, and the mitigation of harm. These practices involve addressing algorithmic bias, ensuring data integrity, safeguarding user consent and data privacy, and promoting inclusive design that considers diverse user needs and societal contexts. Together, XAI and ethical AI create a framework for responsible AI use that aligns with legal, regulatory, ethical, and moral standards to allow organizations to avoid financial and reputational damage, legal risks, and societal harm.

As AI systems become increasingly complex, their decision-making processes often resemble "black boxes," which makes it difficult for them to trace and comprehend how and why specific outcomes are generated. XAI aims to minimize this concern by providing insights into model predictions, enhancing trust, accountability, and fairness. Especially in high-stakes and risky domains such as finance, healthcare, and legal decision-making, where opaque AI models can lead to unintended biases or ethical concerns, the XAI can play an important role. By improving interpretability, XAI supports regulatory compliance, facilitates debugging, and enables stakeholders to make informed decisions based on AI-driven recommendations. XAI is becoming more embedded in decision-making to ensure transparency and accountability of AI and BA systems. Developing AI systems that provide transparent, understandable explanations for their decisions is crucial for ethical considerations and trust in sectors like healthcare and finance. XAI capabilities can improve transparency and explainability and present technical solutions to algorithmic bias and black box problems, but they are lacking in understanding of human perspectives, such as practitioners' and users' expectations, and ensuring ethical AI practices.[4] As AI and BA technologies continue to evolve and impact more aspects of businesses and human life, the integration of explainability and ethical considerations is becoming a technical necessity and a societal imperative to ensure that AI systems contribute positively to human well-being, uphold fundamental rights and values, and generate positive social outcomes.

15.2.7 AI and BA for Sustainability

AI-driven analytics systems are advancing sustainability initiatives and ultimately transforming the sustainability landscape by empowering organizations with AI-powered and BA-assisted tools and techniques to drive informed decision-making, optimize resource use, and promote long-term environmental, social, and economic well-being. Together, AI and BA enable organizations to uncover patterns, forecast trends, and make proactive, sustainability-driven decisions with greater precision and speed through the automation and enhancement of data collection and processing. AI-driven analytics systems play a growing role in examining sustainability factors of planning, performance, risk, and disclosure as related to ESG analytics. Businesses are leveraging AI to monitor supply chain sustainability, track carbon footprints, and assess corporate social responsibility (CSR) initiatives. Utilizing AI-driven analytics for environmental monitoring can predict climate patterns and optimize energy consumption to combat climate change more effectively.

Integrated AI and BA systems enable organizations to advance sustainability across sectors such as healthcare, finance, agriculture, and environmental management in supporting real-time monitoring of sustainability metrics such as carbon emissions, energy consumption, waste management, and supply chain performance, enabling companies to identify inefficiencies, reduce environmental impacts, and improve compliance with regulatory standards. Furthermore, predictive analytics powered by AI allows organizations to anticipate future sustainability risks, adapt to climate-related challenges, and design more resilient and adaptive strategies. For the social dimension of sustainability, AI and BA can be utilized to assess workforce diversity, community engagement, and human rights practices, thereby advancing CSR objectives. In the governance dimension, AI technologies enhance transparency and accountability through data-driven insights and automated reporting, supporting ethical decision-making and stakeholder trust. Thus, the synergy between AI and BA empowers organizations to align profitability with sustainability goals, transition to circular economy models, and create lasting value for all stakeholders, including shareholders, customers, employees, suppliers, communities, society, and the environment. For example, AI-driven analytics systems for chronic kidney disease diagnosis achieved 100% accuracy using ensemble methods, while hybrid models for assessing voice service quality demonstrated high sensitivity and specificity and lower carbon footprints in sectors like healthcare through optimized resource use and reduced waste, which align with Sustainable Development Goals (SDGs).[5]

15.2.8 Quantum AI

Quantum AI represents the next frontier in the AI landscape by integrating the principles of quantum computing with advanced AI algorithms to solve complex problems that are currently intractable for conventional AI systems. Quantum AI computing can solve complex problems exponentially faster than traditional computers, potentially transforming fields like cryptography, materials science, and complex system simulation. While the quantum hardware and algorithms are still maturing, the groundwork for leveraging this power is being laid today by advanced BA. BA prepares the data and problem formulations for the quantum era by refining high-dimensional optimization problems, such as global supply chain routing or molecular interaction datasets, into clean, structured formats that will be executable on future quantum processors. Quantum AI is an emerging field that integrates quantum computing with AI to enhance computational capabilities and solve complex problems beyond the reach of typical AI systems. Quantum AI can process vast amounts of data and perform calculations at unprecedented speeds by leveraging the principles of quantum mechanics, such as superposition, entanglement, and quantum parallelism, and the unique properties of quantum bits or qubits. Combining AI platforms and quantum computations allows for faster training of ML models, enhanced optimization capabilities, and more efficient processing of massive, high-dimensional datasets, and enables exponentially greater computational power compared to traditional binary systems.

Quantum AI holds transformative potential across a wide range of industries, including finance, healthcare, logistics, energy, and cybersecurity, where problems involving complex pattern recognition, combinatorial optimization, and simulation are prevalent. For example, in drug discovery, Quantum AI can accelerate molecular modeling to identify potential treatments with unprecedented speed and accuracy. In financial services, it can enhance risk assessment and portfolio optimization. Furthermore, Quantum AI offers a powerful framework for developing intelligent, adaptive systems capable of addressing these issues more effectively as global challenges become more intricate, such as climate modeling, supply chain disruptions, and energy grid management. While this technology is still in its early stages, with significant potential and challenges in hardware development, algorithm design, and error correction, ongoing advancements suggest that Quantum AI could radically redefine the future of computation and AI, leading to breakthroughs that were previously unimaginable. This has significant implications for optimization, cryptography, drug discovery, financial modeling, and ML. Quantum AI holds the potential to revolutionize areas like deep learning and neural networks by accelerating training processes and improving pattern recognition in large datasets. While still in its early stages, ongoing advancements in quantum hardware and algorithms are gradually paving the way for practical applications, positioning Quantum AI as a transformative force in the future of computing and AI. There is a potential to integrate AI technologies with quantum physics to address complex challenges, such as optimizing quantum algorithms, enhancing quantum communication, and accelerating AI applications through quantum speedups in developing variational quantum algorithms (VQAs) and quantum generative adversarial networks (QGANs) and making valuable contributions to discussions on next-generation computing.[6] Ultimately, AI-driven analytics serves as the critical translation layer between quantum theory and business value.

15.2.9 Neuromorphic Computing

Neuromorphic computing is a cutting-edge approach to computing that mimics the structure and functionality of the human brain to achieve energy-efficient and highly adaptive AI. Unlike traditional von Neumann architectures, which separate memory and processing units, neuromorphic systems integrate computation and memory through artificial neurons and synapses, enabling parallel processing and real-time learning. These systems leverage specialized hardware, such as spiking neural networks (SNNs) and neuromorphic chips, to process information in a manner like biological neural networks. This allows for enhanced pattern recognition, sensory processing, and decision-making with significantly lower power consumption compared to conventional AI systems. Neuromorphic hardware can achieve greater computational efficiency and adaptiveness, particularly for edge computing applications in robotics, autonomous vehicles, healthcare monitoring, and the Internet of Things (IoT) by using spiking neural networks (SNNs), which mimic the way biological neurons communicate through discrete electrical impulses.

Neuromorphic systems can learn and adapt in real time with minimal energy consumption, making them especially suitable for environments with limited power or latency constraints. Moreover, neuromorphic computing holds immense promises for advancing AI by enabling more robust and biologically plausible models of learning and perception. As researchers continue to develop specialized neuromorphic chips, such as Intel's Loihi or IBM's TrueNorth, the field is poised to revolutionize how machines learn and interact with their environment, pushing the boundaries of neuromorphic computing has promising applications in robotics, edge AI, and autonomous systems, offering a pathway toward more intelligent and efficient computing architectures that closely resemble human cognitive abilities. This technique mimics the neural structures of the human brain to create more efficient and powerful AI systems, potentially revolutionizing AI's approach to learning and interacting with the world. Neuromorphic computing has the potential to revolutionize information processing by drawing inspiration from the brain's energy efficiency and computational capabilities to significantly enhance energy efficiency and computational power by leveraging novel materials and nanoscale devices, such as memristors and spintronic oscillators, to emulate neurons and synapses and to achieve brain-like efficiency, with recent advancements demonstrating functional networks of millions of memristors.[7] Despite challenges related to scalability, programming models, and integration with existing AI frameworks, neuromorphic computing stands as a critical step toward achieving more intelligent and energy-efficient computing systems for the future.

15.2.10 AI-Driven Personalization and Customer Insights

AI-driven personalization and customer insights have become integral components of modern business strategies, empowering organizations to deliver highly tailored experiences that resonate with individual preferences, behaviors, and needs. A combination of ML algorithms, NLP, and predictive analytics enables AI to analyze vast and diverse datasets ranging from purchase histories and browsing behavior to social media interactions and demographic information to uncover deep patterns and actionable insights. AI-powered technologies can improve customer analytics by enabling organizations to deliver hyper-personalized experiences. AI-driven analytics systems are expected to (1) anticipate and forecast customer needs using sentiment analysis and predictive modeling, (2) make recommendations based on real-time behavioral data, and (3) foster customer segmentation through advanced clustering and classification techniques. This type and level of tailored insight support more effective marketing, customer relationship management, and product development.

15.2.11 Gemini and Agentic AI Enterprise

AI has undergone a remarkable evolution by transforming from simple rule-based systems to sophisticated, autonomous agents capable of independent reasoning and goal-directed action. Early AI models relied on predefined rules and logic, offering predictable outputs but limited adaptability. As AI advanced, ML presented the ability for systems to learn from data, recognize patterns, and make probabilistic decisions by enabling more flexible and intelligent behavior. The emergence of Agentic AI and Gemini AI enterprises represents the next generation in this evolution. Unlike traditional AI, agentic systems act autonomously, evaluate options, pursue objectives, and make decisions with minimal human intervention. These AI Agentic systems can plan, reason, and adapt dynamically to complex and changing environments that make them powerful tools for automating workflows, enhancing decision-making, and driving innovation across industries. These AI systems are increasingly being designed as autonomous agents capable of reasoning, decision-making, and executing complex tasks. Agentic AI and recently launched Gemini AI Enterprise systems are transforming industries, yet their effectiveness depends largely on how humans interact with them. Prompt engineering explores the emerging discipline of designing, optimizing, and applying prompts to guide AI systems toward accurate, creative, and ethical outputs. Prompt engineering is the art and science of guiding AI systems toward accurate, reliable, and contextually relevant outputs. Google's Gemini technical reporting highlights long-context, multimodal reasoning, important for agents that must read long documents, interpret visual evidence, or track extended task histories.[8] Recent work in embodied and robotics contexts underscores how agentic AI can extend into the physical world, where planning, progress estimation, and tool use become essential.[9] These capabilities empower organizations to undertake tasks that are inherently multimodal (dashboards, scanned invoices, contract PDFs, screenshots, meeting audio), and agents must integrate across modalities to act effectively. The future of Gemini and Agentic AI is not "a chatbot that talks and writes," but a managed, auditable, goal-driven system that can do with prompt engineering and oversight as the practical levers that convert raw model capability into dependable business value.

15.3 Prospects on AI and BA

The prospects of AI and BA are significantly promising, as these technologies continue to reshape the competitive landscape and redefine how organizations generate value in the global and digital economy. As AI and BA technologies continue to advance, businesses that embrace AI-driven analytics will gain a competitive edge in decision-making and operational efficiency by staying ahead of these trends to leverage AI and BA for sustainable growth and innovation. This competitive edge will be built upon a mature BA foundation that transforms data into a formalized, trusted corporate asset. BA will evolve from a support function to a core strategic capability, responsible for governing the data supply chain, ensuring the integrity of insights, and quantifying the ROI of all AI initiatives. The future of AI and BA in daily life is poised for even greater expansion and innovation. Advancements in AI and BA can lead to more autonomous systems capable of complex decision-making and problem-solving and sustainable businesses by reducing the need for human intervention in all business affairs. However, this autonomy will be governed and directed by the strategic frameworks, KPIs, and business rules defined and managed by the BA function. BA will provide the "guardrails" and "destination" for autonomous systems, ensuring they optimize for business outcomes and adhere to ethical and regulatory standards. For example, the integration of AI and BA systems can (1) revolutionize personalized medicine in healthcare by enabling treatments tailored to individuals' genetic makeup; (2) facilitate more immersive and interactive learning experiences through virtual and augmented reality by making education more accessible and customized to learners' needs; (3) make smart homes even more intuitive, where AI anticipates needs and manages the environment with minimal user input; (4) enhance efficiency, creativity, and personalization by profoundly reshaping our daily routines and interactions with technology; and (5) redefine a broad spectrum of industries and societal norms. Ultimately, the convergence of AI and BA is expected to enhance operational efficiency, drive product and service innovation, and uncover new revenue streams by transforming raw data into strategic assets.

The future of AI and BA will become more deeply intertwined with other transformative technologies, including (1) Blockchain, in making data more secure, transparent, and auditable data; (2) Digital Twins, for developing virtual models that use real-time analytics to simulate and optimize business processes; (3) Edge Computing and IoT, for empowering organization to us real-time analytics at the point of data generation; (4) Quantum Computing, which will be intended to solve complex optimization problems and accelerate

AI model training; (5) GenAI, which will automate the synthesis of reports and scenarios from diverse data sources, enabling natural language interaction with complex datasets; (6) Augmented Reality (AR), which will enable immersive, three-dimensional data visualization for collaborative planning and complex system analysis; (7) Intelligent Automation (RPA and AI), which will evolve from task automation to managing entire analytical workflows, from data extraction to insight delivery; and (8) Neuromorphic Computing, which will provide extreme energy efficiency for continuous learning from streaming data in embedded and mobile applications. The expectation is that these technologies will drive a new era of data-driven innovation, fostering smarter, faster, and more strategic decisions across all sectors, from healthcare and finance to retail, manufacturing, and sustainability initiatives. Furthermore, future AI and BA systems must address (1) bias and fairness in AI algorithms; (2) transparency and explainability of BA decisions; (3) the use of AI-driven analytics technologies in sustainability reporting and ESG disclosures; (4) data privacy and compliance with regulations (e.g., GDPR, CCPA); (5) effective and robust governance frameworks to ensure AI and BA are used responsibly and in alignment with societal values; (6) the role of humans as AI and BA platforms in augmenting human capabilities by automating repetitive analytical tasks, supporting complex decision-making, and enhancing creativity and strategic thinking through better insights; (7) strategic and competitive implications of AI and BA technologies for faster innovation cycles, greater customer centricity, improved operational efficiency, and stronger and more effective risk assessment, management and forecasting abilities. (8) Algorithmic Accountability and Auditability, requiring clear documentation of model development, decision trails, and mechanisms for external review to assign responsibility for AI-driven outcomes; (9) Security and Resilience, ensuring AI and BA systems are protected against adversarial attacks, data poisoning, and manipulation that could compromise critical business operations or decision integrity; and (10) Sustainable and Green AI/BA, prioritizing energy-efficient model training and infrastructure to minimize the environmental footprint of large-scale data processing and computation. Overall, the future of AI and BA is transformative, pervasive, and highly dynamic. Organizations must invest in the right technologies, talent, and ethical frameworks to leverage these tools effectively. As AI continues to evolve, its integration with BA will not only enhance performance but also reshape industries, redefine competition, and support sustainable and responsible growth in the digital age.

Ultimately, the next decade of AI and BA integration will be defined by a shift from *analytics-as-reporting* to *analytics-as-decision infrastructure*, where AI systems continuously sense, predict, recommend, and increasingly *act and integrate with BA capabilities*. Three forces are expected to converge: (1) ubiquitous data from digital platforms, IoT, and enterprise systems; (2) rapid advances in ML and GenAI; and (3) organizational demand for faster, more transparent, and more accountable decisions. The integration of these forces empowers organizations to adopt AI capabilities across business structure with broad diffusion of AI and BA capabilities in organizations and continued growth in IT private investment, which will further amplify analytics innovation and competitive pressure.[10] AI-driven analytics systems are becoming the engine that powers faster forecasting, smarter automation, deeper insight generation, and more accountable decision-making across business functions. Organizations are expected to consider AI and BA through technical performance and business outcomes such as cost reduction, revenue growth, risk mitigation, customer retention, and operational resilience by relying on cross-functional fusion teams, combining business experts, analytics professionals, IT engineers, and governance leaders to build analytics solutions aligned with strategy.

15.4 AI and BA Development and Industry Trends

AI and BA have advanced from after-the-fact reporting to continuous to AI-enabled decision support and now toward AI-embedded operations, where models are deployed, monitored, and improved as part of everyday workflows. This development is driven by three forces of technological advancements, adoption of Agentic AI and Gemini AI enterprise, and requirements for governance, security, and measurable business impact. Organizations across different sectors are now able to collect and analyze massive volumes of structured and unstructured data from diverse sources, increasing the scale and scope of analytics-driven transformation. Looking ahead, the democratization of AI and BA tools and the growing emphasis on user-friendly analytics platforms suggest that even small- and medium-sized enterprises (SMEs) will be able to harness these capabilities without needing extensive technical expertise. At the same time, emerging trends such as XAI, AutoML, and augmented analytics will further enhance transparency, usability, and trust in AI-driven insights. A critical future trend is the evolution of BA into "Continuous Analytics," where the traditional cycle of report-request, development, and delivery is replaced by real-time, self-updating data products and living dashboards that proactively alert users to anomalies and opportunities as they emerge. However, to fully realize these prospects, organizations must invest in data governance, digital literacy, and ethical AI practices, ensuring that technological progress is aligned with societal values and stakeholder expectations. Overall, the future of AI and BA is one of continued growth, innovation, and transformation, offering unprecedented opportunities for organizations in all industries to become more intelligent, agile, and sustainable in an increasingly complex and competitive world. Below are some key future development trends.[11]

15.4.1 The Dominance of Composable and Modular Analytics

Traditionally, organizations used descriptive analytics, dashboards, and basic reporting to understand "what happened." With stronger computing power and more data, firms scaled forecasting, classification, and anomaly detection for marketing, credit, fraud, and operations. Today, GenAI is reshaping how analytics is produced and consumed, while augmented analytics automates data preparation and insight generation by expanding BA access to non-technical users. Future BA platforms will be built on composable architectures, where analytics capabilities (data ingestion, transformation, visualization, ML) are modular microservices. This will allow organizations to assemble custom analytics stacks tailored to specific business processes, enhancing agility and reducing vendor lock-in.

15.4.2 The Convergence of BI and Data Science Workflows

The traditional BI of descriptive dashboards) and Data Science of predictive models are integrating to develop platforms that unify these workflows by enabling analysts to seamlessly move from visualizing historical data to building, deploying, and monitoring ML models within the same environment. This enables the democratization of analytics through natural language interfaces, automated insight narratives, and AI-assisted exploration.

15.4.3 Analytics Engineering as a Core Discipline

Augmented analytics reduces technical barriers and speeds up the path from question to insight and action to support broader adoption in functions like finance, audit/risk, marketing, HR, and supply chain. The role of the "Analytics Engineer" will become central, focusing on building reliable, tested, and documented data transformation pipelines (using tools like dbt). This role bridges data engineering and analysis, ensuring that clean, trustworthy data is productized for consumption by the entire organization.

15.4.4 The Rise of Decision Intelligence (DI)

Organizations have used GenAI as an interface layer for BA by summarizing results and generating narratives. BA will shift from primarily providing insights to explicitly modeling and automating decision processes. DI platforms will use a combination of data, AI, and business rules to map, simulate, and optimize the chain of reasoning behind key business decisions, making the link between data and action systematic and auditable. It transforms from building AI and BA models to running model-enabled DI products, which integrate versioning, automated pipelines, deployment, monitoring, and retraining so models remain accurate and reliable over time.

15.4.5 Proliferation of Specialized, Vertical AI–BA Solutions

Instead of generic tools, the market will see an explosion of AI-powered analytics solutions built for specific verticals (e.g., clinical trial analytics for pharma, supply chain resiliency analytics for manufacturing). These solutions will come with pre-trained models and industry-specific data ontologies, dramatically accelerating time-to-value. Competitive advantages of vertical AI–BA solutions come from lifecycle discipline, monitoring drift, testing robustness, managing feedback loops, and ensuring decision outputs remain aligned with business goals.

15.4.6 Embedded and Contextual Analytics

Analytics will increasingly be embedded directly into the operational applications where work gets done (e.g., within CRM, ERP, or field service software). Insights and next-best-action recommendations will be served in the user's workflow context, eliminating the need to switch to a separate analytics portal. AI-driven analytics must be reliable, fair, explainable, secure, and auditable, especially in regulated or high-stakes domains.

15.4.7 The Quantification of ESG and Intangible Assets

Advanced BA will develop robust methodologies to measure and value intangible assets (brand equity, intellectual capital) and ESG performance. This will transform sustainability reporting from a narrative exercise into a rigorously quantified performance management discipline integrated with financial reporting.

15.4.8 Sovereign and Federated Analytics for Privacy

In response to data privacy regulations, federated analytics, where models are trained on decentralized data without it ever leaving its source, will gain prominence. This, combined with privacy-enhancing technologies (PETs), will enable collaborative insights while maintaining strict data sovereignty. The NIST AI Risk Management Framework (AI RMF 1.0) is widely used as a lifecycle structure for governing and managing AI risk (e.g., mapping context, measuring risks, managing controls). NIST also provides cross-sector guidance that extends AI RMF ideas to GenAI risk considerations.[12]

15.4.9 Autonomous Optimization of the Analytics Stack Itself

AI will be applied to manage the analytics infrastructure. This includes AIOps for monitoring data pipeline performance, and meta-learning systems that automatically select the best algorithms, tune parameters, and allocate computational resources for specific analytical tasks, optimizing the cost and performance of the BA function itself. Ultimately, many organizations will report AI use in at least one business function, though fewer have fully scaled it across the enterprise (often due to data readiness, governance, and operating-model gaps).

15.5 Bidirectional Encoder Representations from Transformers (BERT)

BERT is a language representation model that reshaped modern NLP by showing that deep, bidirectional contextual representations learned from large unlabeled corpora can be fine-tuned effectively for many downstream tasks with minimal task-specific architecture changes.[13] BERT builds directly on the transformer encoder architecture that conditions on both left and right context in all layers, which relies on self-attention (rather than recurrence or convolutions) to model relationships among tokens efficiently and in parallel. Therefore, without requiring significant task-specific architecture changes, the pre-trained BERT model may be optimized with just one more output layer to produce state-of-the-art models for a variety of tasks, including question-answering and language inference. BERT uses a multi-layer transformer encoder (Base and Large configurations were introduced in the original paper) where each layer contains multi-head self-attention and position-wise feed-forward networks, with residual connections and layer normalization. The transformer's self-attention mechanism allows each token to attend to all other tokens in the input sequence, supporting strong contextualization and scalability.[14] This innovation enables the model to gain a deep understanding of the context of a word, depending on all its surroundings. For example, the word "booking" can represent either the posting of an accounting transaction or the act of planning, depending on its context.

The BERT language model can differentiate between the meanings of those homographic words with contextualized word embeddings. BERT is pre-trained with an unlabeled dataset of approximately 3.3 billion English words, stemming from open-source books and Wikipedia articles. To understand sentence relationships, the algorithm is trained to predict randomly masked words based on the provided context, as well as next sentences based on their preceding sentences. The resulting model significantly outperforms already sophisticated NLP algorithms by a substantial margin. Given its superior performance, BERT is currently used in Google's search queries and NLP processes, and its effectiveness in classifying the content of corporate disclosures has recently been demonstrated.[15] A major reason BERT became widely adopted is the simplicity of fine-tuning: the pretrained encoder is reused, and a small task-specific head is added (e.g., a classifier on top of [CLS] for classification tasks, or token-level heads for sequence labeling). The entire network is then trained end-to-end on labeled data for the target task. This contrasts with earlier feature-based transfer approaches, and in practice significantly lowered the barrier to achieving strong results across benchmarks. The BERT language model set a new standard for textual analysis algorithms by significantly improving the results for various NLP tasks. FinBERT can be used to classify accounting topics, and AuditBERT can prioritize auditing topics as explained in the following subsections.

15.5.1 FinBERT

FinBERT is pre-trained in financial texts such as corporate filings and analyst reports. FinBERT significantly outperforms alternative models commonly used in finance research. FinBERT can be used in the pretraining of specialized language models. FinBERT is a domain-specific variant of BERT, which is intended for financial sentiment analysis and text mining in accounting and finance disciplines in addressing limits of general-purpose NLP in financial contexts to analyze complex financial text, including earnings forecasts, analyst reports, financial news, and annual (10-K) and quarterly (10 Q) financial reports, which applies to task-specific data and optimizing sentiment classification with labels (positive, neutral, and negative). FinBERT extends the general-purpose transformer encoder by pretraining on finance-centric corpora, enabling a more accurate understanding of financial language nuances such as sentiment, jargon, and specialized syntactic structures that are atypical in general text corpora.[16]

A prominent application of FinBERT is in financial sentiment analysis, where the model is fine-tuned to classify text into sentiment categories (e.g., positive, negative, neutral). FinBERT can achieve significant improvements over traditional ML approaches (like naive Bayes, support vector machines, and long short-term memory models) and generic BERT models on common financial sentiment benchmarks such as Financial PhraseBank. These gains are attributed to FinBERT's ability to correctly interpret financial terms and contextual cues that are subtle yet critical for accurate sentiment interpretation. FinBERT can detect subtle shifts in managerial tone, uncertainty, or optimism within earnings calls and annual reports, providing quantitative sentiment scores that serve as leading indicators of stock volatility, fraud risk, or future performance. This transforms qualitative disclosure into a structured, analyzable dataset.

15.5.2 AuditBERT

Modern auditing faces a rapidly evolving landscape of complex unstructured data (e.g., narrative audit reports, compliance documents, regulatory text) that traditional rule-based systems struggle to analyze efficiently. Consequently, transformer-based language models, particularly those derived from BERT, are increasingly seen as promising tools for augmenting audit analytics and automation. AuditBERT is pre-trained on a large corpus of audit-related texts such as audit reports, financial statements, and regulatory documents with the goal of understanding and generating audit-relevant language with high accuracy and contextual understanding.[17] AuditBERT can address inconsistencies, lack of clarity, and boilerplate language challenges of audit reports. AuditBERT can be fine-tuned to detect and classify critical audit matters (CAMs) from past audit reports using supervised learning, improve consistency in CAM reporting, predict likely CAMs that an auditor should consider, and suggest or generate tailored, non-boilerplate language for CAM disclosures. AuditBERT offers a powerful AI-driven approach to transform how CAMs are identified, crafted, and interpreted. AuditBERT can support the core objectives of auditing standards and the broader push toward enhanced audit transparency in the AI era by improving both the quality (clarity, relevance, comparability) and quantity (coverage of material issues) of disclosures.

Fine-tuned AuditBERT models can continuously monitor management's narratives in quarterly reports or earnings calls, flagging significant deviations from past language or industry norms that may indicate increased risk, aggressive accounting, or obfuscation, thereby enabling a more proactive, risk-based audit approach. AuditBERT, an open-source audit domain LLM, can be developed by fine-tuning a large language model with instruction datasets tailored to multi-level audit tasks (e.g., entity extraction, question answering, document generation). The model can automate preliminary reviews of draft financial statements and footnotes, checking for internal consistency, clarity, and alignment with relevant accounting standards, freeing senior auditors to focus on high-risk judgment areas. AuditBERT can be used in semantic risk detection by identifying latent risk cues in narrative audit documentation or financial disclosures and classifying text segments according to applicable audit standards or regulatory frameworks.

15.6 Generative AI: Concepts, Techniques, and Applications

GenAI represents a paradigm shift in AI, moving beyond predictive analysis to creative synthesis. Unlike traditional analytical models that interpret existing data, generative models—particularly LLMs like GPT-4 and multimodal systems like DALL-E and Sora—create novel content, including text, code, images, and synthetic data. This capability is fundamentally reshaping the landscape of BA, transforming it from a discipline focused on understanding the past and present to one that actively shapes future possibilities. At its core, GenAI relies on techniques like transformer architectures and diffusion models, trained on vast corpora to learn patterns, styles, and logical structures. For business, this translates into several transformative applications: automated generation of reports, marketing copy, and financial summaries; the creation of synthetic datasets for testing and training where real data is scarce or sensitive; and the development of interactive, conversational interfaces for data querying.

The integration of GenAI into BA heralds the era of augmented analytics. Business users will interact with data through natural language conversations, asking complex, multi-layered questions and receiving not just charts but narrative interpretations, strategic hypotheses, and draft action plans. This democratizes insight extraction, allowing non-technical leaders to engage in sophisticated analysis. Furthermore, GenAI will accelerate scenario planning and simulation. Analysts can prompt models to generate detailed, plausible scenarios for market disruptions, supply chain failures, or new competitive threats, enabling stress testing of strategies with unprecedented speed and breadth. However, this power introduces new imperatives for governance and ethical BA. The propensity for GenAI to "hallucinate" or produce biased outputs necessitates robust human-in-the-loop (HITL) validation frameworks. BA teams must establish protocols for verifying AI-generated insights against source data and will become curators of prompt libraries and fine-tuned models to ensure accuracy and brand voice. The future BA function will increasingly manage a portfolio of generative tools—some for creative ideation, others for precise reporting—ensuring the right technology is applied to the right business problem. Ultimately, GenAI does not replace the need for strategic business thinking; it amplifies it. The future competitive advantage will lie with organizations that can most effectively couple human judgment and domain expertise with the creative and synthetic power of GenAI, embedding this partnership into every stage of the analytics value chain from data preparation to decision communication.

15.7 Explainable AI (XAI): From Transparency to Trust in Business Analytics

XAI has evolved from a niche technical concern into a cornerstone of responsible and strategic BA. While early XAI focused on post-hoc techniques like SHAP and LIME to rationalize complex model outputs, cutting-edge developments are shifting toward inherently interpretable architectures and human-centric explanation frameworks that integrate directly into the decision-making workflow. The frontier of XAI is now defined by three key advancements.

15.7.1 Causal AI Integration

Moving beyond correlation, next-generation XAI incorporates causal inference models that explain not just what the model predicts but why in terms of cause-and-effect relationships. This allows businesses to ask counterfactual questions (e.g., "Would this customer have churned if we had waived the fee?") with greater confidence, turning predictive analytics into actionable intervention plans.

15.7.2 Interactive and Iterative Explanation Systems

Modern XAI platforms provide dynamic, real-time explanation interfaces. Business users can interrogate AI recommendations through natural language (e.g., "Why was this loan application declined?"), receive layered explanations, and even adjust model assumptions to see how outcomes change—fostering a collaborative dialogue between human intuition and machine intelligence.

15.7.3 Regulatory-Grade Audit Trails

With regulations like the EU AI Act mandating transparency for high-risk systems, XAI is becoming formalized. New frameworks automatically generate standardized documentation detailing a model's logic, data lineage, confidence intervals, and known limitations, creating an auditable record for compliance and stakeholder reporting.

Looking forward, XAI will converge with Decision Intelligence (DI), evolving from an explainer of outputs to a simulator of entire decision processes. Future systems will not only justify a single prediction but will map and explain the end-to-end impact of an AI-informed decision across the business ecosystem. Furthermore, as GenAI proliferates, explainability for generative models will become critical—requiring new techniques to trace the provenance of AI-generated content, citations, or strategic recommendations back to credible data sources.

For BA, the ultimate trajectory of XAI is the cultivation of strategic trust. It transforms the analytics function from a producer of opaque "black box" insights to a facilitator of transparent, accountable, and defensible decision-making. By embedding explainability into the core of the AI lifecycle—from design to deployment—organizations will unlock greater adoption from cautious stakeholders, more effective human–AI collaboration, and the ability to scale AI responsibly across every business unit.

15.8 Artificial General Intelligence

AGI, which is hypothetical AI possessing human-like cognitive flexibility, reasoning, and self-directed learning across diverse domains, represents the ultimate horizon in technological evolution. While current AI excels at narrow, well-defined tasks (e.g., forecasting sales, detecting fraud, or translating text), AGI aims to integrate these capabilities into systems that can autonomously understand, learn, and act in open-ended business environments without human reprogramming. Cutting-edge developments are gradually bridging the gap between narrow AI and broader cognitive systems. Key research thrusts include:

15.8.1 Foundation Models with Emergent Abilities

Large-scale models like GPT-4 and beyond are exhibiting sparks of generalized reasoning, solving novel problems, transferring knowledge across domains, and engaging in abstract planning. These "emergent abilities" hint at a path toward more adaptable systems, though they remain specialized in linguistic and symbolic tasks.

15.8.2 Neuro-Symbolic AI Integration

The fusion of data-driven neural networks (which excel at pattern recognition) with rule-based symbolic AI (which excels at logic and reasoning) aims to create systems that learn from experience while also manipulating abstract concepts and causal relationships prerequisite for robust, interpretable generalization in business contexts.

15.8.3 Artificial Consciousness and Self-Modeling

While still speculative, research into AI architectures that can form internal models of themselves and their environments—a step toward meta-cognition—could enable AGI to autonomously diagnose failures, optimize its own performance, and align actions with high-level strategic goals.

For BA, the prospect of AGI introduces both profound opportunities and existential considerations. In its mature form, AGI could autonomously manage entire business functions—integrating market analysis, operational execution, financial planning, and innovation pipelines into a unified, self-optimizing system. It could generate entirely novel business models, negotiate complex partnerships, and navigate regulatory landscapes with strategic foresight.

However, the path to AGI also demands a fundamental rethinking of organizational structure, ethics, and value creation. Businesses must consider how to govern systems that may surpass human reasoning in complexity, how to retain meaningful human agency, and how to redefine roles in an economy where cognitive labor is fully automated. The emergence of AGI would likely shift competitive advantage from those with the best data or algorithms to those with the most robust alignment frameworks, ensuring AGI's objectives remain coherent with human values and organizational purpose.

While timelines remain highly uncertain, forward-looking enterprises are already monitoring these advancements through strategic foresight programs, investing in AI safety research, and cultivating adaptive, learning-oriented cultures. The journey toward AGI, even in its incremental stages, will continue to blur the line between tool and collaborator, ultimately challenging businesses to reimagine the very nature of strategy, leadership, and innovation in an age of machine general intelligence.

15.9 Cutting Edge Advancements and Future Outlooks for AI and BA

Cutting-edge advancements in AI and BA are rapidly expanding the boundaries of what organizations can achieve, setting the stage for an era of autonomous, intelligent, and hyper-personalized business operations. Emerging technologies such as GenAI, foundation models, and agentic AI systems are enabling enterprises to automate complex knowledge work, generate dynamic strategic insights, and rapidly prototype solutions with minimal human intervention. Neuro-symbolic AI and XAI are improving interpretability and reliability, allowing firms to integrate advanced analytics into high-stakes decision environments such as auditing, finance, and healthcare with greater assurance and regulatory alignment. Meanwhile, real-time analytics powered by edge computing and IoT ecosystems are transforming operational contexts, from predictive maintenance in manufacturing to adaptive retail pricing and personalized customer engagement. The convergence of AI with digital twins, blockchain, and 5G infrastructure is fostering new capabilities for simulation, traceability, and instantaneous data flows across global value chains. Looking ahead, organizations are expected to adopt enterprise-wide AI orchestration platforms, autonomous decision-making systems, and human–AI collaborative models that embed intelligence into every function. Ethical principles, governance frameworks, and regulatory oversight will shape this evolution by ensuring responsible deployment while unlocking transformative economic and societal value. As these trends mature, AI and BA will ultimately enhance business performance and redefine competitive advantages and the future architecture of digital enterprises.

15.9.1 Real-Time Analytics Powered by Edge Computing and IoT Ecosystems

Real-time analytics powered by edge computing and IoT ecosystems represent one of the most transformative developments in AI and BA, enabling organizations to process, analyze, and act on data at the point of generation rather than relying solely on centralized cloud infrastructures. Edge computing distributes computational power closer to sensors, devices, and machines—dramatically reducing latency, lowering bandwidth demands, and enabling instantaneous decision-making critical for time-sensitive operations. This architectural shift creates a new paradigm for BA, moving analytics from a centralized, retrospective function to a distributed, operational capability embedded directly into business processes. In manufacturing, IoT-enabled machines equipped with edge analytics can detect anomalies, predict equipment failures, and autonomously adjust parameters to maintain optimal performance, as demonstrated in smart factory initiatives by Siemens and Bosch. In healthcare, wearable IoT devices and edge-based analytics allow continuous monitoring of patient vitals by triggering immediate alerts for irregularities, improving chronic disease management, and reducing hospital readmissions. Smart transportation systems use edge analytics to optimize traffic flow, manage autonomous vehicle navigation, and enhance public safety through real-time incident detection. In retail, edge-enabled cameras and sensors support dynamic pricing, inventory tracking, and frictionless checkout experiences, as seen in Amazon Go stores. Moreover, real-time environmental monitoring systems integrate IoT sensors with edge AI to track air quality, water contamination, and climate conditions, informing sustainability and regulatory compliance efforts. The fusion of AI, IoT, and edge computing creates a distributed intelligence layer across physical and digital environments, enabling organizations to achieve unprecedented responsiveness, efficiency, and situational awareness while paving the way for fully autonomous industrial and service ecosystems.

The fusion of AI, IoT, and edge computing creates a distributed intelligence layer across physical and digital environments, enabling organizations to achieve unprecedented responsiveness, efficiency, and situational awareness while paving the way for fully autonomous industrial and service ecosystems. This distributed intelligence fundamentally redefines the role of central BA teams, who must now architect, govern, and continuously refine a federated analytics ecosystem—managing the deployment of edge models, ensuring data quality across thousands of nodes, and synthesizing local insights into a coherent, strategic enterprise-wide picture.

15.9.2 AI with Digital Twins, Blockchain, and 5G Infrastructure

The convergence of AI with digital twins, blockchain, and 5G infrastructure is redefining how organizations model, secure, and operationalize complex systems, enabling unprecedented levels of precision, transparency, and real-time responsiveness. Digital twins of virtual replicas of physical assets, processes, or entire systems leverage AI and advanced simulation to continuously mirror real-world performance, allowing firms to test scenarios, forecast outcomes, and optimize operations without interrupting actual workflows. This AI-powered simulation layer enables predictive what-if analysis at an unprecedented scale, allowing businesses to stress-test new product designs, simulate market disruptions, or optimize entire supply chain networks in a risk-free digital environment before committing physical resources. Companies like Siemens, Boeing, and Unilever use AI-driven digital twins to optimize production lines, reduce defects, and enhance predictive maintenance capabilities. These digital twins evolve from static models into dynamic, learning systems that ingest real-time IoT data, allowing the AI to continuously refine its simulations and predictions, ultimately leading to self-optimizing industrial processes that can anticipate failures and automatically reconfigure for peak efficiency. Blockchain complements these capabilities by providing immutable, decentralized ledgers that enhance trust, traceability, and data integrity across multi-stakeholder ecosystems. When combined with AI analytics, blockchain enables verifiable supply chain transparency, real-time monitoring of ESG compliance, and secure sharing of sensitive digital twin data among manufacturers, regulators, and suppliers. Meanwhile, 5G infrastructure acts as the high-speed, low-latency backbone that enables instantaneous data transmission between physical assets, digital twins, IoT devices, and AI systems. 5G's ultra-reliable low-latency communication (URLLC) is critical for synchronizing high-fidelity digital twins with their physical counterparts in real time, enabling applications where millisecond delays are unacceptable, such as remote surgery guided by a live digital twin or the precise coordination of autonomous mobile robots in a warehouse. In smart cities, 5G-enabled sensors and AI-powered digital twins model traffic patterns, energy consumption, and emergency responses with unprecedented accuracy. In manufacturing, 5G networks support robotic automation, synchronized machine operations, and edge AI deployment at scale. Collectively, the integration of AI, digital twins, blockchain, and 5G creates an interconnected intelligent ecosystem in which data flows seamlessly, decisions occur autonomously, and organizations can innovate faster while maintaining high standards of security, reliability, and operational excellence. This technological stack forms the foundational architecture for Industry 4.0 and the autonomous enterprise, where closed-loop systems of sensing, simulation, verification, and action enable businesses to operate with a level of agility, resilience, and strategic foresight that was previously unimaginable.

15.9.3 Enterprise-Wide AI Orchestration Platforms

Enterprise-wide AI orchestration platforms represent the next frontier in organizational digital transformation, enabling firms to manage, integrate, and scale AI and analytics capabilities across the entire business ecosystem. Unlike isolated ML pipelines or department-specific tools, AI orchestration platforms function as centralized hubs that coordinate data ingestion, model development, training, deployment, monitoring, governance, and lifecycle management. This comprehensive oversight transforms the business of analytics from a fragmented, ad-hoc activity into a standardized, repeatable, and scalable production discipline, ensuring that every AI initiative adheres to corporate standards for quality, security, and strategic alignment. These platforms integrate diverse technologies such as MLOps frameworks, data lakes, cloud services, GenAI APIs, and low-code/no-code interfaces, allowing both technical and non-technical users to participate in AI development. Companies such as IBM (Watsonx), Google (Vertex AI), Microsoft (Azure AI Studio), and Databricks provide orchestration environments that standardize workflows, automate repetitive tasks, ensure version control, and enforce organization-wide governance policies. This unified approach accelerates time-to-value by enabling rapid experimentation, seamless model deployment across business units, and continuous improvement based on real-time performance metrics. Orchestration platforms also incorporate robust governance mechanisms, including bias detection, explainability modules, audit trails, and compliance dashboards to support responsible AI practices aligned with regulatory requirements such as the EU AI Act and emerging U.S. frameworks. This embedded governance automates critical compliance tasks, such as generating standardized documentation for high-risk models, enforcing ethical AI review gates before deployment, and providing immutable audit logs for regulatory inspections, thereby reducing legal and reputational risk. Furthermore, by connecting AI systems with ERP, CRM, supply chain, and operational platforms, enterprises can embed intelligence directly into core business processes, enabling autonomous decision-making, dynamic optimization, and personalized stakeholder engagement. Ultimately, enterprise-wide AI orchestration platforms transform AI from isolated pilot projects into an integrated, scalable, and strategically aligned capability that fuels innovation, operational efficiency, and long-term competitive advantage. They establish the foundational operating system for the intelligent enterprise, enabling businesses to systematically harness their collective data and analytical talent to not only solve discrete problems but to continuously learn, adapt, and evolve in an increasingly dynamic and complex market environment.

15.9.4 Autonomous Decision-making Systems

Autonomous decision-making systems represent a transformative evolution in AI and BA, enabling organizations to move beyond decision support toward fully automated, self-optimizing operations. These systems integrate ML, reinforcement learning, optimization algorithms, and real-time data streams to independently analyze situations, choose optimal actions, and continuously refine decisions based on feedback. This marks a paradigm shift from providing decision-makers with insights to deploying an AI-driven operational layer that acts with strategic intent, creating an "always-on" decisioning capability that operates at machine speed and scale. In supply chain management, autonomous systems dynamically adjust procurement, inventory levels, and logistics routes in response to demand fluctuations, geopolitical shocks, or transportation delays—as seen in Amazon's and DHL's AI-driven logistics networks. In financial services, autonomous trading engines use reinforcement learning to adapt investment strategies in real time, while fraud detection systems autonomously flag, block, and investigate suspicious activities with minimal human intervention. Manufacturing plants leverage autonomous control systems to regulate temperature, pressure, and workflow sequencing, enabling "lights-out factories" with near-continuous production and reduced human oversight, exemplified by advanced operations at Siemens and Fanuc. Customer service is similarly transformed through autonomous conversational agents capable of understanding context, personalizing interactions, and resolving complex service issues without escalation. Ultimately, these systems are increasingly guided by built-in governance mechanisms, ethical constraints, rule-based oversight, explainability modules, and HITL fail-safes to ensure accountability, fairness, and regulatory compliance. A critical development is the emergence of the "Constitutional AI" layer, where autonomous systems are hard-coded with top-level business principles and regulatory boundaries. Every potential action is evaluated not just for business optimization but for alignment with these principles, and any decision approaching a boundary is automatically routed for human review, creating scalable oversight. As autonomous decision-making systems become more sophisticated, organizations will shift from managing discrete analytical models to orchestrating interconnected networks of intelligent agents, enabling a new era of adaptive, resilient, and self-governing digital enterprises. The future enterprise will be architected as a multi-agent system, where strategic objectives are cascaded down to swarms of specialized autonomous agents. The role of leadership and BA will evolve to define these objectives, monitor systemic performance, and intervene only at the highest level of strategic exception, fundamentally redefining organizational agility and competitive resilience.

15.9.5 Human–AI Collaborative Models

Human–AI collaborative models represent a foundational shift in organizational design, emphasizing symbiotic partnerships between human expertise and AI to enhance decision-making, creativity, and operational performance. Unlike models that aim for full automation, collaborative intelligence frameworks intentionally distribute tasks based on complementary strengths: AI excels at pattern recognition, large-scale data processing, and rapid optimization, while humans provide contextual reasoning, ethical judgment, domain knowledge, and socio-emotional intelligence. This deliberate partnership, often termed "augmented intelligence," creates a hybrid cognitive system where the combined output exceeds the capability of either human or machine alone, optimizing for both efficiency and wisdom. This collaboration is evident in auditing, where tools like AuditBERT, GPT-based assistants, and anomaly-detection algorithms guide auditors toward high-risk areas, while human professionals interpret nuances, exercise professional skepticism, and make final judgments. The collaboration follows a structured workflow: AI pre-processes thousands of transactions or documents, surfacing anomalies and drafting preliminary observations; the auditor then investigates these AI-generated leads, applying professional judgment to distinguish between true risk and algorithmic noise, and ultimately authors the final, defensible audit opinion, creating a highly scalable and rigorous assurance process. In healthcare, AI diagnostic systems support physicians by identifying pathologies in imaging or recommending personalized treatment plans, while clinicians integrate these insights with patient histories and ethical considerations. In customer service, AI chatbots handle routine cases and sentiment analysis, escalating complex or sensitive interactions to human agents who offer empathy and discretion. Human–AI collaboration also enhances innovation processes: GenAI accelerates ideation and prototyping, while human teams refine concepts, assess feasibility, and align solutions with strategic objectives. Importantly, organizations must design governance structures, training programs, and workflow protocols that foster trust, transparency, and responsible use of AI. This includes HITL and human-on-the-loop (HOTL) mechanisms that ensure oversight, prevent bias, and maintain accountability. As human–AI collaborative models mature, they will redefine professional roles, augment human capabilities, and create hybrid work systems where humans and intelligent machines jointly drive organizational value, resilience, and long-term innovation. The future organization chart will depict not just human roles, but also the integrated

AI agents and systems that act as force multipliers for each function. Success will be measured by the fluency of this collaboration—the speed and quality of the feedback loop between human intuition and machine intelligence, creating an adaptive enterprise where human creativity is amplified, not replaced, by artificial cognition.

15.9.6 Facial AI Development

Facial AI development has advanced rapidly over the past decade, driven by breakthroughs in computer vision, deep learning, and large-scale data availability, enabling machines to accurately detect, analyze, and interpret human facial features in real time. Early facial recognition systems relied on handcrafted features and statistical methods, but modern models employ CNNs, transformers, and self-supervised learning to achieve unprecedented levels of accuracy and robustness across diverse environments. The frontier is now shifting from two-dimensional image analysis to dynamic, three-dimensional, and temporal modeling, where AI understands facial micro-expressions, physiological signals like heart rate via remote photoplethysmography (rPPG), and behavioral cues over time, creating a much richer biometric and psychometric profile. These technologies support a broad range of applications, including secure authentication (e.g., Apple Face ID), law enforcement identification systems, personalized retail experiences, emotion detection for customer engagement analytics, and telemedicine tools that assess patient stress or pain levels. In the enterprise, Facial AI is being integrated into advanced BA platforms for purposes like secure facility access, monitoring workforce engagement and fatigue in high-risk environments, and powering hyper-personalized marketing in physical stores where cameras analyze shopper demographics and reactions to displays in real-time to optimize store layouts and promotions. Companies such as Microsoft, Google, and SenseTime continue to refine facial AI by incorporating multimodal inputs—such as voice, gesture, and contextual cues—to enhance recognition accuracy and interpretive depth. Despite these advancements, facial AI raises significant ethical, legal, and societal concerns related to privacy, surveillance, algorithmic bias, and civil liberties. High-profile cases involving racial and gender bias in facial recognition have prompted calls for stricter regulation, greater transparency, and improved fairness in model training and deployment. As facial AI technologies evolve, responsible development will require balancing innovation with ethical safeguards, ensuring that systems are accurate, secure, accountable, and aligned with societal values and emerging global regulatory frameworks. The future of enterprise-grade Facial AI will be defined by "Privacy-by-Design" architectures and "Explainable Facial AI" (XFAI) systems that can articulate why a match was made or an emotion was classified, providing audit trails for regulatory compliance. Successful adoption will depend on transparent governance, clear stakeholder communication, and the implementation of facial AI strictly within ethical bounds that respect individual autonomy and prevent mass surveillance, positioning it as a tool for consented enhancement rather than covert control.

15.9.7 Future of Human-Like AI Robots

The future of human-like AI robots lies at the intersection of advanced AI, robotics engineering, cognitive modeling, and human–machine interaction, promising machines that can perceive, reason, communicate, and act with increasing autonomy and social intelligence. Emerging humanoid robots—such as Tesla's Optimus, Boston Dynamics' Atlas, and SoftBank's Pepper—already demonstrate capabilities in mobility, manipulation, speech interaction, and contextual awareness, supported by sophisticated AI systems that integrate computer vision, reinforcement learning, and NLP. The next frontier, often termed "Embodied AI," focuses on grounding AI in a physical form that interacts with the real world, enabling the robot to learn through embodied experience—much like a human child—and develop a practical, common-sense understanding of physics, social norms, and cause-and-effect, which remains a significant challenge for purely software-based AI. As these technologies converge with GenAI, neuro-symbolic reasoning, and emotional computing, future humanoid robots will be able to engage in fluid conversation, learn from real-world experience, collaborate with humans in workplaces, and perform complex tasks in manufacturing, healthcare, logistics, and home environments. In the enterprise, this evolution points toward the deployment of "cobots" (collaborative robots) that can work alongside human teams in factories for assembly, in hospitals for patient lifting and delivery, and in retail for inventory management and customer guidance. These robots will be governed by sophisticated multi-agent AI orchestration platforms that manage fleets of robots, optimizing their collective tasks and ensuring seamless integration with human workflows and existing business systems like ERP and WMS (Warehouse Management Systems). Advances in biomimetic design and smart materials will further enhance dexterity, balance, and adaptability, making robots more capable of functioning safely in human-centered spaces. However, the evolution of human-like AI robots also raises profound ethical and societal questions concerning labor displacement, privacy, dependency, and the psychological implications of human–robot relationships. Ensuring responsible development will require robust governance frameworks, transparency in algorithmic decision-making, HITL oversight, and policies that safeguard human dignity and socio-economic well-being. This will manifest industry-specific safety certifications for humanoid robots, mandatory "black box" recorders for accident investigation, and clear liability frameworks. Business leaders will need to establish ethics boards to oversee robot deployment and ensure that the use of such robots aligns with corporate social responsibility goals and public trust. Ultimately, the future of human-like AI robots is poised to transform work, care, and daily life by expanding human capabilities while demanding thoughtful stewardship to ensure that these powerful technologies serve society in equitable, safe, and ethical ways. The integration of these robots into the enterprise represents the ultimate fusion of physical and digital transformation, creating a hybrid workforce. The long-term strategic implication is the redefinition of productivity and service, where human creativity, strategy, and empathy are amplified by tireless, precise, and adaptable robotic partners, leading to new business models and industries centered around augmented human potential.

15.9.8 Neural Mesh Architecture

Currently used neural networks, while powerful, are inherently static, centralized, and monolithic in design. These characteristics limit their adaptability, scalability, and transparency in dynamic and complex environments. To address these limitations, the Neural Mesh architecture offers a transformative alternative by enabling distributed, adaptive, collaborative, and context-aware AI solutions. The Neural Mesh concept represents a fundamental shift from "model-centric AI" toward "system-centric AI ecosystems," where intelligence emerges from the coordinated interaction of multiple specialized components rather than a single, unified model.[18]

To effectively address the ethical and societal challenges associated with AI platforms, AI solutions and outcomes must adhere to the principles of being Precise, Explainable, and

Provable (PEP).[19] Achieving these principles requires the fulfillment of three critical conditions. First, a new computational paradigm as embodied in the Neural Mesh concept should complement or, where appropriate, replace traditional neural network architectures to enhance the power, precision, and adaptability of AI algorithms. Second, a rigorous methodological framework must be developed to provide mathematically provable evidence regarding the stability, reliability, and performance of AI-driven systems, thereby reducing reliance on purely empirical or experience-based evaluations. Third, future research should prioritize the development of linguistically interpretable and XAI outputs by ensuring that decision-making processes are transparent and understandable to users, regulators, and stakeholders.

The Neural Mesh paradigm is closely aligned with advances in Agentic AI, where autonomous agents coordinate tasks involving planning, execution, and iterative refinement. Under this paradigm, intelligence is distributed across a network of interconnected, semi-autonomous nodes, including agents, models, and analytical modules, where each performs specialized functions such as fraud detection, NLP, and anomaly detection. This decentralized structure reimagines AI systems as collaborative intelligence networks, enhancing flexibility, robustness, and real-time responsiveness.

In the context of forensic accounting, Neural Mesh architecture can integrate multiple specialized nodes, including transaction anomaly detection, textual analysis of disclosures (e.g., ESG-BERT and AuditBERT), behavioral analytics, and entity network analysis. The interaction among these nodes can significantly improve the accuracy and reliability of fraud detection. Similarly, in sustainability analytics, distinct nodes can be dedicated to analyzing environmental metrics, social disclosures, and corporate governance structures by enabling a more comprehensive and dynamic assessment of organizational performance.

15.10 Summary

This forward-looking chapter explores emerging trends in AI, such as GenAI, edge computing, real-time analytics, and quantum computing. This chapter explores the future trajectory of AI, from edge computing to GenAI. Businesses must prepare to adapt to fast-changing technological landscapes and regulatory frameworks. It also discusses how businesses can prepare for ongoing disruptions. This chapter examines the evolving role of AI in shaping the future of business strategy, operations, and innovation. As AI continues to advance, its integration into business models is transforming how organizations operate, compete, and create value. The chapter highlights the key technological trends driving AI's growth, such as ML, NLP, computer vision, and GenAI, and examines their applications across diverse business functions, including marketing, finance, supply chain, customer service, and human resources.

It also discusses the shift from AI as a tool for automation to AI as a strategic partner enabling data-driven decision-making, personalized customer experiences, and agile product development. Emerging areas like AI ethics, explainability, regulatory compliance, and responsible AI are emphasized as essential considerations for long-term sustainability and trust. The chapter explores how businesses can prepare for the AI-driven future by investing in digital infrastructure, upskilling their workforce, fostering innovation ecosystems, and aligning AI strategies with corporate values. Through real-world examples and forward-looking insights, the chapter concludes that the successful adoption of AI will not just be a competitive advantage but a fundamental requirement for resilience, growth, and sustainability in the digital age.

Notes

1 Okeleke, P. A., Ajiga, D., Folorunsho, S. O., & Ezeigweneme, C. (2024). Predictive analytics for market trends using AI: A study in consumer behavior. *International Journal of Engineering Research Updates*, 7(1), 36-49. https://doi.org/10.53430/ijeru.2024.7.1.0032. Available at https://www.researchgate.net/profile/Daniel-Ajiga/publication/383410055_Predictive_analytics_for_market_trends_using_AI_A_study_in_consumer_behavior/links/66cb61b375613475fe7b68ef/Predictive-analytics-for-market-trends-using-AI-A-study-in-consumer-behavior.pdf

2 Okeleke, P. A., Ajiga, D., Folorunsho, S. O., & Ezeigweneme, C. (2024). Predictive analytics for market trends using AI: A study in consumer behavior. *International Journal of Engineering Research Updates*, 7(1), 36-49. https://doi.org/10.53430/ijeru.2024.7.1.0032. Available at https://www.researchgate.net/profile/Daniel-Ajiga/publication/383410055_Predictive_analytics_for_market_trends_using_AI_A_study_in_consumer_behavior/links/66cb61b375613475fe7b68ef/Predictive-analytics-for-market-trends-using-AI-A-study-in-consumer-behavior.pdf

3 Uddin, M. K. S. (2024). A review of utilizing natural language processing and AI for advanced data visualization in real-time analytics. *Global Mainstream Journal*, 1(4), 10.62304. https://doi.org/10.62304/ijmisds.v1i04.185. Available at https://papers.ssrn.com/sol3/papers.cfm?abstract_id=4993556

4 Vainio-Pekka, H., Agbese, M. O. O., Jantunen, M., Vakkuri, V., Mikkonen, T., Rousi, R., & Abrahamsson, P. (2023). The role of explainable AI in the research field of AI ethics. *ACM Transactions on Interactive Intelligent Systems*, 13(4), 1–39. https://doi.org/10.1145/3599974. Available at https://dl.acm.org/doi/full/10.1145/3599974

5 Ojokoh, B. A., Samuel, O. W., Omisore, O. M., Sarumi, O. A., Idowu, P. A., Chimusa, E. R., … & Katsriku, F. A. (2020). Big data, analytics and artificial intelligence for sustainability. *Scientific African*, 9, e00551. https://doi.org/10.1016/j.sciaf.2020.e00551. Available at https://www.sciencedirect.com/science/article/pii/S2468227620302891

6 Zhu, Y., & Yu, K. (2023). Artificial intelligence (AI) for quantum and quantum for AI. *Optical and Quantum Electronics*, 55(8), 697. https://doi.org/10.1007/s11082-023-04914-6. Available at https://link.springer.com/article/10.1007/s11082-023-04914-6

7 Marković, D., Mizrahi, A., Querlioz, D., & Grollier, J. (2020). Physics for neuromorphic computing. *Nature Reviews Physics*, 2(9), 499–510. https://doi.org/10.1038/s42254-020-0208-2. Available at https://www.nature.com/articles/s42254-020-0208-2

8 Gemini 1.5: Unlocking multimodal understanding across millions of tokens of context. March 8, 2024. Available at https://arxiv.org/abs/2403.05530?utm_source=chatgpt.com

9 Google DeepMind. 2025. Gemini Robotics 1.5 brings AI agents into the physical world. September 25, 2025. Available at https://deepmind.google/blog/gemini-robotics-15-brings-ai-agents-into-the-physical-w OpenAI Platformorld/?utm_source=chatgpt.com

10 Stanford Institute for Human-Centered Artificial Intelligence (HAI). (2025). AI Index Report 2025. Available at https://hai.stanford.edu/ai-index/2025-ai-index-report?utm_source=chatgpt.com

11 Amrit, C., & Narayanappa, A. K. (2025). An analysis of the challenges in the adoption of MLOps. *Journal of Innovation & Knowledge*, 10(1), 100637. https://doi.org/10.1016/j.jik.2024.100637. Available at https://www.sciencedirect.com/science/article/pii/S2444569X24001768?utm_source=chatgpt.com

12 National Institute of Standards and Technology. (2024). Artificial Intelligence Risk Management Framework: Generative AI Profile/Companion Resource (NIST AI 600-1). Available at https://nvlpubs.nist.gov/nistpubs/ai/NIST.AI.600-1.pdf?utm_source=chatgpt.com

13 Devlin, J., Chang, M.-W., Lee, K., & Toutanova, K. (2019). BERT: Pre-training of deep bidirectional transformers for language understanding. In *Proceedings of NAACL-HLT*. Available at https://aclanthology.org/N19-1423/?utm_source=chatgpt.com

14 Devlin, J., Chang, M.-W., Lee, K., & Toutanova, K. (2019). BERT: Pre-training of deep bidirectional transformers for language understanding. In *Proceedings of NAACL-HLT*. Available at https://arxiv.org/abs/1810.04805?utm_source=chatgpt.com

15 Huang, A. H., Wang, H., & Yang, Y. (2023). FinBERT: A large language model for extracting information from financial text. *Contemporary Accounting Research*, 40(2), 806–841. https://hai.stanford.edu/ai-index/2025-ai-index-report?utm_source=chatgpt.com

16 Araci, D. (2019). FinBERT: Financial sentiment analysis with pre-trained language models. arXiv:1908.10063. Available at https://arxiv.org/abs/1908.10063?utm_source=chatgpt.com

17 Gu, H., Schreyer, M., Moffitt, K., & Vasarhelyi, M. A. (2024). Artificial intelligence co-piloted auditing. *International Journal of Accounting Information Systems*, 54, 100698. Available at https://www.sciencedirect.com/science/article/abs/pii/S1467089524000319?utm_source=chatgpt.com

18 Researchers consortium in conjunction with Corvinus University of Budapest (CUB), University of Washington (UW), and The Chinese University of Hong Kong (CUHK). (2026). AI next: New paradigm in AI transformation & application. AI Next HURIZONT Project 2025–2026 NKFIH – 2024-1.2.3-HU-RIZONT-2024-00030

19 Researchers consortium in conjunction with Corvinus University of Budapest (CUB), University of Washington (UW), and The Chinese University of Hong Kong (CUHK). (2026). AI next: New paradigm in AI transformation & application. AI Next HURIZONT Project 2025–2026 NKFIH – 2024-1.2.3-HU-RIZONT-2024-00030

Index

Pages in **bold-*italics*** refer to boxes and pages in **bold** refer to tables.